CHALLENGES OF
HUMANISTIC PSYCHOLOGY

CHALLENGES OF
HUMANISTIC PSYCHOLOGY

JAMES F. T. BUGENTAL, Ph.D.

Psychological Service Associates
Los Angeles

McGRAW-HILL BOOK COMPANY
New York, St. Louis, San Francisco
Toronto, London, Sydney

FOR JANE AND JOE

with the hope that one day you will see much of what is written herein as quaintly antique, some of it as importantly pioneering what is coming to realization, and at least a little of it as a still challenging vision of the far frontier of man's potential

PREFACE

What is man, that thou art mindful of him? and the son of man, that thou
visitest him? For thou hast made him a little lower than the angels,
and hast crowned him with glory and honour (Ps. 8:4–5).

*"Like the ant, man has built a complex civilization without
recourse to reason" (Schneirla). "What a piece of work is a man!
how noble in reason! how infinite in faculty! in form and moving
how express and admirable! in action how like an angel! in
apprehension how like a god!" (Shakespeare). "Man is a noble
animal, splendid in ashes and pompous in the grave" (Waller).
"Man is a reasoning animal" (Seneca). "Man is a pliable animal"
(Dostoevski). "Man is the anxiety-avoiding animal" (Becker).
"Man is a military animal" (Bailey). "Man is a social animal"
(Spinoza). "Man is a mere insect, an ant" (Church). "For without
money, George, a man is but a beast" (Percy).*

*Man is the creature that uses abstract thought, that is able to
experience vicariously through words, that hopes, that imprisons his
fellows, that values, that is aware and aware that he is aware, that
cares about the pain he inflicts.*

*All this and much more is man. And humanistic psychology is
directed toward exploring this immensity. I and the authors who
join me in this book and the many others who are loosely grouped
under the name "humanistic psychology" find we are ill content
to be psychologists if psychology is a "nothing-but" process
for reducing us—and all men—to a larger white rat or a
slower computer.*

*Bringing together these chapters to describe the field, the methods,
the content, and—above all—the challenges of humanistic psychology
has been for me a very satisfying and, in all truth, reassuring*

experience. Although I have been in various ways identified with
the development of an orientation to man that cherishes his
unique humanness, it was not until I began this work that I became
aware of the range and depth of people, ideas, and projects which
may properly be included under this banner. Now I know in a
very concrete way that humanistic psychology is rapidly growing
in its strength and in its products.

I began this book in a way which I like to think is humanistic.
I wrote down a list of the living people whose thoughts and writings
I had valued and from whom I had drawn inspiration and mental
sustenance. I was agreeably surprised that this list turned out
to include about seventy-five names. I wrote to these people,
telling them what I proposed. The response was exhilarating:
manuscripts, speeches, reprints, letters of suggestion and
encouragement, and nominations for other writers poured in.
Now I found I could refine the project, deciding we did not need
to include any generally available, previously published items
unless they were peculiarly important to our concerns. One way or
another, we have winnowed down to the present goodly company.
Those who do not appear in the following pages, however, are
as much to be valued as those who do, for their support, their
offered contributions, and—in some cases—their grace in accepting
the editor's judgment which ruled their papers out. Such judgments
were most often made because the balance of the chapters would
be best served by a particular inclusion or exclusion, rather
than because a paper or the ideas it conveyed were found wanting.
Let the reader share the editor's satisfaction: There is many times
over as much "good stuff" in humanistic psychology as will be
found in the following pages.

Plan of Coverage

In this book I have tried to present to psychologists, students,
and the interested general public an array of men, ideas, methods,
and perspectives. Severin's HUMANISTIC VIEWPOINTS IN
PSYCHOLOGY (New York: McGraw-Hill, 1965) served as a
comprehensive position statement to delineate what the humanistic
position protested in behavioristic psychology and to set forth
the programmatic aspirations of the viewpoint. In the present
volume, we seek to build on that foundation and to move beyond
protest to affirmation. Thus our emphasis has been on stating a
philosophic and heuristic position, on examining some of the
research approaches and products, on illustrating humanistic
studies of human experience, and on exploring two areas of
tremendous potential for humanistic psychology which are only
in very limited ways available to the behavioristic position:
the growthful encounters of psychotherapy[1] and basic encounter

[1] It should be recognized that there are so-called psychotherapies of conditioned-
response orientation; however, since for the most part these are procedures for
controlling one person by the efforts of another, they are better called by the name
some of their advocates themselves use, "behavior shaping." Psychotherapy, I
would insist, is a meaningful encounter between two subjects, not between a subject
and an object, in which the subjective experiences of both are crucially important.

*groups and the immense storehouse of the humanities, including
literature, philosophy, religion, the arts, and all man's varied
efforts to understand and improve his own experience.*

*We have been fortunate in both the quality of the material made
available for this book and the caliber of the people writing.
A number of the chapters go beyond reports of what has already
been accomplished and present exciting and promising ventures
into some of the new areas which are so abundantly present to
challenge the humanistic psychologist.*

Acknowledgments

*This book, as is apparent, is the work of many people. Some of
them have contributed the chapters which follow. Some were unable,
for one reason or another, to prepare actual manuscripts for this
book, but have otherwise lent support. They offered ideas, writings,
and nominations of other people to contribute to the volume. We
could not directly incorporate all that was offered, but I certainly
did incorporate and do value the spirit in which so much was
offered me.*

*Three people have particularly helped me with my editing chores.
Alvin A. Lasko, my long-time colleague and dear friend, has
repeatedly given me a most cherished gift: his clear and insightful
thinking and the assurance that he knows I value his utter
candor. This is a rare and beautiful trust. Phyllis Wittenberg has
been unstinting (I started to write "indefatigable," but that is
so clearly not so; more importantly, she has been devoted despite
fatigue) in her skilled and intelligent management of all the
countless details of bringing the manuscript into mechanical form
for publication.*

*And Mary Edith Bugental, my wife, has been beside me with support,
encouragement, and appreciation which constantly renewed my zeal
for humanistic psychology and for humanistic human experience.*

JAMES F. T. BUGENTAL

CONTENTS

CHALLENGES OF
HUMANISTIC PSYCHOLOGY

Part ONE

THE NATURE AND TASK OF HUMANISTIC PSYCHOLOGY

*When any of us are able, on occasion, to step back from the tight
perspectives of our day-to-day living and to take a real look at
ourselves and our lives, we may be filled with either of two strong
emotional responses. Sometimes the feeling is that of anxiety
and vulnerability when we recognize the immensity of all that is and
the minuteness of our own lives—and of all men's lives and their
attainments—within that immensity. Then we may be frightened and
hasten back to our familiar preoccupations, or we may seek some
agency or power to interpose between our nakedness and the world.
Whatever our actions, when we sense that anxiety, we want to do
those things which will increase our potency and give us a greater
sense of being able to contend or harmonize with the world.*

*On other occasions that same long, hard look at our lives, even
that same recognition of the little island of what we know in the
center of the ocean of the unknown, can be the source of quite a
contrasting feeling. At these times, we may derive a sense of awe or
of pride from what this ant, this infinitesimal being called man,
has been able to carve out of emptiness and into meaningfulness.
We sense the fantastic potential in human thought, imagination,
and communication and become aware of the dizzying vastness of*

*possibility that can keep pace with the universe's own immensity,
for only man's thought can hope to match that incredible range.
In the fullness of this emotion, we can be heartened to renew the
endless quest, to press back the limits, and to win yet new continents
and planets for our exploration and development.*

*It will have been evident that—to my mind—either of the strong
emotional responses which I experience on looking with fresh
perspective at our human condition provides a stimulus to further
inquiry and speculation, to observation and hypothesis building,
to experimentation and communication—in short, to what I conceive
to be the scientific (which is to say, the humanistic) endeavor.*

*We shall begin our report on this endeavor by considering the tasks
confronting a humanistic psychology. These are not specific
projects (such as measuring reaction times, studying the psychedelic
reaction, or even trying to understand man's religious impulse).
These tasks are, instead, conceptions of just what man is up to when
he is trying to understand his own nature. Thus in the first chapter,
I shall set out some speculations about the main areas in which our
science must proceed to be most fruitful for a genuine understanding
of what it means to be human, and I shall also present some contrasts
with another major psychological orientation, behaviorism.*

*In the second chapter, Hadley Cantril undertakes to provide a basic
description of what it means to be a human being. This description
is significant in several ways. Note particularly his first postulation:
"Man requires the satisfaction of his survival needs." This, it might
be conceded, is where a mechanomorphic description of man (one
that views life or man in the image of a machine) would end. The
contrast with such "nothing-but" thinking is epitomized when
Cantril goes on to name ten more attributes of being human! Cantril's
list, it will be recognized, provides an overview of quite a different
sort of field from the one that the table of contents of a typical
experimental-behaviorist introduction to psychology, for example,
would describe. Although, of course, the two lists would not be
intended as immediate parallels, it is evident that they are dealing with
very different conceptions of what psychology comprises and with very
different underlying attitudes about human life.*

*This sort of contrast is given additional impetus by Joseph Royce's
exciting yet scholarly analysis in Chapter 3 of the kinds of thinking
appropriate to the psychological enterprise. As he makes clear, the
challenge of this field is such that it warrants and should receive the
full range of man's potential for learning about himself and his world.
The exclusion of intuition, as is customary in much of the regnant
psychology, is clearly a loss to the whole undertaking. Royce
documents the gain to be had by taking off our blinders when he
demonstrates how psychology may profitably interact with the
arts, religion, and history. In doing so, he anticipates matters to
which we shall return in Parts Five and Six.*

*Where Cantril talks about the content of a humanistic psychology,
and Royce about the sorts of thinking appropriate to the study of that
content, in the final chapter of Part One the distinguished novelist*

2

and social philosopher Arthur Koestler directs himself to the central process with which all science and all art are concerned: the act of creation (*the title of his own masterful study of this centrally important human action*). In his analysis of creativity in science, in humor, and in art, Koestler admirably illustrates the very points he is making; for he writes with artistry and with humor, and the product is a scientific contribution in itself: the concept of bisociation.

Thus Part One sets the stage for the chapters to follow. The reader will recognize that we are here undertaking a fresh look at what it means to study the human experience. This fresh look puts greater emphasis on experience than on behavior, on meaning than on causality, on self-realization than on other-manipulation. Part Two will illustrate these contrasts further, as some typically humanistic studies of the human experience are detailed. In subsequent parts, we shall examine some of the methodologies of this orientation and some of their products. Finally, we shall look to two immense fields of research and application (*the distinction is more academic than actual*): growth-promoting encounters and the interaction of psychology and the humanities.

Presently: Partner, Psychological Service
Associates, Los Angeles (since 1953).

Education: Doctor of Philosophy in
psychology from the Ohio State University
(1948).

Current major activities: Practicing intensive
individual and group psychotherapy,
consulting in human relations, and writing
in humanistic and existential psychology.

JAMES F. T. BUGENTAL

Most rewarding project:[1] Trying to develop
group methods for existential confrontation and for facilitating
therapeutic and growth-evoking "follow-through."

Future of humanistic psychology: The probably explosive changes and
expansions in human experience which will almost certainly follow on the
growth of attention to the creative and healthy side of human potential
(in contrast to our emphasis up to now on pathology and repair).

Personal history: Public personnel administration (1941–1944).
Assistant Professor of Psychology at the Georgia School of Technology
(1944–1946) and at the University of California, Los Angeles
(1948–1954). Founded Psychological Service Associates with Alvin
Lasko in 1953. Diplomate in Clinical Psychology, American Board of
Examiners in Professional Psychology. First President of the American
Association for Humanistic Psychology (1962–1963).

Writings: Chiefly in existential-analytic psychology and psychotherapy,
humanistic psychology, and interviewing and counseling methods.
The Search for Authenticity (1965).

Present chapter: Prepared for this volume. (Exercising the editor's
prerogative, I asked all other authors to make substantive statements
and reserved to myself the only straight-out position paper.)

[1] Each author was asked to answer these questions: What project on which you
are engaged do you currently find most rewarding or exciting? What fantasy,
prediction, or speculation about future developments in humanistic psychology
most excites your imagination? The answers are given in brief form with the
headings here shown.

Chapter 1

JAMES F. T. BUGENTAL

THE CHALLENGE THAT IS MAN

Man is the challenge to man. Man, by his very being, provides a fundamental challenge to any pretense to, or system of, knowledge which man may erect. All knowledge is, ultimately, founded on a psychology —conscious or unconscious, implicit or explicit—of the human experience. It is the very ground on which the knower stands. And where one stands makes a difference in what one perceives (or thinks he knows). This is so whether or not one examines or even recognizes that ground.

To make a statement about a distant galaxy is to make a statement about oneself. To propose a "law" of the action of mass and energy is to offer a hypothesis about one's way of being in the world. To write a description of microorganisms on a slide is to set forth an account of human experience. The psychology of the human condition is always the predicating set of assumptions on which all others rest. One says, "I see things out there in such and such a way," neglecting to add what is even more fundamental: "I see them so because I have made such and such presumptions about what it means to see, to describe, to speak, to hear, and so on and on."

We may as well recognize right here that the attempt to circumvent this dependence of all else on an implicit human psychology by introducing instruments does nothing of the kind. It simply adds several more assumptions to our psychology, for at one end of the line is a human observer and reporter, and at the other end is another human listener or receiver of the report.

Now, of course, all this is not new to scientists, whether in the physical or psychological domains, whether behaviorist or humanistic. The difference resides in what one does or the attitude one takes about this predicating human psychology. In an extreme oversimplification, we can say the behaviorist seems to regard it as hopeless and to try to so define his province as to (seem to) detour around it. The humanistic psychologist, in this same exaggerated contrast, accepts this basic subjectivism of all experience as his realm of endeavor.

SCIENCE AND HUMAN EXPERIENCE

Too often scientists and would-be scientists are like the small child after the birthday party who was asked how many people were there. He replied, "There were eleven people and me." Many who would claim the name of psychological scientist seem equally to talk about people without counting themselves in and, most assuredly, without using the evidence of their own

5

experience. Thus they can conceive utopias of happy, bovine people manipulated by a benevolent oligarchy of scientists. They think to describe people without describing themselves and end up having largely missed the picture of people while having writ large their own self-portraits.

By way of recapitulation, let me make quite explicit what it is that I am saying and what the basic psychological dilemma of all science is. At the same time, let me make it quite clear that I intend no metaphor, no extravagance of language or conception, and no heuristic or argumentative point made for emphasis but not intended in all seriousness. I mean, very literally, that any statement we make about the world (the "out there") is inevitably, inescapably, a statement about our theory of ourselves (the "in here"). It may make this somewhat clearer to point out that the astronomer, the physicist, the chemist—as well as the psychologist, the sociologist, the anthropologist—make basic assumptions about such psychological functions as the senses, thinking, the significance of logic, the processes of language, human relationships, communication, motivation, attention, and concentration constantly whenever they observe, record their observations, speculate about meanings, experiment, and write reports.

This recognition, which is the cornerstone of humanistic psychology and which is not unfamiliar to some behaviorists, is in harmony with the thinking of an increasing number of physical scientists. Henry Margenau, in *The Nature of Physical Reality* (1950),[1] says all this in slightly different terms (but perhaps terms even more distressing to tender-minded experimentalists, for he talks about "metaphysics"):

> To deny the presence, indeed the necessary presence, of metaphysical elements in any successful science is to be blind to the obvious, although to foster such blindness has become a highly sophisticated endeavor in our time. Many reputable scientists have joined the ranks of the exterminator brigade, which goes noisily about chasing metaphysical bats out of scientific belfries. They are a useful crowd, for what they exterminate is

[1] References are collected at the end of each chapter.

rarely metaphysics—it is usually bad physics. Every scientist *must* invoke assumptions or rules of procedure which are not dictated by sensory evidence as such. . . . The only answer [to the attempt to avoid assumptions] which carries no metaphysical flavor is that given by the radical empiricist . . . and his answer is palpably wrong . . . (pp. 12–13). Reality does change as discovery proceeds. I can see nothing basically wrong with a real world which undergoes modifications along with the flux of experience (p. 295).

The ultimate subjectivity of all that we call objective is expressed by many writers, from varied backgrounds. Here are two further instances:

> Every intervention to make a measurement, to study what is going on in the atomic world, creates, despite all the universal order of this world, a new, a unique, not fully predictable situation (Oppenheimer, 1954, p. 62).
> Contemporary physics compels the physicist to look upon himself as a subject (Weizsäcker, 1952, p. 200).

Now let us recognize that each of these authors was not necessarily pointing to the same processes toward which I have been directing our attention. But each of them is calling for a recognition that the supposedly "objective" is in fact dependent upon, or subsequent to, other matters which are clearly subjective. These, I am arguing, are—among other things—implicit assumptions about the psychology of human experience and functioning.

To give this matter more point, we may concede that one can deal with these issues about psychological experience and functioning in an objectivist frame of reference—which is what the behaviorist tries to do. However, when he does so, he has once again made subjective assumptions which qualify all his efforts. Only by dealing directly with the matter of one's own subjectivity can a kind of infinite regression be avoided (and even then it is avoided only partially).

There are a number of implications to the recognition of the ultimate subjectivity of all knowledge and all scientific endeavors. Philosophy, logic, religion, and literature each directs attention to some of these implications. Psychology, insofar as it might be separately identified from these related areas, has always been similarly concerned —always, that is, until the behavioristic interregnum.

The revival of humanistic psychology means that scientific attention is once again being directed toward the primacy of the subjective (not to the exclusion of attention to the objective and to behavior, by any means, however). Thus the more fundamental concerns of a psychology of the human experience will once again be explored.

THE TASK FOR HUMANISTIC PSYCHOLOGY

At this time, humanistic psychology is as much distinguished by what it is not or by what it opposes as by what it affirms. However, I think this situation is a growing pain of this reborn orientation rather than a necessary and lasting condition. Indeed, in many ways, this book constitutes an affirmation of a positive content to the humanistic view.

→Humanistic psychology has as its ultimate goal the preparation of a complete description of what it means to be alive as a human being. This is, of course, not a goal which is likely ever to be fully attained;[2] yet it is important to recognize the nature of the task. Such a complete description would necessarily include an inventory of man's native endowment; his potentialities of feeling, thought, and action; his growth, evolution, and decline; his interaction with various environing conditions (and, here, a truly complete psychology of man would subsume all physical and social sciences since they bear on the human experience actually or potentially); the range and variety of experience possible to him; and his meaningful place in the universe.

Recognizing that such an ultimate description is an orienting goal, not an imminently expected attainment, the humanistic psychologist concerns himself with those

aspects of the human experience which have importance in daily living. Thus he will study and seek to increase our understanding of such familiar experiences as love, pain, willing, fearing, hoping, and so on. This is an important point of contrast between the two orientations to psychology: mechanomorphic psychology assumes that it must first find the basic units and laws of human behavior and, with these, build an embracing abstract structure from which understandings of any particular event may be derived. Thus the mechanomorph is impatient with inquiries into naturalistic human experiences and prefers the reductive and abstract. Rather than concerning himself with the relation of a person's pain to his feelings of having power in his own life, he prefers to study the influence of a painful punishment on bar pressing in the rat. Yet such a rejection of subjective inquiry can lead to gross distortions, as is illustrated by Tomkins in Chapter 6.

The humanistic psychologist finds the mechanomorph's restriction to the objective and abstract too limiting. It is, he believes, a tender-minded view of the world which does not really confront the extensity of that which is potential or the influence of the observation process on what is observed. The subjectively oriented psychologist accepts, in contrast, the relentless challenge of a subject matter which he knows he will never be able to encompass fully, finding his reward in his engagement with a meaningful portion of that immensity. Clearly, this is a contrast not only in topics chosen for study but also in actual world views, as Bertalanffy makes evident in Chapter 34.

This same contrast between humanistic and mechanomorphic psychologists is even more clearly discernible when the characteristic "set" or approach to their subject matters is appreciated. The mechanomorphic psychologist is typically concerned to demonstrate that any new human behavior or experience is really *nothing but* a variant on some already known and simpler phenomenon. Indeed, he is habitually entrenched against any proliferation of human phenomena, preferring to try to demonstrate that they are all variations on reinforcement

---

[2] Indeed, we must recognize that the very process of describing the human experience changes that experience and that the more such a description approaches completeness, the more it is apt to be a basis for change in the very experience it describes. This is probably true for all science, but it is particularly true for the sciences that deal with man. Man's awareness about himself acts as a constantly "recycling" agency to produce changes in himself.

schedules and conditioned responses, for example. (Probably it is not really so, but at times he seems to be insisting that the Parthenon is really only stone, the "Mona Lisa" only oil paint, or Beethoven's *Fifth Symphony* only sound waves.)

In contrast, the humanistic psychologist is typically concerned not only to describe the existing way of the human experience but also to ask, "How might it be extended, enriched, or made more meaningful? What more might be potential?" (as Bonner does in Chapter 7). Thus humanistic psychologists (e.g., Otto, in Chapter 13) have often been involved in trying to develop methods for enlarging and enriching human experience. Studies of influences which act to limit our experience (e.g., Harman, in Chapter 33), of the ways of breaking free of these (e.g., Wilson, in Chapter 8, and Mogar, in Chapter 15), and of further potentialities (Clark, in Chapter 27, and Maslow, in Chapter 29, for example) are typical of this attitude. Lasko (in Chapter 26) demonstrates this same broadened perspective from a contrasting point of reference, that of the psychotherapist.

These same concerns have two further extensions. Humanistic psychology is much involved with work in helping people to grow and evolve more fully in realization of their potential. Thus work in psychotherapy (Haigh, in Chapter 22, and Whitaker and Warkentin, in Chapter 25) and in sensitivity training (Rogers, in Chapter 28) is very centrally within the humanistic purview. Second, humanistic psychology is inevitably involved with the social ambience of which it is part. It would be a denial of the very perspective it enunciates to attempt to hold apart from the practical implications of its findings. Thus Lifton, in Chapter 20, and Levine, in Chapter 21, examine vital implications of the war-peace issue which overhangs all human experience today.

Fundamentally, it seems to me, the issue between mechanomorphic and humanistic psychologies may be reduced to a contrast in their views of the nature of man and the orientation of their sciences. Mechanomorphic psychology (psychonomy, in their newer term) views man as an object acted upon from the outside by various forces or driven from within by other forces which are to be characterized chiefly by their relation to the outside (e.g., thirst, hunger, sexual appetite). The regularities in man thus most attract the mechanomorph: instincts, reflexes, conditioned responses, habits, learning. It is all too easy for such an orientation to slip into dismissing irregularities and individual differences as annoying artifacts, chiefly to be accounted for as experimental errors or inadequacies of control and certainly not felt to be ultimately significant. Such thinking soon evolves into a nothing-but orientation in which the intent is to show that all human phenomena are nothing but a minimum number of response processes (e.g., conditioned responses).

The humanistic psychologist has a model of man which contrasts with the mechanomorph's picture at a number of points. Man is viewed as a subject in the midst of his own living, acting on the world, changing himself and all about him. While man's reactiveness is certainly recognized, the humanistic psychologist regards this as less distinctive of the human experience and tends to look to those ways in which humans distinguish themselves from objects, from lower animals, and from one another: conceptual thinking, vicarious experiencing, imagination, communication, invention and discovery, mystical concern and inquiry, artistic creation. The humanistic psychologist discards "nothing but" to ask, "What more may be potential?" Man, thus, is seen to be at an early stage in the evolution of his own possibilities.

This contrast is implicit in Szasz's proposal to regard the moral nature of man as one of his most distinguishing aspects (Chapter 5). The nature of the human being is examined in a complementary fashion by Cantril in Chapter 2, while Severin, in Chapter 16, summarizes the cosmic conception of man which the late Teilhard de Chardin advanced.

Summarizing the Humanistic-Behavioristic Controversy In the competitive and often angry interchanges between dedicated people having contrasting views of the proper place of their lives' work, it is easy for them to become extreme in characterizing either the behaviorist or the humanistic position.

Indeed, there is a delightful gusto to portraying in lurid hues the stupidity or veniality of the experimentalists while reserving all virtue and scientific acumen to the adherents of the subjective and human-centered. Such portraits are caricatures, not characterizations, of course. However, the truer statement is not necessarily the bland, all-encompassing avowal that each perspective is equally valuable and that all psychological work is contributing to a rich eventual synthesis. Caricatures, if they are meaningful, are based on some nuclei of truth. All scientific efforts are not equally valuable, and all science does not automatically contribute to human well-being.

I have very clearly taken sides in this issue between the objectivist and subjectivist approaches to the study of man. I sincerely believe this is such a conflict as may well be termed a battle for man's soul. It is so not because behaviorism is following a blind alley but because it is clearly effective within its frighteningly limited perspective. Paul Tillich said, "Man resists objectification, and if his resistance to it is broken, man himself is broken" (1951, p. 98).

To put the point quite starkly, it makes a very great difference to the world of man and to man's own experience of his life which view of his nature and which orientation to the study of his being is dominant.

The humanistic orientation differs from the behavioristic in a number of ways, but these six points seem to me especially important:

The humanistic psychologist:

1 Disavows as inadequate and even misleading, descriptions of human functioning and experience based wholly or in large part on subhuman species.

2 Insists that meaning is more important than method in choosing problems for study, in designing and executing the studies, and in interpreting their results.

3 Gives primary concern to man's subjective experience and secondary concern to his actions, insisting that this primacy of the subjective is fundamental in any human endeavor. (This is beautifully illustrated by Koestler in Chapter 4.)

4 Sees a constant interaction between "science" and "application" such that each constantly contributes to the other and the attempt rigidly to separate them is recognized as handicapping to both.

5 Is concerned with the individual, the exceptional, and the unpredicted rather than seeking only to study the regular, the universal, and the conforming. (Wilson, in Chapter **8**, strikingly demonstrates the very fundamental importance of this attention to that which is unique in experience.)

6 Seeks that which may expand or enrich man's experience and rejects the paralyzing perspective of nothing-but thinking.

These characterizations flow from a strong sense of concern and conviction about the importance of the issues involved and about the necessity of a more human-valuing perspective (necessity to man's realization of his own potential for evolution and enrichment of experience). I do not believe the characterizations fundamentally to be distorted by this concern; although I may have implicitly painted the behaviorist as more limited or more callous than many individual behaviorists deserve, and the humanistic psychologist as more aware or more altruistic than many individual humanistic psychologists merit.

THE STATE OF THE ART

It is very difficult to assess just how far advanced the development of humanistic psychology may be. There are numerous reasons for this difficulty; among them, two are important to render explicit here. First, there is the recognition of the open-ended nature of the task of humanistic psychology (as described above). This means that any statement of what has been done and what remains to be done is very subjective and very relative to the circumstances under which such a statement is attempted. No absolute measurement is conceivable. Second, it is problematic just what to include within the realm of humanistic psychology. Only in the Balkanized university catalogue can the various forms of observing, thinking about, speculating on, and generalizing about human experience be broken up into packages labeled "literature," "religion," "philosophy," "psychology," and so on. As Wyatt points out (in Chapter 30) and as Greening (Chapter 31) and Kaplan (Chapter 32) clearly demonstrate, the humanities and psychology are generically concerned with the same sorts of issues and observations. This is further illustrated by the contributions of Koestler (Chapter 4) and Wilson (Chapter 8), both of whom are identified primarily as novelists and essayists rather than as formally designated psychologists.

Humanistic psychology is under the apparent handicap that it is little represented in the major American universities and psychological research centers. By and large, these are in the control of mechanomorphic faculties. This is certainly a disadvantage in recruiting new talent into the orientation and helping them to become trained. It is also inconvenient that research funds and facilities are harder for the humanistic psychologist to come by. However, in the long view, these seeming problems may work out to be advantageous. Institutional acceptance and correctness are not notably correlated with creativity and personal dedication. The humanistic psychologist is apt to be such because of strong personal involvement. His research and writing will grow out of genuine concern. New adherents to the humanistic viewpoint will be either those strong-minded, younger members of the profession who have held on to their convictions despite opposing pressures or those mature psychologists who have wearied of the protected and miniature arena of behaviorism and seek the challenging confrontation with living human psychology [as Maslow describes his own experience (1966, pp. xiv–xv)]. In either event, the quality of the recruits to the humanistic viewpoint will often be very high. We shall also receive more than our share of the cranks, the eccentric, the clearly mad, the nonconformist, and so on. This too may well be a good thing in the long run. Creativity does not always wear academic robes or fit comfortably into established procedures and roles.

Humanistic psychology certainly has the advantage that it deals with naturalistic problems (such as that studied by Maurer in Chapter 18), often in everyday language and usually with results that have immediate application (as demonstrated by the Romes in Chapter 19 or the Gibbs in Chapter 17). This means that communication with the vast society which ultimately does much to fashion human outcomes should be more ready. Moustakas so well documents this in Chapter 11.

What humanistic psychology needs urgently now is attention to developing its methods and criteria so that the generality and precision of its products may be better ascertained and demonstrated. Because such a psychologist is more concerned to study a meaningful problem (as notably demonstrated by Charlotte Buhler in Chapter 9) than to find a topic to which to apply a favorite method, he is often less able to observe procedural and statistical niceties. Yet this very concern may help him avoid parochial errors, such as Winthrop demonstrates in Chapter 10. Nevertheless, there is no doubt that the evolution of improved methods for grappling with holistic and naturalistic problems will do much to further this approach. Already these matters are being studied and attacked in a variety of ways. Jourard, in Chapter 12, calls for a sweeping reexamination of our procedures and attitudes in psychological research. Sargent offers a broad-gauge survey of the centrally important area of personality and social psychology in Chapter 14.

Polyani (1958) and Matson (1964) have studied the nature of the scientific enterprise in thorough fashion and with much that aids the humanistic psychologist resulting. Maslow, in the volume cited above (1966), carries the inquiry into the important area of the psychology of the scientific work itself. Rogers has described himself as increasingly concerned to inquire into the philosophy of science and research strategies appropriate to humanistic psychology.

Humanistic psychology, however, needs to be continually aware of how essential is its foundation in philosophy. Royce makes abundantly clear in Chapter 3 that, far from being a limitation, this recognition actually frees psychology to utilize an even wider-ranging approach to its task. Thomas, in Chapter 23, and Shapiro, in Chapter 24, provide eloquent demonstrations of Royce's point that the intuitive and metaphoric may provide unique and valuable data.

CONCLUSION

All the foregoing may be summarized by detailing some of the direct challenges to humanistic psychology (and to man himself). The following seems to me to represent where we are at this stage in the evolution of our discipline:

Humanistic psychology is given the challenge to:

1 Develop adequate methods and criteria for a true science which is yet a human-oriented one.

2 Demonstrate that such a view of man is feasible and is more fruitful in enriching man's life than is a mechanomorphic one.

3 Close the gap with the physical sciences so that man may survive and that he may survive with dignity.

4 Offset the depersonalizing, man-as-object influences of increasing population and mass society so that man may retain and enlarge his domain of subjecthood.

5 Explore the 75 to 90 percent of man's potential which today is largely latent.

In brief, we can say that where behavioristic psychology has taken as its goal the attainment of the ability to describe, to predict, and to control objects (animals: human, and subhuman), humanistic psychology seeks to so describe men and their experiences that they will be better able to predict and control their *own* experiences (and thus, implicitly, to resist the control of others).[3]

REFERENCES

BUGENTAL, J. F. T. Humanistic psychology and the clinician. In L. E. Abt & B. F. Reiss (Eds.), *Progress in clinical psychology*. Vol. 7. New York: Grune & Stratton, 1966. Pp. 223–239.

MARGENAU, H. *The nature of physical reality: A philosophy of modern physics.* New York: McGraw-Hill, 1950.

MASLOW, A. H. *The psychology of science: A reconnaissance.* New York: Harper & Row, 1966.

MATSON, F. *The broken image.* New York: George Braziller, 1964.

OPPENHEIMER, J. R. *Science and the common understanding.* New York: Simon and Schuster, 1954.

POLANYI, M. *Personal knowledge.* Chicago: Univer. of Chicago Press, 1958.

TILLICH, P. *Systematic theology.* Vol. 1. Chicago: Univer. of Chicago Press, 1951.

WEIZSÄCKER, V. V. *The world view of physics.* Chicago: Univer. of Chicago Press, 1952.

[3] See Bugental (1966) for a further discussion of the contrasting images of man held by humanistic and mechanomorphic psychologists.

Presently: Chairman, Institute for International Social Research, Princeton, N.J. (since 1955). Research Associate, Princeton University.

Education: Doctor of Philosophy in psychology from Harvard University (1931), Honorary Doctor of Laws from Washington and Lee University (1949), and Honorary Doctor of Science from Dartmouth College (1960).

Current major activity: Systematic social psychology.

HADLEY CANTRIL

Most rewarding project: A new theory of human motivation.

Personal history: Stuart Professor of Psychology and Chairman of the Department of Psychology at Princeton University (1944–1953; at Princeton since 1936). Expert Consultant to the Secretary of War (1942–1945), to the Office of War Information (1942–1945), and to the Executive Office of the President of the United States (1955–1956). Director of the Office of Public Opinion Research (1939–1957), of public opinion research for the Coordinator of Inter-American Affairs (1939–1940), and of the UNESCO "Tensions Project," Paris (1948). President of the Research Council, Inc., and of the Institute for Associated Research. Past President of the Eastern Psychological Association and of the Society for the Psychological Study of Social Issues.

Writings: Many books and articles, including *The Psychology of Radio,* with G. W. Allport (1935); *The Invasion from Mars* (1940); *The Psychology of Ego-involvements,* with M. Sherif (1947); *Tensions That Cause Wars* (1950); *The Politics of Despair* (1958); *Reflections on the Human Venture,* with C. H. Bumstead (1960); *The Pattern of Human Concerns* (1965); and *Adventures in Policy Research* (1966).

Present chapter: This is a somewhat revised version of the concluding chapter of *The Pattern of Human Concerns,* which also appeared earlier as "The Human Design" in the *Journal of Individual Psychology* (1964, **20,** 129–136). It is included here with the permission of the editor of that journal.

Chapter 2
HADLEY CANTRIL

A FRESH LOOK AT THE HUMAN DESIGN

The human being seems at last to be entering the main body of psychology with a vengeance. For years he has all too often been shorn of his most characteristic attributes, until he has been scarcely recognizable. Variables such as appetites, wants, values, and temperament have been neglected because they are not easily manipulated in the laboratory and can so disturb otherwise neat experimentation. As Henry A. Murray pointed out nearly two decades ago (1948, p. 466), "The main body of psychology started its career by putting the wrong foot forward, and it has been out of step with the march of science much of the time. Instead of beginning with studies of the whole person adjusting to a natural environment, it began with studies of a segment of a person responding to a physical stimulus in an unnatural laboratory environment." One consequence of this false start has been a proliferation of model building which often takes on the aspect of playing games. Another consequence has been an overemphasis by some investigators on a single variable which proves at best tentative and partial after the fad for it has run its course.

It is therefore no wonder that so many students of psychology have found it an insufferably dull subject and that many social scientists and inquiring laymen feel that most of the psychology they read provides them unconvincing, unrewarding concepts from which to choose as they try to give plausible accounts of the behavior of men and women in real-life situations. They sense that somewhere along the line too much of human experience has been left out of account.

It is appropriate, then, for those of us concerned with human experience and behavior in all its subtle ramifications to spell out what seems to us to ring true and what appear to be the demands that the genetically built-in design of the human being imposes on any society, political culture, or enduring social relationship. It is all too easy to neglect the basic functional uniformities which take diverse forms and to leave the accounting or explanation at that level. Differences are often dramatic and simpler to detect than the similarities they may obscure. Here I shall try to orchestrate into some systematic unity the diversities of mankind found in different societies and contexts.

The aspects of "human nature" differ-

13

entiated here are those which seem to me to be pointed to by the data of psychology and by the observations sensitive observers have made of the way people live their lives in a variety of circumstances. I shall try to use a level of accounting appropriate both to an understanding of people and to an understanding of social and political systems. In doing this, some of the absurdities may be avoided that result when a single man-made abstraction, usually devised to account for some single aspect of behavior, is the sole theme song. As the different characteristics of the human design are reviewed here, it must be recognized and emphasized that they all overlap, intertwine, and are interdependent. One must differentiate artificially in order to focus and describe.

Man Requires the Satisfaction of His Survival Needs. Any listing of the characteristics of any living organism must begin here. Neurophysiologists have located and described in a most general way two built-in appetitive systems found in higher animals: one system propelling them to seek satisfying and pleasurable experiences, and the other protecting them from threatening or unpleasant experiences (Cantril & Livingston, 1963). These two systems together can be thought of as the basic forces contained within all human beings, which not only keep them and the species alive as their simple survival needs for food, shelter, and sex are gratified but also are involved in the desire for life itself.

These appetitive systems, of course, become enormously developed, refined, and conditioned—especially in man—as new ways are learned to achieve satisfactions and avoid dangers and discomforts. It has often been noted that unless the survival needs are satisfied, a person devotes himself almost exclusively to a continued attempt to fulfill them, a preoccupation which preempts his energies and repels any concern for other activities. Most people in the world today are still concerned with living a type of life that constitutes well-being on a relatively simple level with what amenities their cultures can provide.

Man Wants Security in Both Its Physical and Its Psychological Meaning to Protect Gains Already Made and to Assure a Beachhead from Which Further Advances May Be Staged. Man wants some surety that one action can lead to another, some definite foothold which provides an orientation and integration through time. People invariably become embittered if they nurse a dream for what they regard as a long time with no signs of it becoming a reality.

In this connection, it should be recalled that the story of evolution seems to tell us that members of every species stake out some territory for themselves within which they can provide for their needs and carry on their living; the size of this territory is dependent on what is required for the survival of the species, and is increased if this will contribute to such survival. In the present era, the territories human beings stake out for themselves are largely bounded by the nation-state, a territorial unit rapidly replacing narrower geographical and psychological identifications. Yet it is doing so just at the time when it is becoming more and more apparent that the concept of nation itself limits and threatens man's development in an age of increasing interdependence and highly developed weaponry.

Man Craves Sufficient Order and Certainty in His Life to Enable Him to Judge with Fair Accuracy What Will or Will Not Occur if He Does or Does Not Act in Certain Ways. People want sufficient form and pattern in life to be sure that certain satisfactions already enjoyed will be repeatable and will provide a secure springboard for takeoffs in new directions.

The conflict of old loyalties with emerging new loyalties in the case of developing people is bound to create uncertainties, doubts, and hesitations. If people become frustrated and anxious enough, they will do almost anything in a desperate attempt to put some order into apparent chaos or rally around new symbols and abstractions that enable them to identify with a new order that promises to alleviate the uncertainties experienced in the here and now.

In stressing process and change, the desire of people to preserve the *status quo* when it has proved satisfying and rewarding and to protect existing forms against alteration must never be overlooked. This craving for certainty would include the satisfactions that come from the sense of stability provided by our habitual behavior —including much of our social and political behavior.

Human Beings Continuously Seek to Enlarge the Range and Enrich the Quality of Their Satisfactions. Man is engaged in a ceaseless quest to extend the range and improve the quality of his satisfactions through the exercise of his creative and inventive capacities. This is, of course, a basic reason why order of any kind is constantly being upset. Whitehead expressed the point eloquently and repeatedly, for example, in his statements that "the essence of life is to be found in the frustrations of established order" (1938, p. 119) and that "the art of progress is to preserve order amid change, and to preserve change amid order" (1929, p. 515).

The distinguished British philosopher John Macmurray has used the phrase "the self as agent" as the title of his book analyzing the role of action in man's constant search for value satisfactions (1957). In a companion volume, he has noted that ". . . human behavior cannot be understood, but only caricatured, if it is represented as an adaptation to environment" (1961, p. 46). The search for an enlargement of satisfactions in the transactions of living can also be phrased as the *desire for development in a direction*, the desire to do something which will bring a sense of accomplishment as we experience the consequences of successfully carrying out some intention and which will thus give us an occasional feeling that our lives are continuous creations in which we can take an active part. During a conversation in Beirut, a wise man once remarked to me that "people are hungry for new and good experiences."

It seems worthwhile to differentiate this search for value satisfactions into two varieties: (1) value satisfactions that are essentially new, different, more efficient, more reliable, more pleasurable, or more status-producing results of activity along familiar and tried dimensions and (2) value satisfactions that are new in the sense of being emergent, a new quality a person discovers or creates himself for the first time. The latter is exemplified in the child who tries

out and relishes new experiences as his own developmental pattern unfolds. The former variety, like the growth on the limb of a tree, builds people out and extends their range, while the latter, like the new growth at the top of the tree, lets them attain new heights and see new vistas. The satisfactions sought by a newly developing people are at first most likely to be of the former type.

The particular value satisfactions man acquires are the result of learning. Some of the values learned will serve as the operative ideals of a people; others will be chiefly instrumental. People in rich countries have learned to want and to expect many aspects of a good life that less favored people have not yet learned are possibilities. From this point of view, one might say that the competition between social and political systems is a competition in teaching people what to want and what is potentially available to them, and then in proving to them in their own private experience that these wants are best attainable under the system described.

Human Beings Are Creatures of Hope and Are Not Genetically Designed to Resign Themselves. This characteristic of man stems from the characteristic just described: that man is always likely to be dissatisfied and never fully "adapts" to his environment.

Man seems continually to hope that the world he encounters will correspond more and more to his vision of it as he acts within it to carry out his purposes, while the vision itself continuously unfolds in an irreversible direction. The whole process is a never-ending one. It is characteristic of man in his ongoing experience to ask himself, "Where do I go from here?" Only in his more reflective moods does a person ask, "Where did I come from?" or "How did I get this way?" Most of the time, most people who are "plugged into" the changing world around them are future-oriented in their concerns.

Human Beings Have the Capacity to Make Choices and the Desire to Exercise This Capacity. Any mechanical model of man constructed by a psychologist or by anyone else is bound to leave out the crucially important characteristic of man as an "appetitive-perceptive agency." Perceptions are learned and utilized by people to provide prognoses or bets of a variety of kinds to weigh alternative courses of action to achieve purposes. Consciously or without conscious awareness, people are trying to perceive the probable relation between their potential acts and the consequences of these acts to the intentions that constitute their goals.

The human nervous system, including the brain, has the capacity to police its input, to determine what is and what is not significant for it, and to pay attention to and to reinforce or otherwise modify its behavior as it transacts in the occasions of living (Cantril & Livingston, 1963). In this sense, the human being is a participant in, and producer of, his own value satisfactions: People perceive only what is relevant to their purposes and make their choices accordingly.

Human Beings Require Freedom to Exercise the Choices They Are Capable of Making. This characteristic of man related to freedom is deliberately worded as it is, rather than as a blanket statement that "human beings require freedom," since the freedom people want is so relative to their desires and the stage of development they have attained. Human beings, incidentally, apparently require more freedom than other species of animals because of their much greater capacity to move about and to engage in a much wider variety of behavior.

It seems true that maximum freedom is a necessary condition if a highly developed individual is to obtain maximum value satisfaction. It is equally true, as many people have pointed out, that too much freedom too soon can be an unbearable burden and a source of bondage if people, like children, are insufficiently developed to know what to do with it. For freedom clearly involves a learning of responsibility and an ability to take advantage of it wisely.

The concept of freedom is essentially a psychological and not a political concept. It describes an individual's opportunity to make his own choices and to act in accord with them. Psychologically, freedom refers to the freedom to experience more of what is potentially available, the freedom to move about and ahead, to be and to become. Freedom is thus less and less determined and more of a reality as man evolves and develops; it emerges and flowers as people learn what it can mean to them in terms of resolving some frustrations under which they are living.

The authoritarian leadership sometimes required to bring about man's awakening and to start him on the road to his definition of progress appears to go against the grain of the human design once man is transformed into a self-conscious citizen who has the desire to exercise the capacity latent within him. The definition of freedom in the Soviet dictionary, *Ushakov,* as "the recognition of necessity" is valid only during those periods in the lives of individuals or the history of a people when they are willing to let others define what is necessary and to submerge their own individuality.

Human Beings Want to Experience Their Own Identity and Integrity (More Popularly Referred to as the "Need for Personal Dignity"). Every human being craves a sense of his own self-constancy, an assurance of the repeatability of experience in which he is a determining participant. He obtains this from the transactions he has with other individuals.

People develop significances they share with others in their membership and reference groups. If the satisfaction derived from and the significance of participation with others cease to confirm assumptions or to enrich values, then a person's sense of self-constancy becomes shaken or insecure, and his loyalties become formalized and empty or are given up altogether. He becomes alienated or seeks new significances, new loyalties that are more operationally real.

People Want to Experience a Sense of Their Own Worthwhileness. This differentiation is made from the desire for personal identity and integrity to bring out the important relationship between this search for identity and the behavior and attitudes of others toward us. A human being wants to know he is valued by others and that others will somehow show through their behavior that his own behavior and its consequences make some sort of difference to them in ways that give him a sense of satisfaction. When this occurs, not only is a person's sense of identity confirmed, but he also experiences a sense of personal worth and self-respect. The process of extending the sense of self both in space and in time appears also to involve the desire that one's "presence" not be limited merely to the here and now of existence, but extend into larger dimensions. These human cravings seem to be at the root of man's social relationships.

People acquire, maintain, and enrich their sense of worthwhileness only if they at least vaguely recognize the sources of what personal identity they have: their family, their friends and neighbors, their associates or fellow workers, their group ties, or their nation. The social, religious, intellectual, regional, or national loyalties formed play the important role of making it possible for individuals to extend themselves backward into the past and forward into the future and to identify themselves with others who live at more or less remote distances from them. This means the compounding of shared experiences into a bundle that can be conceptualized, felt, or somehow referred to in the here and now of daily living, thus making a person feel a functional part of a more enduring alliance. Man accomplishes such feats of self-extension largely through his capacity to create symbols, images, and myths which provide focal points for identification and self-expansion. After reviewing the lessons from history, Muller noted as one of the "forgotten simplicities" the fact that "men have always been willing to sacrifice themselves for some larger cause, fighting and dying for their family, tribe, or community, with or without hope of eternal reward" (1954, p. 392).

Human Beings Seek Some Value or System of Beliefs to Which They Can Commit Themselves. In the midst of the probabilities and uncertainties that surround them, people want some anchoring points, some certainties, some faith that will serve either as a beacon light to guide them or as a balm to assuage them during the inevitable frustrations and anxieties that living engenders.

People who have long been frustrated and who have searched for means to alleviate their situations are, of course, particularly susceptible to a commitment to a new system of beliefs or an ideology that they feel holds promise of effective action.

Beliefs are confirmed insofar as action based on them brings satisfying consequences, and they are denied with growing skepticism if disastrous results consistently occur because they are followed.

Commitment to a value or belief system becomes more difficult among well-informed and sophisticated people who self-consciously try to reconcile what they believe with what they know and what they know with what they believe. In such circumstances, beliefs become more secular and less important as personal identifications.

Human Beings Want a Sense of Surety and Confidence that the Society of Which They Are a Part Holds out a Fair Degree of Hope that Their Aspirations Will be Fulfilled. If people cannot experience the effectiveness of social mechanisms to accomplish some of the potential goals they aspire to, then obviously their frustrations and anxieties mount, and they search for new means to accomplish aims. On the other hand, they make any sacrifice required to protect a society which they feel is fulfilling their needs but which appears seriously threatened.

It cannot be stressed too strongly that any people will become apathetic toward, or anxious about, ultimate goals they would like to achieve through social organizations if they continually sense a lack of reliability in the means provided to accomplish these goals. Obviously, any society that is to be viable must satisfy basic survival needs, must provide security, must ensure the repeatability of value satisfactions already attained, and must provide for new and emerging satisfactions. The effective society is one that enables individuals to develop personal loyalties and aspirations which overlap with, and are congenial to, social values and loyalties and that at the same time takes full account of the wide range of individual differences that exist.

Such a social organization must, too, become the repository of values, must provide symbols for people's aspirations, and must comprise and contain customs, institutions, laws, economic arrangements, and political forms which enable individuals in various ways to give concrete reference to their values in their day-to-day behavior. If the gap between what society actually provides in terms of effective mechanisms for living and what it purports to provide becomes too great, the vacuum created will sooner or later engender the frustrations that urge people on to seek new social patterns and symbols. Whitehead wrote (1927, p. 88):

> The major advances in civilization are processes which all but wreck the societies in which they occur—like unto an arrow in the hand of a child. The art of free society consists first in the maintenance of the symbolic code; and secondly in fearlessness of revision, to secure that the code serves those purposes which satisfy an enlightened reason. Those societies which cannot combine reverence to their symbols with freedom of revision, must ultimately decay either from anarchy, or from the slow atrophy of a life stifled by useless shadows.

Every social and political system can be regarded as an experiment in the broad perspective of time. Whatever the experiment, the human design will in the long run force any experiment to accommodate to it. This has been the case throughout human history. Few would deny that the varied patterns of experiments going on today hold out more promise of satisfying the human condition for a greater number of people than ever before.

REFERENCES

CANTRIL, H., & LIVINGSTON, W. K. The concept of transaction in psychology and neurology. *Journal of Individual Psychology*, 1963, **19**, 3–16.

MACMURRAY, J. *The self as agent.* New York: Harper & Row, 1957.

MACMURRAY, J. *Persons in relation.* London: Faber, 1961.

MULLER, H. J. *The uses of the past.* New York: Mentor Books, 1954.

MURRAY, H. A., et al. *The assessment of men.* New York: Holt, Rinehart and Winston, 1948.

WHITEHEAD, A. N. *Symbolism: Its meaning and effect.* New York: Macmillan, 1927.

WHITEHEAD, A. N. *Process and reality.* New York: Macmillan, 1929.

WHITEHEAD, A. N. *Modes of thought.* New York: Macmillan, 1938.

Presently: Professor and Head of the
Department of Psychology (since 1960)
and Director of the Center for Advanced
Study in Theoretical Psychology at the
University of Alberta, in Edmonton, Canada.

Education: Doctor of Philosophy in psychology
from the University of Chicago (1951).

Current major activity: Research and
administration of the department and the
new Center for Advanced Study in
Theoretical Psychology.

JOSEPH R. ROYCE

Most rewarding projects: Various efforts concerned with theoretical
integration, such as *Toward a Multi-factor Theory of Behavioral
Variability,* a long range, book length effort to "put psychological meat
on the bare bones of factor theory. Empirically, my lifelong project,
Factorial Studies in Comparative Physiological Psychology."

Future of humanistic psychology: "The crucial question is: Can we
evolve methods of analysis, from *within* the humanistic approach
(and not be forced to scientific reductionism), which will add to our
understanding (not necessarily *prediction*) of man and how he behaves?"

Personal history: Associate Professor at the University of Redlands
in California (1951–1960). Associate, Committee on Experimental
Psychology, National Research Council of Canada (1962–1965).
Visiting Professor at the University of Hawaii (Summer, 1964). Canada
Council Senior Research Fellowship for study and travel in Europe
(1965–1966). Associate Editor, *The Psychological Record* and
Multivariate Behavior Research.

Writings: Dr. Royce has written *The Encapsulated Man: An
Interdisciplinary Essay on the Search for Meaning* (1964) and
edited *Psychology and the Symbol: An Interdisciplinary Symposium*
(1965). His journal articles and chapters in books cover as great a
range as that persistent word "interdisciplinary" in his book
subtitles would promise.

Present chapter: This essay is adapted from a portion of "The Present
Situation in Theoretical Psychology," and was a Distinguished Visiting
Lecturer address which Dr. Royce made to the Educational Testing
Service in September, 1965, and to the Banff Conference on Theoretical
Psychology in April of that year. It has not previously been published.

Chapter 3
JOSEPH R. ROYCE

METAPHORIC KNOWLEDGE AND HUMANISTIC PSYCHOLOGY

THREE BASIC WAYS OF KNOWING

Several recent publications (Royce, 1959; Royce, 1964; Sorokin, 1941) have pointed out that there are three basic ways of knowing: empiricism, rationalism, and metaphorism.[1] While there have been many theories of knowledge expounded in the history of philosophic thought, these three "isms" have been dubbed basic because of their fairly direct dependence upon varieties of psychological cognition, on the one hand, and their epistemological testability, on the other hand. This view can be briefly summarized by reference to Table 3–1.

The implication here is that each of these "isms" represents a legitimate approach to reality but that different criteria for knowing are involved. Rationalism, for example, is dependent primarily upon logical consistency; that is, this approach says that we will accept something as true if it is logically consistent and that we will reject something as false if it is illogical. Empiricism says that we know to the extent that we perceive correctly, and metaphorism says

[1] Previous publications referred to the third way of knowing as "intuitionism" and to the underlying psychological process as "feeling." In the present text I refer to the third way of knowing as "metaphorism" and to the underlying psychological processes as "symbolic" and "intuitive."

Table 3–1 Three basic paths to knowledge

COGNITIVE PROCESSES	CORRESPONDING EPISTEMOLOGIES	EPISTEMOLOGICAL CRITERIA
Thinking	Rationalism	Logical-illogical
Symbolizing and intuiting	Metaphorism	Universal-idiosyncratic
Sensing	Empiricism	Perception-misperception

that knowledge is dependent upon the degree to which symbolic and intuitive cognitions lead us to universal rather than idiosyncratic insights. While each of these cognitive processes may lead to error, the implication is that each is also capable of leading to truth. The possibilities of intuitive error, for example, are readily apparent. Equally obvious, at least to psychologists, are the errors of perception. The errors of the thinking process are probably more subtle, but I have been led to believe that they have plagued the efforts of the logicians and mathematicians. Furthermore, we recognize that none of these psychological processes operates independently of the others. That is, one does not think independently of sensory inputs and symbolic and intuitive processes; nor do we perceive independently of intuition and thinking. In short, the

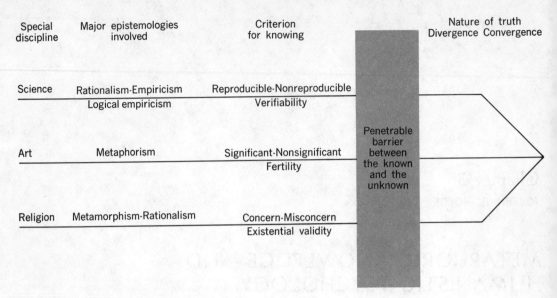

Special discipline	Major epistemologies involved	Criterion for knowing		Nature of truth Divergence Convergence
Science	Rationalism-Empiricism	Reproducible-Nonreproducible		
	Logical empiricism	Verifiability		
Art	Metaphorism	Significant-Nonsignificant	Penetrable barrier between the known and the unknown	
		Fertility		
Religion	Metamorphism-Rationalism	Concern-Misconcern		
		Existential validity		

FIGURE 3–1   Representative special disciplines of knowledge (modified version of Royce, 1964, p. 20).

correspondences indicated in Table 3–1 are oversimplified for purposes of analysis and exposition, but they represent all the known ways that man is enabled to come into contact with reality. The major point I wish to make at this juncture is that man needs to invoke all the available ways of knowing for the best possible grasp of the world but that he tends to be partial to one or the other of these cognitive approaches.

I have developed this theme at some length in a recent book under the title *The Encapsulated Man* (1964), the point being that men of different philosophic commitments (i.e., world views) reflect limited or encapsulated images of reality as a function of their particular epistemological profiles. This state of affairs is particularly apparent if we look at specialists in contrasting disciplines of knowledge, as is indicated in Figure 3–1.

For our purposes I suggest we ignore the right half of this figure and focus on the left-hand portion. It is understood that all three epistemologies are involved in each of the three representative disciplines of knowledge, but it is also clear that each discipline gives greater credence to one or more of

them. The scientist, for example, "thinks," "intuits," "symbolizes," and "senses" as a scientist, but he maximizes the rational and empirical ways of knowing and minimizes metaphoric symbolizing and intuition. Conversely, the artist, who also invokes his entire cognitive repertoire, maximizes the symbolic and intuitive processes at the expense of the thinking and sensory processes. There are, of course, wide variations in the possible permutations and combinations of epistemological profiles; this brief exposition should be taken as relative and typical rather than as absolute and general.

THE EMERGENCE OF HUMANISTIC PSYCHOLOGY

The question "How do we know?" is an old and difficult one for both philosophers and psychologists. But our intuitions, perceptions, and thought regarding symbolic and intuitive knowing are less adequate than our awarenesses of perceptual and rational knowing. Partly because of this and partly because we are products of a sensate-rational culture, we tend to depreciate or at least be wary of the symbol and intuition. On the other hand, we recognize their pervasiveness in all the specialized disciplines of knowledge—the arts, the sciences, and the hu-

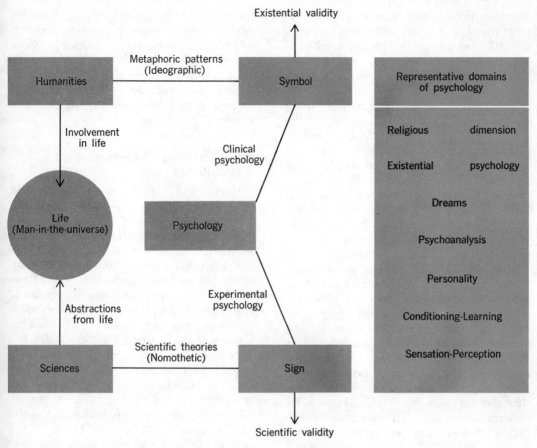

FIGURE 3–2 Psychology at the crossroads.

manities—particularly when we focus on the insights of "great men." The discoveries of Newton and Galileo regarding gravity and the pendulum, the development of new mathematical systems such as the calculus and modern algebra, and the works of art created by a Mozart, a Beethoven, or a Shakespeare reflect a variety of combinations of symbolic and intuitive cognition.

Symbolism and Intuition in Humanistic Psychology In the analysis which follows, I take the position that symbolism and intuition are legitimate ways of knowing, in spite of our ignorance about how they work. Further, I hold that they can be brought into play at any phase of the knowing process and that they have, in fact, manifested themselves to some extent in all domains of psychological study but that their greatest immediate relevance lies in the present emergence of humanistic psychology. Since

humanistic studies are heavily undergirded by the metaphoric epistemology (see Figure 3–1), it follows that any alliance between psychology and the humanities would, by definition, invoke this approach to reality as primary. However, such alliances imply two-way traffic, so that we can anticipate the welding of the empirical-rational epistemologies with the metaphoric approach in coming to grips with psychological problems of a humanistic nature. This means that the symbolic and intuitive insights typical of humanistic thought would eventually be tempered by efforts to provide appropriate empirical tests. More importantly, however, it also implies an openness on the part of the humanistic psychologist to those metaphoric-rational awarenesses which are *not* immediately testable empirically. In another context (Royce, 1965), I develop the theme that the key to the difference between scientific and humanistic psychology lies in the distinction between sign and symbol. This point can be best understood by reference to Figure 3–2.

The purpose of this diagram is to bring out the complementary contributions of the sciences and the humanities to the understanding of life and, particularly, to demonstrate how psychology lies peculiarly at the crossroads between the two cultures. Let us concentrate on the upper half of Figure 3–2. Here we see the humanities as concretely involved *in* life, as opposed to making abstractions *from* the phenomena of life. And, parallel to the ultimate theoretical goal of science, we see that the humanistic disciplines are also ultimately beamed at making overarching statements (i.e., metaphoric-rational) regarding man-in-the-universe. However, and this is the main point, the humanities speak through a symbolic rather than a sign language. Hence, the emerging statements take the form of metaphoric patterns or symbol systems rather than scientific theories, and the truth-giving quality of such statements follows the epistemological criteria of symbols rather than signs (e.g., see Figure 3–1 and note the "fertility" criterion of art and the criterion of existential validity for religion). As used in this context, the essence of the sign-symbol distinction is that the sign reveals a one-to-one correspondence (that is, *A* means *B*, and *not C, D*, and *E*), whereas the symbol provides a one-to-many relationship (that is, *A* may mean *B, C, D*, or *E* or any combination thereof). The multiple meanings of the symbol make the task of empirical analysis extremely difficult, but they open up dimensions of reality which remain unavailable to sign language (Royce, 1965).

The challenge for the humanistic psychologist lies here in the attempt to tap these symbolic dimensions of reality by invoking the knowledge-giving tools of the humanistic trade, on the one hand, and by doing all that is possible to provide empirical tests for whatever is so revealed, on the other hand. But this must be done without the error of reductionism—that is, throwing out as invalid those humanistic insights which are *not* amenable or reducible to empirical confirmation. If the reductionistic error is committed, we simply will not have a humanistic psychology, for we will have reduced it to a (mechanically) scientific or empirical psychology.

CHARACTERIZING A HUMANISTIC PSYCHOLOGY

What might a humanistic psychology look like? It is, of course, too early to tell, but I shall point to several possibilities. As a start, I suggest we supplement the usual schematic conception of the organism-in-the-environment with a conception of man-in-the-universe. Such a schematic view allows us to cast the more philosophic aspects of man's behavior within the traditional definition of psychology as involving organism-environment interactions. The only difference is that we are now operating at the more cosmic level of man-in-the-universe. This business of painting man with such a big brush is typical of the humanistic approach. Also characteristic of the humanities is the effort to unmask the universal by way of the concrete case. Our previous discussion must be kept in mind at this juncture, namely, that such universal-concrete efforts are typically conveyed symbolically rather than via signs. With this as a background, we can now take a look at Figure 3–3.

This diagram shows psychology as the study of man and his behavior rather than as the science of organisms. The purpose behind this heretical, definitional shift is to legitimize symbolic and intuitive cognition (Royce, 1960; Royce, 1965). Such a definition, which appears to be a reactionary move, is actually a forward-looking suggestion in the twentieth century because it demands that we readmit humanistic studies as a way to gain psychological knowledge. Now that we have empiricism as the core epistemology undergirding our discipline, there would seem to be little danger that psychology will regress to a pre-Wundtian stage by making such a move. The solid lines indicate alliances with several humanistic disciplines (shown in solid-line rectangles), the most relevant lying closest to

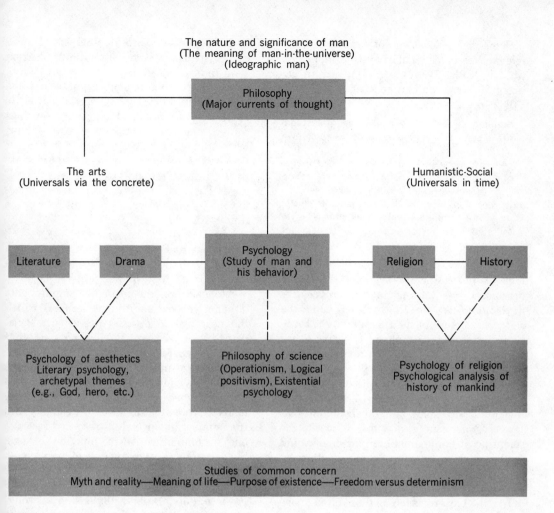

The nature and significance of man
(The meaning of man-in-the-universe)
(Ideographic man)

Philosophy
(Major currents of thought)

The arts
(Universals via the concrete)

Humanistic-Social
(Universals in time)

Literature — Drama — Psychology (Study of man and his behavior) — Religion — History

Psychology of aesthetics
Literary psychology,
archetypal themes
(e.g., God, hero, etc.)

Philosophy of science
(Operationism, Logical
positivism), Existential
psychology

Psychology of religion
Psychological analysis of
history of mankind

Studies of common concern
Myth and reality—Meaning of life—Purpose of existence—Freedom versus determinism

FIGURE 3–3   Psychology and the humanities.

psychology at the center. The broken lines lead to possible areas of humanistic study which are a result of such alliances. The most obvious examples of humanistic study are those indicated out of the alliance with philosophy: philosophy of science, operationism, logical positivism, and existential psychology (for examples of the last, see Royce, 1962, and May, 1961). In other words, philosophy of science and existentialism are seen as the most important currents of thought in contemporary philosophical and theoretical psychology (Royce, 1964). Similarly, the psychology of religion and the psychology of aesthetics are seen as two examples of studies which have resulted from alliances with the indicated humanistic-social and arts disciplines, respectively.

Psychology and the Arts   The defense for the priority given to drama is that its action as revealed on a stage (or on film, on TV, or through another medium) is capable of disclosing a microcosm of man living out his life in the everyday world. It is, in a very real sense, the most behavioral of the art forms. It is also one of the more time-compressed forms of artistic expression. These two points, combined with the fact that the dramatic form ordinarily involves a beginning, a middle, and an end, with a buildup to a conflict which is resolved, provide the psychologist with material which simulates completed or total "lives." Similar material in literature is not as obviously behavioral.

Some of Maslow's recent work is directly relevant here, particularly his thinking on what he calls "being cognition." In an entirely different context, he says, for example (1962, pp. 62–64):

> Sometimes the safety needs can almost entirely bend the cognitive needs to their own anxiety-allaying purposes. The anxiety-free person can be more bold and more courageous . . . anxiety kills curiosity and exploration . . . especially when anxiety is extreme. . . . It seems quite clear that the need to know, if we are to understand it well, must be integrated with fear of knowing, with needs for safety and security.

I see the possibility for a long-range dialogue between the literary picture of man presented by Golding in his provocative novel *Lord of the Flies* (1954) and the scientific picture of man painted by a traditional scientific psychology. It seems to me that complete psychological analyses of literary products such as *Lord of the Flies*, analyzed and empirically investigated à la Maslow and others, could help provide valid insights about man and his behavior patterns. The ensuing dialogue between the scientific and humanistic approaches would further evoke an eventual synthesis, thereby leading to greater understanding between the two.

Mythic patterns such as those cited above have recurred throughout recorded history and have transcended geographical and cultural boundaries as well. Continuing failure on the part of psychologists to study such a rich storehouse of psychologically laden material borders on the foolhardy in the name of scientific purism. Furthermore, the typical sexual reductionism of Freudian psychoanalysis is simply not up to the requirements of the task, and while Jungian analysis may be more promising, contemporary psychologists have not yet given serious thought and effort to the possibilities at hand. For example, of the 4,500 items listed in Kiell's (1963) recent bibliography on psychology and literature, practically all of them involve some kind of psychoanalytic interpretation. Further, possibly as many as one-third of the drama listings deal with *Hamlet*. The majority of the references to psychology per

se concern a very prosaic analysis of audience response to some dramatic production —on radio, on TV, or in films—i.e., a problem in the measurement of public opinion and/or attitude change. There is very little indication that standard approaches, such as content analysis or projective testing, have been adapted for study in this domain or that new techniques of analysis, appropriate to the available material, have been developed. There is, in short, a sad lack of imaginative inquiry in what we might refer to as literary psychology.[2]

Psychology and Religion A similar concern for the symbolic is required for investigation in the psychology of religion, for here we are focusing on the ultimate commitments of man, those commitments around which the meaning of one's existence is built. Penetrating analyses of value, myth, and that which is existentially "real" are all necessary for vital investigation in this area. The typical psychological studies in this area are concerned with such matters as how many people attend church on Sunday and the number of conversions recorded for various denominations as a function of age. Such studies seem to bypass religion almost completely.

A humanistic psychology of religion would not lose Tillich's depth dimension; it would not lose the heart of that which is religious in the name of ease of observation and measurement. In short, contrary to the present dominant positivistic *Zeitgeist*, the humanistic psychological study of religion would deal in whatever way it could with the subjective meaning of life—with that which is existentially valid. Such an approach would begin with ontological anxiety for example, rather than focusing on the easier neurotic anxiety. It takes more "courage to be" (Tillich, 1952) in the face of ontological as opposed to neurotic anxiety for the simple reason that there is no illusion of "cure" in the case of the former variety. The traditional scientific approach to the psychological study of religion, one of the most important and ubiquitous characteristics of mankind, has not yet pene-

[2] Some essays in Part 6 of this volume, The Reunion of Psychology and the Humanities, offer what it is hoped are more imaginative inquiries of the type the author calls for. [Editor]

trated very deeply. It seems to me that the humanistic approach is more likely to probe the "inner man"[3] because of its greater willingness to deal with the fullness of subjective experience via an all-encompassing phenomenology as opposed to a narrow, albeit more rigorous, empiricism.

Psychology and History If we assume, as it seems reasonable to do, that the events of human history are a result of the interdependence between the individual and the culture of his time, then it follows that a more explicit psychological analysis of history is required than has been manifested to date. Because of the overwhelming complexities of life, scholars in all fields oversimplify their domains of study in order to get launched. This approach, however, eventually reveals its simplistic inadequacies. Thus, the study of history has not been of a psychocultural order, but rather it has been dominated by a kind of abstract history of political, economic, and military events —"as if" there were no human organisms generating these changes. There are indications that a psychohistorical alliance would lead to a more complete understanding of the evolution of the human psyche, on the one hand, and to a better understanding of man through time, on the other hand. Toynbee (1946 & 1947), for example, brings psychology to bear in his analyses of the rise and fall of civilizations. A central plank in his approach is the importance of the symbol and the myth as unconscious manifestations of the human spirit. At this juncture his thinking merges with Jung's in their claim that "progress" is crucially dependent upon the validity of symbolic commitments —especially those carrying religious implications. For example, in his concept of "challenge and response," Toynbee indicates that the response to a challenge must eventually become a religious one if the civilization is to survive. Further, Toynbee takes this analysis to the level of the individual personality, particularly the "creative minority" (i.e., the leading artists, scientists, and thinkers of a given epoch), citing this as the source of new values for meeting the challenge of continued existence.

A psychological history is potentially the most empirical of the several humanistic alliances briefly described above, for it can be studied more easily than any of the others within the context of social psychology. However, it does suffer from the fact that behavior as such cannot be observed directly, that it can only be reconstructed from the records and artifacts of the past. Nevertheless, the recent book by Barbu (1960) speaks well for the mutual enrichment which should follow the union of the two disciplines.[4]

SUMMARY AND CONCLUSIONS

Briefly recapitulating, what I have tried to do is assess the present situation in contemporary theoretical psychology in terms of underlying epistemologies (i.e., empiricism, rationalism, and metaphorism). Because of twentieth-century encapsulation within the epistemology of empiricism, contemporary man finds it difficult to be open to symbolic and intuitive cognition.[5] Psychology, as part of the contemporary sensate culture, and psychologists, as part of the contemporary cultural *Zeitgeist*, can also be characterized as superempirical, somewhat at the expense of the rational, and almost completely at the expense of the metaphoric, approaches to reality.

While intuition is involved at all phases of the scientific enterprise, it is minimized as final judge in science. However, metaphoric knowledge is crucial in the humanistic disciplines, and it would assume a dominant position in a humanistic psychology. The possibilities for the evolution of such a development within an expanded definition of psychology were pointed to but not elaborated in detail. Priority was given to alliances with the humanistic disciplines of philosophy, drama, religion, literature, and history.

[4] In Chapter 30, Wyatt explores some of the implications to which Royce here draws our attention. [Editor]

[5] Harman, in Chapter 33, expands on some of the startling implications of this recognition. [Editor]

[3] For a provocative entree to the implied possibilities, see the interdisciplinary round-table discussion edited by Havens (in press).

REFERENCES

BARBU, Z. *Problems of historical psychology*. New York: Grove Press, 1960.

GOLDING, W. *Lord of the flies*. London: Faber, 1954.

HAVENS, J. (Ed.) *A dialogue on religion and psychology*. Princeton, N.J.: Van Nostrand, in press.

KIELL, N. *Psychoanalysis, psychology, and literature: A bibliography*. Madison, Wis.: Univer. of Wisconsin Press, 1963.

MASLOW, A. H. *Toward a psychology of being*. Princeton, N.J.: Van Nostrand, 1962.

MAY, R. (Ed.) *Existential psychology*. New York: Random House, 1961.

ROYCE, J. R. The search for meaning. *American Scientist*, 1959, **47**, 515–535.

ROYCE, J. R. Heretical thoughts on the definition of psychology. *Psychological Reports*, 1960, **8**, 11–14.

ROYCE, J. R. Psychology, existentialism, and religion. *Journal of General Psychology*, 1962, **66**, 3–16.

ROYCE, J. R. *The encapsulated man: An interdisciplinary essay on the search for meaning*. Princeton, N.J.: Van Nostrand, 1964.

ROYCE, J. R. (Ed.) *Psychology and the symbol: An interdisciplinary symposium*. New York: Random House, 1965.

SOROKIN, P. A. *The crisis of our age*. New York: Dutton, 1941.

TILLICH, P. W. *The courage to be*. New Haven, Conn.: Yale Univer. Press, 1952.

TOYNBEE, A. J. *A study of history*. London: Oxford Univer. Press, 1946 & 1947. 2-vol. abridgment.

Presently: Fellow of the Royal Society of Literature.

Most rewarding current activity: "Writing another book."

Most rewarding project: "See above, but for 'rewarding' substitute 'painful.' "

Future of humanistic psychology: "The realization that organisms are many-leveled, self-regulating hierarchic structures, open-ended at both apex and base (base: subatomic level; apex: self-awareness), and that this openness represents freedom, although any attempt to define freedom in logical terms leads to infinite regress."

ARTHUR KOESTLER

Personal history: Born in Budapest, from 1940 on Mr. Koestler has been a resident of England and has become a naturalized citizen of that country. He has worked as a field hand in Palestine, as an architect, as a lemonade vender in Haifa, for a tourist agency, on a survey crew, and as a foreign correspondent. In the last capacity he was assigned to many parts of the world, was the only press representative on the Graf Zeppelin's Arctic expedition, and covered the Republican side in the Spanish Civil War. He was imprisoned by the Spanish Nationalists, by the French, and by the English. His disillusionment with communism has been brilliantly recorded in his novel *Darkness at Noon* (1940) and in his autobiographical books *Arrow in the Blue* (1952) and *The Invisible Writing* (1954).

About ten years ago, Mr. Koestler left writing on political topics and devoted himself once again to the field of his early interest: science and psychology. Mr. Koestler was a Fellow of the Center for Advanced Study in the Behavioral Sciences at Stanford (1965), and he proudly records that he is a "member of the Institute of Patentees and Inventors and Vice-president of the National Dog Owners Association."

Writings: Mr. Koestler's bibliography contains five novels, five volumes of autobiography, one book on the theater, and nine books of essays. In addition to those already mentioned, some of the better known of his works include *The Gladiators* (1939), *Dialogue with Death* (1938), *The Yogi and the Commissar* (1945), *The Sleepwalkers* (1959), *The Lotus and the Robot* (1960), and *The Act of Creation* (1964).

Present chapter: The substance of this essay was originally presented as a lecture given at the Poetry Center in New York City, May 1, 1966. It was intended for "a lay audience, which made it necessary to avoid technical terms and to oversimplify on occasion."

Chapter 4
ARTHUR KOESTLER

THE THREE DOMAINS OF CREATIVITY

This chapter attempts to give a condensed outline of a theory I have set out in detail in a recent book (1964) and to carry that theory the next step. The proposition I shall submit is, in a nutshell, that the conscious and unconscious processes which enter into all three forms of creative activity have a basic pattern in common. And when I speak of *three* forms of creativity, I mean the domains of artistic originality, scientific discovery, and comic inspiration. I believe that all creative activity falls into one or another of these three categories or, more frequently, into some combination of them. If you speak, for instance, of cooking as "creative," you automatically imply that cooking is either an art or a science or both.

As a first step toward describing that pattern, let us try something simple like this: The creative act consists in combining previously unrelated structures in such a way that you get more out of the emergent whole than you have put in. This sounds like making a *perpetuum mobile*, and in a sense it is, because mental evolution, like biological evolution, seems to contradict the second law of thermodynamics, which contends that the universe is running down as if afflicted by metal fatigue. But we will not go into this; instead, let me illustrate by a few schoolbook examples what I mean by combining two previously unrelated structures.

ASSOCIATION AND BISOCIATION

The motions of the tides have been known to man since time immemorial. So have the motions of the moon. But the idea to relate the two, the idea that the tides were due to the attraction of the moon, occurred, as far as we know, for the first time to a German astronomer in the seventeenth century, and when Galileo read about it, he laughed it off as an occult fancy (Santillana, 1953, p. 469). Moral: The more familiar each of the previously unrelated structures are, the more striking the new synthesis and the more obvious it seems in the driver's mirror of hindsight.

The history of science is a history of marriages between ideas which were previously strangers to each other, and frequently considered incompatible. Lodestones —magnets—were known in antiquity as some curiosity of nature. In the Middle Ages they were used for two purposes: as navigators' compasses and as a means to attract an estranged wife back to her husband. Equally well known were the curious properties of amber, which, when rubbed, acquires the virtue of attracting flimsy objects. The Greek word for amber is *elektron*, but the Greeks were not much interested in electricity, nor were the Middle Ages. For nearly two thousand years, electricity and magnetism were considered separate phenomena, in no way related to each other. In 1820, Hans Christian Oersted discovered that an electric current flowing through a wire deflected a compass needle which happened to be lying on his table. At that moment the two contexts began to fuse into one—electromagnetism—creating a kind of chain reaction which is still continuing and gaining in momentum; forever amber.

From Pythagoras, who combined arithmetic and geometry, to Einstein, who unified energy and matter in a single sinister equation, the pattern is always the same. The Latin word *cogito* comes from *coagitare*, "to shake together." The creative act does not create something out of nothing, like the God of the Old Testament; it combines, reshuffles, and relates already existing but hitherto separate ideas, facts, frames of perception, associative contexts. This act of cross-fertilization—or self-fertilization within a single brain—seems to be the essence of creativity. I have proposed for it the term *bisociation*. It is not a pretty word, but it helps us to make a distinction between the sudden leap of the creative act and the more normal, more pedestrian, associative routines of thinking.

The difference between the two could be described as follows. Orderly thinking (as distinct from daydreaming) is always controlled by certain rules of the game. In the psychological laboratory, the experimenter lays down the rule: "Name opposites." Then he says, "dark," and the subject promptly says, "light." But if the rule is "synonyms," then the subject will associate "dark" with "black" or "night" or "shadow." To talk of stimuli in a vacuum is meaningless; what response a stimulus will evoke depends on the game we are playing at the time.

But we do not live in laboratories where the rules of the game are laid down by explicit orders; in normal life, the rules control our thinking unconsciously—and there's the rub. When talking, the laws of grammar and syntax function below the level of awareness, in the gaps between the words. So do certain simple rules of common or garden-variety logic and of courtesy and convention, and also the complex and specialized rules which we call "frames of reference" or "universes of discourse" or "thinking in terms of" this or that—of phys-iological explanations or ethical value judgments. All thinking is playing a game according to fixed rules and more or less flexible strategies. The game of chess allows you a vast number of strategic choices among the moves permitted by the rules, but there is a limit to them. There are hopeless situations in chess when the most subtle strategies will not save you—short of offering your opponent a jumbo-sized Martini. Now in fact there is no rule in chess preventing you from offering your opponent a Martini. But making a person drunk while remaining sober oneself is a different sort of game with a different context. Combining the two games is a bisociation. In other words, associative routine means thinking according to a given set of rules, on a single plane, as it were. The bisociative act means combining two different sets of rules, to live on several planes at once.

THREE KINDS OF REACTIONS

I do not mean to belittle the value of law-abiding routines. They lend coherence and stability to behavior and structured order to thought. But they have their obvious limitations. For one thing, every game tends to become monotonous after awhile and fails to satisfy the artist's craving for self-expression and the scientist's search for explanations. In the second place, the world moves on, and new problems arise which cannot be solved within the conventional frames of reference by applying to them the accepted rules of the game. Then a crisis occurs: The position on the scientist's checkerboard is blocked; the artist's vision is blurred; the search is on, the fumbling and groping for that happy combination of ideas—of lodestone and amber—which will lead to the new synthesis.

The Aha Reaction Karl Buhler has coined a word for that moment of truth, the flash of illumination, when bits of the puzzle suddenly click into place. He calls it the *Aha* experience. One may regard it as a synonym for the "Eureka!" cry. Imagine it written on a blackboard, thus:

| | *Aha* | |

We shall see in a moment the reason for this display. There is an empty panel on each side—for the *Aha* response represents only *one* type of reaction after the bisociative click. There are others. Let me tell my favorite anecdote:

> A nobleman at the court of Louis XV had unexpectedly returned from a journey and, on entering his wife's boudoir, found her in the arms of a bishop. After a short hesitation, the nobleman walked calmly to the window and went through the motions of blessing the people in the street.
> "What are you doing?" cried the anguished wife.
> "Monseigneur is performing my functions," replied the nobleman, "so I am performing his."

Well, some readers will be kind enough to laugh; let us call this the *Haha* reaction:[1]

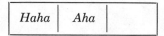

The Haha Reaction

The Logic of Laughter Now let us inquire into the difference between the *Haha* and the *Aha* reactions. Why do we laugh? Let me try to analyze first the intellectual and then the emotional aspect of this odd reaction. The nobleman's behavior is both unexpected and perfectly logical—but of a logic not usually applied to this type of situation. It is the logic of the division of labor, where the rule of the game is the *quid pro quo*, the give-and-take. But we expected, of course, that his reactions would be governed by a quite different logic or rule of the game. It is the interaction between these two mutually exclusive associative contexts which produces the comic effect. It compels us to perceive the situation at the same time in two self-consistent but habitually incompatible frames of reference; it makes us function on two wavelengths simultaneously, as it were. While this unusual condition lasts, the event is not, as is normally the case, perceived in a single frame of reference but is bisociated with two.

But the unusual condition does not last

[1] I owe the term *"Haha* reaction" to Dr. Brennig James's paper "The Function of Jokes" (unpublished), which he kindly sent me.

for long. The act of discovery leads to a lasting synthesis, a *fusion* of the two previously unrelated frames of reference; in the comic bisociation you have a *collision* between incompatible frames which for a brief moment cross each other's path. But whether the frames are compatible or not, whether they will collide or merge, depends on subjective factors, on the attitudes of the audience— for, after all, the colliding or merging takes place in the audience's heads. The history of science abounds with examples of discoveries greeted with howls of laughter because they seemed to be a marriage of incompatibles—until the marriage bore fruit and the alleged incompatibility of the partners turned out to derive from prejudice. The humorist, on the other hand, deliberately chooses discordant codes of behavior or universes of discourse to expose their hidden incongruities in the resulting clash. Comic discovery is paradox stated—scientific discovery is paradox resolved.

Let me return for a moment to our poor nobleman blessing the crowd through the window. His gesture was a truly original inspiration. If he had followed the conventional rules of the game, he would have had to beat up or kill the bishop. But at the court of Louis XV, assassinating a monseigneur would have been considered, if not exactly a crime, still in very bad taste. It simply could not be done; the chessboard was blocked. To solve the problem, that is, to save his face and at the same time to humiliate his opponent, the nobleman had to bring into the situation a second frame of reference, governed by different rules of the game, and combine it with the first. All original comic invention is a creative act, a malicious discovery.

The Emotional Dynamics of Laughter The emphasis is on malicious, and this brings us from the *logic* of humor to the *emotional factor* in the *Haha* reaction. When the expert humorist tells an anecdote, he creates a certain tension which mounts as the narrative progresses. But it never reaches its expected climax. The punch line acts like a guillotine which cuts across the logical development of the situation; it debunks our dramatic expectations, and the tension becomes redundant and is exploded in laughter. To put it differently, laughter disposes of the overflow of emotion which has become pointless, is denied by reason, and has to be somehow worked off along physiological channels of least resistance.[2]

I shall not bore you with physiological explanations because if you look at the coarse and brutal merriment in a tavern scene by Hogarth or Rawlinson, you realize at once that the revelers are working off their surplus of adrenalin by contractions of the face muscles, slapping of thighs, and explosive exhalations of breath from the half-closed glottis. The emotions worked off in laughter are aggression, sexual gloating, conscious or unconscious sadism—all operating through the sympathicoadrenal system. On the other hand, when you look at a clever *New Yorker* cartoon, Homeric laughter yields to an amused and rarefied smile; the ample flow of adrenalin has been distilled into a grain of Attic salt. Think, for instance, of that classic definition: "What is a sadist?" "A person who is kind to a masochist."

The word "witticism" is derived from "wit" in its original sense of "ingenuity." The clown is brother to the sage; their domains are continuous, without a sharp dividing line. As we move from the coarse toward the higher forms of humor, the joke shades into epigram and riddle, the comic simile into the discovery of hidden analogies; and the emotions involved show a similar transition. The emotive voltage discharged in coarse laughter is aggression robbed of its purpose; the tension discharged in the *Aha* reaction is derived from an intellectual challenge. It snaps at the moment when the penny drops—when we have solved the riddle hidden in the *New Yorker* cartoon, in a brainteaser, or in a scientific problem.

The Ah Reaction Let me repeat, the two domains of humor and discovery form a con-

[2] For a review of the theories on laughter, see Koestler, 1964, Chaps. 1 and 2; also Koestler, 1949, part 1 and appendix 2.

tinuum. As we travel across it, from left to center, so to speak, the emotional climate gradually changes from the malice of the jester to the detached objectivity of the sage. If we now continue the journey in the same direction, we find equally gradual transitions into a third domain, that of the artist. The artist hints rather than states, and he poses riddles. So we get a symmetrically reversed transition toward the other end of the spectrum, from highly intellectualized art forms toward the more sensual and emotive, ending in the thought-free beatitude of the oceanic feeling—the cloud of unknowing.

But how does one define the emotional climate of art? How does one classify the emotions which give rise to the experience of beauty? If you leaf through textbooks of experimental psychology, you will not find much mention of it. When behaviorists use the word "emotion," they nearly always refer to hunger, sex, rage, and fear and to the related effects of the release of adrenalin. They have no explanations to offer for the curious reaction one experiences when listening to Mozart or looking at the ocean or reading for the first time John Donne's *Holy Sonnets*. Nor will you find in the textbooks a description of the physiological processes accompanying the reaction: the moistening of the eyes, perhaps a quiet overflow of the lachrymal glands, the catching of one's breath, followed by a kind of rapt tranquillity, the draining of all tensions. Let us call this the *Ah* reaction and thus complete our trinity.

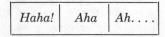

| Haha! | Aha | Ah.... |

Laughter and weeping, the Greek masks of comedy and tragedy, mark the two extremes of a continuous spectrum; both are overflow reflexes, but they are in every respect physiological opposites. Laughter is mediated by the sympathicoadrenal branch of the autonomous nervous system, weeping by the parasympathetic branch. The first tends to galvanize the body into action; the second tends toward passivity and catharsis. Watch how you breathe when you laugh: long, deep intakes of air, followed by bursts of exhalatory puffs—"Ha, ha, ha." In weeping, you do the opposite: short, gasping inspirations—sobs—are followed by long, sighing expirations—"a-a-h, aah" (cf. Koestler, 1964, pp. 271, 284; and, for a bibliography on the psychology and physiology of weeping, pp. 725–728).

SELF-ASSERTION AND SELF-TRANSCENDENCE

In keeping with this, the emotions which overflow in the *Ah* reaction are the direct opposites of those exploded in laughter. The latter belong to the familiar adrenergic hunger-rage-fear category; let us call them the *aggressive-defensive* or self-assertive emotions. Their opposites we might call the *self-transcending* or participatory or integrative emotions. They are epitomized in what Freud called the "oceanic feeling": When you listen to a Bach toccata thundering through the cathedral, you experience that expansion and depersonalization of awareness in which the self seems to dissolve like a grain of salt in a lot of water.

This class of emotions shows a wide range of variety. They may be joyous or sad, tragic or lyrical; but they have a common denominator: the feeling of participation in an experience which transcends the boundaries of the self. That higher entity, of which the self feels a part, to which it surrenders its identity, may be nature, God, the anima mundi, the magic of forms, or the ocean of sound.

The self-assertive emotions are expressed in bodily actions; the self-transcending emotions operate through the passive processes of empathy, rapport, projection, and identification. In laughter, tension is suddenly exploded, emotion debunked; in weeping, it is drained away in a gradual process which does not break the continuity of mood. The self-transcending emotions do not tend toward action but toward quiescence and catharsis. Respiration and pulse rate are slowed down; "entrancement" is a step toward the trancelike states induced by contemplative techniques or drugs. The self-transcending emotions cannot be consummated by any specific, voluntary action. You cannot take the mountain panorama home with you; you cannot merge with the infinite by any exertion of the body. To be "overwhelmed" by awe and wonder, "enrap-

tured" by a smile, "entranced" by beauty—each of these verbs expresses a passive surrender. The surplus of emotion cannot be worked off in action; it can be consummated only in internal, visceral and glandular processes (Koestler, 1964, pp. 285–300).

The participatory or self-transcending tendencies, these stepchildren of psychology, are as powerful and deeply rooted in man's nature as his self-assertive drives. Freud and Piaget, among others, have emphasized the fact that the very young child does not differentiate between ego and environment. The nourishing breast appears to it as a more intimate possession than the toes of its own body. It is aware of events but not of itself as a separate entity. It lives in a state of mental symbiosis with the outer world, a continuation of the biological symbiosis in the womb. The universe is focused in the self, and the self *is* the universe—a condition which Piaget called "protoplasmic consciousness." It may be likened to a liquid, fluid universe, traversed by dynamic currents, the rise and fall of physiological needs causing minor storms which come and go without leaving solid traces. Gradually the floods recede, and the first islands of objective reality emerge; the contours grow firmer and sharper; the islands grow into continents; the dry territories of reality are mapped out; but side by side with it, the liquid world coexists, surrounding it, interpenetrating it by canals and inland lakes, the vestigial relics of the erstwhile symbiotic communion. Here, then, we have the origin of that oceanic feeling which the artist and the mystic strive to recapture on a higher level of development, at a higher turn of the spiral.

ART AND SELF-TRANSCENDENCE

Children and primitives are apt to confuse dream and reality; they not only believe in miracles but also believe themselves capable of performing them. When the medicine man disguises himself as the rain god, he produces rain. Drawing a picture of a slain bison assures a successful hunt. This is the ancient unitary source out of which the ritual dance and song, the mystery plays of the Achaeans, and the calendars of the Babylonian priest-astronomers were derived. The shadows in Plato's cave are symbols of man's loneliness; the paintings in the Altamira caves are symbols of his magic powers.

We have traveled a long way from Altamira and Lascaux, but the artist's inspirations and the scientist's intuitions are still fed by that same unitary source—though by now we should rather call it an underground river. Wishes do not displace mountains, but in our dreams they still do. Symbiotic consciousness is never completely defeated but merely relegated underground to those unconscious levels in the mental hierarchy where the boundaries of the ego are still fluid and blurred—as blurred as the distinction between the actor and the hero whom he impersonates and with whom the spectator identifies. The actor on the stage is himself and somebody else at the same time —he is both the dancer and the rain god.

Dramatic illusion is the coexistence in the spectator's mind of two universes which are logically incompatible; his awareness, suspended between the two planes, exemplifies the bisociative process in its most striking form. All the more striking because he produces physical symptoms—palpitations, sweating, or tears—in response to the perils of a Desdemona whom he *knows* to exist merely as a shadow on the TV screen or as dry printer's ink in the pages of a book. Yet let Othello but get the hiccups, and instead of coexistence between the two planes juxtaposed in the spectator's mind, you get collision between them. Comic impersonation produces the *Haha* reaction because the parodist arouses aggression and malice; dramatic stagecraft achieves the suspension of disbelief, the coexistence of incompatible planes, because it induces the spectator to identify. It excites the self-transcending and inhibits or neutralizes the self-assertive emotions. Even when fear and anger are aroused in the spectator, these are vicarious emotions, derived from his identification with the hero, which in itself is a self-transcending act. Vicarious emotions aroused in this manner carry a dominant element of sympathy, which facilitates catharsis in con-

formity with the Aristotelian definition— "through incidents arousing horror and pity to accomplish the purgation of such emotions." Art is a school of self-transcendence.

We thus arrive at a further generalization: *The* Haha *reaction signals the collision of bisociated contexts; the* Aha *reaction signals their fusion; and the* Ah *reaction signals their juxtaposition.*

This difference is reflected in the quasicumulative progression of science through a series of successive mergers, compared with the quasi-timeless character of art in its continuous restatement of basic patterns of experience in changing idioms. I said "quasi" because it can be shown that this, too, is a matter of degrees, because the progress of science is not cumulative in the strict sense. It is moving in a dizzy, zigzag course rather than in a straight line (Kuhn, 1962; Popper, 1959). On the other hand, the development of a given art form over a period of time often displays a cumulative progression (Gombrich, 1962). I shall return to this in a moment, but first let me briefly mention a few more types of the combinatorial activities which enter into the fabric of art.

BISOCIATIVE STRUCTURES IN ART

When we listen to poetry, two frames of reference interact in our minds: one governed by meaning, the other by rhythmic patterns of sound. Moreover, the two frames operate on two different levels of awareness: the first in broad daylight, the other much deeper down. The rhythmic beat of poetry is designed, in the words of Yeats, "to lull the mind into a waking trance." Rhythmic pulsation is a fundamental characteristic of life; our ready responses to it arise from the depths of the nervous system, from those archaic strata which reverberate to the shaman's drum and which make us particularly receptive to, and suggestible by, messages which arrive in a rhythmic pattern or are accompanied by such a pattern.

The rhyme has equally ancient roots. It repeats the last syllable of a line. Now the repetition of syllables is a conspicuous phenomenon at the very origins of language. The young child is addicted to babbling, "obble-gobble," "humpty-dumpty," and so on. In primitive languages, words like "kala-

kala" or "moku-moku" abound. Closely related to it is association by pure sound. The rhyme is in fact nothing but a glorified pun —two strings of ideas tied together in a phonetic knot. Its ancient origins are revealed in the punning mania of children and in certain forms of mental disorder and in the frequent recurrence of puns in dreams. "What could be moister than the tears of an oyster?" The statement that the oyster is a wet creature and that therefore its tears must be particularly wet would not make much of an impression, but when meaning is bisociated with sound, there is magic. This is what I meant when I said that routine thinking involves a single matrix, whereas creative thinking always involves more than one plane. Needless to say, it is difficult to identify with an oyster, so the reaction will be *Haha,* not *Ah.*

Thus rhythm and meter, rhyme and euphony, are not artificial ornaments of language but combinations of contemporary, sophisticated frames of reference with archaic and emotionally more powerful games of the mind. In other words, creative activity always implies a *temporary regression* to these archaic levels, while a simultaneous process goes on in parallel on the highest, most articulate and critical level: the poet is like a skin diver with a breathing tube.

The same applies, of course, to poetic imagery. Visual thinking is an earlier form of mental activity than thinking in verbal concepts; we dream mostly in pictures and visual symbols. It has been said that scientific discovery consists in seeing an analogy where nobody has seen one before. When in the Song of Songs, Solomon compared the Shulamite's neck to a tower of ivory, he saw an analogy which nobody had seen before; when Harvey compared the heart of a fish to a mechanical pump, he did the same; and when the caricaturist draws a nose like a cucumber, he again does just that. In fact, all combinatorial, bisociative patterns are trivalent—they can enter the service of humor, discovery, or art, as the case may be.

Let me give you another example of this trivalence. Man has always looked at nature by superimposing a second frame on the retinal image—mythological, anthromorphic, scientific frames. The artist sees in terms of his medium—stone, clay, charcoal, pigment—and in terms of his preferential emphasis on contours or surfaces, stability or motion, curves or cubes. So, of course, does the caricaturist, only his motives are different. And so does the scientist. A geographical map has the same relation to a landscape that a character sketch has to a face. Every diagram or model, every schematic or symbolic representation of physical or mental processes is an unemotional caricature of reality—at least unemotional in the sense that the bias is not of an obvious kind, although some models of the human mind as a conditioned-reflex automaton seem to be crude caricatures inspired by unconscious bias.

In the language of behaviorist psychology, we would have to say that Cézanne, glancing at a landscape, receives a stimulus, to which he responds by putting a dab of paint on the canvas, and that is all there is to it. But in fact the two activities take place on two different planes. The stimulus comes from one environment, the distant landscape. The response acts on a different environment, a square surface of 10 by 15 inches. The two environments obey two different sets of laws. An isolated brushstroke does not represent an isolated detail in the landscape. There are no point-to-point correspondences between the two planes; each obeys a different rule of the game. The artist's vision is bifocal, just as the poet's voice is bivocal, as he bisociates sound and meaning.

EXTRACONSCIOUS FACTORS IN DISCOVERY

Let me return for a moment to science. I said at the beginning of this chapter that the essence of discovery is the coagitation, the shaking together, of already existing frames of reference or areas of knowledge. Now we arrive at the crucial question: Just how does the creative mind hit upon that happy combination of ideas which nobody had thought of combining before?

Artists are inclined to believe that scientists reason in strictly rational, precise verbal terms. They do, of course, nothing of the sort. In 1945, a famous inquiry was organized by Jacques Hadamard (1949) among eminent mathematicians in America to find out their working methods. The results showed that all of them, with only two exceptions, thought neither in verbal terms nor in algebraic symbols but relied on visual imagery of a vague, hazy kind. Einstein was among those who answered the questionnaire; he wrote: "The words of the language as they are written or spoken do not seem to play any role in my mechanism of thought, which relies on more or less clear images of a visual and some of a muscular type. It seems to me that what you call full consciousness is a limit case which can never be fully accomplished because consciousness is a narrow thing."

Einstein's statement is typical. On the testimony of those original thinkers who have taken the trouble to record their methods of work, *not only verbal thinking but conscious thinking in general plays only a subordinate part in the brief, decisive phase of the creative act itself.* Their virtually unanimous emphasis on spontaneous intuitions and hunches of unconscious origin, which they are at a loss to explain, suggests that the role of strictly rational and verbal processes in scientific discovery has been vastly overestimated since the age of enlightenment. There are always large chunks of irrationality embedded in the creative process, not only in art (where we are ready to accept it) but in the exact sciences as well.

The scientist who, facing his blocked problem, regresses from precise verbal thinking to vague visual imagery seems to follow Woodworth's advice: "Often we have to get away from speech in order to think clearly." Words crystallize thoughts, but a crystal is no longer a liquid. Language can act as a screen between the thinker and reality. Creativity often starts where language ends, that is, by regressing to preverbal levels, to more fluid and uncommitted forms of mental activity.

Now I do not mean, of course, that there is a little Socratic demon housed in the scientist's or artist's skull who does his homework for him; nor should one confuse unconscious mentation with Freud's primary process. The primary process is defined by

him as devoid of logic, governed by the pleasure principle, apt to confuse perception and hallucination, and accompanied by massive discharges of affect. It seems that between this very primary process and the so-called secondary process governed by the reality principle, we must interpolate a whole hierarchy of cognitive structures, which are not simply mixtures of primary and secondary, but are autonomous systems in their own right, each governed by a distinct set of rules. The paranoid delusion, the dream, the daydream, free association, the mentalities of children of various ages and of primitives at various stages should not be lumped together, for each has its own logic or rules of the game. But while clearly different in many respects, all these forms of mentation have certain features in common, since they are ontogenetically, and perhaps phylogenetically, older than those of the civilized adult. They are less rigid, more tolerant, and more ready to combine seemingly incompatible ideas and to perceive hidden analogies between cabbages and kings. One might call them "games of the underground," because if not kept under restraint, they would play havoc with the routines of disciplined thinking. But under exceptional conditions, when disciplined thinking is at the end of its tether, a temporary indulgence in these underground games may suddenly produce a solution— some farfetched, reckless combination which would be beyond the reach of, or seem to be unacceptable to, the sober, rational mind. The place for the rendezvous of ideas is underground.

Illumination and Catharsis What I have been trying to suggest is that the common pattern underlying scientific discovery and artistic inspiration is a temporary regression, culminating in the bisociative act, i.e., the bringing together of previously separate frames of perception or universes of discourse. I suppose that is what Ernst Kris (1952) meant by his frequently quoted but somewhat cryptic remarks about regression in the service of the ego. The boundaries between science and art, between the *Ah* reaction and the *Aha* reaction, are fluid, whether we consider architecture or cooking or psychiatry or the writing of history.

There is nowhere a sharp break where witticism changes into wit or where science stops and art begins. Science, the hoary cliché goes, aims at truth, art at beauty. But the criteria of truth, such as verification by experiment, are not as hard and clean as we tend to believe, for the same experimental data can often be interpreted in more than one way. That is why the history of science echoes with as many bitter and venomous controversies as the history of literary criticism. Moreover, the verification of a discovery comes after the act; the creative act itself is for the scientist, as it is for the artist, a leap into the dark, where both are equally dependent on their fallible intuitions. The greatest mathematicians and physicists have confessed that, at those decisive moments when taking the plunge, they were guided not by logic but by a sense of beauty which they were unable to define. Vice versa, painters and sculptors, not to mention architects, have always been guided and often obsessed by scientific or pseudo-scientific theories and criteria of truth: the golden section, the laws of perspective, Dürer's and Leonardo's laws of proportion representing the human body, Cézanne's doctrine that everything in nature is modeled on the cyclinder and cone, Braque's alternative theory that cubes should be substituted for spheres; le Courbusier's modulator theory, Buckminster Fuller's geodesic domes. The same goes, of course, for literature, from the formal laws imposed on Greek tragedy to the various recent and contemporary schools—romanticism, classicism, naturalism, symbolism, stream of consciousness, socialist realism, the *nouveau roman,* and so forth—not to mention the intricate rules of harmony and counterpoint in music. The English physicist Dirac, a Nobel laureate, said recently (1963): "It is more important to have beauty in one's equations than that they should fit experiment." The counterpart to this is the statement by Seurat on his pointillist method: "They see poetry in what I have done. No, I apply my method, and that is all there is to it." In other words, the experience of truth, however subjective, must be present for the experience of beauty to arise, and vice versa: An elegant solution of a problem gives rise in the connoisseur to the experience of beauty. Intellectual illumination and emotional catharsis are complementary aspects of an indivisible process.

REGRESSION AND REBOUND

I would like to conclude this discussion with a remark which is no more than a hint, to place the phenomena of human creativity into a wider biological perspective. I have talked of temporary regression, followed by a rebound, as a characteristic of the creative act. Now biologists are familiar with a similar phenomenon on lower levels of the evolutionary scale. I mean the phenomenon of regeneration (Koestler, 1964, pp. 447–474). It consists in the reshaping of bodily structures—or the reorganization of functions—in response to traumatic challenges from the environment. It involves the regression of bodily tissues to a quasi-embryonic state and the release of genetic growth potentials which are normally under restraint in the adult organism—just as in the moment of discovery the creative potentials of the earlier forms of intuitive thinking are released from the censorship of the conscious adult mind. Psychotherapy reflects the same process on a higher level. It aims at inducing a temporary regression in the emotionally traumatized patient in the hope that he will regenerate into a pattern which eliminates the conflict. The creative act could be called a kind of do-it-yourself psychotherapy where the traumatic challenge is intellectual instead of emotional, for instance, new data which shake the foundation of a well-established theory, observations which contradict each other, problems which cause frustration and conflict—or the artist's perplexities in trying to communicate his experiences through the blocked matrices of conventional techniques.

And finally we find the same pattern reflected in the death-and-resurrection motif in mythology, in Toynbee's *Withdrawal and Return,* in Jung's *Night Journey.* Joseph is thrown into a well, Mohammed goes out into the desert, Jesus is resurrected from the tomb, Jonah is reborn out of the belly of the whale. The mystic's dark night of the soul reflects the same archetype. It seems to be a principle of universal validity in the evolution of individuals and cultures.

REFERENCES

DIRAC, P. A. M. Evolution of the physicist's picture of nature. *Scientific American,* 1963, **208** (36), 45–53.

GOMBRICH, E. H. *Art and illusion.* London: Phaidon Press, 1962.

HADAMARD, J. *The psychology of invention in the mathematical field.* Princeton, N.J.: Princeton Univer. Press, 1949.

KOESTLER, A. *Insight and outlook.* New York: Macmillan, 1949.

KOESTLER, A. *The act of creation.* New York: Macmillan, 1964.

KRIS, E. *Psychoanalytic explorations in art.* New York: International Universities Press, 1952.

KUHN, T. H. *The structure of scientific revolutions.* Chicago: Univer. of Chicago Press, 1962.

POPPER, K. R. *The logic of scientific discovery.* London: Hutchinson, 1959.

SANTILLANA, G. DE. *Dialogue on the great world systems.* Chicago: Univer. of Chicago Press, 1953.

Part TWO

THE HUMAN EXPERIENCE

*What are the main ingredients of being human? What is the
world of experiences which lies within each person and yet
which is shared in some measure among all persons?
Humanistic psychology addresses itself to the tasks of
providing meaningful descriptions of this inner world; of
exploring the interrelationships among these aspects, keeping
always within the context of the living, experiencing person;
and of inquiring into the further realms of possible experience
which may be latent within each of us.*

*In Part Two, we shall sample some representative studies of
human experiences. It is yet too early in the revival of man's
study of his own living to attempt a comprehensive survey of
inner experience, but a number of gifted and imaginative
investigators are at work in the field. Four of them are
represented here, and in subsequent sections the reader will
discover other such reports which are doing double service by
illustrating additional aspects of humanistic psychology as well.*

*To return to our opening question—What are the principal
subjective experiences of the human life?—we may recognize that
one of the most pervasive is that of the individual's caring
about what happens in his life. Such formal topics as*

41

96605

"motivation," "drives," "incentives," and so on really have little
to do with the major subjective process of being concerned.
"Attitude," "values," and similar concepts are closer, but this
important area still has been too little explored. Thomas Szasz,
whose fresh perspectives are opening up long-stale areas of
abnormal psychology and psychiatry and whose courageous
enunciations of the meaning of responsibility have exposed the
careless sentimentality underlying much seemingly human concern,
proposes in Chapter 5 that we recognize the fundamental place
of moral issues in the life of modern man.

It is instructive to compare the chapter by Szasz and Chapter
2, by Cantril. Both set forth lists of human concerns, but they do so
from quite different perspectives and with somewhat contrasting
intentions. It is typical of the humanistic orientation that
such differences occur, and in the long run it betokens a fertile
field for innovation and discovery. Sometimes such differences are
only a matter of purpose or outlook; sometimes they are
useful in highlighting conflicting interpretations and thus opening
the way for further inquiry. As a case in point, we may note
that Cantril sees hope as a built-in and positive human attribute,
while Szasz regards it, as the French existentialists do, as
a malignancy.

The next chapter provides an example of the kinds of fresh
insights that an approach which values and employs subjective data
may throw upon familiar topics. In Chapter 6, Sylvan Tomkins
invades the very core of the behaviorist's territory to take a
revolutionary look at the concept of "drive." One might well have
considered that this would be one variable on which the
experimentalists had come close to saying the last word. Yet
Tomkins, by using the fresh perspective of subjectivity, discloses
fundamental fallacies in the way that venerated process has been
conceived. Tomkins's paper is an excellent demonstration that a
psychology that looks only at externals may make as significant
errors as the fabled blind men did with their elephant. Yet Tomkins
is well able to use objective data as well as subjective and resists
any reciprocal tendency to go to the opposite extreme. Indeed, his
paper provides an interesting illustration of yet another feature of
the humanistic orientation: Tomkins draws on both the objective
and the subjective in his marshaling of evidence; he employs both
physiological and psychological data, and he sets up an
experimental-predictive paradigm while yet being sensitive to the
experiential potentialities. His approach contrasts with others in
this book which are more intuitive and heuristic; yet humanistic
psychology welcomes and profits from such diversity. There is no
"party line" of method, style, data, or outcomes. The result is a
diversity which promises much fertility.

Hubert Bonner, in Chapter 7, provides a further contrast in method
and orientation. Bonner, continuing his distinguished
inquiries into the nature of "proactive man," essays a description
of what a more full use of human potential might yield. This
is the sort of presentation that is far too easy to dismiss as merely
an exercise in imagination. (Human imagination, incidentally,

*has been too little appreciated by much current psychology
for the remarkable and unique process that it truly is.) However,
the particular task which Bonner has undertaken is quite a
bit more than it may seem at first inspection. It is a serious attempt
to collate the presently evident possibilities in being human
and to forge a composite that is a truly challenging image of what
man might be and latently is. This is achieved without
recourse to speculation about further but as yet undeveloped
possibilities of human potential (such as some later chapters will
describe, e.g., Chapters 8, 15, 16, and 33). Thus, Bonner, at
once, sets a task for our psychological science and technology and a
challenge for each of us in our own lives.*

*This same dual import may be recognized in Colin Wilson's
fascinating and provocative essay in Chapter 8. Wilson, a social
critic and novelist of the first rank, draws with deep insight
and ready wit on his own subjective experience to make explicit an
aspect of human experience with which we can all identify
but which has largely eluded such explicit formulation and adequate
psychological investigation. No sentimental optimist he, and
yet Wilson unerringly discerns the true essence of being human
and clears away much that is less than human (and which, we might
add, is often the primary if not the exclusive focus of attention
of behaviorism). When he emerges with an ennobled vision of what
may be the potential meaning of being human, he clearly
discerns the vast yet unexplored hemisphere that awaits man's
(and humanistic psychology's) courage and creativity.*

Presently: Professor of Psychiatry at the State University of New York's Upstate Medical Center in Syracuse (since 1956).

Education: Doctor of Medicine from the University of Cincinnati (1944). Certificate from the Chicago Institute for Psychoanalysis (1950).

Current major activities: Teaching and administrative work in the Department of Psychiatry, private practice, and writing.

THOMAS S. SZASZ

Most rewarding project: Further explorations of the historical origins and the moral and social aspects of psychiatric practice.

Personal history: Native of Budapest, Hungary. Came to the United States in 1938. Research Assistant and then staff member at the Chicago Institute for Psychoanalysis (1949–1956). Lecturer at Elgin (Illinois) State Hospital (1952–1954). Visiting Professor of Psychiatry at the University of Wisconsin (1962). Consultant to the Syracuse Veterans Administration Hospital, to the Syracuse Psychiatric Hospital, to the Committee on Mental Hygiene of the New York State Bar Association, and to the Research Advisory Panel of the Institute for the Study of Drug Addiction. Diplomate of the National Board of Medical Examiners and of the American Board of Psychiatry and Neurology.

Writings: Dr. Szasz's reputation could well rest on his publications in psychosomatic medicine, psychoanalytic theory and practice, and the psychology of pain. However, he has opened up a whole area of new social criticism with his fresh perspectives on previously unquestioned concepts and practices in psychology and psychiatry and in their relations with the law. *Pain and Pleasure: A Study of Bodily Feelings* (1957); *The Myth of Mental Illness: Foundations of a Theory of Personal Conduct* (1961); *Law, Liberty, and Psychiatry: An Inquiry into the Social Uses of Mental Health Practices* (1963); *The Ethics of Psychoanalysis: The Theory and Method of Autonomous Psychotherapy* (1965); and *Psychiatric Justice* (1965).

Present chapter: This is an adaptation and modification of a portion of a paper that first appeared in *Comprehensive Psychiatry* (1962, **3**, 268–283). It appears here by permission of the publishers of that journal, Grune & Stratton.

Chapter 5
THOMAS S. SZASZ

MORAL MAN: A MODEL OF MAN FOR HUMANISTIC PSYCHOLOGY

To qualify psychology with the adjective "humanistic" implies at least two things: first, that there are other kinds of psychologies (for example, "abnormal," "physiological," and so forth) from which "humanistic" psychology must be distinguished; and second, that the term "humanistic" labels a more or less clearly identifiable concept or method in psychology.

In common usage, the word "humanistic" means only that its user will, in the endeavor he so labels, attend to or concentrate on, what he regards as the distinctively human aspect of his activity. Thus, we speak of humanistic education to distinguish it from education focused on scientific knowledge and technological skills. In such a context, it is easy to know what is "human": that which concerns man rather than inanimate objects or animals. Since all human (as opposed to animal) psychologies deal with man's ideas and actions, which shall we call "humanistic," and which by some other term? Is gestalt psychology humanistic? Or Freudian psychology? Or Skinnerian psychology? (The list could be expanded at will.) One might surmise that, in each case, the protagonists of any particular "school" might consider their brand of psychology humanistic; if so, they might even wish to withhold this designation from the ideas and practices of their rivals. I think we must frankly recognize this hazard. Like the word "liberal" or "democratic," the term "humanistic" may easily become devoid of all operational meaning, functioning as a rhetorical device for the self-serving interests of whoever uses it.

To avoid or at least minimize this danger, it is necessary that we specify the particular concept of "man" to which we refer when we use this term. I shall try to do this in the present chapter. Of course, it is not necessary that all humanistic psychologists accept my model of moral man as their standard; it is necessary only that they make their own standards also explicit. Only in this way will we be able to measure various schools of psychology against our standard and conclude that this one is, but that another is not, a part of the humanistic stream in the study of man.

THE CONCEPT OF MORAL MAN

The concept of moral man may be best understood by comparing it with other dominant concepts of man.

In the ancient Greek city-states, man—the free citizen, not the slave—was considered chiefly in political terms. This was *homo politicus* or man the political animal.

Man was what he was because of his participation in the affairs of his miniaturized nation. This distinguished him from slaves, barbarians, and animals.

After the establishment of Christianity and until the Enlightenment, it was held that man was what he was because of his relationship to God, Christ, and the church. This was *homo theologicus* or man the religious animal. Man's religious feeling, belief, and action distinguished him from the heathen and from the animal.

With the advent of industrialization arose the concept of *homo economicus* or man the economic animal, well known in the great works of Bentham and Marx. Like the earlier concepts, it described man as he was at a particular time, in a particular society. The production, distribution, and consumption of goods and services—the control of the means of production, capital, and labor—these were the activities that permeated daily life, as a sociopsychological experience. As long as work and rest, money and poverty, and economic exploitation and rebellion against it are the main preoccupations of men, their character or so-called human nature will reflect these interests.

In the course of the last century, the transformation of society—and, in a sense, of man himself—has been especially swift. While political man of the classic Greek tradition is a thing of the past, religious man and economic man are, socially speaking, not entirely outmoded; both are still discernible in modern Western culture. In addition to these concepts of man, others have recently developed, such as biological man, psychological man, and two secularizations of religious man: the obedient servant of the nation-state and his microcosmic counterpart, the organization man.

Moral Man and His Social Context Moral man, as I use this term, designates man in his typically modern state. What is this condition that I claim has given rise to a new concept of man? There are two outstanding facts, one biological and the other social, which have produced a degree of personal freedom unparalleled in human history. Advances in agricultural and industrial technology, in medicine, and in public health have relieved man in Western culture from wasting his energies on the game of mere physical survival. Thus, this question of whether man will survive is replaced by the question: In what manner will man survive? (I disregard here the danger of a nuclear holocaust, against which individual effort alone cannot afford effective protection.)

The second development, which is also relatively recent, is that vast numbers of people are literate and, to an extent, educated. This means that the impact of simple, rule-following types of behavior, such as are transmitted by religious heritage and social custom, is greatly weakened.

Broadly speaking, education and some types of tradition are antagonistic forces in society. Accordingly, both the physicobiological and the sociopsychological circumstances sketched above produce a human condition characterized by the possibility of making choices. To the extent that people have freedom of decision—and to that extent only—they live as moral beings. Thus, I use the term "moral" in the sense of choice or decision-making behavior, not in the sense of following a code of ethics. This viewpoint is not novel. It was clearly defined by Piaget (1932), who called it the morality of the autonomous personality. He contrasted it with the morality of the heteronomous personality, upon whom specified norms of conduct are imposed from without. It is evident that autonomous morality is possible only when there are genuine choices. Moreover, since a person's ability to choose depends in large part on his store of information, his educational experiences will have a decisive effect on his moral stature.

By "education," I mean more than the acquisition of factual knowledge and technical skill. Education in these areas alone produces persons who have been aptly labeled "educated fools." To be educated, a growing child must acquire, by precept and otherwise, a fund of knowledge about human relationships and ethics and about politics and moral sensibilities. In my opinion, lack of education or miseducation (Goodman, 1962) is partly responsible for the important phenomena which Fromm analyzed in his book *Escape from Freedom* (1941).

The gist of Fromm's thesis is that most men, especially in Germany and Italy after the First World War, found responsible decision making too burdensome. Confronted with freedom to choose among various ways of life, men embraced fascism, which promised to free them from this burden. While Fromm analyzed faithfully and well the mechanisms of man's fear of, and escape from, freedom, he did not search deeply enough for the sociocultural and educational reasons for these reactions. However, Fromm's book, and others, like Popper's *Open Society and Its Enemies* (1950), afford striking illustrations of the fact that modern man is a moral animal. One can be afraid of choice or be an enemy of the open society only if there is an opportunity to choose and live in a relatively open society. During most of human history, there were no such alternatives. Society was closed, and it still is for most of the world's population.

The completely open society remains a goal, perhaps a utopian dream. Yet it is undeniable that during recent centuries, and especially since the First World War, the walls that have kept societies closed have weakened and have cracked open here and there. If this continues, without an intervening destruction of the biophysical conditions necessary for human life, then, much as a chick is hatched from a cracked egg, moral man may emerge out of the shell of the closed society.

This essay is an initial exploration of the present, embryonic state of moral man and the social conditions that define his psychological and ethical existence. It is also an inquiry into the human actions that tend, on the one hand, to allow man greater freedom and, on the other, to reestablish subservience to authoritative guidance.

ATTITUDINAL POLARITIES OF MORAL MAN

Autonomy versus Heteronomy The distinction between self-government or self-control and government or control by others is perhaps the fundamental polarity for modern man. While these issues are particularly relevant today, they have been significant to men throughout recorded history. Government of the self by the self or by others has received different emphases in the past. Consider in this connection the juxtaposition of such notions as liberty and slavery, freedom and oppression, heresy and orthodoxy, the open and the closed society, democracy and totalitarianism, inner- and other-directedness, and so forth. Each of these pairs emphasizes a different facet of the polarity of autonomy and heteronomy.

In general, the first term in each pair implies the desirability of enlarging the scope of human self-action. Thus, measures that add to human knowledge are good, for as information increases, so does choice. Similarly, external restraint should be reduced as far as possible because it limits choice and, more importantly, because it limits the expansion of the self and of society.

These values were not always accepted as good. Let us recall the etymology of the word "heresy." It originates from the Greek word *hairesis,* which means "making a choice." Thus, the ability to make decisions independently, considered here as the characteristic capacity of moral man, was regarded as a cardinal sin in medieval Christian theology.

The social practices of Western democracies—and, even more, those of other parts of the world—have fostered both autonomy and heteronomy. Hence, it is not accurate to speak of people "escaping from freedom," if to them "freedom" means the absence of a benevolent leader and hence chaos and loss of direction in life.

Domination versus Submission This polarity is often said to be partly biologically determined. Like other human propensities, man's drive for power is regulated by social processes. The use of force is thus channeled into modes approved by society. The dominance of the male over the female, of one race over another, of one religion or nation over another—each represents traditional human aspirations, encouraged by positive social sanctions. The struggle of the oppressed to become the oppressor is as ancient as mankind. However, the notion that the cycle of domination—submission—domination, so typical of human history, might be both unnecessary and evil is relatively recent.

An illustration of the tendency to accept, as an unalterable "law of nature," the postures of domination and submission is the antifeminine bias of psychoanalytic theory. Although this bias was exposed long ago, it has not been sufficiently recognized that it forms a part of a larger system of a covertly totalitarian, or at least autocratic, ethic.

The "reactionary" features of psychoanalysis have been perceived and exploited by Soviet scholars (Bassin, 1960). These same men, however, have completely ignored the essentially descriptive aspects of Freud's contributions as well as those which foster self-determination, freedom, and personal dignity. [I have dealt with this subject in detail elsewhere (Szasz, 1961; Szasz, 1965).] Psychoanalysis will take its place among the social institutions that have, throughout history, shaped the image of man. The sort of place it takes will be decided by the actual practices of psychoanalysts in three great areas of social action: psychoanalytic practice, psychoanalytic training, and legislative reform based upon (so-called) psychoanalytic recommendations. I believe that depending upon whether psychoanalysis encourages or discourages coercive practices in any or all of these areas, it will contribute to the constriction or expansion of the human personality and, through it, of the human social order.

Meaning versus Futility Man has a need to feel that his existence has "meaning." This need is a consequence of his propensity for symbolizing and a penalty, as it were, for thinking. The need to find meaning in life has been gratified by belief systems, cosmologies, religions, and philosophies of life. The notion of moral man, as developed here, may be compatible with some, but not with all, systems of belief. Thus the idea that man can or should contemplate moral choices and act on his own convictions and responsibilities is contrary to at least some interpretations of traditional Judeo-Christian thought. One purpose of religious codes is to reduce choice in certain crucial areas of life by prescribing the correct actions for typical dilemmas of life such as sex and family relations, aggression, and property.

For many people it is difficult, if not impossible, to accept the idea that life is meaningless. Perhaps this, too, is a matter of education. Because of the megalomaniac significance that man has always attributed to his own conduct, most of us are unfit to approach this issue with equanimity. Although Shakespeare suggested and the existentialists reiterate that life "is a tale told by an idiot, full of sound and fury, signifying nothing," people must live as if this were not true. Indeed, for some people, the meaninglessness or futility of life may itself constitute a meaning—perhaps by the same kind of psychological reversal and reinterpretation which can turn submission into domination, humility into pride, and asceticism into sensuality. In any case, I accept Camus's (1954) thesis that hope is a destructive emotion and that resignation without bitterness, without anger, and without inactivity is the optimal mood for modern man. This is an integral feature of the portrait of moral man. The sophisticated mood of resignation should be contrasted with the angry resentment of the man who finds his God slain in the traffic of scientific society. This reaction is a consequence of his previous self-aggrandizement, which was inherent in his relationship to God and which made him seek meaning in his own life by demeaning the lives of others.

Individuation versus Group Identity The concepts of "individual" and "group" have meaning only in relation to each other. The proposition that man should develop his talents and pursue his interests—in other words, that he should be a "person in his own right" and not merely a "member of a group"—makes sense only in a context in which individual and group are juxtaposed. Similarly, the proposition that man should be a well-functioning member of an integrated team rather than a solitary individual also depends on a juxtaposition of individual and group, of "selfish interests" and "social interests."

In the modern industrial society, more than ever before, the work situation exerts a constant pressure on people to become at once individuated and yet cooperative. Men must learn complex skills, and in order to practice them successfully, they must also make them their own. This requires a high degree of personal self-development. At the same time, however, the pressures to cooperate and to be a member of the team are also operative. Indeed, some observers—such as William H. Whyte, Jr., in his book *The Organization Man* (1956)—have claimed that the pressure to conform, to be unindividuated, is at an all-time high.

The observations of Whyte and others are valid, but I would like to suggest a different interpretation. Social pressures toward conformity, and the alleged conformity itself, are more noticeable and perhaps more painful today than they were in the past because of the powerful opposing pressures toward individuation. In the Middle Ages, for example, the pressures toward conformity were virtually unopposed. I doubt that the pressures toward conformity are greater now than in the past. It seems rather that society as a whole and people individually are torn by strong and opposing forces. Conformity, like capitalism, has been with us for a long time. As management must now contend with labor organizations and capitalism with communism, so the forces of collectivism are now more evenly matched by those of individualism.

What is the evidence for this view? To most scholars, the concept of individualism is closely connected with the philosophy of the Enlightenment. It is necessary to remember, however, that in the eighteenth century, individualism was an individualistic affair. In those days, being an individual required the help of others—servants, if not actually slaves—who, in turn, could not aspire to be individuals themselves. Thus, the self-development of one person could be attained only by encroaching on the educational and sociopolitical *Lebensraum* of others.

In contrast, today, because of large-scale dependence on the machine rather than on human help, individualism has become a mass affair. Never before in human history have so many people been so free of political and religious coercion. While this development has, in my opinion, been largely beneficial for human nature, it has also

resulted in complications unforeseen by men like Voltaire, Rousseau, Hume, and Locke. Individuation as a large-scale social value, almost as a mass commodity, has made it necessary for many people, rather than for just a few, to live relatively autonomously —that is, with mutually adjustive, contractual arrangements. These mechanisms are personally more costly than the use of fixed-role definitions, established by institutional criteria and handed down by tradition.

Socialization versus Alienation In a culture such as ours, socialization does not mean simply learning to get along with others. Unfortunately, this belief has wide currency and has had far-reaching effects on American education. Nevertheless, it remains a fact that if a person wishes to get along in the contemporary world, he must learn a great many skills. These begin with walking and talking and proceed at a rapid pace during the first two decades of life. Even after young adulthood, most people find it necessary to learn and relearn. Often this process continues until old age and death.

We must remember that in the process of acquiring complex skills—such as learning to play the piano, write a novel, or construct a new machine—we undergo a process of *both* socialization and desocialization. The reasons for this paradox are not hard to find. Each complex learning experience is a step in socialization because it provides the learner with symbols and tools for exchange with others. Thus, social interdependencies, such as between composer and performer or writer and reader, develop. Stated teleologically, we could say that the purpose of socialization is to bring about the "right" kinds of interdependencies among people.

And yet acquiring complex skills tends to result also in desocialization and, potentially, in alienation. This is a consequence of the fact that skills tend to make people self-reliant and independent of others. For example, once a baby learns to walk, he does not require a mother or mother substitute to carry him around. This progressive "desocialization" from the mother and father takes place as the child becomes "socialized" into the adult role defined by the mores of his society.

Furthermore, it seems that learning and skill acquisition are desocializing influences in an even more profound sense. They involve more than exchanging one kind of interdependence, as between infant and mother, for another, as between husband and wife. A high degree of development in the use of symbols and skills leads also to a diminished need for other people. The reasons for this are twofold: First, such a person is self-reliant to more than an ordinary degree. Hence he does not need the help of others. Second, he has largely exchanged symbols and skills for human companions. Hence not only may he endure solitude, but he may actually crave and enjoy it. Illustrative of this condition are the "ancients" in George Bernard Shaw's play *Back to Methuselah* (1947). These men are caricatures of superlatively well-differentiated individuals. In our terms they are asocial because they neither require nor desire much from anyone. The amount of social transaction in which they engage approaches nil. A man like Einstein offers a less extreme but more realistic example of the desocializing effect of symbolic sophistication. He remarked that the solitude which had been painful to him in his youth became essential and enjoyable in later life.

In this connection, I want to mention a common contemporary problem, closely related to the issues of learning, skill, and performance. It is the development of anxiety and tension in a person, not because he lacks skills to meet social demands, but rather because he appreciates the discrepancy between his actual performance and his potential ability. Once people acquire knowledge and skills, they develop the need to use them. If knowledge or skill cannot be utilized, frustration results and becomes a source of suffering.

Educated women bear the brunt of this problem today. If they are married and have small children to care for, they often feel like caged animals. It is not only that they must perform the unchallenging and dreary tasks of homemaking. What may be most distressing is the fact that because of these drudgeries, they lack opportunities to exercise their previously acquired skills. Sometimes, women attempt to solve this problem by trying to attend to two, three, or more tasks simultaneously. These are the women who are, or try to be, mothers, homemakers, wives, and professional persons all at the same time. The success or failure of such nearly superhuman efforts depends on many factors: the physical health and personal vitality of the particular woman, her mental makeup, her educational and socioeconomic status, the kinds of help available to her both at home and at work, and so forth.

In less obvious and perhaps less extreme forms, many persons of both sexes and of all ages are subject to frustrations of this kind. A society that fosters rather than minimizes problems of this type manifests a powerful ambivalence toward the value of individualism.

CONCLUSIONS

Traditionally, the word "moral" has been used to characterize a person who lives up to the teachings or correctly obeys the regulations of his particular moral code. Thus, a person labeled a "good Jew," a "good Christian," or a "good American" is one who makes the rules of a particular ethical system his own and follows them, as we say, faithfully.

The conception of moral man here proposed is the antithesis of this traditional view. Instead, I maintain that that man is "moral" who considers all moral laws and principles to be anything but self-evident. His attitude toward ethics is skeptical and questioning. He must increasingly examine moral alternatives and make moral choices in the conduct of his life.

The fundamental principle governing the conduct of moral man was well articulated by Reichenbach (1951, p. 141) when he wrote: "The power of reason must be sought not in the rules that reason dictates to our imagination but in the ability to free ourselves from any kind of rules to which we have been conditioned through experience and tradition."

REFERENCES

BASSIN, F. V. A critical analysis of Freudianism. *The Soviet Review*, 1960, **1**, 27–44.

CAMUS, A. *The rebel*. New York: Knopf, 1954.

FROMM, E. *Escape from freedom*. New York: Holt, Rinehart and Winston, 1941.

GOODMAN, P. *Compulsory miseducation*. New York: Horizon Press, 1962.

PIAGET, J. *The moral judgment of the child*. New York: Free Press, 1932.

POPPER, K. R. *The open society and its enemies*. Princeton, N.J.: Princeton Univer. Press, 1950.

REICHENBACH, H. *The rise of scientific philosophy*. Berkeley, Calif.: Univer. of California Press, 1951.

SHAW, G. B. *Back to Methuselah: As far as thought can reach*. Fair Lawn, N.J.: Oxford Univer. Press, 1947.

SZASZ, T. S. *The myth of mental illness*. New York: Hoeber-Harper, 1961.

SZASZ, T. S. *The ethics of psychoanalysis*. New York: Basic Books, 1965.

WHYTE, W. H., JR. *The organization man*. New York: Simon and Schuster, 1956.

Presently: Director of the Center for Research in Cognition and Affect at the City University of New York (since 1964) as a Research Professor under a National Institute of Mental Health Career Award.

Education: Doctor of Philosophy in philosophy from the University of Pennsylvania (1934).

Current major activity: Construction of a general theory of personality.

SILVAN S. TOMKINS

Most rewarding project: A study of the relationship between the rise and fall of civilizations and the predominant affect or emotion of the society as expressed in the varying frequency of different emotionally toned words.

Future of humanistic psychology: The prospect of a closer integration of humanistic psychology and the social sciences and literature.

Personal history: Research Assistant (1936–1943), Instructor (1943–1946), and Lecturer (1946–1947) at Harvard University. Research Associate at the College Board (1947–1948). Professor of Psychology at Princeton University (1947–1964). Consultant to the Educational Testing Service (since 1947) and to the Philadelphia Psychiatric Hospital (since 1957).

Writings: Dr. Tomkins's major work is *Affect, Imagery and Consciousness,* Volumes I and II (1962 and 1963). He also contributed to the theory and method of apperceptive projection, publishing a book entitled *Thematic Apperception Test* (1946) and his own *Tomkins-Horn Picture Arrangement Test* (1955 and 1956). He edited *Contemporary Psychopathology* (1943) and *Computer Simulation of Personality,* with S. Messick (1963). The former was issued in a revised edition as *Psychopathology* (1958) under the joint editorship of Dr. Tomkins, C. Reed, and I. Alexander.

Present chapter: This is an adaptation of an invited address delivered at the meetings of the Eastern Psychological Association in Philadelphia, April 16, 1964.

Chapter 6
SILVAN S. TOMKINS

HOMO PATIENS: A REEXAMINATION OF THE CONCEPT OF DRIVE

My theme[1] is *homo patiens*, passionate, suffering, caring, feeling man. Early on, the human being identified himself as an actor and as a knower. But why did he act, and for what did he desire knowledge? In a dimly lit cave one night after the day's work had been done, one of our more reflective forebears wrinkled his forehead, scratched his beard, and, in wonder and perplexity, began the study of human motivation. His answer to the fundamental question—What do human beings really want?—was the same answer that was to be given for some few thousand years, up to and including Hull and Freud. That answer was, and for not a few still is, that the human animal is driven to breathe, to eat, to drink, and to engage in sex—that the biological drives are the primary sources of motivation of all animals, not excluding man. The clarity and urgency of hunger, of thirst, of anoxia, and of lust provided the basic paradigm that captured the imaginations of all theorists.

Protests against this paradigm have been perennial, but none of its competitors has had its hardiness.

This is a radical error. The intensity, the urgency, the imperiousness, the "umph" of drives is an illusion. The illusion is created by the misidentification of the drive "signal" with its "amplifier." Its amplifier is the affective response which is ordinarily recruited to "boost the gain" of the drive signal.

Some Examples Consider anoxic deprivation. Almost any interference with normal breathing will immediately arouse the most desperate gasping for breath. Is there any motivational claim more urgent than the demand of one who is drowning or choking to death for want of air? Yet it is not simply the imperious demand for oxygen that we observe under such circumstances. We are also observing the rapidly mounting panic ordinarily recruited whenever the air supply is suddenly jeopardized. The panic amplifies the drive signal, and it is the combination of drive signal and panic which we have mistakenly identified as the drive signal.

[1] This work was supported in whole by a Public Health Research Career Award from the National Institute of Mental Health, 1–K6–MH–23, 797–01.

We have only to change the rate of anoxic deprivation to change the nature of the recruited affect which accompanies the anoxic drive signal. Thus, in the Second World War, those pilots who refused to wear their oxygen masks at 30,000 feet suffered a more gradual anoxic deprivation. They did not panic for want of oxygen. They became euphoric. It was the affect of enjoyment which the more slowly developing anoxic signal recruited. Some of these men, therefore, met their deaths with smiles on their lips.

Consider next that most imperious, primary drive of sex. Surely the tumescent, erect male is driven. Surely the tumescent sexual organ is the site of both the sexual urge and sexual pleasure. So it is, but just as we misidentify panic and the anoxic signal, so here we have misidentified the tumescence of the sexual drive with the affect of excitement. Excitement is ordinarily recruited as an amplifier of the sexual drive signal. Still, no one has ever observed an excited penis. It is a man who is excited and who breathes hard, not in the penis, but in the chest, the esophagus, the face, and the nose and nostrils. Both the sexual urge and the sexual pleasure of intercourse are ordinarily as amplified by excitement as anoxia is amplified by panic.

The potency of the sexual drive is notoriously vulnerable to the learned recruitment of affect which inhibits sexual satisfaction. If one learns to feel ashamed or afraid of sexuality, tumescence may become impossible, and the potent primary drive becomes impotent. To be fully sexually aroused and satisfied, one must be capable of excitement as well as tumescence. The contribution of affect to complete sexual satisfaction is nowhere clearer than in those who report unimpaired sexual pleasure and even orgasm but who, nonetheless, complain of lack of sexual satisfaction. What can it mean when the genitals are tumescent and yield sexual pleasure from mutual stimulation, which produces mutual orgasm, and yet both partners report that they are sexually unfulfilled and dissatisfied? Sexual intercourse repeated with the same partner is vulnerable to such attenuation of satisfaction whenever the decline in novelty of the interpersonal relationship is such that excitement can no longer be sustained. Those who are generally bored with each other may also be unable to become sexually excited even when they are capable of stimulating tumescence and orgasm. Excitement is no more a peculiarly sexual phenomenon than panic is unique to anoxic deprivation.

THE AMPLIFICATION MECHANISMS

The relationship we have postulated between the drive system and the affect system must also be postulated between both of these and nonspecific amplifying systems, such as the reticular formation. This and other amplifier circuits serve both motivational and nonmotivational systems. The words "activation" and "arousal" have tended to confound the distinction between amplification from affects and the nonspecific amplification of any neural message, be it a sensory, a motor, a drive, or an affect message.

Amplification is the preferable, more generic term, since it describes equally well the increase or decrease in gain for any and every kind of message or structure. The terms "activation" and "arousal" should be abandoned because of their affective connotations.

It is now clear from the work of Sprague, Chambers, and Stellar (1961) that it is possible by appropriate anatomical lesion to produce a cat who is active by virtue of intact amplifier structures but who shows little affect and, conversely, to produce a cat who is inactive and drowsy but who responds readily with affect to mild stimulation.

Thus it appears that after interruption of much of the classical, lemniscal paths at the rostral midbrain, the cat shows . . . little attention and affect, despite the fact that the animal is wakeful and active and has good motor capacity. . . . These cats are characterized by a *lack of affect*, showing little or no defensive and aggressive reaction to noxious and aversive situations and no response to pleasurable stimulation or solicitation of affection by petting. The animals are mute, lack facial expression, and show minimal autonomic responses. . . . Without a patterned afferent input to the forebrain via the lemnisci, the remaining portions of the central nervous system, which include a virtually intact reticular formation, seem incapable of elaborating a large part of the animal's repertoire of adaptive behavior. . . . In contrast to this picture, a large reticular lesion sparing the lemnisci results in an animal whose general behavior is much like that of a normal cat except for chronic hypokinesia or drowsiness and for strong and easily aroused affect to mild stimulation (pp. 172-173).[2]

Both drives and affects require nonspecific amplification, but the drives have insufficient strength as motives without concurrent amplification by both the affects and the nonspecific amplifiers. Their critical role is to provide vital information of time, of place, and of response—where and when to do what—when the body does not know how to help itself otherwise. When the drive signal is activated, we learn first when we must start and stop consummatory activity. We become hungry long before our tissues are in an emergency state of deficit, and we stop eating, because of satiety, long before the tissue deficit has been remedied.

Localization   But there is also information of place and of response—where to do what. When the drive is activated, it tells us a very specific story—that the "problem" is in the mouth in the case of hunger, farther back in the nose and throat and chest if it is an oxygen drive, in the urethra if it is the urination drive, at the anal sphincter if it is the defecation drive. This information has been built into the site of consummation, so the probability of finding the correct consummatory response is very high. That this information is as vital as the message *when* to eat can be easily demonstrated.

Let us suppose that the hunger drive were "rewired" to be localized in the urethra, and the sex drive localized in the palm of the hand. For sexual satisfaction, the individual would first open and close his hand and then reach for a wide variety of "objects" as possible satisfiers, cupping and rubbing his hand until orgasm. When he became hungry he might first release the urethra and urinate to relieve his hunger.

If this did not relieve it, he might use his hands to find objects which could be put inside the urethra, depending on just how we had rewired the apparatus. Such an organism would be neither viable nor reproductive. Such specificity of time and place of the drive system, critical though it is for viability, is nevertheless a limitation on its general significance for the human being.

AFFECTS: THE PRIMARY HUMAN MOTIVES

It is the affects, rather than the drives, which are the primary human motives. This primacy is demonstrated first in that the drives require amplification from the affects, whereas the affects are sufficient motivators in the absence of drives. One must be excited to be sexually aroused, but one need not be sexually aroused to be excited. To motivate any man, it is quite sufficient to arouse either excitement or joy or terror or anger or shame or contempt or distress or surprise.

Second, in contrast to the specificity of the space-time information of the drive system, the affect system has those more general properties which permit it to assume a central position in the motivation of man. Thus, the affect system has generality of time rather than the rhythmic specificity of the drive system. Because the drive system is essentially a transport system, taking material in and out of the body, it must impose its specific temporal rhythms strictly. One cannot breathe only on Tuesday, Thursday, and Saturday, but one could be happy on Tuesday, Thursday, and Saturday and sad on Monday, Wednesday, and Friday.

In contrast to the necessary constraints of a system which enjoys few degrees of freedom in transporting material in and out of the body, there is nothing inherent in the structure of the affect mechanism which limits its activation with respect to time. One can be anxious for just a moment or for half an hour, for a day, for a year, for a lifetime, or never; one can be anxious only occasionally now, though much more frequently some time ago, or conversely.

There are structures in the body which

are midway between the drive and affect mechanisms. Thus the pain receptors on the back of my hand are as site-specific as any drive. If I were to place a lit cigarette on the skin of my hand, I would experience pain. But the pain mechanism is similar to the affect mechanism in its time generality. There is nothing in the nature of the pain receptors which requires that they be stimulated rhythmically or that they ever be stimulated, and there is nothing which will prevent them from being stimulated whenever I happen to have an accident.

Affect Generality The affect system permits generality of object. Although one may satisfy hunger with Chinese, American, or Italian food, it must be some variety of edible object. Not so with any affect. There is literally no kind of object which has not been linked to one or another of the affects. In masochism, man has even learned to love pain and death. In Puritanism, he has learned to hate pleasure and life. He can invest any and every aspect of existence with the magic of excitement and joy or with the dread of fear or shame or distress.

Affects are also capable of much greater generality of intensity than drives. If I do not eat, I become hungrier and hungrier. As I eat, I become less hungry. But I may wake mildly irritable in the morning and remain so for the rest of the day, or one day I may not be at all angry until quite suddenly something makes me explode in a rage. I may start the day moderately angry and quickly become interested in some other matter and so dissipate my anger.

Affect Density Not only are both the intensity and duration of affects capable of greater modulation than is possible for drives, but so is their *density*. By "affect density," I mean the product of intensity times duration. Most of the drives operate within relatively narrow density tolerances. The consequences of too much variation of density of intake of air is loss of consciousness and possible death. Compared with drives, affects may be either much more

casual and low in density or much more monopolistic and high in density. By virtue of the flexibility of this system, man is enabled to oscillate between affect fickleness and obsessive possession by the object of his affective investments.

Affects in Combination Not only may affects be widely invested and variously invested, but they may also be invested in other affects, combine with other affects, intensify or modulate them, and suppress or reduce them. Neither hunger nor thirst can be used to reduce the need for air, as a child may be shamed into crying or may be shamed into stopping his crying.

The basic power of the affect system is a consequence of its freedom to combine with a variety of other components in what may be called a *central assembly*. This is an executive mechanism upon which messages converge from all sources, competing from moment to moment for inclusion in this governing central assembly. The affect system can be evoked by central and peripheral messages from any source, and in turn it can control the disposition of such messages and their sources.

PRIMACY OF FACIAL EXPRESSION

If the affects are our primary motives, what are they and where are they? Affects are sets of muscle and glandular responses located in the face and also widely distributed through the body, which generate sensory feedback which is inherently either "acceptable" or "unacceptable." These organized sets of responses are triggered at subcortical centers where specific "programs" for each distinct affect are stored. These programs are innately endowed and have been genetically inherited. They are capable, when activated, of simultaneously capturing such widely distributed organs as the face, the heart, and the endocrines and imposing on them a specific pattern of correlated responses. One does not learn to be afraid or to cry or to be startled, any more than one learns to feel pain or to gasp for air.

Most contemporary investigators have pursued the inner bodily responses, after the James-Lange theory focused attention on their significance. Important as these undoubtedly are, I regard them as of secondary importance to the expression of emotion through the face. The relationship between the face and the viscera is analogous to that between the fingers and the forearm, upper arm, shoulders, and body. The fingers do not "express" what is in the forearm or shoulder or trunk. They lead rather than follow the movements in these organs to which they are an extension. Just as the fingers respond both more rapidly and with more precision and complexity than the grosser and slower-moving arm to which they are attached, so the face expresses affect, both to others and to the self via feedback, which is more rapid and more complex than any stimulation of which the slower-moving visceral organs are capable. There is, further, a division of labor between the face and the inner organs of affective expression similar to that which exists between the fingers and the arm. It is the very gross and slower-moving characteristic of the inner organ system which provides the counterpoint for the melody expressed by the facial solo. In short, affect is primarily facial behavior. Secondarily it is bodily behavior, outer skeletal and inner visceral behavior. When we become aware of these facial and/or visceral responses, we are aware of our affects. We may respond with these affects, however, without becoming aware of the feedback from them. Finally, we learn to generate, from memory, images of these same responses which we can become aware of with or without repetition of facial, skeletal, or visceral responses.

Taboos on Eye-to-eye Intimacy If we are happy when we smile and sad when we cry, why are we reluctant to agree that smiling or crying is primarily what it means to be happy or sad? Why should these be regarded as "expressions" of some other, inner state? The reasons are numerous, but not the least of them is a general taboo on sharing this knowledge in eye-to-eye intimacy.

The significance of the face in interpersonal relations cannot be exaggerated. Not only is it a communication center for the sending and receiving of information of all kinds, but because it is the organ of affect expression and communication, it is also necessarily brought under strict social control. There are universal taboos on looking too directly into the eyes of the other because of the likelihood of affect contagion, as well as escalation; because of the unwillingness to express affect promiscuously; and because of concern lest others achieve control through knowledge of one's otherwise private feelings. Man is primarily a voyeuristic animal, not only because vision is his most informative sense, but also because the shared eye-to-eye interaction is the most intimate relationship possible between human beings. There is in this way complete mutuality between two selves, each of which is simultaneously aware of the self and the other. Indeed, the intimacy of sexual intercourse is ordinarily attenuated, lest it become too intimate, by being performed in the dark. In the psychoanalytic myth, the crime of the son in witnessing the "primal scene" is voyeuristic, and Oedipus is punished, in kind, by blindness.

The taboo on the shared interocular experience is easily exposed. If I were to ask you to turn to another person and stare directly into his eyes while permitting him to stare directly into your eyes, you would become aware of the taboo. Ordinarily we confront each other by my looking at the bridge of your nose and your looking at my cheekbone. If our eyes should happen to meet directly, the confrontation is minimized by glancing down or away, by letting the eyes go slightly out of focus, or by attenuating the visual datum by making it ground to the sound of the other's voice, which is made more figural. The taboo is not only on looking too intimately but also on exposing the taboo by too obviously avoiding direct confrontation. These two strategies are taught by shaming the child for staring into the eyes of visitors and then shaming him a second time for hanging his head in shame before the guest.

Only the young or the young in heart are entirely free of the taboo. Those adults whose eyes are caught by the eyes of another in the shared interocular intimacy may fall in love on such an occasion or, having fallen in love, thereby express the special intimacy they have recaptured from childhood.

THE PRIMARY AFFECTS

If the affects are primarily facial responses, what are the major affects? I and my colleagues have distinguished eight innate affects. The positive affects are (1) *interest* or *excitement*, with eyebrows down, stare fixed or tracking an object; (2) *enjoyment* or *joy*, the smiling response; and (3) *surprise* or *startle*, with eyebrows raised and eye blink. The negative affects are (1) *distress* or *anguish*, the crying response; (2) *fear* or *terror*, with eyes frozen open in fixed stare or moving away from the dreaded object to the side and with skin pale, cold, and sweating and with trembling and hair erect; (3) *shame* or *humiliation*, with eyes and head lowered; (4) *contempt* or *disgust*, with the upper lip raised in a sneer; and (5) *anger* or *rage*, with a frown, clenched jaw, and red face.

Innate Activators of Affects Viewing these as innately patterned responses, are there also innate activators of each affect? Inasmuch as we have argued that the affect system is the primary motivational system, it becomes critical to provide a theory of the innate activators of the affect system. Consider the nature of the problem: The innate activators had to include the drives as innate activators but *not* to be limited to drives as exclusive activators. The neonate, for example, must respond with innate fear to any difficulty in breathing, but must also be afraid of other objects. Each affect had to be capable of being activated by a *variety* of unlearned stimuli. The child must be able to cry at hunger or loud sounds as well as at a diaper pin stuck in his flesh. Each affect had, therefore, to be activated by some general characteristic of neural stimulation, common to both internal and external stimuli, and not too stimulus-specific like a releaser. Next the activator had to be correlated with biologically useful information. The young child must fear what is dangerous and smile at what is safe. Next the activator had to "know the address" of the subcortical center at which the appropriate affect program is stored—not unlike the problem of how the ear responds correctly to each tone. Next, some of the activators had not to habituate, whereas others had to be capable of habituation; otherwise a painful stimulus might too soon cease to be distressing and an exciting stimulus never be let go—like a deer caught by a bright light. These are some of the characteristics which had to be built into the affect mechanism's activation sensitivity. The most economical assumption on which to proceed is to look for communalities among these varieties of characteristics of the innate alternative activators of each affect. This I and my associates have done, and we believe it is possible to account for the major phenomena with a few relatively simple assumptions about the general characteristics of the stimuli which innately activate affect.

Differences in Affect Activation We would account for the differences in affect activation by three general variants of a single principle—the density of neural firing or stimulation. By "density," we mean the number of neural firings per unit time. Our theory posits three discrete classes of activators of affect, each of which further amplifies the sources which activate them. These are stimulation increase, stimulation level, and stimulation decrease. Thus, there is provision for three distinct classes of motives—affects about stimulation which is on the increase, about stimulation which maintains a steady level of density, and about stimulation which is on the decrease. With respect to density of neural firing or stimulation, then, the human being is equipped for affective arousal for every major contingency. If internal or external sources of neural firing suddenly increase, he will startle or become afraid, or he will become interested, depending on the suddenness of increase of stimulation. If internal or external sources of neural firing reach and maintain a high, constant level of stimulation, which deviates in excess of an optimal level of neural firing, he will respond with anger or distress, depending on the level of stimulation. If internal or external sources of neural firing suddenly decrease, he will laugh or smile with enjoyment, depending on the suddenness of decrease of stimulation.

The general advantage of affective arousal to such a broad spectrum of levels and changes of level of neural firing is to make the individual care about quite different states of affairs in different ways. It should be noted that, according to our views, there are both positive and negative affects (startle, fear, interest) activated by stimulation increase but that only negative affects are activated by a continuing unrelieved level of stimulation (distress, anger), and only positive affects are activated by stimulation decrease (laughter, joy). This latter, in our theory, is the only remnant of the tension-reduction theory of reinforcement. Stimulation increase may, in our view, result in punishing or rewarding affect, depending on whether it is a more or less steep gradient and therefore activates fear or interest. A constantly maintained high level of neural stimulation is invariably punishing inasmuch as it activates the cry of distress or anger, depending on how high above optimal levels of stimulation the particular density of neural firing is. A suddenly reduced density of stimulation is invariably rewarding, whether, it should be noted, the stimulation which is reduced is itself positive or negative in quality. Stated another way, such a set of mechanisms guarantees sensitivity to whatever is new, to whatever continues for any extended period of time, and to whatever is ceasing to happen. In Figure 6–1, I have graphically represented this theory.

Thus any stimulus with a relatively sudden onset and a steep increase in the rate of neural firing will innately activate a startle response. As shown also in Figure 6–1, if the rate of neural firing increases less rapidly, fear is activated, and if still less rapidly, interest is innately activated. In contrast, any sustained increase in the level of neural firing, as with a continuing loud noise, would innately activate the cry of distress. If it were sustained and still louder, it would innately activate the anger

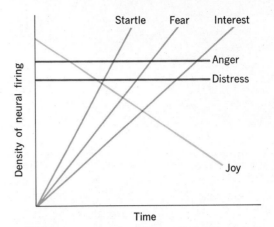

FIGURE 6–1 Graphical representation of a theory of innate activators of affect.

response. Finally, any sudden decrease in stimulation which reduced the rate of neural firing, as in the sudden reduction of excessive noise, would innately activate the rewarding smile of enjoyment.

CONCLUSION

In conclusion, the affect system provides the primary blueprints for cognition, decision, and action. Man is responsive to whatever circumstances activate positive and negative affects. Some of these circumstances innately activate the affects. At the same time, the affect system is also capable of being instigated by learned stimuli. The human being is thus urged by nature and by nurture to explore and to attempt to control the circumstances which evoke his positive and negative affective responses. It is the freedom of the affect system which makes it possible for the human being to begin to implement and to progress toward what he regards as an ideal state—one which, however else he may describe it, implicitly or explicitly entails the maximizing of positive affect and the minimizing of negative affect.

REFERENCE

SPRAGUE, J. M., CHAMBERS, W. W., & STELLAR, E. Attentive, affective and adaptive behavior in the cat. *Science*, 1961, **133**, 165–173.

Presently: Professor of Psychology at the Ohio Wesleyan University (since 1947).

Education: Doctor of Philosophy in psychology from the University of Chicago (1949).

Current major activity: Teaching and writing within a humanistic orientation to personality and social psychology.

Most rewarding projects: A new book, *Psychology for Our Time,* and a special honor and appointment: Centennial Professor at the American University in Beirut, Lebanon (1966–1967).

HUBERT BONNER

Future of humanistic psychology: Looks for epochal developments in the study of creativity and of ethical and aesthetic values.

Personal history: Born in Rolitz, Austria, and now a United States citizen. Assistant Professor of Philosophy at North Michigan University (1931–1933). Director of Student Personnel and Instructor in Psychology at Gogebic College (1933–1938). Lecturer at the University of Chicago (1940–1945). Dr. Bonner has been a Visiting Professor at Columbia University (1953–1955, 1956), at the University of Missouri (1953), and at the Ohio State University (1959–1961).

Writings: *Social Psychology: An Interdisciplinary Approach* (1953); *Group Dynamics: Principles and Applications* (1959); *Psychology of Personality* (1961); and *On Being Mindful of Man* (1965). Presently he is at work on *Psychology for Our Time* and on a new edition of his *Social Psychology.*

Present chapter: This chapter was prepared especially for this volume. The ideas it so poetically presents are part of *On Being Mindful of Man.*

Chapter 7
HUBERT BONNER

THE PROACTIVE PERSONALITY

Every psychologist who aims to present a scientific view of the human personality finds himself in a predicament. The more general or nomothetic his description of man is, the more he is impelled to ignore man's uniqueness. This statement holds with special force regarding the problem of psychological types. As a scientist, the psychologist must organize his knowledge of man into more or less stable categories, called *psychological types*. But the moment he classifies man into types, he calls attention to human similarities. Yet, if there is one thing that stands out in the endless research on human behavior, it is that no two human beings are exactly alike.

This difficulty can be reduced if we think of human types not as independent personality categories but as styles of intentional behavior. Every healthy human being approaches life situations in a characteristic manner, which is his unique way of perceiving and controlling himself and the social world which he inhabits. Among such styles of behavior, the best known are introversion and extraversion.

Since my aim in this paper is not to add to the existing typologies but to gain insight into human beings, I shall hypothesize not only that are we all introverted and extraverted in different circumstances but also that we are all proactive—that is, possessed of some degree of forward movement—in different life situations. The degree and extent of proaction will depend on the degree and extent of encouragement or suppression of the natural forward movement of the healthy organism. In this view, I am assuming that, just as we are all born with some degree of intelligence and that this intelligence varies from very high to very low, so we are all endowed with some degree of intentional forward thrust, or proaction. Like intelligence, proaction can be modified by circumstances and by the individual's effort to transform himself in the light of his individual abilities and social conditions.

METHOD AND POINT OF VIEW

The term "method" implies nothing pretentious and no rigorous technique of measurement; for the subject matter of my discussion is not amenable to formulation in measurement terms. It is broadly scientific and accepts information from any source if it expands our field of inquiry, does not go counter to well-established facts, and does not serve as a barrier to the understanding of the living human individual. More affirmatively, it is a way of studying the human being by means of an interrelated descriptive phenomenology, self-anchored perception, and immediate cognition. Each of these will now be amplified.

Descriptive Phenomenology Phenomenology holds that all human knowledge is based on *lived* experience. It deals with both empirical facts and emerging possibilities. It is the act of immediate absorption in experience as such. As a form of experiential knowledge, phenomenological psychology presupposes consciousness as a basic and central process. This consciousness is an act by means of which objects, persons, and situations present themselves and through which they are apprehended as being what they are. Accordingly, we can know the world of objects and persons only by means of conscious experience. Conscious experience thus gives us access to whatever exists. And since neither life nor consciousness is fixed but always in the making, phenomenological and proactive psychology must always be tentative. It cannot hold anything as permanently established; for psychology, like life itself, has a Rilkean quality in which every ending is but another beginning.

Self-anchored Perception This form of investigation is based on the conviction, validated by distinguished students of human conduct, that although a plenitude of subjects or cases may in some circumstances be

desirable, it is in fact neither necessary nor crucial (Skinner, 1959). The self-anchored mode of research holds that a careful consideration of the single case is often sufficient for the establishment of truth in psychology. More important, this view maintains that a person carefully observing his own subjective experience can add substantial and dependable insight into the nature of human behavior (Bonner, 1965; Stephenson, 1961). The psychologist with the gift of imagination knows that there are occasions when, in order to comprehend the nature of human nature, there is no substitute for his own human nature. Experience has taught him that often he can understand human beings only by means of his own humanity.

Immediate Cognition Although this is a less threatening and less disparaging term than "introspection," and especially "intuition," it has the quality of being holistic, of seeing things in wholes. It refers to the fact that normally our experience comes to us in the form of immediate understanding of totalities. Except in mental disorders, man's experience comes to him in more or less integrated form, and the more integrated he is as a person, the more dependable are his holistic observations of human behavior. He understands the meaning of other persons' conduct because he is himself a human being.

METHODOLOGICAL IMPLICATIONS
When skillfully integrated by a perceptive psychologist, descriptive phenomenology, self-anchored perception, and immediate cognition are valuable means to the understanding of proactive man. Since proactive man, as we shall see, is a life totality, not a partitioned mechanism, his integrated nature can be disclosed most adequately by means of the "methodology" which I have briefly described.

The general point of view in this study, then, is a broadly scientific humanism. It interprets psychological phenomena "experimentally," that is, as "provisional tries." This point of view is similar to that of John Dewey (1929), who many years ago defined thinking as a form of inner or conceptual experimentation. Such an approach makes room for self-observation as well as the observation of other people's behavior, including all those psychological phenomena, such as love, moral responsibility, creativity, and self-transformation, which, although important characteristics of the proactive personality, are excluded from traditional psychology.

A VIEW OF PROACTIVE MAN

I have said that we are all proactive in some degree. But the extent of the natural forward movement of each individual depends on two important circumstances, namely, the degree of facilitation or suppression provided by the human world in which he lives and his courage to face unstructured situations. Those who live in the past and immediate present feel secure because both temporal dimensions provide them with the safety which comes from knowing what they must do. A repressive socialization will hardly make for an adventurous individual or stimulate in him the freedom to make his own decisions. Proaction is at a low ebb in those persons who, having undergone a restrictive and often arbitrary socialization, have not cultivated the courage to face the consequences of their individual decisions.

To clarify the nature of the proactive style, it is necessary, therefore, to examine the roles of freedom and anxiety in the formation of the proactive personality.

Freedom and Anxiety I shall not engage in a dispute over the possibility of individual choice, for there are both logical and empirical evidences to substantiate a limited indeterminism in both man and nature. Far more important than quibbling over its possibility is examining its place in the life style of the proactive individual.

Whenever man is faced with the need to reach a decision on vital issues, especially those which relate to his own and other people's destinies, he experiences various degrees of anxiety. Freedom of choice involves the fear of unpredictable consequences. Both the proactive and the less forward-directed individuals experience anxiety in the face of freedom and an unstructured life situation. But the proactive individual, by virtue of his strong desire for new experience and his capacity to assimilate and control anxiety, becomes anxiety's master instead of its slave.

The paradox of intentionality, of forward movement, is that, although anxiety is induced by the unpredictability of human events, the more numerous and far-reaching an individual's choices are, the more satisfaction is in store for him when he gains control over his own conduct. He can say truly of himself that he *lives* instead of *being lived*. He can now view life not as a "useless passion" but as something he can love and enjoy.

Freedom, then, in the sense of making his own choices and reaching his own decisions regarding the person he wants to become, is a powerful psychological incentive of the proactive individual. And, although he is profoundly conscious of life's gratuity and the anxiety which it generates, he prefers the uncertainty of an unpredictable future to the security of a stable existence. This is the record of the "nonadjusted" person, the intense and turbulent individual, the broadly creative human being. It is a style of life that terrifies the less adventurous spirit, and thus its rarity on the continuum of human existence is understandable.

In a sentence, the proactive individual, although facing the same randomness and unpredictability of future events as the rest of us, can mitigate their effects upon himself through bold imagination, moral courage, and a determined effort to see what lies hidden behind his psychological horizon.

Aesthetic View of Life The proactive individual approaches life with a marked sense of form and symmetry, beauty and harmony. He evaluates experience by his individual standard of fitness rather than by utilitarian categories. Like creative persons generally, he trusts less what he knows and does than he trusts aesthetic experience in the making.

In his aesthetic perceptions, as in his loving encounter with the central others in his life, he comes as close as human beings possibly can to blending into a unity the fragments of his existence. By means of his sensitive awareness of all things beautiful, the proactive individual succeeds in transforming the strains and distresses of daily living into a tragic vision of life's possibilities. Living not alone by cold reason but also by aesthetic feeling, the proactive individual can abandon himself to the sensuous and sensual nature of his being, without victimizing himself by conventional and harmful self-accusation.

The intensely aesthetic meaning of his life impels the proactivert to validate truth by affective as well as rational predicates. His style of life confirms what thoughtful men have always known, that healthy human feelings are a necessary basis for understanding and validating truth. For him, facts alone can never be the final ground for truth; they must be allied with aesthetic judgment to make them true and meaningful.

Reference needs to be made to the proactivert's tragic vision of life's possibilities. This is a marked characteristic of his aesthetic style of life. It refers to his seeking of a perfection which is becoming, but never achieved. This tragic sense enables the proactive individual to feel the poignancy and gratuitousness of life, without yielding to cynicism and despair. At such a moment he can succumb to silent grief, and yet give grateful expression to the feeling that life is not wholly destitute of nobility and beauty.

Idealization My description thus far clearly shows that the proactive individual guides his life by ideals of his own choosing and making. However, it is a matter of great importance to distinguish between healthy and neurotic idealization. Neurotic idealization is a condition of self-deception. The individual in this condition strives to *appear* to be what he is not. It is important

for him that others *believe* that he is a certain type of individual, even though he may deviate markedly from the image of himself which he is trying to project. Morally speaking, the neurotic person is hypocritical or insincere—"inauthentic," as the existentialists would say. He is a slave to the image which he compulsively projects, and he wastes his psychological energies in trying to be faultless, a condition which he cannot reach. In him the anxiety which is the lot of all of us is a function not of his awareness of life's imperfectibility or of the awesomeness of human choice but of the fear that others will see through his counterfeit self.

While he is in this state of chronic defense, the neurotic individual is incapable of forward movement. He cannot choose or make decisions, for these entail risk regarding the unpredictable future. His fears are not proofs of his existence, not self-confirmatory, but lead to an intensification of his neurotic condition, of his fear of self-exposure.

The proactive individual, on the other hand, is relatively free of crippling self-deceptions. Although he strives mightily to transform himself in the light of his own ideal of who he wants to be, he finds self-validation only in actualizing what he potentially is.

In short, proactive idealization is the envisioning of ourselves as being different from what we are. Rather than being an act of self-deception and self-falsification, idealization is the process through which the healthy person generally and the proactive individual in particular become authentic persons.

Creativity In his approach to life, the proactive man is essentially creative. By this word I do not confine myself to artistic and scientific productions or to special skills or uncommon gifts, but I refer to the broader meaning of optimal psychological functioning in the form of self-actualization, constructive imagination, and intuitive perception of new relationships where none were perceived before. But the word has application also in the former sense, for I have found a high incidence of proaction in artists and creative scientists (Bonner, 1965).

The creative aspects of the proactive style reveal themselves in easily recognizable personal characteristics, of which the following seem at the present stage of my concern with the problem to be the most prominent.

First and practically without exception, the proactive man is moved by a strong need for individuation, for being himself as a person. If people are often intimidated by him or find him incomprehensible, it is because they are baffled by his relative unconcern for social adjustment, which they interpret as a form of eccentricity. Were they to look beyond this superficial layer of his being, they would find that his individuation is firmly grounded in the pursuit of excellence. Being moved by this exacting standard, he does not readily adapt himself to the commonplace, and for this reason the less proactive persons cannot fit him into conventional categories.

Second, not finding fulfillment in the existing canons of taste, the proactive man is constantly in pursuit of new values or a fresh reconstruction of the old ones. Transcendence of past accomplishments, both in others and in himself, is therefore another characteristic of the creative, proactive human being. This generates not only tensions in himself but also anxiety in others, which compounds his seeming threat to those who are baffled by his individuality. But instead of being maladjusted in the conventional sense by his transcendence of existing values, he finds increasing personal integration in "adjusting" himself to a world which he himself has largely created.

Finally, the creative individual, almost without exception, has a high degree of intellectual and emotional turbulence. This psychic unrest must never be confused with the emotional agitation and distress of neuroticism for, unlike the unproductiveness of the latter, it is an important source of creative and novel reconstruction.

Self-transformation Being essentially forward-thrusting, future-oriented, and broadly creative, the proactive individual is constantly engaged in the task of making of himself a "better" human being. In his own

eyes this is the most arduous and difficult of all creative acts for, in becoming what he wants to be, he must not only strive unrelentingly toward the ideal of what he wants to become but also transcend the molding power of his past. The degree of his success in achieving these objectives is a measure of his capacity to change himself from what he was yesterday into what he can be tomorrow.

Many a person, born in humble and culturally impoverished circumstances, has outgrown his past and become an individual of exceptional character and achievement. It is not necessary to cite dramatic cases of this transformation, such as Benjamin Franklin and Abraham Lincoln. The world is full of unsung instances. The latest in a long series is Jean Genet, as described by Sartre (1963). Although he had lived a life of crime and sexual perversion and had spent many years in prison, Genet succeeded in overcoming his past and directing his life toward an artistically creative future. He has become deeply aware that in his acts of choice about his own life he has freed himself from the destructive forces of his past. He has "cured" himself in the sense that he has transcended his prior reactive life and directed himself proactively toward a future of superior literary creations.

The proactive person, then, like every healthy and creative individual, resists engulfment by custom and rigid habits, the impairing force of narrow enculturation, and all barriers to a free and active forward movement of his personality. He has both the will and the capacity to resist external pressures toward conformity and to transform himself in the light of his personal goals and values. He is that individual who strives to attain a more free and creative state for himself and his fellow human beings. He exemplifies in his style of living the belief that the future of man is largely of his own making. He validates the view that man is possessed of a creative selfhood.

In fine, proactive man is that being who

more than any other human being strives to make of himself a work of art.

CONCLUSION

In this paper I have tried to present as precise a description of the proactive personality as present evidence and discussion permit. It reveals that the proactive person, like all persons, is not an achievement but a process of becoming. It shows him to be what in a general way every superior human being is: an idealist, an innovator, and one who does not fit comfortably into the conventional social scheme.

The proactive man, finally, combines in himself the defiance of a Prometheus and the self-surrender of a Job, in his own unique way. Prometheus was defiant, to be sure; yet his defiance was not willful, but a strong determination to fulfill his proactive being. Job did not meekly resign himself to an arbitrary fate, but expressed trust in his power of endurance. Each had faith in his ability to make himself into a better human being. Together their characters express the Nietzschean view that man is that being who must continually surpass himself.

REFERENCES

BONNER, H. *On being mindful of man.* Boston: Houghton Mifflin, 1965.

DEWEY, J. *The quest for certainty.* New York: Putnam, 1929.

SARTRE, J.-P. *Saint Genet: Actor and martyr.* (Tr. by G. Frechtman.) New York: George Braziller, 1963.

SKINNER, B. F. A case history in scientific method. In S. Koch (Ed.), *Psychology: A study of a science.* Vol. 2. *General systematic formulations, learning and special processes.* New York: McGraw-Hill, 1958. Pp. 359–379.

STEPHENSON, W. Scientific creed—1961: The centrality of self. *Psychological Record,* 1961, **11**, 18–25.

Presently: Author and essayist.

Education: Schools in Leicester (England).

COLIN WILSON

Current major activities: "I divide my time equally between writing books about my 'new existentialism' and writing novels. I find the latter an important way of illustrating the former. My new existentialism comes from a recognition that the continental variety (of Sartre, Heidegger, and so on), because of its pessimistic premises, has ended in a cul-de-sac and is therefore as unproductive as the equally paralyzed philosophy of logical positivism and language analysis."

Most rewarding project: "This 'phenomenological existentialism' offers the prospect of the most exciting breakthrough that has ever happened to the human race."

Future of humanistic psychology: "Someone has defined existentialism as a study of 'man's alienation from the source of power, meaning, and purpose.' Would it not be fantastic if phenomenology could actually take steps toward the solution of such an ultimate problem? For me the lines of research pursued by Maslow and Cantril—Maslow's evolutionary psychology and Cantril's transactionism—are not merely closely related; they are fundamentally identical. My own phenomenology steals shamelessly from both, as well as from Michael Polanyi, who has also influenced both."

Personal history: British civil service for eighteen months. Worked at dishwashing, and ditchdigging, in a coffee bar, in a plastics factory, and in offices. Lecturer in various American universities (1961 forward). Visiting Professor at Hollins College, in Virginia (1966–1967); at the University of Washington, Seattle (Fall, 1967); and at Purdue University (Spring, 1968).

Writings: The "Outsider" series, consisting of *The Outsider* (1956), *Religion and the Rebel* (1957), *The Stature of Man* (1958) (English title: *The Age of Defeat*), *The Strength to Dream* (1962), *Origins of the Sexual Impulse* (1964), and *Beyond the Outsider* (1965). An outline of the basic ideas of this series is contained in *Introduction to the New Existentialism* (1966). Mr. Wilson is also the author of eight novels, including *Ritual in the Dark* (1960) and *The Glass Cage* (1966) and of studies of Rasputin and Shaw. A "preliminary autobiography," *Voyage to a Beginning,* is due to appear in England in 1967.

Present chapter: This inquiry into human potentiality was prepared for the present volume.

Chapter 8
COLIN WILSON

EXISTENTIAL PSYCHOLOGY:
A NOVELIST'S APPROACH

It is slightly embarrassing to find myself in this company of scientists and psychologists. I am a novelist, and I consider myself an existentialist philosopher. I happen to believe that there are certain things you *cannot* say in a treatise on philosophy which you *can* say in a novel.

There is a certain danger in being nothing but a thinker. Consider: At the time I am beginning this chapter, I should be writing a novel. I have got well into this novel—a kind of psychological thriller concerned with the "dark room" and sensory deprivation—and I don't like to leave it. Because I have got myself into a kind of *creative* flow: The people and events have got me so interested that this interest has become self-perpetuating. It increases without much conscious effort on my part. Now if I spend a couple of hours on this essay, I shall find that I have narrowed down my senses and cut myself off from this source of "inspiration." My mind puts on its thinking harness, and at the end of a couple of hours, it can't get it off; it is stuck. Let me be clear, I am not denying that this thinking is also a creative process. But it puts my Pegasus into a tighter harness and gives him a heavier cart to pull. My intellect is like an oil derrick that tries to drill down to subconscious regions of my mind, to release the same secret flow of vitality and affirmation that I may experience on a spring morning or on seeing a pretty girl or while listening to music.

All this lands me in the heart of my subject. (The novel will have to wait until to-morrow.) I am a phenomenologist, and my philosophical work is closely related to that of Husserl and Merleau-Ponty. But I have never yet opened a book on phenomenology that stated clearly the nature of its central obsession. Let me try this.

THE ROBOT AND I

I am writing this on an electric typewriter. When I learned to type, I had to do it painfully and with much nervous wear and tear. But at a certain stage a miracle occurred, and this complicated operation was "learned" by a useful robot whom I conceal in my subconscious mind. Now I only have to think about what I want to say; my robot secretary does the typing. He is really very useful. He also drives the car for me, speaks French (not very well), and occasionally gives lectures at American universities.

He has one enormous disadvantage. If I discover a new symphony that moves me deeply, or a poem or a painting, this bloody robot promptly insists on getting in on the act. And when I listen to the symphony for the third time, *he* begins to anticipate every note. He listens to it automatically, and I lose all the pleasure. He is most annoying when I am tired, because then he tends to take over most of my functions without even asking me. I have even caught him making love to my wife.

My dog doesn't have this trouble. Admittedly, he can't learn languages or how to type, but if I take him for a walk on the cliffs, he obviously experiences every time just as if it is the first. I can tell this by the ecstatic way he bounds about. Descartes was all wrong about animals. It isn't the animals who are robots; it's us.

There are times when I wonder whether I can really afford my robot. He costs so much to run, far more than my car. Admittedly, it is all my fault. When I was in my teens, I had a strongly scientific bent. And I so hated being a teen-ager, a churning mass of emotions and embarrassments. I was like a man learning to skate, wasting a vast amount of energy and getting covered with bruises. So I set out to develop the robot, just as a factory manager would call in an efficiency expert. Soon he had things under control. He learned how to turn my emotional problems into symbols and equations and how to avoid some of the really destructive emotions that sometimes used to consume my energies like a forest fire. I soon found that I could think usefully and continuously, for hours on end if necessary. I could concentrate my mind on a problem with the precision of a microscope. I began to write books, and the books were accepted, which made life much easier. The trouble was that he became *too* damned efficient. It was all very nice being able to think efficiently and sort out my emotional problems. But life became so much duller. His obsessive tidiness used up so much time and energy. I would sometimes go for a country walk, and I couldn't hear the birds because his machinery was chattering along like an old typewriter. In a sense, he became my jailer. In my childhood, I was always having marvelous experiences of freedom. Sometimes just coming out of school in the afternoon would make me burst with sheer joy, the feeling, "I'm *free* —how lovely everything is." Now, with this efficient, interfering robot, I have such experiences only once a year. When I threaten to get rid of him, he always points out reasonably that he saves me all kinds of unpleasant experiences too. And I suppose, looking back on it, this is true. One tends to remember the nice moments of childhood, but there were so many nasty ones. He said to me only the other day, "Wilson, you're a fool. When I took you over, you were a stupid adolescent. You didn't really enjoy life because you disliked yourself too much. Well, you must admit you like yourself much more now. Why, because of me, you're more *godlike*—let's not be shy of the word."

I got to thinking about this. It was obviously true. I wouldn't go back to my childhood for worlds. It was a nasty, beastly time, and I hated it. And although I envy the way my dog rushes around on the cliffs, I wouldn't really like to be a dog either. I thought, "There must be *some* way out of this stupid situation I've got myself into. There must be some way of outwitting this robot. After all, he's only a machine."

It's really an interesting problem. Man has reached his present position on the evolutionary ladder because he is a tool-making animal, a machine-making animal . . . in fact, a robot-making animal. But his sheer cleverness is proving to be his downfall (although I wouldn't have you suppose I am pessimistic about the issue). It is the same with my library. I started off with half a dozen books, and it didn't really matter where I kept them; I could always put my hand on a book when I needed it. Then I got carried away and began buying them by the dozen. I put shelves up all over the house. But I found I had to devote more and more time to keeping them in order, and finally I had to devise a kind of a cataloguing system. Even so, it often costs me an hour to find a book. It's the same principle as when you're having a complicated argument, and you keep losing the thread of the argument and have to ask, "What was I saying?" This never happens when you're discussing baseball.

But when I was discussing this with my robot the other day, he made a good point. He said, "You're blaming me for all this, but it's your own fault. It's a case of the bad workman blaming his tools. I'm only your tool. You made me. And the reason I'm so unsatisfactory is that I'm such a crude piece of work. The real trouble is that you're lazy and self-indulgent. You complain that I take over when you're listening to a symphony. All right, take me to pieces and introduce some more complicated circuits. As to your complaints about the energy I waste, I've never heard anything more dishonest. *You're* in control of the energy supply, not me. By using the proper channels, you can get as much as you like." "But what *are* the proper channels?" I asked him, but he just shrugged and said, "Don't be so damned lazy. Think it out for yourself."

The Saint Neots Margin Let me underline this last point with an autobiographical digression. I promise it won't be too irrelevant.

Some years ago, I was hitchhiking up the Great North Road out of London, on my way to Peterborough. I was in a state of utter boredom and discouragement. It was a hot, dusty, Saturday afternoon, and there was little traffic on the roads. What made it worse was that I didn't much want to go to Peterborough. It was a rather dreary "duty" call. And I wasn't much looking forward to going back to London either, since I had a particularly boring job at the time. So I was bursting with ennui and resentment—a feeling of total life rejection. If I'd had a bottle of whisky, I'd have got drunk and slept under the hedge.

After half an hour or so, a lorry stopped for me. This didn't improve my temper at all; I just thought it was about damned time. But after he'd been going for about twenty minutes, there was a knocking noise from his gearbox. He explained that he would have to stop at the next garage and get it fixed. So when he stopped, I got out and walked on. I was in such a state of boredom I didn't even feel annoyed about the inconvenience.

I wandered on for another half hour, getting hotter and more disgusted with life. Finally, another lorry stopped for me. Again, I didn't feel grateful; I was too tired. But after the lorry had been chugging along for twenty minutes or so, an odd coincidence occurred: There was the same knocking noise from inside *his* gearbox. This seemed too much; I felt that fate was persecuting me. The driver told me he'd have to drop me off at the next garage. However, he found that if he dropped his speed to about 20 miles an hour, the knocking noise stopped. The moment he got above that

speed, it started again. So he got his speed up to about 19½ miles, and we found that this seemed OK. He was as anxious to get to Peterborough as I was and didn't want to stop. So we both sat there, straining our ears for any sign of the knocking noise and keeping our fingers crossed. Finally, the driver said, "I think we'll make it if we stick at this speed. It can't be anything serious."

As he said this, I felt a great burst of elation. And then I caught myself feeling it, and thought, "This is absurd. Half an hour ago, you were in a state of total disgust with life. Well, nothing has happened. It isn't as if you've found a £5 note or something. All that has happened is that *a threat of inconvenience has arisen, and now the threat has been removed.* So you're back where you started, and yet you are suddenly aware of your freedom!"

I saw I'd hit on an idea of profound importance. Why hadn't it given me pleasure when a lorry had stopped for me? There is obviously an area of the human psyche that can be stimulated by pain (or inconvenience) and *yet not by pleasure.* I recognized there in the lorry, that without involvement, commitment, participation—call it what you will—but without any emotional stake in what is going on, boredom leads to apathy, which may soon mount to utter distaste for life. So forcibly did this recognition come home to me that I named it by our location at the time—in the town of Saint Neots in Huntingdonshire—the "Saint Neots margin." It is basically an extremely familiar idea. It refers to that state of mind—of boredom, resentment, life devaluation—that we fall into so easily. Auden caught it when he wrote:

Put the car away; when life fails
What's the good of going to Wales?

"When life fails. . . ." That's the problem. Give people peace and quiet, and they soon want to commit suicide. Let a threat of inconvenience arise, and suddenly they're enjoying life again. I remember the early days of the war in England, how happy everybody was. And yet there is something quite mad about this peculiarity of human nature. It is like buying a powerful car and discovering that it will do 90 miles an hour *in reverse* and only 20 miles an hour going forward.

Now what happened to me, passing through Saint Neots, is obviously the answer to the robot problem. I had let myself get into a state of boredom and resentment. The threat of inconvenience made me snap out of it. It is true: our energies are almost infinite. But when there is no challenge, no threat, present, we tend to fall into a state of *sleep*. And in sleep, the robot takes over. It is a kind of vicious circle.

FREEDOM: "THE ORGASM EXPERIENCE"

But having considered this negative side of the problem—the robot—let us take a look at its other aspect. My sudden flashes of freedom have a revelatory nature. I am inclined to refer to these moments as the "orgasm experience"—understanding, by this, not merely the sexual orgasm, but any kinds of similar experience, due to music, poetry, a spring morning, your first Martini of the evening. [Maslow (1962) calls these "peak experiences," but for the moment, I will stick to my own terminology.] Consider the meaning-content of these orgasm experiences and what they have in common. It will reveal, I believe, some very important conclusions.

To begin with, let us merely try to describe what happens in the orgasm experience. There can be no doubt whatever that the first word that comes to mind is "freedom."

When my six-year-old daughter has finished her bath, she is inclined to leave the sponge where you can knock it on the floor. And unfortunately, it is usually sopping with water, so that it squelches and makes a nasty wet mess. So if I see the sponge on the side of the bath, I place my index finger on it and press it gently. If it is full of water, the water appears in the depression around my finger. I cannot tell whether the sponge is full of water just by looking at it.

This image describes something else about the orgasm experience. What happens is that my "mechanical threshold," my robot levels, have been pushed lower for a moment, and the freedom comes bubbling out. *In my ordinary, everyday state of consciousness, I am not aware of my freedom;* I can't see it or feel it, any more than I can see the water in the sponge.

Another interesting observation arises from all this. In my ordinary state of consciousness, the word "me" refers to me, the personality—me, Colin Wilson. In the orgasm experience, I suddenly realize that this "me" isn't me at all; *he is a robot.* The me called "Colin Wilson" is entirely mechanical. The "real me" is not mechanical; it is pure freedom. Pure freedom and energy, power to change my life, to do what I like. This is why in the orgasm experience, visible objects become so intensely beautiful. It is not the robot seeing them anymore. It is the real "you."

This, incidentally, is what mysticism is all about. Blake called the robot the "spectre," but it is all the same thing.

The Princeton "black-room" experiments (Vernon, 1963) only underline these points. I am 99 percent machine or robot. Most of my consciousness tends to be a mechanical affair. If a sudden emergency—or stimulus—arises, my "free" levels quickly take over. But in the black room, the robot part of me says, "No emergency present—may as well go to sleep." Sleep is the opposite of the orgasm experience, of the experience of freedom. But even when the body has had its fill of sleep after twenty hours in the black room, the robot continues to repeat mechanically, "No emergency present; may as well sleep." So the black room artificially induces the opposite of the freedom experience. And the longer you stay in it, the heavier the burden of consciousness becomes. Your only salvation under the circumstances would be to use your brain—to think, to develop ideas, to feel, if possible. But the darkness has you hypnotized or, rather, has the robot hypnotized. (Hypnotism is the science of taking command of the robot.)

Consciousness and Habit At this point I'll be autobiographical again for just a moment.

In my teens I read a lot of poetry. But there were whole days when poetry left me cold, particularly after a really boring and frustrating week at the office (I left school at sixteen). Sometimes, on a Sunday, I'd spend the whole day trying to snap out of this dreary state of coldness, of indifference. Yet it would be like trying to start a car when you've flooded the carburetor. Keats, Shelley, Wordsworth, Rupert Brooke —all would fail to touch me. Then sometimes, toward evening, it would seem that my sheer mental exhaustion was doing the trick. A warm glow would begin to pervade my brain. And then suddenly it was expanding, way beyond "everyday consciousness." It was as if a thick fog was lifting and revealing distant views of immense beauty. Occasionally these poetic experiences would rise to the level of genuine mystical insight. I was all freedom; it was like a sexual orgasm that could burn steadily for hours instead of seconds. There was a sense that human notions of good and evil are absurdly stupid and limited, based upon our spoiltness, our laziness.

These experiences left me with one certainty. Consciousness may be 99 percent mechanical. But it is that other 1 percent that counts. That 1 percent, by continuous effort, can gradually subdue the other 99 percent. It is a long and painful job, like pushing a stalled car uphill. Yet a point comes where you get over the top, and away you go. Sartre (1936) insists that consciousness is entirely mechanical, that its changes are mechanical changes, like the movements of the tides, sucked by the moon —that the sea has no power to move itself. He is a liar. It is hard work, but it can be done. It could be done a lot more easily if we understood the mechanism of the robot.

This examination of the robot is called *phenomenology*, and its basic techniques were laid down by Edmund Husserl (1912). At this point I should try to express how I see phenomenology. Every phenomenologist has a different approach.

If I am watching a weight lifter, I am aware of his effort; I can see it in the straining muscles, in the sweat on his forehead. I am aware that he has every *intention* of raising the weight. There is nothing me-chanical about it; he is intensely aware of every ounce of effort that it is costing him.

When I was learning to type, I had the same agonized awareness of my intentions. But after months of practice it became a habit. Now if anyone saw me using this typewriter, they might think *I* was a machine, I am doing it so quickly and efficiently. But I'm not a machine. In spite of appearance, I *intend* every word that I type (allowing for misprints). Luckily most of my "intentions" have been passed on to my robot. They have become mechanical. They are still intentions, but they are mechanical intentions. I am no longer painfully aware of them, as the weight lifter is aware of his intentions.

Consciousness is composed largely of mechanical intentions, habits. But they must not be mistaken for mechanisms. A mechanical intention is not a mechanism; it is half-and-half. When the sun comes up in the morning, that is a mechanism; it doesn't intend to. When my consciousness returns in the morning, that is partly a mechanism, but it is very largely my conscious intention. (The confusion here arises over the word "consciousness." We tend to use it as a kind of antonym of the "unconscious." In the sense in which it is used in phenomenology, consciousness *is* the mind—"conscious" and "subconscious.")

These habit mechanisms are "laborsaving devices." They are intended to leave the conscious mind free for more important problems. And it is here that the problem arises. There is a whole number of reasons why we don't use consciousness to attack more important problems. To begin with, we get lazy. This is one of the more usual consequences of having laborsaving devices. Secondly, the habit mechanisms work so swiftly and efficiently that, before we know where we are, a "problem" is being solved by habit, before new problems come along. So we get bored. Third, and most important, we tend to forget that a mechanical intention is not a mechanism. We start to take consciousness for granted. So the mind starts to get compartmentalized—just as a big business tends to get "departmentalized," with each department working in relative isolation, only dimly aware of the others. What is here most important is that I don't allow this to happen. The boss should keep coming out of his office at the top of the building and taking a stroll around the works.

To put this in another way, consciousness is made up of intentions. Most of them are mechanical; a small number are conscious. And one gets a "balance of power" situation in consequence. If too many of the intentions get "mechanized," consciousness becomes robotic, automatic; you even *see* automatically; you stop *feeling*. In this situation—as I discovered in my teens—a real mental effort will change the balance of power and restore the necessary level of freedom to consciousness. It can be done purely instinctively, by what Blake calls "mental fight." Or it can be done far more consciously, by the various disciplines of phenomenology which consist in isolating intentions.

External Stimulation and Internal Intentionality It takes only a little thought to see that this matter of freedom is one of our most basic values. When you call a man a "moron," you mean that he strikes you as largely mechanical, a robot—the vacant gaze, the automatic movements, and so on. (The word "zombi" catches this even more distinctly—the robotic movements.) On the other hand, when you look at a highly intelligent and sympathetic person, you feel his freedom; you *see* it in his eyes.

The life of every animal is a continuous interaction with its environment. When I take my dog on the beach and throw a ball, he becomes twice as alive. If he is lying on the rug and I am reading, he promptly falls asleep because there is nothing to keep him interested. He *needs* the outside world to keep him alive and interested. The life in him simply wilts and collapses when the world doesn't present him with something to do.

The same kind of thing happens when a man of sixty retires to the country cottage he has always dreamed about—and is dead

within a year of sheer boredom and inactivity. He has no inner resources to fall back on.

At first sight, the black-room experiments seem to justify the worst kind of pessimism about human nature. What Sartre said about his café proprietor in *Nausea* (1938), "When his café empties, his head empties too," seems to be true of everybody. In the last analysis, there is not so much difference between Einstein and my dog. We are all dependent on external stimuli.

But then, consider a very simple and obvious matter: the sexual stimulus. Most animals need the smell of the female in heat to excite them sexually. Men have gone one stage further. They don't need the smell of estrus; the sight of a naked woman serves the same purpose.

But unlike any other animal in the world, man can also become sexually stimulated without the actual physical presence of the sexual object. That is, he can use his imagination to produce the sexual stimulus, even to the point of orgasm. We regard masturbation as a slightly shameful subject; but, viewed phenomenologically, it is one of man's greatest glories. He has such remarkable control over his *sexual intentions* that the presence of the physical object is unnecessary.

The Saint Neots margin problem can now be stated with more precision. If you peer into the darkness to distinguish some vague object, you are increasing the intentionality of your act of seeing. If you concentrate on some interesting problem, you are increasing the intentionality of your intellectual perception. And if you simply happen to be feeling healthy and optimistic on a spring morning, you can increase the general intensity of your consciousness by simply opening your senses; in this case, *all* the intentions are affected.

The one thing that human beings want above all others is the moment of freedom, of orgasm, of intense and ecstatic happiness —in short, a change in the quality of consciousness. Yet we leave this important function to our robot levels. Under circumstances of comfort the robot tends to take over. A man might spend years in prison dreaming of freedom. Yet within twenty-four hours of leaving the jail, he has lost his freedom. The intention he had directed toward freedom has vanished because he is outside the jail. The robot quickly takes over; consciousness yawns and goes to sleep. Freedom vanishes. In a paradoxical sense, he was freer in jail.

All this sounds pessimistic, but that is to miss the point entirely. For if you think about it for a moment, you will see that man is superior to the animal—in freedom —precisely because of the robot. Although an animal is never at the mercy of the robot, it has no freedom because it is stuck in the present. The whole purpose of the robot is to give man a certain *continuity of existence*, to save him from the meaninglessness of living in a perpetual "present."

FACULTY X

This brings me to my final point, and the one with which I shall undoubtedly arouse most dissension.

When I was a child I was always fascinated by sheets of water. If I went out on a long bus trip, I used to keep my nose glued to the windowpane in case we went over a bridge. Water always produced in me a strange and ecstatic excitement. But if the bus ever stopped near the water, I was always disappointed because there was nothing you could *do* about that strange desire. If I stared fascinated in a sweetshop window, I knew exactly what I wanted to do with the sweets. But what can you do with a sheet of water?

At about the age of thirteen, I came across a passage in Dr. Johnson's *Rasselas* (1759) that struck me as important. The prince remarks: "Man has surely some latent sense for which this place affords no gratification, or he has some desires distinct from sense that must be satisfied before he can be happy." That last part sounded like a description of my problem with the sheets of water. Yeats (1939) had made the same remark, speaking in a poem about a waterfall that he loved, yet knowing that if he touched it, it would be only "cold stone and water."

At a later period I christened this "latent sense" or desire distinct from sense "faculty X." It seemed to me that all poetry and mysticism prove that man indeed possesses some faculty that he hardly ever makes use of. It woke up when Proust tasted the biscuit dipped in tea. It is the freedom experience. It accounts for that feeling of, "Of *course*, how obvious!" in the orgasm experience.

I was also particularly fascinated by a couple of experiences described by Strindberg that seemed to reveal yet a new dimension of faculty X. On one occasion he was sitting in a café with a friend and trying to describe to the friend a conversation that had taken place some weeks previously in another café. He started to describe the other café in detail and suddenly found himself sitting there. Or rather, he was sitting in both cafés at once, with an odd effect of double exposure. The odd thing was that a door had appeared in a place where previously there was only a wall, and people were walking in and out of it—total strangers. With an effort Strindberg dismissed the hallucination and brought himself back to "reality," that is, the first café. Yet it is a pity that he didn't take special note of the strangers and check up on whether they were really coming into the other café at that moment.

On another occasion Strindberg was ill and was longing to be with his family. He imagined the room with such intensity that he suddenly found himself standing in it (although it was many hundreds of miles away). His mother-in-law was playing the piano and looked up and saw him. When a moment later he disappeared, the old lady quickly wrote him a letter describing the "apparition" and asking him whether he was well; she was afraid it was a precursor of death.

This appears to be a case of the Proustian experience taken a stage further, and it may well explain the many well-authenticated cases of apparitions of the living. However, I do not insist on it. It merely seemed to me, on reading these experiences of Strindberg (who was half insane when he had them), that his abnormal mental state had stimulated the normally latent faculty X.

But in view of what has been said above, it can be seen that there is no need to posit some faculty X. The moment man began to develop symbol memory, language, and so on, he had begun to create a new faculty. His very continuity is a new faculty, a new dimension of his being.

The Spirit-Body Duality In a brilliant passage in his autobiography, Wells (1934) compared men to the earliest amphibians, prehistoric creatures who wanted to become land animals but who possessed only flippers for moving around on land. After a short time on land, they had to get back to the sustaining medium of the sea. This, it seems to me, describes man's present position. His natural sphere is freedom, the world of the mind (which Teilhard de Chardin calls the *noosphere*).[1] The problem is that he has insufficient control of the robot. And yet Shaw (1921) once remarked about evolutionary change, "The brain will not fail when the will is in earnest." The concept of faculty X has a certain importance in that it gives us a sense of something to strive for. A philosopher like Gilbert Ryle (1949), who insists that the old mind-body dichotomy is due to a confusion of language, may be right in many ways; but in the ultimate sense he is wrong. For there *is* a dichotomy, between our robot levels and our freedom.

If I happen to be reading a book like Wells's *Outline of History* (1920), I experience an odd sensation. To begin with, I become aware that I am not all that unique. There have been millions of species before man. I am merely a member of a species. One day, man may be as extinct as the dinosaur. I become aware of myself as a grain of sand on a universal beach.

At the same time, this humility is checked by an interesting reflection. I may be a mere grain of sand, but I am quite unlike all other animals in one important respect. My body may be doomed to die, but here is my mind, hovering over the page, contemplating eons of history with total objectivity. Physically speaking, I am a limited

[1] See Severin's description of Teilhard's concept of the noosphere in Chap. 16 of this book. [Editor]

human being. Mentally speaking, I am as timeless and impersonal as the stars. I am a mind grasping the universe objectively, and it doesn't matter whether I am a duke or a dustman, a human being or a Martian, a man or a woman. For the time being I have transcended my everyday, "human" aspects and have become a kind of immortal. Or, to use Husserl's language, I have placed the "world" in brackets and become aware of myself as a transcendental ego.

It has been Husserl's achievement to give a new meaning to the spirit-body duality and to bring a new unifying principle into philosophy. Its full implications are so enormous that there are very few phenomenologists who have even started to grasp them. But let me try to outline them.

We develop "intentions" as we develop a taste for foreign cooking. (In fact, such a taste *is* an intention.) If I pick up a difficult philosophical article, I have to force myself to read it. Six weeks later I may have grasped so many of its implications that next time I see the name of the philosopher on an article, I seize it with interest and devour it. My "interest" was an *intention* which I developed, as I might develop a taste for olives. In a year's time my interest in this philosopher may be so deep as to seem a natural appetite.

According to Husserl all our appetites, all our intentions, are developed in this way; none are "natural." But they are passed on to our preconscious regions as habits, until we are no longer aware of them as intentions. Husserl's disciplines enable us to reexcavate these habits and to realize them as living intentions. This, in turn, takes away our boredom, our tendency to let familiarity breed contempt.

But it can be seen that what phenomenology has done is to restore primacy to the will, as in the philosophy of Nietzsche or Shaw. In revealing mechanisms to be buried intentions, it suggests the possibility that the answers to all the fundamental problems of the human psyche may be disclosed in terms of *willed intentions* instead of mechanisms. This should bring a certain simplicity into some of the classical psychological problems—for example, in the psychology of sex, where no one has ever been able to suggest how to draw a line between "normal sexuality" and "perversions," i.e., between instincts and intentions. According to the Husserlian view, "instinct" is a misnomer; sex is simply a series of intentions, buried at different levels, and therefore more or less accessible to limited everyday consciousness. Again, Saint Augustine remarked, "What is time? When I do not ask the question, I know the answer" (Wittgenstein, 1953). Naturally; for the level of everyday consciousness that asks the question has no contact with the level of human intentionality concerned with time consciousness.

Beyond the Robot In short, the word "robot" is also a misnomer in this connection. He is actually composed of compacted layer upon layer of willed intentions.

A metaphysician might leap to the question of whether our birth and death may not be interpreted as willed intentions. This hardly concerns us here. We are concerned solely with the new picture of psychology that emerges from Husserl. In a sense, it could be likened to a kind of archaeology. When I speak of "myself" in the everyday sense, I am speaking of the uppermost layer of willed intentions. One layer below these lies the realm of my acquired habits: typing, speaking French, reading, etc. Another two or three layers down lie my sexual intentions, which can actually be studied *as* willed intentions if I develop a certain skill in descriptive analysis. The archaeological equivalent of these layers would be Troy or Babylon. And below these lie the mental equivalents of the Miocene, the Jurassic, the Carboniferous. Up to a few hundred years ago, man's historical knowledge was limited; now he can look back over a hundred million years of life. But his psychological knowledge is still in its crude, prehistoric state. The mind's archaeology must be made accessible to present consciousness: In this direction lies man's development.

CONCLUSION

It can be seen that I consider the basic problem to be that of the dead weight of consciousness. (I am here using the word in the phenomenological sense of the whole mind.) Man is in his paradoxical, neurotic, highly dangerous position because he has given too much of the control to the robot. If he is to have any real freedom, if freedom is to be more than a word that is mocked by the realities of politics and human weakness, then man must gain control over consciousness in a real sense. He has some slight control at the moment, but the muscle is undeveloped through lack of use. It will remain undeveloped while he is half asleep and unaware of its existence. His tendency to laziness—and mechanicalness—is the great obstacle. He must set out to develop this "muscle" (which we might call faculty X) as consciously as a marksman sets out to develop a good aim. Man has to strive consciously to change the balance of power between his robot levels and his conscious intentions. His most valuable weapon is Husserlian phenomenology.

The hypotheses I've been describing, I might add parenthetically, should have some interesting repercussions on existential philosophizing. For example, philosophers have traditionally treated the problems of man's contingency—his proneness to illness, accident, and death—as an absolute. But we know that a man in a state of "freedom," in the "peak experience," can stay awake as long as he likes. Sleep seems to be largely a mechanism of the robot. Everyone has noticed how difficult it is to stay awake when he is bored and how difficult it is to fall asleep when he is stimulated, intellectually or physically. Research on cancer indicates that it is partly a psychosomatic illness: that it tends to be a concomitant of psychological defeat, of surrendering to the robot. It is even conceivable that men who have managed an ultimate change of the psychological balance of power might discover that death, like sleep, is to a large extent a mechanism of the robot.

All this is speculation. What matters is that phenomenology has, so to speak, endowed human evolution with a conscious intention. It has revealed that man's incorrigible craving for optimism and purpose can be justified on basic epistemological grounds. Moreover, there is a practical point of application. There is an amusing story about Sartre, that after the war he would arouse audiences to fever pitch of enthusiasm by telling them, "You are free; go out and claim your freedom." But the enthusiasm never lasted for more than a few hours because the audiences never knew what to *do*—where to make a start.

Phenomenology *is* the start. It is also a direction. We face the absurd possibility that the creature we have called "man" does not yet exist.

REFERENCES

AUDEN, W. H. *Poems.* London: Faber, 1933.

HUSSERL, E. *Ideas.* London: G. Allen, 1912.

JOHNSON, S. *Rasselas: Prince of Abissinia,* 1759.

MASLOW, A. H. *Toward a psychology of being.* Princeton, N.J.: Van Nostrand, 1962.

RYLE, G. *The concept of mind.* London: Hutchinson, 1949.

SARTRE, J.-P. *The transcendence of the ego.* New York: Noonday Press, 1936.

SARTRE, J.-P. *Nausea.* London: John Lehmann, 1938.

SHAW, G. B. *Back to Methueselah: As far as thought can reach.* Fair Lawn, N.J.: Oxford Univer. Press, 1947.

STRINDBERG, J. A. *Legends: Autobiographical sketches.* London: Melrose, 1912.

TEILHARD DE CHARDIN, P. *Le phenomene humaine.* Paris: Editions de Seuil, 1955.

VERNON, J. A. *Inside the black room.* London: Souvenir Press, 1963.

WELLS, H. G. *Experiment in autobiography.* London: Golancz, 1934.

WITTGENSTEIN, L. *Philosophical investigations.* Fair Lawn, N.J.: Oxford Univer. Press, 1953.

YEATS, W. B. Under Ben Bulben. In *Last poems and two plays.* Dublin: Cuala Press, 1939.

Part THREE

RESEARCH AREAS AND METHODS

*Humanistic psychology is in the paradoxical position of having at
once a tremendous range of available methods for its work
and yet a serious methodological problem. The result is that there
is a very chaotic condition in the whole field and that a great
deal of subjective judgment is involved in trying to sort out that
which is truly creative and productive from that which is
simply clever or well intentioned. It is not a situation which offers
comfort to those who like their lives and their science orderly
and their decisions depersonalized. Yet it is, withal, a scene with
much ferment and potential. Evolution and genuine growth
are not especially characterized by being neat or tidy.*

*Humanistic psychology has a tremendous range of available
methods. This is so because all the fields of study by which man has,
from earliest times, tried to inquire into his own nature and
destiny are available: Philosophy, religion, history, literature, art,
and all other fields make an overwhelming array. Prayer,
meditation, mystical insight, magic, contemplation, naturalistic
observation, introspection, interviews, experiments, surveys
—all these and more are possible tools to the task.*

*Yet, it is evident, where there is such profusion there must be—and
indeed there is—much confusion, contradiction, and ambiguity.
Therein lies the paradoxical position of humanistic psychology, and
thus here is its methodological problem. At root, the issue is
chiefly that of developing adequate criteria for evaluating all that is
offered. Yet that is not so simple as it seems. An objective
psychological science can operate reasonably well by placing almost
exclusive reliance on the criterion of regularity: It seeks to
find those abstractions about behavior which will be as universally
true as possible, that will not be changed by individuals,
time, location, or any other influences. Then it seeks those regular
processes of change which have the same universality.
Obviously in carrying out such a program, all that is irregular tends
to be excluded from study.*

*A psychology concerned with subjective experience and the
expansion of possibilities cannot employ the sole
criterion of regularity with such singleness. It is not enough to
know those aspects of human phenomena which are constant (and*

which, for that very reason, are often least significant to the person). Rather, we must seek those conditions under which variations from the expected and predictable will occur. To know how many times the average person must repeat a list of nonsense syllables before he is able to reproduce it is but a beginning. Too often psychological experimentation seems to have made it the end of inquiry, leaving as implicit any further development. It is much more to the point of exploring human potential to go on to inquiry into the conditions under which different people will learn and observe principles of equity in their relations with others.

In Parts One and Two, we have already begun to see some of the varied approaches and products of humanistic psychology. We saw the use of philosophic analysis, of introspection, of logical deduction, of physiologic observation and reasoning, and of creative intuition. In Part Three, we shall sample further as we deal directly with issues of method and approach in humanistic science.

Charlotte Buhler, in Chapter 9, carries forward her distinguished work on the very difficult task of attempting to study the human life as a whole. Providing us with a scholarly review of such efforts, she demonstrates how such an embracing orientation opens up challenging and rewarding perspectives on the scientific undertaking and on the human experience with which it concerns itself. These perspectives are illustrated as she gives attention to such concepts as self, intentionality, will, and choice. Significantly, Buhler finds the work of intensive psychotherapy at once—and indistinguishably—a research methodology and an ameliorative endeavor.

In Chapter 10, Henry Winthrop calls our attention to the inevitable subjectivity of investigations into human phenomena. His analysis of the "black-box model" does much to make evident the limitations of this once popular "game" of psychological science. When we referred above to the paradoxical situation in humanistic psychology with respect to methodology, we indicated the need for criteria by which to discriminate the value of the wealth of material that is available. It is through just such analyses as Winthrop here makes that this task is forwarded.

Some psychologists seem concerned that, without their present preoccupation with statistics, the science will get lost in the personal experiences of a few "clinical types" and lose its important touch with that which is general. For such concerns, Clark Moustakas offers a dramatic and convincing antidote in his concept of "heuristic research" (Chapter 11). This is an excellent example of the point made at the end of the first chapter when we called on humanistic psychology to so describe human experience as to help men understand and better control their own experiences. The striking way in which Moustakas has been able to do just that is important to note, as is the clear implication of how this may aid men to change and to better their experiences in other areas also.

In psychology we speak of the people we study as "subjects," when actually far too often they are treated as objects, as things rather than persons. Sidney Jourard regards this situation as fraught with immense significance, for he shares the belief of most humanistic psychologists that a person's subjective interpretation of his experience does much to determine what behavior he will produce. This is, of course, the opposite of the black-box thinking which Winthrop analyzed. Jourard, in Chapter 12, calls on psychologists to recognize that their subjects are indeed subjects and partners in the scientific enterprise, a proposal with truly revolutionary potential.

Probably one of the clearer products of man's preoccupation with deficiency which we noted in the first chapter has been an overconcern with pathology, with what is wrong and disturbed in human experience. It is startling to recognize the full implications of the fact that we have no contrasting word for that all-too-familiar term "trauma."

Herbert Otto (in Chapter 13) has recognized this situation and has set out to do something about it. In the concept of the "Minerva experience," he has given us a way of speaking of those occasions in our lives when we experience the benign, the creative, and the growth-evoking. Moreover, Otto has developed a facile method for seeking out such events and has discovered what we might have expected but what had not previously been developed: that there is a very real constructive benefit from recovering such memories. Again it should be evident how often in humanistic psychology research and application are intertwined.

Stansfeld Sargent, in Chapter 14, provides us with the sort of comprehensive perspective which can do so much to aid in the continuous task of orienting our efforts effectively. Central areas for humanistic psychology are, of course, the human personality and the whole realm of interpersonal life which we call social psychology. Sargent suggests six criteria for looking at theories and conceptual structures in these fields. Here, then, is another tool for the task with which we were concerned above: reducing the plethora of material in some useful and meaningful way. Sargent's humanistic criteria help us to examine presently available theories—a task upon which he begins—and prepare the way for more embracing and creative further developments.

We have made the point several times in these pages that humanistic psychology is ill content with the reduction of human experience to its most routine, mechanistic, and limited aspects. We are seeking the "more" that may be potential to man. One of the more exciting developments of recent years in this way has been the discovery of the psychedelic experience and the sorts of demonstrations and hypotheses about its meaning that it has generated. It is far too early to reach any conclusions about the relative balance of benign and malignant influences of the various psychedelic substances. What is clear is that they are powerful indeed and that they have opened up truly fundamental and vital issues about what it may mean to be human and alive. Robert Mogar, in Chapter 15, provides a distinguished survey of the literature on the psychedelics and emerges with a new and powerful demonstration of the tremendous significance of the attitude of a person toward his own experience. Thus further support is given to the view Jourard advanced and to the recognition implicit throughout this book that psychology neglects the subjective in human life only at the expense of neglecting one of the primary phenomena of its field.

In Part Four, we shall be examining some representative research findings. These will overlap, of course, with some of the materials dealt with in this part, but they will serve also to illustrate additional methods available to the humanistic psychologist and further difficulties in evaluating and collating the great mass of material at hand. Needless to say, the final two parts—dealing with psychotherapy and the humanities— will probably do more to add to our sense of the immensity of the task than to reassure us of its imminent solution.

Presently: Private practitioner of psychotherapy and Assistant Clinical Professor of Psychiatry at the University of Southern California Medical School (since 1950).

Education: Doctor of Philosophy in psychology from the University of Munich (1918).

Current major activities: In addition to her work as a psychotherapist, she continues her long and distinguished career of research and writing.

CHARLOTTE BUHLER

Most rewarding project: Writing a book about the "fulfillments and failures of life."

Future of humanistic psychology: Dr. Buhler hopes for, and works toward, the general recognition and acceptance of the humanistic approach to psychological problems.

Personal history: Born in Berlin, Germany, Dr. Buhler came to the United States in 1940. Associate Professor of Psychology at the University of Vienna (1922–1938). Director of Child Guidance Clinics in Vienna, London, and Oslo. Fellow of the Rockefeller Foundation (1924–1925, 1935). Professor of Psychology at St. Catherine College (1940–1941). Chief Clinical Psychologist at the Minneapolis General Hospital (1942–1945) and at the Los Angeles County General Hospital (1945–1953). Diplomate in Clinical Psychology of the American Board of Examiners in Professional Psychology. President of the American Association for Humanistic Psychology (1965–1966).

Writings: Her first book, *Fairy Tales and the Child's Fantasy*, was published in 1918 and went through five editions (fairly typical of her work). She has written in both English and German, and her writing has been translated into Hungarian, Polish, French, Spanish, Swedish, Russian, Norwegian, Dutch, Icelandic, Danish, Portuguese, Italian, Finnish, and Hebrew. Among her books are *The First Year of Life* (1930); *Rorschach Standardization Studies*, with her husband, Karl Buhler, and D. W. Lefever (1948 and 1952); *Childhood Problems and the Teacher* (1952); *Values in Psychotherapy* (1962); and *Psychology in the Life of Our Time* (1965). Currently she is editing, with Fred Massarik, *The Human Course of Life in Its Goal Aspects*.

Present chapter: This chapter has been especially prepared for this book.

Chapter 9
CHARLOTTE BUHLER

HUMAN LIFE AS A WHOLE AS A CENTRAL SUBJECT OF HUMANISTIC PSYCHOLOGY

In the gradual process by which those who now represent humanistic psychology came together as a group, they were (and are still) groping for a clarification of the issues that united them. From various presentations (Kelly, 1965; Maslow, 1965; May, 1965; Rogers, 1965; Shoben, 1965), it is evident that humanistic psychologists see both the *objectives* and the *methods* of psychology differently from the way they are viewed in much of the mainstream of scientific psychological research as it is today.

MAN IN HIS WHOLENESS

There is more agreement with regard to the objectives of humanistic psychology than with regard to method. *Man in his wholeness* is generally seen as the humanistic psychologist's concern. In describing the essential characteristics of man when seen as a whole, various authors emphasize different points. Maslow (1965) stresses the aspects of "purposefulness" and of "self-transcendence." May (1965) sees the main characteristic in man's having "intentionality," both in the sense of "meaning" as well as in the sense of "movement toward something." Rogers (1965), influenced by Polanyi (1958), conceptualizes the whole-

ness as a "pattern of relationships" representing a "hidden reality."

The question is how to come to grips with this whole. This leads to the problem of *method*: What would be the method enabling the psychologist to comprehend the individual whole in a manner that would be scientifically acceptable?

The discussion about this question reintroduces the old dispute between *ideographic* and *nomothetic* sciences, as it took place at the beginning of this century between Dilthey (1961) and his contemporaries.[1] While at the time no conclusive arguments were presented, now for the first time we find in Polanyi's systematic presentation a thorough enough analysis of scientific methodology. In his book *Personal Knowledge* (1958), he shows in a lucid way the difference of procedure in the study of a *machine* as contrasted with the study of a *person*. Beyond this, he also shows conclusively the objectivity and therefore the scientific justification of what he calls research by way of "participating experience." He gives careful deliberation to the problem of this method. In the study of persons, he says, it is necessary that the

[1] Wyatt, in Chap. 30, also examines some of the current extensions of this issue. [Editor]

researcher become a participant in the studied individual's experience. This seems to make it a more "subjective" procedure. However, he proceeds to show, personal participation does not make our understanding necessarily subjective. "Comprehension," on the basis of personal participation, according to him, "is neither an arbitrary act nor a passive experience, but a responsible act claiming universal validity. Such knowing is indeed objective in the sense of establishing contact with a hidden reality" (p. vii). This "hidden reality" is an "existing framework of knowledge" within which we operate. Our "perception prefigures all our knowing of things." "Why do we entrust the life and guidance of our thoughts to our conceptions? Because we believe that their manifest rationality is due to their being in contact with domains of reality, of which they have grasped one aspect" (p. 104). Although, admittedly, "science" (unlike history) is concerned with regularities and not with unique events, "this is true only up to a point." Regularities can be outweighed by "systematic interest," when facts can be shown in a "scholarly context" (p. 137).

Matson, in identifying with these statements, speaks of the "understanding of personal experience in its complementary wholeness" (1964, p. 241). He also quotes the psychiatrist Viktor von Weizsäcker for the way he combines the "understanding" of the person with objective treatments and techniques. In his system of "medical anthropology," all objective diagnoses and specifications are rendered secondary to the task of comprehending the patient as a whole person, a unique and irreducible subject. On the basis of this "inclusive" understanding, Weizsäcker believes, the complementary tasks of objective treatment and technique may proceed without danger of that fragmentation of the person in which his identity is destroyed. "The smooth functioning of the objective practitioner lasts just as long as there is a self-understood relation between doctor and patient, unnoticed because unthreatened. But if the *de facto* assent to this relation falls away, then the

objectivity is doubtful and no longer of use" (von Weizsäcker, quoted in Matson, 1964, p. 239).

Understanding versus Explaining This brings us to the lengthy debates about *understanding* as against *explaining* psychology, which took place at the beginning of this century between the *geisteswissenschaftlichen* and the *naturwissenschaftlichen* psychologists in Germany. Dilthey and Spranger, Brentano and Husserl laid the groundwork for the conceptualization of what "understanding" psychology was about. They worked out the difference between "causal processes" and "meaningful relations." "Understanding," says Dilthey, "is the rediscovery of the I in the Thou" (1961, p. 67). Several humanistic psychologists have identified with this method of understanding in their theory as well as in their psychotherapy, and they feel particularly strengthened by the foundation which Polanyi gives to their procedure. However, not all those who operate with the concept and method of understanding are as concerned as Polanyi with the validation of their findings and procedure. Allport (1942) discussed these problems carefully with respect to documentary material, as will be reported below.

The requirements of this validation are still under debate. Polanyi sees the judgment of competence proceeding from a framework of commitment and a scholarly context. Matson (1964) sees validation in the complementary use of intersubjective participation and objective observation, as exemplified in Weizsäcker's procedure.

The Study of the Individual All along, while the validity of the ideographic method was debated, others proceeded with psychologically oriented biographical studies of individuals. There were three main types of such studies around the beginning of the century. One type concerned itself with the individual's personality as such. William James, Havelock Ellis, A. L. Baldwin, and Henry Murray were representatives of this view. A second group was made up of the psychoanalytically orientated biographies which began with Freud's study in 1910 of Leonardo da Vinci. These studies sought to "explain" historical figures in Freudian terms. Garraty (1957) quotes Lewis Mumford and Clement Wood as having supported this approach. A third group, which had its roots in studies of human development and whose members made their main contributions between 1882 and 1931, included Preyer, Hug-Hellmuth, Bernfeld, and myself. Working with diaries of infant and adolescent development and experience, this line of research related the individual's history to the life cycle. It is the line of research which has had renewed attention in recent years and which I shall report on in detail below.

In that period of the twenties and thirties, during which the mainstream of documentary material was introduced into psychology, Gordon Allport began to interest himself in a systematic and critical investigation of the problem of methodology with respect to this kind of data. Specifically in his outstanding monograph entitled *The Use of Personal Documents in Psychological Science* (1942), he investigated the validity of the individual case technique. In discussing the ideographic as against the nomothetic approach, he came to the conclusion that the most rigid scientific procedures of understanding, prediction, and control can be achieved as well ideographically as nomothetically. Furthermore, he found that nonquantitative as well as quantitative indicators of credibility of documents are available and that critical tests of science are met by personal documents properly handled.

In his book *Pattern and Growth in Personality* (1961), Allport discusses systematically the methodological problems of sizing up an individual life history and sets up certain rules and criteria for the adequate usage of such a life history.

THE LIFE CYCLE AS A CENTRAL SUBJECT OF HUMANISTIC PSYCHOLOGY

"Every psychological theory contains within it an implicit image of man" (Shoben, 1965). In comparing various images, it might be said that the behavioristic vision of man is that of a conditioned behavioral system; the psychoanalytic image of man is that of a basically driven creature who secondarily rises to become an adapted member of society. In humanistic psychology, however, man is seen as a person who lives with purpose and intent (C. Buhler, 1933; C. Buhler, 1959a; May, 1965). At first in a vague way and later with increasingly clear awareness of himself and of the world around him, he activates his own potentials with the triple purposes of bringing them to actualization or realization (Fromm, 1941; Goldstein, 1939; Horney, 1950), accomplishing certain things in the world outside, and, by doing so, finding fulfillment in life (C. Buhler, 1959a). In this procedure, he expresses himself creatively in the pursuit of self-transcendent goals (Frankl, 1957; Maslow, 1962). Under the best of circumstances, his own personal needs might be essentially satisfied within the framework of these pursuits (Horney, 1950).

These basic hypotheses lead on to a number of further assumptions. One is that for an adequate realization of his own potentials, a person must have a "growth motivation" instead of a "deficiency motivation" (Maslow, 1955). Bugental (1965), who replaces the genetic conception implied in Maslow's thinking by an existential orientation, wants "actualization" understood "as the full and *authentic being* in the world, which transcends any substantive limit or characterization" (p. 213, italics added).

Those who conceive of actualization as at least in part a developmental process assume first a vaguely perceived and tentatively expressed and then a gradually increasingly clarified and fully developed image of the person's own self (C. Buhler, 1962; Erikson, 1959). This development leads to a comprehensive awareness of the person's own existence in the present, past, and future (C. Buhler, 1933; C. Buhler, 1959a). The self-realization in self-transcendent goals is experienced as a "meaningful" life (C. Buhler, 1933; Frankl, 1957; Maslow, 1962). The implications of this concept of meaningfulness are much debated.

In 1922, E. Spranger wrote that he requested psychology's return to the study of meaningful existence as against meaningless reactions. In this definition of "meaning," he calls it a constituent of a valuable whole. Karl Buhler (1927) debates this tie-up of meaning and value. He defines meaningfulness as relatedness to a purpose and to intentionality but not to value. Something that is meaningful is a contributory constituent of a teleological whole; the relation is that of a word to a sentence or of a mechanical part to a machine.

Something that is *meaningful to our lives* would be, according to this definition, *a constituent part of our lives as wholes.* In other words, those experiences are meaningful without which our lives would be incomplete.

This again implies that a person who thinks of his experiences in terms of their meaningfulness has intentionality toward his life as a whole. Case studies (C. Buhler, 1967) show that intentionality need not be conscious. It is also found that this directive is not operative in every kind of person.

Assuming now that there are people who live their lives with intentionality toward the wholeness of their existence, psychology needs a new theoretical frame and new methods to approach the study of this subject. As far as the theoretical frame is concerned, wholeness of the personality has to be considered not only horizontally but also longitudinally. We must have concepts and methods to encompass the whole of the life cycle as well as the whole of personality.

The Problem of the "Ego" and the "Self" It seems very unlikely, as Sanford (1965) assumes, that "we can do no better" than to use the Freudian concepts of id, ego, and superego, and the dynamics they imply, as sufficient tools to work with when it comes to questions of the life cycle. Even within the rank and file of psychoanalysts, the question of an "integrating core" of the personality has been brought up and the "self" considered in this role. "Classical Freudians," says Munroe (1955, p. 362), "are offended by any implication that they do not deal with the self, with the person-as-a-whole. They do, of course—both in their actual handling of patients and in ultimate theory. But they disapprove of taking the self as a primary psychological unit." From Carl Jung and Karen Horney up to Erik Erikson, the self is brought into play without ever being clarified.

In the more recent development of ego psychology, which for many has replaced classical Freudianism, the ego is supposed to play the role of an integrative as well as a directive principle which others see in the self. The ego psychologist's conceptualization of the self, on which particularly Hartmann has been working, is that of "one's own person" as an object rather than a subject. This own person or self is what the "goals set by the ego, in contradistinction to aims of the id or of the superego, center around" (Hartmann, 1964, p. 136). Murphy (1958), for example, conceives of the self in this sense of an object which the individual builds up gradually and of which the child becomes aware at a certain stage. Allport (1961), on the other hand, sees the self under the double aspect of the perceived and the perceiver. As the latter, it is "some kind of core in our being" (p. 110).

Strong emphasis on the self as the core has been put forward by Horney (1945; 1950). To her, the self is the representative of the person-as-a-whole and its integrative agent. This "real self" will under favorable conditions help the human individual to realization of his best potential or else to self-realization (Horney, 1950). This is essentially Erich Fromm's point of view.

In all this, the question of the nature of this self remains unresolved. As Munroe (1955) complains, it is unclear how this kind of an entity operates and what kind of an entity it is.

In deviating from the ego psychologist's usual thinking of the self as an object, Erik Erikson sets up tentatively the concept of *self-sameness* as the nucleus of personal identity and of a core process of the self's development.

I assume the self to be a core system, whose development I see in four directions: (1) the development of what we want for ourselves, (2) the development of what we believe we owe to others and to the world at large, (3) the development of our self-expression and self-realizing potentials, and (4) the development of our self-evaluation

(C. Buhler, 1959b). In other words, I believe that certain *basic tendencies* interact and are integrated in this core system. I called these basic tendencies *need-satisfaction, self-limiting adaptation, creative expansion,* and *upholding the internal order.* This core system's thrust into life is that *intentionality* with which the individual strives toward a hoped-for *fulfillment.* In the ideal case, this is identical with the realization of the individual's best potentials.

Intentionality, Will, and Choice In what might be called a parallel development to humanistic psychology, new concepts were brought forth by those who developed the modern existential philosophy into psychologically and psychiatrically applicable systems. Their emphasis is not on goals and development, but on *being,* on man's consciousness of, and responsibility for, his existence (May, Angel, & Ellenberger, 1958). The "never-lost kernel" of man's existence is in this view "his power to take some stand" (May, 1965, p. 3). In taking this stand, man makes use of and expresses his freedom. It is the moment of decision, in which man becomes truly human (Tillich, 1952),

In this decision, according to May, a will is expressed. If the choice is made toward meaningful goals, it represents a person's intentionality. Intentionality, in May's definition, is "the capacity by which we constitute meanings in life" (1965). Meaning, to May, is a pattern; meaningful is what opens up "world designs" (May et al., 1958, p. 201).

Choices and decisions are made by the "I." Bugental (1965) prefers the concept of the I to that of the self because ". . . the true *Self*-as-doer, the I, is a radically different process from the object of perception, the *Self*-as-object, or the *Me*" (p. 203). He wants to avoid this duplicity of meanings of the self. This I is "combined awareness and choice" (p. 204). In this combined functioning, it may be considered a comparable system to the above-defined self as a core, although he conceives of it as a process, not as a substantive entity.

Also in Bugental's theory, it is a basic postulate that man is intentional. It ". . . is the basis on which he builds his identity" (p. 12), and he does so "through having purpose, through valuing, and through creating and recognizing meaning" (p. 12). Of primary value in human life is, according to Bugental, living in accordance with, and as part of, how things really are (p. 14). This value is called *authenticity*: ". . . we are authentic to that degree to which we are at one with the whole of being (world)" (p. 33).

Intentionality in these theories is seen as relating the individual to the whole of his being and of the world. In my own theory, it relates the individual also to the whole of his life and is more concretely involved with his development and with the buildup of his experiences. In all these theories, the meaningfulness of the individual's experience is considered of the essence.

In considering the life cycle as the frame within which the operation of human intentionality has to be understood, I find it essential to establish some further concepts related to it, especially and before all the concept of *goal.*

Motivation in the past decades' theorizing was seen almost exclusively in terms of needs and need satisfiers. Little attention was paid to the goals. Insofar as there was any thinking about goals, two theoretically opposite basic assumptions were to be found in the literature. One was Goldstein's (1939) hypothesis that goals are basically inherent in drives; the other was Hartmann's theory that goal direction is determined by perception, however underdeveloped this may be at the beginning. Therefore, any anticipation of the future as incorporated in any intention toward a goal is to him "one of the most important achievements of early ego development" (Hartmann, 1964, p. 40).

I developed a theory, based on infant observations and general considerations, that we must assume "a principle which represents the living being's expansiveness and creativity, implying an active outgoing force, directivity, intent with positive anticipation, preparedness to cope . . ." (C. Buhler, 1954, p. 640). The accomplishing of something, somehow, somewhere, is the inherent goal of the activity drive in this conceptualization. This does not, of course, preclude the fact that from almost the first moment of activity on, the impact and gradually increasing awareness of the environment may modify, determine, and even replace the original goal disposition.

The ultimate goal development is a complex resultant of many factors. In a study now in preparation (Buhler & Massarik, 1967), the factors contributory to goal setting are categorized as the structural codeterminant (that is, biological growth and decline) as well as age; the genetic, the dynamic, and the sociocultural codeterminants; and the selective and integrative factor.

It is this selective and integrative factor which sets up certain goals as *values*, that is, preferred and believed-in intents. It is one of the most widely spread assumptions of humanistic psychologists that appropriately established values, that is, values bringing out the individual's best potentials, enhance self-realization (e.g., Maslow, 1954).

Phases of the Life Cycle This self-realization through realization of valued goals takes place during the life cycle. A systematic study of the multiplicity of pursued goals requires a frame of reference. In trying to establish such a frame, I hypothesized five phases of what I called *self-determination to fulfillment by setting up life goals* (C. Buhler, 1933): First, there is a phase before life goals are set up (zero to about fifteen years; this is generally true, but actually there are cases in which valid life goals are set up in childhood). Second, there is a phase of preliminary, programmatic self-determination (fifteen to twenty-five). Third, there is a phase of finite, specified self-determination (twenty-five to forty-five). Fourth, there is a phase of self-assessment regarding attained or failed goals (forty-five to sixty-five). Fifth, there is an individually varying phase with a return to any of the previous orientations prevailing (after sixty-five).

On the basis of later studies, the further assumption was added that in each of these phases, one or more of the four basic tendencies prevails: the need-satisfying and adaptive tendencies in the first phase, creative expansion in the second and third phases, and the tendency to establish inner order in the fourth phase. The figures and distributions of these categories are all very schematic and may actually vary a great deal.

The frame of reference discussed here is based on the empirically established concept of life being lived as a whole by a fully developed person. This person who lives with intentionality assesses at different periods, and particularly toward the end, his successes and failures and his total fulfillment.

Another frame of reference for the life cycle as a whole was offered by Erikson (1959). Erikson conceives of the life cycle as composed of eight phases in the development of the individual's ego identity: (1) trust versus mistrust, (2) autonomy versus shame and doubt, (3) initiative versus guilt, (4) industry versus inferiority, (5) identity versus identity diffusion, (6) intimacy versus isolation, (7) generativity versus self-absorption, and (8) integrity versus disgust and despair.

While Erikson does not use the concept of self-realization, actually he also describes what could be called phases and stages of it. Also, Erikson assumes an end stage which is related to the person's life as a whole. He speaks of it as "an acceptance of one's own and only life cycle," as against that nonacceptance which results from an individual's contempt of himself. These are assessments and resultants which in his theory, however, are not related to an initial directive or intentionality.

In a large number of studies in which life-cycle data are assembled, these are related to the biological frame of reference of growth and decline. There the individual's life is seen not as a whole, but in phases. The aging individual's satisfaction or dissatisfaction is not so much viewed in its relationship with his foregoing life, but rather in terms of an adjustment or maladjustment to the given situations. This is, for example, Havighurst's (1952) orientation in his outline of success or failure in accomplishing the developmental tasks during the life cycle.

HUMANISTIC PSYCHOLOGICAL RESEARCH TECHNIQUES

Modern social psychology and modern developmental psychology have put out an enormous amount of interesting life-cycle data. They are obtained in test, questionnaire, and interview studies and have furnished us with a large number of descriptions of behavior, inner experiences, and products occurring during different phases of human development. The material is, generally speaking, statistical and based on group studies. While providing useful information, the orientation of these studies is, however, not in accord with the humanistic psychologist's concern for life as a whole. His focus is on the individual as a whole and on the understanding of the person, not on facts as such. This means that the humanistic psychologist's research subject is the individual, seen in the completeness of his personality and his life cycle. This leads us back to the initially discussed problem of the validation of individual interview and biographical techniques, which seem to be the only ones that give access to the individual as a whole.

We are only at the beginning of this development. At this time in new research, a number of different techniques are proposed, most of which share the idea of *participating experience*, which represents the most outstanding recent trend in humanistic as well as existential psychotherapy and research. In saying "psychotherapy and research," I mean to indicate that these two are seen as complementing each other in a new way. The reason is that while biographical techniques offer the comprehensive view of life as a whole, and while interview material may provide data of an actual participating experience, neither of these two resources opens up that depth of penetration which we obtain in psychotherapy. With his interviews, the psychotherapist does not cover exactly the lifetime of a patient, but often he covers a long enough stretch of time to gain a comprehensive understanding of his patient's life-cycle structure. Psychotherapy, therefore, appears to be the most appropriate technique for this modern research which, through participating experience, tries to understand in depth an individual's self-direction within the total frame of his life cycle.

This approach presupposes, of course, that such participating experience and the understanding occurring in it are considered by these new schools to be not only a research vehicle but also the most effective therapeutic method. This is brought out in a number of studies, with the emphasis being put on different aspects of this procedure. In a way, this is opposite to that psychoanalytic technique in which the analyst sits in his "ivory tower" or is a "blank screen." It is also quite different from Rogers's original, completely nonintervening technique, as Gendlin pointed out (1962).

In the humanistic and existential perspective, the psychotherapeutic encounter is, in Maslow's (1962) terms, a "synergistic relationship," and in Bugental's words, a "shared experience." Most pronouncedly this view is emphasized by Gendlin (1962) in his studies on personality change. In picking up Rogers's statement that something happens in an individual when he is fully understood, Gendlin goes on to show that, for a time, only within the experience of this understanding relationship can the individual's self-process take place. By "self-process," he means an interaction of the individual's feelings with his own behavior.

The problem of the way the therapist will express his own participating self in this procedure is obviously handled quite differently by different therapists, as is the problem of the degree to which he will express it. No comparative studies are yet available as to how and how far this participating therapist reveals himself as a person. The analysis of precisely what the therapist wants to accomplish is thus far also incomplete. There is agreement on the goal to help the patient "change"—to help him drop his defenses and see himself as he is. To support these purposes come the emphases on the patient's access to his own feelings and on the "interaction of the individual's feelings with his own behavior" (Gendlin, 1962).

Still controversial at this point is the problem of how new and more appropriate self-realizing directives become activated in a patient's life. It is quite generally agreed that the generating of the "willpower," to use May's (1965) term, or else of the patient's self-direction toward new goals is not necessarily the consequence of the change.

Here, then, the concepts of the therapeutic "encounter" and of the therapist's "engagement," "involvement," or "dialogue" come into play. Just what all these terms imply is still vague. Bugental (1965, p. 30) suggests that the way Moustakas (1962) refers to the experience between two individuals presumes a willingness to risk one's understanding of one's life with the other. In this mutual understanding, the therapist's own values may be revealed, not necessarily in terms of a suggestion to identify with them, but as exemplifying self-direction (C. Buhler, 1962).

Jourard (1964) suggests that most important in the therapeutic relationship is the therapist's serving as a model of authenticity for the patient. This means that the therapist's personality becomes a factor in the process, depending on the degree to which it is allowed to be evident. This assumption needs to be considered, as against the impact of transference. As Bugental says, the mature psychotherapist will seek "to discriminate that which is authentic in his encounter with the patient from that which is distortedly carried over from the patient's past" (1965, p. 150).

A valid impact of the therapist's personality and value orientation will not be expected before the patient is free enough to see himself and his therapist realistically and to make choices of directions for himself.

Psychotherapy based on participating experience is thus still in the stage of experimentation. However, even at this stage, the evidence of the available data is that with this procedure, a penetrating understanding is gained which will be of basic significance for that humanistic psychological research which we are trying to perfect today.

REFERENCES

ALLPORT, G. W. *The use of personal documents in psychological science.* New York: Social Science Research Council, 1942.

ALLPORT, G. W. *Pattern and growth in personality.* New York: Holt, Rinehart and Winston, 1961.

BUGENTAL, J. F. T. *The search for authenticity.* New York: Holt, Rinehart and Winston, 1965.

BUHLER, CHARLOTTE. *Der menschliche Lebenslauf als psychologisches Problem. (The human course of life as a psychological problem.)* Leipzig: Hirzel, 1933.

BUHLER, CHARLOTTE. The reality principle. *American Journal of Psychotherapy,* 1954, **8**, 626–647.

BUHLER, CHARLOTTE. *Der menschliche Lebenslauf als psychologisches Problem.* (2nd ed.) Göttingen: Vlg. f. Psych., 1959. (a)

BUHLER, CHARLOTTE. Theoretical observations about life's basic tendencies. *American Journal of Psychotherapy,* 1959, **13**, 561–581. (b)

BUHLER, CHARLOTTE. Genetic aspects of the self. *Annals of the N. Y. Academy of Science,* 1962, **96**, 730–764.

BUHLER, CHARLOTTE, & MASSARIK, F. (Eds.). *Humanism and the course of life: Studies in goal-determination.* New York: Springer, 1967.

BUHLER, K. *Die Krise der Psychologie.* Jena: G. Fischer, 1927. American edition, *The crisis of psychology.* Cambridge, Mass.: Schenkman, 1967.

DILTHEY, W. *Pattern and meaning in history.* New York: Harper Torchbooks, 1961.

ERIKSON, E. H. *Identity and the life cycle.* New York: International Universities Press, 1959.

FRANKL, V. E. *The doctor and the soul.* New York: Knopf, 1957.

FROMM, E. *Escape from freedom.* New York: Holt, Rinehart and Winston, 1941.

GARRATY, J. A. *The nature of biography.* New York: Knopf, 1957.

GENDLIN, E. T. *A theory of personality change.* New York: Wiley, 1962.

GOLDSTEIN, K. *The organism.* New York: American Book Co., 1939.

HARTMANN, H. *Essays on ego psychology.* New York: International Universities Press, 1964.

HAVIGHURST, R. J. *Developmental tasks and education.* (2nd ed.) New York: Longmans, 1952.

HORNEY, K. *Our inner conflicts.* New York: Norton, 1945.

HORNEY, K. *Neurosis and human growth.* New York: Norton, 1950.

JOURARD, S. M. *The transparent self: Self-disclosure and well-being.* Princeton, N.J.: Van Nostrand, 1964.

KELLY, G. A. The threat of aggression. (Presented at First Invitational Conference on Humanistic Psychology, Old Saybrook, Mass., 1964.) *Journal of Humanistic Psychology,* 1965, **5**, 195–201.

MASLOW, A. H. *Motivation and personality.* New York: Harper & Row, 1954.

MASLOW, A. H. Deficiency motivation and growth motivation. In R. M. Jones (Ed.), *Nebraska motivation symposium, 1955.* Lincoln, Nebr.: Univer. of Nebraska Press., 1955.

MASLOW, A. H. *Toward a psychology of being.* Princeton, N.J.: Van Nostrand, 1962.

MASLOW, A. H. Humanistic science and transcendent experiences. (Presented at First Invitational Conference on Humanistic Psychology, Old Saybrook, Mass., 1964.) *Journal of Humanistic Psychology,* 1965, **5**, 219–227.

MATSON, F. *The broken image.* New York: George Braziller, 1964.

MAY, R. Intentionality: The heart of human will. (Presented at First Invitational Conference on Humanistic Psychology, Old Saybrook, Mass., 1964.) *Journal of Humanistic Psychology,* 1965, **5**, 202–209.

MAY, R., ANGEL, E., & ELLENBERGER, H. F. (Eds.) *Existence: A new dimension in psychiatry and psychology.* New York: Basic Books, 1958.

MOUSTAKAS, C. E. Honesty, idiocy and manipulation. *Journal of Humanistic Psychology,* 1962, **2**, 1–15.

MUNROE, RUTH. *Schools of psychoanalytic thought.* New York: Holt, Rinehart and Winston, 1955.

MURPHY, G. *Human potentialities.* New York: Basic Books, 1958.

POLANYI, M. *Personal knowledge.* Chicago: Univer. of Chicago Press, 1958.

ROGERS, C. R. Some thoughts regarding the current philosophy of the behavioral sciences. (Presented at First Invitational Conference on Humanistic Psychology, Old Saybrook, Mass., 1964.) *Journal of Humanistic Psychology,* 1965, **5**, 182–194.

SANFORD, N. Will psychologists study human problems? *American Psychologist,* 1965, **20**, 192–203.

SHOBEN, E. J., JR. Psychology: Natural science or humanistic discipline? (Presented at First Invitational Conference on Humanistic Psychology, Old Saybrook, Mass., 1964.) *Journal of Humanistic Psychology,* 1965, **5**, 210–218.

SPRANGER, E. *Lebensformen.* (3rd ed.) Halle: Niemeyer, 1922. American edition, *Types of men.* (Tr. by P. Pigors.) New York: Steckert, 1928.

TILLICH, P. *The courage to be.* New Haven, Conn.: Yale Univer. Press, 1952.

Presently: Professor and Chairman of the Department of Interdisciplinary Social Sciences at the University of South Florida (since 1963).

Education: Doctor of Philosophy in psychology, philosophy, and sociology from the New School of Social Research (1953).

Current major activities: Teaching, writing, and research.

Most rewarding project: Preparation of an interdisciplinary work dealing with the impact of science and technology on society and tentatively titled *Ventures in Social Interpretation*, to appear in 1967.

HENRY WINTHROP

Future of humanistic psychology: "The restoration of the recognition that the inner life of man is as important psychologically as those elements in his behavior which have been stressed by a radical empiricism in psychology."

Personal history: Economic Consultant under New York State and United States Civil Service programs (1936–1952). Director and Lecturer in Philosophy and Social Science of the Muhlenberg Adult Education Forum in New York City (1943–1947). Lecturer in Industrial and Personnel Psychology in the New York City Civil Service in-training program (1948). Assistant Professor of Psychology at the Richmond Professional Institute (1953–1954), at Hollins College (1956–1957), and at the University of Wichita (1957–1960). Research Consultant to the Washington Public Opinion Laboratory (1951–1966). Member of the Scientific Advisory Board of the Institute for Cybercultural Research (1965). Trustee of the Commission for Research into the Creative Faculties of Man.

Writings: A prolific contributor to scholarly journals around the world, Dr. Winthrop is an editor on, and regular contributor to, the following: *Journal of Human Relations, Journal of Humanistic Psychology, Journal of Existentialism, Darshana International* (India), *Sociologia Religiosa* (Italy), *Fibonacci Quarterly* (mathematics journal), *Journal of Education* (India), and seven others.

Present chapter: This is an adaptation of a paper originally published under the title "Cultural Determinants of Psychological Research Values," in the *Journal of Social Psychology* (1961, **53**, 255–269). It appears here with the permission of the *Journal Press*.

Chapter 10

HENRY WINTHROP

CULTURAL FACTORS UNDERLYING RESEARCH OUTLOOKS IN PSYCHOLOGY

The type of problem an investigator sets himself is often conditioned by a cultural frame of reference and, at the same time, by some of the prevailing values which are implicitly and uncritically accepted by the culture. Since a culture has a *Lebenstyl* of its own, it may slant the type of problem chosen by the investigator and weight the type of outcome he expects. In a very real sense, the cultural (and frequently a subcultural) frame of reference may actually determine both the form and the content of an investigator's null hypothesis.

CULTURAL BIAS ILLUSTRATED

To illustrate the point, consider a Russian and an American investigator, both of whom may wish to study farm morale as a function, respectively, of the communist and democratic ways of life. Having developed, let us say, an identical scale for the measurement of farm morale, each studies the change in morale scores as a function of increasing size of farm, using a series of successful farms of different sizes. The variation in size may, of course, refer to acreage or farm population or both. We shall assume that in both investigations, both variables were involved. The American investigator's null hypothesis might be that there is no difference in morale as a function of increasing individuality, interpreting the magnitude of indi-

viduality to be directly proportional to farm size. The Russian investigator's null hypothesis is likely to be that there is no difference in morale as a function of "togetherness," interpreting the magnitude of togetherness to be directly proportional to farm size. It is right here—at the beginning of the investigation, when assumptions are being made uncritically—that the cultural bias takes its toll, for the American investigator who bends with the bias of his culture would probably be inclined to accept the unexamined notion that individuality can express itself in terms of the entrepreneurial ambition to concentrate land, labor, and capital in one's own hands. The Russian investigator, just as susceptible to distortion by cultural bias, would be inclined to see similar concentrations as an expression of collective, communist mentality and outlook, indicating a sense of community or *Gemeinschaft*, as opposed to untempered capitalistic, pre-Marxian individuality.

Assuming that the investigators obtain the same results, so that the null hypothesis is rejected, the first will draw the conclusion that success at farming is a function of individuality, and the second that it is a function of togetherness, both investigators reflecting cultural bias. Both investigators find that morale scores increase with the increase in size of farm. The first investigator then draws the conclusion that the rise in rural morale (as a result, presumably, of success at farming) is a function of individuality in the institutional expression of farming activity. Individuality here is defined strictly in terms of the increasing size of farm units operated successfully. The second investigator draws the opposite conclusion, namely, that rural morale (following success in farming activities) is a function of the communal expression of agricultural activity. The communal spirit is here likewise defined strictly in terms of the increasing size of farm units which are being managed efficiently and which are therefore highly productive.

Faults in Design and Assumptions The design and the assumptions are clearly faulty. They are faulty for several reasons. Let us set forth some of these reasons below.

1 Such concepts as *individuality*, expressed through the provision of social opportunity and freedom of enterprise, and *collective consciousness*, expressed through the social demand that community needs be achieved through the concerted action of groups, have to be defined for a wider context than that of agricultural activity. Furthermore, they have to be defined *prior* to any effort to translate them into forms which are strictly appropriate only for an agricultural milieu.

2 The group observed by the American investigator may be as large as—and, perhaps, even larger than—the Russian group. However, the controlling "social images" are *cognitive maps*, which are a product of the culture, and which prompt the American investigator to see the farmhands and other employees of the American entrepreneur as passive servants of the farm owner, who alone is responsible for accomplishing the tasks and solving the problems of farm management. On the other hand, in the Soviet milieu, these same tasks of management are seen by the Soviet investigator as executed through group processes, and the problems which arise are seen always as collectively solved. The cognitive maps in both cases are collections of "fictions."

3 The American investigator imputes some special meanings to the concept of *democracy*. First, democracy is equated ambiguously with individuality. Second, individuality is equated with the allowable, institutional expressions of economic activity for private gain. Third, that behavior in agricultural activity which successfully promotes private gain and which is only one possible mode of expression of individuality is allowed to act as proxy for all possible institutional expressions of individuality in a democracy. Fourth, the increase in morale scores as a function of the scale of agricultural operations is probably more basically proportional to returns per capita than to any other single factor, but these scores are then interpreted so as to confirm indirectly the superiority of the "democratic way of life."

The same sort of fallacies likewise trap the Soviet investigator, who implies a special meaning to the concept of the "communist way of life" through a series of glib and sliding intellectual operations. First, the communist way of life is defined *ad hoc* by the Soviets as *grazhdanstvennost*, a term which refers to the whole complex of sentiments which relate the individual to communist society. *Grazhdanstvennost* is a sort of official Soviet humanism which recognizes the acceptance of the Soviet way of life as a form of salvation as well as a form of recantation and purgatory for indigenous counterrevolutionaries and fallen-away Communists. The stress is on fidelity to the group. It is *grazhdanstvennost* which makes defendants in Soviet treason trials wallow publicly in guilt and remorse. Therefore, in *grazhdanstvennost*, one automatically adopts group-think and togetherness.

The Soviet investigator defines all behavior which takes place in the pursuit of successful agricultural activity as a communal expression of *grazhdanstvennost*. Here again, all such behavior is only one possible mode of expression of a collective ethos. It therefore cannot be taken gratuitously as something which can do service for, and justice to, a whole complex of milieus which would have to be invoked if the superiority of *grazhdanstvennost* over individuality is to be tested scientifically. Finally, the Soviet investigator, like his American counterpart, jumps to the conclusion that the increase in morale scores constitutes the *experimentum crucis* of his investigation. By this I mean that the fact that increasing large-scale farm operations in the U.S.S.R. (which reflect an increasing use of technology) result in increasing size of morale scores is then taken to indicate the superiority of the communist way of life.

In both cases we are presented with clear-cut evidence of the manner in which a prevailing social psychology, expressed uncritically, not only operates to determine the manner in which an investigation is designed but also operates to distort the findings which come to light.

Animal Psychology and Experimenter Bias   In connection with the effects of cultural determinants and prevailing social psychologies upon one's mode of thinking in the conduct of investigations in the behavioral and social sciences, a humorous comment from Bertrand Russell will be appropriate here. I regret that I have long since lost the source of this quotation, but that loss will in no way reduce its appositeness. Russell comments as follows:

> The manner in which animals learn has been much studied in recent years, with a great deal of patient observation and experiment. Certain results have been obtained as regards the kinds of problems that have been investigated, but on general principles, there is still much controversy. One may say broadly that all the animals that have been carefully observed have behaved so as to confirm the philosophy in which the observer believed before his observation began. Nay, more, they have all displayed the national characteristics of the observer. Animals studied by Americans rush about frantically, with an incredible display of hustle and pep, and at last achieve the desired result by chance. Animals observed by Germans sit still and think, and at last evolve the solution out of their inner consciousness. . . .

And presumably Russell might have added that the animals observed by an Englishman do not waste time looking about for a satisfactory solution, but eventually muddle through, while those observed by a Russian solve their problems by the application of orthodox proletarian ideology with, I suppose, eminently satisfactory dialectical results. Russell continues:

> To the plain man, such as the present writer, the situation is discouraging. I observe, however, that the type of problem which a man naturally sets to an animal depends upon his own philosophy, and that this probably accounts for the differences in results. The animal responds to one type of problem in one way and to another in another; therefore the results obtained by different investigators, though different, are not incompatible. . . .

THE "BLACK-BOX" MODEL

Russell's quip is not without some basis in reality. One evidence of it is well known to most psychologists, who are familiar with the fact that the European cultural climate has been conducive to *verstehen* and to the development of personalistic terms focusing on *la vie intérieure*. The American cultural climate, on the other hand, has fostered an obsessive desire to make a break with the "mentalistic" pattern, even at the cost of denying the need to deal scientifically with events of the inner life. It is the black-box approach which is more congenial to many American psychologists and a good many investigators in English-speaking countries who are strong adherents of the British empirical tradition. Such an approach is part of the cultural bias which has come down to us both from the giants of British philosophy, like Hobbes, Locke, and Hume, and from British associationists in psychology, like Hartley. A fundamental bias present but too infrequently emphasized in the black-box approach is a penchant for simplicity in explanation. Too often it is felt that if a simple explanation will work, then that explanation must be the true one. Since a black-box approach achieves a tremendous oversimplification by neglecting the existtence and contributory functions of unobserved, perceptual organizations, the derived simplicity may prove *ultimately* to be deceptive. In effect, the bias involved represents an overuse of the approach expressed in the principle of parsimony, in which a theoretician is cautioned to use as few explanatory entities as possible.

Limitations of Black-box Thinking   It should be obvious, however, that a black-box approach, no matter how successful it proves to be over a substantial period of time, may sooner or later reach the limits of its explanatory and predictive power. Nature has clearly provided man and the vertebrates with a central nervous system and neuromuscular processes for participation in types of behavior to which such structures are surely necessary, even if not sufficient.

This is a point of view which perhaps can be shared by centrists, gestalt psychologists, organismic psychologists, transactionalists, and other types of holistic thinkers in psychology. Sooner or later, behavior to which these central structures are maximally relevant will be investigated, and the black-box approach is likely to prove decreasingly relevant as such behavior becomes pinpointed. The virtues and the limitations of the black-box approach have been ably and rather briefly described by Ashby (1958). Whether a black-box approach will be adequate for the roles played by feeling, sympathy, empathy, motivation, directive values, all forms of cognitive patterning, and similar considerations remains to be seen. In fact, limitations on the black-box approach are recognized even within cybernetic theory. There we say that central structures and their functions can be deduced from protocol data *up to an isomorphism*. Said differently, our deductions are successful only to the extent that a new system (and its behavior) can be shown to be a member of a class of systems whose internal structures and functions are already well understood or whose behavior, at least, is fairly similar. Our point here, however, is to note that the black-box approach does reflect a cultural bias and a professional value in the form of preference for a given research bias, regardless of the eventual degree of success which that research bias may achieve.

OTHER RESEARCH AREAS

Often, however, the setting of a professional problem is less subtly dependent upon the *Zeitgeist*. Experiments in conformity behavior, such as those performed by Asch (1952), yield results which unquestionably suggest group influence as a major factor. In an other-oriented culture like ours, such results may be frequent. Would we have gotten them from an experimental group of arch-individualists? We cannot know until we have a valid measuring device for individuality and have repeated experiments of

this sort upon high scorers in that attribute. If we did not get similar results, perhaps we should have to conclude that Asch had paid insufficient attention to the personality variable. On the other hand, in a culture which encouraged fierce individuality, *failure* to get such results would be likewise due to social conditioning. The investigator in an individualist culture would be forced to conclude that conformity to the culture was operative there too but that it was conformity to the ideal of fierce independence of judgment. The standard deviation of judgments of line length in retrials would, in such a setting, be likely to increase. My point, however, in all this is that the decision to investigate problems of this type reflects an implicit preference for investigating behavior determined by socially built-in habits of a sort which are not generally admired in a critical context.

Personal Investment There are, of course, many other problem specialties of interest to the social psychologist which, I am convinced, would betray a set of values if the roots of the investigator's interests could be probed deeply enough. In fact one would be hard put to defend the proposition that the choice of problem made by an investigator is a random affair. Familiarity with one's colleagues makes it abundantly clear that most psychologists have vested values in the problems they choose for investigation and often, indeed, in the outcomes as well. Who among us is not familiar with the psychologist who pounces gleefully upon the hoped-for outcome when it is obtained but who strains vigorously for an explanation which will leave the issue in doubt if the outcome is not in the expected direction? I do not say that the average social psychologist functions like the average lawyer, setting out to prove what he has already decided is the case. I do say, however, that at times he strains somewhat at his explanations, influenced without doubt by his phenomenal bias with all the values that bias carries in its train.

The Nature-Nurture Debate Finally, let us observe the manner in which the nature-nurture controversy furnishes an area in which the values of psychologists line up according to sentiment. I do not want to commit myself here to one or the other emphasis or to the conviction that the joint play of both will probably yield the best account of human behavior. Some evidence can be brought forward on either side of this hoary controversy, and some evidence is available to indicate the obvious interplay of both factors, though with differing emphases. Some of the evidence brought forward in support of one side or the other is ambiguous. Many experimental designs are shoddy. Often significant variables are omitted, or suppressor variables are neglected. For these reasons, a well-crystallized position is inappropriate. However, most American psychologists, regardless of supporting evidence for the various possible positions already mentioned, are strongly inclined toward an environmentalistic approach and will prefer to account for as much behavior as possible in terms of learning theory.

CULTURAL ROOTS OF EXPERIMENTER BIAS

What is not always well recognized is the degree to which the environmentalist sentiment is part of the *Zeitgeist*. Under the influence of the British empiricists and the Enlightenment thinkers, the Founding Fathers introduced into our early national outlook the strong faith that similarities in education and environmental opportunities could produce similarities in talents among men. These sentiments, introduced long before the advent of a science of genetics, were reinforced by the opportunities open to all sorts of oppressed peoples who sought refuge in the New World from the tyrannies of the Old or who merely sought their fortunes here. Opportunities which arose in the conquest of a lush continent and success in attaining religious freedom, wealth, or education—all of which would have been permanently denied by the more rigid class structures of the Old World—spread the conviction that potentially one man was as good as another. The enveloping quality of this outlook is impressed forcibly on any careful reader who saturates himself in de Tocqueville (1956). This conviction, aided and abetted by the faith in the possibilities of universal education in a democracy, gave to all forms of environmentalism an easy headway socially, culturally, and pedagogically.

It did not take long, particularly with the rise of behavioristic influences in psychology, for the deep and abiding faith in the all-powerfulness of the environment to take root, doubly so as theory in the behavioral sciences sought to break the shackles of a hereditarianism concerning human subjects which was more an article of faith or an expression of individual and class snobbery than anything else. For many decades now, the environmentalist bias has been dominant in academic circles.[1] Some behavioral scientists maintain it as a result of objective research and a dispassionate acquaintance with the relevant literature. Others have imbibed it with their academic mother's milk, so to speak, adopting the theoretical coloring and sentiments of their academic progenitors. Such an attitude does the problem little justice in intellectual depth and does the writings of geneticists even less.

CONCLUSION

The considerations discussed in this chapter reflect an attempt to indicate some of the ways in which professional research in the behavioral and social sciences, but particularly psychology, can be influenced by cul-

[1] To some extent the environmentalistic outlook is being balanced by an increasing recognition of the degree to which behavior may have biological substrates, whether genetic or otherwise. For professional psychologists, the extent to which biology may be highly relevant to human behavior has been richly laid out in a recent volume edited by Koch (1962; see particularly the paper by David and Snyder). A brief, popular, and stimulating survey of some of the relations of biology to human behavior has been furnished by Rosenfeld (1965), and the genetic possibilities which may be available for influencing human behavior have been briefly and interestingly discussed by Rostand (1959). There is no dearth of professional material on the degree to which genetic factors may be related to human behavior. The important point in this connection, however, is that the pendulum is swinging back a little in the direction of the recognition of biological factors in behavior and performance. This tends somewhat to reduce the excesses of an uncritical environmentalism in the behavioral sciences.

tural determinants and a prevailing social psychology. It is important that the behavioral scientist recognize that culture-free research in many contexts—especially those which arise for research in social psychology, personality theory, motivation, etc.—is sometimes more difficult to achieve than culture-free intelligence tests. Other examples of cultural determinants of research exist, and I have explored these elsewhere (Winthrop, 1961). The important consideration to be stressed here, however, is that if we recognize the existence of such prospective bias in its many forms, research can be considerably improved, and conflicts among schools and points of view in psychology may be considerably reduced. Such a reduction should help to promote an increased tolerance for newly emerging viewpoints in psychology. A humanistic psychology should be able to profit considerably from such increased tolerance.

REFERENCES

ASCH, S. *Social psychology.* Englewood Cliffs, N.J.: Prentice-Hall, 1952.

ASHBY, W. R. General systems theory as a new discipline. In L. Von Bertalanffy & A. Rapoport (Eds.), *General systems yearbook.* Vol. 3. Ann Arbor, Mich.: Society for General Systems Research, 1958. Pp. 1–6.

DAVID, P. R., & SNYDER, L. H. Some interrelations between psychology and genetics. In S. Koch (Ed.), *Psychology: A study of a science.* Vol. 4. *Biologically oriented fields: Their place in psychology and in biological sciences.* New York: McGraw-Hill, 1962. Pp. 1–50.

DE TOCQUEVILLE, A. *Democracy in America.* (Abridged ed.) New York: Mentor Books, 1956.

KOCH, S. (Ed.) *Psychology: A study of a science.* Vol. 4. *Biologically oriented fields: Their place in psychology and in biological sciences.* New York: McGraw-Hill, 1962.

ROSENFELD, A. Will man direct his own evolution? *Life,* 1965, **59** (14), 96–111.

ROSTAND, J. *Can man be modified?* New York: Basic Books, 1959.

WINTHROP, H. Cultural determinants of psychological research values. *Journal of Social Psychology,* 1961, **53,** 255–269.

Presently: At the Merrill-Palmer Institute of Human Development and Family Life in Detroit, Michigan.

Current major activity: At the time he responded to this question, Dr. Moustakas was putting the finishing touches to *The Authentic Teacher: Sensitivity and Awareness in the Classroom* (1966).

Most rewarding project: "My summer at Merrill-Palmer is primarily a time for meditation, self-reflection, reading, and discovery. I find these unscheduled hours of silence and self-communion rewarding and exciting experiences which I look forward to each new day," Dr. Moustakas replied last year.

CLARK MOUSTAKAS

Future of humanistic psychology: "Genuine communication based on ethical and moral values leading to imaginative, creative, individual growth in an authentic community of persons."

Personal history: Clark Moustakas is a creative man who resists being put into conforming modes. He does not provide eager editors with the usual biographical material. Instead, he simply lists some of the many places he has taught as a lecturer or workshop leader. These include temporary appointments at Wayne State University (1949 and 1950), Washington State University (1951), Syracuse University (1952), Arizona State University (1963), Indiana State College (1963), and Brigham Young University (1965). In addition, he has conducted workshops and seminars for colleges and universities, professional groups, and state educational departments from coast to coast.

Writings: Moustakas is a sensitive, introspective, and fertile writer. His books include *Psychotherapy with Children* (1959), *The Alive and Growing Teacher* (1959), *Loneliness* (1961), and *Creativity and Conformity* (1966). He has edited *The Self* (1956) and *Existential Child Therapy* (1966).

Present chapter: This essay has not previously been published.

Chapter II
CLARK MOUSTAKAS

HEURISTIC RESEARCH

The impetus for writing this essay came from several sources: my own growing dissatisfaction with conventional research as a means to study significant problems, issues, and processes with reference to man and human experience; the questions of my students and colleagues; and my wish to clarify with others my own research philosophy and perspective before accepting appointments as a research consultant.

Rather than listing a series of research concepts and abstractions which would be fragmented, mechanical effort and which I would approach unenthusiastically, I have decided to explore an actual research experience which distinguishes the discovery process from that of verification and corroboration. In this presentation, I shall outline the significant dimensions of what I am calling *heuristic research*, that is, a research approach which encourages an individual to discover and methods which enable him to investigate further by himself.

Because of its recent significance and its impact on my own awareness and way of life, I have chosen my study of loneliness (1961) to express and illustrate the nature and meaning of heuristic research.

Sources of the Study My study of loneliness had no design or purpose, no object or end, and no hypotheses or assumptions. While I was faced with a question or problem (whether or not to agree to major heart surgery which might restore my daughter to health or result in her death) in the beginning, I was not inquiring into the nature or meaning of loneliness and its impact on the individual in modern society. However, the urgency for making this critical decision plunged me into the experience of feeling utterly alone and cut off from human companionship. The entire process of facing the terror and consequences of major heart surgery or an uncertain future and a premature death initiated my search into loneliness. At first, the search was a search into my own self, looking deeply within, trying to discover and be aware, trying to find the right way to proceed, and experiencing a sense of isolation when each path or journey ended with a question mark.

Experiences of lonely self-reflection came at unexpected moments, in the midst of a crowd of people, in response to a word or phrase in conversation. Many different kinds of situations evoked an inner process of doubt, uncertainty, and isolation. Sometimes I awakened in the night, and being overwhelmed by images and feelings and thoughts, I tried to draw from deep down within myself a single answer, a single direction, which would utilize in an integrated form all the data—my experiences with my daughter, talks with physicians, and published reports on heart surgery. The initial journey was an attempt to discover the one true way to proceed; it involved a process of self-inquiry, which was not planned but simply happened, which was not carefully sampled but occurred spontaneously at unexpected times and places. While no answer came to the problem of surgery, I became aware that at the center of my world was a deep and pervasive feeling of loneliness. With this feeling came the tentative realization that loneliness is a capacity or source in man for new searching, awareness, and inspiration—that when the outside world ceases to have a meaning, when support and confirmation are lacking or are not adequate to assuage human suffering, when doubt and uncertainty overwhelm a person, then the individual may contemplate life from the depths of his own self and in nature. For me, this was a discovery that in a crucial and compelling crisis, in spite of comfort and sympathy from others, one can feel utterly and completely alone, that, at bottom, the experience of loneliness exists in its own right as a source of power and creativity, as a source of insight and direction, as a requirement of living no matter how much love and affirmation one receives in his work and in his relationships with others.

Thus the beginning steps of my research into loneliness (which at the time I did not know I was researching) involved not a question of the nature of loneliness, not a question of its restorative, creative, or destructive impact on the individual, but a struggle and search into another problem. Much later I realized that loneliness is often experienced by men who must make crucial decisions that will have major consequences in the lives of other men. Through inner exploration and study, I sought to find a solution which would integrate the facts

into one clear pattern. The significance of inner searching for deeper awareness as a relevant step in research is cogently expressed by Polanyi (1964, pp. 10–14) in his book *Science, Faith and Society*:

Scientific knowing consists in discerning Gestalten that are aspects of reality. I have here called this "intuition"; in later writings I have described it as a tacit co-efficient of a scientific theory, by which it bears on experience, as a token of reality. Thus it foresees yet indeterminate manifestations of the experience on which it bears.

Every interpretation of nature, whether scientific, non-scientific or anti-scientific, is based on some intuitive conception of the general nature of things. . . . But in spite of much beautiful work . . . we still have no clear conception of how discovery comes about. The main difficulty has been pointed out by Plato in the *Meno*. He says that to search for the solution of a problem is an absurdity. For either you know what you are looking for, and then there is no problem; or you do not know what you are looking for, and then you are not looking for anything and cannot expect to find anything. . . . A potential discovery may be thought to attract the mind which will reveal it—inflaming the scientist with creative desire and imparting to him intimations that guide him from clue to clue and from surmise to surmise. The testing hand, the straining eye, the ransacked brain, may all be thought to be labouring under the common spell of a potential discovery striving to emerge into actuality.

Experiences in meditation and self-searching, in intuitive and mystical reachings, and in hours and hours of silent midnight walking paved the way to a formulation of my study of loneliness, a formulation which emerged clearly during my observations of hospitalized children. In the hospital I began to see how lonely feelings impelled young children to seek a compassionate voice and a warm, friendly face; I began to see how young children separated from their parents could often be more completely involved in the struggle with loneliness than in the painful experiences connected with illness and surgery; I began to see how children separated from their parents underwent a period of protest and resistance against separation, against the mechanical actions and fixed faces and gestures of the hospital combine. I also observed a gradual deterioration of protest, rebellion, and self-assertion and, in their place, a deep sense of isolation, lonely weeping, withdrawal, depression, and numbness. In general, I witnessed a basic, pervasive feeling of dehumanization, which sought to repress lonely feelings and the whole range of human emotions that characterize the alive and growing child.

THE TOTAL PERSON AS A RESEARCH METHOD

When I saw that these dimensions of loneliness were almost totally ignored, misunderstood, and misinterpreted by hospital aides, nurses, and doctors, I decided, using the hospital situation and my own intuitive awareness as a beginning, to try to understand loneliness, how it fitted into the perceptions and behavior of hospitalized children, and the way in which it existed in myself and others. I decided to listen to the experiences of children in the hospital with objectivity and warmth, not taking notes and making records and thus objectifying, but keeping the focus of my interest on the experience of loneliness itself, on the essence of the experience through the person's rendering of it and relating of it. Objectivity, in this connection, means seeing what an experience *is* for another person, not what causes it, not why it exists, not how it can be defined and classified. It means seeing attitudes, beliefs, and feelings of the person as they exist for him at the moment he is experiencing them, perceiving them whole, as a unity. I set out to know the meaning of loneliness, not by defining and categorizing, but by experiencing it directly and through the lives of others, as a simple reality of life in the way that Moore (1903, p. 7) describes reality in *Principia Ethica*:

My point is that "good" is a simple notion, just as "yellow" is a simple notion; that, just as you cannot, by any manner of means, explain to any one who does not already know it, what yellow is, so you cannot explain what good is. Definitions of the kind that I was asking for, definitions which describe the real nature of the object or notion denoted by a word, and which do not merely tell us what the word is used to mean, are only possible when the object or notion in

question is something complex. You can give a definition of a horse, because a horse has many different properties and qualities, all of which you can enumerate. But when you have enumerated them all, when you have reduced a horse to his simplest terms, then you can no longer define those terms. They are simply something which you think of or perceive, and to any one who cannot think of or perceive them, you can never, by any definition, make their nature known.

Thus I set out to discover the meaning of loneliness in its simplest terms, desiring to perceive the experience of being lonely in its absolutely native state. At the same time, I knew from my own experiences and from my conversations with hospitalized children that loneliness itself could not be communicated by words or defined in its essence, that loneliness could not be known except by persons who are open to their own senses and aware of their own experiences. I set out to discover the nature of lonely experience by intimate encounter with other persons. A quotation from Polanyi's (1958, pp viii–6) *Personal Knowledge* may clarify this point:

To say that the discovery of objective truth in science consists in the apprehension of a rationality which commands our respect and arouses our contemplative admiration; that such discovery, while using the experience of our senses as clues, transcends this experience by embracing the vision of a reality beyond the impression of our senses, a vision which speaks for itself in guiding us to an ever deeper understanding of reality—such an account of scientific procedure would be generally shrugged aside as out-dated Platonism: a piece of mystery-mongering unworthy of an enlightened age. Yet it is precisely on this conception of objectivity that I wish to insist. . . . Into every act of knowing there enters a passionate contribution of the person knowing what is known, and . . . this coefficient is no mere imperfection but a vital component of his knowledge.

Entering into the Experience My way of studying loneliness, in its essential form, was to put myself into an open, ready state, into the lonely experiences of hospitalized children, and to let these experiences become the focus of my world. I listened. I watched. I stood by. In dialogue with the child, I tried to put into words the deep regions of his experience. Sometimes my words touched the child in the interior of his feelings, and he began to weep; sometimes the child formed words in response to my presence, and thus he began to break through his numbness and the dehumanizing impact of the hospital atmosphere and practice. At this point, loneliness became my existence. It entered into every facet of my world—into my teaching, my interviews in therapy, my conversations with friends, my home life. Without reference to time or place or structure, somehow (more intentionally than accidentally) the theme came up. I was clearly aware that exhaustively and fully, and in careful manner, I was searching for, studying, and inquiring into the nature and impact of loneliness. I was totally involved and immersed in this search for a pattern and meaning which would reveal the various dimensions of loneliness in modern life. This was research in the sense of a close searching and inquiring into the nature of a reality of human experience. I was certainly not studying loneliness simply as an intellectual or academic question, in a detached manner, but rather in an integrative, living form; becoming part of the lonely experiences of others; being within lonely moments in living; being involved, committed, interested, concerned, while at the same time aware of an emerging pattern and relatedness. Facts, knowledge, insights were accumulating as I listened and later recorded and studied; but, at the same time, there were intuitive visions, feelings, sensings that went beyond anything I could record or think about or know in a factual sense. At the center of the lonely existence were ineffable, indescribable feelings and experiences, a presence which I felt in a unified and essential way. I had gone "wide open," at moments ceasing to be a separate individual, but wholly related to the other person, leaving something behind of my own intuitive vision and comprehension while, at the same time, taking something away—very much in the

manner that Steinbeck and Ricketts (1941) approached their study of the *Sea of Cortez*:

Let's see what we see, record what we find, and not fool ourselves with conventional scientific strictures—in that lonely and uninhabited Gulf our boat and ourselves would change it the moment we entered. By going there, we would bring a new factor to the Gulf. Let us consider that factor and not be betrayed by this myth of permanent objective reality. If it exists at all it is only available in pickled tatters or in distorted flashes. "Let us go," we said, "into the Sea of Cortez, realizing that we become forever a part of it; that our rubber boots slogging through a flat of eelgrass, that the rocks we turn over in a tide pool, make us truly and permanently a factor in the ecology of the region. We shall take something away from it, but we shall leave something too." And if we seem a small factor in a huge pattern, nevertheless it is of relative importance. We take a tiny colony of soft corals from a rock in a little water world. And that isn't terribly important to the tide pool. Fifty miles away the Japanese shrimp boats are dredging with overlapping scoops, bringing up tons of shrimps, rapidly destroying the ecological balance of the whole region. That isn't very important in the world. And six thousand miles away the great bombs are falling on London and the stars are not moved thereby. None of it is important or all of it is.

Thus I entered into a formal study of loneliness, taking into it my own growing awareness, the discovery of myself as a lonely person, my experiences in the hospital, and my many moments, conversations, dialogues, and discussions with other persons —children in school settings who spoke freely and openly and wrote themes expressing their lonely experiences; parents and young adults in therapy who struggled and found it painful to speak of loneliness but who, once initiated in this journey, were able to recapture and create in a living sense moments of the past and current feelings of isolation and solitude; and friends and colleagues who could reveal the intimate depth of lonely experiences. I steeped myself in a world of loneliness, letting my life take root and unfold in it, letting its dimensions and meanings and forms evolve in its own timetable and dynamics.

The Use of the Literature The study was culminated in my readings of published reports on loneliness and lonely experiences. But this was a point near the end, not at the beginning, where it might have acted to predispose and predetermine and color my own growing awareness. I began to study volumes of biography and autobiography of individuals who dramatically exemplified lonely lives. Among other persons, those who captured my interest were Emily Dickinson, Abraham Lincoln, Woodrow Wilson, Benedict Arnold, and Ned Langford. I also followed the lonely experiences of Herman Buhl in his journey to the highest peak of the Himalayas, Admiral Byrd alone on an advanced base in Antarctica, Saint-Exupéry lost in the desert, and other persons involved in extreme situations of isolation. I studied the autobiographical volumes of Hiss and Chambers, as well as many political analyses of their confrontation and its implications, including the numerous volumes of the House Unamerican Activities Committee and the ten volumes of the trial transcript, to see more fully the lonely consequences of infamy and mass public rejection. I discovered additional nuances of the meaning of loneliness from the studies of Frieda Fromm-Reichmann of the loneliness of mental patients, Margaret Wood's *Paths of Loneliness*, Eithne Tabor's *Songs of a Psychotic*, Karl Menninger's *Love against Hate*, David Riesman's *Lonely Crowd*, Erich Fromm's *Escape from Freedom*, Thomas Wolfe's *Hills Beyond*, Sullivan's *Interpersonal Theory of Psychiatry*, and the numerous articles and reports appearing in newspapers and journals, accounts which could be understood both as attempts to escape and overcome loneliness and as evolutions of deeper sensitivity and awareness which enabled unique and creative expressions of loneliness in poetry, music, literature, and other art forms.

When a pattern began to emerge with reference to the nature and function of loneliness in individual experience and in modern living, the formal study came to an end. At this point the framework and detail, the clarification of loneliness, had been formed; it was possible to differentiate and refine its meaning, to expand and illustrate its nature and relevance in human experience. Thus what started as a hospital study of loneliness became an extended research into the phenomenon of loneliness. The conditions and factors which initiated and characterized the study were as follows: (1) a crisis which created a question or problem; (2) a search of self in solitude, from which emerged a recognition of the significance of loneliness both as a creative urging and as a frightening and disturbing experience; (3) an expanding awareness through being open to lonely life and lonely experiences, through watching, listening, and feeling, and through conversation, dialogue, and discussion; (4) a steeping of myself in the deeper regions of loneliness, so that it became the ingredient of my being, the center of my world; (5) an intuitive grasping of the patterns of loneliness, of related aspects and different associations, until an integrated vision and awareness emerged; (6) further clarification, delineation, and refinement through studies of lonely lives, lonely experiences, and published reports on loneliness; and (7) creation of a form, a manuscript, in which to project and express the various forms, themes, and values of loneliness and in which to present its creative powers, as well as the anxiety which it arouses in discontent, restlessness, and boredom, and the strategies used in attempting to overcome and escape loneliness.

HUMAN VALIDATION

Since the publication of *Loneliness*, I have received approximately five hundred letters which verify and validate my portrayal of loneliness in modern life—its nature, its beauty, and its terror. My correspondents confirmed the meaning and essence of loneliness which had emerged from my research; each of these persons portrayed the uniqueness of lonely experience and its powers in drawing upon untouched capacities and resources, in evolving new creations, and in expanding awareness, sensitivity, and compassion, as well as the extreme pain, grief, despair, and impotency which often accompany the urge to discover, to answer the challenges and problems of living, to face genuinely and authentically separation, illness, and death. I have selected five letters as illustrations of response and confirmation:

1 Today I read your book, *Loneliness*. It was one of those rare experiences that seem to come "just in time." Somehow I wanted you to know that I appreciated your sharing with me the "feelings and insights" expressed in this book—for you see it is not just a book but a kind of communication not often experienced.

The greatest value I received from sharing this communication was that when circumstances of life seem to be taking from us our right to be then we must re-affirm our faith in our own being and refuse to be pushed aimlessly along. Thank you for giving some impetus to this re-affirmation.

2 Having just completed your book *Loneliness*, I must thank you for such an articulate and sensitive presentation of basic truths relating to human suffering. Since the sudden and premature death of my husband in September, 1959, and the agonizing period following it when, primarily motivated by the two babies I had been left to rear alone, I struggled to retain sanity, I have had a deep interest in loneliness, its causes, its effects. Your book clarified a number of matters for me.

3 I read your beautifully written book of *Loneliness* and was very impressed with its truthfulness. I do believe, however, that the subject matter has been expounded many times by many writers and authors, but because of the lack of a formal education I never realized that anyone could possibly see me in these dimensions. I think I know the meaning of this subject as well as, if not better, than most. I need no formal education for this. I have lived, associated myself with, become drawn toward the lonely, and know readily those who are. P.S. I am a janitor. I also work in a print shop. Please forgive the informality.

4 I read those parts which I felt a need to read from *Loneliness* during Christmas vacation. I was deeply affected by the experiences I was able to share. I picked the book up again and read and was surprised at the wonderment of being able to experience as though never before these same journeys through loneliness.

I felt that my very feelings were caught up and understood by the author—that a friendly someone could write what I had felt, but hadn't been able to express in words.

I gained something from this reading, partly that I don't have to feel that being lonely is wasteful—that I don't have to be busy every minute, to be a complete person. Before I was afraid to be lonely, afraid I was just wasting precious time and afraid that I wasn't adequate enough within myself.

For someone who usually rambles endlessly on when affected by something I can't really think of anything else to say, perhaps later, right now I'm still experiencing it.

5 Not long ago I talked to a group of people with considerable feeling in my presentation, pointing their attention to the need to be individual and independent centers for living, each man in his own. I had been able to suggest that this was an avenue also to deepest companionship and significant social value. After my lecture, I noticed that the group disbanded quickly and individuals went off by themselves, not even coming up to me as they usually do. My first impulse was to feel that my lecture had fallen flat. Later I learned that the opposite was the case with several of the group, at least. People are hungry to be their own authorities in basic life matters and, spurred by my own expression in these matters, they wanted it all the more, meaning they had to leave me to *my* own, too.

I need not tell you that I think you are doing just the right thing in forming your experience as you are doing. The vacuum of "being," if not filled with the substance of life-realized in depth (as you are doing), will gain so much power that our people will collapse inwardly in the clutter of their own psychic debris.

The loneliness each man feels is his hunger for life itself, not only life in his being, but life in the being of creation, past, present and future. Your book allows the reader to recognize his own vacuum which is the first step to appreciation of its filling. Had you left your own vacuum uncomposed in expression, you would have left others with nothing (a disparate emptiness); composing it, you gave others not only a chance of recognizing their own, but also a way of composing a view of one's emptiness as one visualizes the cup in a ring, inviting the placement of the pearl of great price. It is the yearning that makes fulfillment possible in the most elemental ranges. It is death present within life, without which there could not be life.

CONCLUSION

While the subject of the research was loneliness, I have tried to portray the research process itself from its initial steps to its final phases. I now believe in such a process of searching and studying, of being open to significant dimensions of experience in which comprehension and compassion mingle; in which intellect, emotion, and spirit are integrated; in which intuition, spontaneity, and self-exploration are seen as components of unified experience; in which both discovery and creation are reflections of creative research into human ventures, human processes, and human experiences. In conclusion, I quote several passages which I believe are relevant to this study of heuristic research. Some of the effects of such an approach [selected from an essay by Rogers (1964, pp. 20–22)] are as follows:

In the first place it would tend to do away with the fear of creative subjective speculation. As I talk with graduate students in the behavioral sciences this fear is a very deep one. It cuts them off from any significant discovery. They would be shocked by the writings of a Kepler in his mystical and fanciful searching for likenesses and patterns in nature. They do not recognize that it is out of such fanciful thinking that true science emerges. . . .

A second effect would be to place a stress on disciplined commitment, disciplined *personal* commitment, not methodology. It would be a very healthy emphasis in the behavioral sciences if we could recognize that it is the dedicated, personal search of a disciplined, open-minded individual which discovers and creates new knowledge. No refinement of laboratory or statistical method can do this. . . .

Another effect would be that it would permit a free rein to phenomenological thinking in behavioral science, our effort to understand man and perhaps even the animals from the inside. It would recognize that no type of hypothesis has any special virtue in science save only in its relationship to a meaningful pattern which exists in the universe. . . .

Another and more general effect would be that if the picture of science I have tried to suggest gains some general acceptance in our field then it would give a new dignity to the science of man and to the scientist who commits himself to that field. It would keep the scientist as a human being in the picture at all times, and we would recognize that science is but the lengthened shadow of dedicated human beings.

REFERENCES

MOORE, G. E. *Principia ethica.* New York: Cambridge Univer. Press, 1903. Paperback edition, 1959.

MOUSTAKAS, C. *Loneliness.* Englewood Cliffs, N.J.: Prentice-Hall, 1961.

POLANYI, M. *Personal knowledge.* Chicago: Univer. of Chicago Press, 1958.

POLANYI, M. *Science, faith and society.* (First Phoenix ed.) Chicago: Univer. of Chicago Press, 1964.

ROGERS, C. R. Some thoughts regarding the current philosophy of the behavioral sciences. Unpublished paper, Western Behavioral Sciences Institute, La Jolla, Calif., 1964.

STEINBECK, J., & RICKETTS, E. F. *Sea of Cortez.* New York: Viking Press, 1941.

Presently: Professor of Psychology at the University of Florida at Gainesville (since 1958).

Education: Doctor of Philosophy in psychology from the University of Buffalo (1953).

Current major activities: Teaching, with concurrent research and part-time practice in psychotherapy.

Most rewarding projects: Completing a book on some humanistic trends in psychology and continuing research in self-disclosure.

SIDNEY M. JOURARD

Future of humanistic psychology: "I envision, and am trying to bring into being, 'institutes for the study of man.' These would be cross-disciplinary and would aim not at making man more predictable and manipulable but rather at discovering and evoking more of his possibilities. Related to these institutes would be centers where people could go to discover and realize more of their possibilities and where experiments in living could be carried out."

Personal history: Born in Canada, and became a United States citizen in 1951. Instructor at the University of Buffalo (1948–1951). Assistant Professor of Psychology at Emory University (1951–1956). Assistant Professor of Psychiatry at the University of Alabama Medical School (1956–1957). Private practice in Birmingham, Alabama (1957–1958). Sometime consultant to the National Office of Vital Statistics and to the Peace Corps. President of the American Association for Humanistic Psychology (1963–1964). Special United States Public Health Service fellowship (1964–1965), during which time Dr. Jourard studied in Europe, chiefly in England, and gave lectures at Oslo University, Oxford, Cambridge, and London and before the British Psychological Society meeting in Aberdeen.

Writings: Dr. Jourard has been interested in such matters as body cathexis, self-disclosure, the concept of "wellness," the psychotherapist himself, and inspiritation. He has published *Personal Adjustment: An Approach through the Study of Healthy Personality* (1958) and *The Transparent Self: Self-disclosure and Well-being* (1964).

Present chapter: The basic ideas in this essay were presented by Dr. Jourard in his lectures in Europe. He has reworked the paper extensively for its first publication here.

Chapter 12
SIDNEY M. JOURARD

EXPERIMENTER-SUBJECT DIALOGUE: A PARADIGM FOR A HUMANISTIC SCIENCE OF PSYCHOLOGY

The image of man that emerges from traditional experimental psychology is of a "determined" being, subject to the controlling influences of assorted variables. This is not at all an image of man with which we can gladly identify. Indeed, one of the aims of a humanistic science of psychology is to liberate man from the constraining or inciting pressures of "determiners." A humanistic psychologist, like his less humanistic colleague, is concerned to identify factors that affect man's experience and action, but his aim is not to render man predictable to, and controllable by, somebody else. Rather, his aim is to understand how determining variables function, in order that man might be liberated from their impact as he pursues his own free projects.

In pursuing the project of developing a humanistic research methodology for psychology, the hypothesis occurred to me that the aspect which human subjects show to psychological experimenters may be an artifact of the typical relationship established by the researchers with their subjects. If people show only certain of their possibilities to investigators who relate to human subjects in a prescribed, impersonal way, it is possible that if a different and mutually revealing kind of relationship between experimenters and subjects were established,

different facets of the latters' beings would be disclosed. Perhaps a more valid image of man might emerge if research done in the past were repeated in the context of mutual knowledge and trust.

I have begun to explore the possibility of replicating typical psychological experiments, first in the impersonal way their designers conducted the studies, and then in the context of greater openness and mutual knowing between the psychologist and his subjects. Some of my students likewise are exploring in this vein. The remarks that follow give a more detailed consideration of the rationale for such replication and an introduction to some preliminary findings. At this stage, we are only beginning a project that may take many years and many collaborators to bring to fruition.

TWO KINDS OF ENCOUNTERS

Ultimately, we come to know something or somebody if that being *shows itself* to us. If we are dealing with stones, animals, stars, or viruses, the problem of knowing calls first for making contact with the object of study and then for devising means of getting it to disclose its mysteries. Natural scientists have shown incredible ingenuity in this task.

They have devised gadgets which reveal previously inaccessible aspects of the being of all kinds of phenomena: Xrays, telescopes and microscopes, transducers, and recorders of light, sound, and movement. This equipment has enabled scientists to find answers to questions they pose about the being of things, objects, and processes in the world.

To know the being of *man* is a different problem. Existentialists have said that man is the being whose being is *in question*, i.e., not fixed. Man chooses his projects and thereby produces his own being. He chooses his ways to be in the world, and upon how he has chosen to be will depend the aspects of his being that he will show to anyone who happens to be looking. One choice open to him is whether he will show himself at all or choose to hide in a cave. Another option is whether he will aim to reveal his experience, his "being-for-himself," to another person or seek to conceal and misrepresent it.

If a man chooses to be fully known, he will show himself freely to another man, in all possible ways. His behavior, which is the "outside"[1] of his being-for-himself (his experience), is unintelligible, however, unless he provides the observer with the key. Behavior is actually a code—or, better, a cipher—analogous to Etruscan writing or Egyptian hieroglyphics. It is the embodiment of a meaning assigned to it by the one who behaves. The observer can guess at this meaning, but the key rests with the behaver himself. The behavior carries out his intentions, his goals, and his projects. It is the goal of the action which gives it meaning. Yet it is precisely aims and goals that people seek most strongly to conceal from others, fearing that if the intentions were known, the other person might interfere. Machiavelli knew this when he advised his Prince to conceal his ultimate aims from his subjects. They were to be kept mystified.

[1] Compare Teilhard de Chardin's concept of the "without" and the "within" of being, as summarized by Father Severin in Chap. 16 of this volume.

People will disclose their aims and the ways they construe the world only to those whom they have reason to trust. Without the trust and goodwill, a person will conceal or misrepresent his experience, hoping thus to mystify the other and to get him to misconstrue the action that is visible.

Encounters That Mystify Suppose a young man is attracted to a pretty girl. At first, she is indifferent to his display of manly charms. He then tries to change her experience of him, in the hope that she will ultimately change her behavior toward him. What he does before her is the expression of his intent: "I want her to tumble for me." But he does not say this to her directly. If he did, it might frighten her away. Instead, he pretends he has no such wishes. He tries to appear as the kind of young man in whose physical presence she will want to stay. Once he wins her attention, he may start the next stage of his secret project. He will speak of jazz and Bach, philosophy and baseball. Then, he may remark about her lovely complexion and hair. His hand, apparently by accident, brushes against her shoulder, and she does not pull away. He suggests they go somewhere for a drink. There, he invites her to tell him about herself, and he seems to listen to every word with rapt attention.

Viewed from an abstract perspective, this encounter between the boy and the girl may seem a mystifying one. He tries to mislead her as to his intentions. He is "on the make," and he tries to manipulate her experience and action so that she will behave in the service of *his* goals, not her own. When a person is thus on the make, he will show aspects of himself that aim at persuading or influencing the other. The other person has been reduced from the status of a person to the status of an object, a manipulandum, something to be used if it is useful and neutralized or changed if it is not.

There is another kind of encounter that people may undertake in order to fulfill different aims. This is *dialogue*.

Encounters That Reveal In genuine dialogue (Buber, 1958), each experiences the other as a person, as the origin and source of his intentional acts. Each participant aims to show his being to the other *as it is for him*. Transparency (Jourard, 1964), not mystification, is one of the goals. It matters little whether the dialogue is nonverbal or verbal or whether it occurs between a philosopher and his pupil, a therapist and his patient, a parent and child, or two friends. The aim is to show oneself in willful honesty before the other and to respond to the other with an expression of one's experience as the other has affected it. Dialogue is like mutual unveiling, where each seeks to be experienced and confirmed by the other as the one he is for himself. Such dialogue is most likely to occur when the two people each believe the other is trustworthy and of goodwill. The threat that motivates people to conceal their intentions and experience in manipulative encounters is absent in dialogue. The aims that make the action of each intelligible to the other will be fully revealed.

Now, I would like to examine the relationship between an experimenter and his subject in the light of these analyses of the two kinds of encounters.

EXPERIMENTER-SUBJECT RELATIONSHIP: MANIPULATION OR DIALOGUE?

The usual encounter between a psychological researcher and his subject has more in common with the example of the young man on the make than it has with dialogue. The experimenter wants something from the subject, but he wants to keep him partly mystified as to what it is. Moreover, he does not want to frighten the subject away, so the psychological researcher often cloaks his intentions with camouflage. If he "tips his hand," he may influence the subject and bias the findings. He tells the subject as little as he can when the latter appears in the laboratory.

Actually, in some ways a research psychologist tries to impersonate a machine by depersonalizing himself. He tries to be invisible or to be "constant." He seldom tries to find out from his subject just how that person experiences him, the researcher, either perceptually or in his fantasy.

Failure of the Impersonal Model Increasingly, workers are finding that this effort to eliminate bias is failing. Rosenthal (1963) and Orne (1962), among others, are showing that when a psychologist is with a human subject he functions not unlike a subtle propagandist or attitude and action manipulator. They have shown that the data gotten from subjects (that is, the subjects' disclosures encoded in words or in nonverbal behavior) can be likened to expressions of compliance on the part of the subjects to confirm the psychologist's hypotheses about people of that sort. In fact, it seems to me that human subjects, to the extent that they are free, will please a researcher and confirm just about any of his hypotheses; witness the many confirmations of radically conflicting hypotheses. A person truly can choose a being, in the laboratory, that will uphold or refute his *experience* (fantasy or perceptual) of what the researcher wants him to show.

We researchers may be victims of the same myopia that has long afflicted physicians, preventing them from realizing that many diseases are actually *iatrogenic*—outcomes of the doctor-patient relationship. Laing and Esterson (1964) have shown, for example, that schizophrenia—its symptoms as recorded in textbooks—is (at least in part and perhaps fully) a function of the disconfirming attitudes of relatives and physicians toward the patient's experience of his world, as well as a way of being which is evoked by the mental hospital milieu itself. It is known that instances of invalidism have occurred because a doctor implied to a patient, "Your heart is not as healthy as it might be."

In research, we have recognized the "social-desirability" variable (Edwards, 1957). It has been investigated, and techniques have been proposed to bypass it or to make allowances for it. We have recognized subjects' tendencies to misrepresent their experiences in order to produce some desired image of themselves in the mind of the investigator. So we have invented tests and traps to catch their conscious and unconscious deceptions, e.g., the "Lie" and K scales on the MMPI (Minnesota Multiphasic Personality Inventory). We have utilized projective tests in the hope that a person will unwittingly reveal hidden aspects of himself. What we may not have realized is that a subject in a research project is no fool. He knows that many times his future career may depend upon how he appears through test and experimental findings. So he has a vested interest in such misrepresentation. It is very sane for him to protect himself. He has no guarantee, at least in his experience, that his responses will help the psychologist to help *him* (the subject) fulfill himself more fully. Our commitments as experimenters and as testers and the settings in which we work sometimes make it insane for a person to uncloak himself.

The Dyadic Effect Research in self-disclosure (Jourard, 1964) has amply shown that what a person will disclose to another is a function of many variables, including the subject matter to be disclosed, the characteristics of the person, the setting in which disclosure is to take place, and—more important—the characteristics of the audience person. The most powerful "determiner" of self-disclosure appears to be the willingness of the audience person to disclose *himself* to the subject to the same extent that he expects the subject to confide his own experiences. I have termed this the *dyadic effect*. It asserts, as a general principle, that "disclosure begets disclosure." Now this is not, by any means, the only condition under which a man might reveal his experience to another. He will often disclose himself unilaterally, without reciprocation, when he believes that it serves his interests to do so. This is what happens, for example, in much psychotherapeutic interviewing. The patient discloses much more about himself than the therapist does, on the implicit promise that if he does so, his lot will be improved.

It is necessary to ask whether the rela-

tionship between the experimenter and his subject is such that a dyadic effect can occur. Is it anything like dialogue? Do the laboratory setting and the typical relationship between an investigator and his human subject provide the conditions for the fullest, most authentic disclosure of self by the latter, whether in words, in writing, or by means of action of unequivocal, revealed meaning?

In most psychological investigations, the psychologist is a stranger to the subject. It is hoped that the subject is naive, unselfconscious, and willing to disclose himself, verbally or behaviorally and only through his responses, which are to be recorded on objective machines. Perhaps some people enter a laboratory in that spirit. Probably some infants and children are ready and willing to trust and to show themselves in that manner. However, I am convinced that the people who serve in psychological studies quickly become sophisticated and learn to play their parts. They are often taught what their part is by older, more experienced subjects who have served in many studies. This is also what happens to newcomers to a prison or mental hospital. The "old pros" show the ropes to the novices. I have ample reason to suspect that many subjects rattle off their performances before a researcher in a cynical way, giving him much "data" to carry off with him, away from people, to the calculating room. There the psychologist conducts complex analyses of variance and writes up his findings as part of his dialogue with his colleagues. But the people he is arguing about, the subjects, may be out in the pubs telling their cronies about how they "put one over."

Not only do we not provide human subjects with a setting and a relationship within which authentic self-disclosure can take place, but we also limit their vocabulary. Thus we limit our subjects' disclosures. We note only their GSR (galvanic skin response) reading or their questionnaire responses or the marks they leave on an event recorder. We ignore as irrelevant all the other possible means by which a person could show us what the laboratory conditions and the experiment have meant to him. We appear not to be interested in grounding our psychology on his experience. Rather, we want only to account for variance in the one kind of message we got from him and his fellow subjects. This message is just a response: serialized, fragmented, quantified. We assume that such responses have the same experiential meanings for each of the subjects or assume that whatever meanings the responses have for them are irrelevant. This is, I think, a mistake.

We can do something about this and, moreover, do it in the spirit of experimental inquiry. We can begin to change the status of the subject from that of an anonymous *object* of our study to that of a *person*, a *collaborator* in our enterprise. We can let him tell the story of his experience in our studies in a variety of idioms. We can let him show what our stimuli have meant to him through his manipulations of our gadgetry, through his responses to questionnaires, with drawings, and with words. We can invite him to reveal his being. We can prepare ourselves so that he will want to produce a multifaceted record of his experiencing in our laboratories. We can show him how we have recorded his responses and tell him what we think they mean. We can ask him to examine and then authenticate or revise our recorded version of the meaning of his experience for him. We can let him cross-examine us to get to know and trust us, to find out what we are up to, and to decide whether he wishes to take part. Heaven knows what we might find. We might well emerge with richer images of man.[2]

PRELIMINARY DIALOGUE-BASED REPLICATIONS

My students and I have made a beginning in reperforming experiments in the kind of relationship climate I have been describing. However, I would like to see such studies done by more workers to see which "classes of response" and which "psychological functions" are affected by the interpersonal context of dialogue and which are not.

Here is a progress report on what we have done so far toward discovering whether the dialogic quality of the relationship between researcher and subject makes a difference.

One of my students, W. R. Rivenbark (1963–1964), varied the way in which he conducted interviews with subjects. Under one set of conditions, he responded to the subjects' self-disclosures with disclosures of his own which reported true experiences of his that were comparable to those of his subjects. Subjects interviewed under these conditions—as opposed to the conditions under which the interviewer was technically competent but impersonal and anonymous—reported that they liked the interviewer and the interview more and that they saw the interviewer as more human and more trustworthy, and they indicated that they would like to be interviewed by him again.

Rivenbark also conducted a simple word-association test, presenting words from the list given by Rapaport (1946) in his *Diagnostic Psychological Testing*. His procedure was as follows: He gave some general, impersonal instructions to his subjects, letting them know what he expected from them. Then, he gave them one-half of the words from the list. Next, he gave them an opportunity to disclose themselves to him in writing, in response to questions, or in mutually revealing dialogue. After this, he administered the rest of the words and secured the subjects' responses. Finally, he made a rating of the degree to which he judged that good rapport and willingness to be open existed in his relationship with each person. He did not ask the subjects to do this. Then, he studied the reaction times of the subjects in response to the stimulus words. There were no differences in mean reaction time or in the kind of responses given between groups differentiated in terms of the way they disclosed themselves to the experimenter, that is, in writing, in response to spoken questions, or in dialogue. Rivenbark did find, however, that there was a significant correlation (rho of .68) between his ratings of "goodness of rapport" and

See the striking corroboration of Jourard's views, by the Romes in Chap. 19. [Editor]

the mean *increase* in reaction time between the first administration of stimulus words and the last.

We have no idea just now of what this finding means in terms of psychodynamics. It does show that either the experimenter's or the subject's experience of the relationship between them—in this case, the experimenter's—was related to differences in the objective outcome of the experiment. True, there is much wrong, from a methodological viewpoint, with this study, but it is a beginning at the kind of replication discussed above.

Subject's Attitudes about Confiding Rivenbark conducted still another exploratory study, this time directed toward people's views as to how trustworthy psychologists and their tools are. He prepared a list of fifteen possible confidants to whom, or settings within which, one might reveal intimate and personal data about himself. He asked twenty-five male and thirty female college students to rank these confidants or settings according to how willing they would be to confide fully under such circumstances. His findings, expressed as median ranks, are shown in Table 12–1.

Significantly, the research psychologist was ranked ninth. Anonymous research questionnaires were ranked fifth by women and seventh by men. This investigation may be thought of as similar to the work of public relations firms engaged to determine the "public image" of their clients. Though I dislike the term "image" in this context, I feel justified, on the basis of these data, in urging all research psychologists to seek to earn an authentically higher rank as prospective recipients of the disclosures of their subjects.

Importance of Responsiveness Another student, W. J. Powell, Jr. (1964), did a doctoral dissertation which was more carefully controlled than Rivenbark's exploratory study. He conducted interviews with college students, asking them to make themselves as fully known to him, the interviewer, as they cared to. He carefully controlled all extraneous variables and compared the increase in self-disclosure (using an operant-conditioning design) that occurred when, on the one hand, he responded to the students' disclosures with authentic disclosures of his own (in contrast to "reflecting" the feeling or content of their disclosures) and when, on the other hand, he responded with expressions of approval and support. He found that "approving, supporting" responses did not increase the students' disclosures at all. Reflection and restatement of their disclosures resulted in an increase in disclosures of negative self-statements, but did not affect positive, self-enhancing expressions. Self-disclosure from the researcher was associated with significant increases in the subjects' disclosures of both positive and negative self-references.

Another student, Miss Lee Reifel (1965–1966) conducted an interview with a girl whom she had never met, in the context of a game we invented, called "Invitations." The questions or topics for disclosure were

Table 12–1 Students' readiness to confide in different settings*

SETTING	MALE RANK	FEMALE RANK
Tell a radio or TV audience	15	15
Tell a stranger on a bus or train	14	14
Tell at a cocktail party with friends and strangers present	13	12
Write on an application for a job or club membership	12	13
Write in an autobiography for publication	11	11
Tell in a bull session with friends	10	10
Tell an interviewer for scientific purposes	9	9
Write in a letter to a friend	8	8
Write in an anonymous questionnaire for scientific purposes	7	5
Tell a priest or minister	6	6
Tell a psychotherapist	5	2
Write in a secret diary	4	7
Tell closest parent	3	4
Tell best same-sex friend	2	3
Tell best opposite-sex friend or spouse	1	1

* Taken from Rivenbark, 1963–1964.

typed on cards, and the rules were that the subject could ask the interviewer any question that she was willing to answer herself, and vice versa. In this interview, the girl became incredibly involved and revealed literally all she had to reveal. Miss Reifel disclosed much about herself, too. By the end of the interview, which lasted several hours, they knew each other very well indeed. In another interview, Miss Reifel began by using the cards as a guide, to "get acquainted" with a female student. However, for the first half of the session, she confined herself to asking questions only. The girl was to answer if she chose, but Miss Reifel would not explain or disclose more. Then Miss Reifel changed the rules and began to disclose herself truthfully regarding each question before she asked it of the student. The transformation in terms of openness and extent of self-disclosure on the part of the girl was remarkable.

TOWARD GREATER EXPERIMENTAL VALIDITY

We are continuing with this kind of research, still in the spirit of exploration. There are many technical problems to solve in a replication project of the sort we have begun. We shall need to learn better how to rate or measure the degree to which mutually self-revealing dialogue is being attained in any given relationship between a researcher and his subject. But we begin with a simple either-or discrimination between the impersonal researcher and the one who engages in a mutually revealing conversation before the experiment. More refined measures can be evolved with experience.

It would be helpful, in attempting replications in dialogue of representative experiments, if experimenters were trained to be more versatile in interacting with human beings. Perhaps we could insist that they be nice people, capable of entering into close, confiding relationships with a broad range of people. To be "nice" does not mean to be softheaded or unreliable in one's calculation of results. Training in experimental design, physiology, and statistics is no guarantee that one is qualified to interact in a confirming and evocative way with

another person. I believe we can no longer afford to ignore the effect of the experimenter on the experience and behavior of the subject. We can no longer afford to divert nice, tenderhearted humanitarians into clinical work and leave the research for hard-nosed, hardhearted, impersonal folk. If an experimental psychologist is unpleasant and threatening in the eyes of others, it might be better to confine him to the calculating room or else let him contact human subjects only when the design for the experiment calls for an impersonal investigator. If a person has gone into psychology to get away from people, let him design experiments, build equipment, analyze data, run computers, and so on. We need all the versatility we can get in psychology.

At least, however, when we want to find out how people behave and disclose themselves under more permissive interpersonal conditions, let the one who encounters the subjects be someone who, by training and by commitment, is able to enter into dialogue. How strange that good animal psychologists view their animal subjects like individual persons, worthy of respect, while experimental psychologists frequently treat their human subjects as if they were anonymous animal objects! It is already known that "gentled," tame animals show different behavioral and physiological characteristics from those shown by nongentled or "wild" ones ("wild" means, here, defensive and hostile in the presence of humans). Yet many of our subjects are assumed to be tame and trusting when, in fact, they are wild. Genuine dialogue may prove to be the appropriate context for research in *human* (free) beings. When the experimenter-subject relationship varies, we might expect the subjects' responses to stimuli to vary. It is appropriate to consider the question: What will man prove to be like when he is studied by an investigator who consents to be studied by the subject?

If we do no more than study the effects of various modes of experimenter-subject relationship on the outcome of psychological experiments, and if we do this systematically, while including dialogue as one of the relationship modes, we shall have enriched our psychological knowledge considerably. Just as important, we may have taken a step toward reconciling the conflict between humanistic and nonhumanistic orientations to our discipline.

REFERENCES

BUBER, M. *I and thou*. New York: Scribner, 1958.

EDWARDS, A. L. *The social desirability variable in personality assessment and research*. New York: Dryden Press, 1957.

JOURARD, S. M. *The transparent self: Self-disclosure and well-being*. Princeton, N.J.: Van Nostrand, 1964.

LAING, R. D., & ESTERSON, A. *Sanity, madness and the family*. Vol. 1. *Families of schizophrenics*. London: Tavistock, 1964.

ORNE, M. T. On the social psychology of the psychological experiment: With particular reference to demand characteristics and their implications. *American Psychologist*, 1962, **17**, 776–783.

POWELL, W. J., JR. A comparison of the reinforcing effects of three types of experimenter response on two classes of verbal behavior in an experimental interview. Unpublished doctoral dissertation, Univer. of Florida, 1964.

RAPAPORT, D., et al. *Diagnostic psychological testing*. Vol. 2. Chicago: Year Book Publishers, 1946.

REIFEL, LEE. Unpublished research, Department of Psychology, Univer. of Florida, 1965–1966.

RIVENBARK, W. R. Unpublished research, Department of Psychology, Univer. of Florida, 1963–1964.

ROSENTHAL, R. On the social psychology of the psychological experiment. *American Scientist*, 1963, **51**, 268–283.

Presently: Associate Professor in the Graduate School of Social Work and Director of the Human Potentialities Project at the University of Utah (since 1960).

Education: Master of Social Work from Tulane University (1950), Doctor of Philosophy in the sociology of the family and clinical psychology from Florida State University, in Tallahassee (1952), and Master of Science in community mental health from the Harvard School of Public Health (1955).

Current major activities: Teaching and research.

HERBERT A. OTTO

Most rewarding project: "We are in the process of trying out some promising new methods designed to tap human potential."

Future of humanistic psychology: "The unfolding of man's vast possibilities and latent capacities."

Personal history: Born in Berlin, Germany, of American parents. Came to the United States in 1939. Medical social worker at Charity Hospital in New Orleans (1950–1951). Assistant Professor of Mental Health Education at the University of Georgia (1952–1960). Formerly Consultant to the Georgia Department of Public Health and the Georgia Department of Education. Consultant to the Utah State Council on Aging and the Utah Department of Public Instruction. President of the Utah State Conference on Social Welfare (1962–1963).

Writings: *The Development of Theory and Practice in Social Casework,* with Nina Garton (1964), and *Guide to Developing Your Potential* (1967) are Dr. Otto's books. He also edited *Explorations in Human Potentialities* (1966) and *Human Potentialities: The Challenge and the Promise* (1967). His articles have centered around marital and premarital counseling, spontaneity training, personal and family strengths, and human potentialities. He is the author of a test, *The Otto Pre-marital Schedules,* and accompanying guide, *Manual for Pre-marital Counseling* (both 1961).

Present chapter: Dr. Otto prepared this survey, a part of the Human Potentialities Research Project, especially for this book.

Chapter 13
HERBERT A. OTTO

THE MINERVA EXPERIENCE: INITIAL REPORT

In the background of every person is a web of highly formative positive experiences charged with deep emotional meaning. These I have called "Minerva experiences."[1] My hypothesis is that these experiences have a great deal to do with the way an individual grows and develops and with the network of his strengths and potentialities. The uncovering and recall of Minerva experiences can make psychic energy available by increasing self-understanding and by providing clues to strengths and potentialities, some of which may be latent or hidden.

THE NATURE OF THE MINERVA EXPERIENCE

Although there are some similarities, the Minerva experience concept differs from Abraham Maslow's concept of "peak experiences," which he defines as follows: "The word peak experience is a generalization for the best moments of the human being, for the happiest moments of life, for experiences of ecstasy, rapture, bliss of the greatest joy" (1963, p. 117). An essential difference is that Minerva experiences are defined as *a network of highly formative and growthful experiences, having strongly positive affective components and playing a dominant role in the genesis of personality resources, and thus significantly affecting personality development.* Maslow's research into peak experiences adds to and deepens our understanding of Minerva experiences, a more inclusive construct.

The Human Potentialities Project follows the mainstream of humanistic psychology and the humanistic orientation by pursuing "an ultimate concern with and valuing of the dignity and worth of man and an interest in the development of the potential inherent in every person. Central in this view is the person as he discovers his own being and relates to other persons and to social groups" (Buhler & Bugental, 1965). Significantly also, the Minerva experience concept, as presented here, is a part of humanistic psychology's attention to the growth end of the personality continuum, or to what Maslow calls "B-Process," as opposed to "D-Process" (1962).

Begun in 1959 at the University of Georgia, the Human Potentialities Project[2] has been conducted since 1960 under the auspices of the Graduate School of Social Work of the University of Utah. The

[1] The recall of these positive experiences, the Minerva experience method, was developed in 1963 as a part of the Human Potentialities Project at the University of Utah. The method is named after Minerva, Roman goddess of health and wisdom, who sprang fully armored from the head of Jupiter.

[2] Research is carried on within the framework of laboratory groups which are offered by the University of Utah Division of Continuing Education.

research is based in part on the pioneering thinking of Murphy (1961), Maslow (1954), Fromm (1960), and Rogers (1961). The approach at the University of Utah has been essentially holistic, focusing on the whole man and the development of his interrelated potentialities.

One contribution from psychoanalysis is the hypothesis that during his formative years, every person undergoes a series of traumatic experiences which are repressed and forgotten and which become part of his unconscious. A task of the therapist is to help the patient explore his unconscious and to discover and work through these traumatic incidents so that they can be more successfully integrated into the life experience. In this way, energy formerly invested in repression of traumatic material is made available, leading to a healthier ego structure and libido economy. Similarly, it is our hypothesis that these positive, creative incidents, which we call Minerva experiences, are as important as, if not more important than, traumatic incidents.

Examples The following are examples of Minerva experiences taken from tape recordings of laboratory groups:

> During this time—about nine years of age—I was prepared for confirmation by a learned and deeply religious man, Dean Ramsey. The trip to the cathedral was long—clear across town. I remember the lesson on vestments and eucharistic articles with great vividness. We were in his study, a great paneled room, lined with books. The dean showed us all the chasubles—the richness of color, the fabrics, the magnificence of the appliqué, the delicacy of the embroidery—the carving of the walnut bishop's crosier, the metalwork are still with me. The explanation he gave us of the significance of the historical vestiture, in terms of their symbols of the virtues of our Lord, I still recall. *A great part of my life today is directed toward this constant apprehending of man's creative efforts to communicate the transcendent element in his life* —in words, and above all in religious art. Furthermore, my enjoyment of textures—in natural elements, in fabrics, in modern art— is very keen. *Both facets had their beginnings, I think, in that afternoon's lesson.*

> *   *   *

This incident I remembered of the teacher opening the window, and we sang to the birds—I still have a good feeling toward birds, and I, of course, am not a member of the Audubon Society, but there is a fellow at work that is, and I like to go talk to him about the birds; and if I see a certain bird, I like to go and ask him what type it is. If I go to the farm at Mirror Lake, I observe some hill cranes; and I reported them to this fellow, and every year I report when I return —and so forth. I have always had a good feeling, since then, toward birds and outdoor life.

> *   *   *

There is another incident that I can recall that has made me, what would you say, unafraid to tackle mechanical jobs—repairing, for instance, my refrigerator or washer at home or at work. I was the engineer on testing a big rock mill, and everybody seemed to be afraid to touch it; but I wasn't afraid to make a modification on it—and I could see it work. I believe that stems back to when I was seven or eight and I bought a bicycle, and I took the brake apart. I believe it was a Morrow Brake, and if you remember those brakes—all the parts that used to be in there. . . . I was sitting on the cellar steps trying to fix this brake, and I was washing it —and my father came along and looked at it and saw all those parts and said, "Do you think you can get it back together?" And I said, "Yeah." I worked on it for awhile, and then I wrecked it—and it sat there for a couple of days; and my father asked me what I was going to do with it. And I said, "Well, I don't know." And he got a can and gathered up all of the parts and put them in the can. He didn't say a word. He just took them all downtown and had it put back together. He didn't bawl me out or anything. He could have set a pattern there where I would have been afraid to tackle mechanical things, but he left a good feeling in my mind —even though I failed. Now I am not too afraid to tackle any mechanical thing, although that is not particularly my line. I remembered I redesigned a part—so it doesn't bother me to try.

USE OF THE MINERVA EXPERIENCE METHOD

The Minerva experience method has been used largely as a group method, although this concept may also have application to individual treatment programs.

Procedure First, Minerva experiences (hereafter referred to as ME's) are defined, and then the method is described in detail.

The decision whether to use the ME method is then made by the total group. When the group elects to use this method, all members are assigned to think about and "go back into their childhood" to uncover such ME's. It has been found that if an assignment is given, most group members will make an effort to recall these experiences in the period between sessions. Only about 10 percent of group participants have difficulty recalling *any* ME's. Therefore, as a part of the assignment, the instructions are given: "If you have difficulty recalling any Minerva experiences, it might be helpful to write down on a sheet of paper all the injurious, hurtful experiences which you have had, the traumatic incidents or the most unhappy moments in your life. This can help you to recall experiences." About one-half of those initially unable to recall any ME's are helped by this suggestion. Approximately 60 percent of the remainder will recall some ME's of their own while group members are sharing theirs.

During the session following the assignment, a layer-removal or "onionskin" procedure is used to foster recall of ME's. A chart is placed on the blackboard reading: "Ages fifteen to eighteen," "Ages ten to fourteen," "Ages six to nine," "Ages three to five," and "Below three years." Use of this chart fosters the recall. Participants are urged, "Let your minds and memory wander freely or free-associate," and are told to begin by recalling ME's at the top of the chart, between ages fifteen and eighteen. They are requested not to voice aloud experiences recalled from an earlier period unless the experience is so important that they wish to share it right away.

Whenever a participant finishes sharing an experience, the person in charge asks the following questions: "At about what age would you place this experience—can you recall anything else about the experience?" and "How do you feel this experience has been formative—what has this experience meant to you in relation to your personal development?" There is some evidence that asking the individual to identify or to make an attempt to identify the age at which the experience took place makes him better able to "build a map" of his past experiences both sequentially and chronologically, and this seems to facilitate recall. Often a triggering phenomenon can be observed, as the sharing of an experience stimulates the recall of forgotten incidents in other group members.

When there is a marked decline in the recall of ME's or when the group has reached the bottom of the chart, the person conducting the group states that he will describe some odors (or experiences with smell), as this has been found to facilitate greatly the recall of early memories, often leading to the uncovering of ME's. He then recites (using his own free flow of associations) in a manner similar to the following: "The smell of the hot sun on sand, of a wet dog coming in from the rain, of the seashore and seaweeds, of bread or cookies baking, of freshly mown hay." Participants usually interrupt with exclamations indicating they have new recollections. These are then shared and explored in relation to possible ME's. The description of odors (an appeal to one of the most primitive and basic senses) at times produces a flow of memories and associations and can be used a number of times repeatedly. As a final step, the following question is raised: "What clues to your strengths and potentialities do you now have, and what are the implications of this experience?" The group then spends some time integrating material which has been uncovered, deepening insights, and relating their discoveries to the aims and goals which they wish to achieve in the group.

A Study of Minerva Experiences Virginia Husband (1966), under my direction, conducted a study designed to determine the nature, scope, and use of the ME. Three groups were selected from six who had used the ME method. A criterion in the selection of groups using the ME was the technical fidelity of tape recordings obtained of the ME. Two groups were chosen for study because they were in session at the time and could be observed in vivo. Members of the latter two groups were invited to participate in interviews outside of class in order that ME's not recalled or verbalized during the sessions could be shared. Nine women and six men volunteered and were interviewed.

ME's from group sessions and interviews were transcribed on 3- by 5-inch cards, which were then analyzed and sorted. The following categories of ME's were distinguished and defined:

1 Significant relationships with parents

2 Significant relationships with grandparents

3 Significant relationships with siblings

4 Significant relationships with relatives

5 Significant relationships with peers, friends, and others

6 Related to achievement and/or recognition

7 School-related, not having to do with recognition or achievement

8 Religion-related

9 Music-related

10 Nature-related

11 Animal-related

12 Food-related

13 Nostalgia: recall of often fragmentary but pleasant memories of past

14 Other experiences and combinations

Findings A total of 249 ME's were collected and categorized. Of these, 125 were collected from tape recordings of group interaction, and 124 from interviews with 14 volunteers. The interview situation elicited eight ME's per person, as compared with three ME's per person during class time. It was found that the average number of ME's per participant did not differ significantly between the sexes. The 14 categories previously described were ranked by the number of ME's in each category. The majority, 165 ME's (66 percent), fell into the four highest-ranking categories, namely achievement and recognition, nature-related, relationships with others, and relationships with parents. Another 62 ME's (25 percent) occurred in the five middle categories, relationships with relatives, nostalgia, religion-related, relationships with siblings, and miscellaneous. The other 22 ME's (9 percent) were distributed among the remaining five categories.

The achievement-and-recognition category elicited twice as many ME's (67) as were found in each of the next highest categories, namely, nature-related (33) and relationships with others (33). Husband concluded that one reason for the large number in the nature-related category may have been that the person in charge stimulated recalls in the participants by sharing some delightful memories of his own in regard to nature. Husband observed, "Participants derived a particular pleasure from recalls in this category."

Analysis of the number of ME's retrospectively assigned to various age groupings revealed an interesting pattern: The highest number of ME's (73) was reported for the six- to nine-year-old age group. This suggests that the first three school years are an important source of formative experiences. The next highest total (68) was found in the fifteen- to eighteen-year-old age group, with the ten- to fourteen-year-old age group ranking third. There was a decline in the number of ME's as age decreased. In the three-year-old and under age group, there were only 13 recalls.

Since the achievement-and-recognition category contained the largest number of ME's, an analysis of this category was undertaken: It is of interest that in 57 ME's the recognition or sense of achievement was felt by participants to originate directly or indirectly from other people, mostly adults. In only 10 ME's was the self the source of a sense of achievement or recognition. The most significant differences between male and female perceptions of ME's were demonstrated in the achievement-and-recognition category. Men reported achievement and recognition as positive, formative experiences almost three times as frequently as women. The next most significant differences between male and female perceptions were demonstrated in the relationship categories. Thirteen men reported a total of fifteen ME's, as compared with thirty women reporting eighty ME's within the five relationship categories. This is almost 2½ times as many ME's reported by women as by men. This seems to indicate the importance of peer relationships in filling needs of women. Of all male ME's reported in the relationship categories, 67 percent fell within the relationships-with-parents category, whereas only 28 percent of the female ME's fell within this group.

GENERAL RESULTS AND IMPLICATIONS

A number of conclusions emerge based on the use of the ME method over a three-year period with eight groups: (1) In most instances, participants identify as ME's incidents which characteristically have strong emotions associated with them. (2) Other group members in most instances are more clearly aware of the part played by a particular experience in relation to the personality development of the person than the individual describing the ME. Often the impact of a particular ME on the whole future course of a person's life appeared in dramatic relief. (3) So-called normal or healthy persons experience considerable difficulty in recalling significant material from childhood. There are extensive gaps and difficulties in establishing chronology. This difficulty of recall seems in part to be responsible for the relatively low number of ME's reported within the group and during interviews. (4) Approximately 15 to 20 percent of the group members routinely and spontaneously reported a significant upsurge in energy during the week following the ME recall, as well as "very positive feelings about life and living." (5) There have been several instances of a dramatic change in attitude toward parents as a result of the ME recall. Some group members who had comparatively little contact with their parents or who had felt emotionally isolated from them reestablished warm and vital relationships following the ME recall. Many other members routinely made such remarks as, "My parents were much nicer to me than I gave them credit for." (6) There are indications that the uncovering and working through of trauma leads to easier recall of ME's. One almost gets the impression that the trauma rests as a heavier stratum on top and keeps the ME's from emerging.

I undertook an analysis of tape-recorded group reactions to the ME recall, using the same and the next following session. Reactions of the participants to the experience were overwhelmingly favorable. Most comments focused on the positive nature of the experience. ("It was a good experience. It made me feel wonderful.") The next highest number of remarks indicated a shift in perceptions of the gestalt of childhood experiences. ("I used to think that my childhood was mostly negative—this made me change my mind.")

Values and Potentials Evaluation to date reveals that the ME method holds considerable promise for the identification and development of latent strengths. Participants recall strong interests and skills which were present in childhood and much enjoyed but which, for one reason or another, were forgotten or not utilized during subsequent life experience. Often a resurgence of interest and a desire to develop an ability or skill is evident following ME recall. In many instances, the group encourages such development and verbalizes latent strengths if the participant does not take the initiative or seems unaware. ("Have you done anything with your whittling since that happened?" "Maybe sculpting or wood carving is something you have a talent for.") Thus, individual potential may be developed as a direct result of the experience.

There is also evidence that the method enhances self-confidence and generally has ego-supportive values. This is expressed by one participant: "I felt full of pep and energy after we used the method. It makes you feel better about yourself, and you like people better." Improved self-images and self-concepts were indicated by a number of participants who, in their final evaluation of the class, identified their experiences with the method as a turning point in their developments. "After Minerva I really changed. I bought a new dress and wig, got some confidence, and changed jobs. My relations with my mother improved. I just wish Father hadn't died two years ago."

An interesting use of the method was made with a small group of parents whose children had been referred for social services because of school adjustment problems. This was primarily an educational group with some emphasis on group discussion.

Following use of the ME method, parents stated that they had a much better idea of the type of growthful and positive experiences they could provide for their children. Based on current pilot use of the method in diverse settings, it has application to a wide range of clinical, educational, and personnel development programs.

Rogers (1962) has pointed out that man's basic disease is too little self-love. Is it possible that the recovery of ME's is a first and necessary step for the building of the self-love which is of the very essence of health? Is the recovery and integration of the web of ME's one of the prime requisites for the full flowering of a healthy ego? To what degree does the unfolding of ME's bring greater flexibility and strength to the ego structure? In the sense of the foregoing, does the ME method have preventive implications for the healthy and comparatively well-functioning person? Finally, at what particular times and to what extent can the method best be used so that it becomes a highly effective and joyous trigger experience in the actualizing of potential? These are some of the questions which await further exploration.

REFERENCES

BUHLER, CHARLOTTE, & BUGENTAL, J. F. T. (Informational brochure.) San Francisco: American Association for Humanistic Psychology, 1965.

FROMM, E. *Man for himself.* New York: Holt, Rinehart and Winston, 1960.

HUSBAND, VIRGINIA. Personality strengths analysis. Unpublished master's thesis, Univer. of Utah, 1966.

MASLOW, A. H. *Motivation and personality.* New York: Harper & Row, 1954.

MASLOW, A. H. Notes on being-psychology. *Journal of Humanistic Psychology,* 1962, **2** (2), 47–71.

MASLOW, A. H. Fusions of facts and values. *American Journal of Psychoanalysis,* 1963, **23**, 117–181.

MURPHY, G. *Human potentialities.* New York: Basic Books, 1961.

ROGERS, C. R. *On becoming a person.* Boston: Houghton Mifflin, 1961.

ROGERS, C. R. Niebuhr's "The Nature and Destiny of Man." In S. Doniger (Ed.), *The nature of man in theological and psychological perspective.* New York: Harper & Row, 1962.

Presently: Clinical psychologist in the Neuropsychiatric Service of the Veterans Administration Hospital at Phoenix, Arizona (since 1956).

Education: Doctor of Philosophy in psychology from Columbia University (1940). Postdoctoral training in clinical psychology at UCLA and the Sepulveda Veterans Administration Hospital in Los Angeles (1955–1956).

S. STANSFELD
SARGENT

Current major activities: In the fall of 1966, Dr. Sargent was a seagoing Professor of Psychology on Chapman College's University of the Seven Seas. At home in Phoenix, in addition to his post at the hospital, he conducts a private practice.

Future of humanistic psychology: "I am sanguine about the long-range prospects for humanistic psychology because I think it represents the most mature and realistic orientation. It includes the good and the beautiful as goals for research, as well as the true. To the humanistic psychologist, values and feelings are perhaps the most significant data of all."

Personal history: Dr. Sargent has taught at Adelphi College (1931–1932), at the Central YMCA College (now Roosevelt University) in Chicago (1935–1940), and at Barnard College and Columbia University (1940–1955). He became an Associate of Professional Psychological Services, a private group practice in 1958. President of the Society for the Psychological Study of Social Issues (1954–1955), of the Arizona State Psychological Association (1961–1962), and of the American Association for Humanistic Psychology (1966–1967).

Writings: *Basic Teachings of the Great Psychologists* (1944, and revised in 1965 with Kenneth Stafford) and *Social Psychology*, which has gone through three editions, the last two of which were done with R. C. Williamson (1950, 1958, 1966). Dr. Sargent edited *Culture and Personality: Proceedings of an Interdisciplinary Conference*, with M. W. Smith (1949), and "Anti-intellectualism in the United States," with T. Brameld (*Journal of Social Issues*, 1955, **11**, No. 3).

Present chapter: This essay was prepared especially for this volume.

Chapter 14
S. STANSFELD SARGENT

HUMANISTIC METHODOLOGY IN PERSONALITY AND SOCIAL PSYCHOLOGY

What are the important humanistic criteria for evaluating theories and research in the broad area of personality and social psychology? By now, fortunately, humanistic psychologists seem to agree well enough so that their major emphases can be outlined. The following categories are suggested:

1 BREADTH AND INCLUSIVENESS. To what extent does the viewpoint under consideration encompass man in relation to his world, his *weltanschauung*, his philosophy of life, his past and future, as well as his present cultural frame of reference?

2 SOCIAL ORIENTATION and sensitivity. How clearly spelled out is man's relation to his fellow men and his interaction with them? Is there concern for what Adler called *"Gemeinschaftsgefühl"*—feeling for mankind? Are people regarded as ends rather than as means?

3 FOCUS ON THE EXPERIENCING PERSON. Does the theory or viewpoint have regard for subjective reactions, particularly feelings? That is, is it phenomenological? This would include concepts like the self-image, self-esteem, and the unity or integrity of the personality.

4 CONCERN WITH HIGHER HUMAN QUALITIES. These are often neglected in the psychologist's preoccupation with problems of adjustment. Although views would vary, such higher human qualities would include love, creativity, spontaneity, autonomy, sympathy, empathy, openness to stimuli, transcendence, and the like.

5 CONSIDERATION OF VALUES, GOALS, AND PURPOSES. Is man regarded as *proactive*,[1] or future-seeking, rather than as merely *reactive*? Is he thought to be capable of self-actualization?

6 METHODOLOGY. Is the theory or research problem-oriented rather than technique-oriented? Is the method well adapted to the problem or task, or is it the same method which is being used without question for all kinds of research?

Which theories of personality and social behavior come close to meeting these humanistic criteria? Let us review some of their high points, beginning with the psychoanalysts.

BREADTH AND INCLUSIVENESS

Sigmund Freud not only plumbed the unconscious but also looked into much of man's history and institutional life—all without the aid of recent research in anthropology and other social sciences. His studies

[1] See Chap. 8, by Hubert Bonner, for an expanded treatment of this concept. [Editor]

of Moses, Leonardo, and many phases of art, religion, and history are well known. His contribution to social psychology is also important; it has been considered to cover five areas: socialization of the individual, family structure and dynamics, group psychology, the origin of society, and the nature of human culture (Hall & Lindzey, 1954, p. 165).

Carl Jung, even more than Freud, was noted for the catholicity of his interests: history, mythology, classics, archaeology, anthropology, and religion. His more spiritual aspirations were probably best expressed in *Modern Man in Search of a Soul* (1933), largely a protest against what he considered the negative or animalistic trends in Freud.

Alfred Adler, although not as historically or philosophically inclined, seemed more aware than Freud and Jung of the social and economic conditions of his times. Commenting on this, Murphy suggests that ". . . Adler's was the first psychological system in the history of psychology that was developed in what we should today call a social-science direction" (1949, p. 341).

Among the neoanalysts, *Erich Fromm* is outstanding as to breadth of orientation. *Escape from Freedom* (1941) is a historical and cultural, as well as a psychological, study. His theory of personality is even more socially oriented than Adler's. Fromm's concept of "social character" and his book *The Sane Society* (1955) bespeak his great interest in the sweep of human culture and the problems of contemporary society.

Kurt Lewin's field theory elaborated the gestalt viewpoint so that it applies to theories of both personality and social behavior. His breadth of interest is suggested not only in his personality and group-dynamics studies but also in his concern for cultural reconstruction, marriage conflict, and minority-group problems (1948). The often forgotten *J. F. Brown* pioneered in drawing on sociological and political science data, as well as psychological data, and in attempting to synthesize psychoanalysis and field theory. He analyzed the effects of national, church, social-class, and minority-group membership character and applied his theories to the analysis of democracy and of both fascist and communist dictatorships (1936).

At least three other theorists deserve mention here. *Gordon Allport* is perhaps the best known and most eclectic of students of personality. With wide philosophical, scholarly, and international interests, he is interdisciplinary in approach. As Hall and Lindzey put it (1957, p. 260):

> For many years he has inveighed against encapsulating psychology within the walls of the laboratory, and his work in the fields of prejudice and international relations are among the more fruitful examples of the application of psychology to social issues. It is interesting to note that with many other theorists who have emphasized strongly the uniqueness and individuality of human behavior there is an underlying pessimism on Allport's part concerning the ultimate power of psychological method and theory to unravel the mystery of human behavior. The enigma posed by the complex individual is too great to be completely understood through the earth-bound methods and conceptions of the psychologist.

Important to personality and social psychology, as well as to other fields of psychology, *Gardner Murphy* has advanced a "biosocial" theory of personality. Exploring the biological, psychological, and social approaches to the subject, he made strides toward integrating them. For good measure, in his major volume, *Personality* (1947), he ended with a section called "Individual and Group," which deals with such varied topics as economic determinism, ethos, history as the proving ground, and the fitness of culture for personality. With his broad and eclectic tendencies, Murphy seems practically a field theorist.

Henry A. Murray is noted for his focus upon "lives-as-wholes" and for his exploration of all aspects of human experience. His organismic and field-theory approach has been called "personology." Like Murphy and Allport, his preference is interdisciplinary, and his studies cover many cultures and many phases of our own, from myths to *Moby Dick,* and from science to Satan (White, 1963).

SOCIAL ORIENTATION

Much more than other psychoanalysts, *Adler* stressed man's primarily social motivation. Social interest and style of life in relation to others were two of his cardinal concepts. But Adler did more: "By endowing man with altruism, humanitarianism, co-operation, creativity, uniqueness, and awareness, he restored to man a sense of dignity and worth that psychoanalysis had pretty largely destroyed. . . . Adler offered a portrait of man which was more satisfying, more hopeful, and far more complimentary to man" (Hall & Lindzey, 1957, p. 125).

Fromm too espouses a humanistic kind of psychoanalysis. He sees existing society as frustrating to man's basic social needs and proposes a "sane society" more suited to his human condition. This society might be called "humanistic communitarian socialism," he suggests. It is a society "in which man relates to man lovingly, in which he is rooted in bonds of brotherliness and solidarity, rather than in the ties of blood and soil; a society which gives him the possibility of transcending nature by creating rather than destroying, in which everyone gains a sense of self by experiencing himself as the subject of his powers rather than by conformity, in which a system of orientation and devotion exists without man's needing to distort reality . . ." (1956, p. 314).

Lewin, both in his personality theory and in his group dynamics, stressed the great importance of the social field, considered both objectively and subjectively. His well-known studies of group decision and of group atmospheres were based upon his keen sensitivity to the whole social situation and the complex interpersonal relations present. *Murray's* conception of personality gave a very prominent part to social determinants and to "interpersonal proceedings." He dealt with group membership, role, and situational determinants, which operate interdependently along with constitutional or biological determinants (Murray & Kluckhohn, 1953).

Probably social sensitivity has been given most attention by those with a therapeutic orientation. *Sullivan* (1947) conceived of personality and of psychiatry in terms of interpersonal relations; he dealt with psychotherapy primarily in terms of the processes of communication. Both *Rogers* and *Maslow* think of psychotherapy as a warm and close human relationship. Rogers has

spelled out in detail the nature of the interpersonal relations underlying successful therapy: The therapist must be genuinely himself, must freely accept the client, must be sensitively and empathically aware of the client's experiences, and must be able to communicate to the client that he understands his feelings and experiences (1957, pp. 95ff.). Maslow cites examples of therapeutic improvement arising from good interpersonal relations without benefit of special training, techniques, or theory; for him, good human relations are *ipso facto* therapeutic. "Certainly we need not be afraid as professionals of putting into the hands of amateurs these important psychotherapeutic tools: love for other human beings and respect for other human beings. . . . Love and respect are forces almost always for good and not for harm" (1954, pp. 320-321).

FOCUS ON THE EXPERIENCING PERSON

The phenomenological viewpoint goes back at least to *Adler,* who stressed self and consciousness in his "individual psychology." Consciousness of self and self-esteem form important aspects of *Allport's* conception of personality. As he put it: "Until the child has a fairly definite conception of himself as an independent person, he cannot conceptualize his relationship to the surrounding world and hence lacks the subjective nucleus for the development of his own personality" (1937, p. 160). *Lecky,* in his *Self-consistency* (1951), treated the self as a unity which gives purpose and continuity to living. *Sherif* and *Cantril* brought in the term "ego-involvement" as a constellation of ego attitudes which "determine the more or less enduring character of one's personal identity" (1947, p. 4). *Hilgard* proposed that the well-known mechanisms of adjustment imply a self-reference and are not understandable unless we adopt a concept of the self. He suggested it be called the "inferred self" and be investigated in the laboratory (1949).

Lewin, of course, had distinguished sharply between the objective and the psychological environment, stressing the significance of the subjective interpretation since the objective environment cannot be perceived per se. This phenomenological view was featured even more by *Snygg* and *Combs*, who stated that *"all behavior, without exception, is completely determined by and pertinent to the phenomenal field of the behaving organism"* (1949, p. 15). Of recent theorists in social psychology, *Festinger* seems closest to a phenomenological view. His theory of social comparison assumes that people evaluate their opinions and abilities by comparing them with others', which has many implications for social action. His theory of cognitive dissonance insists that we strive to reduce felt dissonances between cognitions (1962).

Among psychotherapists, *Rogers* has been consistently phenomenological. Each person has a private world of experience, to which he reacts for better or worse as if it were reality. In the client-centered therapy situation, every effort is made by the therapist to understand the client's perceptions and feelings—his changing world of experience—with the aim of guiding him toward a more realistic conception of himself and of his world (1951).

It might be added that behaviorists, most learning theorists, and all objectivists are particularly opposed to the phenomenological viewpoint. They see it as fuzzy, qualitative, and suspect because it is reachable via introspection. Rather than bothering with such "unscientific" data, they prefer to leave them out of their calculations. How they handle subjective matters in their own personal lives is seldom made clear. Presumably they are to be dealt with by some nonscientific approach such as philosophy, art, or religion, but certainly not by a *science* such as psychology!

CONCERN WITH HIGHER HUMAN QUALITIES

More than Freud or even Jung, *Adler* emphasized the creative, cooperative, and altruistic nature of man. Similarly, *Fromm* spoke of man's urge for transcendence, his need to rise above his animal nature. He

wrote *The Art of Loving* in order to show "that love is not a sentiment that can be easily indulged in by anyone, regardless of the level of maturity reached by him." He sought to convince the reader "that all his attempts for love are bound to fail, unless he tries most actively to develop his total personality, so as to achieve a productive orientation" (1956, p. vii).

With his belief in the uniqueness of the individual and his principle of functional autonomy, *Allport* might be expected to discuss higher qualities in man. Many current theories, he laments, "are based largely upon the behavior of sick and anxious people or upon the antics of captive and desperate rats. Fewer theories have derived from the study of healthy human beings, those who strive not so much to preserve life as to make it worth living. Thus we find today many studies of criminals, few of law-abiders; many of fear, few of courage; more on hostility than on affiliation; much on the blindness in man, little on his vision; much on his past, little on his outreaching into the future" (1955, p. 18). This view parallels that of *Maslow,* who has called on psychology not to restrict itself to man's weaknesses but to study his strengths, to study not *deficiency* but *growth* motivation, not defense but growth (1962).

Nor are these voices in the wilderness. Others are speaking out. *Murray* has vigorously protested the narrow specialization of psychology. *Goldstein* (1939) and others with an organismic view have inveighed against analyzing the organism into small bits and thus losing sight of the whole—the integrated and organized personality. *Murphy's Human Potentialities* (1958) calls for freeing intelligence through breaking the mold of custom and culture, as we strive creatively to bring about emergence of new forms of organization.

CONSIDERATION OF VALUES, GOALS, AND PURPOSES

Many theorists of personality and social behavior have been greatly concerned with values. All psychologists are familiar with the Allport-Vernon scale for the measurement of basic values. *Maslow* has called for a "science of values" and not long ago edited a volume entitled *New Knowledge in Human Values. Charlotte Buhler* has explored the significance of values in psychotherapy and their role in personality development as well as in personality theory (1962).

Closely related to values is the view of man as an organism reaching for the future rather than simply acting out the past or present. One recalls *Jung's* early concern with causality and teleology, i.e., with the past and the future. Both views are necessary for the complete picture, but the fact remains that civilized man is unique in his striving for self-actualization. *Adler's* theory of the creative self is similar; it includes a goal and an active seeking for the goal. *Murray* has spoken of "serial programs" and of "ordination" to cover the making of plans and the working toward distant goals. *Lewin's* "level of aspiration" may be considered a short-term version of the same concept: setting up goals and reaching for them. *Hubert Bonner's* recent book, *On Being Mindful of Man: Essay toward a Proactive Psychology* (1965), centers about the psychological processes of intentionality and "proaction." Proactive psychology, he says, "contrasts sharply with the two dominant approaches to human behavior: the poetic mythology of psychoanalysis and the mindless technology of behaviorism. Both present us with a very one-sided view of man. One describes man as a blind victim of his past, the other, as a driven creature of habits" (p. 6). He later quotes Allport in the same vein: "People, it seems, are busy leading their lives into the future, whereas psychology, for the most part, is busy tracing them into the past" (p. 37).

Self-actualization or self-realization became an important part of the theories of *Goldstein, Maslow,* and *Rogers.* For Goldstein, self-actualization was at once the master motive and the creative aspect of man's life. For Rogers, the human being has one basic tendency: "to actualize, maintain and enhance the experiencing organism" (1951, p. 487). Maslow has developed his concept most thoroughly in his study of self-actualizing people. He finds them to be people who accept themselves; who are spontaneous, autonomous, and creative; and who have a quality of detachment and democratic character structure (1954).

He later investigated what he called "cognition of Being" in the peak experiences and the creative activities of self-actualizing people. These studies provided further data on the functioning of mature and healthy human beings, as compared with what he called the "psychopathology of the average" (1962).

METHODOLOGY

In many ways the crux of the issue between the humanistically inclined and other psychologists is methodological. The former tend to be problem-oriented; the latter are technique-oriented in that they stick to one or two research techniques and have little use for others. In fact, many of the technique-oriented investigators shun personality and other complex areas because they cannot be dealt with easily and neatly by the favored means. Where experimentation and quantitative treatment of data are followed strictly, one is likely to find a limited conceptualization of personality and social behavior. Let us cite some examples.

W. H. Sheldon's constitutional or morphological approach to personality is widely known (Sheldon & Stevens, 1942). He stressed the temperamental or biological aspects of the subject and was not much concerned with the attitudinal or social sides, except insofar as they enter as details of viscerotonia, somatotonia, or cerebrotonia. He paid little attention to the phenomenological side, to the self, or to creative qualities in personality. Sheldon's method was morphological classification and measurement, which he improved greatly, with statistical treatment of results.

A follower of B. F. Skinner, *R. W. Lundin* (1961) recently published a book called *Personality: An Experimental Approach.* He begins by defining personality as "the branch of the general field of learning which studies in particular those processes significant to human adjustment." The subsuming of personality under the head of learning, along with his experimental emphasis, no doubt contributes to

Lundin's lack of interest in social orientation, creativeness, or such "intervening variables" as values and purposes.

Another approach to personality and social behavior is furnished by factor analysis. Central factors or traits are educed from correlational treatment of batteries of questionnaires or other measures. The prolific *Raymond Cattell* (1950) has come up with a large number of personality traits (both "source" and "surface" traits) and several types of social behavior. He cannot be called narrow in scope; Cattell is willing to bring in concepts such as the self or sentiments, and has introduced new terms such as "syntality" into the psychological vocabulary. Perhaps the main criticisms of this approach, in the eyes of the humanistically inclined, are the loss of the individual as a person—as a unique gestalt—and the artificiality of the categories when applied to any given individual. It may be added that the traits which boil out of a factor analysis always reflect the particular measures used; when another set of measures is employed—e.g., a different battery of personality tests—the resulting pattern of factors may not be the same. Yet both may be referred to as "the" factors or components of personality.

The humanistic objection to orthodox research methods is not that they have no merit but that despite the researcher's confidence in his techniques, they fail to portray the essence of the personality or social behavior. It may be argued that the humanistic psychologist has not done much better. Surely, however, criticism of existing inadequacies is the first step toward discovering new and better techniques. As Barker (1965) says, we need to enter the scientific arena ourselves and devise methods for studying the uniquely human qualities in which we are interested.

Actually we have many models, some of them implicit in the earlier discussion of humanistic categories. *Lewin* was most ingenious in setting up real-life situations for the testing of significant theoretical and practical issues. *Sherif* began his studies of norms in the laboratory and gradually ex-

tended his research more and more widely into the community. *Rogers* devised new ways for evaluating the subtle qualitative changes occurring in the course of psychotherapy. After insisting that psychology should study healthy and mature personalities, *Maslow* proceeded to do pioneering research in this direction. *Allport* and *Murray*, focusing on individuals, have been productive in trying out new approaches to personality. Many other independent and original investigators could be mentioned, such as Charlotte Buhler, Rollo May, Andras Angyal, Anthony Sutich, J. F. T. Bugental, Clark Moustakas, Sidney Jourard, and Hubert Bonner.[2]

CONCLUSION

In a word, we of humanistic persuasion —just like all scientific and professional people—have the right and the duty to point out the errors and inadequacies of those we consider biased, narrow, or merely limited. But we should not stop there; this is but a beginning. Our task is to provide better conceptualizations, more inclusive theories, and more ingenious and adequate research techniques. In the frustratingly complex domain of personality and social psychology, this confronts us with a real challenge.

REFERENCES

ALLPORT, G. W. *Personality: A psychological interpretation*. New York: Holt, Rinehart and Winston, 1937.

ALLPORT, G. W. *Becoming*. New Haven, Conn.: Yale Univer. Press, 1955.

BARKER, E. N. A program of research in humanistic psychology. Paper read at American Association for Humanistic Psychology, Chicago, September, 1965.

BONNER, H. *On being mindful of man: Essay toward a proactive psychology*. Boston: Houghton Mifflin, 1965.

BROWN, J. F. *Psychology and the social order*. New York: McGraw-Hill, 1936.

[2] In the reference list which comes at the close of this chapter, the following items are helpful as general sources: Deutsch & Krauss, 1965; Karpf, 1932; Maddi, 1963; Schlien, 1963; and Wepman & Heine, 1963.

BUHLER, CHARLOTTE. *Values in psychotherapy*. New York: Free Press, 1962.

CATTELL, R. B. *Personality: A systematic theoretical and factual study*. New York: McGraw-Hill, 1950.

DEUTSCH, M., & KRAUSS, R. M. *Theories in social psychology*. New York: Basic Books, 1965.

FESTINGER, L. *A theory of cognitive dissonance*. New York: Harper & Row, 1962.

FROMM, E. *Escape from freedom*. New York: Holt, Rinehart and Winston, 1941.

FROMM, E. *The sane society*. New York: Holt, Rinehart and Winston, 1955.

FROMM, E. *The art of loving*. New York: Harper & Row, 1956.

GOLDSTEIN, K. *The organism*. New York: American Book Co., 1939.

HALL, C. S., & LINDZEY, G. Psychoanalytic theory and its applications to the social sciences. In G. Lindzey (Ed.), *Handbook of social psychology*. Reading, Mass.: Addison-Wesley, 1954.

HALL, C. S., & LINDZEY, G. *Theories of personality*. New York: Wiley, 1957.

HILGARD, E. R. Human motives and the concept of self. *American Psychologist*, 1949, **4**, 374–382.

JUNG, C. G. *Modern man in search of a soul*. New York: Harcourt, Brace & World, 1933.

KARPF, FAY B. *American social psychology*. New York: McGraw-Hill, 1932.

LECKY, P. (Edited and interpreted by F. C. Thorne.) *Self-consistency: A theory of personality*. New York: Island Press, 1951.

LEWIN, K. *Resolving group conflicts*. New York: Harper & Row, 1948.

LEWIN, K. *Field theory in social science*. New York: Harper & Row, 1951.

LUNDIN, R. W. *Personality: An experimental approach*. New York: Macmillan, 1961.

MADDI, S. R. Humanistic psychology: Allport and Murray. In J. M. Wepman & R. W. Heine (Eds.), *Concepts of personality*. Chicago: Aldine, 1963.

MASLOW, A. H. *Motivation and personality*. New York: Harper & Row, 1954.

MASLOW, A. H. (Ed.) *New knowledge in human values*. New York: Harper & Row, 1959.

MASLOW, A. H. *Toward a psychology of being*. Princeton, N.J.: Van Nostrand, 1962.

MURPHY, G. *Personality: A biosocial approach to origins and structure*. New York: Harper & Row, 1947.

MURPHY, G. *Historical introduction to modern psychology*. New York: Harcourt, Brace, & World, 1949.

MURPHY, G. *Human potentialities*. New York: Basic Books, 1958.

MURRAY, H. A., & KLUCKHOHN, C. L. (Eds.) *Personality in nature, society and culture*. New York: Knopf, 1953.

ROGERS, C. R. *Client-centered therapy*. Boston: Houghton Mifflin, 1951.

ROGERS, C. R. The necessary and sufficient conditions of therapeutic personality change. *Journal of Consulting Psychology*, 1957, **21**, 95–103.

SCHLIEN, J. M. Phenomenology and personality. In J. M. Wepman & R. W. Heine (Eds.), *Concepts of personality*. Chicago: Aldine, 1963.

SHELDON, W. H., & STEVENS, S. S. *The varieties of temperament*. New York: Harper & Row, 1942.

SHERIF, M., & CANTRIL, H. *The psychology of ego-involvements*. New York: Wiley, 1947.

SNYGG, D., & COMBS, A. W. *Individual behavior*. New York: Harper & Row, 1949.

SULLIVAN, H. S. *Conceptions of modern psychiatry*. Washington, D.C.: W. A. White Foundation, 1947.

WEPMAN, J. M., & HEINE, R. W. (Eds.) *Concepts of personality*. Chicago: Aldine, 1963.

WHITE, R. W. (Ed.) *The study of lives: Essays on personality in honor of Henry A. Murray*. New York: Atherton, 1963.

Presently: Associate Professor of Psychology at San Francisco State College (since 1963).

Education: Doctor of Philosophy in psychology from the State University of Iowa (1960).

Current major activity: "Exploring and attempting to understand altered states of consciousness induced by a variety of means and for a variety of purposes."

Most rewarding project: Developing methods of expanding and cultivating individual awareness for humanistic purposes.

ROBERT E. MOGAR

Future of humanistic psychology: "Bringing the insights of humanistic psychology to bear on the life experience of 'everyman.' "

Personal history: Teaching and Research Assistant at the State University of Iowa (1956–1959). Psychology Intern at the Veterans Administration Psychiatric Clinic in Des Moines (1959–1960). Instructor and Counseling Psychologist at Pennsylvania State University (1960–1961). United States Public Health Service Post-doctoral Fellow at Mount Zion Psychiatric Clinic and Stanford University (1961–1963). Research Consultant to the International Foundation for Advanced Study and to the Mendocino (California) State Hospital.

Writings: Dr. Mogar is by way of becoming one of the major critics of psychedelic theory and research. He has at least a dozen publications in this field, including "Personality Changes Associated with Psychedelic (LSD) Therapy," with C. Savage (*Psychotherapy: Theory, Research & Practice*, 1964, **1,** 154–162); "Current Status and Future Trends in Psychedelic Research" (*Journal of Humanistic Psychology*, 1965, **5,** 147–165); and "Psychedelic Drugs and Human Potentialities," in H. A. Otto (Ed.), *Explorations in Human Potentialities* (1966).

Present chapter: This thoroughgoing review and critique was prepared especially for the present volume.

Chapter 15

ROBERT E. MOGAR

PSYCHEDELIC (LSD) RESEARCH: A CRITICAL REVIEW OF METHODS AND RESULTS

Since the discovery of LSD-25 in 1943, close to two thousand professional journal articles on the subject have appeared, together with a rash of commentary in the mass media. Despite its brief history, many thousands of people have ingested the drug and reported experiences ranging from the most heavenly to the hellish. Clearly, the increasing attention and controversy generated by this recent addition to the psychedelic family indicate a remarkable degree of fascination with altered states of awareness—among the general public as well as among scientists and psychotherapists.

Such widespread attraction suggests that the promise *and* fear evoked by LSD are symptomatic of larger issues within our culture. This possibility gains support from both current research with LSD and the aura surrounding its informal use, which, interestingly, is concentrated among college-level people.

In contrast to its initial link with insanity and dire warnings of adverse reactions, many investigators are currently exploring constructive uses of this powerful agent and its relation to man's most illuminating experiences. Experimental applications of LSD include the treatment of emotional disorders, the study of higher mental processes, and the similarity of psychedelic experiences to such phenomena as creative thinking; hypnotic, mystical, and dream states; identity crises; and naturally occurring nadir and peak experiences. As with countless other innovations, the controversy and sensationalism surrounding LSD have decreased as knowledge and familiarity have increased.

Despite significant shifts in the direction and results of LSD research, a number of *genuine* issues remain unresolved. Granted the drug experience holds considerable promise as a therapeutic and scientific tool, how shall we regard "consciousness expansion"? Do psychedelic experiences facilitate attitudes and behavior that conflict with our cultural values, social mores, and personal aims? Who shall have access to these drugs, and for what purpose? Do their increasing popularity and ready availability pose ethical, social, or legal problems? It is apparent that questions concerning psychedelic agents touch upon some of the major dilemmas of our time and that consensus on these issues will not soon be forthcoming. Accumulated facts cannot settle questions' of value. However, by examining the evidence currently available, it is possible to clarify problems and increase our understanding of them.

The Psychedelic Phenomena There is general agreement on the major subjective and behavioral effects induced by LSD. Experimental and clinical studies have consistently found a lowered response threshold for both internal and external stimuli (Mogar, 1965b). All the senses, particularly sight and hearing, are more sensitive to incoming sensations. This is especially so with weaker sensations or aspects of one's environment which are always present but generally ignored. Similarly, awareness of internal, normally unconscious events increases. In short, perception under LSD is greatly intensified and takes place on a wider screen. Less filtering of experience occurs; less is screened out of consciousness. Temporarily freed from "word prisons," thinking is less cluttered with abstractions and conventional symbols. As in normal imagination and dream states, the relative flatness of verbal conceptual thinking is suspended in favor of richly colored, multidimensional visual imagery in constant motion.

In addition to changes in perception and thinking, one's usual orientation to space, time, and self is greatly altered. Spatial relations shift, forming myriad configurations and patterns. Time may "stand still" or greatly accelerate, consistent with the events being experienced. Body boundaries and the distinction between self and nonself become less definite, so that the person feels more intimately a part of his surroundings. Also prominent are the intensified emotional reactions that typically occur.

On a purely descriptive level, these are the major effects of LSD on human beings. More specific reactions are dependent on factors other than the drug's chemical properties or its direct physiological effects. As with any substance ingested by humans, psychological and social factors play a crucial role. The psychedelic experience may be interpreted as a self-fulfilling prophecy. What one expects to happen has a direct bearing on what actually does happen. How a person verbalizes the experience will reflect his beliefs and attitudes, as well as the cultural climate in which he lives.

Earlier investigators gave LSD to normal subjects, hoping artificially to produce schizophrenic symptoms. At that time it was thought that LSD might be the key to understanding severe forms of mental illness. In many cases LSD did induce hallucinations, delusions, anxiety reactions, and other disturbing effects. However, it soon became apparent that the subject's fear of the drug, the psychiatrist's expectation of producing a psychotic state, and the barren laboratory setting were contributing greatly to the adverse reactions. Despite these unfavorable conditions, many subjects still experienced profound insights, perceptions of extraordinary beauty, and feelings of love and joy. Unlike the psychotic patient, most LSD subjects were usually aware that their visions and novel experiences had an unreal quality and did not confuse them with external reality.

STRATEGIES OF PSYCHEDELIC RESEARCH

Despite the mass of published reports on the effects of LSD in man and animals, results have been contradictory even within species far less complex than man. In addition to the unresolved medico-legal-social issues, systematic study of human reactions to LSD has been plagued by a host of methodological problems associated with greater organic complexity, shortcomings of currently available measuring devices, the ubiquity of individual differences, lack of an adequate theoretical model, and the influence of nondrug factors such as set and setting.

As with *any* therapeutic agent, the major psychological and behavioral effects, both during and subsequent to the LSD-induced state, are not drug-specific. The nature, intensity, thematic content, and aftermath of the experience are the resultants of com-

Laboratory Studies	Clinical Studies
1 View the drug as a stressor capable of simulating psychoticlike behavior ("psychotomimetic" orientation)	**1** View the drug as a liberator which facilitates accurate perception and insight ("psychedelic" orientation)
2 Focus on the direct effects of the drug shortly after ingestion	**2** Focus on behavior changes subsequent to, rather than during, the drug experience
3 Systematically manipulate drug variables such as dose and frequency of administration rather than extradrug variables	**3** Manipulate subject characteristics (e.g., diagnosis) and vary drug variables unsystematically
4 Pay minimal attention to nondrug variables (e.g., set and setting) and individual differences (e.g., personality)	**4** Pay greater attention to variables associated with the context of drug administration (e.g., preparation of subject, setting)
5 Use more objective, quantitative, precise indexes of drug effects (e.g., EEG, reaction time)	**5** Use more global, subjective, qualitative indexes of drug effects (e.g., therapists' ratings)
6 Apply operationally defined criteria of behavioral change measured against predrug performance levels (e.g., paired-associate learning task)	**6** Apply clinical, less operational criteria of behavioral change (e.g., decrease in psychic pain, increase in marital harmony)
7 Employ nonclinical, "naïve," randomly selected subjects	**7** Use selected clinical samples of subjects or sophisticated volunteers
8 Obtain results which indicate various kinds and degree of performance impairment	**8** Obtain results which indicate various kinds and degree of performance enhancement

plex transactions between the subject's past history and personality, the expectancies of both subject and administrator, and the physical and psychological setting in which the experience takes place. Importantly, most of these determinants can be intentionally arranged or manipulated so as to foster either a propitious or a stressful experience. In the search for invariant, or drug-specific, reactions, much of the reported research to date has failed to assess, control, or systematically vary the relevant nondrug variables.

The bulk of published reports in professional journals have been of two kinds: (1) laboratory studies of the physiological and behavioral effects during the period immediately following ingestion of the drug (three to eight hours) and (2) clinical studies of the therapeutic efficacy of LSD either as an adjunct to orthodox therapies or as a primary means for producing rapid personality change. A number of distinctive features have characterized these two major lines of investigation. These are summarized in the table above.

It should be emphasized that these two research paradigms are mutually exclusive, yield opposite findings, and neatly accommodate well over five hundred studies. Clearly, some basic conceptual and

methodological fallacies underlie both strategies. From a historical perspective, the legacy of Newtonian science and physicalistic notions of illness and treatment characterize this work. The major conceptual fallacy, usually implicit, is the assumption that only drug-specific effects are real, valid, and lawful. Nonspecific variables that are difficult to define and measure rigorously are deemed random, insignificant, and sources of error. Methodologically, this assumption results in the use of artificial and often meaningless control groups, arbitrary distinctions between real and placebo reactivity, and inappropriate applications of the double-blind procedure.

Although laboratory and clinical studies are dissimilar in almost all respects, both approaches consider the drug's pharmacological properties the major determinants of physiological, behavioral, and/or subjective changes. Stated differently, the drug per se is assumed to be the most important independent variable under study. The effects of nondrug variables have generally been ignored, minimized, or estimated *post hoc*. The few studies employing a control group have either randomized or attempted to equalize nondrug variables. Laboratory studies attempt to eliminate the effects of such variables in both groups (double-blind design), while clinical studies match groups at minimal or "optimal" levels of various nondrug variables. Controlled or uncontrolled, laboratory or clinical, LSD studies have almost invariably interpreted psychosocial variables as "confounding" or "biasing" the results.

The sole purpose of the control group has been to assess the effects of the one "valid" class of independent variables (drug factors) and control the effects of "extraneous" variables (collectively termed the "placebo effect"). It is most ironic that in clinical terms, these extraneous classes of variables are precisely those considered the major determinants of response to psychotherapy, namely, patient variables, therapist variables, situational variables, and therapist-patient interaction variables. With reference to psychotherapy, the nonspecific-extraneous-placebo fallacy has been well stated by Shapiro (1964, p. 56): "The placebo is defined as the psychological elements in treatment; psychological elements constitute psychotherapy; therefore, psychotherapy is a placebo."

The "No-treatment" Control Group

The limited value of the double-blind design for evaluating psychotropic drugs has become increasingly apparent in recent years (Tuteur, 1958). For similar reasons, the usefulness of inert and active placebos has also been seriously questioned (Ditman, 1963). Central to the documented short-comings of these control devices is the major conceptual fallacy stated above, namely, the untenable assumptions concerning specific and nonspecific variables. Recent findings indicate that it is impossible to isolate a "pure" drug effect (Lyerly, Ross, Krugman, & Clyde, 1964), that no substance is entirely "inactive" (Shapiro, 1964), and that double-blind studies are seldom truly double-blind (Barsa, 1963). In addition to its methodological flaws, Rickels (1963) concludes that the double-

blind design is clinically impractical, medically unsound, and too rigid for psychiatric research. He further notes, "While uncontrolled studies are easily influenced by the optimistic and enthusiastic bias of the investigator, it should be realized that controlled clinical trials may be just as easily influenced by the negative, pessimistic attitude of the investigator" (p. 544).

These observations parallel recent developments in psychotherapy research. For example, Strupp (1960) considers the therapist's personality almost inextricably interwoven with his technique and questions the possibility of separating them experimentally. Similarly, Goldstein's (1962) careful critique of control studies disclosed a basic fallacy in the "therapy" versus "no-therapy" design, since "nonspecific therapy" was always operative in the control group.

It is apparent that attempts to assess the effects of a drug or a method of psychotherapy in a psychosocial vacuum are futile. In the same sense that the causes and treatment of emotional disorders are nonspecific, the potential therapeutic effects of LSD are also nonspecific. Like all psychotherapies and most medical treatments, there is nothing intrinsically therapeutic about LSD that cannot be negated (or enhanced) by so-called nonspecific variables.

Real versus Placebo Effects

Current re-evaluations of the placebo concept have been strongly influenced by the advent of psychotropic drug therapies. Another equally important factor has been the acceptance of psychotherapy as a legitimate form of treatment. As evidenced by the work of Frank (1961), Goldstein (1962), and Shapiro (1964), the main features of the placebo effect are essential ingredients of effective psychotherapy (e.g., positive therapist-patient expectancies). Consistent with these developments, revisions of the placebo concept have taken two directions. One would redefine the specific-nonspecific distinction. According to this view, the "nonspecific" rubric should be restricted to unidentified variables which affect the dependent variable, but are not clearly delineated as yet, and which therefore cannot be measured, controlled, or manipulated.

The other trend in current thinking

would retain the traditional specific-nonspecific distinction, but readily accepts placebo effects as "real" and "valid." Many writers have observed that the benefits of placebos are and always have been very real. "It is not such benefits which are new to medicine, only recognition that such benefits actually exist" (Goldstein, 1962, p. 207). However, there is far from complete acceptance of placebos as *legitimate* aspects of medical and psychological treatment. Contrary views presently in vogue are amply documented by Shapiro (1964) and strongly evident in psychedelic research. The problem is further complicated by the tendency to define the placebo so that one's own therapy is excluded. For example, psychotherapists and psychoanalysts often consider drug and convulsive treatment to be placebo treatments but frequently deny the possibility that psychological treatment might be in the same category. Surgeons might include the aforementioned treatments in the definition but exclude surgery (Shapiro, 1964.).

Similar biases in defining placebo effects differentiate laboratory and clinical studies of LSD. The striking polarities in psychedelic research reflect and underscore the real versus placebo dilemma. The major issues involved are especially well focused in this work because the therapeutic use of LSD bridges the gap between medical treatment and psychotherapy. Consistent with the holistic approach to illness and treatment, psychedelic therapy highlights the arbitrary but well-entrenched distinctions between specific and nonspecific factors, true and error variance, and drug therapy and psychotherapy.

One-dimensional Therapy Developments in research design and methodology have failed to keep pace with the holistic nature of most treatments. Rather than designing a paradigm to fit the treatment, the treatment is often bent to fit an outmoded paradigm. "Goodness of fit" between experimental design and psychedelic therapy has been particularly poor, in part because of its ambiguous status as a psychopharmacological treatment. Unfortunately, the variable-in-a-vacuum ideal of drug research has taken precedence over the multidimensional design preferred in psychotherapy research.

Exclusive manipulation of the single "valid" independent variable distorts and oversimplifies the therapeutic process. It also restricts hypothesis testing to variations of the rhetorical outcome question, "Does it work?" A further weakness is the unacknowledged cluster of experimental biases which usually accompany this strategy. As detailed earlier, these biases result in an artificial straining at a neutral or even a negative attitude. The presumed objectivity achieved is more apparent than real since the direction of bias is merely reversed, not eliminated. The obtrusive demands of the double-blind study disrupt meaningful regularities (e.g., in therapist-patient expectancies), creating instead a synthetic Hawthorne effect. Rosenthal (1963) and his coworkers have amply demonstrated the ubiquitous influence of experimenter bias even in animal studies. Regarding therapy research, it seems apparent that the null hypothesis is often desirable as a design characteristic, improbable as an experimenter attitude, and merely absurd as a therapist expectation.

The Independent-variable Complex Rather than disrupting the treatment process in order to isolate one special status variable, a more fruitful approach to psychedelic therapy would be to acknowledge at the onset that the *known* factors affecting patient change are multidimensional and intimately related and have comparable status ("specific," "real," "valid"). Research in psychedelic therapy requires a conceptual model that permits systematic study of different types of patients exposed to different kinds and levels of the relevant drug *and* nondrug conditions. At the methodological level, experimental design and/or statistical procedures must allow for covariance and interaction as well as manipulation and control. In other words, the use of factorial designs is strongly indicated. Only factorial designs meet the necessary requirements for relating outcome to the complex patterning of independent variables. Unlike the single-variable model, hypothesis testing becomes more comprehensive and meaningful. Instead of "Does it work?" the factorial design makes it possible to ask, "When it works, why does it?" and "When it does not, why not?" In these terms, the many faces of "it" (drug-nondrug variable patterning) will eventually serve as a basis for prognosis and/or optimizing the treatment process.

The Placebo Effect Revisited The cardinal features of the drug-induced state suggest that patient expectancies constitute a major determinant of response to LSD. More generally, Krasner (1962) considers the placebo effect (the emotional state of trust, "faith," positive expectancy) the common element in *all* influencing processes, including psychotherapy. Krasner's analysis represents an extension of the trends described earlier toward "legitimizing" the placebo effect and specifying its parameters. Consistent with this view, placebo reactivity does not indicate feigned illness and correlates positively with both favorable prognosis and favorable outcome (Goldstein, 1962). Of particular relevance to psychedelic therapy is the failure to identify consistent placebo responders; i.e., the placebo effect tends to be situation- or treatment-specific. Shapiro (1964, p. 55) notes that ". . . a drug may be a good placebo stimulus for some patients; psychotherapy may be a good placebo stimulus for other patients."

The growing body of evidence indicating that the placebo effect is instrumental in effecting patient change tends to confirm Frank's (1962, p. 9) observation: "There is no independent, objective criterion for the truth of any interpretation in psychotherapy. . . . The therapeutic effect of an interpretation depends not on its truth but on whether both therapist and patient believe it to be true."

In psychedelic therapy, the greatly heightened susceptibility of the patient to both internal and external sources of influence underscores the importance of therapist-patient compatibility. Although the relevant dimensions of therapist-patient congruence have yet to be specified in psyche-

delic research, it seems safe to assume that some consensus is necessary "between the kind of help the patient is seeking and the kind of help the therapist is able to provide" (Wallach & Strupp, 1960, p. 321). This implies an explicitly or implicitly shared belief that the treatment will be effective.

Although major changes in the patient's value-belief system are a common result in psychedelic therapy (Unger, 1964), the extent to which this represents a "convergence" between patient and therapist is presently unknown. The degree of such convergence may be primarily a function of the patient's relative susceptibility to internal (latent beliefs) and external (therapist beliefs) sources of influence. Since it has become apparent that one man's treatment (healer or patient) is another man's placebo (healer or patient), all forms of therapy should seek to maximize congruence between patient complaint and healer treatment.

PSYCHEDELIC AND RELATED STATES

Probably the most significant and exciting research of the past decade has occurred in the areas of dream activity, sensory deprivation, creativity, hypnosis, and the psychedelic drugs. Viewing this work as occurring within a broader cultural context, one convergent finding seems of major significance, namely, that richness of imagination and so-called regressive experiences are not the exclusive privilege of madmen and artists. Instead, recent evidence indicates quite conclusively that under favorable circumstances most people can greatly expand their experiential horizons without sacrificing effectiveness in dealing with conventional reality.

The significant parallels among relatively independent lines of investigation are most striking (Mogar, 1965a). Each of these phenomena (psychedelic, dreams, creativity, sensory isolation, and hypnosis) has traditionally been associated with the negative, bizarre, and abnormal. Until relatively recently, dreams and hypnosis have generally been linked with magic and the occult. Similarly, "hallucinogenic" drug states, sensory confinement, and inordinate creativeness have strong historical associations with defective character and insanity. As a result, these classes of experiences have typically been treated as isolated phenomena, discontinuous with other psychological processes and inexplicable in terms of known principles.

A second significant parallel concerns the remarkable subjective and behavioral similarities of these experiences. Consistent findings in research on hypnotic, psychedelic, and dream states; certain phases of the creative process; as well as sensory and dream deprivation indicate an almost complete overlap of major effects. Reported commonalities include significant alterations in perception, dominance of sensation and imagery over verbal-associative thinking, relaxed ego boundaries, changes in bodily feelings, and the suspension of conventional reality orientation to space, time, and self.

Theoretical accounts of these psychological changes have also run parallel. Whether self-induced or situationally induced by means of fatigue, drugs, or some form of stress, such states have typically been viewed as regressive, infantile, or primitive and as indicating sudden loss of ego control and the eruption of unconscious forces. Until recently, the effects have been interpreted as disturbing, quasi-psychotic, or depersonalizing. Consistent with these interpretations, persons prone to altered states of awareness have generally been described as poorly adjusted, suggestible, irrational, passive, and low in ego strength (Mogar, 1956a).

Perhaps the most important parallel concerns the current direction of research in these areas. Recent studies reveal a discernible shift away from investigating the condition or phenomenon per se, focusing instead on the situation- or subject-determined variables. This significant turning point calls attention to the key importance of the psychosocial context in which these experiences are inextricably embedded. Related to this new research strategy, recent findings and shifts in theorizing about altered states of consciousness have taken a more positive turn.

As a case in point, the aftereffects of dream deprivation, both positive and negative, vary widely across subjects. Dement

(1960) found that ". . . the kinds of alterations represent extensions or revelations of tendencies native to the individual personality" and that their form, degree, and dynamic meaning are influenced by the setting and by interpersonal transactions. Similarly, recent findings indicate that the nature and intensity of hypnotic experiences are strongly influenced by the sociopsychological milieu, particularly the mutual expectancies of subject and experimenter (Sarbin & Lim, 1963).

The same trends are found in sensory-deprivation research. There is considerable evidence indicating that greatly reduced sensory input can impair or facilitate mental functioning, depending on the particular interaction of set, setting, and personality. Leiderman (1964, p. 229) found that ". . . with the element of fear removed, the imagery of sensory deprivation becomes like the imagery of daydreams, quite familiar and usually not anxiety-producing." The direction of thinking in this area is perhaps best summed up by Suedfied (1964, p. 4). Noting that some experimentally isolated subjects reveal striking creativity in solving problems, he poses the question, "What would happen if creative behavior were externally reinforced by the experimenter?"

A number of studies have demonstrated that personality differences are as important as set and setting in determining response to LSD. Mogar and Savage (1964) found that post-LSD changes were related to personality styles and modal defense patterns. The results indicated that subjects with a well-defined but flexible self-structure responded most favorably to the drug, while those with either underdeveloped or overly rigid ego defenses responded less favorably. Similar differential findings have been obtained recently in work with sensory deprivation and hypnosis (Mogar, 1965a). Particularly relevant to the psychedelics is the finding that positive visual imagery during isolation correlates highly with (1) intellectual flexibility, breadth, and richness; (2) freedom from emotional disturbance and constriction; and (3) acceptance of one's passive, feminine side (Holt & Goldberger, 1961).

A host of studies have found that hypnotic susceptibility is negatively correlated with neuroticism and placebo responsiveness and positively correlated with emotional stability. Although generally unrelated to personality, independent work by Shor (1962) and Aas (1963) indicates a consistently high relationship between hypnotizability and the frequency of naturally occurring altered states, particularly ecstatic and peak experiences. The range of personal-history experiences inventoried in these studies was characterized by constructive use of regression, tolerance for logical paradoxes, willingness to relinquish ego control, and ability to suspend disbelief or to adopt an "as if" attitude. It is worth noting that these correlates of hypnotic susceptibility are also associated with propitious psychedelic states, certain phases of creativity, and self-actualization.

Current findings and theorizing in the various areas considered here can be summarized briefly. Whether self-induced, stress-induced, or drug-induced, altered states of consciousness will be welcomed and valuable rather than feared and harmful to the degree that the sociopsychological demands of such experiences are congenial to the "kinetic" needs and values of a given individual. This view is consistent with recent developments in personality theory, particularly the current emphasis on latent creative potential and self-actualizing tendencies. Stated simply, theoretical innovations recognize that greater access to unconscious resources is a cardinal feature of psychedelic, creative, and other novel perceptual experiences, as well as of psychosis. In contrast to hallucinatory states, it is being recognized that creative or revelatory experiences involve a *temporary* and *voluntary* breaking up of perceptual constancies, permitting one "to shake free from dead literalism, to re-combine the old familiar elements into new, imaginative, amusing or beautiful patterns" (Holt & Havel, 1960, p. 304).

THE PSYCHEDELIC ETHIC

The major application of LSD today is to *treat* mental illness rather than to *produce* it. Although results are presently inconclusive, psychedelic therapy is apparently effective with a wide range of emotional disorders. Impressive improvement rates have been consistently reported in both individual and group therapy and by investigators throughout the world. Particularly noteworthy are the positive results obtained with cases highly resistant to the usual forms of therapy. Chronic conditions that have responded favorably to LSD include alcoholism, sexual deviations, criminal psychopathy, childhood schizophrenia, drug addiction, and adolescent behavior disorders (Mogar, 1966).

Psychedelic therapy has been characterized by two major viewpoints and methods of administration: One emphasizes the use of LSD periodically and in small doses as an adjunct to orthodox psychotherapy (Freudian orientation). The other major approach employs LSD in a single, high dose, producing an intense and prolonged state of expanded consciousness (psychedelic orientation). Applied in this manner, LSD serves as a catalyst for inducing rapid and profound changes in the subject's value-belief system and in his self-image. While recognizing the therapeutic effects of LSD, this latter technique places greater emphasis on its more unique potentialities, namely, as a means of facilitating creative insight and self-realization. Rather than freedom from emotional symptoms, the primary objective of the psychedelic experience becomes a major reevaluation of one's beliefs and life outlook. In short, the first method is essentially illness-oriented (Freudian); the second, health- or growth-oriented (psychedelic).

When employed as an adjunct to Freudian therapy, the beneficial effects of LSD are usually associated with reduced defensiveness, reliving of childhood memories, and increased awareness of unconsciousness motives. In contrast, when used as a primary means for producing an intense and profound self-confrontation, emphasis is usually placed on the transcendental quality of the experience, the resynthesis of basic values and beliefs, and major changes in the way one perceives himself and his world. Thus, Freudian and psychedelic therapists interpret LSD experiences quite differently, but consistently with their techniques and purposes.

Broader Extensions of the Psychedelic Ethic

These two points of view have counterparts in every area of contemporary psychology and psychiatry. The traditional view adheres to the Freudian ethic: the beliefs that present behavior can be understood and future conduct predicted from a knowledge of the past (scientific determinism), that health and happiness are synonymous with the absence of neurosis, and that altered states of consciousness and intense emotional reactions are signs of mental disturbance. The Freudian ethic is currently being challenged by what I shall call the *psychedelic ethic*: the beliefs that scientific determinism is inadequate as a personal philosophy or world view, that man has the capacity to transcend his past at every moment, that psychological health requires more than the absence of illness, and that a meaningful personal identity must be continually created through self-exploration and passionate commitments.

Current trends in psychotherapy clearly reflect the basic premises of the psychedelic ethic. Foremost among these are the humanistic viewpoint in psychology and the increasing influence of existentialism in psychology and psychiatry. Both views recognize that the nature of human discontent in a technological (and affluent) society is undergoing rapid and profound change. The search for identity and meaning, the decline of traditional values and religion, and the advent of science as a way of life have become dominant themes of modern existence. One result has been a decline in the conventional forms of neurosis.

While certainly unhappy and unfulfilled, the person seeking private, outpatient therapy today is generally *not* unproductive or crippled with neurotic symptoms. Many writers have described the typical patient as one who is relatively free of physical complaints, emotional conflicts, and failures of achievement. Instead, the central struggle for an increasing number of successful, well-adjusted people seems to be "a loss of meaning in life, an absence of

purpose or a failure of faith" (Schofield, 1964). Modern discontent tends to take the form of alienation—in William Barrett's terms, alienation from God, from nature, from the human community, and ultimately from self. While recognizing that the person with problems in personal identity and life outlook needs help, some writers consider the psychotherapist ill equipped for such a *priestly* task. Yet it has been said that if science is the new religion, then psychotherapy is its place of worship.

In view of the apparent incompatibility between modern discontent and traditional psychotherapy, it is certainly less than a coincidence that the majority of people attracted to LSD fit the above description. Their lives lack what the psychedelic ethic promises, namely, passion and meaning in an impersonal, objective world. It would be indeed ironic if the agent of scientific man's salvation should appear in the form of a synthetic drug—a secular version of the cosmic joke. Substances with LSD properties have been known and ingested throughout man's history and in all parts of the world. Typically they have been taken as medicines or at religious ceremonies. Indeed, recognizing that ills may afflict the spirit as well as the body, some cultures used them for both curative and religious purposes. Could it be that in his quest for significance, man has come full circle?

These observations are consistent with recent findings in LSD studies. Savage and his coworkers (1966) gave almost four hundred volunteer subjects a high-dose LSD experience. One-third of this group expressed problems of an existential nature and revealed minimal emotional disturbance according to test data and psychiatric diagnosis. As a result of their stable life situations and freedom from neurotic symptoms, these subjects were more likely to grapple with ultimate problems during the LSD experience. Surrounding the central issue of self-identity, questions of love, death, creation, and rebirth and of the resolution of life paradoxes received frequent attention. Tests taken two and six months after the experience indicated that most subjects were aware of more meaning and purpose in life, greater aesthetic sensitivity, and a sense of oneness with nature and humanity. Decreases were found in values pertaining to material possessions, social status, and dogmatism.

Peak and Nadir Experiences Since most of these subjects were psychologically sophisticated, it is noteworthy that the frequency of experiences of a transcendental nature is apparently as great in "naïve" prisoners and alcoholics (Unger, 1964). Such commonalities are not surprising in view of the key role played by universal and personal symbolism in psychedelic experiences and the relatively weak role of the conscious self (including verbal facility, accumulated knowledge, and intelligence). What seems to be affected by subject differences is the *content* of the experience, rather than its *form* or *intensity*.

Differences in thematic content were found among subjects with diverse cultural backgrounds. For example, wide individual differences were demonstrated with respect to content in the frequent experience of unity. However, the fact that the majority of subjects experienced a sense of unity or oneness seems far more significant than whether the unity was felt with self, nature, the universe, God, or some combination of these. This is merely another way of saying that to the degree an individual can verbalize the experience, he will draw on his own particular semantic framework and belief system.

These findings suggest that the profundity or intensity of a psychedelic experience is more crucially related to subsequent change than thematic content. More specifically, the hypothesis currently being tested is that subsequent transformations in values, personality, and conduct are a function of the experience's intensity—positive, negative, or both. In other words, painful experiences can be as personally revealing and permanently beneficial as experiences of great joy and beauty.

The hypothesis that a profound psyche-delic experience, regardless of emotional valence, can serve as a catalyst for rapid personal growth is consistent with current interpretations of both nadir and peak experiences. Concerning nadir experiences, Erikson's analysis of the postadolescent identity crisis has recently been extended to include periodic "crisis of maturation" (Kahn, 1963), naturally occurring "desolation experiences" (Laski, 1961), and the therapeutic value of "existential crises" (Bugental, 1965). These writers emphasize that, although painful, a personal crisis is (1) not pathological, (2) a critical choice point in life necessitating a "leap of faith," (3) an essential condition of growth and psychological change, and (4) often a catalyst for an emerging inner conviction or new awareness. The potential value of nadir experiences has been well stated by Forer (1963, p. 280): "Crisis as a psychological experience is a part of any creative effort, scientific, artistic, therapeutic or inter-personal."

Concerning positive revelatory experiences, Maslow (1964) views religious, mystical, or transcendental states as special cases of the more generic "core-religious" or peak experience described as the hallmark of highly self-actualized people. Similarly, the extensive research on creativity by MacKinnon (1964) and his coworkers indicates that the truly creative person is distinguished by his capacity for "transliminal" experiences. The transliminal experience is characterized by an illuminating flash of insight occurring at a critical threshold of the conscious-unconscious continuum. As MacKinnon describes it, the transliminal state bears a striking resemblance to the more inclusive peak experience. Maslow (1964) suggests that psychedelic drugs may offer a means of producing a controlled peak experience under observation, particularly in "nonpeakers."

CONCLUSION

The rival prophecies of the Freudian ethic and the psychedelic ethic are readily detectable in the mass of commentary on LSD. Does the drug experience mimic insanity or produce "instant Zen"? Is it infantile or illuminating, ego-destroying or "an existential encounter of decisive proportions"? The ambivalence expressed in these representative views is merely another symptom of the major tensions of our time. Reactions to LSD, positive and negative, reflect the traditional schism in Western culture between science and humanism, reason and imagination, the abstract and the poetic. By means of psychedelic and other high-impact experiences, many people hope to resolve these artificial polarities at least within themselves. Such is the promise, if not the fulfillment, of consciousness-expanding drugs.[1]

REFERENCES

AAS, A. Hypnotizability as a function of nonhypnotic experiences. *Journal of Abnormal and Social Psychology*, 1963, **66**, 142–150.

BARSA, J. A. The fallacy of the "double-blind." *American Journal of Psychiatry*, 1963, **119**, 174–175.

BUGENTAL, J. F. T. The existential crisis in intensive psychotherapy. *Psychotherapy*, 1965, **2**, 16–20.

DEMENT, W. The effects of dream deprivation. *Science*, 1960, **131**, 1705–1707.

DITMAN, K. S. Psychotomimetics: Pharmacodynamic and psychotherapeutic properties. *Proceedings of Western Pharmacological Society*, 1963 **6**, 13–27.

FORER, B. R. The therapeutic value of crisis. *Psychological Reports*, 1963, **13**, 275–281.

FRANK, J. D. *Persuasion and healing.* Baltimore: Johns Hopkins Press, 1961.

FRANK, J. D. Introduction. In H. H. Strupp & L. Luborsky (Eds.), *Research in psychotherapy.* Vol. 2. Washington, D.C.: American Psychological Association, 1962.

GOLDSTEIN, A. P. *Therapist-patient expectancies in psychotherapy.* New York: Macmillan, 1962.

HOLT, R. R., & GOLDBERGER, L. A. Assessment of individual resistance to sensory alteration. In B. E. Flaherty (Ed.), *Psychophysiological aspects of space flight.* New York: Columbia Univer. Press, 1961.

HOLT, R. R., & HAVEL, J. A method of assessing primary and secondary process in the Rorschach. In Marie Rickers-Orsiankina (Ed.), *Rorschach psychology.* New York: Wiley, 1960.

KAHN, E. On crises. *Psychiatric Quarterly*, 1963, **37**, 1–9.

KRASNER, L. The therapist as a social reinforcement machine. In H. H. Strupp & L. Luborsky (Eds.), *Research in psychotherapy.* Vol. 2. Washington, D.C.: American Psychological Association, 1962. Pp. 61–94.

LASKI, M. *Ecstasy.* London: Crescent Press, 1961.

LEIDERMAN, P. Imagery and sensory deprivation. *Proceedings of the Third World Congress in Psychiatry*, 1964, 227–231.

LYERLY, S. B., ROSS, S., KRUGMAN, A. D., & CLYDE, D. Drugs and placebos. *Journal of Abnormal and Social Psychology*, 1964, **68**, 321–327.

MACKINNON, D. W. Creativity and transliminal experience. Paper read at American Psychological Association, Los Angeles, September, 1964.

MASLOW, A. H. *Religions, values, and peak experiences.* Columbus, Ohio: Ohio State Univer. Press, 1964.

MOGAR, R. E. Current status and future trends in psychedelic research. *Journal of Humanistic Psychology*, 1965, **5**, 147–166. (a)

MOGAR, R. E. Search and research with the psychedelics. *ETC: Review of General Semantics*, 1965, **22**, 393–407. (b)

MOGAR, R. E. Psychedelic drugs and human potentialities. In H. A. Otto (Ed.), *Explorations in human potentialities.* Springfield, Ill.: Charles C Thomas, 1966.

MOGAR, R. E., & SAVAGE, C. Personality change associated with psychedelic (LSD) therapy. *Psychotherapy*, 1964, **1**, 154–163.

RICKELS, K. Psychopharmacological agents: A clinical psychiatrist's individualistic point of view. *Journal of Nervous and Mental Disorders*, 1963, **136**, 540–549.

ROSENTHAL, R. On the social psychology of the psychological experiment. *American Scientist*, 1963, **51**, 268–283.

SARBIN, S., & LIM, D. T. Some evidence in

---

[1] Harman, in Chapter 33, develops some of the further implications which reside in the results of the psychedelic investigations. [Editor]

support of the role-taking hypothesis in hypnosis. *International Journal of Clinical and Experimental Hypnosis*, 1963, **9**, 98–103.

SAVAGE, C., FADIMAN, J., MOGAR, R. E., & ALLEN, M. The effects of psychedelic therapy on values, personality, and behavior. *International Journal of Neuropsychiatry*, 1966, **2**, 241–254.

SCHOFIELD, W. *Psychotherapy: The purchase of friendship*. Englewood Cliffs, N.J.: Prentice-Hall, 1964.

SHAPIRO, A. K. A historic and heuristic definition of the placebo. *Psychiatry*, 1964, **27**, 52–58.

SHOR, R. E. Validation and cross-validation of a scale of self-reported personal experiences which predict hypnotizability. *Journal of Psychology*, 1962, **53**, 55–75.

STRUPP, H. H. Nature of psychotherapist's contribution to treatment process. *Archives of General Psychiatry*, 1960, **3**, 219–231.

SUEDFELD, P. Toward greater specificity in evaluating cognitive and attitudinal changes in sensory deprivation. Paper read at American Psychological Association, Los Angeles, September, 1964.

TUTEUR, W. The double-blind method: Its pitfalls and fallacies. *American Journal of Psychiatry*, 1958, **114**, 921–922.

UNGER, S. M. Mescaline, LSD, psilocybin, and personality change. In D. Solomon (Ed.), *LSD: The consciousness-expanding drug*. New York: Putnam, 1964.

WALLACH, M. S., & STRUPP, H. H. Psychotherapists' clinical judgments and attitudes toward patient. *Journal of Consulting Psychology*, 1960, **24**, 316–323.

Part FOUR

SOME RESEARCH PRODUCTS

Because the name "humanistic psychology" has only recently begun to have currency, there is a tendency to think of work in this field as of similarly recent origin. Of course, this is quite inaccurate. Psychologists and others have been conducting research and writing in this perspective throughout man's history, and each of the authors in this volume certainly was at work well before the name was adopted.[1] In Part Four, we shall sample some typical and varied products of humanistic research. In choosing these, I have tried to illustrate something of the range of the field and to complement the other chapters by dealing with methods or topics not sufficiently represented there.

[1] The term "humanistic psychology" may well have a longer history, but its current usage seems to stem chiefly from two papers which appeared in *Etc.*, both of which bore the title "Toward a Humanistic Psychology." Hadley Cantril wrote the first of these in the Summer, 1955, issue (pp. 278–298), and Abraham H. Maslow wrote the second in the Autumn, 1956, issue (pp. 10–22). "Humanistic psychology" was one of several names (others were "orthopsychology" and "self-psychology") considered for a new journal which Anthony Sutich undertook to edit and publish with the encouragement of Maslow and others. The first issue of the *Journal of Humanistic Psychology* appeared in the spring of 1961. Shortly thereafter, the American Association for Humanistic Psychology was initiated, again with the initiative of Sutich and Maslow.

As Royce demonstrated in Chapter 3, there is a rich area for
inquiry at the intersection of theology and psychology
and within the realm of philosophical psychology. In all ages some
of man's most penetrating analyses of his own nature
have been interwoven with his speculations on the nature of the
universe of which he finds himself a part. Whether the
theorizer was theistic or atheistic or simply unconcerned with the
issue of a divinity, it has been impossible validly to
separate questions of meaning from questions of human experience.
Teilhard de Chardin is coming to be recognized as one of
the great philosophical thinkers of our time, and his concept of
evolution may be seen as one of the seminal perspectives
on man in the world. Father Frank Severin has devotedly studied
Teilhard's thought, and in Chapter 16 presents a concise
and highly readable précis of those aspects most immediately
relevant to humanistic psychology. He well presents
Teilhard's concept of the noosphere, which is, I think, especially
evocative, for here the point which has been made several
times in these pages—that man's awareness introduces a totally new
dimension—is given an elegant and courageous expansion.

Jack and Lorraine Gibb have for many years studied how a group
forms, grows, and declines. They have, in the process,
come to an appreciation of this fundamental unit of human life,
which permits them to speak with authority when they
describe the basic dimensions of group life. Here, as so often, we
are at a border area between that which might be
deemed pure science and that which is applied in significance;
yet again we see how a psychology of human experience
draws from both sources and feeds back immediately pertinent
products to both. In Chapter 17, the Gibbs deal with trust
and fear and provide descriptions of group processes which clearly
interrelate with the consideration of basic encounter groups in
Part Five (see especially Chapter 28, by Rogers).

In Adah Maurer's inquiry into children's conceptions of God
(reported in Chapter 18), we have a study that is superficially like
many inventories of attitudes performed in child and
educational psychology. What distinguishes this report is Maurer's
clear participation with her subjects and her concern to go
beyond a mere tabulation of answers to the life meanings of those
answers. Certainly these features are not unique, but they
are very significantly characteristic of the humanistic orientation.

There is an understandable tendency to think of clinical, one-to-one
work as typically humanistic, and of large-scale investigations
as more behavioristic and impersonal. This presumption
is apt to be even stronger when the large-scale study makes central
use of a computer in its design. For these reasons it is
especially satisfying to see the work of Beatrice and Sydney Rome,
which they describe in Chapter 19. Going directly to the
heart of the same appreciation which Sidney Jourard described in
Chapter 12, they provide a dramatic confirmation of the
difference in outcome when the people with which one works are
treated as genuine subjects rather than objects. Their

results, arising from a context of "robots" and "programs," clearly illustrate the difference between the human potential when it is tapped in an atmosphere of trust and when it is neglected (in this case by design, but far too often by default).

Comments similar to those made above about Maurer's study may be made about Robert Lifton's monumental work on death imagery and the emotional dynamics of the response to death, which is summarized in Chapter 20. The scale of the investigation is, of course, immensely greater; yet here again one may sense a thoroughgoing scientific perspective seeking answers, even answers to questions painful to ask. Yet the embracing concern is not simply to report the findings but to take the further and challenging step to confront what those answers mean in our living experience. Men generally are reluctant to study death, but Americans especially are prone to push away their part in what Lifton rightly calls the "Hiroshima disaster." This shutting down of awareness is a dangerous process, as Lifton observes, which occurred in the disaster itself but which is not limited to such extreme circumstances. We would do well to heed the warning implicit in his comments.

Louis Levine is also deeply concerned about the kinds of issues which Lifton raises. He recognizes the fundamental role of experience in relation to behavioral change, and he asks in Chapter 21 whether men are subjectively ready for peace. In his discussion, he accepts the difficult task of trying to assess what our ways of thinking must be if we are to have hope for genuinely achieving and maintaining peace. What emerges is a challenge to man himself. This is humanistic psychology at its most characteristic: involved in vital human affairs and trying to bring to bear the insights of science and an informed and trained human mind.

Although we thus conclude this part, which is devoted particularly to illustrating research products, the final two parts carry this task on. In those occasions when men come together to try to improve their personal conditions, however those occasions are named, and in the literature, art, and other humanistic endeavors through which man expresses his deeper meanings and strivings, we have the active arena in which humanistic psychological science and application are very much engaged.

Presently: Professor of Psychology, Saint Louis University (since 1939).

Education: Master of Arts from Catholic University (1939). (Father Severin is a Jesuit and took his seminary training at Saint Louis University.)

Current major activity: Teaching psychology.

Most rewarding project: The preparation of supplementary humanistic materials for courses in psychology.

FRANK T. SEVERIN

Future of humanistic psychology: "I look to the development of adequate methods for dealing with humanistic problems on an empirical basis."

Personal history: At Saint Louis University, Father Severin served for a time as Assistant Dean of Arts and Sciences (1945–1950) and as Director of Counseling Services (1950–1955).

Writings: *Humanistic Viewpoints in Psychology* (1965), which Father Severin edited, was probably the first American book to use the term "humanistic psychology" in the title and to make a general position statement for this revitalized orientation. However, he had been preparing for this for some time by writing humanistically oriented supplements to a popular, mechanomorphic textbook in psychology. He published these in 1957 and 1961. In 1966 he brought out the most recent, this time using the distinguishing adjective in the title for the first time: *Humanistic Supplement to Clifford T. Morgan and Richard A. King, "Introduction to Psychology."*

Present chapter: This chapter was prepared especially for this book. In fact, it was prepared twice! When difficulties arose over copyright restrictions, Father Severin rewrote the entire chapter in record time and with remarkable lucidity.

Chapter 16
FRANK T. SEVERIN

THE HUMANISTIC PSYCHOLOGY
OF TEILHARD DE CHARDIN

The human mind thirsts for understanding. The more it learns about the universe, the more importunate become its demands to penetrate the mysteries that remain. If it is true that love creates love, it can be said with even greater confidence that knowledge breeds knowledge. One felicitous insight is all that is needed to weld together a whole host of isolated facts and scientific observations into a comprehensive explanation. The theories of gravitation, atomic radiation, wave mechanics, and relativity are but a few examples. A century ago Charles Darwin electrified the world with his vision of natural history that traced man's origin through the intervening animal species to a primordial organism. Almost at a glance the seemingly unrelated pieces of life's mosaic fell into place to reveal a design of unmatched elegance and consistency. But more important still, he had discovered a unifying thread in nature.

A BROADENED CONCEPTION OF EVOLUTION

In retrospect it seems only natural that someone, pondering the sweeping success of evolution in biology, would ask why the concept could not be pushed still further. Is it not possible that the laws pertaining to life are but a special case of more general laws governing the whole universe—laws which if known would remove the apparent discontinuities between pure energy, subatomic particles, molecules, living cells, animals, and man? Even consciousness, the products of thought, and human society could be included. Such is the breathtaking hypothesis Pierre Teilhard de Chardin proposed to himself in *The Phenomenon of Man* (1965).

THE UNITY OF NATURE

The universe around us, he observes, constitutes a gigantic atom which holds together in such a way as to be comprehensible only when taken as one piece. Breaking off fragments of matter for study in isolation from the rest will never uncover its true nature. The laws at work are on a scale so vast as to escape detection by anyone who looks at less than the total picture. From top to bottom, from within to without, there is a marvelous unity crying out to be discovered, and nowhere is it more apparent than in the origins of man.

At every level of evolving reality, certain processes occur in a definite sequence: first *divergence*, and then *convergence*, followed by the *emergence* of a more complex and autonomous form of development. This pattern is clearly illustrated in the case of animals. Invariably a new life form, shortly after its appearance, gave rise to a large cluster of separate species, most of which lost their creative drive by overadapting to special environmental conditions. Like the scholarly mind that becomes overcommitted to one idea or bogged down in methodology, they lacked the freedom of action required to discover unique solutions to their problems without sacrificing flexibility. The branch in each whorl that eventually succeeded in becoming the leading shoot of evolution was the one remaining relatively small and unspecialized. Instead of squandering its resources in developing a complex structure adapted to only one purpose, it concentrated its energy by folding inward on itself until a state of creative instability had been reached. Then a new and more highly organized form of life emerged with a degree of consciousness corresponding to its inner organization. Thus was born the law of recurrence or the law of complexity-consciousness, which Teilhard[1] extended to the whole universe in a most original manner.

Once in possession of the key to evolution he was able to advance another step. The way this key has consistently operated in past ages sets the pattern for further developments. To predict what man will be like, structurally as well as psychologically,

[1] When not using the full form of his family name (Teilhard de Chardin), he regularly referred to himself as Teilhard (rhymes with "they are"), never as Chardin or de Chardin.

in future millennia, it is necessary only to extend the curve of evolution a little further. Later in the chapter we shall return to this topic, after sketching the genetic history of matter in some detail.

THE *WITHIN* OF THINGS

Teilhard noted that physics, for all its power and precision, is self-limiting in its understanding of the universe because it neglects an entire dimension of matter (p. 163).[2] It looks only at the *without* of things, the external aspect whose behavior is completely determined by *tangential* energy. Although this is the only type of energy at present recognized by the physical sciences, a *radial* or *psychic* energy must be postulated to give evolution its forward thrust. The latter is reciprocally related to the second dimension of cosmic stuff, the *within*, which provides the basis for all forms of consciousness.

Some of Teilhard's readers may protest that the study of energy belongs to physics. If there is a radically new form of energy, why have physicists not discovered it? He replies that physics has, indeed, shown that different levels or spheres exist in nature and that certain factors dominating the activity of one level are scarcely perceptible at another. What biologist would be concerned about the infinitesimal increase in the mass of an animal running at full speed, although it is known that any change in velocity affects this property of matter? In atomic physics the situation is just the reverse. At extreme velocities this phenomenon crowds out most other considerations to become a determining factor. Theoretically the mass of even a subatomic particle becomes infinite as its velocity approaches the speed of light.

Similarly the influence of molecules is not confined to the minute circumference assigned to them by textbooks, but extends to the limits of space. From this point of view each atomic nucleus is an actual center of the universe, although nothing would be gained by using such a frame of reference. A single particle in the Milky Way exerts so feeble a gravitational force on the solar sys-

[2] All page numbers refer to *The Phenomenon of Man* (1965).

tem that no one would attempt to measure what it does to the earth's orbit. Scientists think differently about the valence of atoms entering into chemical combination. On this level of activity the effects of unit charges are magnified until they become visible.

The same is true of radial energy. Although inorganic substances give no hint of its activity, the existence of consciousness in the higher life forms cannot be ignored. Even the most objectively oriented scientist who may not wish to judge about the awareness of others has the evidence of his own immediate perception. Without consciousness there would be no sensation, no thought, no knowledge. It constitutes the focal point of every manifestation of the self and every emotion. Although subjectively experienced, consciousness is nonetheless an empirical fact that cannot be easily disavowed even by those psychologists who are inclined to do so.

Teilhard was not a party to this dispute, but he asks a relevant question: What would have happened had physicists closed their eyes to the unlawful behavior of radium because it seemed a queer exception to the well-established principle of atomic stability? They would never have learned what radioactivity was trying to tell them about the constituents of matter. The *within*, or consciousness, is clamoring just as loudly to be heard in testimony to the fundamental unity of nature. The fact that consciousness is most clearly visible only in man does not brand it as an aberrant function that need not be represented in a model of the universe. We have, instead, another example of a universal phenomenon hidden beneath the exceptional. If consciousness is present in the leading branch of the evolutionary tree of life, gradually diminishing expressions of it must be found in all the lower limbs, reaching a point where the roots contact inorganic matter. Atoms and molecules contain a potential consciousness which becomes actualized in proportion to the complexity of arrangements of the parts in a living being. In other words, beneath the mechanical layer of matter, which has been analyzed with such precision by physicists, lies a deeper biological and psychological layer so attenuated as to escape through the meshes of their methodology. Yet its presence must be postulated in order to explain what has happened in the course of evolution. Whether we refer to it in terms of the *within*, consciousness, or spontaneity, we are speaking of one and the same thing (pp. 56–57).

The Place of Consciousness in a Mechanistic Universe In spite of the fact that everything in the universe is either living or pre-living, a mechanistic science of matter is still possible for the reasons given above. The law of complexity-consciousness working silently in every sphere of reality guarantees that the quality of the *within* will correspond to the organization of its structural components. If a mammal has greater learning capacity than the amoeba, it is because complexification and consciousness are but two aspects of one and the same phenomenon. The simpler substances studied by most physical sciences possess only a minuscule of *within* whose embryonic influence is completely overwhelmed by the determining nature of the dominant tangential energy. For all practical purposes the behavior of elemental matter corresponds point by point to its *without* dimension. Only when complexification has reached a critical stage can spontaneity break through the surface to reveal itself.

In such a world picture a mechanistic universe combined with freedom involves no contradiction. Both components of matter are omnipresent, and nowhere more than in man is their interaction discernible. Mind is both dependent upon, and independent of, metabolic processes. Every conscious experience, whether it be a fleeting thought or an ardent wish, must be purchased by the expenditure of physical energy. Still we are faced with the dilemma that consciousness is not restricted by the calories that nourish it. Like the fixed notes of the musical scale, the same calories can sustain an infinite diversity of intellectual harmonies. " 'To think we must eat.' But what a variety of thoughts we get out of one slice of bread!" (p. 64).

Whatever welds together the internal and external dimensions of matter, it is a most unusual bond—one that allows mutual interdependence while still providing a measure of autonomy. One way to resolve the paradox is to assume that the corresponding radial and tangential energies are components of a single physical energy.[3] The first impulse is to look to physics for a model of how they operate, perhaps through some type of direct transformation. On second thought this solution appears to be seductively simple. Besides the autonomy mentioned above, there is a quantitative disproportion between input and output in their transactions. For these reasons alone, if for no other, the hypothesis is untenable. Whatever the solution, physical energy should be considered a complex phenomenon functioning on different levels. Such a formulation does not resolve all the difficulties, but it does meet the demands of both matter and consciousness, liberty and determinism without violating the fundamental unity of the universe.

A corollary to this theory views all physical science as a continuum rather than a series of disconnected disciplines. Psychology, the extension and further development of biology and ultimately of physics, occupies the highest level. Its framework is broad enough to accommodate with ease all the characteristic modes of human behavior. There is no need for the psychologist to disclaim mental activities as part of his subject matter or to reduce them to mechanical processes. Consciousness is as genuinely a part of science as matter is.

THE EVOLUTION OF REFLECTIVE CONSCIOUSNESS

In Teilhard's world vision it is man's conscious life that unlocks the mystery of all

that has happened in natural history (p. 281). Whether we trace backward its development from one species to another to rudimentary beginnings in matter or whether we proceed in the reverse order, the conclusion is the same: Evolution is not a random process. It has followed privileged lines which can be identified by the paleontologist (pp. 142, 220). The moment we focus attention on the progressive sharpening of awareness instead of thinking exclusively in terms of body structure, evolution ceases to appear as a hodgepodge of disconnected processes. At the core of matter is an irrepressible, irreversible tendency to find expression in ever-clearer forms of consciousness until it passes over the threshold of reflective thought. From this point onward a new type of elaboration occurs.

The actual fulfillment of this inherent tendency in the universe has not come easily. Under the relentless impetus of directed chance, nature groped for a solution.[4] After the first appearance of life each phylum proliferated in a multitude of forms, as if trying out every possibility. The less successful organisms either ceased to exist or entered blind alleys from which retreat became impossible. The diminutive size and ungainly exoskeleton of insects, for example, have forced the drive toward reflective consciousness into a rigid mold of instinctive behavior. In spite of such failures, one branch at each cluster on the tree of life outstripped its rivals by developing a greater degree of immanent spontaneity.

A noteworthy phenomenon in evolution consists in the appearance of thresholds from time to time, such as the granulation of energy into subatomic particles or the birth of vital activity. Another climax was reached when reflective consciousness became possible through progressive complexification of the brain. The whole nature of the organism was transformed, causing it to implode upon itself in a flurry of abstraction, invention, and reasoned choice far beyond the capabilities of other animals. The sudden appearance of some unique organi-

[3] Lest the reader imagine that Teilhard is presenting a nontheistic interpretation of the universe, a word of explanation seems appropriate. Here, as throughout the whole of *The Phenomenon of Man,* Teilhard repeatedly calls attention to his frame of reference as a scientist. He deals only with phenomena or appearances, neither affirming nor denying what theologians or philosophers may have to say about creation or the ultimate nature of man. Such questions lie beyond the scope of natural history and cannot be resolved by its methods.

[4] Although phrases such as these seem to raise the question of teleology, Teilhard was not postulating on an a priori basis the direction that evolution must necessarily take. He was merely reading the history of evolution as it is written in the fossil remains that have been discovered.

zation of the magnitude of life or reflective consciousness produces a discontinuity in evolution. Whatever follows can be understood only in terms of this new phenomenon, not in terms of what preceded it. Man, as a consequence, is qualitatively different from the life forms below him on the phylogenetic scale. Not only is he an individualized organism, but he is also a *person*.

The Meaning of Consciousness With the advent of reflection, evolution entered a new stage. Quite obviously the earlier pressures for animals to differentiate into endless varieties sharply declined in intensity. There is little need to search endlessly for a goal already attained. Even in man the physical phase of evolution is practically complete. His limbs may lengthen somewhat, his wisdom teeth and appendix disappear altogether, but there is little likelihood of essential structural changes or even of increase in learning capacity. What has happened is that once the *within* aspect of the cosmic stuff reached this "boiling point," it became the dominant factor in evolution (p. 277). The great leap forward into reflective consciouness was accomplished with only minor alterations in the anthropoid brain and skeleton. For the first time in natural history an explosive expansion of psychic life occurred which was disproportionate to the structural changes involved. In all other animal phyla the development of the brain can be used as a scale for measuring the degree of spontaneity, autonomy, and flexibility of behavior. This yardstick is no longer sufficient now that life has passed through its second threshold. "To unravel the structure of a thinking phylum, anatomy by itself is not enough: it must be backed up by psychology" (p. 176). Trying to understand man's mental processes in terms of other animals is as futile as making a list of chemicals below the threshold of life to explain the vital functions of a plant. While the plant may indeed contain these chemicals, it is the unique *new organization* that accounts for the striking difference between life and nonlife. Evolution from this point onward is almost entirely a function of reflective consciousness. Man, himself, has "grasped the tiller of evolution" (p. 250). Whether or not he steers a straight course toward his ultimate destiny will depend in no small measure upon how well he understands his own responsibilities in the matter.

Earlier it was noted that the same pattern of evolution occurs at every stage of development from the inorganic elements to man. Hence it can be seen that anthropogenesis (the evolutionary birth of mankind) is but a continuation of biogenesis, which is in turn an extension of cosmogenesis. Clearly then the laws of biology continue to apply to evolution even after it enters the psychological and social spheres. We are still dealing with natural history (p. 208).

THE NOOSPHERE

Undoubtedly one of Teilhard's unique contributions is the notion of a noosphere. To understand this construct it is necessary to remember that evolution does not take place uniformly throughout space, but only on the surface of planets. The earth is composed of an outer crust, or geosphere, enclosing a heated liquid core. On and near its surface various forms of life exist which collectively form the biosphere. Encompassing the whole as an outer membrane is the noosphere, or layer of thought. This recent addition to the earth's structure results from the unique way in which the law of complexity-consciousness applies to man. The variation does not constitute an exception. Rather it points up the preponderant role of thought in evolution at this rarefied level. Whereas all other newly emerging phyla immediately broke up into a number of distinct species, in Homo sapiens this did not occur. Mutual infiltration of neighboring cultures and intermarriage never ceased, regardless of the social and ethnic differences that developed in isolated groups of people. A powerful magnet was at work forcing the frayed strands of the phylum to converge: the ability to think and to communicate ideas and feelings. Pictured in this collective way, the mass of mutually shared thought and experience of mankind around the globe constitutes an invisible layer no less real than the air we breathe.

The Neolithic Age furnishes an excellent

example of the genesis and structure of the noosphere. Like our own it was a critical period, for it witnessed the birth of civilization. Within an incredibly short time, from a geological point of view, man forsook the nomadic life of a hunter to divide up the earth and strike root in permanent settlements. With few guidelines to follow, he set to work to fashion a complex web of rights, duties, and laws. It was a period of great inventiveness and feverish research. Virtually every approach to property rights, marriage arrangements, and moral behavior seems to have been tried. Not only did agriculture and stock breeding replace the chase, but almost every domestic animal, fruit, and grain we depend upon today was selected and empirically improved during this time. Skill in pottery and weaving was soon followed by metalworking and picture writing. As trade routes developed, ideas and traditions were exchanged as freely as the objects of commerce. Out of this shared knowledge were spun the first spidery elements of the noosphere. In time it would encircle the globe, as population pressures and an adventurous spirit induced men to venture farther and farther away from their original base of operation until they took possession of all the earth (pp. 203–206).

Economic changes in the modern world, combined with the intellectual and social awakening of the masses, have greatly accelerated the growth of the noosphere. Minds are mutually stimulated by close proximity to one another, and each advance in the noosphere serves as a stimulus for new ideas.

THE FURTHER EVOLUTION OF MAN

Joined together as men are in their thinking, there is no danger of being swallowed up as individuals into some monolithic collective mind of the future. Personality, far from being abbreviated by its participation in the noosphere, is actually accentuated. Who is more individualistic, the literate or the illiterate man? The person with six years of elementary education or the college graduate? The more profoundly one shares

in the accumulated wisdom of mankind, the greater is his capacity to emerge from the human collectivity as a unique personality.

Teilhard welcomed the growing trend toward automation. Instead of demeaning man, machines free his mind from the slavery of routine labor, so that he can devote himself to works of greater inventiveness. Unlike other species which are forced to develop parts of their bodies as tools, man builds an endless variety of industrial and mechanical contrivances. Scientific instruments, computers, and other aids to research amplify his effectiveness in wresting from nature its best-kept secrets. What is even more significant, any notable intellectual or technical advance anywhere in the world swiftly becomes the possession of all society through the magic of modern communications.

Looking more closely at the maturing noosphere, this time with an eye trained to recognize the law of convergence, we can detect a gradual closing in of the human phylum on itself, like the petals of a day-blooming water lily after sunset. Forces at work even now in the more highly developed countries should cause us to expect that, as people become better educated and enjoy more leisure, whole populations will become vitally interested in understanding the world in which they live. The hero, even for the man in the street, will be the person who has wrenched a new secret from nature rather than the athlete with good reflexes or the entertainer. Knowing will seem more personal and vastly more important than the feverish drive to acquire many possessions. A new awakening is taking place: a change in thought which, without changing our bodies, is making us new creatures (pp. 215, 280).

The Place of Love Humanity, while at work in this way building its composite brain, is also developing a heart. Little by little we are learning that nothing but love can gratify and fulfill what lies deepest within us. The paradox, "He who would save his life must lose it," sounds totally unrealistic; yet it is verified by everyone who falls deeply in love. At no time does he come into possession of himself so completely as when lost in the love of another. The same contradictory feat of achieving unity without detriment to individual personality is seen daily on a smaller scale in the enthusiastic cooperation of the members of a ball club who enjoy playing together or in the total concentration of a surgical team fighting desperately to save the life of a patient. Is it too much to expect that the embryonic power of loving possessed by man today will, in its maturity, embrace all people and the whole earth?

While full achievement of this utopian goal is no doubt millions of years distant, some small beginnings are even now visible in a world torn by the paroxysm of just discovering itself. The organization of the UN, the aid extended to underdeveloped countries, and interest in the opinions of the common man are but a few examples.

We are so accustomed to think of love in terms of the joy or sorrow it brings that we have lost sight of its evolutionary significance. Love is not exclusively human. Gradually diminishing forms of the same affinity that draws human beings together can be found lower on the tree of life. The gregariousness, mating, and parental instincts of mammals are clear expressions of subhuman love. Below the threshold of life, analogies of love are too obscure to be perceptible, but were it not for the propensities of molecular elements to unite, love would not appear at the higher levels. What we are dealing with here is a characteristic of the *within* aspect of matter: a property of the same radial energy that gives evolution its forward thrust.

The Emergence of a New Man We have already seen that evolution invariably follows a definite sequence: divergence and convergence, followed by the emergence of a new and more highly developed being. In terms of the law of recurrence, the noosphere represents psychic convergence in human evolution, thus pointing to a new emergence, another threshold, on the distant horizon. When man has passed through this threshold, he will be so changed psychologically as to deserve a new name. No longer will each individual feel that his own needs and interests conflict with those of the group, but like the colonies of one-celled animals that preceded the appearance on earth of more complex organisms, whatever affects one member will be seen to affect all the rest (pp. 250–251).

Thus a superorganism with a collective mind is in the process of formation. It will bring all mankind together in a focus: a center of centers, or *omega point*, which is also personal (p. 306). Such union will not absorb the individual as the sea absorbs a drop of water. Rather, he will become more visible than before because the union of parts in an organism emphasizes their distinctness. Teilhard believed that the evolutionary future of man gives the lie to radical individualistic and racial philosophies (p. 246). It is only in union with others that man finds self-fulfillment, not in isolation.

If biology is to comprehend such realities it must add a new dimension (p. 247). Other sciences have advanced by introducing additional categories whenever they came to a dead end in an outgrown intellectual framework. Geometry, beginning with the obvious notion of size, was eventually forced to accept the incommensurables "e" and "π" as being as fully understandable as whole numbers. Calculus would never have been able to meet the needs of modern science without constantly conceiving new functions. Physics, too, had no choice but to accept the strange model of wave mechanics in order to account for the unusual behavior of light. Before biology can generalize to the whole of life, some way must be found to incorporate those collective aspects which formerly could be ignored. The noosphere is a synthesis which in the last resort can be defined only as mind. If the evidence adduced for it seems modest, we should remember that from a single track in a cloud chamber, physicists infer the presence of invisible atomic particles having fantastic amounts of energy. Similarly, in order to be consistent in applying the principles of evolution to an emerging world conceived as coherent, we are led to acknowledge the reality of the noosphere and the omega point.

Anyone tempted to think that the human race is daily becoming more fragmented rather than more integral should remember that a million years were required to pass from the stage of ape-man to man. Considering the relatively short time that a unified world has appeared possible, we should not be surprised that man is "still at loggerheads with himself" (p. 255).

Modern Man and the Challenge of the New Man Teilhard believed that modern disquiet is due largely to man's sudden confrontation with an evolutionary space-time explanation of the universe. Modern man feels like a newborn infant opening his eyes to the world for the first time: Everything seems strange and terrifying. For centuries he had grown accustomed to the comfort of a narrow intellectual outlook that neatly arranged small segments of knowledge in isolated categories. Now he must rearrange his whole inner world, finding a new equilibrium for all its contents. A single mental index no longer suffices, for everything is related to everything else and must be appropriately cross-referenced. But more upsetting still is the growing awareness of his own responsibility for the continued progress of evolution. This is almost as distressing as being required to take the controls of an airliner in flight without the advantage of previous instruction; yet psychological and social evolution cannot attain their goals unless he freely chooses to cooperate. Is he willing to pay the price? Will he endure the anxiety and birth pangs of bringing a superhumanity into being?

What Teilhard feared most was the ennui of uncommitted persons and philosophies that picture the world as absurd. Mankind might decide that the task of pushing the world forward is too heavy and threatening to undertake; he might go on strike against the noosphere (pp. 306–307). Appealing to the average individual to make painful personal sacrifices so that the species may come to full florescence millions of years from now is not likely to be effective. People may begin to repeat seriously what Mark Twain said in jest: "What has posterity ever done for me?" From a practical point of view, he postulated the conditions necessary to motivate not just a few idealistic individuals but

the mass of humanity to work toward such distant goals.

The first condition is that we should be assured of a chance to fulfill ourselves in some manner to the limits of our potentialities, whether this be done directly or indirectly, as individuals or as members of a group. A second condition concerns continued conscious existence after death. Man can now glimpse what is in store for him in future millennia provided that he is willing to expend the effort and to make the personal sacrifices necessary to push evolution of the species to this pinnacle of perfection. The prospect of a total death that would blot out all hope of sharing in this supreme consummation of human nature would effectively destroy his motivation. Thus the mainspring of evolution would be broken.

CONCLUSION

As a species the human race is little more than a newborn infant. Judging from other life forms that have run their course in past ages, man can look forward to an adulthood of scores of million years before reaching the omega point. During that entire period, his intellectual, psychological, and social evolution will continue at an ever-quickening pace in an atmosphere of growing mutual esteem and affection. Imagine if you can, Teilhard asks, what man will be like psychologically even a million years from now. The possibilities that lie ahead are as unimaginable as outer space, toward which the farthest galaxies are speeding.

REFERENCES

FRANCOEUR, R. T. *The world of Teilhard.* Baltimore: Helicon, 1961.

RAVEN, C. E. *Teilhard de Chardin: Scientist and seer.* New York: Harper & Row, 1962.

TEILHARD DE CHARDIN, P. *The future of man.* New York: Harper & Row, 1965.

TEILHARD DE CHARDIN, P. *The phenomenon of man.* (2nd ed.). New York: Harper & Row, 1965.

TRESMONTANT, C. *Pierre Teilhard de Chardin: His thought.* Baltimore: Helicon, 1959.

Presently: Jack is Resident Fellow, and Lorraine is Research Associate, at the Western Behavioral Sciences Institute in La Jolla, California (since 1961).

Education: Jack took a Doctor of Philosophy degree at Stanford University (1943), while Lorraine received a Master of Arts from Syracuse University (1946).

JACK R. and LORRAINE M. GIBB

Current major activities: Both are at work on *The Emergent Group: A Study of Trust and Freedom,* a book which will summarize their fifteen-plus years of research and practice with groups.

Most rewarding project: Although Lorraine gives first priority to her family (including two sons), both agree that their work in further developing and refining their TORI method of personal development is the central professional concern of their lives right now. TORI stands for Trust-Openness-Realization-Interdependence, the variables they have shown to be most relevant to the enrichment of the human experience.

Future of humanistic psychology: Jack says, "Humanistic psychology has the seeds and potential for contributing to the general cultural revolution that is now going on." Lorraine adds, "Someday parents, as well as professionals in various fields, may discover new ways of family 'management,' living, and child rearing which will be more satisfying, rewarding, and creative."

Personal histories: Jack: Associate Professor of Psychology at Brigham Young University (1937–1946) and at Michigan State University (1946–1949). Professor of Psychology and Director of the Group Process Laboratory at the University of Colorado (1949–1956). Director of Research at the National Training Laboratories (1958–1961). President of the American Association for Humanistic Psychology (1967–1968).

Lorraine: Dean of Women at Carroll College (1946–1949). Assistant Director of Student Activities at the University of Colorado (1949–1952). Research Associate for the Office of Naval Research Program on Defensive Behavior within Groups (1956–1962).

Writings: Together they have written *Dynamcs of Participative Groups,* with Grace N. Platts (1951); *Applied Group Dynamics* (1953); and a number of articles. Jack, in addition, has written *Explorations in Human Relations Training,* with L. P. Bradford and R. Lippitt (1953), and has edited, with L. P. Bradford and K. D. Benne, *T-group Theory and Laboratory Method* (1964). He also wrote several chapters for that volume.

Present chapter: This chapter was prepared especially for the present book.

Chapter 17

JACK R. and LORRAINE M. GIBB

HUMANISTIC ELEMENTS IN GROUP GROWTH

Some groups seem to grow. They appear healthy—and seem to get more healthy as time goes on. In such groups the human being seems to emerge as having great worth and great potential. It is difficult to separate feelings of personal growth and well-being from feelings of membership and interdependent fulfillment. Members of the group feel free, emergent, and creative.

Some groups appear to stagnate. They seem unhealthy. Members may speak defensively about their membership. In such groups the human being may appear as less than he is, as having little worth and little potential. Members may wonder whether the group is ever really going to amount to much or whether it will ever accomplish its aims. Members may feel restricted by the demands of the group. Persons may feel that they give more to the group than they get from it.

What distinguishes sick from healthy groups is a significant question. For most of us, groups are important elements in the structure of our culture. Some groups grow, and become, in a sense, actualized. Other groups progress slowly or fail to develop in meaningful dimensions. Therapy groups can provide a setting for therapy and remedial help, or they can be useless to the members. Classroom groups can be environments where growth and learning are easy, or they can be of little help and actually inhibit such growth. YMCA clubs can be climates which foster healthy spirituality and character formation, or they can hamper such formation. Families, regardless of such variables as economic welfare or presence or absence of fathers, can foster healthy growth in parents and children, or they can be festering grounds for juvenile delinquency, neurotic habits, or unhappiness. Research

teams can be creative atmospheres for innovation and productivity, or they can lead to mediocrity, stagnation, and low productivity.

Research Base of Observation In our research on group growth,[1] we have obtained a revealing and even inspiring view of man as he might become, and we have had occasional glimpses of groups in peak experiences of sustained creativity and trust, i.e., group actualization. These group experiences have occurred most often (1) when groups have been in sensitivity training in semiweekly sessions for eight or nine consecutive months, (2) when groups have been in around-the-clock "marathon" sessions for 90 to 120 hours with little or no sleep, or (3) when groups have been in twelve-hour sessions daily for twelve or thirteen consecutive days. In our experience, this optimal growth occurs most frequently in groups which have no professional leader present and in which emergent and interdependent strength is maximized.

Under these conditions, the groups are qualitatively different from the groups usually met in natural settings. The groups attain and often maintain states of creativity, depth of communication, and trust that are impressive and memorable, both to those participating and to those observing. We have seen this state of affairs in occasional

[1] Since 1951 the authors have conducted a series of experimental and field studies designed to investigate longitudinal changes in small groups, particularly as these changes are associated with the arousal and maintenance of defensive or productive behavior. These studies were financed mainly by a series of grants from the Group Psychology Branch of the Office of Naval Research.

natural groups in organizational settings, usually after the group has undergone a training experience of appropriate duration and intensity.

Group and Person Potentials Research from several different disciplines has indicated that man grows at a fraction of his potential growth rate. This underdevelopment is even more startling when one examines the growth rate of groups in our culture. In our research program, we made systematic observations of groups in natural settings— YMCA clubs, management teams, national boards, therapy groups, work groups, and families. We made use of a number of methods in comparing the groups under depth training with natural groups: group interviews, individual depth interviews, coded group observations, questionnaires, expert opinions, and analysis of taped recordings (Gibb, 1955; Gibb, 1963; Gibb, 1964).

In this chapter, we shall present informal summaries of our general impressions from the longitudinal research and of our conclusions about a humanistic theory of personal and group growth.

Our impression is that man's capacity for creativity, happiness, and personal growth is greatly underrated, both by himself and by many scientists who study man. Behavioral scientists in evaluating potential have looked at persons and groups in the natural setting and judged what they might become. It is as if, wishing to determine how well men could hit golf balls, we lined up fifty average adult males at a golf tee, had each hit two balls, measured the distances, and concluded that the average man's driving potential was 30 yards. After practice and effort, perhaps the average man could hit the ball 155 yards. However, after experiencing a refined instruction process, the average person could possibly be trained to hit the ball 225 yards. The above analogy is relevant to the testing of the group's capability for creative growth. There is a qualitative difference between the average management team in the usual organizational

setting and the same group after it receives the kind of training that is now possible. This significant fact has led to a new look at human potential in persons and groups, to new organizational theories, and to new theories of individual and group development.[2]

BASIC DIMENSIONS OF GROUP LIFE

The process aspects of the group, *qua* group, are a relatively recent object of scientific study. Knowing little about groups and often fearing them, man has sometimes felt that they were a hindrance to human growth. It now seems likely that man can reach new satisfactions and significant functional levels of living in group action.

Our research indicates four significant dimensions in which groups differ. These dimensions are interdependent, and as yet we have no clear comprehension of that interdependence, but we do have some convincing evidence of the relevance of each of these factors in group growth, health, or actualization.

Groups differ in (1) the degree of *reciprocal trust* among members; (2) the *validity, depth, and quality of the feedback system*; (3) the degree of *directionality toward group-determined goals*; and (4) the degree of *real interdependence in the system*. A schematic picture of these four variables is given in Table 17–1. Let us examine each of these factors in some detail.

THE FORMATION OF TRUST

Trust is the pacemaker variable in group growth. From it stem all the other significant variables of health. That is, to the extent that trust develops, people are able to communicate genuine feelings and perceptions on relevant issues to all members of the system. To the degree that trust is present, people are able to communicate with themselves and others to form consensual goals. To the degree that trust is pres-

[2] The burgeoning area of group life is dealt with from several perspectives in this book: See Haigh (Chapter 22), Thomas (Chapter 23), Shapiro (Chapter 24), Clark (Chapter 27), and Rogers (Chapter 28). [Editor]

Table 17–1 Personal and group growth

KEY AREAS OF SOCIAL BEHAVIOR	DIRECTIONS OF PERSONAL GROWTH	DIRECTIONS OF GROUP GROWTH
Climate (membership)	Acceptance of self; acceptance of others	Climate of trust; climate of support
Data flow (decision making)	Awareness (input); openness (output)	Valid feedback system; consensual decision making
Goal formation (productivity)	Goal integration in self; self-determination; self-assessment	Goal integration in group; group determination and assessment of goals
Control (organization)	Interdependence (inner, emergent control and value system)	Interdependence (inner, emergent control and norm system)

nt, people can be truly interdependent. Each of the four group-growth variables is dependent upon the prior variable in the hierarchy. Feedback is dependent upon trust. Goal formation is dependent upon feedback and trust. Interdependence is dependent upon goal formation, feedback, and trust.

As is indicated in Table 17–1, the four factors in group growth are related to parallel factors in personal growth. There is some agreement among psychologists on the criteria of mental health in personal growth.[3] There is considerably less agreement among group scientists on the criteria of group health and development. The schema outlined here provides a framework for analyzing group actualization.

The Dynamic of Fear The most impressive dynamic of early group life is the presence of fear. Fear grows out of distrust. We tend to fear events, people, and stimuli for which

See a helpful analysis of contemporary agreement and disagreement on criteria of personal growth in Jahoda (1958).

we feel we have no adequate response. Many factors in the new or immature group increase the normal residual fear that all people share. Great uncertainty increases fear, and individuals have many ways of trying to reduce this uncertainty. They put other people into categories which they feel they can understand and predict. "If I know she is a nurse, then I know what nurses are like and can respond to what I know they will do." They get the group to agree upon some ground rules. "If we take turns talking around the circle, then I know when my turn comes." Individuals also try to find out what the other members think of them and about the world.

Some of these efforts to lessen uncertainty are unsuccessful, while others are fairly effective. Even if I can reduce the ambiguity in my own perceptual world, this gets shattered when I realize that growth in me and in the group can come only with ambiguity, tension, conflict, and unfreezing. I cannot truly become safe from my fears by building my perceptual world into safe and predictable categories.

Growth turns out to be something more.

The group in its early stages will attempt to cling to and create fragile structural stabilities to reduce fear. These apparently secure structures turn out to be made of sand. A group may assign a timekeeper so that one person will not monopolize the group; it may appoint a chairman, or it may decide in what order people will speak. This supposedly "rules in" order and control and "rules out" chaos and threatening situations.

For some people, moving quickly lessens fear by reducing the tension and turmoil of decision making in depth. "Let's do anything," "Let's get something done," "We are wasting time," and other impatient expressions aimed at speeding up direct movement are common in the early stages of group development. Later observations show that these frantic demands for movement are fear-based.

Other Group Evidences of Fear Politeness and formality are early indications of fear.

Politeness prevents retaliation, keeps people at a safe distance, makes it unnecessary to face members in such a way that intimidating negative feelings would be revealed, discourages the other person from giving negative feedback, and in general serves the unanalyzed needs of the fearful person.

Another response to fear in early stages of group life is the use of humor. It is ambiguous enough to serve as a presumably safe camouflage for hostile feedback to another person. Humor tends to encourage people to keep things from getting too sentimental, too intimate, and too close to embarrassing or painful exposure or confrontation. By using humor, a person can "hedge his bets" and deny the hostile intent if the listener accuses him of being unfriendly.

In its early stages, the group is sometimes work-addicted. The group can avoid fearsome confrontation, interpersonal conflict, and exposure by hard, safe work upon a seemingly legitimate task. Groups can make long lists, engage in routine tasks, and attempt to look busy to themselves and others, in order to avoid depth relationships. A group may engage in an unending warm-up session, talking in an apparently serious, work-oriented vein about the factors determining today's weather. Of course, all the defense mechanisms are relevant here.

People who are afraid distrust the motivations of other members and tend to step in and try to control the situation in order to prevent those whom they fear from exerting prior influence. This is often done in subtle ways, such as nominating a less feared person to be chairman. This apparent cleanly motivated act can hopefully be seen as selfless and group-oriented rather than as a disguised manipulation for control.

Signs of Group Growth Thus, fear and distrust characterize behavior in the early stages of group development. As groups grow, these fears gradually become reduced. Trust grows. People learn to tolerate greater degrees of ambiguity. They become more spontaneous and less cautious. Members make allowances for greater differences, both in themselves and in others. People are allowed to hold a wider variety of opinions. They are permitted to be themselves—to dress differently, to be unpredictable, and perhaps even to be disloyal. The boundaries of acceptance widen. Whereas in the early stages of development, the group boxes in or punishes persons who deviate from the group norms, in the later stages, nonconformists are encouraged. Radical ideas are used to test reality or to create new solutions. Deviation is perhaps even welcomed as a creative contribution to possible group productivity.

Fear reduction allows people to feel and to express publicly the warmth that wells up. People are able to show affection in a number of spontaneous, often gestural, ways without the need for exaggerated or showy expressions. There is a great deal of warmth in the group. In addition, there is an easy expression of "I feel this way," on the assumption that other members will permit the voicing of individualistic feelings. It is also common to hear people spontaneously say and feel "we," rather than "you." (The use of "you" in referring to the group is a sign of membership denial.)

The problem of trust formation is the problem of attaining membership. One achieves genuine belonging by trusting himself and the group. The critical index of group health is trust development. As the group grows, fear decreases and trust increases. Thus, group actualization is a process of attaining increasingly higher levels of trust.

COMMUNICATION AND DECISION MAKING

In the early stages of group development the customary fear and distrust make it difficult for a valid feedback system to occur, for people to talk honestly with one another and for the group to integrate these feeling and perception data into appropriate decisions for the group.

The processes of ambiguity, strategy, facade building, and gamesmanship, mentioned in the earlier paragraph as resulting from fears, also tend to reduce the effectiveness of the communication system

With the presence of fear and the lack of trust, there is little encouragement for open exploration of one's own inner world of motivations and attitudes. People give off mixed messages: There is a difference between facial expression and verbal content, between tone of voice and what one says, between what one has courage enough to say in a subgroup and what one says publicly in the total group, and between what one says the first time and what one says when challenged to repeat or clarify the message. Thus, such differences further increase the distortion of data.

In low trust, a great number of concealing skills develop. People become adept at consciously or unconsciously withholding feelings. Especially in situations of actual or supposed power differences, the weaker person, the person lower in the hierarchy, or the person with the lowest status may deliberately treat a disliked person with great friendliness in order to cover his real negative feelings. Secretaries may develop complicated strategies for seeming busy. Using facades, bosses may camouflage favoritism or degrees of differential feelings about employees.

People spread rumors in order to test reactions. This feedback distortion is used to hurt others or to explore the depth of feeling. There are elaborate skills for learning one's way in the maze of distortion in the usual organization.

A common process which suppresses relevant information in the group is the ignoring of known or suspected experts. People are jealous of those with knowledge and are suspicious of their motives. The expert is frequently articulate and persuasive, so he overstates his case in an imposing manner and rebreeds resentment and resistance. Thus, there are many reasons why people with information are discouraged from sharing it.

Another source of distortion occurs because of inadequate methods of problem solving. In its early stages, the group seldom adequately defines the problem, and because problem definition may cause conflict, the participants find it safer to philosophize about nonpersonal items.

As the group develops, the members learn that it is possible to deal with many deep-seated feelings and concerns without undue fear and anxiety about being hurt. The participants discover that, although long-withheld feelings are sometimes disturbing to everyone present, the alternative of holding back the feelings has even worse consequences for the group. It becomes clear to the group that feelings can, in a genuine sense, be integrated into work, creativity, and problem solving.

Effective groups, with development, are able to develop consensual decision making about significant problems that the group faces. This is the payoff of data processing and the feedback system of the group.

GOAL FORMATION AND PRODUCTIVITY

Group health is related to the integration of group goals. Unhealthy groups are unable to decide what they want to be or want to do. Lacking an adequate system of communication, members may not know that they, as a group, are not doing what they want to do. The difficulties in goal formation arise rather directly from partial data processing, which in turn grows out of fear and distrust. When members distrust the motivations of other members, it is difficult to share goals in a meaningful way. The problem that the group faces is somehow to create out of the available data a satisfying goal which would adequately include the real goals of the members and which would be more fulfilling than any of the half-verbalized goals that the individuals have.

One of the early errors that groups make is to force the expression of a few goals that come "off the top of the head," separate these into some alternatives, and then vote on a goal. This process necessitates a compromise, so that participants often feel that they are now doing something less satisfying than they would have done alone. They say that they are going along to satisfy others, to appear flexible, to avoid being seen as stubborn or rebellious, and to please authorities. In our early research, we found a high "reservation score" in early stages of group growth; that is, a large number of members were seen by the rest of the group as consenting, but were found (when data were later gathered by better means such as depth interviews) to have a number of unverbalized reservations about the decisions that had been made by the group (Gibb, 1963).

Coercion and Resistance One error made by unhealthy groups is the attempt to impose control mechanisms and to verbalize public goals before the group has worked through its fears and data-processing problems. Verbal, anxious, or dominant people are prone to do this. For various reasons, weak, uninterested, or nonverbal individuals often go along with these coercive members. Members combat persuasion by using various forms of resistance, often little understood by the high persuaders. Thus, members, consciously or not, will be withdrawn and apathetic and will show a low commitment to verbalize any goals. Then, too, there are those who really do not know what they want to do. Perhaps because they have so often gone along with persuasive or dynamic leadership, they have never developed the capacity to examine their own goals and plan life activities that will accomplish these aims.

One of the first tasks in training groups or teams in natural situations is to learn to examine the motivations of individuals. This may be a lengthy task, calling for long-dormant skills and feelings. The general stagnation of self and the lack of personal identity in our withdrawn culture are evident in immature groups. In the developing group, members can seek their identity; they can learn to explore previously half-formulated desires, repressed wishes, and formerly unrealizable goals in an atmosphere of trust and listening. Sharpening of this inner quest takes place in the caring group.

The apparent reverse of apathy is a condition of frenetic work at tasks that the group uses to respond to duty motivations, loyalty to the organization, compulsive

needs, and the desire to prove to themselves and to others that they can work hard. This busywork can easily be misunderstood and seen as productive or creative work.

Public Goals and Real Goals A common error is the declaring of public "motherhood-and-the-flag" kinds of goals. There is no real commitment to these goals, and they are used as a cover-up. Learning groups, for instance, will set up as a goal a two-hour discussion of foremen training because this seems like something that the company would want or that the group should be interested in. In reality, though, the people come to the meeting to complain about the company, air personal grudges, or get a vacation, or because of a whole variety of motivations that are unrelated to the public statement.

When a group of people have worked through the fear, trust, and data-flow problems to the point where they can communicate in high trust or "speak the truth in love," it is possible to work to a reasonable consensus on major problems of goal formation and decision making.

The members integrate tasks, groups, and individual goals. (We are assuming that all people are achievement-motivated and that work, when self-determined, is intrinsically satisfying.) In order for personal and group needs to be met, the group must select a task and make some kind of visible progress toward accomplishing it. In effective groups, *esprit de corps,* individual satisfaction over group achievement, and commitment to the group are vital. Group members must also feel some sense of belonging, fulfillment, self-worth, influence, and linkage to whatever goals are currently important to them as individuals. As high trust and a valid communication system develop, it becomes possible to mesh these needs in satisfying ways without undue group pressures to conform for the sake of conformity. The creation of this state of affairs gives people a sense of freedom.

A well-known vice-president of one of America's largest corporations once said, after observing a T-group in a highly cooperative session, that he had never seen a group in which people listened to one another so deeply and were so well able to integrate what they said into a creative and satisfying discussion. He was so impressed that he had a deep emotional experience just observing the session! A minister stated, after spending a day in such a group, "This is the first time that I have ever really had a religious experience!" When the average organization works at from 20 to 40 percent effectiveness, it is a dramatic and memorable occasion to see a group working at a 70 percent efficiency level. Those of us who have seen participative groups in action, both in training and in the natural organizational setting, are aware of the exciting and awesome potential of people who are engaged in creative interaction on group-initiated tasks. Group actualization occurs with the productive integration of deeply personal needs into a genuine consensus on goals. The group continues to form goals that are a creative synthesis of personal goals—new, exciting, and fulfilling (Gibb, 1961a; Gibb, 1965).

CONTROL SYSTEMS AND ORGANIZATION

Most all of us in the process of socialization develop authority and influence problems that stem from our early relations with our parents and teachers. When a group of people meets in the early stages, problems of mutual influence become immediately visible to the observer and to the more sensitive members. This is true of all groups, whether their purpose is work or recreation. Distrust, distorted communication, and imposed or ambiguous goals tend to make these feelings more severe and to limit growth.

One of our T-groups, composed of upper-middle management people from governmental, industrial, educational, and religious organizations, was discussing what seemed to be an innocent problem of whether or not to take a coffee break. The issue was brought up by a member in the first three minutes of the opening session as an apparently harmless and minor goal. The member's proposal was followed by a few, apparently frivolous, comments about the absence of cream, some mild wishes for tea, some weak resistance to taking time from the group for an unnecessary break, a few jokes, and laughter. This then led a few of the more vigorous members to try to push for a quick decision. These tactics snowballed into a mild resistance, and a long conversation developed. The discussion became more heated and continued for two hours and twenty minutes, until the group was actually late for lunch and yet still deadlocked about whether to waste time taking a morning coffee break! People shouted, developed hurt feelings, withdrew occasionally to sulk, and argued violently about apparently trivial issues. The group broke up at someone's suggestion and went to lunch. After lunch, one of the observers interpreted the discussion as a power struggle. This meaning was violently rejected by those engaged in the fight, but three days later, the group laughed together in recognition that it had been just that.

In undeveloped groups we often see such camouflaged and displaced battles for power and authority. Members are aware to various degrees of these interpersonal feelings in themselves and others. When communication and trust are low and facades are high, people pretend that there is no struggle, that the argument is "purely intellectual," that mixed feelings toward powerful members are inevitable and nonintrusive, and that there is nothing they can do about the matter.

Feelings of Impotence A sense of powerlessness or impotence is a dominant characteristic of the early life of groups. Because people seldom listen, because the group has a difficult time finding a satisfying direction, and for a number of other reasons explored above, individuals in the group feel that it is very difficult to influence other individuals or "the group." Both the quiet and the talkative people have these feelings.

Resistance to induction takes many forms. The aggressive, high initiators are responded to with apathy or passive listening. Persuasion leads to resistance. Quiet, low-status, mild people are often ignored and thought to be idealists or uninterested in initiation. A recent study indicated that, in general, during the early stages of group life, members thought that unusually restrained people were stupid, uninterested, afraid, or lazy! Another factor that leads to the feeling of powerlessness is the tendency of people, especially during the early fear and distrust stages, to be suspicious of the motivations of other people. Thus, our study indicated that quiet members thought that the aggressive members were insecure, manipulative, domineering, and showing off their knowledge! It is also true that some of the noninitiators saw the initiators as helpful, full of ideas, and courageous. Some of the talkative members saw quiet individuals as good listeners, flexible, and courteous. As people trust and communicate better, the initiators are more apt to be seen as wanting to help, and the quiet members are more apt to be seen as receptive listeners. Ironically, in early stages the same behavior is viewed as dominance, manipulation, or uninterested resistance (Gibb, 1959; Gibb, 1961b; Gibb, 1964).

When people are afraid and feel powerless to influence their own important development or goal setting, they try to sway the group in a number of ways. People may not wish to admit to themselves or to the other members of the group that they do desire to influence, because this unrelieved need for power, as such, is looked down on in our aspiring-to-be-democratic society. Direct influence efforts are fairly easy to deal with, but camouflaged or devious attempts are more difficult for the group to examine and handle. Covert strategies are used by individuals with varying degrees of consciousness. Some may deliberately try to use strategies and manipulative gimmicks. Others may unconsciously use tricky means of getting their way (Gibb, 1961a).

Sometimes the opposition may be conscious and take the form of strategies such as appointing committees, using parliamentary maneuvers, calling for a summary, or apparently innocent or useful list making, in order to prevent an impending decision that is being pushed by a person who is thought to be seeking power.

Desires to influence are apparently characteristic of all of us. These needs are troublesome only when they are covered up and are thus difficult for the group to handle or when they are denied (although overpowering because of fear and anxiety), so that the group cannot deal with the behavior for what it is. The wish to influence and be influenced is a productive and creative one and is necessary for group growth.

The Fear of Uncontrolled Groups   Groups in early stages of development seem unmanageable. This gives rise to the feeling that special procedures are necessary to control the group. The organization tries rules, regulations, appointed leaders, span of control, parliamentary procedure, channels of communication, tight organization, and "articles of war" formally to control the behavior of people in groups. It seems to members that it would be unthinkable for the group to operate without strong formal leadership and regulations. Thus, tight controls arise which tend to be self-deceiving. People resist the rules by various forms of displaced rebellion, by apathy, or by a kind of unimaginative obedience. Conflict, spontaneity, and vigorous interplay are all productive in a high-trust and high-feedback situation. These factors, however, produce disruptions and unproductive organizations in a low-trust and low-feedback condition.

Another state of affairs characteristic of the early stages of group life and related to control and organization may be the calm of the orderly, obedient, peace-at-any-price atmosphere. The deadly politeness may be interpreted by members or observers as productive work. "Sweetness and light" can be a cover-up for the group's uncertainty about the handling of the control and authority problems.

Permissiveness is another uncertain concept in this connection. What is called "permissiveness" may be many things. In low-trust and low-communication groups, it may be a kind of unrelated, undigestible disorder in which people look as if they are doing what they want to do, but are in fact responding to impulse, play, and resistance. Lacking formal leadership, the group is thus confused and structureless. Permissiveness in high-trust, high-feedback groups can be realized in exciting, spontaneous, and playful integration of creative efforts in the group. Opponents of permissiveness are thinking about low-trust groups, while the advocates of permissiveness are thinking about the high-trust situation that occurs in the relatively well-developed group.

It has been our observation that developed groups can operate in a leaderless situation without formal, prepared agenda, without organizational coercion in the formal sense, and without the parliamentary procedures which are thought to make decision making easier.

EXTRINSIC SOLUTIONS TO GROUP PROBLEMS

Because of low trust and low communication, groups have invented mechanisms for solving the problems on these four dimensions. A legal system of formal laws has been invented to solve the fear and distrust problem. Membership requirements such as college entrance examinations and racial and religious codes for housing, clubs, and jobs have been developed.

A great many mechanisms have been produced to solve the low-communication, poor-data-flow problems. Communication channels are organized. Parliamentary procedures which guarantee minimal opportunity for people to talk are set up. Formal rules for making decisions by majority vote are used. Company newspapers, written memoranda, multiple copy systems, and many tools of the communications and public relations profession have arisen.

Various mechanisms are devised during the early stages of group development to solve the passivity toward the goal-formation dimension. Most of these involve the artificial creation of motivation by extrinsic reward systems: competition, grades, piecework, and praise and merit systems.

All these mechanisms are control systems which arise as a result of recognition of membership, decision, and motivation problems. Mechanisms for handling control problems, of course, are also used. Rules of way, bargaining contracts, codes of gentlemen, punishments for nonconformity, formal job prescriptions, and tables of organizations are all examples. As groups grow, the necessity for these formal control systems disappears.

Conflict Conflicts will occur in living and in active and creative people. Resolving the conflict, by finding alternatives that are creative solutions rather than deadening compromises, can be a productive process. The motivation to build something new can come from the dissatisfaction revealed by the discord. The deliberate creation of conflict is likely to occur in the early stages of group development, when frantic leaders have no other way for creating excitement or when playful members are bored. However, when conflict does exist, the best way to handle it is to look at it and resolve it. The mature group is able to do this. A process analysis of the way the conflict arose and was solved is potentially meaningful and is likely to be cathartic. The aftermath of conflict can also be productive. People can learn about themselves, about the group, and about the reality of the world by the way that they, as individuals or as a group, have handled the discord.

CONCLUSION

Groups are often unhealthy and add little to the lives of their members. Such groups might well be discontinued or certainly changed. Grouping can become a fetish, and many groups are preserved long beyond their day. As we have seen, signs of ill health include undue fear and distrust, inadequate and distorted communication, undigested and dysfunctional goal systems, and unresolved dependency problems.

Groups *can* be healthy. Groups can be

creative, fulfilling, and satisfying to all their members. We have seen groups that can be appropriately described as actualizing. Such groups develop a high degree of trust, valid communication in depth, a consensual goal system, and a genuine interdependence. Our research has shown promising data that provide a way for therapists, parents, managers, and teachers to aid in the process of creating groups which are in themselves healthy organisms and which provide a climate for member growth and fulfillment (Gibb, 1964; Gibb, 1965). It is such groups that can provide the framework for a better world.

REFERENCES

GIBB, J. R. Factors producing defensive behavior within groups. II. *Annual Technical Report, Office of Naval Research*, Contract Nonr–1147(03), NR 170–226, 1955.

GIBB, J. R. Factors producing defensive behavior within groups. VI. *Final Technical Report, Office of Naval Research*, Contract Nonr–2285(01), 1959.

GIBB, J. R. Defensive communication. *Journal of Communication*, 1961, **11**, 141–148. (a)

GIBB, J. R. Defense level and influence potential in small groups. In L. Petrullo & B. M. Bass (Eds.), *Leadership and interpersonal behavior*. New York: Holt, Rinehart and Winston, 1961. Pp. 66–81. (b)

GIBB, J. R. Factors producing defensive behavior within groups. VII. *Final Technical Report, Office of Naval Research*, Contract Nonr–3088(00), 1963.

GIBB, J. R. Climate for trust formation. In L. P. Bradford, J. R. Gibb, & K. D. Benne (Eds.), *T-group theory and laboratory method*. New York: Wiley, 1964. Pp. 279–309.

GIBB, J. R. Fear and facade: Defensive management. In R. E. Farson (Ed.), *Science and human affairs*. Palo Alto, Calif.: Science and Behavior Books, 1965. Pp. 197–214.

JAHODA, MARIE. *Current concepts of positive mental health.* (A report by the Joint Commission on Mental Illness and Health.) New York: Basic Books, 1958.

Presently: Psychologist in the Fairfield (California) School District (since 1964) and Lecturer in the University of California Extension Division at Davis.

Education: Master of Arts in educational psychology from the University of Chicago (1957).

Current major activities: School psychology and serving as the editor of the *Bulletin of the Society for the Study of Human Existence.*

ADAH B. MAURER

Most rewarding project: Working on "a book by and for teachers anent the emotionally disturbed child in the classroom (as distinct from clinic cases) to help close the cultural gap by reducing the sadistic aspects of corporal punishment, sarcasm, and belittling that destroy so many spirits during the vulnerable growing years."

Future of humanistic psychology: "A scientific psychology so thoroughly permeated with humanistic ideas that the need for a separate movement eliminates itself."

Personal history: Counselor at the Hyde Park High School in Chicago (1957–1960) and at the Chicago Psychiatric Foundation (1960–1961). School Psychologist with various California school systems (since 1962). Mrs. Maurer has a son who is a computer scientist at the University of California, a daughter, and three grandchildren.

Writings: Mrs. Maurer's writings couple the humanistic and the impertinent delightfully: "Peter Pan Is Undernourished" (*Chicago Schools Journal*, 1960, **41**); "Did Little Hans Really Want to Marry His Mother?" (*Journal of Humanistic Psychology*, 1964, **4**, 139–148). She has also been a consistent student of children's attitudes about death: "The Child's Knowledge of Non-existence" (*Journal of Existential Psychiatry*, 1961, **2**, 193–212); "Adolescent Attitudes toward Death" (*Journal of Genetic Psychology*, 1964, **105**, 75–90); and "Maturation of Concepts of Death" (*British Journal of Medical Psychology*, 1966, **39**, 35–41).

Present chapter: The study here reported has not previously been published, although it is clearly related to Mrs. Maurer's studies of children's concepts of, and attitudes toward, death.

Chapter 18

ADAH B. MAURER

CHILDREN'S CONCEPTIONS OF GOD

Freud's (1918, p. 242) speculation that every man's God is modeled after the father of his childhood is not directly susceptible of proof or disproof, nor does it in that form afford an access into the dynamics of childhood. We may wonder, however, whether the converse is true. Does the child's definition of God reveal the essence of his relationship with his parents?

Allport (1950) suggests two possibilities: that a child's reaction to the God idea may be an authentic welling up of a basic emotion or, if he has been instructed in the routine performance of small gestures and short recitations at mealtime and bedtime, that his reply may be a memorized statement of dubious personal significance. It may be that children's attitudes are a combination of inculcated teaching and experiential projections, but this would not preclude their being of significance in understanding a child and his relations with his parents. This investigation proposes to explore these ill-defined areas to determine whether any universals emerge and whether or not questioning about God might prove to be a useful clinical tool.

Previous Studies Very little research has been done on this subject. Graebner (1960) tested 977 children in Lutheran parochial schools with drawings representing the various attributes of God. The replies indicated some tendency for the older and brighter children to show less personal involvement, to give more atypical answers, to admit they did not know, and to give flippant or impudent answers. At the same time, these children tended to see God as forgiving and caring oftener than the younger and duller children did. The latter gave more replies describing God as punishing. The younger children in many instances gave as many "right" answers as the older, and some children who were tested in both the sixth and the eighth grades scored less acceptably to their religious teachers the second time.

Among 360 families in Tennessee, according to Nunn (1964), those families who utilized threats that God would punish the disobedient child were significantly associated with low income, lack of affection, demands for conformity to unquestioned authority, and weak, powerless, and ineffectual personalities. The effect upon the children was to increase self-blame but not to internalize values. Compliance under threatening surveillance was found not conducive to the development of a conscience.

Sex differences appeared in a related study by Strang (1964). In 1,000 essays on the meaning of "good" and "bad," boys' reasons for being good were found to be desire for peer approval, fear of punishment, and hope for reward, in that order. Girls listed religious influences, peer preferences, and reward possibilities. Thus

173

popularity and reward proved common incentives, but punishment avoidance is masculine, as God pleasing is feminine.

METHOD AND SUBJECTS

The present study was started when a number of conspicuous examples of spontaneous projection came to light in my own work. Thus a child's response to "What is God like?" contained clear-cut confirmation of known family dynamics. The competent son of an Air Force captain answered with obvious pride, "He's in command of the whole world!" reflecting a boastfully true attitude toward his father. In contrast, another seven-year-old, the stepson of an often punitive unemployed workman, replied to the same question, "Sometimes He comes down and hits you." The "comes down" indicates clearly that he had in mind a figure residing up above, typically for this age in the sky, but the activity ascribed to the deity characterized male authority as he had experienced it. Less obvious was the response of a five-year-old girl, the second of six in a closely knit family of very modest accomplishments. She said, "He made us because He wants us to be His friends," and after a pause she added, "Because He didn't have no friends." The mother of this family expressed the same thought directly: "We don't mix much," she said; "we have each other."

Since these examples confirmed the psychoanalytic dictum that the child identifies the attributes of God in his earthly father, and since the children in a secular setting did not iterate instructed verbalisms, the investigation was continued. The form of the question was changed after some experimentation. "What is God like?" seemed to restrict the full range of possible responses. It also implied a personification that was too embodied to encompass all possible definitions of God. "Tell me about God," spoken in a confidently expectant manner and repeated in a somewhat coaxing tone if necessary, was included as a routine part of psychological interviews with 184 children (53 girls and 131 boys) between the ages of five and twelve.

The sample was somewhat heavily weighted with slow learners and children with mild behavior problems who had been referred to the school psychologist. Economically, all the families from which they came were lower-middle class; geographically, they lived in a burgeoning, tract-ringed small city. Religious affiliation was predominantly Protestant, many belonging to small sects. About 90 percent of the families were white; about half had migrated from the old South or Oklahoma within the parents' lifetime. Most were ambitious, independent, respectable, and employed. None of these factors were used as variables; they are mentioned in order to locate the test population in its niche in the American scene.

Assessment of Replies Categorizing the replies was attempted in two ways: first according to philosophic descriptions of the attributes of the deity, and second empirically, according to what the children actually said. As it turned out, these two methods showed some overlap but also much divergence.

The attributes of God drawn up by the Lutheran Education Association were "creator," "eternal," "holy," "just," "merciful," "omnipotent," "omnipresent," "omniscient," and "promise keeper" (Graebner, 1962, p. 19). Only one of these appeared with any regularity in my sample. "Creator," expressed in many ways, constituted 37 per cent of the replies. An eight-year-old said, "He's the one made the world and made us, made animals, trees, coconuts, and all kinds of stuff." The difference between created and manufactured articles is not clear to the five-year-old: "He makes trees, sun, clouds. He makes furniture."

"Does He make furniture?"

"Yes."

"And toys, houses, chairs, roofs, books and schools?"

"Oh, no, not books!"

But there the congruence between the two studies between expectation and actuality dropped off sharply. Even the most generous translation of childishly inadequate expressions resulted in few mention of the remaining qualities. "Eternal," as such, was not mentioned, although the concept did appear once as, "He will never die." Five children reported that "He rose from the dead," but for sixteen others, "He died," or "They put Him on a cross." One earnest six-year-old became bug-eyed with excitement: "He got killed!" Immortality of the self seemed to concern more of the children than God's eternality. Eight of them spoke of going to heaven "when you die." But if all mention of heaven, living forever, and arising from the dead could be taken to mean some dim, childish understanding of God as eternal, a mere 17 percent thought to speak of it.

"Holy" was mentioned twice; "just" and "merciful" not at all. "Omnipotent," if one includes many doubtful terms such as "king," "magic," "ruler," "lots of powers," and "He can do anything He wants to," had impressed ten. "Omnipresent" appeared three times. One child rolled his eyes and whispered, "He's right here, right now, listening to everything we say!" "Omniscient" could not be construed from anything any child said, with the single exception of a Catholic altar boy who recited, "He knows all things," while staring at the ceiling. As for "promise keeper," there were only three instances, and those seriously qualified, e.g., "If you ask Him for something, He just might do it, if He happened to feel like it."

Second Analysis An empirical sorting seemed to promise more enlightenment in this hedged and often taboo topic. Four qualities stood out in almost equal proportion: "creator," "provider," "disciplinarian," and "friend" (see Table 18–1). About one-third of the children gave at least a part of their response to some statement that could be subsumed under each one of these. All the miscellaneous remainder, including "don't know" and unique and strange replies, constituted little more than another one-third.

"Provider" was poorly differentiated from "creator," especially by the younger children. Besides confusing living things with man-made articles, they used "made" and "gave" interchangeably. "I think . . . God . . . He's very nice. He's the one gives us all the cars and buses. He made all the animals, trees, churches, suitcases. He makes us jackets, clothes, stoves, and all sorts of things." "Provider" also includes many expressions of God as helper and caretaker: "God helps people. He gives them food and water." "He helps you, makes your body grow." "He's our Father; when we get sick He takes care of us, sends us to the hospital." "He gave me to my mother and father to keep for Him, something like a baby-sitter, sort of."

The difference in emphasis upon the powerful strength of the creator of the world and the gentle kindness of the helper who provides suitcases and sandwiches appears to be sex-linked to a certain extent. Girls place the helping aspects first by a wide margin; boys, the creative aspects. Differences also extend into seeing God as lawmaker, judge, and punisher. Boys place this function second after creator; girls give it last place, a finding that confirms Strang's (1964) data about the differing motivations for moral conduct.

God as lawmaker and judge constituted the most revealing set of responses, forming a continuum from teacher of ethics to executioner, with no central tendency. Age seemed not to be a factor in ethical judgment. The quality of the kindergarteners' replies was consistently on as high a level as that of older children's. A six-year-old of average intelligence said, "He helps us when we pray and to be good." An average twelve-year-old said, "He makes sure we say our prayers and helps us with things and like that." Toward the other end of the scale, a six-year-old, "When children are

Table 18–1 Attributes of God as given by boys and girls ages five to twelve, in answer to, "Tell me about God."

CATEGORY	PERCENT WHO REPLIED THUS WHOLLY OR IN PART		
	BOYS (131)	GIRLS (53)	ALL (184)
Creator	40	28	37
Helper	31	51	36
Judge, lawmaker	37	24	33
Friend	22	30	23
Miscellaneous	43	28	38

Table 18–2 Children's views of God as arbiter of ethics

ROLE OF DEITY	CASES	EXAMPLE	AGE
Teacher	3	"He teaches people to love their neighbors as well as their-selves."	8
Helper	7	"He helps us to be good."	5
		"God helps us and keeps us good."	10
Pacesetter	5	"He wants you to be nice."	6
Lawmaker	4	"We should obey His rules and you shouldn't disobey your mother."	9
Naysayer	6	"Our Lord doesn't agree with evil."	12
		"He doesn't like us to hit anybody."	7
Sufferer	6	"If you be bad, He'll go away!"	7
		"If you do bad, it hurts Him too."	10
Thunderer	4	"God gets angry and gets mad too when you stay home from work."	6
Punisher	5	"If God don't like you, gonna punish you."	7
Condemner	5	"When they be nasty, He goes under the ground; gets the Devil after 'em."	6
Murderer	1	"He'll kill you if you're bad."	10
Destroyer	2	"He'll destroy it [the world] by water next time."	12
		"... the fire next time."	11

no good, the Devil comes and burns them up." A twelve-year-old put it this way: "If we don't do good, we go you know where!" As with age, intelligence seems not to correlate with replies on this continuum, except that in the most ethical groups, all three boys who mentioned concern for others were found to have IQs well above average. Otherwise, bright, average, and dull were scattered over almost the whole

range. No really good minds ranged as low as the last four—the punishment groups—but the samples here presented are too small to permit one to come to any firm conclusions in this regard.

Parent-Child Relation and Child's Answers
The factor that differentiates those who are familiar with gentle controls from those whose first reactions are to think of God as angry and violent is neither age nor intelligence. Rather, it is emotional stability versus aggressiveness. A first-grade boy whose head was covered with scars, who needed glasses but whose parents refused to permit him to have them, and who suffered from pica so much that his teacher kept cookies for him in a vain effort to substitute these for the chalk, paste, crayons, and paper he continually ate, answered the question about God with a very angry, "I don't know anything about God!" When the request was repeated, he shouted in what was an unmistakable imitation of his mother's tone: "You don't listen to your mother; you listen to the Devil!" Then he looked up coyly and added confidentially, "If you listen to Jesus, the Devil gets mad."

Yet control by nonviolence does not always result in a happy, effective child. A desperate, defeated eight-year-old girl looked up with a puzzled frown: "God?" The request was repeated. "Cry," she said at last. After much coaxing she added, "God cries if you did something wrong." Armed with this hint about the parent performance, I was able to break through the barrier of noncommunication to offer the needed suggestions about child rearing.

The fourth group of concepts about God also suggests a relationship to the parents. "Nice" is an omnibus word to children used along with "real good" to describe any adult who is not a downright ogre. Expressing affection either toward or from a higher power in a casual, friendly fashion was found not to overlap expressions of fear of punishment, nor was it found among the very shy. A few less common ways of describing this life style: "God, well, He's my favorite God. ...." "He's a good guy; heaven's a good guy too." Predictably, statements of loving came oftener from girls, but in no case was such an expression more than an introduction to a fuller statement.

There remains the miscellaneous category. Verbalisms or garbled versions of Sunday school or catechism lessons sometimes succeeded in blocking an expression of affect. "He shed His life on us," seemed to stem in part from *America the Beautiful*. It conveyed awe, dependence, and mystery in about equal proportions, but little else. "Jesus got a long beard, and His hair hangs down," describes with pictorial literalness a picture or an icon and gives no indication of family interaction, if indeed there was any for that boy. The epitome of noncommunication was the identification of God by the foulmouthed first-grader who answered eagerly: "That's the man nobody's supposed to talk about cause that's bad words." Such verbalisms probably should not have been accepted as the final statement from the child. Follow-up in the manner of Piaget, whose persistent questioning left no doubt about how much each child really understood, would have determined whether some of these and similar iterations did carry symbolic loadings.

Attempted verbal conformity by two determined rebels had been raised to a high art as a defensive weapon. One, so disruptive that he could not be contained in any organized group, neither school nor Scouts, intoned, "We must serve, loyal, trustworthy and obey!" The second, a survivor of a slum abandonment who had lived by his wits for several months before placement, rattled off a long speech that began, "He made us to be good boys and girls and obey your parents and do your work so you can get a good education, so you can be a good citizen and get a good job. You want to learn how to read, write, spell, subtraction, borrowing. . . ." Both of these children were pseudoretardates, active, belligerent, and clever at maintaining their own distorted integrity against the massive assaults of a determined battery of school and clinical specialists.

Others among the miscellaneous projected themselves into Biblical stories, identifying with one or another of the characters. An eleven-year-old, heavy, clumsy, overcautioned, spoke thus: "He rose on the third day. He hung on the cross. He fell three times before He got there." Another eleven-year-old, enuretic, overtutored, and nagged, told the same story with another emphasis: "He picked Jesus for His son, and when Jesus got hung He made a great big flood and wiped out that city." Certainly the information that the first boy knew he had poor motor coordination and that the second wet the bed in retaliation did not wait upon the use of the story of Jesus as a projective technique. Nevertheless, these instances illustrate the almost limitless ways in which stories can be manipulated to fit personal idiosyncrasies and how religious stories are particularly adaptable as background for the projection of personal and secret concerns.

Even when the child replies with an apparently irrelevant digression (or perhaps particularly then), the mention of the diety tends to tap the deepest confusions and needs. Billy could not sit still. His mother claimed helplessness and pleaded for aid since he could not even sit still to watch television. She denied pertinent history for many sessions until led in a direction suggested by Billy's explanation of God: "You have to say your prayers. Tells you how to go to sleep. I have trouble to go to sleep. I have trouble to go to the bathroom. That's the trouble." Eventually the whole hideous story poured out. Billy had been sexually assaulted while still an infant and was so badly torn that he had had to be kept in a body cast for many months after surgical repair. Bowel movements and the sitting posture continued to be painful, but medical attention was not sought for fear of having to recite the shameful story again.

CONCLUSIONS

Children's statements about God fell into no one pattern. Equally emphasized aspects of God were "creator," "protector," "punisher," and "friend" and a miscellaneous category as large.

The hypothesis that the relationship children feel they have with God is the same as their relationship with their parents was only partly confirmed, possibly because questioning was brief and defensive verbalisms were not always probed for deeper meaning. However, fully three-fourths of the replies did supply "direction signals" toward understanding family dynamics. This seemed due largely to a lack of differentiation among the functions of society, of our ancestors, of the immediate parents, and of an ultimate source. Because infantile egocentrism has little depth perception, all things outside the self seem equally remote.

The lack of a maturational factor in determining replies suggests that children absorb very early the dominant ethico-religious pattern of their family and cling to the same attitude, at least until adolescence.

Sex differences were marked. Qualities of the deity emphasized by girls were helpfulness and affection, while boys were more impressed with creativity and law making.

Intelligence did not conspicuously affect replies, except that ethical consideration for others was confined to the brightest.

Age differences, up to twelve, were found in vocabulary and in lesser naïveté about causality, but not in emotional tone. Older children often referred to Biblical figures, projecting themselves into the stories.

Religious teaching or lack thereof (four claimed, "Don't know, don't go to church") seemed not to obliterate expressions of emotional relationships except in those cases where correctness was used as a cover for total rejection of all authority.

Children's understandings of the deity are more complex and idiosyncratic than psychoanalytic theory has heretofore held.

REFERENCES

ALLPORT, G. The individual and his religion. New York: Macmillan, 1950.

FREUD, S. Totem and taboo. (Tr. by A. A. Brill.) New York: Moffat, Yard, 1918.

GRAEBNER, O. E. Child concepts of God. Yearbook, Lutheran Education Association, 1960, **17**.

NUNN, C. Z. Child-control through a "coalition with God." Child Development, 1964, **35**, 417–432.

STRANG, RUTH. Children's moral concepts: A tentative taxonomy. Education (Boston), 1964, **85**, 67–77.

Presently: Social scientists in the research directorate of the System Development Corporation in Santa Monica, California (since 1955).

Education: Beatrice received her Doctor of Philosophy degree in philosophy from Radcliffe College and Harvard University in 1955, while Sydney received his from Harvard University in 1941. Both studied philosophy at the Sorbonne and Collège de France also.

BEATRICE and
SYDNEY ROME

Current major activity: Humanistic research on large social organizations with live subjects in a computer-based laboratory.

Most rewarding project: "Formulating the next-generation Leviathan methodology to advance a humanistic-experimental science of large social organizations."

Personal histories: Beatrice: Member of Philosophy Department, College of William and Mary (1946–1955); System Development Corporation, (initially RAND Corporation) (1956).

Sydney: Special Research Associate in the Harvard Psycho-Acoustic Laboratory (1941–1942). Head of the Project Information Section in the research laboratory of the Polaroid Corporation (1942–1944). Administrative Coordinator of the research laboratory and Assistant to the President of the Sonotone Corporation (1944–1946). Lecturer at the New School for Social Research (1946). Member of Philosophy Department, College of William and Mary (1946–1955). At System Development Corporation the Drs. Rome have conceived, designed, developed, and administered the Leviathan project (which is described in their chapter here).

Writings: The Romes continue their contributions to philosophy as well as producing a steady stream of articles on their Leviathan program. Beatrice Rome wrote *The Philosophy of Malebranche: A Study of His Integration of Faith, Reason and Experimental Observation* (1963), and the Romes together edited *Philosophical Interrogations* (1964). Meantime, they have written a number of descriptions of their program—e.g., "Leviathan: An Experimental Study of Large Organizations with the Aid of Computers," in R. V. Bowers (Ed.), *Studies on Behavior in Organizations* (1966, pp. 257–311).

Present chapter: This presentation was written especially for this book.

Chapter 19
BEATRICE and SYDNEY ROME

HUMANISTIC RESEARCH
ON LARGE SOCIAL ORGANIZATIONS

THE LEVIATHAN METHOD

Over the past few years, we have been developing and perfecting a unique method studying the organization and government of large social organizations.[1] Our method, called *Leviathan,* comprises a humanistic theoretical framework, a system of computer programs, a series of experimental simulations in a laboratory (Figure 19–1), a repertory of experimental controls, and quantitative measurements of organizational performance. The simulations are conducted over a period of three months. They employ from twenty to thirty human subjects, who interact with hundreds of robots and with one another through a computer that operates on line and in real time. This humanistic-operational method enables us to help individual people to combine into effective, coherent, highly authentic social organizations and permits us to carry out experiments on the evolving social organisms.

We shall describe our conceptual framework, explain how we translate this framework into a program of experimental research, and discuss the history and outcome of two series of Leviathan experiments.

[1] Development of the formal and quantitative theoretical aspects of the Leviathan research program has been supported in part by the U.S. Air Force Office of Scientific Research (Information Sciences Directorate), of the office of Aerospace Research under Contract No. AF 49(638)–1188.

CONCEPTUAL FRAMEWORK

A Humanistic Approach Our conceptual framework for the study of large social organizations begins with a double affirmation. First, we affirm (neither deny nor reduce) what is distinctively human: Persons are (or can be) autonomous, freely creative, responsible, goal-oriented, active, intentional processes. These conational, volitional, telic processes, moreover, are self-transcendent. In *time,* human individuals reach beyond their immediate, specious now toward futurity; in *reality,* they reach beyond the historical-temporal finite to the infinite; in *community,* they reach beyond the separate ego to dialogue, to *I-Thou* communion and mutual participation—they seek to live and move and engage their being with others. As Buber writes: "Man exists anthropologically not in his isolation, but in the completeness of the relation between man and man; what humanity is can be properly grasped only in vital reciprocity" (1965, p. 84).

Second, we affirm that when humans do thus reach beyond themselves and become socially intertwined and interrelated, another distinctive and irreducible kind of reality can be discerned: corporate social organization. Corporate beings are just as truly real per se as humans are; they are not ontologically derivative from individuals. To be sure, social organizations mani-

181

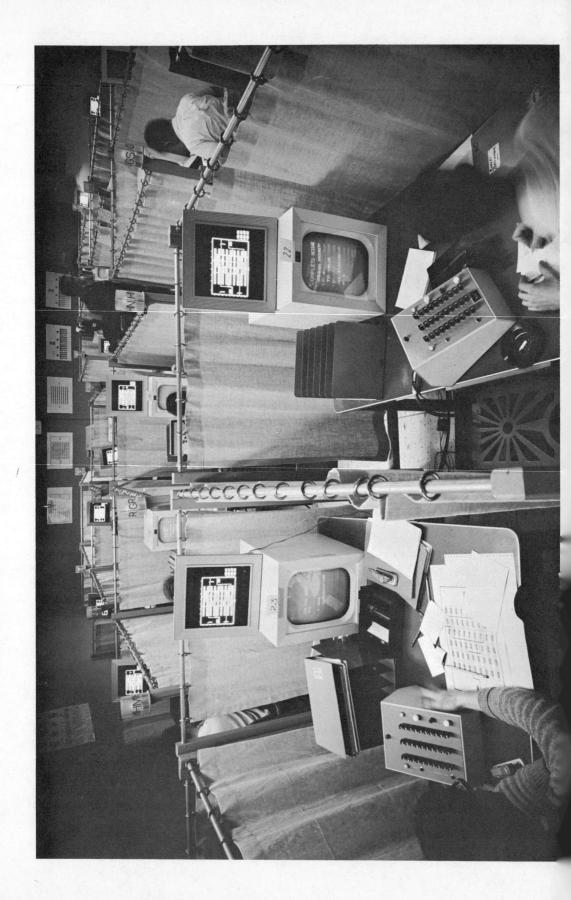

festly contain—even literally consist of—their individual human members and the social relations among these persons, and they are invented, established, and sustained by their members. But once launched, social organizations are more than mere multiplicities of selves or alters. They are ultimately real, have characteristic properties, and act in characteristic ways. Thus our double affirmation: Distinctively human and social beings both irreducibly exist, each in his or its own right, with neither having ontological primacy over the other.

Hierarchy Hence we have a paradox: Organizational life is made possible through the ontological reality of persons, but persons are not solipsists; they exist in and with others. This means that the ontological reality of organizations, in turn, makes possible the reality of persons. Persons are persons in virtue of existing in corporate social worlds. The two kinds of ultimate reality—corporate social identity and personal individual identity—interpenetrate each other. Each provides the raw material (social transactions) which the other synthesizes.

A dialectical, relational process resolves the tension and circularity of this paradoxical interinvolvement of the individual and the social—this is the hierarchical process. Hierarchy fuses individual and social identities into single nexuses, without dissolving the ultimate autonomy and irreducibility of either kind. What is social hierarchy?[2]

[2] Hierarchies of this kind present problems of fundamental importance for modern symbolic logic. A theoretical discussion of the failure of contemporary logic to represent their structure is contained in our "Formal Representation of Intentionally Structured Systems" (B. K. Rome & S. C. Rome, 1960). Earlier discussions are contained in our address to the Metaphysical Society of America, "Some Speculations concerning Intentionally Structured Systems" (B. K. Rome & S. C. Rome, 1956), and in the article "Some Formulae for Aesthetic Analysis" (S. C. Rome, 1954).

FIGURE 19–1   Leviathan laboratory operation in 1964. Twenty-one subjects, enacting officers' roles in a hierarchy of command, communicate with one another and with their robots by means of computer-tied push buttons and displays.

"Hierarchy" packs together a cluster of concepts. At minimum, a hierarchy is a tree structure. But a social hierarchy is more than just a tree; it is a complex organization. It includes different kinds of functional systems, each of which has its proper mission. These specialized partial systems are at once autonomous, interdependent, and overlapping. Each functional system exhibits a plurality of levels—levels of authority, of responsibility, and of accomplishment. These subordinate levels within a partial system are also at once autonomous, interdependent, and overlapping. Throughout a hierarchy there are diverse offices, each with status, role, prerogatives, spheres of influence, and effectiveness. The offices are knit together into the articulated functional systems by crisscrossing networks of interpenetrating authority, responsibility, communication, and information flow.

Thus, a hierarchy is a multiplicity of individual components pyramided together in a network of interrelationships and interinvolvements. But it is much more. By "hierarchy," we mean a united, single entity, self-contained, with a boundary or envelope. We do not mean a collection, aggregate, or combination of individual components taken distributively; we mean a solidary fusion. The ultimate components, individual persons, on the other hand, do not vanish into some undifferentiated blob or mass. Through self-transcendent transactions and intentional acts, autonomous persons in an organization relate themselves to one another by establishing, enrolling themselves in, and maintaining their hierarchy. A hierarchy, then, is an articulated, structured process, with many nexuses of unification and a recognizable social identity. It is an integral social individual, and it has a proper name, for example, the Air Force Office of Scientific Research.

A hierarchically structured social organism, moreover, exists in a maze of environments that challenge, buffet, exploit, and sustain it and its subsystems. At the same time, it provides its own inner environments to its subordinate subsystems. Within its envelope, its many agents influence one another; they also bargain, compete, and come to terms with one another.

Throughout a hierarchy, all leadership activities are bimodal. On every level, within and across every functional system, roles and offices merge and participate in one another's decisions, loyalties, and knowledge. There are no clear-cut lines of separation between leader and led, supervisor and supervised, initiator and follower. Policy, decisions, and evaluations can flow downward from the top; they can also be born on every intermediate level or swell from below.

Finally, a hierarchy is not simply a static, formal, morphological, or logical skeleton or pattern. It suffers the bite of time. Hierarchy is a process, a dialectical drama of tension and relaxation, of crises and stabilities. It has a history and a real future. It is open to change, growth, and decay. It can succeed and flourish, and it can fail and decline.

Decision The fate of every corporate hierarchy is therefore constantly at stake. Choice is the pivot of its existence. First, choice is inescapable. Commitments are constantly being made, even if only by default, by large numbers of individuals within an organization, acting in their official capacities and in the name of the organization. Second, the importance of choice does not lie merely in acts of commitment and dedication as such, but also in the modes, contents, and consequences of these acts. For social organizations, as for individual persons, transcendence is of the essence. With each organizational decision, what is at stake is not merely an organization's own present and future but the present and future of every individual now within it and to come, of every other organization on which it impinges, and of the total community in which it acts. Third, choice involves the continual renunciation of possibilities. Claims, obligations, and opportunities press in unending streams on the organization, originating from multiple sources without and from all levels within. How the organization goes about selecting from among all its possible futures and how it goes about

structuring, reconciling, exploiting, and creatively integrating its decisions into a total program of corporate action continually determine whether and what it shall become.

Hence corporate identity is, on every occasion, a matter of degree and of unending, never-completed struggle and striving. When choices are made inadequately, the hierarchy is threatened with some degree of dissolution, of loss of integration, of submergence of identity under the welter of internal and external competition. When, however, a corporate hierarchical process functions adequately, integrally, and responsibly, the organization tends to realize its potentialities. It may then be said to function in a highly *authentic* way.

Authenticity A hierarchical organization acts "authentically" to the extent, first of all, that, throughout the hierarchy, its decision makers adequately assess its internal and external environments: What is unalterably thrust upon them at each moment, beyond their capacity to alter? What are the organization's physical and human limitations, and what are its contingencies and risks? What claims and demands are being laid on the organization and its officers by components and individuals within the organization and by other hierarchies and other individuals? In addition to appraising these constraining conditions and limiting forces of organizational action, the corporate officers must also adequately appraise their freedoms, their potentials for action, and their corporate opportunities: Are they mobilizing their organization's human and physical resources adequately? What appropriate innovations can they effect and at what costs? What hitherto unenvisaged alternatives can they formulate? What can they inspire their organization to contribute to their community, nation, society?

A hierarchy, furthermore, should do more than merely appraise or assess itself and its environments. It should also face up to these, make decisions, and continually act. Such behavior also determines the organization's degree of authenticity: Does the leadership fail to acknowledge, and is it unwilling to remedy, failures? Is it blind to the inevitability of risk and error, failing to confront these or to convert them into opportunities? Does it retreat from responsibility, fail to shape organizational policy, let drift the organization's destiny, and remain indifferent to the organization's place in, and obligations to, society? Or do the leaders continually and sensitively reexamine, revise, readapt, and reaffirm corporate procedures, policies, norms, strategies, obligations, contributions, objectives, and achievements, as concrete conditions and situations require?

A hierarchical organization, in short, like an individual person, is "authentic" to the extent that, throughout its leadership, it accepts its finitude, uncertainty, and contingency; realizes its capacity for responsibility and choice; acknowledges guilt and errors; fulfills its creative managerial potential for flexible planning, growth, and charter or policy formation; and responsibly participates in the wider community.

Accomplishment Thus far we have stressed the notions of direction and path, of the *way* of corporate existing. Our emphases on choice, decision, commitment, and dedication, however, all point beyond organizational activity to that which organizations accomplish. For an organization to be dedicated or committed is for it to have particular, concrete uses, ends, and services. Doing, making, and performing must all express themselves: "The deed becomes proof of conviction" (Baeck, 1948, p. 56). The activity must congeal, come to fruit, yield something other than itself, even if this something is only another process. Organizational existence issues in denotable, describable, palpable *work*, in organizational performance. The importance to corporate life of such work in progress is signalized by the fact that many organizations identify themselves with their principal service or product—the World Health Organization, the Federal Bureau of Investigation, the United States Steel Corporation, for example. Furthermore, organizational effort must yield not only a product or a service but also a valuable product or a valuable service. "Fruitfulness alone does not suffice; the test is the quality of the fruit brought forth."[3] For indeed, from the worth or value or utility of an organization's product or service are derived

the importance and seriousness of its decisions, its striving, and its choices.

In our conceptual framework, accordingly, we pinpoint two kinds of organizational activity—acts of choosing and acts of producing—and two kinds of excellence —authenticity of the choosing and effectiveness of the producing.

PROGRAM OF EXPERIMENTAL RESEARCH

Research Objectives The foregoing conceptual framework establishes our program of experimental research. We bring very large organizations into simulated life in our laboratory. We attempt to grow and develop highly effective organizations and to grow and develop highly authentic organizations.

Our basic hypothesis is that the two kinds of organizations are closely related: The more authentically an organization acts, the more effective is its system performance. Conversely, the more effectively it performs, the more authentic will its choices be. This two-sided hypothesis is not a tautology. There are many alternative ways for an organization to be authentic and many ways to be effective, and from highly authentic organizational activity many kinds of effective performance can issue.

Excellence, however, is almost never an accident. Spinoza's words apply: "All things excellent are as difficult as they are rare" (1951, p. 271). The achievement of excellence by any large organization must surely be related to how it conducts itself. The relation between *modes of functioning* and *effectiveness* in large organizations, then, is an open and important question that can be decided only empirically, by testing.

Our research objective is to determine whether organizations that meet our criteria of high authenticity are exceptionally effective and whether unusually effective organizations qualify as highly authentic. Accordingly we ask: How *do* highly effective organizations actually carry on their hierarchical and governing activities? Are there distinct modes of coordination characteristic of different levels of accomplishment, given specific internal and external environmental

[3] Attributed by Martin Buber (1958, p. 6) to Rabbi Yaacob Yitzchak, the "Seer" of Lublin (d. 1815).

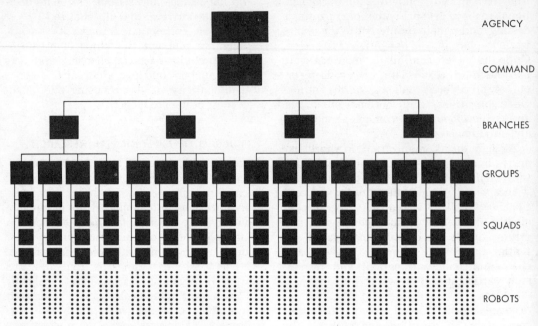

AGENCY

COMMAND

BRANCHES

GROUPS

SQUADS

ROBOTS

FIGURE 19–2   Six-level hierarchy simulated in
the 1963 and 1964 Leviathan
experiments.

conditions? Can interrelationships be established between modes of executive transaction and bureaucratic accomplishment? What are these, and how do they operate?

Given this research objective, we shall now explain how we have translated our humanistic conceptual framework into overt operations in a computer-based laboratory—how we formulated our simulations, what experimental techniques we used, and how we conducted our initial experiments.

Laboratory Simulation: The Concrete Myth
For our experiments, we designed, produced, and adapted a system of computer programs to represent a six-level hierarchy with the formal structure shown in Figure 19–2. With our subjects, we adopt the myth that this bureaucracy is the Intelligence Communications Control Center in the National Intelligence Agency. At the lowest level are the enlisted personnel, 704 robots that exist in the computer programs. The robots are grouped into sixty-four working squads. Directing the squads are live officers plus their staff assistants. The live officers are the sixteen group leaders, four branch heads, and the commanding officer. The entire center reports to the National Intelligence Agency. Graduate students enact the roles of the live officers. The National Intelligence Agency is simulated by the experimenters.

Our myth asserts that this center receives intelligence communiqués from all parts of the world; its mission is to process these quickly and efficiently, but in accordance with their degree of importance, and then to transmit them to various governmental agencies. In this way, the environment of the center is defined. This environment consists of (1) consumers who lay competing demands upon the center for prompt service or output and who demand that the communiqués be filtered in accordance with their importance to the competing consumers; (2) the senders of communiqués, who supply the center with its input, that is, the raw materials for its productive work, and who themselves also assess the importance of the contents of the communiqués; (3) the center's own inner formal and extraformal web of relations channels of communication, and internal criteria for evaluating communiqués; and (4) the center's supervening, embedding authority, the National Intelligence Agency.

The subjects' task is to manage their center. This managerial mission can be broad and varied, from establishing long-range policies and contingency plans to erecting norms and mechanisms for adjudicating internal and external conflicts and grievances and to exercising the more narrowly technical controls—allocating their resources of robot manpower, setting production quotas, assigning priorities, and dispatching the communiqués through the center.

During an experiment, the officer-subjects transact their managerial responsibilities and obligations in three modes of communication: (1) face-to-face conversation in small or large groupings, around a conference table—this mode usually takes place at the option of the subjects and at times of their own choosing, but the duration of the conference is limited by the experimenters; (2) handwritten messages which couriers deliver to addressed subjects in their individual private offices; and (3) messages composed by the subjects over the computer—these are constructed in ordinary English by means of push buttons and computer-driven displays (see Figure 19–1), recorded by the computer, displayed on addressees' display scopes, and delivered in printed form to senders and recipients for future reference.

It goes without saying that all communication from live officer-subjects to the robots in the computer takes place by means of the push buttons and display scopes, but again in natural English.

Laboratory Simulation: Abstract, General Elements The Leviathan laboratory simulation is supported by a complex, very large system of computer programs.[4] Whereas the simulation, as operated by the subjects in the laboratory, is concrete and specific, the computer programs that support the simulation have been designed and executed in

entirely general terms. Hence it is possible to simulate different varieties of large bureaucracies with them, e.g., the management of a school system, of a United Nations project office, or of an industrial manufacturing plant.

The complete generality of the computer programs, furthermore, guarantees that the basic formulation that underlies all our simulations is abstract and general. Hence the results of experiments performed with any one concrete, specific myth are, without further refinement, generalizable to many other possible concrete organizations.

In point of fact, seven basic elements essential to all large hierarchical organizations are incorporated in the computer programs: (1) structures of formal authority and (2) a technological or productive system, with (3) a productive task; (4) continual interaction with competing, impinging external environments; (5) a hierarchically structured system of information feedback reports to assess the effectiveness of system and component performance; and (6) various communication media that (7) permit and invite policy formation and decision making in both formal and extra-formal contexts. These seven basic elements of bureaucracy, accordingly, underlie any specific Leviathan myth and any concrete laboratory simulation.

Experimental Controls What happens in the ongoing life of simulated social hierarchies issues, as in the real world, partly from within, from their own immanent self-determination, and partly from without, from how their environments impinge upon them. But in the laboratory, the environmental influences that help shape the growth of organizations can be rather rigorously structured and controlled. As experimenters, therefore, we can direct and cultivate the evolution of a simulated bureaucracy to a great extent.

Conduct of Experiments Not everything is under the experimenter's control, however. Indeed, a major feature of a Leviathan laboratory simulation is its dialogic character.

---

[4] The Leviathan computer programs have been realized principally by Mildred Almquist and Robert E. Krouss.

Subjects and experimenters act as two distinct social forces that mutually influence each other during the progress of an experiment.

As the subjects, in their roles as officers, manage and control their intelligence center, they provide us with clues to their organizational development. They do so in two ways: first by discussing, coordinating, organizing, and planning their actions, and second by making their technological system perform. Both types of subjects' responses are constantly monitored. With respect to subjects' interactions or transactions, some are directly observed from behind one-way glass and are recorded on sound tape, some are incorporated in handwritten messages, and others take place over the computer and are observed and recorded through it. With respect to technological performance, this all takes place exclusively over the computer. It is measured precisely and quantitatively, at both component and system levels, in terms of temporal flow of work, filtering of more important from less important work, distribution of flow over the processing network, productivity, utilization of resources of robot energy, and the like.

As an experiment progresses, we continually seek evidence that the subjects are moving both to more authentic action and to more effective performance. We attempt to assess which tendencies are likely to inhibit the subjects' twofold development and which are likely to further it, and accordingly we either resist or encourage the directions in which the subjects are developing. This we do by enacting the roles of suppliers, consumers, supervening bureaucratic authority, and impinging cultural influences. Thus an ever-progressing spiral is established between subjects and experimenters, in which a mutual monitoring or balancing-counterbalancing interaction takes place. Each thrust attempted by the experimenters can be assessed by the subsequent conduct and achievement of the subjects.

Our efforts toward eliciting ever-greater organizational authenticity do not imply that we have fixed preconceptions concerning what forms authenticity necessarily must take. Authenticity does not consist in some ultimate quality or set of qualities which can be scaled, calculated, and mathematically optimized.[5] The criteria of authenticity offered above have all been heuristic only; each criterion subsequently has to be applied in the concrete given context of responsible choice.

HISTORY OF TWO EXPERIMENTAL RUNS

Thus far, two large-scale series of Leviathan experiments have been performed, the first in 1963 and the second in 1964. Each series spanned more than 120 laboratory hours and consisted of five consecutive runs. The conduct and accomplishments of the two groups were strikingly different, as we shall see.

With both groups we used developmental techniques that, taken one by one, were for the most part similar in kind and in aim. These techniques helped to set the scene, identify the unique wholeness of the organization, provide a systemic point of view, and define the policies toward which the organization does and should aspire— in short, these techniques help to develop the group's corporate identity or image, what some call the "organizational charter," and to enhance its corporate authenticity. Fewer varieties of techniques were used in 1963 than in 1964, however, and were introduced more gradually; and the spiral of dialogic interaction that emerged between subjects and experimenters in 1963 was very different from that in 1964. We attribute the differences in the conduct and accomplishments of the 1963 and the 1964 subjects to the differences in the manner in which we, as experimenters, intervened.

[5] Cf. John Wild's reply to Brand Blanshard's query in *Philosophical Interrogations* concerning the existence of "natural tendencies" and his answers to our questions concerning the ethics of freedom and the notion of an "authentic monster": "Questions of this sort forget the finiteness of human existence, which is limited always by suffering, physical and social dependence, conflict, guilt, chance and death. These limits cannot be adequately understood as determinate properties of the human organism which require fixed kinds of action for a natural realization" (B. K. Rome & S. C. Rome, 1964, pp. 123–131).

The First 1963 Experiment From the outset of our 1963 experiments, deliberately minimal instruction was provided to the subjects. In their first formal meeting, following quick self-introductions, they were exposed, by our briefing officer,[6] to an organization chart; they were told the names of the offices on the chart; they were told what the chart represented; and they were made sketchily aware of the technological or productive system and of the productive task of the center. Thereupon, with no further guidance or training concerning their managerial roles in the system of their goals, obligations, or mission, the subjects were plunged into the uncharted task of managing the center.

Thus the experimental setting for initiating the 1963 subjects into their responsibilities was one of almost total ignorance and uncertainty. No genuine dialogic encounter had taken place between subjects and experimenters. No explicitly stated demands, commands, directives, or covenantal obligations were laid upon the subjects. In the language of Buber, our 1963 subjects were treated more as manipulable objects than as genuine partners in an I-Thou confrontation.

During the first ten simulated days of operation, system performance was initially low and continued to fall, until it became nearly extinct. Then we intervened with three steps:

1 We convened the subjects in a face-to-face debriefing, conducted by the briefing officer.

2 The briefing officer presented to the subjects exactly the same feedback information that they had already received, but now trended over the entire course of previous play and aggregated to the total system level.

3 The briefing officer repeatedly gave the subjects a single but direct exhortation: "Emphasize the system point of view!"

Before the close of the session, cries could be heard: "Seems each branch is just looking after its own." "To hell with *you*, Jack, I'm all right." "I don't think it's the problem between the groups and their branches.

6 The 1963 Leviathan briefing officer and laboratory manager was Richard Knight.

I think it's the *interbranch* communication which is causing the problem." With this new awareness of the need for reciprocal, interdependent action, of the responsibility of each to be his brother's keeper, the subjects resumed operations. Thereafter, they achieved improvements in performance ranging between 250 and 300-plus percent.

Subsequent 1963 Experiments In the four subsequent 1963 experimental runs, we progressively enriched the systemic and normative elements of the simulation by successively taking the following steps:

1 We forced the subjects to reorganize their administrative structure in such a way as to promote a deeper understanding of their responsibilities to one another and of potential contributions to the total organization's objectives.

2 We introduced quantified "crisis scenarios" to induce a sense of common threat.

3 We eliminated almost all computer-generated quantitative information feedback at the component levels, but provided overall system reports and component failure reports. This served to encourage the subjects to try to improve system performance, while, at the component levels, they could continue to manage by exception, that is, try to avoid failures.

4 Next, we again forced the subjects to reorganize in such a way as to cut the line command between branch and group levels. This compelled greater cross-level and intergroup coordination and communication.

5 Finally, we introduced into the computer-based intercommunication language sets of prestructured reasons which the subjects could use to justify their command decisions and which therefore served as cues to elicit more responsibility in their decision making.

Each of these successive steps resulted in appreciable improvement in system performance. After the sixtieth simulated day, however, the 1963 subjects reached a ceiling in their ability to improve. We concluded that the 1963 group could not advance further without accomplishing what in Biblical terms would be called a "turning": They would have to purge themselves of their established bureaucratic habits and aspirations and embrace radically different values and objectives and a radically different organizational charter. Since our contracts with the subjects were running out, we terminated the 1963 experiments at the close of the ninety-eighth simulated day and resolved to start again with a new group.

Initiation of the 1964 Subjects For our 1964 experiments, we created a radically new initiatory setting. Unlike the swift, abrupt, icy, directionless, and minimally instructive initiation of the 1963 subjects, the introductory treatment of the 1964 subjects was prolonged, intensive, solicitously attentive, directed, and comprehensively informative.

Starting with the first experimental session and continuing intermittently over sixteen laboratory hours, the subjects received a series of elaborate technical briefings. Each subject received his briefing individually, in the privacy of his own office, by means of a computer-based teaching machine that he operated at his own pace and under his own control. The briefings addressed and spoke directly to him: "Make the next display appear . . . ," "You will view . . . ," "You now know . . . ," "Use. . . ."

The very first briefing declared the purpose of each subject's presence in the laboratory: "You are here to enact the role of an officer in a military communications processing center." It continued by unfolding the nature, structure, and organization of his center, and it developed fully the subject's overall responsibilities, obligations, authority, and power. Subsequent briefings spelled out in detail the technical operations and multiple controls of the center.

By thus unfolding the total bureaucratic scene, the teaching machine served to make each subject aware that he was being invited to enter into a community of responsibility with his fellow participants in the adjoining offices; he was not alone.

To further this sense of community, at the end of each briefing sequence, the subjects—now become officer-trainees—assembled in face-to-face meeting to discuss among themselves the contents of their briefings.[7] To facilitate learning, to give point and focus to their conversations, to promote active cooperation in a useful task right from the start of the experimental series, and to enable them to come to know something of one another's potentialities, they were requested to construct in these meetings a jointly agreed-upon glossary of terms occurring in the briefings. At the officer-trainees' own initiation and request, these glossary-making sessions were conducted under a succession of temporary chairmen and recording secretaries, elected by the subjects themselves in voice votes.

In the course of this training period, the officer-trainees received ample warning that, in due time, they were to be given the opportunity, and were expected, to elect permanent officers from among themselves, who would manage their center. Just before the indoctrination period was ended, this election took place in three successive, ever-narrowing winnowings of candidates.

Throughout their induction, subjects were encouraged by the briefing officer to raise technical questions with him or to communicate directly, by means of handwritten messages, with the technical staff of their embedding agency, the National Intelligence Agency, actually enacted, of course, by ourselves as experimenters. Unlike the briefing officer in the 1963 experiments, who deliberately served as a "noisy" channel of communication between subjects and experimenters, the briefing officer in 1964 made elaborate preparations in advance for his involvements with the subjects. As a consequence, he was able to provide intensive technical guidance, while carefully protecting the experimental design. Moreover, he was able to establish the boundaries of technical question raising on the part of the subjects, in such a way that the very boundaries became spurs to the subjects to use their own initiative and to decide matters for themselves. To each carefully timed "No comment" or "Use your own judgment" on his part, the subjects responded with warm laughter and an attitude of "Let's think it out for ourselves."

[7] Briefing officer and laboratory manager in 1964 was Stanley Terebinski.

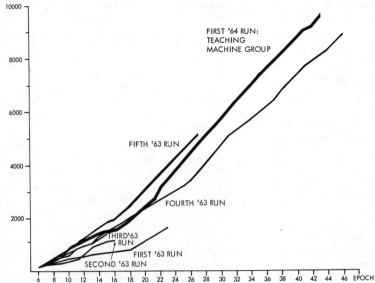

FIGURE 19–3 Cumulative productivity of the
first 1964 run compared with
that of the 1963 runs.

Throughout these initiation rites, and indeed thereafter, the briefing officer conveyed a sense of prophetic mission, of having been called upon to perform a significant service, and in turn, of calling upon the subjects to share this enterprise. As revealed in postexperimental interviews, from the moment of selection and arrival the subjects came to see themselves as participants with the experimenters in a joint, serious, significant endeavor, not just as paid employees in some alien researcher's experiment.[8]

A subsequent minute analysis of the 3,000 utterances made by the individual subjects during the period of indoctrination and of the events that took place therein indicates that a very rapid series of transformations occurred in the group. This period began with twenty-eight separate "alters"—individual subjects almost all unknown to one another—and, sixteen phases later, culminated in a nascent but strongly cohesive, highly enthusiastic, and solidary group, set and ready to take over the management of the center.

Performance and Organizational Conduct in 1964 Performance of this group in the very first 1964 experimental run is shown in Figure 19–3, wherein it is compared with the achievements of the 1963 group in all its five successive runs. Right from the start, the cumulative productivity of the 1964 group was as good as, or better than, that of the 1963 group, except in its very best performance. Indeed, the performance of the 1964 group began near where that of the 1963 group terminated! We attribute these marked initial gains to the mode in which the 1964 group was indoctrinated.

As the 1964 experiments subsequently ran their course, the performance of the 1964 group continued to rise. It was still rising when we terminated! As a matter of fact, we were unable to establish what, precisely, could be defined as a ceiling on the 1964 subjects' ability to perform. Eventually, their performance rose to levels twice those of *any* 1963 performance, although their economic resources were not increased over those of the 1963 group.

[8] See related discussion by Jourard in Chapter 12. [Editor]

The 1963 and 1964 groups differed markedly not only in achievement but also in organizational conduct. The 1963 group, in reaching its ceiling on performance, seemed also to have reached a limit on developing its managerial activities. In contrast, the 1964 subjects began at once to invent ways of transacting their bureaucratic process, starting with their first face-to-face meeting as a working group in training. The sixteen distinct phases through which the 1964 group developed during the indoctrination sessions were only the beginning of a most intensive subsequent elaboration of hierarchical process. Examples are:

1 The 1964 group spontaneously created many new administrative functions—administrative aids to the commanding officer and to the branch heads, a technical aid to devise optimal contingency strategies for allocating manpower resources in times of crisis, an assistant to plot and report on trends in output, roving specialists whose task was to move from office to office in order to solicit key data and to offer technical advice, tutors for incompetents, and specialists who lectured the others in areas of their specialization.

2 The 1964 group voluntarily undertook many new responsibilities beyond official obligations—many members arrived early; many members remained late for technical discussions; other members arranged for private strategy sessions outside the laboratory environment; and some brought from home written plans and suggestions for improving performance and the center's activities.

3 Right at the start of their managerial operations, the 1964 subjects successfully overruled their commanding officer when he suggested that all communications go through official channels, and they thus established free access to one another, both formally and informally. They held lengthy conferences in groups of all sizes—commanding officer and branch officers, branch officers and group heads, group heads with a common responsibility, or all meeting as a committee of the whole. Conflicts and debates were lively and frequent, but these were almost all quickly resolved, and usually they allowed the commanding officer the final word.

4 Few actions were taken without carefully preplanned preparation and discussion, but also frequently the management, both as a whole and individually, deliberately made trial-and-error probes.

5 The 1964 group elaborated many extra-formal roles: elder statesman, sagacious counselor, technical expert. Equally it developed factions, lobbies, and other social mechanisms for weathering internal moral crises.

6 Whereas the 1963 group preferred to operate with far less and far simpler computer-produced information feedback reports than they could actually have received, the 1964 group constantly welcomed additional information. This group, moreover, put the feedback information reports to more subtle use. The 1963 group used reports of failures within the technological system (exception reports) to "put out fires" but the 1964 group used the identical reports as prearranged triggers to call into operation contingency plans that they had previously established in anticipation of possible failures.

Thus, throughout their entire history, the 1964 subjects, in contrast to those in 1963, operated as a farsighted, long-range policy-planning group that subordinated administrative control to positive, risk-taking, innovative command objectives. It faced its contingencies and errors, accepted responsibilities, and fulfilled, to a high degree, its creative managerial potential. We therefore infer that the 1964 group realized a more highly authentic hierarchical process than the 1963 group.

CONCLUSION

Data analysis of both series of experiments is still in progress. On the basis of evidence already culled, nevertheless, it appears that our hypothesis concerning the reciprocity between degree of authentic organizational behavior and level of organizational performance has received preliminary but vivid experimental corroboration. This hypothesis will be put to more explicit testing in a series of experiments projected for 1967 to 1969.

No less important than the experimental support for our basic hypothesis is the confirmation of our Leviathan methodology: Our 1963 and 1964 experiments demonstrate, by the fact that they have been successfully performed, that the organization and government of large social hierarchies can now be both humanistically conceived and experimentally investigated and, moreover, that a humanistic-operational science of organizational behavior is now possible.

REFERENCES[9]

BAECK, L. *The essence of Judaism.* New York: Schocken, 1948.

BUBER, M. *For the sake of heaven.* Cleveland: World Publishing, 1958.

BUBER, M. *The knowledge of man.* (Ed. by M. Friedman.) New York: Harper & Row, 1965.

ROME, BEATRICE K., & ROME, S. C. Some speculations concerning intentionally structured systems. Address to Plenary Session, Metaphysical Society of America, March 24, 1956. (Document SP–14, System Development Corporation, Santa Monica, Calif., 1956.)

ROME, BEATRICE K., & ROME, S. C. Formal representation of intentionally structured systems. In A. Kent (Ed.), *Information retrieval and machine translation.* New York: Interscience, 1960.

ROME, BEATRICE K., & ROME, S. C. *Philosophical interrogations: Interrogations of Martin Buber, John Wild, Jean Wahl, Brand Blanshard, Paul Weiss, Charles Hartshorne, Paul Tillich.* New York: Holt, Rinehart and Winston, 1964.

ROME, S. C. Some formulae for aesthetic analysis. *Review of Metaphysics,* 1954, **8**, 357–365.

SPINOZA, B. The ethics. In R. H. M. Elwes (Ed. and Trans.), *The chief works of Benedict de Spinoza.* Vol. 2. New York: Dover, 1951.

[9] Current documentation of the Leviathan project is contained in Herold, V. P., *Bibliography of Project Leviathan Documents.* Document TM–983/000/02, System Development Corporation, Santa Monica, Calif., 1966.

Presently: Foundations' Fund for Research in Psychiatry Associate Professor in the Department of Psychiatry of the Yale University School of Medicine (since 1961).

Education: Doctor of Medicine from the New York Medical College (1948).

Current major activity: At work on a comprehensive, book-length report on his studies of the Hiroshima disaster.

ROBERT JAY LIFTON

Personal history: Interned at the Jewish Hospital of Brooklyn (1948–1949). Psychiatric Residency at the State University Medical Center at New York and in the Veterans Administration program at Northport and Brooklyn (1949–1951). Psychiatrist in the Air Force in this country, in Korea, and in Japan (1951–1953). Research Associate of the Asia Foundation (1954). Member of the faculty of the Washington School of Psychiatry (1954–1955). Research Psychiatrist at the Walter Reed Army Institute of Research (1956). Research Associate in Psychiatry and Associate in East Asian Studies at Harvard University (1955–1961). Research Associate in Psychiatry at Tokyo University (1960–1961). Diplomate of the National Board of Medical Examiners (1949). Candidate of the Boston Psychoanalytic Institute (1957–1960). Consultant of the Behavioral Sciences Study Section of the National Institute of Mental Health (since 1962). Member of the Council on East Asian Studies, Yale University (since 1964).

Writings: "Youth and History: Individual Change in Postwar Japan" (*Daedalus*, 1962, **91**, 172–197); "Psychological Effects of the Atomic Bomb in Hiroshima: The Theme of Death" (*Daedalus*, 1963, **92**, 462–497); and "Individual Patterns in Historical Change: Imagery of Japanese Youth," in D. McK. Rioch (Ed.), *Disorders in Communication*, Vol. 42, *Proceedings of the Association for Research in Nervous and Mental Disease* (1964). Dr. Lifton is also the author of *Thought Reform and the Psychology of Totalism: A Study of "Brain-washing" in China* (hard cover, 1961; paperback, 1963).

Present chapter: This is an adaptation and abridgment of a paper with a similar title which was first presented at the American Psychiatric Association in Los Angeles, May 7, 1964, and was published in *Psychiatry* (1964, **27**, 191–210). It appears here with permission of William Alanson White Psychiatric Foundation, Inc., holders of the world copyright.

Chapter 20

ROBERT JAY LIFTON

ON DEATH AND DEATH SYMBOLISM:
THE HIROSHIMA DISASTER

The larger a human event, the more its significance eludes us. In the case of Hiroshima's encounter with the atomic bomb —surely a tragic turning point in man's psychological and historical experience— the meaning is perhaps only now beginning to reveal itself. Yet the event has much to teach us that is of considerable value in our struggles to cope with a world altered much more than we realize, and made infinitely more threatening, by the existence of nuclear weapons. In this chapter I shall describe a portion of a larger study of the psychological effects of the atomic bomb in Hiroshima.[1] I shall focus upon what I believe to be the central psychological issue in both the actual disaster and its wider symbolism—the problem of death and dying. The work represents a continuation of an

The study was supported by research funds from the Department of Psychiatry, Yale University. Colleagues and friends from the various divisions of Hiroshima University (particularly the Research Institute for Nuclear Medicine and Biology), the Hiroshima City Office, and many other groups in the city lent indispensable help in making arrangements; and Miss Kyoko Komatsu and Mr. Kaoru Ogura provided skillful and dedicated research assistance throughout. I have published one earlier, more general paper on the work (Lifton, 1963a), and the present chapter draws upon a more comprehensive book-length report now in preparation.

effort, begun ten years ago, to develop a modified psychoanalytic research approach to broad historical problems.

There are many reasons why the study of death and death symbolism has been relatively neglected in psychiatry and psychoanalysis. Not only does the subject arouse emotional resistances in the investigator— all too familiar, though extraordinarily persistent nonetheless—but it confronts him with an issue of a magnitude far beyond his empathic and intellectual capacities. Yet whatever the difficulties, the nuclear age provides both urgent cause and vivid stimulus for new efforts to enhance our understanding of what has always been man's ineradicable problem. Certainly no study of an event like the Hiroshima disaster can be undertaken without some exploration of that problem.

I conducted the study over a six-month period, from April to September, 1962, mostly in Hiroshima itself. It consisted primarily of individual interviews with two groups of atomic-bomb survivors: one group of thirty-three chosen at random from the list of more than ninety thousand survivors (or *hibakusha*),[2] and an additional

[2] *Hibakusha* is a coined word, which is by no means an exact equivalent of "survivor" (or "survivors"), but means, literally, "explosion-affected person"

group of forty-two survivors specially selected because of their prominence in dealing with atomic-bomb problems or their capacity to articulate their experiences—including physicians, university professors, city officials, politicians, writers and poets, and leaders of survivor organizations and peace movements.

Interviews generally lasted two hours, and I tried to see each research subject twice, though I saw some three or four times, and others just once. They were conducted in Japanese, with a research assistant always present to interpret; the great majority (particularly with subjects in the randomly selected group) were tape-recorded, always with the subject's consent. While I attempted to cover a number of basic questions with all research subjects, I encouraged them to associate freely to whatever ideas and emotions were brought up.

I wish to explore in this paper the psychological elements of what may be referred to as the permanent encounter with death which the atomic bomb created within those exposed to it. I shall discuss, in sequence, four different stages of experience with death, that is, four aspects of this encounter. Under examination, therefore, will be shared individual responses to an atmosphere permeated by death. Then, in the latter portion of the chapter, I will attempt to suggest a few general principles in the difficult area of the psychology of death and dying, essentially derived from this investigation but by no means limited to the Hiroshima experience.

IMMERSION IN DEATH

The immersion in death directly following the bomb's fall began with the terrible array of dead and near-dead in the midst of which each survivor found himself. Important here was the extreme sense of surprise and unpreparedness. Survivors were unpre-

pared because, following an air-raid alarm, an all-clear signal was sounded just a few minutes before the bomb fell; because of the psychological sense of invulnerability all people tend to possess, even in the face of danger; and because of the total inability of anyone to anticipate a weapon of such unprecedented dimensions. The number of deaths, both immediate and over a period of time, will probably never be fully known. Variously estimated at from 63,000 to 240,000 or more, the official figure is usually given as 78,000, although the city of Hiroshima estimates 200,000. The enormous disparity is related to the extreme confusion at the time, to differing methods of calculation, and to underlying emotional influences, quite apart from mathematical considerations, which have at times affected the estimators. But the point here is that anyone exposed relatively near the center of the city could not escape the sense of ubiquitous death around him—a result of the blast itself, of radiant heat, and of ionizing radiation. For instance, if a survivor was within 1,000 meters (0.6 miles) from the hypocenter and out of doors (that is without benefit of shielding from heat or radiation), more than nine-tenths of the people around him died; and if he was unshielded at 2,000 meters (1.2 miles), more than eight of ten people around him were killed. For those indoors, mortality was lower; but even then, in order to have even a 50 percent chance of escaping both death and injury, one had to be about 2,200 meters (1.3) miles from the hypocenter.[3] Therefore, the most significant psychological feature at this point was the sense of a sudden and absolute shift from normal existence to an overwhelming encounter with death.

Psychic Closing-off This encounter with death was so overwhelming that many would have undoubtedly been unable to avoid psychosis were it not for an extremely widespread and effective defense mechanism which I shall refer to as *psychic closing-off*

(or people) and conveys in feeling a little more than merely having encountered the bomb and a little less than having experienced definite physical injury from it.

[3] See particularly Oughterson and Shields (1956) for detailed studies of early mortality. Other sources for overall mortality estimates are listed in Lifton (1963a, p. 492). Without here attempting to enter into the complexities of mortality estimates, one may say that it is significant that Japanese estimates are consistently higher than American ones

In the face of grotesque evidences of death and near-death, people—sometimes within seconds or minutes—simply ceased to feel. They had a clear sense of what was happening around them, but their emotional reactions were unconsciously turned off.

A physicist, observing this process in himself, compared it to an overexposed photographic plate. A clerk who witnessed others dying around him at a temporary first-aid area reached a point where "I just couldn't have any reaction. . . . You might say I became insensitive to human death." And a woman writer described "a feeling of paralysis that came over my mind."

The unconscious process here is that of closing oneself off from death itself; the controlling inner idea, or fantasy, is, "If I feel nothing, then death is not taking place." Psychic closing-off is thus related to the defense mechanisms of denial and isolation, as well as to the behavioral state of apathy. But it deserves to be distinguished from these in its sudden global quality, in its throwing out of a protective symbolic screen which enables the organism to resist the impact of death, that is, to survive psychologically in the midst of death and dying. It may well represent man's most characteristic response to catastrophe: one which is at times life-enhancing or even, psychologically speaking, life-saving but which at other times, particularly when prolonged and no longer appropriate to the threat, is not without its own dangers. Certainly the investigator of nuclear disaster finds himself experiencing a measure of such closing-off, as indeed does the reader of an account such as this one.[4]

Effective as it is, psychic closing-off has its limitations, even as a protective reaction. It cannot succeed in entirely neutralizing either the threatening stimuli from without or those from within—the latter taking the

[4] In my previous paper (Lifton, 1963a), I referred to this defensive maneuver as "psychological closure" and mentioned some of its wider implications for survivors, its necessity for me in carrying out the investigation, and its relationship to attitudes concerning nuclear weapons in general. The term "psychic closing-off," however, more directly conveys the threefold process involved: numbing of affect, symbolic walling-off of the organism, and abrupt disconnection in communication between inner and outer worlds.

form of self-condemnation, guilt, and shame. For at the very beginning of the atomic-bomb experience, a need was initiated in each survivor for justifying his own survival in the face of others' deaths, a form of guilt which has plagued the survivors from then on and to which I shall return. Here I shall say only that the quick experience of self-condemnation intensified the lasting imprint of death created by this early phase of atomic-bomb exposure. Contained within this imprint was something very close to witnessing in actuality that which ordinarily takes place only in psychotic fantasy, namely, an end-of-the-world experience. Normally a projection of inner psychological "death" onto the outside world, the process was here reversed, so that an overwhelming external experience of near-absolute destruction became internalized and merged with related tendencies of the inner life.

A type of memory which symbolizes this relationship of death to guilt appears in what I have called the *ultimate horror*—a specific image of the dead or dying with which the survivor strongly identifies himself and which evokes in him particularly intense feelings of pity and self-condemnation. The scene may include his own family members, anonymous people in particularly grotesque physical array, or, as was frequent, pitiful images of women and children, universal symbols of purity and vulnerability, and especially so in Japanese culture.

INVISIBLE CONTAMINATION

The second encounter with death took the form of invisible contamination. After the bomb fell—sometimes within hours or even minutes, often during the first twenty-four hours, and sometimes during the following days and weeks—many *hibakusha* began to notice in themselves and others a strange form of illness. It consisted of nausea, vomiting, and loss of appetite; diarrhea with large amounts of blood in the stools; fever and weakness; purple spots on various parts of the body, caused by bleeding into the skin (purpura); inflammation and ulceration of the mouth, throat, and gums (ora-pharyngeal lesions and gingivitis); bleeding from the mouth, gums, nose, throat, rectum, and urinary tract (hemorrhagic manifestations); loss of hair from the scalp and other parts of the body (epilation); and extremely low white blood-cell counts when these were taken (leukopenia)—these symptoms in many cases taking a progressive course until death. Such manifestations of irradiation and the fatalities associated with them aroused a special terror in the people of Hiroshima, an image of a weapon which not only instantaneously kills and destroys on a colossal scale but also leaves behind, in the bodies of those exposed to it, deadly influences which may emerge at any time and strike down its victims. This image was made particularly vivid by the delayed appearance of these radiation effects—often two to four weeks after the bomb fell—in people who had previously seemed to be in perfect health, externally untouched by atomic-bomb effects.

No one at first had any understanding of the cause of the symptoms, and in the few medical facilities that were still functioning, isolation procedures were instituted in the belief that they were part of some kind of infectious gastrointestinal condition.[5] Ordinary people also suspected some form of epidemic, possibly in the nature of cholera. But very quickly, partly by word-of-mouth information and misinformation about the atomic bomb, people began to relate the condition to a mysterious "poison" emanating from the weapon itself. Whatever their idea of cause, survivors were profoundly impressed, not only by the fact that others were dying around them, but by the way in which they died—a gruesome form of rapid bodily deterioration which seemed unrelated to more usual and "decent" forms of death. They were struck particularly by the loss of scalp hair, by the purple spots on the skin, and (whether or not this was always true) by the way in which victims ap-

peared to remain conscious and alert almost to the moment of their death.

The psychological aspects of the second encounter with death may thus be summarized as follows: There was a fear of epidemic contamination to the point of bodily deterioration; a sense of individual powerlessness in the face of an invisible, all-enveloping, and highly mysterious poison (and in regard to this mysteriousness, there has been some evidence of psychological resistance toward finding out the exact nature of radiation effects); and a sense, often largely unconscious and indirectly communicated, that this total contamination—seemingly limitless in time and space—must have a supernatural, or at least more-than-natural, origin, must be something in the nature of a curse upon one's group for some form of wrongdoing that had offended the forces which control life and death. This latter formulation was occasionally made explicit in, for instance, survivors' Buddhistic references to misbehavior in previous incarnations; it was implicit in their repeated expressions of awe, in the elaborate mythology (only a portion of which I have mentioned) that they created around the event, and in their various forms of self-condemnation relating to guilt and punishment as well as to shame and humiliation.

"A-BOMB DISEASE"

The third encounter with death occurred with later radiation effects, not months but years after the atomic bomb itself, and may be summed up in the scientifically inaccurate but emotionally charged term "A-bomb disease." The medical condition which has become the model for A-bomb disease is leukemia, based upon the increased incidence of this always fatal malignancy of the blood-forming organs, first noted in 1948 and reaching a peak between 1950 and 1952.[6] The symptoms of leukemia, more-

[5] For a vivid description of these reactions in one of the hospitals that remained functional, see Hachiya (1955).

[6] For extensive studies of delayed physical aftereffects of radiation, see the series of technical reports of the Atomic Bomb Casualty Commission (an affiliate of the United States National Academy of Sciences—National Research Council, functioning with the cooperation of the Japanese National Institute of Health of the Ministry of Health and

over, rather closely resemble those of acute radiation effects, both conditions sharing various manifestations of blood abnormalities as well as the more visible and dreaded purple spots and other forms of hemorrhage, progressive weakness, and fever. Leukemia, however, unlike acute irradiation, inevitably results in death.

Psychologically speaking, leukemia—or the threat of leukemia—became an indefinite extension of the earlier "invisible contamination." And individual cases of leukemia in children have become the later counterpart of the "ultimate horror" of the first moments of the experience, symbolizing once more the bomb's desecration of that which is held to be most pure and vulnerable—childhood itself. Indeed, Hiroshima's equivalent of an Anne Frank legend has developed from one such case of leukemia in a twelve-year-old girl, Sadako Sasaki, which occurred in 1954; her death resulted in a national campaign for the construction of a monument (which now stands prominently in the center of Hiroshima's Peace Park) to this child and to all other children who died as a result of the atomic bomb.

Beyond their own sense of impaired body image, survivors carry the fear that this impairment will manifest itself in subsequent generations. The issue of genetic effects from the A-bomb is also controversial and unresolved. Fortunately, studies on comparative populations have revealed no increase in abnormalities among children of survivors. But it is widely known that such abnormalities can be caused by radiation, and there are again the problems of variation in medical opinion (some Japanese pathologists think that some evidence of increase in genetic abnormalities exists), and of lurid,

Welfare), as recently summarized in "Medical Findings and Methodology of Studies by the Atomic Bomb Casualty Commission in Atomic Bomb Survivors in Hiroshima and Nagasaki," in "The Use of Vital and Health Statistics for Genetic and Radiation Studies," *Proceedings of the Seminar Sponsored by the United Nations and the World Health Organization,* held in Geneva, Sept. 5–9, 1960, A/AC 82/Seminar, United Nations, New York, 1962, pp. 77–100. Additional Japanese and American studies are cited in Lifton (1963a, pp. 489–493).

sometimes irresponsible, journalistic reports. There is, moreover, one uncomfortably positive genetic finding among significantly exposed survivors, that of a disturbance of sex ratio of offspring, the significance of which is difficult to evaluate. Still another factor in the survivors' psychological associations has been the definite damage from radiation to children exposed *in utero,* including the occurrence of microcephaly with and without mental retardation; this phenomenon is, scientifically speaking, quite unrelated to genetic effects, but ordinary people often fail to make the distinction.

Thus, at this third level of encounter with death, the sudden "curse" becomes an enduring taint—a taint of death which attaches itself not only to one's entire psychobiological organism but to one's posterity as well. Although in most cases survivors have been able to live, work, marry, and beget children in more or less normal fashion, they have the sense of being involved in an endless chain of potentially lethal impairment which, if it does not manifest itself in one year—or in one generation—may well make itself felt in the next. Once more elements of guilt and shame become closely involved with this taint. But the whole constellation of which they are part is perceived not as an epidemiclike experience but as a permanent and infinitely transmissible form of impaired body substance.

IDENTIFICATION WITH THE DEAD

The fourth level of encounter with death is a lifelong identification with death, with dying, and with an anonymous group of "the dead." Indeed, the continuous encounter with death, in the sequence described, has had much to do with creating a sense of group identity as *hibakusha,* or survivors. But it is an unwanted, or at best ambivalent, identity, built around the inner taint I have discussed and symbolized externally by disfigurement, that is, by keloid scars, which, although possessed by only a small minority of survivors, have come to represent the stigmata of atomic-bomb exposure.

Survival Priority   Each survivor had to face a central conflict of this *hibakusha* identity: the problem of what I have come to speak of as "survival priority"—the inner question of why one has survived while so many have died, the inevitable self-condemnation in the face of others' deaths. For the survivor can never, inwardly, simply conclude that it was logical and right for him and not others to survive. Rather, I would hold, he is bound by an unconscious perception of organic social balance which makes him feel that his survival was made possible by others' deaths: If they had not died, he would have had to; and if he had not survived, someone else would have. This kind of guilt, as it relates to survival priority, may well be that most fundamental to human existence. Also contributing greatly to the survivor's sense of guilt are feelings (however dimly recalled) of relief, even joy, that it was the other and not he who died. And his guilt may be accentuated by previous death wishes toward parents who denied him nurturance he craved or toward siblings who competed for this nurturance, whether this guilt is experienced directly in relationship to the actual death of these family members or indirectly through unconsciously relating such wishes to the death of any "other," however anonymous.

In ordinary mourning experiences, and in most ordinary disasters, there is considerable opportunity to resolve this guilt through the classical psychological steps of the mourning process. But with the atomic-bomb disaster, my impression was that such resolution has been either minimal or at best incomplete. As in other mourning experiences, survivors have identified themselves with the dead (in this case, with the latter both as specific people and as an anonymous concept) and have incorporated the dead into their own beings; indeed one might say that survivors have imbibed and incorporated the entire destruction of their city and, in fact, the full atomic-bomb experience. But they have found no adequate ideological interpretation—no spiritual explanation, no "reason" for the disaster—that might release them from this identification and have, instead, felt permanently bound by it. They have felt compelled virtually to merge with the dead and to behave, in a great variety of ways, as if they too were dead. Not only do they judge all behavior by the degree of respect it demonstrates toward the dead, but they also tend to condemn almost any effort which suggests strong self-assertion or vitality—that is, which suggests life.

The *hibakusha* identity, then, in a significant symbolic sense, becomes an identity of the dead—taking the following inner sequence: "I almost died; I should have died; I did die, or at least am not really alive; or if I am alive, it is impure for me to be so, and anything I do which affirms life is also impure and an insult to the dead, who alone are pure." Of great importance here, of course, is the Japanese cultural stress upon continuity between the living and the dead, but the identity sequence also has specific relationship to the nature of the disaster itself.[7]

GENERAL PRINCIPLES

Through the experiences of Hiroshima survivors, we have been thrust into the more general realm of the interrelationship between the anticipation of death and the conduct of life. It is an interrelationship that has been recognized and commented upon by generations of philosophers, though mentioned with surprising infrequency in psychiatric work. There are many signs that this psychiatric neglect is in the process of being remedied,[8] and indeed the

[7] The point of view I wish to suggest about cultural factors in this response—and in other responses to the disaster—is that they are particular emphases of universal tendencies. Here, for instance, survivors' identification with the dead reflects a strong Japanese cultural tendency related in turn to a long tradition of ancestor worship, but this cultural emphasis should be seen as giving a special kind of intensity to a universal psychological pattern. Thus, "extreme situations" such as the Hiroshima disaster, through further intensifying culturally stressed behavior patterns, throw particularly vivid light upon universal psychological functions.

[8] Among recent psychiatric and psychological studies of death and death symbolism, see Eissler (1955), Feifel (1959), and Brown (1959). In addition, a good deal of research is now in progress. See, for instance, Weisman & Hackett (1961), and Schneidman (1963).

significance of problems in this area so impresses itself upon us in our present age that matters of death and dying could well serve as a nucleus for an entire psychology of life. But I shall do no more than state a few principles which I have found to be a useful beginning for comprehending the Hiroshima experience, for relating it to universal human concerns, and for examining some of the impact upon our lives of the existence of nuclear weapons. Attempting even this much is audacious enough to warrant pause and examination of some rather restraining words of Freud, which are made no less profound by the frequency with which they have been quoted in the past (1957, p. 89):

> It is indeed impossible to imagine our own death; and whenever we attempt to do so we can perceive that we are in fact still present as spectators. Hence the psychoanalytic school could venture on the assertion that at bottom no one believes in his own death, or to put the same thing another way, that in the unconscious every one of us is convinced of his own immortality.

These words, which were written in 1915, about six months after the outbreak of the First World War, have found many recent echoes. Merleau-Ponty, the distinguished French philosopher, has said, "Neither my birth nor my death can appear to me as my experiences. . . . I can only grasp myself as 'already born' and 'still living'—grasping my birth and death only as pre-personal horizons" (1963, p. 31).

Profound as Freud's words are, it is possible that psychological investigations of death have been unduly retarded by them, for they represent the kind of insight which, precisely because of its importance and validity, must be questioned further and even transcended. I believe it more correct to say that one's own death—or at least one's own dying—is not entirely unimaginable, but can be imagined only with a considerable degree of distance, blurring, and denial; that we are not absolutely convinced of our own immortality, but rather *have a need to maintain a sense of immortality* in the face of inevitable biological death; and that this need represents not only the inability of the individual unconscious to recognize the possibility of its own demise but also a compelling universal urge to maintain an inner sense of continuous symbolic relationship over time and space to the various elements of life. Nor is this need to transcend individual biological life mere denial (though denial becomes importantly associated with it). Rather, it is part of the organism's psychobiological quest for mastery, part of an innate imagery that has apparently been present in man's mind since the earliest periods of his history and prehistory. This point of view is consistent with the approach of Campbell (1959), the distinguished student of comparative mythology, who has likened such innate imagery or "elementary ideas" to the "innate releasing mechanisms" described by contemporary ethologists. It also bears some resemblance to Otto Rank's stress upon man's long-standing need of "an assurance of eternal survival for his self" and to Rank's further assertion that "man creates culture by changing natural conditions in order to maintain his spiritual self" (1958).[9]

The Sense of Immortality It is my view that the sense of immortality of which I speak may be expressed through any of several modes. First, it may be expressed biologically—or, more correctly, biosocially—by means of family continuity, living on through (but in an emotional sense with) one's sons and daughters and their sons and daughters, by imagining (however vaguely and at whatever level of consciousness) an endless chain of biological attachment.

Second, a sense of immortality may be achieved through a theologically based idea of a life after death, not only as a form of "survival" but even as a "release" from pro-

[9] In developing his ideas on the "inherited image," Campbell (1959, pp. 30–49, 461–472) follows Adolf Bastian and C. G. Jung. Otto Rank (1958, pp. 62–101) develops his concepts of man's quest for immortality through the literary and psychological concept of the "double as immortal self." While I do not agree with all that Rank and Campbell say on these issues (I would, in fact, take issue with certain Jungian concepts Campbell puts forth), their points of view at least serve to open up an important psychological perspective which sees the quest for immortality as inherent in human psychology and human life.

fane life burdens into a "higher" form of existence.

Third, and this is partly an extension of the first two modes, a sense of immortality may be achieved through one's creative works or human influences—one's writings, art, thought, inventions, or lasting products of any kind that have effects upon other human beings.

Fourth, a sense of immortality may be achieved through being survived by nature itself: the perception that natural elements —limitless in space and time—remain. I found this mode of immortality to be particularly vivid among the Japanese, whose culture is steeped in nature symbolism, but various expressions of Western tradition (the romantic movement, for instance) have also placed great emphasis upon it. It is probably safe to say—and comparative mythology again supports this—that there is a universal psychic imagery in which nature represents an "ultimate" aspect of existence.

These psychological modes of immortality are not merely problems one ponders when dying; they are, in fact, constantly (though often indirectly or unconsciously) perceived standards by which people evaluate their lives. They thus make possible an examination of the part played by death and death symbolism during ordinary existence, which is what I mean by the beginnings of a death-oriented psychology of life. I shall for this purpose put forth three propositions, all of them dealing with death as a standard for, or test of, some aspect of life.

Death as a Standard for Life   These three are: First, death is anticipated as a severance of the sense of connection—or the inner sense of organic relationship to the various elements, and particularly to the people and groups of people, most necessary to our feelings of continuity and relatedness. Death is therefore a test of this sense of connection in that it threatens us with that which is most intolerable: total severance. Indeed, all the modes of immortality mentioned are symbolic reflections of that part of the human psychic equipment which protects us from such severance and isolation.

Another expression of the threat to the sense of connection represented by death is the profound ambivalence of every culture toward the dead. One embraces the dead, supplicates them, and creates continuous rituals to perpetuate one's relationship to them and (as is so vividly apparent in the case of the Hiroshima survivors) to attenuate one's guilt over survival priority. But one also pushes away the dead—considers them tainted and unclean, dangerous and threatening—precisely because they symbolize a break in the sense of connection and threaten to undermine it within the living. These patterns too were strongly present in Hiroshima survivors (and can be found in general Japanese cultural practice), although less consciously acceptable and therefore more indirectly expressed. Indeed, in virtually every culture the failure of the living to enact the rituals necessary to appease the dead is thought to so anger the latter (or their sacred representatives) as to bring about dangerous retribution for this failure to atone for the guilt of survival priority.

Second, death is a test of the meaning of life, of the symbolic integrity—the cohesion and significance—of the life one has been living. This is a more familiar concept, closely related to ideas that have long been put forth in literature and philosophy, as well as in certain psychoanalytic writings of Freud, Rank, and Jung; and it has a variety of manifestations. One is the utilization of a *way* or *style of dying* (or of anticipated dying) as an epitome of life's significance. An excellent example of this is the Japanese *samurai* code, in which a heroic form of death in battle on behalf of one's lord (that is, a death embodying courage and loyalty) was the ultimate expression of the meaning of life.[10] Various cultures and subcultures

[10] The *Hagakure*, the classical eighteenth-century compilation of principles of *Bushido* (the way of the *samurai*), contains the famous phrase: "The essence of *Bushido* lies in the act of dying." And another passage, originally from the *Manyoshu*, a poetic anthology of the eighth century: "He who dies for the sake of his Lord does not die in vain, whether he goes to the sea and his corpse is left in a watery grave or whether he goes to the mountain and the only shroud for his lifeless body is the mountain grass. This is the way of loyalty" (Bellah, 1957, pp. 90–98).

have similarly set up an ideal style of dying, rarely perfectly realized, but nonetheless a powerful standard for the living. The anticipation of dying nobly, or at least appropriately—of dying for a meaningful purpose—is an expression of those modes of immortality related both to man's works (his lasting influences) and to his biosocial continuity. And I believe that much of the passionate attraction man has felt toward death can be understood as reflecting the unspoken sense that only in meaningful death can one simultaneously achieve a sense of immortality and articulate the meaning of life.

The foregoing may suggest some of the wider meanings of the concept of the survivor. All of us who continue to live while people anywhere die are survivors, and both the word and the condition suggest a relationship which we all have to the dead. Therefore, the Hiroshima survivors' focus upon the dead as arbiters of good and evil and as invisible assigners for guilt and shame is by no means as unique as it appears to be at first glance. For we all enter into similar commitments to the dead, whether consciously or unconsciously, whether these commitments are to specific people who lived in the past or to the anonymous dead, or whether they relate to theological or quasi-theological ideas about ties to the dead in another form of existence or to more or less scientific ideas about a heritage we wish to affirm or a model we wish to follow. In fact, in any quest for perfection there is probably a significant identification with the imagined perfection of the dead hero or heroes who lived in the golden age of the past. Most of our history has been made by those now dead, and we cannot avoid calling upon them, at least in various symbolic ways, for standards that give meaning to our lives.

Third, death, in the very abruptness of its capacity to terminate life, becomes a test of life's sense of movement, of development and change—of sequence—in the continual dialectic between fixed identity on the one hand and individuation on the other. To the extent that death is anticipated as absolute termination of life's movement, it calls into question the degree to which one's life contains, or has contained, any such development. Further, I would hold that a sense of movement in the various involvements of

life is as fundamental a human need, as basic to the innate psychic imagery, as the countervailing urge toward stillness, constancy, and reduction of tension, which Freud (1955) (after Barbara Low) called the "nirvana principle."[11] Freud referred to the nirvana principle as the "dominating tendency of mental life" and related it to the "death instinct"; but I would prefer to speak instead of polarizing psychic tendencies toward continuous movement and ultimate stillness, both equally central to psychic function. Given the preoccupation with, and ambivalence toward, death since mankind's beginnings, Freud's concept of the death instinct may be a much more powerful one than his critics will allow. At the same time, it may yield greater understanding through being related to contemporary thought on symbolic process and innate imagery, rather than to older, more mechanistic views on the nature of instinct.[12]

To express this human necessity for a sense of movement, I find it often useful to speak of "self-process" rather than simply of "self." And I believe that the perpetual quest for a sense of movement has much to do with the appeal of comprehensive ideologies, particularly political and social ones,

---

[11] Cholsy (1963) has pointed out that Freud (and presumably Barbara Low), in employing this terminology, misunderstood the actual significance of nirvana—to which I would add that nirvana (whether the ideal state or the quest for the state) probably involves various kinds of indirect activity and sense of movement, and not simply ultimate stillness.

[12] See, for instance, Langer (1948), Campbell (1959), Boulding (1956), Barnett (1963), and Portmann (1964). What Freud refers to as the "death instinct" may well be an *innate imagery* of death which the organism contains from birth; which becomes in the course of life further elaborated into various forms of conscious knowledge, fear, and denial; and which interacts with other forms of innate imagery relating to life enhancement (sexual function, self-preservation, and development) as well as to mastery. From this perspective, the need to transcend death involves the interrelationship of all three of these forms of imagery —death, life enhancement, and mastery—with that of mastery of great importance.

since these ideologies contain organized imagery of wider historical movement and of individual participation in constant social flux. Yet ideologies, especially when totalist in character, also hold out an ultimate vision of utopian perfection in which all movement ceases because one is, so to speak, *there.*

The psychic response to a threat of death, actual or symbolic, is likely to be either that of stillness and cessation of movement or that of frenetic, compensatory activity. The former was by far the most prominent in the Hiroshima situation, though the latter was not entirely absent. The psychic closing-off which took place right after the bomb fell was, in an important sense, a cessation of psychic motion—a temporary form of symbolically "dying"—the purpose of which was to protect the individual from the threat of more lasting psychological "death" (psychosis) posed by the overwhelming evidence of actual physical death. And the same may be said of the later self-imposed restraint in living which characterizes the "identity of the dead," an identity whose very stillness becomes a means of carrying on with life in the face of one's commitment to death and the dead. But there were occasional cases of heightened activity, usually of an unfocused and confused variety, even at the time of the bombing. And later energies in rebuilding the city—the "frontier atmosphere" that predominated during much of the postwar period—may also be seen as a somewhat delayed intensification of movement, though it must be added that much of this energy and movement came from the outside.

Can something more be said about these propositions concerning death and about the various modes of immortality, as they apply specifically to the nuclear age? I believe that from these perspectives we can see new psychological threats posed by nuclear weapons—right now, to all of us among the living.

Concerning the first proposition, that death is a test of our sense of connection, if we anticipate the possibility of nuclear weapons being used (as I believe we all do in some measure), we are faced with a prospect of being severed from virtually all our symbolic paths to immortality. In the postnuclear world, we can imagine no biological or biosocial posterity; there would be little or nothing surviving of our works or influences, and theological symbolism of an afterlife may well be insufficiently strong in its hold on the imagination to still inner fears of total severance. Certainly in my Hiroshima work I was struck by the inability of people to find adequate transcendent religious explanation—Buddhist, Shinto, or Christian—for what they and others had experienced. This was due partly to the relatively weak state of such theological symbolism in contemporary Japan, but perhaps most fundamentally to the magnitude of the disaster itself. And whatever the mixed state of religious symbolism in the rest of the world, there is grave doubt as to whether the promise of some form of life after death can maintain symbolic power in an imagined world in which there are none (or virtually none) among the biologically living. This leaves only the mode of immortality symbolized by nature, which I found to be perhaps the most viable of all among Hiroshima survivors—as expressed in the Japanese (originally Chinese) proverb quoted to me by several of them: "The state may collapse, but the mountains and rivers remain." And with all the other modes of immortality so threatened, we may raise the speculative possibility that, independent of any further use of nuclear weapons, one outcome of the nuclear age might be the development of some form of natural theology (or at least of a theology in which nature is prominent) as a means of meeting man's innate need or a sense of immortality.

Concerning the second proposition, relating to the meaning and integrity of life, we find ourselves even more directly threatened by nuclear weapons. As many have already pointed out, nuclear weapons confront us with a kind of death that can have no meaning. There is no such thing as dying heroically, for a great cause, in the service of a belief or a nation—in other words, for a palpable purpose—but rather only the prospect of dying anonymously, emptily, without gain to others. Such feelings were prominent among Hiroshima survivors both at the time of their initial immersion in death and during the months and years following it. They could not view their experience as purposeful, in the sense of teaching the world the necessity for abandoning nuclear weapons, but rather saw themselves as scapegoats for the world's evil, as "guinea pigs" in a historical "experiment," or else as victims of a war made infinitely more inhuman by the new weapon. Part of their problem was the difficulty they had in knowing whom or what to hate, since, as one of my colleagues put it, "You can't hate magic." They did find in postwar Japanese pacifism an opportunity for organized rechanneling of resentment into a hatred of war itself; this was of considerable importance, but has by no means resolved the issue. The only consistent "meaning" survivors could find in all the death and destruction around them was in the application of an everyday expression of East Asian fatalism—*shikataganai* ("It can't be helped")—which is a surface reflection of a profoundly important psychological tendency toward accepting whatever destiny one is given. But however great the psychological usefulness of this attitude, one can hardly say that it enabled survivors to achieve full mastery of their experience. And concerning the question of the "appropriateness" of anticipated death, Hiroshima survivors were the very antithesis of what are termed "predilection patients". Rather than being ready for death, they found its intrusion upon life to be unacceptable, even absurd; and when seeming to embrace death, they were really clinging to life.

But considering the destructive power of present nuclear weapons (which is more than a thousandfold that of the Hiroshima bomb), and considering the impossibility of a meaningful nuclear death, is not life itself deprived of much of its meaning? Does not nuclear death threaten the deep significance of all our lives? Indeed, the attraction some feel toward the use of nuclear weapons might be partly a function of this meaninglessness, so that in a paradoxical way they want to "end it all" (and perhaps realize their own end-of-the-world fantasies) as a means of denying the very emptiness of the nuclear death toward which they press.

Here the principle of individual suicide as an attempt to deny the reality of death[13] is carried further to encompass nuclear suicide-murder as an attempt to deny the threat to meaningful human existence posed by these weapons.

And finally, in relationship to the proposition of death as a test of life's sense of movement, I think the matter is more ambiguous, though hardly encouraging. There is a sense in all of us, in greater or lesser degree, that nuclear weapons might terminate all life's movement. Yet there is also, at least in some, a strange intensity and excitement in relationship to the confrontation with danger which nuclear weapons provide, and this, it might be claimed, contributes to a sense of movement in present-day life. But this exhilaration—or perhaps pseudoexhilaration—is less a direct function of the nuclear weapons themselves than of the universal historical dislocation accompanying a wider technological revolution. In other words, there is in our world an extraordinary combination of potential for continuously enriching movement and development of self-process, side by side with the potential for sudden and absolute termination. This latter possibility, which I have called the *potentially terminal revolution*,[14] has not yet been seriously evaluated in its full psychological consequences, and whatever its apparent stimulus to a sense of movement, one may well suspect that it also contributes to profound listlessness and inertia that lurk beneath.

I am aware that I have painted something less than an optimistic picture, concerning both the Hiroshima disaster and our present relationship to the nuclear world. Indeed it would seem that we are caught in a vicious psychological and his-

---

[13] Eissler (1955, pp. 65–67) notes the frequently observed psychological relationship between suicide and murder and goes on to speak of suicide as the "result of a rebellion against death," since "for most suicides the act does not mean really dying" but is rather a means of active defiance of, rather than passive submission to, death.

[14] See Lifton (1963b, pp. vii–ix).

torical circle, in which the existence of nuclear weapons impairs our relationship to death and immortality and in which this impairment to our symbolic processes in turn interferes with our ability to deal with these same nuclear weapons. But one way of breaking out of such a pattern is by gaining at least a dim understanding of our own involvement in it. And in studying the Hiroshima experience and other extreme situations, I have found that man's capacity for elaborating and enclosing himself in this kind of ring of destructiveness is matched only by his equal capacity for renewal. Surely the mythological theme of death and rebirth takes on particular pertinence for us now, and every constructive effort we can make to grasp something more of our relationship to death becomes, in its own way, a small stimulus to rebirth.

REFERENCES

BARNETT, S. A. Instinct. *Daedalus*, 1963, **92,** 564–580.

BELLAH, R. N. *Tokugawa religion.* New York: Free Press, 1957.

BOULDING, K. *The image: Knowledge in life and society.* Ann Arbor, Mich.: Univer. of Michigan Press, 1956.

BROWN, N. O. *Life against death: The psychoanalytic meaning of history.* Middletown, Conn.: Wesleyan Univer. Press, 1959.

CAMPBELL, J. *The masks of God: Primitive mythology.* New York: Viking, 1959.

CHOLSY, M. *Sigmund Freud: A new appraisal.* New York: Philosophical Library, 1963.

EISSLER, K. R. *The psychiatrist and the dying patient.* New York: International Universities Press, 1955.

FEIFEL, H. (Ed.) *The meaning of death.* New York: McGraw-Hill, 1959.

FREUD, S. Beyond the pleasure principle. In *The standard edition of the complete psychological works.* Vol. 18. London: Hogarth, 1955. Pp. 7–64.

FREUD, S. Thoughts for the times on war and death. In *The standard edition of the complete psychological works.* Vol. 14. London: Hogarth, 1957. Pp. 273–302.

HACHIYA, M. *Hiroshima diary.* (Tr. by W. Wells.) Chapel Hill, N.C.: Univer. of North Carolina Press, 1955.

LANGER, SUSANNE. *Philosophy in a new key.* New York: Mentor Books, 1948.

LIFTON, R. J. Psychological effects of the atomic bomb in Hiroshima: The theme of death. *Daedalus*, 1963, **92,** 462–497. (a)

LIFTON, R. J. *Thought reform and the psychology of totalism.* New York: Norton, 1963. (b)

MERLEAU-PONTY. Phenomenologie de la perception. (Tr. by Arleen Beberman.) In "Death and my life," *Review of Metaphysics*, 1963, **17,** 18–32.

OUGHTERSON, A. W., & SHIELDS, W. *Medical effect of the atomic bomb in Japan.* New York: McGraw-Hill, 1956.

PORTMANN, A. *New paths in biology.* New York: Harper & Row, 1964.

RANK, O. *Beyond psychology.* New York: Dover, 1958.

SCHNEIDMAN, E. S. Orientations towards death: A vital aspect of the study of lives. In R. W. White (Ed.), *The study of lives.* New York: Atherton, 1963.

WEISMAN, A., & HACKETT, T. P. Predilection to death: Death and dying as a psychiatric problem. *Psychosomatic Medicine*, 1961, **23,** 232–256.

Presently: Professor of Psychology at San Francisco State College (since 1951).

Education: Doctor of Philosophy in psychology from Stanford University (1950).

Current major activity: "Conducting research, studying, and writing in the general area of the preservation and enhancement of human rights and liberties. This is being done within the context of our democratic ideology, and my major interests center about reducing the disparity between the ideology of democracy and its practice."

LOUIS S. LEVINE

Most rewarding project: "I am presently most concerned with the question of how environments can be developed which will contribute optimally to the development of the individual. An organizing concept is that of *place*, which is a combined physical-social-psychological concept involving the sense within the individual of congruity between his immediate environment and himself."

Future of humanistic psychology: Hopeful that the human dimensions may be given consideration not only in the field of psychology but in social planning and governmental practice as well.

Personal history: At the Veterans Administration Hospital in Palo Alto, California, Dr. Levine was first an interne (1946–1948) and later Supervisor of Training (1949–1951). Visiting Professor at Yeshiva University in New York (1965–1967). Consultant of the Center for Study and Research in American Liberties at Columbia University (since 1966). Diplomate in Clinical Psychology of the American Board of Examiners in Professional Psychology. President of the California State Psychological Association (1962–1963).

Writings: *Personal and Social Development: The Psychology of Effective Behavior* (1963); "San Francisco and Civil Rights: A Community Study" (an occasional paper of the Center for the Study of Democratic Institutions) and numerous papers on educational psychology, school guidance programs, and related matters. Currently in press is a new book, *Developing Democratic Behaviors in Young Children*; a further volume, *The Psychologist Talks with Teachers,* is in preparation.

Present chapter: This chapter was adapted for the present volume from a presentation at a symposium on world peace held at San Francisco State College, April 30, 1963.

Chapter 21
LOUIS S. LEVINE

SOME PSYCHOLOGICAL PREREQUISITES FOR PEACE

For the most part, preparations for peace have been discussed in terms of power and politics. People, as such, have generally not been considered relevant in these discussions. In this chapter, I shall maintain that people, as such, *are* relevant to deliberations about preparedness for peace. By "peace," I do not mean the absence of all conflict or competition—I mean simply the elimination of war as a means of settling international disputes.

The three issues appropriate to our topic are best expressed as questions. Affirmative answers to these questions suggest that we are ready to cooperate in establishing the conditions of world organization and world law essential to a world without war. Negative responses to these questions suggest that we are not prepared for peace.

The first question relates to *what* people think: Do we possess the cognitive categories essential for thinking about peace and the conditions basic to its attainment? The other two questions relate to *how* people think. The second question: Is it possible that our psychological need for an enemy can be redirected so that our thoughts and behaviors can lead to preparations for peace, or at least not lead to violence? And the last question: Do we have the degree and quality of compassion that the times require?

COGNITIVE CATEGORIES NECESSARY TO PEACE

We begin by thinking about thinking: Do we possess the cognitive categories essential for thinking about peace and the conditions basic to its attainment? We are all aware that thought involves a process whereby images, sensations, and feelings mysteriously combine to represent events past, present, and future. The symbolic process that allows man to consider his future is accomplished in part through the grouping of symbols into abstract categories on the basis of their perceived common qualities. These cognitive categories themselves vary in their degrees of abstraction, that is, in their degrees of distance from the concrete elements close to us or, more properly, close to our sensory receptors. Some cognitive categories are, in fact, not far removed from immediate sensory experience. Consider, for example, the category "vegetable." The things to which we assign the category "vegetable" have a substantive reality: They can be touched, smelled, and tasted. The cognition "freedom" constitutes a far more abstract category.

Most cognitive categories required for considering the conditions essential for relinquishing war as a means of resolving international disputes not only are highly abstract but also have been outside the life experiences of most of us. Albert Einstein stated, "The unleashed power of the atom has changed everything except our ways of thinking. Thus we are drifting toward a catastrophe beyond comparison. We shall require a substantially new manner of thinking if mankind is to survive" (1946).

If we are to think of peace, what new cognitive categories do the present and future require? Obviously there are the categories that relate to the technological aspects of modern warfare: ICBMs, antimissile missiles, nuclear reactors, and the like. Then there are those categories which relate to nuclear war itself: fallout, radiation sickness, fire storms, overkill, and so on. We require the tools of thought necessary to comprehend the meaning of 60 million, 80 million, or even 200,000 (one estimate of the number killed at Hiroshima). Lacking cognitive categories required for the future, we rely upon those which have served us in the past. This is particularly true when we move away from categories relating to warfare and destruction to those more abstract categories required in thinking about the conditions essential to the elimination of war.

Changing Our Categories Consider, for example, the complexity and the level of abstraction of the categories essential to the establishment and maintenance of a system of world law in which sovereign national states have relinquished nuclear weapons and in which there is some organizational entity with the power to inspect and destroy armaments beyond a specific destructive potential. Our present thought categories ill equip us to contemplate this proposal or others of a similar nature. At another level, consider the categories which are appropriate to the struggle between East and West. Some political scientists view the East and West as one system within which there are two identifiable subsystems, the East and the West. If we accept this formulation, we need cognitive categories that enable us to think about the reciprocal interaction of East with West and the significance of occurrences within either subsystem to the other subsystem.

The distinction between the present condition and that which existed twenty years ago is that man either has reached or is approaching the point where his capacity for destruction requires categories to replace those such as "winning a war." We ask, then, does he, in fact, have the cognitive categories required for thinking of new relationships and structures between nations, structures necessitated by the destructive capacity which he has at his disposal?

Preconceptions about Man's Nature With respect to the question of *what* men think, we turn to the categories which they utilize in thinking of themselves. In this connection we are perhaps at a point where we must abandon some of the guiding fictions we found convenient in the past. These pertain to the categories of thought which rule out the possibilities of a world without war. Although they may be resorted to at different levels of sophistication, such categories restrict the image of man to that of an aggressive animal whose murderous impulses are brought under control only by threat of retaliation. The thought categories which combine to produce the belief that war is inevitable because the nature of man is basically aggressive and destructive are particularly inappropriate to the present situation. They belie the value of seeking an end to war. They are not reflective of man and his nature.

Whether man is by nature aggressive and destructive or whether these behaviors constitute partial reactions to the frustration occasioned by the thwarting of his needs and wishes is a debate that has waged long and fiercely in the literature of both philosophy and psychology. Whether man acquires his aggressive potential genetically or as the result of learning, it cannot be denied that the history of man is a record of warfare, brutality and inhumanity. But man's history also records his potentialities for cooperative and constructive action and his humanistic endeavors. The salient point here is that, although he may be impulsive, aggressive, irrational and violent, a total characterization of man must also include his capacity to control his destructive impulses and to act rationally. Man has the capacity to redirect aggressive impulses into constructive channels; he can find reasonable solutions to the problems besetting him, whether such problems are personal or international. He is able to delay gratification, to plan for the future and to take advantage of past experience. Such central characteristics of the human being must also be taken into account in any predictions about his future (Levine, 1963, p. 482).

Men in Relation to One Another Finally, there are those categories which enable man to think of himself in relation to other men. These categories pertain to the primary group with whom the individual identifies. These categories have changed from family to tribe to nation, as man has moved through time. Now we are at the point where man must develop the necessary cognitive categories to think of his loyalties to all men— to life—and to the development of structures in which he can live without resort to violence.

We ask a last question before turning away from issues of cognitive categories. Is attention directed in the public schools to the development of cognitive, categories *appropriate* to the problems confronting the human race today? Are the cooperative, accepting, and compassionate behaviors of elementary school children being consistently reinforced, or is the trend rather toward a mechanized, utilitarian mode of education that is geared more and more to the production of the technologists required in a warfare state? A close examination of the patterns and trends of education at all levels suggests that the commitment is to past practices, *not* to the principles which can be translated into new cognitive categories relevant to a peaceful future.

THE NEED FOR AN "ENEMY"

We have touched on the need for new cognitive categories to enable man to think about his future. Now let us turn to the question of *how* he uses the categories available to him. Let us consider the use made of the category "enemy" and its utility in stress situations. We can term this category "the need for an enemy."

We all recognize that we need our friends. We recognize that this need to be close to, to be loved by, and to be near those with whom we feel safe is of great

importance. Yet as we view the affairs of nations, it seems that there is another psychological function being served by the need we have for our enemies.

Having an enemy protects us against the anxiety that stems from ambiguity. It enables us to substitute definition for doubt and certainty for confusion. We can attribute our frustration and fear not to our own shortcomings and limitations but rather to someone "out there"—a someone or a nation—that has done something to us, is doing something to us, or will do something to us. By having an enemy, we are spared the agonies of self-confrontation. By having an enemy, an individual and a nation can more readily integrate their resources; disparate tendencies are brought together, and energies that otherwise might be dissipated in a variety of pursuits and directions become mobilized. Energies are focused, and the question of what to do is easily resolved. All that is required is that the enemy be destroyed.

Russian-American Mirror Images At an international level, Bronfenbrenner (1961) made an extremely important observation, namely, that the Russians and the Americans hold "mirror" views of each other; that is, they each impute similar motives to the other, views which reflect a standard characterization of the "enemy" more than accurate perceptions of each other. In each country, for example, there is the common perception that the leadership of the other does not represent the people and that there is widespread dissatisfaction. The mirror belief prevails that the form of government in each country would be overthrown if the people were able to express their will and that it is only the fear of reprisal that prevents revolution. Each side perceives the other as the aggressor; each believes that the other government exploits and deludes the people. Each side believes the other cannot be trusted and that its policies verge on madness.

It might seem that we may be more able, in a psychological sense, to get along without our friends than without our enemies. However, we must note that when the psychological need for an enemy is great, the likelihood of misperceiving the intentions and behaviors of the enemy is also great. Proponents of a preemptive war, who would destroy themselves rather than abandon their perceptions of the enemy, are hardly able to think or act in ways congruent with the values to which they nominally subscribe, namely, the survival of the democratic ideal. This is but one example of the irrationality that is a by-product of an excessive need for an enemy.

Such an excessive need for an enemy is built into the cognitive categories that we learn as we grow up. One example of this would be the idea that the Indians were bad and the white men were good, an idea popularized and reinforced by movies and television. It has to do with the cognitive categories that allow nations to pride themselves on a narrow provincialism, in which all that is home-grown is topnotch and all that is foreign is second rate. It has to do with a materialistic orientation in which wealth and power itself are kings. Thus we will see as our enemies those who have less than we and who wish for more, for surely they covet what we have, and certainly they will attempt to divest us of our wealth. Partly, the excessive need for an enemy derives from the personal frustrations experienced when lives do not go the wished-for way and when there is a great need to blame, to point the finger and say, "It is your fault, not mine." Here is where national frustrations, derived from the presence of competitive powers of great strength, intermingle with personal frustrations to provide a context—a cause— and a devil.

The greater the need for the devil, for the enemy, the greater the probability that thought process will stray from reality and the greater the likelihood of self-deception and misperception. Thus, how people think depends in part upon the degree to which having an enemy removes the discomfort associated with their own failures, shortcomings, and guilts. However, there are enemies we could attend to, but in so doing, our discomfort would increase and our anger convert to compassion. These

enemies are our ignorance and our arrogance, our apathy, our lethargy and our laziness, our biases and our prejudices; and finally, our enemy is the personal neuroses that chain us to immobility, to inertia, to lack of interest, and ultimately to the denial of the significance of life itself.

THE NEED FOR COMPASSION

In the context of how men think, I want to speak now about the third question of whether we have the degree and quality of compassion that the times require. Compassion as a moral, ethical, and spiritual issue holds a central position in the humanistic doctrines of all the great religions. Consider the following, for example [cited by Tussing (1959, p. 24)]:

> Hatred is not diminished by hatred at any time. Hatred is diminished by love; this is the eternal law (Buddhism).
>
> Therefore, all things whatsoever ye would that men should do to you, do ye even so to them (Christianity).
>
> Confucius was asked: "Is there one word that sums up the basis of all good conduct?" And he replied, "Is not 'reciprocity' that word? What you yourself do not desire, do not put before others" (Confucianism).
>
> No one is a true believer until he loves for his brother what he loves for himself (Islam).
>
> Do not unto others that which is hateful to you (Judaism).

From the past which has provided our ethical structures, we have expressed in many tongues and in a variety of codes the idea that we should treat others as we would have them treat us. What has been an ethical injunction now becomes the key issue of our survival. The compassion which we can direct toward other persons and other nations is nothing less and nothing more than the compassion we feel toward ourselves.

The notable lack of compassion that marks the attitudes, behaviors, and politics of many persons reflects the minimal value held for oneself and one's commitment to life and to love. The extremist in our midst, irrespective of his persuasion, evidences a notable lack of respect for the dignity and humanity of those with whom he disagrees. This singular lack of compassion on the part of any extremist, whether he be a prominent leader or a local rabble-rouser, will have appeal to those whose personal devils inflict such torment that it can be relieved only when hate rules out reason.

Finally, we ask who can stand against the raging tide of war? The answer is, only those who are psychologically prepared for peace: those who have ideas, compassion, and clarity of vision; those who have the courage to confront the "realists" with reality, the reality that force begets only force and that violence begets but violence, the reality that whatever security is achieved from now on will depend not on missiles but rather on the main sources of our strength—our morality and our minds.

REFERENCES

BRONFENBRENNER, U. The mirror image in Soviet-American relations. *Journal of Social Issues*, 1961, **17**, 45–56.

EINSTEIN, A. *The New York Times*, May 25, 1946.

LEVINE, L. S. *Personal and social development: The psychology of effective behavior.* New York: Holt, Rinehart and Winston, 1963.

TUSSING, L. *Psychology for better living.* New York: Wiley, 1959.

Part FIVE

THE GROWTHFUL ENCOUNTER

In the two decades since the Second World War, the field of
psychotherapy has had an astonishing growth and development. It
has evolved from a relatively minor ameliorative effort
chiefly employed with the very ill emotionally or the very wealthy
and self-preoccupied to a commonplace part of the experience
of the upper-middle class, a frequent palliative of the veteran, a
status symbol of the young intellectual, and a burgeoning
professional and scientific arena. Concurrently, fundamental
questions about the meaning of psychotherapy as a
social phenomenon and about the implications of its products
are being asked.

Two of the most profound of these questions are deceptively simple
on the surface: (1) What is it that psychotherapy tries to
do? (2) How is it that one person can help another person at all
with what is so personal and subjective?

From the first of these questions flows the realization that the
traditional concepts of mental illness and health are
riddled with contradictions and built-in presumptions many of
which are surely fallacious. Further, there is the increasing
appreciation that the human potential is seldom deeply mined and
that nearly everyone could profit from aid in realizing more
of his life. Finally, there is the fundamental disclosure that man
and his society are deeply in need of revitalizing—whether
that be deemed a psychological, a social, or a theological task.

The second question concerns how one person can help another.
Here, too, the implications are extremely pervasive. The
concepts of human relatedness and communication are opened up
anew by this inquiry. The failure of so many of our social
institutions—family, education, religion—to keep pace with man's

*needs today is highlighted, and the truly explosive potential
of human relationship and human concern is beginning to be grasped.*

*In Part Five, we shall examine some of these implications of our two
questions in a variety of ways. As we do so, the reader will
observe that old lines of distinction are becoming increasingly hazy:
Individual versus group therapy, psychotherapy versus
education, abnormal versus normal, psychology versus religion,
emotional encounter versus training, doctor or leader versus patient
or student—these and other contrasting terms are no longer
so clearly distinguishable.*

*Gerard Haigh presents, in Chapter 22, an embracing perspective on
human relatedness that draws on individual and group
therapy, on sensitivity training, and on literature. In all these, he
finds common threads which speak of the importance of
relationship, of the threat of alienation, of the loss in incongruence,
and of the fulfillment in absorption into one's living and
genuine interpersonal encounter.*

*Hobart Thomas deals with many of the same sorts of experiences
as he explores within his own awareness in Chapter 23.
Using, as many therapists do today, an existential perspective,
Thomas demonstrates a modern introspectionism which
supplements other forms of inquiry and richly fills
in our understanding of important human experiences. I say
"modern" introspectionism because there is no attempt made in this
use of the subjective to specify the basic structures of all
men's experiences; rather the goal is, as Thomas illustrates, to find
a language which will illuminate and communicate so that
experience may change and grow. Nor does modern introspectionism
of this kind deny the role of other methods (such as are
illustrated in the chapters by the Romes, by Lifton, and by others);
rather, it seeks to supplement these.*

*In Chapter 24 Stewart Shapiro avails himself of the introspective
approach to present a candid and penetrating account of a
psychotherapist's inner experience. Here is a wealth of psychological
material which could be obtained in no other way except
through the courage, self-discipline, and insight of a trained and
sensitive scientist-professional. Without such information,
any account of group processes would seem thin and incomplete.
With it, the possibilities open up of increasing our
effectiveness, improving our training, and enriching our
appreciation of being human.*

*Many of these same comments may be made about Carl
Whitaker's and John Warkentin's analysis of the therapist's function
as a prototype in Chapter 25. It is evident in this discussion—as
in other chapters in this section—how much the old concept of
therapeutic detachment is being discarded. This is a clear instance
of the evolution which is occurring in the human sciences, in
which the place of the subjective is increasingly being appreciated
and the gap between scientist and subject or therapist and
patient is constantly narrowing.*

As long as the illness concept was central to psychotherapy, "symptoms" and "disordered behavior" were the focus of the treatment efforts. How much this is changing is well evidenced by Alvin Lasko in Chapter 26. While recognizing that behavioristic psychology is working with human objects and endeavoring to shape them into forms deemed desirable, Lasko makes abundantly evident how different that sort of enterprise is from a humanistic and value-centered psychotherapy. Here, again, the concern for the subjective experience outweighs the attention to external behavior.

James Clark describes in Chapter 27 some of the profound experiences which may emerge from the encounters of sensitivity training. In keeping with Tillich and other modern theologians, Clark regards the resulting attention to ultimate concerns as truly religious. The possibilities of building this tie between psychology and religion into a source of renewal for the religious experience is but one of the implications that he draws out.

For a variety of reasons, what is coming to be called the basic encounter group is receiving increasing attention. Among those reasons are the recognized economic limits on individual therapy, the evident impactfulness of the group on individuals within a short span of time, and the great proliferation in forms of groups, methods of using them, and kinds of products achieved. Carl Rogers, in Chapter 28, brings to bear his masterful observational and conceptual talents on the phenomenon of the basic encounter group. He discerns and illustrates a series of basic processes or phases which such groups go through and which seem importantly related to their products. Clearly, this analysis is a major contribution to the study of these groups, but it is more than that: It is an important contribution to the study of human relationships as well.

Abraham Maslow first enunciated the concept of "self-actualization" in 1954. Since then the concept has become an important part of the psychological language. In Chapter 29 Maslow undertakes to describe some of the behaviors which lead toward self-actualization. This is the sort of translation of the abstract into the concrete which may do much to keep humanistic psychology's ideas vital and evolving. A purely abstract system may so readily become crystallized and removed from daily concerns; the test in the crucible of actual practice may serve to winnow the viable from the sterile.

In the final part, we shall move from the ferment of psychotherapy and basic encounter groups to the perspective of the humanities. I do not mean to imply that the latter are inactive; quite the contrary, the humanities often expose harshly and dramatically the lacunae in man's own humanity. But the humanities do offer, many times, a certain freshness and inclusiveness of perceptive which can do much to illuminate the concerns of humanistic psychology.

Presently: Partner, Psychological Service Associates in Los Angeles (since 1963).

Education: Doctor of Philosophy in psychology from the University of Chicago (1950). Postdoctoral fellowship in clinical psychology at the Menninger Foundation (1955–1957).

Current major activity: "As a psychotherapist I work with individuals, with couples, and with groups. I reach toward encounter with these people, disclosing as much of myself as I dare."

GERARD V. HAIGH

Most rewarding project: "Residential basic encounter groups in which I risk encounter with six to twelve people in a no-exit structure for sustained periods of time. If we get through enough of our 'hang-ups,' we are sometimes able to 'turn on,' achieving ecstatic states without the use of drugs. Through these groups, I catch a glimpse of what human communities might become with an increasing emphasis on awareness expansion and upon the quality of consciousness."

Personal history: Instructor and Counselor at the University of Chicago (1948–1950). Assistant Professor of Psychology at Springfield (Massachusetts) College (1950–1955). Associate Psychologist at the Menninger Clinic (1957–1958). Associate Professor of Psychology at Arizona State University (1958–1963). Lecturer at the University of California, Los Angeles. Diplomate in Clinical Psychology of the American Board of Examiners in Professional Psychology. Los Angeles Society of Clinical Psychologists Post-doctoral Training Faculty.

Writings: Dr. Haigh has been interested in group processes for some time and, while writing in other areas also, has continually developed this area: "Multiple Therapy as a Method for Research and Training in Psychotherapy," with W. Kell (*Journal of Abnormal and Social Psychology,* 1950, **45**, 659–666); "The Learning of Subject Matter in Teacher-centered and Group-centered Classes," with W. Schmidt, (*Journal of Educational Psychology,* 1956, **47**, 295–301); "Human Relations Training in the Peace Corps" (*Journal of Social Psychology,* 1966, **68**, 3–13); "Psychology and Retreats: Frontier for Experimentation," with J. F. T. Bugental (in R. J. Magee (Ed.), *Call to Adventure,* in press).

Present chapter: The essay which follows has not previously been published, although it is related to his paper "Learning Theory and Alienation" (*Psychotherapy: Theory, Research and Practice,* 1965, **2**, 147–150).

Chapter 22
GERARD V. HAIGH

PSYCHOTHERAPY AS INTERPERSONAL ENCOUNTER

Humanistic psychology should be able to turn to the literature on psychotherapy in order to find a model for growthful encounter. After all, psychotherapy is specifically designed to facilitate personal growth and moreover utilizes the medium of an interpersonal relationship for inducing such growth. However, discovery of a useful model within the field of psychotherapy is complicated by the diversity of viewpoints about the therapeutic process. Some therapists state with conviction that psychotherapy is essentially behavior control. Others state with equal certainty that psychotherapy is reorganization of impulse defense configurations. Still others say that psychotherapy is directed toward the realization of one's potential as a person.

The simplicity of such forthright statements about the nature of psychotherapy is disturbed by the side effects of an inordinate amount of communication which exists among psychotherapists. Therapists in the different schools are forever entering into intercourse with one another and losing their purity. As a consequence, a great deal of bastardization ensues. For example, many depth analysts are becoming existentialists; many Rogerians are becoming relationship therapists; some behaviorists are talking about the importance of the concept of self. Hardly anybody has the decency to remain for any length of time in one category; thus anything I might say about one school today may have

already been refuted by one of its exponents yesterday. Or, if not already refuted, it will certainly be refuted tomorrow by a statement which I have not anticipated.

This state of disorder in the broad field of psychotherapy is a close replication of the intrapsychic field of the individual therapist who stops being a therapist at any given moment and asks himself, "What am I doing and why?" Writing this chapter has forced me to ask myself these questions, and I have been immediately precipitated into the state of disorder which seems to be the natural resting state of my mental processes. I struggle in the midst of this disorder to find some fixed points. I reach toward the raw data for the significant incident to learn what is going on and why:

A woman's eyes fill with tears as she reports a childhood incident with her mother. She looks up at me with an embarrassed smile. I do not smile back, but nod in a manner which in retrospect I would want to be seen as "understanding." What am I doing? I am not responding to the smile, which expresses her ridiculing reaction to her tears. I am responding with interest and understanding to her very tears. I am, in short, applying a selective reinforcement schedule. I am a behaviorist.

A man tells me that he feels as if he were in an elevator stuck between floors and that he is fighting off a rising tide of fear. I tell him that I hear the beginnings of terror which he feels in being cut off from people. I am reflecting his feelings back to him, reporting to him my understanding of his phenomenal field. I am a client-centered therapist.

A man comes in wearing dark glasses and reports that he has a viral infection of the retina which may cause him to lose the sight of one eye. Later in the session, while he is discussing his turbulent relationship with his wife, he says, "I wish I couldn't see her." I pounce upon this, ask him whether he heard what he has just said, press him as far as he can go with this potential opening into the unconscious, my own awareness spinning with images and thoughts related to the Oedipal complex, repression, somatization, and the like. I am trying to communicate an interpretation. I am a depth therapist.

I am each of these and more at different times. But who am I really? The label "eclectic" comes to mind. It makes for a bad taste in my mouth. It seems to mean partial acceptance of everything—commitment to nothing. I seek a more pervasive and abiding sense of meaning for coping with the unordered flux of my experience as a therapist.

I presently find a central meaning in my thinking about psychotherapy in the concept of growthful interpersonal encounter. In the remainder of this chapter, I shall discuss the nature and the significance of encounter and the process by which it occurs, using examples from individual and group psychotherapy and from literature.

ALIENATION AND ABSORPTION

The search for interpersonal encounter is a central human quest. Perhaps the most pressing existential crisis of our age is the pervasive sense of aloneness which so many of us feel so much of the time. Henry, who described himself as trapped in an elevator between floors, was expressing such a sense of aloneness. At another time, he said that he felt as if he were wrapped up in a cocoon with splotchy gray walls through which he could see the world but dimly. Henry is a bright, young executive who is unusually efficient in his job. He is well liked by a fairly large circle of men and women, both at work and in his social life. Clearly, Henry's sense of aloneness does not reflect the absence of people in his life. How then could he experience separateness from others so intensely?

Some of the most penetrating analyses of aloneness may be found in the novels of Camus.[1] In *The Fall* (1956), he tells of one man's discovery of his aloneness. Camus describes the man as initially an outstandingly successful lawyer who maintains a reputation for nobility of character and generosity of purpose by defending the poor and the downtrodden in court. In his personal life, he never misses an opportunity to give up his seat to a woman in a bus or to help a blind person cross the street. He is a witty conversationalist and much sought after socially. As a lover, he is pursued by the most beautiful women of Paris.

Then, an incident occurs which completely shatters the lawyer's life. He is returning in the early morning hours from a delightful rendezvous with his current mistress. While crossing the bridge, he sees a young woman standing at the railing and staring at the water below. He notes the slender nape of her neck nestling into her coat collar and feels a warmth toward the girl. He walks past her and a moment later hears a splash. He stops stock still without turning. He hears a cry and braces himself not to move. There are a few more cries, and then stillness. Slowly he walks away, informing no one.

The lawyer cannot shake the memory of this incident. Through it he realizes that despite his sociable and humanitarian appearance, he is emotionally cut off from people. He does not really care enough to permit himself to get involved. He is essentially isolated from the world. He, like Henry, is encapsulated, isolated, alienated.

Absorption In marked contrast with the experience of being encapsulated is the experience of openly and fully being in the

[1] Greening, in Chap. 31 of this book, deals at length with Camus and his treatment of alienation. [Editor]

world, of being completely absorbed. The following accounts seem to describe such experiences.

Kazantzakis, in *Report to Greco*, describes an incident that occurred when he was about three years old, involving a girl of four (1965, p. 47):

> She rose then, took me by the hand, and brought me inside. Her mother was away the entire morning; she hired out as a charwoman. Without losing a moment, we took off our socks, lay down on our backs, and glued our bare soles together. We did not breathe a word. Closing my eyes, I felt Emine's warmth pass from her soles to mine, then ascend little by little to my knees, belly, breast, and fill me entirely. The delight I experienced was so profound that I thought I would faint. Never in my whole life has a woman given me a more dreadful joy; never have I felt the mystery of the female body's warmth so profoundly. Even now, seventy years later, I close my eyes and feel Emine's warmth rise from my soles and branch out through my entire body, my entire soul.

Barron, in *Creativity and Psychological Health,* gives an account of a painter's experience under the influence of psilocybin, from which the following has been excerpted (1963, pp. 250–251):

> My concern was with the immediate and what had preceded a particular mark on the page or what was to follow seemed quite irrelevant. When I finished a drawing I tossed it aside with a feeling of totally abandoning it and not really caring very much. . . . I was far better able to isolate the significant and ignore that which, for the moment, seemed insignificant and I was able to become much more intensely involved with the drawing and with the object drawn. I felt as though I were grimacing as I drew. I have seldom known such absolute identification with what I was doing—nor such a lack of concern with it afterward. Throughout the afternoon nothing seemed very important beyond what was happening at the moment. . . .

Also from Barron (1963, p. 254), an excerpt from a graduate student's report of a group experience under psilocybin:

> The faces of other people became clear and beautiful and open. . . . Their faces looked bright and strong, like those of archangels. I could look at them without fear or shyness and with frank admiration and adoration. . . . People looked naked, shed of a fog of dissimulations, anxieties, hypocrisies. Everyone was true to his own self and no one was ashamed.

These descriptions all involve intense concentration upon a here-and-now event. They involve direct immersion in the world, immersion in which prejudgments tend to be suspended, permitting new ways of perceiving to emerge. This immersion tends to be experienced as transactional, with apparent loss of boundaries between the self and the world. The past and the future seem to fade out of awareness. So does any potential audience for whom one might perform, as the person becomes completely absorbed in the immediate experience.

Social Programming and Alienation Experiences of feeling encapsulated and experiences of being absorbed are vastly different from each other. Somewhere between these two extremes, most of us live the greater part of our waking hours. During psychotherapy, the quality of a person's experience tends to move from some degree of alienation in the direction of complete absorption. How do such changes occur? An understanding of the change process is facilitated by a prior understanding of the nature and origin of the condition of alienation.

Camus so penetratingly depicts the experience of aloneness of the lawyer in *The Fall* as to expose some essential aspects of this condition. Some two or three years after the drowning which was described, another incident occurs which ultimately shatters the man. After winning an important verdict in court, he is alone, feeling contented with himself. He stops to light a cigar, and in the darkness he hears a laugh. Startled, he looks around but sees no one. He hears it again, more faintly. It dies off in the distance, and he assumes it must have come from someone on a boat passing by on the river. But he cannot shake the memory of the laugh from his mind.

Putting these two incidents together, the lawyer is shocked into the recognition that he has been faithfully following a program in regard to his behavior which has no dependable congruence with his own inner experience. In standing by while the girl drowned, he discovered that he did not really care about people. He became aware of tipping his hat to a blind person whom he had helped across the street and realized that the whole action was intended for an audience. It became apparent to him that most of his actions followed a script written by society, that he was in fact almost completely programmed. Apart from the program, he experienced himself as an empty organism, a hollow man. His discomfiture over the innocent laugh in the dark reflected his apprehension about being seen through, about having his incongruence recognized. His first reaction to the possibility that someone might see through his programmed behavior to his inner experience (or lack of experiencing) was one of humiliation.

Incongruence This Western culture of which we are a part, like every culture, develops in each of us a programmed self which exists in varying degrees of congruence in relation to our own inner experience. The process of interpersonal repression operates to maintain conformity with the program. An incident in the movie *Lawrence of Arabia* illustrates the kind of difficulty one may encounter in attempting to defy the program and express his own experience. In this incident, Lawrence describes to a group of officers how he was forced to kill a man whose life he had previously saved. Then he says that the difficult part of it was that he enjoyed killing him. The officers look away in silence. By such simple but tremendously impactful acts as this, interpersonal repression tends to be maintained; the individual learns not to disclose his inner experience.

The struggle between interpersonal repression and interpersonal disclosure is illustrated by the following incident, which occurred in a group therapy session:

> One of the members, Arnold, says that he usually tends to feel inferior with people and that he feels hurt when people do not seem to notice him. His eyes fill with tears as he says this. Another member, Paul, says that he does not like to be a crybaby. When he gets this kind of feeling, he gives himself "a kick in the ass" and gets out and does something about it. A third member, Helen, says that she never feels hurt anymore. She tends to recognize people for what they are and not to expect friendliness from everybody.

Thus, Arnold congruently disclosed his inner feeling. Paul discloses that he also has such feelings but then goes on strongly to affirm the validity of the social program for dealing with them. Helen reveals that she is effectively programmed, not only at the level of overt behavior, but also at the level of inner experience. In coming to terms with these markedly different forms of expression, each member of the group had to find a position for himself along the continuum of interpersonal repression–interpersonal disclosure.

The existential essence of most problems brought into psychotherapy derives out of incongruence between the programmed self and authentic experience. Robert, for example, is a responsible, work-oriented person who does not waste time, who makes decisions, and who gets things done. He attacks all problems rationally and maintains a Victorian elegance in his life style. But when, during a therapy session, he found himself on the brink of feeling anger and of crying, he felt so humiliated that he dashed out of the office. Thus he struggled to cover up his anger and his tears in order to ward off anticipated humiliation.

This fear of being humiliated is a major force maintaining interpersonal repression. The maintenance of interpersonal repression leads to the pervasive sense of aloneness which characterizes our age. There is in each of us the need to have our own uniqueness seen by others, to be recognized as a person. We are like the child trick-or-treating on Halloween who was all dressed up in a costume, complete with mask, but who could not bear to remain anonymous and pulled aside his mask almost immediately, each time he visited another person. But even though we have the same urge to be known, we adults have been carefully programmed not to remove the mask.

Interpersonal Encounter The antidote to alienation is interpersonal encounter. We seek encounter through relationships, but many of our relationships contain a great deal of interpersonal repression and permit little or no encounter. A therapeutic relationship is one in which the repression is systematically handled with the purpose of removing blocks to self-disclosure, and it is thus one in which encounter may potentially occur.

We are accustomed to focusing on blocks in the patient, but when psychotherapy is conceptualized as interpersonal encounter, it becomes equally relevant to examine blocks in the therapist as a valid part of the total therapeutic process. The following incident centers around a block in the therapist and illustrates movement from alienation to an intense state of contact and absorption. It is presented in the words of the therapist himself. The incident occurred during a three-day residential basic encounter group[2]:

> I found myself becoming increasingly anxious in the group, toward the end of the second day. I felt more and more out of it. My responses to group members became increasingly mechanical. I was aware of this, so I spoke less and less, letting my co-therapist take over more and more.
>
> I felt so estranged that I stayed away from the party which the group held on the second night. I lay in bed trying to shut out the blare of the party music and trying to master my anxiety. I knew it had something to do with my relationship with one of the women in the group. I determined to talk about this in the group.
>
> The next morning I asked the group for some time, and I told them about my anxiety. In talking about it, the anxiety began to be replaced by shame, and the shame seemed to be in relation to feelings of tenderness,

affection, and sexual attraction to this woman. I felt like a lover toward her. I was very apprehensive in revealing these feelings, thinking them inappropriate for a therapist, and expecting that I would be censured for them. I had difficulty meeting the eyes of group members, but I deliberately looked at each person and felt accepted by each in turn. Then I noticed that my anxiety had completely disappeared and that what I felt was excitement. From then on, I was swinging! I was able to tune in on each person who expressed himself. My responses were deeply impactful. I was able to be open and direct with the woman who had generated my anxiety. We had a deeply intimate exchange in the group, communicating as much with our eyes as we did with our words.

> Afterward, I went down to the seashore and walked alone among the rocks. I felt vibrantly alive. I saw a large wave shatter on the rocks, and as the spray leapt into the air, I laughed aloud with joy. I spent about an hour in ecstatic communion with nature.

This example begins with an anxiety state which was apparently derived from incongruence between the therapist's role image of himself, on the one hand, and his feelings toward a patient, on the other. The social programming by which he was controlled defined these feelings as socially unacceptable. A concomitant of the anxiety was a progressively increasing degree of alienation from the group and thus from his entire social world during this period of time. The anxiety dissolved in the experience of shame as the suppressed feelings were discovered and disclosed. Tacit group acceptance led to the dissolution of shame feelings, and the predominant feeling tone became one of excitement. Openness of the therapist to his own feelings made it possible for him to be open to the group members and to their feelings. This in itself represented the making of contact where before there had been alienation. The contact with the woman became one of deep absorption, replacing a previous reaction of general avoidance. Concomitant with the openness to self and the openness to others, the therapist also experienced an openness to the

---

[2] See especially the chapters by the Gibbs (17) and by Rogers (28) for expanded descriptions of encounter groups. [Editor]

physical world which is similar in immediacy and absorption to that of the painter described earlier.

CONCLUSION

A model for growthful encounter which may be found in psychotherapy involves a process which moves from alienation toward absorption. Alienation produces the sense of aloneness which is a predominant experiential anguish dealt with in a humanistically oriented psychotherapy. Alienation itself is a product of incongruencies between social programming and experiential reality. Incongruent social programs are maintained via neurotic anxiety and the threat of shame. When the participants in a therapeutic relationship reach for encounter with one another, they must risk self-disclosure, with its attendant shame and anxiety. To the extent that they achieve encounter, with its attendant acceptance and absorption, their shame tends to dissolve, and the anxiety tends to turn into excitement. Such encounter involves and enhances openness to self, openness to the other, and openness to the world at large.

This look at a humanistic approach to psychotherapy suggests that the ingredients for growthful encounter must include the possibility of going into and through the experience of shame, of transmuting anxiety into excitement, of dealing with incongruencies between social programming and experiential reality, and of utilizing all these as part of a total process which moves from alienation toward absorption.

REFERENCES

BARRON, F. *Creativity and psychological health.* Princeton, N.J.: Van Nostrand, 1963.

CAMUS, A. *The fall.* New York: Random House, 1956.

KAZANTZAKIS, N. *Report to Greco.* New York: Simon and Schuster, 1965.

Presently: Professor and Chairman of the Department of Psychology at Sonoma State College in Rohnert Park, California (since 1961).

HOBART F. THOMAS

Education: Doctor of Philosophy in psychology from Stanford University (1951).

Current major activities: (When he answered the editor's question, Dr. Thomas was "gliding up the Rhine, while conducting a group of eighteen people on a basic encounter tour of Europe.") More generally, he is currently quite caught up with setting up and getting under way at Sonoma State College a master's degree program in humanistic psychology.

Most rewarding project: "I enjoy most moving into the frontier areas of human growth and creativity. I believe that we have within our scope, ways of fostering creativity and ways of being in tune with ourselves, others, and the total life process. To me, our experiments with encounter groups offer both promise and great challenge."

Future of humanistic psychology: "Personal fulfillment for every man, so that all of us can experience and enjoy the game—playing our parts in the great symphony, being in tune and 'with it' at every moment."

Personal history: Professor of Psychology at San Francisco State College (1951–1961) and Coordinator of the Counseling Center there (1955–1956). Staff member of the Western Training Laboratory in Group Development (1955–1956). Staff Psychologist at the Sonoma County Mental Hygiene Clinic (1957–1959). Part-time private practice in clinical psychology (since 1958). He directed conferences on existential psychology in 1962, 1963, and 1965.

Writings: Not a prolific writer, Dr. Thomas has been concerned with trying to give expression to the subtleties of the person's experience in basic encounter groups. "Self-actualization through the Group Experience" (*Journal of Humanistic Psychology*, 1964, **4**, 39–44) is an example.

Present chapter: This chapter grew out of some earlier, unpublished writing that the author had been working on.

Chapter 23

HOBART F. THOMAS

AN EXISTENTIAL ATTITUDE IN WORKING WITH INDIVIDUALS AND GROUPS

Several years ago, when I became a member of the American Academy of Psychotherapists, I was asked to declare my orientation as a therapist. Although the bulk of my professional training had been with Freudian and Jungian therapists, and although I had been considerably influenced by Carl Rogers, I could not classify myself as Freudian, Jungian, or Rogerian. Neither did I feel right about the term "eclectic." Frankly, without a great deal of thought and in spite of the fact that I did not have much scholarly background in existential writings, I declared my orientation as existential. Now, a number of years later, despite a built-in repugnance for labels, I have chosen to stay with my original choice. I shall attempt in this paper to describe what existential psychology means to me.

CHARACTERISTICS OF AN EXISTENTIAL APPROACH

First of all, I believe it is safe to say that existential psychology is not a school or system in the sense that, say, psychoanalysis is. Most people prefer to think of it as an attitude, a point of view, or an approach. In my opinion, one of the most important advantages of this point of view is that it enables me to view man not as a fixed object but as a being in a constant state of becoming. Once man becomes aware of himself in the moment, he is free to change. For instance, suppose I tell a lie and then admit that I have lied. The very act of being aware that I had lied and admitting this means that I am telling the truth. I then am free to become something else. If, on the other hand, I choose to classify myself as a liar, I remain fixed as a liar. The act of classifying people into categories such as feebleminded, delinquent, or psychotic tends to make the possibility of behavioral change more difficult. Time and time again in psychotherapy, I have observed that the moment the person faces himself with all his formerly denied negative, shadowy features and allows himself to view things as they are, he is free to change. When one has participated in such growth experiences, one is most hesitant to classify and diagnose. Man is not an object to be labeled and manipulated but an organism of unknown potential.

Here-and-now Emphasis In order for growth and the development of one's potential to occur, the individual needs to face himself as he is at each moment. So, in addition to the emphasis on becoming, the existential attitude asks the question: What exists right now? I often think of this as "tuning in" on my experience. If we do this seriously, we are obligated to take the bitter with the sweet, the hate with the love, the doubt with the certainty, the boredom with the excitement; we must face the possibility that life may have no meaning as well as the possibility that so-called prosaic events are pregnant with the most exquisite meanings, the possibility of God or no God at all. There are both theists and atheists who are considered to be existential in their viewpoints. What then is the common denominator? To me, it is the willingness to use one's own experience as the final authority for truth. This I see as both a humble and a proud attitude—humble in the sense that man can say, "I don't know," and proud in the sense that he also says, "I shall find out for myself." If one adopts this attitude, he tends to shun abstractions which have little to do with experience. He is also less inclined to accept things on someone else's say-so. He adopts a kind of "show me" attitude. He assumes that anything which is within the realm of human experience, no matter how unorthodox, is fair game for his concern and study.

Such a perspective will include all kinds of private and subjective material often shunned by the more "proper" behavioral scientists. Existential psychotherapy aims toward helping the person to perceive and understand his inner world, to see himself as he is, and to rely upon himself with constant emphasis on the present, the here and the now. Rogers (1961) maintains in his process analysis of psychotherapy that as the client progresses in therapy, he moves into a more fluid condition and lives more fully in the moment, being more aware of his immediate feelings. Other therapists, such as Perls (Perls, Hefferline, & Goodman, 1951), with gestalt therapy use active methods to bring the person into the present. These include such techniques as having a person act out the various parts of a recent dream in the attempt to show that the dream is actually a part of the living reality of the present. I see the gestalt approach as representing a more active and direct attempt to focus on the here and now. Even though the method differs from Rogers's, the goal of living in the present is similar.

While the existential approach does not deny the relevance of certain past or anticipated future events, it attempts to deal only with those aspects of past and future which have bearing on the problem that is now present. As a therapist I find it important to ask: What is this person's most significant problem right now?

I recall a client with whom I once worked who came into the office one day complaining that she was constantly forgetting things, misplacing valuables, leaving lights turned on and doors unlocked, and so on. She made some attempts to analyze this behavior and to understand its significance. This seemed to lead nowhere, and I merely sat and waited. Gradually she became more serious, and tears welled up in her eyes as she allowed herself to face what was really concerning her at the moment. Suddenly she said that she was struck with how very much alone she was. She had never married, and at that moment she faced the prospect of spending the rest of her life alone. She saw the initial complaints of forgetfulness as mere trivialities, attempts to sidetrack her from facing the most dismal prospect, her loneliness. This was reality. It could not be denied or analyzed away. When we faced together the depths of her despair, she was then free to look at some of the other aspects of her situation in a more realistic light. Although she did not have a husband, she did have family and friends who could offer her richness in human relationships. While her situation was far from perfect, she had the courage to face it and make the most of it. It seemed to me that in moments of deep despair, the significant healing force is the therapist's willingness to move with the client into the depths in facing what often appears to be an insoluble problem.

SOME EXISTENTIAL ISSUES

Whereas reductive approaches in therapy attempt to explain away such feelings a love, fear of actual death, or religious experiences by reducing them to drives such as sexuality or unresolved dependency needs, the existential approach is more inclined to consider that many of these experiences have validity in themselves and are not necessarily reducible to something else. While the experience of love, for instance, may include erotic components, we cannot reduce all forms of love to sexuality per se. Also, the fact that someday each of us will die is a part of reality with which we must come to terms. These are existential problems, facts of life that are taken seriously by the therapist. This is not to say that analysis and the reductive approach do not have a place in existential therapy. Rather than being ends in themselves, however, they become the means of bringing the person into closer contact with his experience. It seems to me that if the therapist and client are constantly attuned to what is going on in the present, insights tend to occur spontaneously. My experience has been that the less the therapist pushes for events from the client's past, the more likely it is that relevant past events will be recalled. Most psychotherapists are well aware that clients who go into the past and deal with their childhoods may be attempting to escape present reality. Again, the significant question is: What is the *real* problem?

Sometimes a significant aspect of the problem is the individual's avoidance of responsibility for his actions. Glasser (1962) discusses several incidents at the Ventura School for Delinquent Girls which illustrate this point. When girls claimed that they were at the school because they were emotionally disturbed, he quickly helped them become aware of the fact that they were really there because they had broken the law (Ch. 3). An important aspect of therapy is the therapist's refusal to allow the client to use emotional disturbance as an excuse for not facing responsibility.

Although psychopathology has been emphasized in traditonal psychotherapy, I find that it is equally important to work with the person's healthy side. In my own therapeutic experience, even the most seriously disturbed individual has disclosed a healthy fragment of self to which one can appeal.

I recall a particularly difficult situation in working with a delusional individual with both suicidal and homicidal tendencies which he discussed and almost acted upon. We faced these terrible feelings together, moving at one point to the very brink of suicide. At another time, we also faced the even more terrifying possibility that he might commit homicide. Both of these acts were within his power to commit, and we both realized that the choice was his. In addition to these negative aspects, there was another side. This individual, disturbed as he was, still was able to maintain a responsible job, actually manifested love for his family along with violent hate, and saw me as a friend he could trust. There was no guarantee that at some point he would not act upon the violent impulses that were a part of him. (Nor is there such a guarantee for any of us.) I can say, however, that he was able to face some of the most distressing aspects of himself and still live, finding that there were also aspects of life which made it worthwhile.

Open-ended Conceptualization Another aspect of the existential approach which I value most highly is its open-ended view of the human being. This stands in sharp contrast to traditional psychoanalytic theory and method. In his development of psychoanalysis, Freud extended the concept of man which existed at that time by including sexuality as a dominant motivating force. This obviously was a necessary and important development, and few who have even the slightest understanding of human behavior would deny this. The basic error, it seems to me, comes when we take sexuality or any other drive and use it as a basis for explaining all behavior. The existential attitude tends to place less stress on systematization than many approaches but greatly values openness to experience. Openness means here that one approaches a situation with few preconceived ideas or theories as to how to explain it or how to predict its outcome. This may be effected by asking myself first, "What is going on in this situation? Just what am I experiencing?" and by letting myself move into the existent feelings in a given situation. I deemphasize the question "Why?" since asking a person to explain why he did something usually results only in rationalization of behavior, not understanding. I have found that my most important insights have occurred when I was able to be intensively involved in my experience at a given moment and when I allowed myself to be open to myriad possibilities. In therapy I have found that the more I attempt to probe for specific information, the less anything important seems to happen. If, on the other hand, people are involved in a meaningful relationship, insights and understandings occur spontaneously, and there is a feeling of rightness about them.

LIVING WITH UNCERTAINTY

One pays a price for this attitude, however. Part of the price is living with uncertainty and unpredictability of outcome. I experience this a good deal of the time in the classes I teach. Learning is a two-way process, and as a teacher I must participate in many of the struggles of the learner. Along with my students, I must also risk failure—failure in the sense of not measuring up to expectations, either my own or those of others. If one is to help another, he must be prepared to go all the way himself and be willing to face at least as much in himself as he asks others to face in themselves.

The reward for such an attitude is that, in my experience, one becomes more intensively involved with life. As one learns to experience the pangs of pain, he also learns to experience real joy. There is more opportunity for the thrill of discovery and less chance for things to go stale.

The existential attitude in no way offers to remove anxiety and suffering. If, however, we are able to face ourselves honestly, we may be able to be anxious and suffer for the right, rather than the wrong, reasons. Phobias and other "unreal" fears are usually a means of avoiding more basic prob-

lems of existence. Rather than making specific theoretical assumptions about the basis of the phobia, the existential therapist will be interested in exploring what it means to the individual and how the individual is using it as a means of avoiding facing his own life problems. I would specifically be concerned with such questions as: Is this person living authentically in his present situation? Is he avoiding certain responsibilities? Is he blocking his potential for a more complete life for himself?

I recall a client who complained of an intense fear of speed and high places which was most pronounced when she and her husband went skiing. In the course of therapy, she explored some of the origins of this fear which related to early traumatic events. She went beyond the understanding of some of the past origins, however, by seeing what her phobia meant in terms of the present and her general outlook on life. Actually she was a rather sensitive, artistic person and really quite inept at athletics. She became aware in our sessions together that she spent a good deal of her life trying to please her husband by engaging in outdoor activities such as skiing, boating, and tennis, often at the expense of developing some of her creative, artistic, and basically more introverted potentials. She saw her fear of speed as a symbol of letting herself be pulled apart by others rather than living her own life. With this recognition she was then able to be herself rather than attempting to live up to what she perceived to be her husband's and other people's expectations of her.

THE SEARCH FOR MEANING

Beyond the mere attempt to alleviate neurotic suffering is the problem of how each individual finds meaning in his own life. It seems to be generally recognized that a chief characteristic of modern man, particularly in Western civilization, is a feeling of meaninglessness (boredom and lack of involvement). The "coolness" of the "beat generation" is one example of this. I do not pretend to know all the reasons for this. I suspect that such things as material affluence, the breakdown of traditional values, the disillusionment men experience when they find that most of the answers of the various authorities do not satisfy them, and the loss of contact with basic realities, such as useful work, are involved. It is a rather appalling, synthetic state of affairs when we have to slow production to make work for people, produce merchandise which will wear out prematurely, and spend billions of dollars in advertising in order to convince people to buy things they do not need. Charles Schulz, in a clever *Peanuts* cartoon, captured the modern loss of contact with basic realities most poignantly for me: When Lucy's friend complains to Charlie Brown that there is nothing to do, he suggests that she go jump in a big pile of leaves. She seems to think this is a pretty good suggestion, puts on her coat, and goes outside and walks around awhile. Pretty soon she comes back to Charlie Brown and asks him, "Where does one go to purchase a pile of leaves?"

I am sure that the answer to such problems is not simply a matter of all of us moving to the country. What does seem to be crucial to me is this: If there is an answer to the problem of meaning in my life, it does not lie out there someplace, but within me. Life does not present me with meanings. Life merely *is*. The meaning, the true zest for living, comes from full involvement with life. Frankl (1962), in his description of life in a Nazi concentration camp, shows how, in even the most ghastly situations imaginable, it was still possible for him to find meaning and value in his life.

In order for me to find meaning in my life, it is important that I be as fully aware as possible of the ongoing stream of experience: The one fact that for me stands beyond all doubt is my own experience. The feelings that I now have as I sit at my desk writing, the various impressions that pop in and out of awareness, are realities that I cannot doubt. *They are*. I also find that in my encounter with my fellow human beings, others seem to have experiences we can mutually share. I may find, then, that other persons apparently feel as I do about some things. They, too, enjoy some of the same music or painting. They, too, suffer from feelings of inadequacy. They, too, experience love and hate. The honest exchange of experiences between people offers a basis for true intimacy, free of the pretenses and facades which tend to isolate us from ourselves and others.

Barriers to Relationship Unfortunately, we often become removed from true encounter with our fellow human beings. We adopt specialized roles such as teacher, professor, superintendent, doctor, policeman, judge, parent. Since we all tend to have expectations as to how people in these various roles are supposed to act, it often occurs that in order to play a given role we may have to act differently from the way we feel. The teacher, perhaps for sensible reasons, does not explode with anger at the principal because of what appears to be an unreasonable request for lesson plans. The student, perhaps for equally sensible reasons, does not tell the teacher what a horrible drag he finds the class to be. The judge or the lawyer may be trapped into actually promoting an injustice by acting quite legally. My point here is that in carrying out our various social roles and doing what we may conscientiously feel to be a responsible job, we may unconsciously lose a good deal of the true self in the bargain. Somewhere in the course of events our most valuable feelings often get lost in the shuffle.

Because of this split of the person from his feelings, both we ourselves and other people lose some very important data. If the principal or plant superintendent were able to face the facts and had means of discovering just how the people for whom he was responsible *really* felt about things and if he were also able to involve them in mutually meaningful planning, for example, then there would be a possibility for positive change to occur. If the teacher were able to establish a classroom climate in which the student was free to express his feeling that the course is a horrible drag at times, then it might happen that the teacher and the student together could do something about the course. In being able to explore feelings together, it is likely that the people involved become aware of the fact that the responsibility for a good show is a shared thing. No one person can or should carry the burden alone.

ESTABLISHING A CLIMATE FOR GROWTH

I am personally very much concerned with the problem of how to deal with this fundamental split in the human being. We have within our present knowledge the means of establishing conditions under which it would be possible for people to become able to act more "of a piece," more congruently, and to be less alienated from their feelings. Those of us in the psychology department at Sonoma State College and others throughout the country in the past several years have been experimenting with special group situations which are designed to facilitate more authenticity in human relations.[1] So far, the initial results of these experiments have been most intriguing. We find that in specially set-up climates, people seem to be able to face themselves more openly and honestly within a relatively short period of time, to rely more on themselves and less on external authority for answers, to be willing to deal with conflict, and to become more accepting of themselves and other people. We also find that facing oneself can be a disturbing prospect. I suspect that we become disturbed, first of all, when we discover we may be different from the original image we held of ourselves or that there are aspects to us that we have refused to recognize. For example, a person may become aware that he is capable of being mean to others on occasion, even though he thinks of himself as a fairly decent person. He may also discover that it is possible for him to experience deep feelings of love for a person even though he may feel emotionally committed to another person. These experiences, which may contradict formerly held concepts of who he is, often make it necessary for him to reexamine and reorient himself. There is also a different source of threat. In some cases, I have found that

when people have had the experience of living fully and intensively, they then sense more acutely the gap between what they are most of the time and what they are capable of becoming.

We still have much to learn about the implications of this approach. There are both encouraging and somewhat sobering implications, to say the least. I feel that we are really putting to the test the hypothesis that, given a climate of freedom, each person is most likely to determine what is best for him. To pursue this course necessitates what I choose to call an attitude of trust in the nature of things. It is a movement toward openness, toward life with all that it has to offer. It is a willingness to search diligently for one's own truth, one's own way, and to follow it. It is also a readiness to alter one's course freely when experience seems to indicate new and challenging courses of action.

Also implicit in this attitude is a faith in man's potential to find within his own experience deep and significant meanings to his existence. My experience in working with people thus far leads me to believe that the individual who is relatively open and aware, with "all antennae functioning," in tune with himself and life, is most likely to act in a trustworthy manner. He may err, but if he is in touch with his experience, he is in a position to correct his errors.

So this is where I stand as of now. I find that one of the most challenging and exciting tasks for me as a psychologist is the search for greater awareness for myself and others who choose to engage in this endeavor so that we may gain a fuller appreciation of life.

REFERENCES

FRANKL, V. E. *The doctor and the soul.* New York: Knopf, 1962.

GLASSER, W. *Reality therapy: A new approach to psychiatry.* New York: Harper & Row, 1962.

PERLS, F. S., HEFFERLINE, R. F, & GOODMAN, P. *Gestalt therapy.* New York: Julian Press, 1951.

ROGERS, C. R. *On becoming a person.* Boston: Houghton Mifflin, 1961.

[1] See the discussions by Rogers (Chapter 28), Haigh (Chapter 22), and Clark (Chapter 27). [Editor]

Presently: Codirector of Western Psychological Center, Encino, California (since 1956).

Education: Doctor of Philosophy in clinical psychology from the University of Southern California (1950).

Special interests: Dr. Shapiro has wide-ranging interests, which include writing fiction, plays, and poetry; giving attention to psychologists as people ("their growth, authenticity, intimacy, etc."); innovations in role playing, personality theory, and treatment techniques; marital and family therapy; and many other areas.

STEWART B. SHAPIRO

Personal history: With two colleagues, Dr. Shapiro organized and directed for its first six years one of the first group practices in psychology, the Los Angeles Psychological Service Center (1950–1956). He has been active in both the academic and the industrial worlds as a consultant and teacher: Sensitivity Trainer at UCLA (since 1962). Management Consultant to Non-Linear Systems, the unique organization in Del Mar, California (1964), in which A. H. Maslow and J. V. Clark have also worked. Consultant to Los Angeles County Probation Department (1951–1953), to Mt. Sinai Hospital (1964–1965), to the Episcopal Church Home for Children (1965), and to the UCLA Peace Corps training program (1965). Assistant Professor of Psychology at Los Angeles State College (1950–1955) and at San Fernando Valley State College (1963–1964). Lecturer in the UCLA Graduate School of Business Administration (since 1965). Diplomate in Clinical Psychology of the American Board of Examiners in Professional Psychology.

Writings: Dr. Shapiro produced an unusual training resource in *Six Modern Therapies,* tape recordings of psychotherapy sessions conducted by six noted therapists. He wrote a student's guide and an instructor's manual to accompany these. He has also been developing an approach to therapy in a series of papers: "A Theory of Ego Pathology and Ego Therapy" (*Journal of Psychology*, 1962, **53**, 81–90); "Ego Therapy in Action: A Case Study" (*Psychological Reports*, 1962, **11**, 821–831); "Transactional Aspects of Ego Therapy" (*Journal of Psychology*, 1963, **56**, 479–498); "Orienting Patients to Ego Therapy" (*Journal of Psychology*, 1964, **59**, 315–318); and "Resistance to Ego Therapy" (*Psychological Reports*, 1966, **18**, 703–712).

Present chapter: The ideas in this essay were originally presented to the Graduate Students Forum in the School of Education at UCLA in April, 1965. They have not previously been published.

Chapter 24
STEWART B. SHAPIRO

MYSELF AS AN INSTRUMENT

I wonder about myself as an instrument. This might sound like a somewhat inhuman way of putting it. After all, I am a human being, not a machine. The major premise of this paper is, however, that my human-beingness is my best instrumentality. What I really mean by an "instrument" is the capability of my guts, my body, and my computer-brain to pick up subtle cues given by other people, the environment, and myself as I encounter people and move through the world.

Yet this definition leaves something to be desired. It refers to only one kind of instrument, a recording instrument. Not only do I pick up cues, but I also decode them, translate them, and I express myself. I am a message sender as well as a recorder. I suppose I am just as much a computer, too, as a recorder, and I am also a musical instrument. Not only do I try to listen to the music as well as the words that people say, but I also sometimes play a tune myself on the instrument. My tune could be my pattern of feelings expressed, my voice, my facial expression, a sigh or frown, or it could be something less tangible for which others might have to listen, even disregarding my words. I often tell people, "Listen for the music, not the words."

At this point, it might be agreed that I am several instruments: a recorder and a player as well as a computer and collator. But before I go any further, there may be questions about who tunes these instruments and who directs them.

FUNCTIONS OF MYSELF AS AN INSTRUMENT

I have found repeatedly that some of my wildest free associations (from left field) are to be listened to and respected. I find this upon sitting down with any group of people, but particularly at professional staff meetings, in sensitivity training, in group therapy, and in individual therapy. I now listen to my inner stirrings, my fantasies, the thoughts that sometimes pass quickly through my mind and sometimes seem obsessive. This has become second nature to me. I guess my third ear has been tuned over and over again in my training and practice as a psychotherapist, husband, father, son, man, and so forth. However, there seems to be some sort of strange collation that goes on with all the diverse data which my computer receives. This collation process seems largely conscious, but sometimes quite hazy; it makes the most sense when certain thoughts repeat themselves in an orderly sequence, a pattern. For example, I find myself vaguely uncomfortable in greeting and saying goodbye to one group of patients. It is as though we have a silent pact that each meeting is something special and each parting a crisis, perhaps representing life and death for all of us.

At times it is difficult to know which self is my instrument. Perhaps all my selves are. Since I am a person who holds that there is more than one psychological self (Shapiro, 1962), it seems reasonable to cast the question in this form: How does my subself system function when I am operating as an instrument? Do the daydreaming associations, stray thoughts, perceptions, and feelings come from my child self? Are they monitored or filtered by my chairman or parental subselves? More of this later.

At first glance it seems wise to specify which kinds of responses I am talking about when I speak of myself as an instrument. As I suggested before, I am more likely a battery of instruments, some measuring voltage, some heat and light, some amperage, some magnetism, some electrical resistance, and so on. Some of these instruments give off signals as well as receiving them, and some coordinate the messages. When my guts record seismographic tremors, are they within the same phenomenological ball park as, say, an interesting thought with no particular affect? Does a particular tune running through my head mean roughly the same thing as visual imagery that strikes me when I am immersed in a therapy group?

Responding as a Whole On second thought, perhaps it does not make so much sense to categorize my instrumentation. Maybe the integration or synthesis of all these data, differing as they do in range, sensory modality, clarity, consciousness, and still other ways—perhaps this is the key to understanding myself as an instrument. Certainly, when I perceive or feel an integrated picture (with sound track, to be sure), it comes out as a whole, albeit sometimes strange, thought. I have found repeatedly that these whole responses are helpful to me and to others in finding out what is going on in a group or interpersonally or within me. For instance, if a group looks tired, it is usually a cue to me that there is a kind of infectious, often silent, shared depression. Sometimes it is the very first few of these concatenations, in the very beginning of a session, which seem most prophetic. Subtle changes in seating positions or postures usually cue me that something different from usual is happening.

Often at the end of a session, after all the data are in, the first few impressions and associations are validated. This validation at the end of the session takes place in a more complete and meaningful way, in the context of the total session. For example, in a student group which looked tired at the start, it developed later that there was a great deal of anger at certain professors in the school but a sense of futility and separation from these authority figures. At the same time the group was beginning to feel separation anxiety because the time for termination was approaching. On further discussion it developed that many of the group members felt both angry and sad about my forthcoming separation from them. Discovery of the displacements of these feelings to me from other professors led to an awareness of the genuine sadness about leaving me and one another.

In spite of some success in using my instruments, I worry about my instrument self. One of the reasons I worry is that I am subject to variation. In instrument terms, I have reliability problems. My instrument self and its performance also have a circular connection with my self-esteem. At times I seem to be constantly off in my reactions to certain people or on a certain evening or when certain emotions are in the air. At other times it is not the way I receive that troubles me but the way I send messages.

Validations and Contradictions To me, experiencing the world and making sense of the world are two prepotent drives in man. If my instinctive machinery is not validated, then I am not validated. I can not make sense of my world, and this can be very upsetting. It is like a bad tape recording which I have to discard. Nevertheless, this bad recording can be most helpful for the reason that I often feel compelled to replay the situation in question. Thus, I go over and over certain puzzling interpersonal or group encounters. I look for more data. I try to synthesize and make sense of the data I had originally. In doing this I often do what Harrison (1965) calls "elaborating the opposites." Cognitive dissonance is produced by a contradictory situation. My instruments tell me *one* thing, and social consensus tells me something quite different.

To reduce this dissonance I sometimes search for a creative thought or two which may show both of us to be wrong and yet right at the same time. It takes an explanation of the data on a higher conceptual level to accomplish this. The point is that my feel for a situation is not mutually exclusive with what appears to be the opposite social interpretation of what happened. But we do need a higher-level concept to explain the so-called contradiction.

Some examples may be pertinent at this point. In one weekend therapy group which I recently conducted, I and several other people experiencing intense emotion in a peak experience were perceived as phony by others on the periphery of the group. It seemed as though they could not experience these emotions in this situation. These bits of data came consistently from several people. This was not new to me. I had been called "phony" before, and my so-called phoniness took many different forms. Sometimes I have been confronted as follows: "Stew, you're always the therapist. Even your emotions are calculated. Everything you do and say is clinical. It's all run through your calculator." Another form of this criticism is that I am an actor putting on a performance. "You should have majored in theater arts, not psychology. Everything you do is for dramatic effect."

These data appear consistently and in many groups, particularly in the first four or five meetings, before the people get to know me. How can I reconcile these data with my own perceptions of myself as non-phony, sincere, authentic, and self-disclosing?

In the particular weekend group I described, I responded to the charge of phoniness in the following way: "Yes, you're right. I am a phony, sometimes. Yes, I see myself as 70 percent real and 30 percent phony. What I did tonight was probably artificial, but it was real too." This reply seemed to have a very integrative effect on me as well as on the finger pointers. Had I denied their charge completely, I think they would have gone on believing that my role-playing methods were just games and that my emotions were not real. I admitted and actually felt that they were

correct. But by bringing in the conception of my complexity, of the fact that there is more than one side to me, I pointed out that one could be both real and phony. Thus I demonstrated that the same person at the same time could be several ways. I formed a higher-order synthesis of the opposites.

Controlled Spontaneity Another experience yielded what I now call "controlled spontaneity." In an electronics firm, I was conducting a task-oriented T-group with foremen and bench supervisors in the fabrication department. During the first session of this sensitivity training, I expressed anger at one of the foremen for his sarcasm and because he interrupted me on several occasions. He was shocked that I could be angry with him. Certainly he could not believe that I was only more than faintly irritated with him. He, and others in the group, after they recovered from their initial shock, regarded my anger as a technique to shake up the group and get things going. However, several of the group members kept coming back to my anger, not knowing what to make of it. When I was asked point-blank about my feeling—whether it was put on as a technique or really sincere—I said something like the following: "Sure I was mad at Norm. No, I wasn't putting it on just to shake up the group." Was it a technique? "Yes, in a way." I told them that I believed that direct expression of full feeling, at the time it is felt, is helpful to such a group, particularly when it comes from a trainer and is expressed toward one of the group leaders. They wanted to know when it was really me and when it was just the trainer role I was performing. I said it was both. I use my emotion. What I feel, I express in the service of the job. What I have learned is to let such feelings go instead of sitting on them. It was guided spontaneity, like a guided missile. (This reply also served to model self-disclosure for the group.)

In the above example, a contradiction was resolved, and later when I expressed feelings, positive or negative, the group usually felt I was being honest *and* being a trainer. "Yes, that's him all right—hard to take sometimes, but that's what he feels, *and* he is doing his job as a trainer."

Premature Expression I have found that trouble also occurs when I express a feeling or thought when it is still nascent, sometimes long before it is fully formed or felt. Since I regard myself as a battery of instruments, my various signals may be not only contradictory, but also at different latency levels. Let me cite an example of this. In a married couples' sensitivity training group in which my wife and the wife of the other trainer participated, I assumed the responsibility of assigning pairs to spend some time together. I arranged male-female, nonspouse pairs. During the pairing time, I felt some subtle discomfort relating to the basis on which I had chosen the pairs. When the total group of fourteen reconvened, I decided to air this vague discomfort. I talked about it and reflected aloud, saying that I felt guilty because I had chosen an attractive woman with whom to pair, and at the same time I had paired my wife with the least attractive (in my opinion) man in the group. Upon confessing this I feared my wife's jealousy and anger.

My wife did become angry, and so did most of the group. Particularly stung was the man I considered safe and unattractive enough not to be a threat to me when paired with my wife. Most of the group was furious with my manipulating. They said I should have disqualified myself from setting up the pairs and that I was just using my own pair partner to get at my wife (i.e., to make her jealous). In this example, I aired my vague discomfort at having manipulated a situation, but I think my more basic apprehension was about the whole idea of pairing per se. I doubt that I intended to make my wife jealous or to hurt the feelings of her partner. I think the so-called manipulating was to minimize the deep threat which nonspouse pairing represents to me. Here I was all too willing to confess guilt, before a stronger and more fundamental feeling of anxiety emerged. The group took my premature cue and reacted strongly, and, I might add, away from the theme of moral conditioning, threat of new experience, and possessiveness.

A much briefer example of this premature expression involves my saying impulsively to someone, "I like you," or "I perceive you as a strong person," when I am only faintly aware of these thoughts or feelings. Perhaps a stray thought, very fleeting and weak in intensity, flits through my mind, and I express it. "I don't know why, but for a second there you sounded like a criminal." The problem is that very shortly after, I will experience a much stronger feeling of the opposite. I will feel a strong dislike for the person I said I liked, or I will perceive the "strong person" as very weak. I suppose I could verbalize each of these shifts as they occurred, but that would be very difficult to do.

To correct for this tendency of mine, I sometimes deliberately hold back my impressions or feelings until they become much stronger. This is somewhat like the principle of a Quaker meeting: You are silent until you really have something to say. While this has the disadvantage of inhibiting complete spontaneity, it has the advantage of correcting my battery of instruments and obtaining more reliable and valid readings.

THE INSTRUMENT AND SUBSELF THEORY

But the underlying question is: Reliable and valid for what and according to whom? I suppose the answers go back to subself theory (Shapiro, 1962). A more reliable and valid reading most of the time can be traced to a more reasonable (adult) reading or a more parental reading. Primary-process impressions, such as may be produced in free association in psychoanalysis, can usually be assigned to the inner child subself. Often this is the destructive or natural inner child, as distinguished from the good or adapted inner child.

In my opinion, messages from the child subselves need to be heeded if an individual is to be whole and aware of himself in depth. Often it is only through the inner child that we are aware of beauty or pain in human life. The child subselves also speak in symptom language or body language. I regard symptoms as messages of distress, and I try to teach my clients as well as myself not to disregard symptoms but to listen to them. A rapid heartbeat, an acid stomach, or a sudden coughing spell may be my best indication that I am trying to signal myself or others. The task here is to use my decoding instrument on messages which my recording instrument's pick up in code.

Still another consideration in exploring myself as an instrument involves preverbal and prelogical thinking. Sometimes a gesture, a facial expression, or a body movement is a far more eloquent and sensitive expression of my feeling than mere words. Then, too, these expressions are not always conscious, and I may need others to read my instruments for me by pointing out what is on my face or in my person.

Since I value artistic expression and peak experiences as spiritual or religious phenomena in interpersonal relationships, I am curious about myself as an instrument during peak experiences. In these situations, whether positively or negatively ecstatic, I feel as though my soul is hanging out. Characteristic of the sensory modalities in peak experiences is their receptivity and almost complete openness to stimuli of any kind. It is as though my instruments were operating on a reserve battery, a hidden source of strength and validity. It could be thought of as universal human spirituality. At these times I rarely question myself as an instrument because my instrument self is so fused with my total being.

CONCLUSION

To summarize, I have considered various aspects of myself as a group of instruments: a recorder, a collator, and a transmitter. I have learned to respect my inner messages, and I often try to express them because they can be helpful in varied therapeutic situations. Considering myself as a battery rather than a single instrument seems useful and also helps to explain complex, contradictory, and otherwise complicated readings and sendings. However, at times the overall pattern of impressions, without categorization, is most important. Still, there are problems with myself as an instrument. Some of these are nonvalidation and loss of self-esteem, premature expression of impressions, and inability to read my own meters. However, by elaboration of the opposites, sometimes by restraining fleeting impressions, and by having others help me to read myself, I am often able to overcome these handicaps.

Subself theory (Shapiro, 1962) holds that the natural child self, primary process, is at the heart of many of the deeper messages but that these are often monitored by adult and parental subselves. Symptom messages, prelogical and nonverbal impressions, and peak experiences were also discussed as various conditions of myself as an instrument.

REFERENCES

HARRISON, R. Cognitive models for interpersonal and group behavior: A theoretical framework for research. *Explorations in Human Relations Training and Research.* Washington, D.C.: National Training Laboratories, N.E.A., 1965.

SHAPIRO, S. B. A theory of ego pathology and ego therapy. *Journal of Psychology,* 1962, **53,** 81–90.

Presently: Dr. Whitaker is Professor of Psychiatry at the University of Wisconsin (since 1965), and Dr. Warkentin is a Staff Psychiatrist at the Atlanta Psychiatric Clinic (which he helped to found in 1953).

Education: Carl received a Doctor of Medicine (1936) and a Master of Arts in psychology (1941) from Syracuse University. John earned his Doctor of Philosophy in psychology from the University of Rochester (1938) and a Doctor of Medicine from Northwestern University (1942).

Current major activities: Both are much involved in studying, practicing, and teaching couple's and family therapy.

CARL A. WHITAKER

Most rewarding projects: Carl: Proving that the cotherapist need not be a professional expert but can be naïve and yet be tremendously useful. John: Editing the journal, *Voices: The Art and Science of Psychotherapy*.

Future of humanistic psychology: Carl: A chemical breakthrough to worlds within ourselves resulting in almost unlimited creativity. John: More understanding of the almost magical capacity of people to respond to one another, possibly including extrasensory perception.

Personal histories: Carl: Instructor in Psychiatry at Syracuse University (1939–1940) and at the University of Louisville (1940–1944). Director of the Department of Psychiatry at the Oak Ridge Hospital (1944–1946). Professor and Chairman of the Department of Psychiatry at Emory University College of Medicine (1946–1955). President of the American Academy of Psychotherapists (1962–1964). John: Psychiatrist at Walter Reed Hospital and at Oak Ridge, Tennessee (1943–1946). Chief of the Neuropsychiatric Service at Lawson Veterans Administration Hospital (1946–1949). Professor of Psychiatry at Emory University (1949–1953). President of the American Academy of Psychotherapists (1959–1960) and of the Georgia Psychiatric Association (1966–1967).

Writings: Drs. Whitaker and Warkentin have contributed separately and jointly to such areas as schizophrenia, multiple therapy, innovations in therapeutic practice, and the training of psychotherapists. With Thomas Malone, Carl wrote *The Roots of Psychotherapy* (1953). He edited *Psychotherapy of Chronic Schizophrenia* (1958). John wrote the chapter on anality in the latter book (1958) and "The Involvement of the Professional Therapist," with Malone and Whitaker, in A. Burton (Ed.), *Case Studies in Counseling and Psychotherapy* (1959, pp. 218–256).

JOHN WARKENTIN

Present chapter: This is a revision of a paper which the authors originally prepared when they were working together at the Atlanta Psychiatric Clinic, a site of much innovative and humanistic thinking in psychology and psychiatry. It has not been previously published.

Chapter 25
CARL A. WHITAKER and JOHN WARKENTIN

THE THERAPIST AS A PROTOTYPE

The young graduate student and his wife had been in couple's psychotherapy for approximately twenty hours. The initial move in therapy was made by the wife, who established a seductive relationship with the therapist within the first two or three interviews which faded within the next two or three interviews. The husband seemed unaware of this and certainly not very jealous. There was much talk about their battles at home and about the distance between them; yet there was a quiet sense of how significant they were to each other. Following her initial approach, the wife became a silent or almost silent observer of the restless interaction between the therapist and her husband. He was a petulant, whining, dependent little boy whose bursts of rebellion were associated with blaming the therapist for his sense of impotence. In between, he exuded a kind of bizarre admiration of the therapist, couched in the philosophic and poetic terms of his training. He talked about his fluttery heart when he saw the therapist on the street, his panic for fear he would see the therapist undressed in the swimming area of the gym, and his general feeling of anxiety about members of the older generation. He repeatedly tried to fix the responsibility for his lack of progress on the therapist's unwillingness to push him or on the therapist's lack of interest.

The therapist did, indeed, lack interest. This man was boring, and his dreamy projection of the therapist's 9-foot stature in comparison with his own "Tiny Tim" feeling gave the whole situation a gross sense of unreality. Gradually this changed in quality. The patient gradually became more con- vinced that he was not going to spring full-grown out of therapy and that maybe he would have to go on living with his inadequacies. Because of the impasse quality, the therapist invited a consultant into the interview and discussed the situation described above. It suddenly seemed clear that the wife's little-girl quality was one of the things that kept her partner from being masculine. There was a fairly remarkable clearing between that interview and the next, and the couple decided that they would end in three more visits. The death of the young student's image of the therapist as himself twenty years hence was a healthy, although painful, experience for him. Almost from the first, he had been denying himself as a person and denying the therapist as a person. Now he was free to talk about his inadequacies as reality and to talk to the therapist as a person. The prototype was dying.

A discussion of psychotherapy may be concerned with the process, the functioning of the patient, or the function and the person of the therapist. We will place the emphasis of the present chapter on a consideration of the person of the therapist as it affects his functioning. We will become involved only incidentally in aspects of the therapeutic process as such or in the patient's function as such. We will discuss the subject on an informal level, in part because it will be obvious that we must be autobiographical in derivation.

The Significance of Technique It may seem presumptuous to disregard the technique of psychotherapy. However, our intent is to define those denominators which are a stratum below technique and to deal with those intangible factors in psychotherapy which operate in the success of a therapist, independently of his specific method. A more compelling consideration is the fact that patients get better with therapists who utilize extremely diverse methods.

We question the concept that success is based on the use of techniques or on the therapeutic role. The power of the feeling relationship between therapist and patient seems more significant than the technique of either in dealing with the other. Regardless of method, they each seek the therapeutic relationship in order to satisfy profound inner needs. It should be accepted by both that the patient will have priority in being a parasite in the relationship. A major problem for the therapist, therefore, is how he can yield to his emotional functioning without making his participation of such a nature that the process serves primarily his own residual needs. We, and others, have found it useful to approach this question by accepting the therapist as being a prototype to the patient as well as being a real person. We challenge the current emphasis on what the therapist does. What he is, especially in terms of his unconscious, seems much more important for the success of treatment.

We have three concepts to present. The first relates to assigning a name to a complex factor in the effectiveness of the therapist, i.e., "prototype." The second states that this prototype factor necessitates continued growth in the therapist as a person. He may be able to develop his methodology to the point where it needs little modification, but such stabilization is not adequate to the development of the intuitive function which underlies the process of being a prototype for the patient. Third, it is this prototype use of the therapist which makes ending possible and essential: possible, because the death of the prototype is like the ending of a fantastic dream in contrast with the loss of a real-life friend; and essential, since the patient becomes a child in this dream and is bound to the therapist unless he can conclude and complete the dream in relation to that particular therapist as prototype.

THE CONCEPT OF "PROTOTYPE"

In using the term "prototype," we are trying to bring into focus a concept which has to do with the functioning of each one of us but which is so ghostlike that this function permeates our relationships with little awareness or with only momentary and hazy awareness. By "prototype," we mean not merely an example or ideal in the usual sense, but rather a pattern for all of life, as exemplified in our cultural attitudes about certain charismatic persons like Churchill or Gandhi. A prototype need not be a person; perhaps even undercurrents of our culture itself could be conceived of as prototypes. We want to emphasize as prototypes particularly those models which are moving forces in our living and which we adopt without deliberate intent. Perhaps our most significant prototype is the introjected primordial parent, the presexual parent, combining the nurturing mother and the protective father.

In therapy, it is as if the patient develops a fantasy image which combines the qualities of previous prototypes and the inner qualities of the immediate therapist. The therapist as a prototype may even come to represent the patient's entire world; hence the abysmal quality of his panic in the face of possible desertion by the therapist. If this concept is accurate, then one of the essential objectives of the good therapist is to accept himself as prototype to the patient. Yet simultaneously he must be able to be himself, a maturing person. The therapist is a transference object. He is a symbolic source of nourishment and a symbol of authority. He is a teacher of interactional patterns, of cause and effect, and of those unique laws of personal relations which contrast with public relations. He is also a person, with all the implications of that omnibus term.

Yet in one sense, the therapist may be thought of as a hallucination which makes apparent to the patient facets of life which he did not see previously. The patient likely to experience only those feeling tones which the therapist experiences with comfort. In other words, the extent of the p tient's emotional experience in therapy is directly related to the therapist's freedom with the violence or intimacy of his own childlike emotions. The therapist is thus both a positive and a negative model, and it is important that he be able to "give first" or "go first." The patient's feeling of safety and trust in the therapist is related to a certainty that the therapist can enjoy in the patient those aspects which he has already accepted within himself.

Centrality of the Therapist as a Person This makes the therapist himself the pivot around which the therapeutic process centers. The patient orients himself in his utilization of therapy to those areas within which the therapist is most capable of giving. In fact, the patient is so perceptive that he may orient himself to one of the specific areas in which the therapist is at that time growing as a "patient" (i.e., a person). The patient is intuitively aware of the therapist's unconscious functioning in a manner similar to the intuitive capacity of animals and children to recognize emotional acceptance or rejection. The patient is aware because he had similar childhood capacities which have become unavailable to him in the bind of reality and culture. With an adequate therapist, the patient will dare to loosen his hold on reality and function more and more on the level of his own unconscious. This therapeutic creativity increases as he finds himself acceptable to the therapist, and that acceptance is the limiting factor. The critical question is: Can the therapist relate to the patient's unconscious and simultaneously face the "patient" factors in himself, i.e., be emotionally transparent? The inner experience of the therapist in any given interview constitutes the biggest limitation on the patient's experience in that interview. Thus, it is not possible for the therapist to accept the "role" of being permissive to the patient. He will not be able to permit emotional outbursts on the part of the patient unless he can permit emotional explosions within himself. Thus, true permissiveness is conditional upon a level of emotional participation which is possible only if the therapist has been a patient and is being a person.

Whether the therapist is useful to the pa-

tient seems to have to do with both the maturity of the therapist as a person and the availability of the therapist's unconscious. The patient brings to the therapy the function of making the therapist symbolic, but this is lost unless the therapist can "be." For example, the schizophrenic patient may overwhelm the therapist who has not experienced help with his own psychotic self; the patient is simply disillusioned once again in his efforts to find an adequate prototype. The template was faulty. The extent of the harm done to the patient, however, is limited to an interference with the potential therapeutic value which the therapist might have had. The harm is limited by the patient's amazing capacity to protect himself against the immature therapist. A more serious threat is the experienced therapist who carefully avoids any extensive commitments because he knows the depth of involvement possible. By contrast, the naïve therapist plunges fully into the therapeutic experience before he is aware of the tremendous abyss that threatens to engulf him and which he may, at best, barely be able to struggle through. This may be one reason why he succeeds where the old professional, who avoids the stress, does not. Once the patient is involved, the therapist who does not commit himself immobilizes the patient's growth by denying access to that capacity, which the patient nonetheless senses. It is as if the patient becomes a child, accepts the therapist as a prototype, and is then frozen in this relationship with the therapist as master.

The therapist as prototype can be of little functional use unless he is willing to go to the limits of his own capacity as an integrated person with each patient. Technical expertise is no substitute for this personal commitment. Only as the therapist accepts himself as a "patient" in this situation can the patient declare himself. The patient can feel acceptance of his irrational self only as the therapist accepts the irrational component in himself. For example, this "growing edge" may be manifested when the therapist expresses verbally an inner impulse which seems out of context and unrelated to anything except the therapist's own fantasy life. Often the patient can sense such acceptance without any apparent verbal or behavioral manifestation. In any case, unless the therapist pushes his own limits in that situation, the patient does not dare to exceed his own self-imposed restrictions. We are increasingly convinced that the only aspect of prototype which has major emotional value for the patient is the irrational component of the integrated therapist.

The Therapist as a Patient We have discussed above some of the prerequisites of the therapist as a person, the most essential of which is that he has himself been a "successful" patient. Inasmuch as his residual immaturities influence the course of his functioning with patients, his continued maturing is a necessity to doing adequate therapy. As indicated above, we are firmly convinced that the dynamics and the pathology of the therapeutic process are both centered in the person of the therapist. However, his patients may provide a deep impetus to the further development of his own capacities. It is not enough that the therapist strive to help others acquire that which he has himself learned; the learning process must be going on in the therapist if he is to help initiate it in the patient.

It might be postulated that the completely mature person would be incapable of functioning as a therapist because his motivations for the emotional effort involved would have been lost. Actually, it seems to me that the professional therapist has, in one sense, entered upon the vocation of "being a patient," and his function as therapist is always dependent upon his capacity to change (just as any expert must continue his learning). If it becomes impossible for him to ask for help with his residual immaturities, he then loses the capacity to be a therapist. We may now define the patient as a person who sees the limitations of his capacities, and the therapist as one who is more and more aware of the unlimited nature of his potential and who has an increasing interest in the realization of it. The therapist must be able to recognize and accept the offer of help from the patient.

In psychotherapy, it is more important for the patient to know the therapist as a person than for the therapist to know the patient. When it becomes necessary for the therapist to know his patient, this need is occasioned by the therapist's excessive need for help. In general, the flow of help is in the direction of the greater need, as recognized by both patient and therapist and as responded to by the capacity of the other person to give. If one analyzes a single interview, he can observe the seesaw movement of therapist factors in one and of patient factors in the other, as they provide for the continual deepening of the relationship.

If an impasse develops, whether it is momentary or continues for years, the therapist is responsible for resolving it. On occasion, however, the patient may resolve such an impasse by accepting his own therapeutic capacity as the necessary ingredient for further progress. Each realizes that such a reversal is merely an intermission; yet it is surprising how easily the return to the original pattern takes place. The basis for this "righting reflex" has to do with the patient's recognition of his increased safety and power. Now he is free to demand of the therapist. In the overall sense, the "taking" of the patient is great, but while the by-product which the therapist takes is minimal in comparison, it is of great importance.

Perhaps the most important factor in the therapist as a person is his belief that the patient can grow in emotional capacity. The therapist's own continued growth constitutes the only valid basis for a belief that patients are treatable. In a similar sense, the therapist's capacity to separate when a relationship has achieved what is possible forms the basis for the manner in which each patient ends.

DEATH OF THE PROTOTYPE

We have tried to show, through some consideration of our own therapeutic work, how the professional therapeutic process involves the projection of the patient's previous prototype onto the therapist as a person. Utilizing the learnings from our professional function, we now come to the "death of the prototype" as the means by which the patient becomes able to inherit his own adequacy.

The nature of the separation of the patient from the therapist is of such major significance that it conditions the final value which the therapy has for both. This separation has customarily been called *ending*, usually referring to the cessation of interviews. Actually the term is inadequate if we think of therapy as a phase in the process of living rather than as an entity in itself.

During the process of therapy, it is our professional effort to establish a relationship which is so profound (and even primitive) that it will replace all earlier prototypes. The intensity of the relationship can be proportionately greater if it is clear to the therapist that he functions as a prototype, with the eventual goal of helping the patient to grow away from him. We believe that the superimposition of the patient's perception of the therapist as a person on his perception of the therapist as a prototype is the dynamic basis which enables the patient to shed his pseudoadult facade during the therapeutic process. At the conclusion of therapy, the patient's realization that the therapist is a person makes possible the release of the patient from his involvement with the prototype.

The discussion of ending must deal with the increasing significance of the therapist as a person, concomitant with his diminishing significance as a prototype. This is brought about by the patient's satisfaction of his infantile needs to the point where he realizes that the therapist is to some degree seeing him, the patient, as a prototype. If the therapist is willing to accept this patient-type view of himself even to a minimal degree, the patient is offered the opportunity to be a person and a prototype to the therapist. He then invites the therapist to be a peer, and when the therapist in his professional function denies this, the patient in retaliation destroys the last remnant of the therapist as a prototype and begins the process of relating to others as persons. The therapist is then faced with his own grief at parting.

If, however, the therapist should deny his own patient factors, the patient may still end knowing full well that in taking from the therapist he has been helpful but feeling the same grief which the therapist feels at the separation. The therapist has helped the patient grow up to the point where the patient feels mature enough to help the therapist. The patient may go away disappointed if the therapist has so little respect for his growth and stature that he is unable to take freely that which the patient offers.

CONCLUSION

The patient originally comes to the therapist with the fear that he will become dependent, as he once was on his original parent. With the death of the prototype, the patient kills all previous prototypes to the extent to which they were incorporated in the therapist. This makes the residual prototype needs in the patient relatively harmless, so that he may relate more freely to any person. Now, in relating to those people who have some prototype values to him, he establishes a reciprocal relationship in which reversal of function is so easy that it has little of the restrictive character of the professional relationship. He has ended with a professional therapist and is increasingly able to call upon the therapeutic capacities of any individual. In any such casual meeting there may develop a brief but profound response to his living in that moment, and he is free to offer similar resources in return.

Presently: Partner, Psychological Service Associates, Los Angeles (since 1953).

Education: Doctor of Philosophy in psychology from the Ohio State University (1952).

Current major activity: Individual psychotherapy.

Most rewarding project: "Trying to become aware of what is."

ALVIN A. LASKO

Future of humanistic psychology: "A fantasy and a tentative prediction: Humanistic psychology may become a major factor in the lives of people generally."

Personal history: Alvin Lasko was an accountant for a number of years before he returned to college to prepare himself for the field of psychology. Assistant Professor of Psychology at the University of California, Los Angeles (1952–1955). Founded Psychological Service Associates (with James F. T. Bugental, 1953). Human relations training for educational institutions, business, and industry, and the UCLA Graduate School of Business Administration. Former President of the Los Angeles Society of Clinical Psychologists and of the Southern California Psychological Association. Diplomate in Clinical Psychology of the American Board of Examiners in Professional Psychology.

Writings: (The editor begs leave to insert a personal word here: Alvin Lasko has, so far as I know, not published any work before the present chapter. He is, instead of being a writer, a reader and thinker of unusual depth and dedication. I, personally, and not a few others who have published regularly, have often profited by Dr. Lasko's creative insights, penetrating criticisms, and genuine valuing of others' efforts. He gives much support and help to others, is happy when they take and develop his ideas, and does not need to assert paternity.)

Present chapter: This is a revision of a paper originally presented at the American Psychological Association meetings in Los Angeles, September, 1964.

Chapter 26
ALVIN A. LASKO

PSYCHOTHERAPY, HABITS, AND VALUES

"The moment one inquires about the sense or value of life, one is sick." So said Freud (Jones, 1957, p. 465). At the risk of giving my Freudian friends evidence of what they have only suspected, I shall now inquire into just such issues and try to show why I believe that it is the therapist's primary task to deal with the value systems of his patient, rather than with his habits or behaviors.

I would like to start by pointing out that the formulation "habits *versus* values," although commonly made, unnecessarily polarizes some issues and beclouds others. It is my contention that values and habits are reflections of conceptualizations that are on different levels of discourse. The concept of "habit" reflects an objective, positivistic conceptualization, whereas the concept of "value" is experiential and phenomenological. The approach to therapy in terms of habit and reinforcement takes behavior as the basic datum of concern, together with the conditions under which behavior is brought about, maintained, and changed. On the other hand, a value orientation has as its base and as its fundamental datum the experience of a living person.

What is involved here is a contrast between two philosophic positions: the habit approach, oriented to the positivistic position, and the value approach, oriented to a phenomenological and an existential position. The attack on the habit approach often resorts to a kind of name-calling or subtle moralizing by pointing out that this approach deals with the individual as a sort of robot and neglects those very aspects that make him human. And it is often pointed out that the individual is not seen in his wholeness and that his feelings are completely neglected. Such arguments, it seems to me, are beside the point. The therapeutic position that is chosen will depend on the assumptions that are made and the goals that are sought.

The Habit Approach When treatment is conceptualized as a process in which the therapist determines the character of the behaviors that get the individual into difficulty and the kinds of behavior required to avoid the difficulty, then it seems to me that a habit approach not only is warranted but also may be most effective. This position assumes that the kind of behavior required

247

is clearly known and that the goals are to eliminate certain behaviors and substitute others. Such an approach, as has been demonstrated by the application of reinforcement approaches (Eysenck, 1960; Rotter, 1954; Wolpe, 1958) to some kinds of clinical situations, *can* be effective.

The Value Approach However, under conditions such as generally prevail in individual therapy in noninstitutional settings, the central focus must, by the very nature of the therapy situation, be on the ways the individual regards himself and his world. We are forced into a phenomenological frame of reference, into dealing with the experience of the individual; and we must recognize that the experience of the individual is organized by the value system he holds. By "value," I mean that which the individual regards as enhancing to his existence. The fact that man is capable of regarding or being aware of himself and of what may enhance his existence is the crucial aspect that dictates a value approach for the task of the psychotherapist. It is this self-awareness that constitutes the essential human condition.

The value approach—the existential approach—sees an experiencing being who is capable of recognizing his own experience (his own conditioning, if you like) and of making choices based on this recognition. The self-recognition of one's own conditioning or past experience gives rise to the recognition that the outcome of action based on such past experience is at best only a probability surrounded by contingency. The individual experiences this circumstance as one evoking the fear and anxiety of choice. The habit approach sees only the conditioning and fails to recognize the essential human quality of being aware of one's own conditioning.

FUNCTION OF THERAPY

It is the function of therapy from a value standpoint to aid the patient in recognizing how it is that he lives in the world, with himself and with others (Buhler, 1962). How he lives depends on the values he holds—what he sees as enhancing to his existence. The existential or value therapist is basically interested in aiding his patient to become aware of his value system, of how he has organized his experience to enhance and to defend his existence. It is my contention that when the patient becomes aware of how he lives, of what he values, and of what his conditionings are, then the basis for a value reorganization and change will be established.

I say that a *basis* for value reorganization and change is established, rather than that the change or reorganization itself occurs, because whether either occurs depends on the patient's willingness to risk and to make an act of commitment. It is precisely at this point of risking and making a commitment that the recognition of the phenomenologically enhancing and defensive character of the patient's value system determines the particular quality and nature of the value-oriented therapist's participation. Fundamentally, as the patient becomes aware of his value system, of his way of organizing experience, he becomes aware of his identity. As this awareness begins to lead to a value reorganization, an identity crisis is precipitated. It is the authentic presence of the therapist, his presence as a person, which is the crucial aspect in fostering the self-determined growth of the individual and which supports letting go of the old identity, the old value patternings.

By way of contrast, the habit or reinforcement therapist decides which behaviors are the cause of the presenting difficulties and which new behaviors must be substituted for these. He then proceeds to act, says Krasner (1961), as a "social reinforcing machine" with the intent of eliminating the undesirable behavior and encouraging the desirable. The difficulty with this formulation lies, I believe, in the determination of which behavior to reinforce and which to leave alone or to reinforce negatively. Such a determination lies outside the habit or reinforcement theoretical system; that is, what behaviors are to be *valued* is a question outside the system. If such valuation is not taken into account systematically, the therapist's choice of what to reinforce will be an unconsidered reflection of his own values, of what *he* considers enhancing. If he recognizes this danger without really meeting the value issue, he will be forced to determine the behaviors that he will positively or negatively reinforce by reference to those institutions he, the therapist, represents, consciously or unconsciously.

GOALS OF THERAPY

If the goals of therapy are construed in terms of helping people become more fully functioning, more self-determining and autonomous, the habit approach based on principles of reinforcement is a self-contradiction and incompatible with such goals. It seems to me that inherent in the habit-reinforcement position are certain assumptions which deny the very concept of a self-determining, autonomous person. In this approach the individual is seen as a set of habits that are established, maintained, and changed by social reinforcement which, by definition, originates outside himself. This implicitly systematizes and limits the conceptualization of therapy goals—and all forms of human interaction, for that matter —as other-directed or other-determined. It is most certainly a gross oversimplification, but it appears to me that a habit-reinforcement way of thinking is usually basic to the approach to change in an authoritarian society. Similarly, it is not surprising that in such a society a value approach—an existential approach centering around the concepts of autonomy, commitment, and choice—is neglected or rejected.

The existential therapist, working from a value position, has his goals directed explicitly toward aiding the patient to become aware that he is not in the control of others, that he is not limited to behaving so as to avoid external punishment or to gain gratification in terms of how he is viewed by others (Bugental, 1965). The patient is helped to recognize that he can become aware of his own conditionings, which are the experiences of the past, and that he can make choices that are applicable to the present.

SOME SOCIAL AND POLITICAL IMPLICATIONS

In a stable, highly structured society where habitual ways of doing things yield a minimally satisfying way of life, a habit approach would seem to be possible and feasible. This is so because under these conditions past learnings are a sufficient basis for "adjusted" behavior. The choice of a habit approach to the understanding of behavior and its change may be seen as a consequence of a profit- or power-oriented society organized on principles of mass production and mass consumption. This follows because only under conditions of relatively certain behavior predictability, can such a society function. However, in a rapidly changing, person-oriented, affluent society, where the individual's behavior must be constantly changing also, an approach which stresses autonomous values is required to provide the flexibility and creativity that is essential to growth and well-being.

Another setting in which the same forces are at work is the college campus. I believe that it is the failure of those who determine policy in our colleges and universities to recognize and take into account the need to shift from a habit to a value approach that, at least conceptually, is reflected in the student revolts against depersonalized educational processes. In the same way, the seemingly senseless rioting among the dispossessed of our society may grow from similar roots.

CONCLUSION

I began my discussion with Freud's quotation, "The moment one inquires about the sense or value of life, one is sick." It appears to me that once man achieves a fairly regularly full belly, this is exactly the kind of question he does ask. It may be that this is sickness, but, if this is so, being truly human is a sickness. The capacity of man to be aware of himself, which was originally a means to survival, may become a burden when survival is assured. Vaihinger (1966)[1] has suggested that when the means exceed the requirements of the ends for which they were designed, they become ends in them-

[1] My introduction to Vaihinger was through an article by Paul S. Frey, entitled "Vaihinger's Law on Existential Inquiry," which was published in the *Journal of Existential Psychiatry*, 1964, **4**, 237–243, and the concluding section reflects Dr. Frey's influence.

selves. He further suggests that man's self-awareness represents a particular case of this general principle. Like Parkinson's (Osborn, 1957) ever-expanding bureaucracies, the ever-expanding ruminative redundancies of self-awareness reflect both the curse and the glory of being human. Be that as it may, man's ability to be aware of himself (and even aware of what has brought about his being as he is) must be seen as basic to his being human. It follows then that the value system, by which the person organizes his awareness of self and the world, dictates that the therapist's task must be to deal primarily with values.

REFERENCES

BUGENTAL, J. F. T. *The search for authenticity.* New York: Holt, Rinehart and Winston, 1965.

BUHLER, CHARLOTTE. *Values in psychotherapy.* New York: Free Press, 1962.

EYSENCK, H. J. *Behavior therapy and the neuroses.* New York: Pergamon Press, 1960.

JONES, E. *The life and work of Sigmund Freud.* Vol. 3. New York: Basic Books, 1957.

KRASNER, L. The therapist as a social reinforcement machine. *Research in Psychotherapy,* 1961, **2,** 61–94.

OSBORN, R. C. *Parkinson's law.* Boston: Houghton Mifflin, 1957.

ROTTER, J. B. *Social learning and clinical psychology.* Englewood Cliffs, N.J.: Prentice-Hall, 1954.

VAIHINGER, H. *The philosophy of "as if."* (2nd ed.) New York: Barnes & Noble, 1966.

WOLPE, J. *Psychotherapy by reciprocal inhibition.* Stanford, Calif.: Stanford Univer. Press, 1958.

Presently: Associate Professor of Business Administration and Chairman of the Behavioral Sciences Area of the Graduate School of Business Administration at the University of California, Los Angeles. Also Associate Research Behavioral Scientist in the Institute of Industrial Relations at UCLA (since 1961).

Education: Doctor of Business Administration in organizational behavior from Harvard University School of Business (1958).

JAMES V. CLARK

Current major activities: Teaching, consulting, and research in applied humanistic behavioral science; mainly in large organizations such as businesses, school systems, and religious organizations.

Most rewarding project: Two related projects: "The explication and development of a field of practice I am calling 'task group therapy' and trying to spell out a system for existential behavioral science."

Future of humanistic psychology: Dr. Clark believes that "people in positions of great responsibility will be (and are) the first to see the practical necessity for humanistic values by which to guide their enterprises and that this fact will come more and more to influence academic values and practices."

Personal history: Warrant Officer in the United States Maritime Service (1944–1947). Social Planning Consultant to the Community Chest of San Francisco (1950–1952). Operations Manager of the United Fund of San Francisco (1952–1954). Research Associate in Human Relations and then Assistant Professor of Business Administration at Harvard University (1956–1961).

Writings: *Education for the Use of Behavioral Science* (1962) and *Organizational Behavior and Administration: Cases, Concepts and Research Findings,* coauthored with Paul R. Lawrence et al. (1961). Dr. Clark has expressed his fresh and cross-disciplinary perspective in articles in psychological, sociological, and business journals.

Present chapter: This chapter represents thinking on the interrelations between human relations training and religious experience which has interested Dr. Clark for some time but which he here publishes for the first time.

Chapter 27
JAMES V. CLARK

TOWARD A THEORY AND PRACTICE
OF RELIGIOUS EXPERIENCING

SENSITIVITY TRAINING AND RELIGIOUS DEVELOPMENT

I am engaged in the practice of working as a professional in so-called sensitivity training groups. More recently these are coming to be called "basic encounter"[1] groups, and the term has much merit, for the longer I work in such settings, the more I see man as grappling with and toward some of the most profound aspects of his existence. Specifically (and very much to my surprise, for I had rejected organized religion like many other intellectuals), I have discovered for myself how deep man's needs for religious experience are. Time and again I have seen persons unfold in a way that has forced me to conclude that sensitivity training is indeed a religious enterprise. I am even more surprised to find myself thinking it is the *most* religious enterprise of which I know. Now I mean something quite specific by "most religious": I mean that the probability of people connecting with their own capacities for love and power is greater in such groups than elsewhere.

[1] See Rogers' extensive examination of basic encounter groups in Chapter 28, the Gibbs' analysis in Chapter 17, and the discussions of such groups by Haigh in Chapter 22 and Thomas in Chapter 23. [Editor]

Placed in the environment of one of these groups, people seem, in their own ways, to go through the development of a religion. Although the revelations and the symbols used in each individual's faith and witnessing have their own unique content for each person, the process each person goes through appears similar to the development of any religion. It is thus the case that sensitivity training offers both a technology for the creation of meaningful religious development and an unparalleled laboratory for the study of the necessary elements of religious experience itself. In this chapter, I shall discuss both these aspects.

WHAT PEOPLE IN GROUPS SAY

To communicate a flavor of what I am seeing and responding to, let me share some quotations from groups I was in as I wrote this chapter:

AN ELECTRONICS VICE-PRESIDENT, AGED FORTY-SEVEN:
You, your—all of a sudden, John—I have worked with you for five years, and all of a sudden, right now, this minute, I see that you are a creature. *You* are a *creature*.

A CHINESE BANKER AND PHILOSOPHER, AGED FORTY-FIVE:
I have studied philosophy all my life, and now, right now, I feel the hands of Christ

are upon me. You—your hands are the hands of Christ.

A MANAGEMENT CONSULTANT, AGED THIRTY-FIVE:
I *saw* this old man today in our afternoon group. He is a, a *jerk*. He is a fundamentalist, and he is *proud* of it. And I, I (*crying*) *loved* him. I loved him. I love him.

A MANAGEMENT CONSULTANT, AGED THIRTY-SEVEN:
Since our last meeting, I have been so *excited*. I can hardly breathe. It seems like *I* can do *any*thing. It's like I turned myself inside out.

A MALE SCHOOLTEACHER, AGED FORTY:
My God, look at Frances! That face! Her face! What's happened to her?! She, she, she's the Buddha. She's beautiful.

A MALE PSYCHOTHERAPIST, AGED FORTY-SIX:
I can't look at you. It is like I am blinded by your face. You—it's—you're the sun! I can't look at you. It's like all the sorrow and all the beauty of the whole human race is in your face. *I'm* in your face! *I'm* the sun. I'm, I'm—I am beautiful. (*Cries.*)

A FEMALE PROBATION OFFICER, AGED THIRTY-TWO:
I saw in that moment when I chose to love, that I must love, now. It is *me* to love. I have spent my love like it's penny ante, like I had a dollar when I started and now I am thirty-two and I have a pot with 97 cents under my bed. I need not to have 85 cents left when I am seventy.

A BEHAVIORAL SCIENCE PROFESSOR, AGED THIRTY-FOUR:
I feel like a goddam ape! I have never felt like this before. Look at my fist. I just walked around hitting the wall with it. God, that felt good. I feel like any woman in the world could be mine if I wanted her.

A LAWYER, AGED THIRTY-FOUR:
It's like I am on two ladders, like I *must* be on two ladders. One is my family and the other is the men I work with. And I am on these ladders and looking up, and at the top, at the top (*cries*), is a big light and it's "Eli!" (*Cries, smiles.*) You know, I was brought up a good orthodox boy, and I never saw God before. I never did.

SOME DETERMINANTS OF RELIGIOUS EXPERIENCE IN GROUPS

How does this happen? This is not the place to go deeply into the theories being developed to understand sensitivity training,[2] but certainly at least three aspects of the experience can be identified as having a considerable impact on the outcome: (1) the impetus toward connection, growth, and development that brings people to these groups; (2) the power of human interaction at once to meet man's need for connection and his need for self-actualization; and (3) the conviction and skill of the professional in designing the experience and in helping it unfold.

These groups consist of people who come seeking something. Usually they are students, managers, executives, or professional people—people who do not define themselves as patients, and yet who come on a quest. They come seeking a greater, richer, and more connected experiencing of themselves which they cannot describe. The professional trainers know, however, that regardless of the ways in which members define themselves, they are treating their group members in a complex and deeply human sense. And they know that in treating those who are succeeding in this society, they are often treating those who are failing. Often, that is, they are treating those who are succeeding in internalizing the valuelessness, the deadness, the objectifying of others, the "marketing orientation" of society. Nevertheless, it is these professionals' faith that such people can, under appropriate conditions, experience the exhilaration of discovering and expressing their own love and power with one another. When this happens, people develop a sense of themselves as *in* their universe. And if it is their universe, they develop the need to relate to it.

The second ingredient in sensitivity training that bears on religious development has to do with the power of human interaction simultaneously to meet man's needs for love and for self-actualization. Those of us working in these groups have learned that if we hold people in a small group situation with no assigned parameters long enough, there

[2] See, for example, Clark (1963) and Culbert (1966, Ch. 2).

are only two ways out—withdrawal into distance or extension outward toward expressing more love and power. More often than not, a person expands when he is confronted —for forty or fifty hours—by a dozen or so other people in a circle; with no imposed task to fly into; no hierarchy to bind, contain, and ritualize love and power; and a skilled professional to' help in the expression of the feelings generated in such an experience. He becomes aware of the unrealistic limits that both he and his environment have imposed on him; he expands beyond them, and he begins the process of sensing his own personal limits at that moment in time. He comes to see that these limits are there because he feels too much fear at the thought of choosing to step through them. But, when he can sense himself as *choosing* to remain inside his own limits, he begins to develop an important sense of mastery. He can, in a phrase, resist holding out to others the false hope that he has no limits.

Knowing what one cannot give, one is able to offer what he *can* give. Knowing what one can give leads to a genuine experiencing of interdependence. And this experiencing leads to, and is almost the same as, the *valuing* of interdependence. People come to see that the prizing of others—the mystical, terrifying, deep, religious, expansive experience of knowing that no man is an island—and the valuing of a personal and social ethic of interdependence have been too rare in their world. They want more of it.

I have already touched on the third important ingredient in sensitivity training viewed as religious experience: the trainer and his skill both in designing the experience and in facilitating the expression of the feelings it generates. What trainers do, specifically, is still very much under investigation.[3] In my experience, there is an immensely important ingredient that has not been investigated: the trainer's faith in human beings' capacities to encounter all varieties of profound anxiety and to master them. ("Master" does not mean "deny.") Such faith emerges only in people who have a great deal of experience with their own

and others' anxiety. And such experience is achieved only by people who have an engulfing passion to be in the presence of their own and others' developing personhood. When one is grasped by this passion, he has a need to fulfill himself through the experience of being in the presence of another person who is, to use the Jungian term, "individuating." Because he has this need, he is willing to use his own power to bring it about. Depending on his own personality and other important factors of the moment, he may express this power through either restraining or expressing himself. Regardless of his specific behavior, though, it is his need to feel fulfilled in the presence of another self-realizing person that seems to have a powerful effect on the outcome of the group.[4]

INTERACTION AND RELIGIOUS DEVELOPMENT

Regardless of with whom it takes place, trainer or member, it is the revelation of the *I* to the other and the other to the *I* that is the core healing and redemptive activity in the sensitivity training group. It is so because the more one member of the relation meets his need for self-actualization, the more the other does.[5]

To me this form of relation is the highest form of human interaction. As each gets what he needs, each grows. I believe it was Tillich who observed that we come to know our own ego only through the resistance of another. He was pointing to half the circle of interdependence I am pointing to here. Martin Buber was making a similar point when he said (1965, p. 71) that it is "from one man to another that the heavenly bread of self being is passed."

To put this whole point in yet a different way and thus to state the central observation of this essay, the mutually revelatory

[4] Spiegelman (1965) has discovered the same phenomenon in the two-person therapy situation.

[5] For a fuller discussion of this point, see Rogers (1961, Ch. 18) and Clark (1963). For some measurements of it, see Clark & Culbert (1965) and Culbert (1966).

[3] See, for example, Culbert (1966) and Peters (1966).

relation is the medium in which all the central elements of religious experience emerge almost at once. These elements are a *revelatory experience*, the development of *transcendent values* such that the person values facing toward the content of his revelation, *faith* in Tillich's sense (1957) of developing an internal ultimate concern with the external ultimate seen only in symbols, and *witnessing*, by which I mean acting—moving toward or in some way expressing one's ultimate concern.

Rereading the quotations presented earlier in this chapter, one may see—both in the words and in the "ring" of the words—that these elements are often present, evoked by the interpersonal experiences of the members. Revelation is evident in the sudden and powerful new visions of themselves and of others which the speakers describe. Implicit in many of the statements is the emergence of a transcendent valuing of the experience. Faith, the development of an ultimate concern with the ultimate, is involved with the infinite and is expressed through symbols rather than signs: "Christ," "the Buddha," "the sun," "Eli."

The central evidence of witnessing is the fact that most of these statements were made intensely and directly to the other in the relation. To have a revelatory experience about someone and to speak it to him is one thing. To have it and not to speak it to him is quite another. The one witnesses; the other simply partakes.

EXISTENTIAL GUILT AND EXISTENTIAL SHAME

The avoidance of existential confrontation is a central function of neurosis (Bugental, 1965, Ch. 17). To relate, one must set oneself at a distance (Buber, 1965, pp. 59–71), and to set oneself at a distance is to confront existential aloneness. Buber has shown (1965, pp. 121–148) that existential guilt is the guilt of not having affirmed another, of not having answered another's plea for community, of not having entered an I-Thou relationship. Existential guilt, then, is clearly an important determinant in one's

coming to value and create relation, for such guilt can often be expiated only by the establishment of relation in the here and now.

Existential shame, on the other hand, is the shame of not experiencing oneself as an actor, as a creator, as—to use Bugental's term (1965, pp. 203–208)—an "I process." We experience existential shame as we are aware of having treated ourselves only as recipients of power and not also as expressors of it.

The kind of experience people in sensitivity training groups have is one which is better designed than any other I know of to allow for the experiencing of both existential shame and existential guilt, and both are manifestly important for man to experience. The prevalence of neurotic guilt and neurotic shame attests to both the difficulty we have in experiencing their existential counterparts and the lack of opportunity for such experiencing. The kinds of experiences in the quotations in this paper are the only ones I know of in any educational environment whatever which will facilitate the experiencing of these extremely important ingredients of the human experience.

Moreover, people do not emerge from this experiencing unchanged. They emerge with the commitment and the capacities to avoid a great deal of existential guilt and shame by choosing to avoid the situations which would give rise to them. People (not all people, by any means, but a substantial number) emerge with a profound desire to make choices, choices to move toward and to create again the kind of relationship in which they had the experience. And they sense themselves as being *able* to create that kind of relation. In so doing, they illustrate a deep and integrative religious insight.

To *be* religious is to experience onself as *creating* God's presence.[6] When Adam did not answer, he, for that moment, destroyed God. To create God's presence is a joy and a

[6] My agnostic readers can translate this and all similar phrases into internal frame-of-reference phraseology. Wherever else God may or may not exist, He exists internally in the experiencing of Him. To me, it is at least poetic to omit the cumbersome internal frame-of-reference language. Moreover, such language overlooks the importance of relating oneself as a subject to an object.

duty of each human being, and the speakers in our quotations seemed to realize this. It is a joy and duty because we are doing what we need to do for our own creation. When man avoids experiencing himself as a creator, he sins against his own basic nature, and in that sense it is his duty to place himself in relation to the other who is presenting himself. Certainly central points of Buber are that God presents Himself through the other and that it takes an *I* to create a *Thou*. When another "secretly and bashfully watches for a silent Yes" (Buber, 1965, p. 71) and when we move toward him and respond to him with our "I-ness," we create him. And, if God is presenting Himself through the human other, we create Him. When this happens we are awed and exhilarated to discover that our looking and speaking have for us created God. We have discovered the kingdom of heaven where it is.

Such awe can be so overwhelming that it can take the form of terror (as the mystics know), the terror of being fused with, and engulfed in, the infinite. That experience *is* terrifying, all the more so when we *feel* that the infinite is within us and that our capacities to create are awesomely limitless. It is in part to avoid this terror that many have been attracted to religious organization at face value, without understanding or valuing its symbolic nature. If one is looking for it, one certainly can find there a set structure to avoid both the terror of creating God and the existential shame of not doing so. If a person concentrates solely on trying to alter and eliminate a fixed array of characteristics—the presence of which he believes will prevent him from being rewarded at some future time—then he may be a culturally acceptable person, he may do many gentle and fine things, and he may even contribute much to eliminating some bad things from the world, but he does nothing directly to create the other who can reciprocally create him. As a result he sins. He stands existentially guilty and existentially shameful.

Of course, each of us who avoids the terror of feeling himself as a prime mover, as an actor, as a creator, certainly deserves compassion, but compassion is different from failing to recognize our sins, and there is precious little opportunity for us either to know these basic sins or to seek redemption. If God is created in the encounter between our *I* and the other, then to avoid that creation for the terror of it or for any other reason is to put other gods before Him. Specifically, it is to put the idolatrous god of set structure before the terrifying and exhilarating act of creating. And redemption exists only in the creation of encounter.

To experience oneself as creating God in this way, one needs not only the desire to do it but some capacity to symbolize the act. One must face toward the creating act in order to move toward it, and therefore he must have a something to face toward. As I have said above, that something is a symbol for the ultimate. Faith is the centering act of the personality (Tillich, 1957). It is the unconditional focusing on and toward the ultimate as seen in symbol.

For a person unconditionally to center himself toward the ultimate, its symbols must be unreservedly his own. Regardless of its origin, he must have taken it utterly and completely into himself, as did the group members who felt the hands of Christ and who saw the face of Buddha and "Eli." Because the symbols of religious organization are not our own originally, we are quite correct (in a developmental sense) to reject them. And most intellectuals and professionals have. Indeed, it appears that most people have. But we are left needing an experience in which we can develop our own symbols. It may well be that later on we will see in culturally more widespread symbols, such as that of Christ on the cross, even deeper and more meaningful expressions of the object of our ultimate concern. If that happens, though, it will be because we chose to substitute the new symbol for one of our own. It was our own because it came to us in our own revelation. In fact it is quite likely that the symbol was an emotional memory of the encounter in which the revelation occurred.

SUMMARY

To summarize, religious development is contingent upon the centering act of faith, the act of developing an unconditional concern with the ultimate. But this cannot occur without a revelation that has allowed us to experience ourselves as *engaged* with the infinite. It is only then that we will come to *value* our facing it and moving toward it, our faith and our witnessing. And we will come to value only as we have experienced something we *want* again and again. Organismically, when we have engaged and been engaged by the other, we know we need it.

It is in this sense, then, that those concerned with religious development can find in this new, growth-oriented technology of sensitivity training a surprising ally. There is reason to believe that the pedagogy of religious experience has advanced far beyond what many religionists are aware of.

By the same token, those few scientists who are not afraid to look for the natural and growthful tendencies of man under conditions where such can be observed may also find in sensitivity training a living laboratory. It is no accident that the anthropologists have been comfortable about stating the uniformity of religious experience; they have observed man as he really lives. I predict such comfort for psychologists when they observe under the proper conditions.

And finally, I hope my colleagues in the practice of sensitivity training can come to see that organized religion is not inherently and irrevocably antireligious, as they may have thought. What would our society look like if every church and temple in America centered around encounter groups? Such a vision is possible, I know, for whenever I have conducted sensitivity training experiences for religious organization leaders, they have come to see vividly the profound relevance of sensitivity training for their life and work. Time and again these growthful and humble people—bishops, priests, ministers, and the like—have told sensitivity training professionals that in these groups they have seen Christ and God in ways they never thought possible.

They have seen Him where Martin Buber told us all to look, between man and man. They have seen Him where Paul Tillich told us all to look, in our own depths (Tillich, 1962, p. 63). But they *have* seen Him because they were in an educational experience in which they could face one another and reveal their beingness. The existence of such an educational experience seems good news indeed.

REFERENCES

BUBER, M. *The knowledge of man.* New York: Harper Torchbooks, 1965.

BUGENTAL, J. F. T. *The search for authenticity.* New York: Holt, Rinehart and Winston, 1965.

CLARK, J. V. Authentic interaction and personal growth in sensitivity training groups. *Journal of Humanistic Psychology*, 1963, **3**, 1–13.

CLARK, J. V., & CULBERT, S. A. Mutually therapeutic perception and self-awareness in a T-group. *Journal of Applied Behavioral Science*, 1965, **1**, 180–194.

CULBERT, S. A. Trainer self-disclosure and member growth in a T-group. Unpublished doctoral dissertation, Univer. of California, Los Angeles, 1966.

PETERS, D. Identification and personal change in laboratory training groups. Unpublished doctoral dissertation, Massachusetts Institute of Technology, 1966.

ROGERS, C. R. *On becoming a person.* Boston: Houghton Mifflin, 1961.

SPIEGELMAN, J. M. Some implications of the transference. *Spectrum Psychologiae*, Festschrift for C. A. Meier on his sixtieth birthday. Zurich: Rascher Verlag, 1965.

TILLICH, P. *Dynamics of faith.* New York: Harper Torchbooks, 1957.

TILLICH, P. *The shaking of the foundation.* London: Pelican Books, 1962.

Presently: Resident Fellow at the Western Behavioral Sciences Institute in La Jolla, California (since 1964).

Degrees: Doctor of Philosophy from Teachers College at Columbia University (1931). Doctor of Humane Letters from Lawrence College (1956).

Most rewarding project: "I am currently most excited about the possibility of the basic encounter group as a means of facilitating positive change in persons and their behavior. Also I would like to see more use made of such groups in education. I feel progress must be made in the philosophy of the behavioral sciences if we are to get out of the mechanistic rut of the Newtonian model of science, which still serves for most psychologists."

CARL R. ROGERS

Future of humanistic psychology: "I think that humanistic psychology will be playing an increasingly large role in the thinking of young people, especially young behavioral scientists. I believe we are, and I hope that we will deserve to be, the 'wave of the future.' "

Personal history: Psychologist-Director of the Child Study Department of the Society for the Prevention of Cruelty to Children in Rochester (1928–1939). Director of the Rochester Guidance Center (1939–1940). Professor of Psychology at Ohio State University (1940–1945), at the University of Chicago (1945–1957), and at the University of Wisconsin (1957–1963). Vice-president of the American Orthopsychiatric Association (1941–1942). President of the American Association for Applied Psychology (1944–1945), of the American Psychological Association (1946–1947), and of the American Academy of Psychotherapists (1956–1958). Distinguished Scientific Contribution Award from the American Psychological Association (1956). Fellow of the American Academy of Arts and Sciences (since 1961). Fellow of the Center for Advanced Study in the Behavioral Sciences (1962–1963).

Writings: Dr. Rogers's books include *Measuring Personality Adjustment in Children* (1931); *Counseling and Psychotherapy* (1942); *Client-centered Therapy* (1951); *Psychotherapy and Personality Change*, with others (1954); and *On Becoming a Person* (1961).

Present chapter: Written to try to capture in a naturalistic way some of the trends which occur in a group experience. This essay has not previously been published.

Chapter 28
CARL R. ROGERS

THE PROCESS OF THE BASIC ENCOUNTER GROUP

I would like to share with you some of my thinking and puzzlement regarding a potent new cultural development—the intensive group experience.[1] It has, in my judgment, significant implications for our society. It has come very suddenly over our cultural horizon, since in anything like its present form it is less than two decades old.

I should like briefly to describe the many different forms and different labels under which the intensive group experience has become a part of our modern life. It has involved different kinds of individuals, and it has spawned various theories to account for its effects.

As to labels, the intensive group experience has at times been called the *T-group* or *lab group*, "T" standing for training laboratory in group dynamics. It has been termed *sensitivity training* in human relationships. The experience has sometimes been called a *basic encounter group* or a *workshop*—a workshop in human relationships, in leadership, in counseling, in edu-

cation, in research, in psychotherapy. In dealing with one particular type of person—the drug addict—it has been called a *synanon*.

The intensive group experience has functioned in various settings. It has operated in industries, in universities, in church groups, and in resort settings which provide a retreat from everyday life. It has functioned in various educational institutions and in penitentiaries.

An astonishing range of individuals have been involved in these intensive group experiences. There have been groups for presidents of large corporations. There have been groups for delinquent and predelinquent adolescents. There have been groups composed of college students and faculty members, of counselors and psychotherapists, of school dropouts, of married couples, of confirmed drug addicts, of criminals serving sentences, of nurses preparing for hospital service, and of educators, principals, and teachers.

The geographical spread attained by this rapidly expanding movement has reached in this country from Bethel, Maine (starting point of the National Training Laboratory movement), to Idyllwild, California. To my personal knowledge, such groups also exist in France, England, Holland, Japan, and Australia.

In their outward pattern these group experiences also show a great deal of diversity.

[1] In the preparation of this paper I am deeply indebted to two people, experienced in work with groups, for their help: Jacques Hochmann, M.D., psychiatrist of Lyon, France, who has been working at WBSI on a U.S.P.H.S. International Post-doctoral Fellowship, and Ann Dreyfuss, M.A., my research assistant. I am grateful for their ideas, for their patient analysis of recorded group sessions, and for the opportunity to interact with two original and inquiring minds.

There are T-groups and workshops which have extended over three to four weeks, meeting six to eight hours each day. There are some that have lasted only 2½ days, crowding twenty or more hours of group sessions into this time. A recent innovation is the "marathon" weekend, which begins on Friday afternoon and ends on Sunday evening, with only a few hours out for sleep and snacks.

As to the conceptual underpinnings of this whole movement, one may almost select the theoretical flavor he prefers. Lewinian and client-centered theories have been most prominent, but gestalt therapy and various brands of psychoanalysis have all played contributing parts. The experience within the group may focus on specific training in human relations skills. It may be closely similar to group therapy, with much exploration of past experience and the dynamics of personal development. It may focus on creative expression through painting or expressive movement. It may be focused primarily upon a basic encounter and relationship between individuals.

Simply to describe the diversity which exists in this field raises very properly the question of why these various developments should be considered to belong together. Are there any threads of commonality which pervade all these widely divergent activities? To me it seems that they do belong together and can all be classed as focusing on the intensive group experience. They all have certain similar external characteristics. The group in almost every case is small (from eight to eighteen members), is relatively unstructured, and chooses its own goals and personal directions. The group experience usually, though not always, includes some cognitive input, some content material which is presented to the group. In almost all instances the leader's responsibility is primarily the facilitation of the expression of both feelings and thoughts on the part of the group members. Both in the leader and in the group members there is some focus on the process and the dynamics of the immediate personal interaction. These are, I think, some of the identifying char-

acteristics which are rather easily recognized.

There are also certain practical hypotheses which tend to be held in common by all these groups. My own summary of these would be as follows: In an intensive group, with much freedom and little structure, the individual will gradually feel safe enough to drop some of his defenses and facades; he will relate more directly on a feeling basis (come into a basic encounter) with other members of the group; he will come to understand himself and his relationship to others more accurately; he will change in his personal attitudes and behavior; and he will subsequently relate more effectively to others in his everyday life situation. There are other hypotheses related more to the group than to the individual. One is that in this situation of minimal structure, the group will move from confusions, fractionation, and discontinuity to a climate of greater trust and coherence. These are some of the characteristics and hypotheses which, in my judgment, bind together this enormous cluster of activities which I wish to talk about as constituting the intensive group experience.

As for myself, I have been gradually moving into this field for the last twenty years. In experimenting with what I call *student-centered teaching*, involving the free expression of personal feelings, I came to recognize not only the cognitive learnings but also some of the personal changes which occurred. In brief intensive training courses for counselors for the Veterans Administration in 1946, during the postwar period, I and my staff focused more directly on providing an intensive group experience because of its impact in producing significant learning. In 1950, I served as leader of an intensive, full-time, one-week workshop, a postdoctoral training seminar in psychotherapy for the American Psychological Association. The impact of those six days was so great that for more than a dozen years afterward, I kept hearing from members of the group about the meaning it had had for them. Since that time I have been involved in more than forty ventures of what I would like to term—using the label most congenial to me—*basic encounter groups*. Most of these have involved for many of the mem-

bers experiences of great intensity and considerable personal change. With two individuals, however, in these many groups, the
experience contributed, I believe, to a psychotic break. A few other individuals have
found the experience more unhelpful than
helpful. So I have come to have a profound
respect for the constructive potency of such
group experiences and also a real concern
over the fact that sometimes and in some
ways this experience may do damage to individuals.

THE GROUP PROCESS

It is a matter of great interest to me to
try to understand what appear to be common elements in the group process as I
have come dimly to sense these. I am using
this opportunity to think about this problem, not because I feel I have any final
theory to give, but because I would like to
formulate, as clearly as I am able, the elements which I can perceive at the present
time. In doing so I am drawing upon my
own experience, upon the experiences of
others with whom I have worked, upon the
written material in this field, upon the written reactions of many individuals who have
participated in such groups, and to some
extent upon the recordings of such group
sessions, which we are only beginning to tap
and analyze. I am sure that (though I have
tried to draw on the experience of others)
any formulation I make at the present time
is unduly influenced by my own experience
in groups and thus is lacking in the generality I wish it might have.

As I consider the terribly complex interactions which arise during twenty, forty,
sixty, or more hours of intensive sessions,
I believe that I see some threads which
weave in and out of the pattern. Some of
these trends or tendencies are likely to appear early and some later in the group sessions, but there is no clear-cut sequence in
which one ends and another begins. The
interaction is best thought of, I believe, as
a varied tapestry, differing from group to
group, yet with certain kinds of trends evident in most of these intensive encounters
and with certain patterns tending to precede
and others to follow. Here are some of the
process patterns which I see developing,

briefly described in simple terms, illustrated
from tape recordings and personal reports,
and presented in roughly sequential order.
I am not aiming at a high-level theory of
group process but rather at a naturalistic
observation out of which, I hope, true
theory can be built.[2]

Milling Around As the leader or facilitator
makes clear at the outset that this is a
group with unusual freedom, that it is not
one for which he will take directional responsibility, there tends to develop a period
of initial confusion, awkward silence, polite
surface interaction, "cocktail-party talk,"
frustration, and great lack of continuity.
The individuals come face-to-face with the
fact that "there is no structure here except
what we provide. We do not know our purposes; we do not even know one another,
and we are committed to remain together
over a considerable period of time." In this
situation, confusion and frustration are natural. Particularly striking to the observer is
the lack of continuity between personal expressions. Individual A will present some
proposal or concern, clearly looking for a
response from the group. Individual B has
obviously been waiting for his turn and
starts off on some completely different tan-
gent as though he had never heard A. One

[2] Jack and Lorraine Gibb have long been working on
an analysis of trust development as the essential
theory of group process. Others who have contributed significantly to the theory of group process
are Chris Argyris, Kenneth Benne, Warren Bennis,
Dorwin Cartwright, Matthew Miles, and Robert
Blake. Samples of the thinking of all these and
others may be found in three recent books: Bradford, Gibb, & Benne (1964); Bennis, Benne, &
Chin (1961); and Bennis, Schein, Berlew, & Steele
(1964). Thus, there are many promising leads for
theory construction involving a considerable degree
of abstraction. This chapter has a more elementary
aim—a naturalistic descriptive account of the
process.
[See Chapter 17 of the present volume. In that discussion, Jack and Lorraine Gibb present a synopsis
of their theory to which Rogers refers above. The
chapters by Haigh (22), Thomas (23), and Clark
(27) also deal with aspects of the basic encounter
group. —Editor]

member makes a simple suggestion such as, "I think we should introduce ourselves," and this may lead to several hours of highly involved discussion in which the underlying issues appear to be, "Who is the leader?" "Who is responsible for us?" "Who is a member of the group?" "What is the purpose of the group?"

Resistance to Personal Expression or Exploration During the milling period, some individuals are likely to reveal some rather personal attitudes. This tends to foster a very ambivalent reaction among other members of the group. One member, writing of his experience, says:

> There is a self which I present to the world and another one which I know more intimately. With others I try to appear able, knowing, unruffled, problem-free. To substantiate this image I will act in a way which at the time or later seems false or artificial or "not the real me." Or I will keep to myself thoughts which if expressed would reveal an imperfect me.
>
> My inner self, by contrast with the image I present to the world, is characterized by many doubts. The worth I attach to this inner self is subject to much fluctuation and is very dependent on how others are reacting to me. At times this private self can feel worthless.

It is the public self which members tend to reveal to one another, and only gradually, fearfully, and ambivalently do they take steps to reveal something of their inner world.

Early in one intensive workshop, the members were asked to write anonymously a statement of some feeling or feelings which they had which they were not willing to tell in the group. One man wrote:

> I don't relate easily to people. I have an almost impenetrable facade. Nothing gets in to hurt me, but nothing gets out. I have repressed so many emotions that I am close to emotional sterility. This situation doesn't make me happy, but I don't know what to do about it.

This individual is clearly living inside a private dungeon, but he does not even dare, except in this disguised fashion, to send out a call for help.

In a recent workshop when one man started to express the concern he felt about an impasse he was experiencing with his wife, another member stopped him, saying essentially:

> Are you sure you want to go on with this, or are you being seduced by the group into going further than you want to go? How do you know the group can be trusted? How will you feel about it when you go home and tell your wife what you have revealed, or when you decide to keep it from her? It just isn't safe to go further.

It seemed quite clear that in his warning, this second member was also expressing his own fear of revealing *him*self and *his* lack of trust in the group.

Description of Past Feelings In spite of ambivalence about the trustworthiness of the group and the risk of exposing oneself, expression of feelings does begin to assume a larger proportion of the discussion. The executive tells how frustrated he feels by certain situations in his industry, or the housewife relates problems she has experienced with her children. A tape-recorded exchange involving a Roman Catholic nun occurs early in a one-week workshop, when the discussion has turned to a rather intellectualized consideration of anger:

Bill: What happens when you get mad, Sister, or don't you?
Sister: Yes, I do—yes I do. And I find when I get mad, I, I almost get, well, the kind of person that antagonizes me is the person who seems so unfeeling toward people—now I take our dean as a person in point because she is a very aggressive woman and has certain ideas about what the various rules in a college should be; and this woman can just send me into high "G"; in an angry mood. *I mean this.* But then I find, I. . . .
Facil.:[3] But what, what do you do?
Sister: I find that when I'm in a situation like this, that I strike out in a very sharp, uh, *tone*, or else I just refuse to respond—"All right, this happens to be her way"—I don't think I've ever gone into a tantrum.
Joe: You just withdraw—no use to fight it.

---

[3] The term "facilitator" will be used throughout this paper, although sometimes he is referred to as "leader" or "trainer."

Facil.: You say you use a sharp tone. To *her*, or to other people you're dealing with?
Sister: Oh, no. To *her*.

This is a typical example of a *description* of feelings which are obviously current in her in a sense but which she is placing in the past and which she describes as being outside the group in time and place. It is an example of feelings existing "there and then."

Expression of Negative Feelings Curiously enough, the first expression of genuinely significant "here-and-now" feeling is apt to come out in negative attitudes toward other group members or toward the group leader. In one group in which members introduced themselves at some length, one woman refused, saying that she preferred to be known for what she was in the group and not in terms of her status outside. Very shortly after this, one of the men in the group attacked her vigorously and angrily for this stand, accusing her of failing to cooperate, of keeping herself aloof from the group, and so forth. It was the first *personal current feeling* which had been brought into the open in the group.

Frequently the leader is attacked for his failure to give proper guidance to the group. One vivid example of this comes from a recorded account of an early session with a group of delinquents, where one member shouts at the leader (Gordon, 1955, p. 214):

> You will be licked if you don't control us right at the start. You have to keep order here because you are older than us. That's what a teacher is supposed to do. If he doesn't do it we will cause a lot of trouble and won't get anything done. [Then, referring to two boys in the group who were scuffling, he continues.] Throw 'em out, throw 'em out! You've just *got* to make us behave!

An adult expresses his disgust at the people who talk too much, but points his irritation at the leader (Gordon, 1955, p. 210):

> It is just that I don't understand why someone doesn't shut them up. I would have taken Gerald and shoved him out the window. I'm an authoritarian. I would have told him he was talking too much and he had to leave the room. I think the group discussion ought to be led by a person who simply will not

recognize these people after they have interrupted about eight times.

Why are negatively toned expressions the first current feelings to be expressed? Some speculative answers might be the following: This is one of the best ways to test the freedom and trustworthiness of the group. "Is it really a place where I can be and express myself positively and negatively? Is this really a safe place, or will I be punished?" Another quite different reason is that deeply positive feelings are much more difficult and dangerous to express than negative ones. "If I say, 'I love you,' I am vulnerable and open to the most awful rejection. If I say, 'I hate you,' I am at best liable to attack, against which I can defend." Whatever the reasons, such negatively toned feelings tend to be the first here-and-now material to appear.

Expression and Exploration of Personally Meaningful Material It may seem puzzling that following such negative experiences as the initial confusion, the resistance to personal expression, the focus on outside events, and the voicing of critical or angry feelings, the event most likely to occur next is for an individual to reveal himself to the group in a significant way. The reason for this no doubt is that the individual member has come to realize that this is in part *his group*. He can help to make of it what he wishes. He has also experienced the fact that negative feelings have been expressed and have usually been accepted or assimilated without any catastrophic results. He realizes there is freedom here, albeit a risky freedom. A climate of trust (Gibb, 1964, Ch. 10) is beginning to develop. So he begins to take the chance and the gamble of letting the group know some deeper facet of himself. One man tells of the trap in which he finds himself, feeling that communication between himself and his wife is hopeless. A priest tells of the anger which he has bottled up because of unreasonable treatment by one of his superiors. What should he have done? What might he do now? A scientist at the head of a large research department finds the courage to speak of his painful isolation, to tell the group that he has never had a single friend in his life. By the time he finishes telling of his situation, he is letting loose some of the tears of sorrow for himself which I am sure he has held in for many years. A psychiatrist tells of the guilt he feels because of the suicide of one of his patients. A woman of forty tells of her absolute inability to free herself from the grip of her controlling mother. A process which one workshop member has called a "journey to the center of self," often a very painful process, has begun.

Such exploration is not always an easy process, nor is the whole group always receptive to such self-revelation. In a group of institutionalized adolescents, all of whom had been in difficulty of one sort or another, one boy revealed an important fact about himself and immediately received both acceptance and sharp nonacceptance from members of the group:

George: This is the thing. I've got too many problems at home—uhm, I think some of you know why I'm here, what I was charged with.
Mary: I don't.
Facil.: Do you want to tell us?
George: Well, uh, it's sort of embarrassing.
Carol: Come on, it won't be so bad.
George: Well, I raped my sister. That's the only problem I have at home, and I've overcome that, I think. (*Rather long pause.*)
Freda: Oooh, that's *weird*!
Mary: People have problems, Freda, I mean ya know. . . .
Freda: Yeah, I know, but *yeOUW*!!!
Facil. (*to Freda*): You know about these problems, but they still are weird to you.
George: You see what I mean; it's embarrassing to talk about it.
Mary: Yeah, but it's O.K.
George: It *hurts* to talk about it, but I know I've got to so I won't be guilt-ridden for the rest of my life.

Clearly Freda is completely shutting him out psychologically, while Mary in particular is showing a deep acceptance.

The Expression of Immediate Interpersonal Feelings in the Group Entering into the process sometimes earlier, sometimes later, is the explicit bringing into the open of the feelings experienced in the immediate moment by one member about another. These are sometimes positive and sometimes negative. Examples would be: "I feel threatened by your silence." "You remind me of my mother, with whom I had a tough time." "I took an instant dislike to you the first moment I saw you." "To me you're like a breath of fresh air in the group." "I like your warmth and your smile." "I dislike you more every time you speak up." Each of these attitudes can be, and usually is, explored in the increasing climate of trust

The Development of a Healing Capacity in the Group One of the most fascinating aspects of any intensive group experience is the manner in which a number of the group members show a natural and spontaneous capacity for dealing in a helpful, facilitative and therapeutic fashion with the pain and suffering of others. As one rather extreme example of this, I think of a man in charge of maintenance in a large plant who was one of the low-status members of an industrial executive group. As he informed us, he had not been "contaminated by education." In the initial phases the group tended to look down on him. As members delved more deeply into themselves and began to express their own attitudes more fully, this man came forth as, without doubt, the most sensitive member of the group. He knew intuitively how to be understanding and acceptant. He was alert to things which had not yet been expressed but which were just below the surface. When the rest of us were paying attention to a member who was speaking, he would frequently spot another individual who was suffering silently and in need of help. He had a deeply perceptive and facilitating attitude. This kind of ability shows up so commonly in groups that it has led me to feel that the ability to be healing or therapeutic is far more common in human life than we might suppose. Often it needs only the permission granted by freely flowing group experience to become evident.

In a characteristic instance, the leader and several group members were trying to be of help to Joe, who was telling of the almost complete lack of communication between himself and his wife. In varied ways members endeavored to give help. John kept putting before Joe the feelings Joe's wife was almost certainly experiencing. The facilitator kept challenging Joe's facade of "carefulness." Marie tried to help him discover what he was feeling at the moment. Fred showed him the choice he had of alternative behaviors. All this was clearly done in a spirit of caring, as is even more evident in the recording itself. No miracles were achieved, but toward the end Joe did come to the realization that the only thing that might help would be to express his real feelings to his wife.

Self-acceptance and the Beginning of Change

Many people feel that self-acceptance must stand in the way of change. Actually, in these group experiences, as in psychotherapy, it is the *beginning* of change. Some examples of the kind of attitudes expressed would be these: "I *am* a dominating person who likes to control others. I do want to mold these individuals into the proper shape." Another person says, "I really have a hurt and overburdened little boy inside of me who feels very sorry for himself. I *am* that little boy, in addition to being a competent and responsible manager."

I think of one governmental executive in a group in which I participated, a man with high responsibility and excellent technical training as an engineer. At the first meeting of the group he impressed me, and I think others, as being cold, aloof, somewhat bitter, resentful, and cynical. When he spoke of how he ran his office it appeared that he administered it "by the book," without any warmth or human feeling entering in. In one of the early sessions, when he spoke of his wife, a group member asked him, "Do you love your wife?" He paused for a long time, and the questioner said, "OK, that's answer enough." The executive said, "No. Wait a minute. The reason I didn't respond was that I was wondering if I ever loved anyone. I don't think I *ever* really *loved* anyone." It seemed quite dramatically clear to those of us in the group that he had come to accept himself .as an unloving person. A few days later he listened with great intensity as one member of the group expressed profound personal feelings of isolation, loneliness, and pain, revealing the extent to which he had been living behind

a mask, a facade. The next morning the engineer said, "Last night I thought and thought about what Bill told us. I even wept quite a bit by myself. I can't remember how long it has been since I have cried, and I really *felt* something. I think perhaps what I felt was love."

It is not surprising that before the week was over, he had thought through new ways of handling his growing son, on whom he had been placing extremely rigorous demands. He had also begun genuinely to appreciate the love which his wife had extended to him and which he now felt he could in some measure reciprocate.

In another group one man kept a diary of his reactions. Here is his account of an experience in which he came really to accept his almost abject desire for love, a self-acceptance which marked the beginning of a very significant experience of change. He says (Hall, 1965):

> During the break between the third and fourth sessions, I felt very droopy and tired. I had it in mind to take a nap, but instead I was almost compulsively going around to people starting a conversation. I had a begging kind of a feeling, like a very cowed little puppy hoping that he'll be patted but half afraid he'll be kicked. Finally, back in my room I lay down and began to know that I was sad. Several times I found myself wishing my roommate would come in and talk to me. Or, whenever someone walked by the door, I would come to attention inside, the way a dog pricks up his ears; and I would feel an immediate wish for that person to come in and talk to me. I realized my raw wish to receive kindness.

Another recorded excerpt, from an adolescent group, shows a combination of self-acceptance and self-exploration. Art had been talking about his "shell," and here he is beginning to work with the problem of accepting himself, and also the facade he ordinarily exhibits:

> Art: I'm so darn used to living with the shell; it doesn't even bother me. I don't even know the real me. I think I've uh, well, I've pushed the shell more away here. When I'm out of my shell—only twice—once just a few minutes ago—I'm really me, I guess. But

then I just sort of pull in the [latch] cord after me when I'm in my shell, and that's almost all the time. And I leave the [false] front standing outside when I'm back in the shell.

Facil.: And nobody's back in there with you?

Art (crying): Nobody else is in there with me, just me. I just pull everything into the shell and roll the shell up and shove it in my pocket. I take the shell, and the real me, and put it in my pocket where it's safe. I guess that's really the way I do it—I go into my shell and turn off the real world. And here: that's what I want to do here in this group, ya know, come out of my shell and actually throw it away.

Lois: You're making progress already. At least you can talk about it.

Facil.: Yeah. The thing that's going to be hardest is to stay out of the shell.

Art (still crying): Well, yeah, if I can keep talking about it, I can come out and stay out, but I'm gonna have to, ya know, protect me. It hurts; it's actually hurting to talk about it.

Still another person reporting shortly after his workshop experience said, "I came away from the workshop feeling much more deeply that 'It is all right to be me with all my strengths and weaknesses.' My wife has told me that I appear to be more authentic, more real, more genuine."

This feeling of greater realness and authenticity is a very common experience. It would appear that the individual is learning to accept and to *be* himself, and this is laying the foundation for change. He is closer to his own feelings, and hence they are no longer so rigidly organized and are more open to change.

The Cracking of Facades As the sessions continue, so many things tend to occur together that it is difficult to know which to describe first. It should again be stressed that these different threads and stages interweave and overlap. One of these threads is the increasing impatience with defenses. As time goes on, the group finds it unbearable that any member should live behind a mask or a front. The polite words, the intellectual understanding of one another and of relationships, the smooth coin of tact and cover-up—amply satisfactory for interactions outside—are just not good enough. The expression of self by some members of the group has made it very clear that a deeper and more basic encounter is *possible*, and the group appears to strive, intuitively and unconsciously, toward this goal. Gently at times, almost savagely at others, the group *demands* that the individual be himself, that his current feelings not be hidden, that he remove the mask of ordinary social intercourse. In one group there was a highly intelligent and quite academic man who had been rather perceptive in his understanding of others but who had not revealed himself at all. The attitude of the group was finally expressed sharply by one member when he said, "Come out from behind that lectern, Doc. Stop giving us speeches. Take off your dark glasses. We want to know *you*."

In Synanon, the fascinating group so successfully involved in making persons out of drug addicts, this ripping away of facades is often very drastic. An excerpt from one of the "synanons," or group sessions, makes this clear (Casriel, 1963, p. 81):

Joe (*speaking to Gina*): I wonder when you're going to stop sounding so good in synanons. Every synanon that I'm in with you, someone asks you a question, and you've got a beautiful book written. All made out about what went down and how you were wrong and how you realized you were wrong and all that kind of bullshit. When are you going to stop doing that? How do you feel about Art?

Gina: I have nothing against Art.

Will: You're a nut. Art hasn't got any damn sense. He's been in there, yelling at you and Moe, and you've got everything so cool.

Gina: No, I feel he's very insecure in a lot of ways but that has nothing to do with me. . . .

Joe: You act like you're so goddamn understanding.

Gina: I was *told* to act as if I understand.

Joe: Well, you're in a synanon now. You're not supposed to be acting like you're such a goddamn healthy person. Are you so well?

Gina: No.

Joe: Well why the hell don't you quit acting as if you were.

If I am indicating that the group at times is quite violent in tearing down a facade or a defense, this would be accurate. On the other hand, it can also be sensitive and gentle. The man who was accused of hiding behind a lectern was deeply hurt by this attack, and over the lunch hour looked very troubled, as though he might break into tears at any moment. When the group reconvened, the members sensed this and treated him very gently, enabling him to tell us his own tragic personal story, which accounted for his aloofness and his intellectual and academic approach to life.

The Individual Receives Feedback In the process of this freely expressive interaction, the individual rapidly acquires a great deal of data as to how he appears to others. The "hail-fellow-well-met" discovers that others resent his exaggerated friendliness. The executive who weighs his words carefully and speaks with heavy precision may find that others regard him as stuffy. A woman who shows a somewhat excessive desire to be of help to others is told in no uncertain terms that some group members do not want her for a mother. All this can be decidedly upsetting, but as long as these various bits of information are fed back in the context of caring which is developing in the group, they seem highly constructive.

Feedback can at times be very warm and positive, as the following recorded excerpt indicates:

Leo (*very softly and gently*): I've been struck with this ever since she talked about her waking in the night, that she has a very delicate sensitivity. (*Turning to Mary and speaking almost caressingly.*) And somehow I perceive—even looking at you or in your eyes—a very—almost like a gentle touch and from this gentle touch you can tell many —things—you sense in—this manner.
Fred: Leo, when you said that, that she has this kind of delicate sensitivity, I just felt, *Lord yes!* Look at her eyes.
Leo: M-hm.

A much more extended instance of negative and positive feedback, triggering a significant new experience of self-understanding and encounter with the group, is taken from the diary of the young man mentioned before. He had been telling the group that he had no feeling for them, and felt they had no feeling for him (Hall, 1965):

Then, a girl lost patience with me and said she didn't feel she could give any more. She said I looked like a bottomless well, and she wondered how many times I had to be told

that I *was* cared for. By this time I was feeling panicky, and I was saying to myself, "My God, can it be true that I can't be satisfied and that I'm somehow compelled to pester people for attention until I drive them away!"

At this point while I was really worried, a nun in the group spoke up. She said that I had not alienated her with some negative things I had said to her. She said she liked me, and she couldn't understand why I couldn't see that. She said she felt concerned for me and wanted to help me. With that, something began to really dawn on me, and I voiced it somewhat like the following. "You mean you are all sitting there, feeling for me what I say I want you to feel, and that somewhere down inside me I'm stopping it from touching me?" I relaxed appreciably and began really to wonder why I had shut their caring out so much. I couldn't find the answer, and one woman said: "It looks like you are trying to stay continuously as deep in your feelings as you were this afternoon. It would make sense to me for you to draw back and assimilate it. Maybe if you don't push so hard, you can rest awhile and then move back into your feelings more naturally."

Her making the last suggestion really took effect. I saw the sense in it, and almost immediately I settled back very relaxed with something of a feeling of a bright, warm day dawning inside me. In addition to taking the pressure off of myself, however, I was for the first time really warmed by the friendly feelings which I felt they had for me. It is difficult to say why I felt liked only just then, but, as opposed to the earlier sessions, I really *believed* they cared for me. I never have fully understood why I stood their affection off for so long, but at that point I almost abruptly began to trust that they did care. The measure of the effectiveness of this change lies in what I said next. I said, "Well, that really takes care of me. I'm really ready to listen to someone else now." I *meant* that, too.

Confrontation There are times when the term "feedback" is far too mild to describe the interactions which take place, when it is better said that one individual *confronts* another, directly "leveling" with him. Such confrontations can be positive, but frequently they are decidedly negative, as the following example will make abundantly clear. In one of the last sessions of a group, Alice had made some quite vulgar and contemptuous remarks to John, who was entering religious work. The next morning, Norma, who had been a very quiet person in the group, took the floor:

Norma (*loud sigh*): Well, I don't have *any* respect for you, Alice. *None!* (*Pause.*) There's about a hundred things going through my mind I want to say to you, and by God I hope I get through 'em all! First of all, if you wanted us to respect you, then why couldn't you respect *John's* feelings last night? Why have you been on him today? Hmm? Last night—couldn't you—couldn't you accept—*couldn't you* comprehend in any way at all that—that *he felt* his unworthiness in the service of God? Couldn't you accept this, or did you have to dig into it today to find something *else there*? And his respect for womanhood—he *loves* women—yes, he does, because he's a real person, but you—you're not a real woman—to me—and thank God, you're not my mother! ! ! ! I want to come over and beat the hell out of you ! ! ! I want to slap you across the mouth so hard and —oh, and you're so, you're many years above me—and I respect age, and I respect people who are older than me, *but I don't respect you, Alice. At all*! And I was so *hurt* and *confused* because you were making someone else feel *hurt* and *confused*. . . .

It may relieve the reader to know that these two women came to accept each other, not completely, but much more understandingly, before the end of the session. But this *was* a confrontation!

The Helping Relationship outside the Group Sessions No account of the group process would, in my experience, be adequate if it did not make mention of the many ways in which group members are of assistance to one another. Not infrequently, one member of a group will spend hours listening and talking to another member who is undergoing a painful new perception of himself. Sometimes it is merely the offering of help which is therapeutic. I think of one man who was going through a very depressed period after having told us of the many

tragedies in his life. He seemed quite clearly, from his remarks, to be contemplating suicide. I jotted down my room number (we were staying at a hotel) and told him to put it in his pocket and to call me anytime of day or night if he felt that it would help. He never called, but six months after the workshop was over he wrote to me telling me how much that act had meant to him and that he still had the slip of paper to remind him of it.

Let me give an example of the healing effect of the attitudes of group members both outside and inside the group meetings. This is taken from a letter written by a workshop member to the group one month after the group sessions. He speaks of the difficulties and depressing circumstances he has encountered during that month and adds:

I have come to the conclusion that my experiences with you have profoundly affected me. I am truly grateful. This is different than personal therapy. None of you *had* to care about me. None of you had to seek me out and let me know of things you thought would help me. None of you had to let me know I was of help to you. Yet you did, and as a result it has far more meaning than anything I have so far experienced. When I feel the need to hold back and not live spontaneously, for whatever reasons, I remember that twelve persons, just like those before me now, said to let go and be congruent, to be myself, and, of all unbelievable things, they even loved me more for it. This has given me the *courage* to come out of myself many times since then. Often it seems my very doing of this helps the others to experience similar freedom.

The Basic Encounter Running through some of the trends I have just been describing is the fact that individuals come into much closer and more direct contact with one another than is customary in ordinary life. This appears to be one of the most central, intense, and change-producing aspects of such a group experience. To illustrate what I mean, I would like to draw an example from a recent workshop group. A man tells, through his tears, of the very tragic loss of his child, a grief which he is experiencing *fully*, for the first time, not holding back his feelings in any way. Another says to him, also with tears in his eyes, "I've never felt so close to another human being. I've never before felt a real physical hurt in me from the pain of another. I feel *completely* with you." This is a basic encounter.

Such I-Thou relationships (to use Buber's term) occur with some frequency in these group sessions and nearly always bring a moistness to the eyes of the participants.

One member, trying to sort out his experiences immediately after a workshop, speaks of the "commitment to relationship" which often developed on the part of two individuals, not necessarily individuals who had liked each other initially. He goes on to say:

> The incredible fact experienced over and over by members of the group was that when a negative feeling was fully expressed to another, the relationship grew and the negative feeling was replaced by a deep acceptance for the other. . . . Thus real change seemed to occur when feelings were experienced and expressed in the context of the relationship. "I can't *stand* the way you talk!" turned into a real understanding and affection for you the *way* you talk.

This statement seems to capture some of the more complex meanings of the term "basic encounter."

The Expression of Positive Feelings and Closeness As indicated in the last section, an inevitable part of the group process seems to be that when feelings are expressed and can be accepted in a relationship, a great deal of closeness and positive feelings result. Thus as the sessions proceed, there is an increasing feeling of warmth and group spirit and trust built, not out of positive attitudes only, but out of a realness which includes both positive and negative feeling. One member tried to capture this in writing very shortly after the workshop by saying that if he were trying to sum it up, ". . . it would have to do with what I call confirmation— a kind of confirmation of myself, of the uniqueness and universal qualities of men, a confirmation that when we can be human together something positive can emerge."

A particularly poignant expression of these positive attitudes was shown in the group where Norma confronted Alice with her bitterly angry feelings. Joan, the fa-cilitator, was deeply upset and began to weep. The positive and healing attitudes of the group, for their own *leader*, are an unusual example of the closeness and personal quality of the relationships.

Joan (*crying*): I somehow feel that it's so *damned* easy for me to—to put myself *inside* of another person and I just guess I can feel that—for John and Alice and for you, Norma.
Alice: And it's *you* that's hurt.
Joan: Maybe I am taking some of that hurt. I guess I am. (*crying*.)
Alice: That's a wonderful gift. I wish I had it.
Joan: You have a lot of it.
Peter: In a way you bear the—I guess in a special way, because you're the—facilitator, ah, you've probably borne, ah, an extra heavy burden for all of us—and the burden that you, perhaps, you bear the heaviest is— we ask you—we ask one another; we grope to try to accept one another as we are, and —for each of us in various ways I guess we reach things and we say, *please* accept me. . . .

Some may be very critical of a "leader" so involved and so sensitive that she weeps at the tensions in the group which she has taken into herself. For me, it is simply another evidence that when people are real with each other, they have an astonishing ability to heal a person with a real and understanding love, whether that person is "participant" or "leader."

Behavior Changes in the Group It would seem from observation that many changes in behavior occur in the group itself. Gestures change. The tone of voice changes, becoming sometimes stronger, sometimes softer, usually more spontaneous, less artificial, more feelingful. Individuals show an astonishing amount of thoughtfulness and helpfulness toward one another.

Our major concern, however, is with the behavior changes which occur following the group experience. It is this which constitutes the most significant question and on which we need much more study and research. One person gives a catalog of the changes which he sees in himself which may seem too "pat" but which is echoed in many other statements:

I am more open, spontaneous. I express myself more freely. I am more sympathetic, empathic, and tolerant. I am more confident. I am more religious in my own way. My relations with my family, friends, and co-workers are more honest, and I express my likes and dislikes and true feelings more openly. I admit ignorance more readily. I am more cheerful. I want to help others more.

Another says:

Since the workshop there has been a new relationship with my parents. It has been trying and hard. However, I have found a greater freedom in talking with them, especially my father. Steps have been made toward being closer to my mother than I have ever been in the last five years.

Another says:

It helped clarify my feelings about my work, gave me more enthusiasm for it, and made me more honest and cheerful with my coworkers and also more open when I was hostile. It made my relationship with my wife more open, deeper. We felt freer to talk about anything, and we felt confident that anything we talked about we could work through.

Sometimes the changes which are described are very subtle. "The primary change is the more positive view of my ability to allow myself to *hear*, and to become involved with someone else's 'silent scream.' "

At the risk of making the outcomes sound too good, I will add one more statement written shortly after a workshop by a mother. She says:

The immediate impact on my children was of interest to both me and my husband. I feel that having been so accepted and loved by a group of strangers was so supportive that when I returned home my love for the people closest to me was much more spontaneous. Also, the practice I had in accepting and loving others during the workshop was evident in my relationships with my close friends.

DISADVANTAGES AND RISKS

Thus far one might think that every aspect of the group process was positive. As far as the evidence at hand indicates, it appears that it nearly always is a positive process for a majority of the participants. There are, nevertheless, failures which result. Let me try to describe briefly some of the negative aspects of the group process as they sometimes occur.

The most obvious deficiency of the intensive group experience is that frequently the behavior changes, if any, which occur, are not lasting. This is often recognized by the participants. One says, "I wish I had the ability to hold permanently the 'openness' I left the conference with." Another says, "I experienced a lot of acceptance, warmth, and love at the workshop. I find it hard to carry the ability to share this in the same way with people outside the workshop. I find it easier to slip back into my old unemotional role than to do the work necessary to open relationships."

Sometimes group members experience this phenomenon of "relapse" quite philosophically:

The group experience is not a way of life but a reference point. My images of our group, even though I am unsure of some of their meanings, give me a comforting and useful perspective on my normal routine. They are like a mountain which I have climbed and enjoyed and to which I hope occasionally to return.

Some Data on Outcomes What is the extent of this "slippage"? In the past year, I have administered follow-up questionnaires to 481 individuals who have been in groups I have organized or conducted. The information has been obtained from two to twelve months following the group experience, but the greatest number were followed up after a three- to six-month period.[4] Of these individuals, two (i.e., less than one-half of 1 percent) felt it had changed their behavior in ways they did not like. Fourteen percent felt the experience had made no perceptible change in their behavior. Another fourteen percent felt that it had changed their behavior but that this change had disappeared

[4] The 481 respondents constituted 82 percent of those to whom the questionnaire had been sent.

or left only a small residual positive effect. Fifty-seven percent felt it had made a continuing positive difference in their behavior, a few feeling that it had made some negative changes along with the positive.

A second potential risk involved in the intensive group experience and one which is often mentioned in public discussion is the risk that the individual may become deeply involved in revealing himself and then be left with problems which are not worked through. There have been a number of reports of people who have felt, following an intensive group experience, that they must go to a therapist to work through the feelings which were opened up in the intensive experience of the workshop and which were left unresolved. It is obvious that, without knowing more about each individual situation, it is difficult to say whether this was a negative outcome or a partially or entirely positive one. There are also very occasional accounts, and I can testify to two in my own experience, where an individual has had a psychotic episode during or immediately following an intensive group experience. On the other side of the picture is the fact that individuals have also lived through what were clearly psychotic episodes, and lived through them very constructively, in the context of a basic encounter group. My own tentative clinical judgment would be that the more positively the group process has been proceeding, the less likely it is that any individual would be psychologically damaged through membership in the group. It is obvious, however, that this is a serious issue and that much more needs to be known.

Some of the tension which exists in workshop members as a result of this potential for damage was very well described by one member when he said, "I feel the workshop had some very precious moments for me when I felt very close indeed to particular persons. It had some frightening moments when its potency was very evident and I realized a particular person might be deeply hurt or greatly helped but I could not predict which."

Out of the 481 participants followed up by questionnaires, two felt that the overall impact of their intensive group experience was "mostly damaging." Six more said that it had been "more unhelpful than helpful." Twenty-one, or 4 percent, stated that it had been "mostly frustrating, annoying, or confusing." Three and one-half percent said that it had been neutral in its impact. Nineteen percent checked that it had been "more helpful than unhelpful," indicating some degree of ambivalence. But 30 percent saw it as "constructive in its results," and 45 percent checked it as a "deeply meaningful, positive experience."[5] Thus for three-fourths of the group, it was *very* helpful. These figures should help to set the problem in perspective. It is obviously a very serious matter if an intensive group experience is psychologically damaging to *anyone*. It seems clear, however, that such damage occurs only rarely, if we are to judge by the reaction of the participants.

Other Hazards of the Group Experience
There is another risk or deficiency in the basic encounter group. Until very recent years it has been unusual for a workshop to include both husband and wife. This can be a real problem if significant change has taken place in one spouse during or as a result of the workshop experience. One individual felt this risk clearly after attending a workshop. He said, "I think there is a great danger to a marriage when one spouse attends a group. It is too hard for the other spouse to compete with the group individually and collectively." One of the frequent aftereffects of the intensive group experience is that it brings out into the open for discussion marital tensions which have been kept under cover.

Another risk which has sometimes been a cause of real concern in mixed intensive workshops is that very positive, warm, and loving feelings can develop between members of the encounter group, as has been evident from some of the preceding examples. Inevitably some of these feelings have a sexual component, and this can be a matter of great concern to the participants

[5] These figures add up to more than 100 percent since quite a number of the respondents checked more than one answer.

and a profound threat to their spouses if these feelings are not worked through satisfactorily in the workshop. Also the close and loving feelings which develop may become a source of threat and marital difficulty when a wife, for example, has not been present, but projects many fears about the loss of her spouse—whether well founded or not—onto the workshop experience.

A man who had been in a mixed group of men and women executives wrote to me a year later and mentioned the strain in his marriage which resulted from his association with Marge, a member of his basic encounter group:

> There was a problem about Marge. There had occurred a very warm feeling on my part for Marge, and great compassion, for I felt she was *very* lonely. I believe the warmth was sincerely reciprocal. At any rate she wrote me a long affectionate letter, which I let my wife read. I was *proud* that Marge could feel that way about *me*, [Because he had felt very worthless.] But my wife was alarmed, because she read a love affair into the words—at least a *potential* threat. I stopped writing to Marge, because I felt rather clandestine after that.
>
> My wife has since participated in an "encounter group" herself, and she now understands. I have resumed writing to Marge.

Obviously, not all such episodes would have such a harmonious ending.

It is of interest in this connection that there has been increasing experimentation in recent years with "couples workshops" and with workshops for industrial executives and their spouses.

Still another negative potential growing out of these groups has become evident in recent years. Some individuals who have participated in previous encounter groups may exert a stultifying influence on new workshops which they attend. They sometimes exhibit what I think of as the "old pro" phenomenon. They feel they have learned the "rules of the game," and they subtly or openly try to impose these rules on newcomers. Thus, instead of promoting true expressiveness and spontaneity, they endeavor to substitute new rules for old—to make members feel guilty if they are not expressing feelings, are reluctant to voice criticism or hostility, are talking about situations outside the group relationship, or are fearful of revealing themselves. These old pros seem to be attempting to substitute a new tyranny in interpersonal relationships in the place of older, conventional restrictions. To me this is a perversion of the true group process. We need to ask ourselves how this travesty on spontaneity comes about.

IMPLICATIONS

I have tried to describe both the positive and the negative aspects of this burgeoning new cultural development. I would like now to touch on its implications for our society.

In the first place, it is a highly potent experience and hence clearly deserving of scientific study. As a phenomenon it has been both praised and criticized, but few people who have participated would doubt that *something* significant happens in these groups. People do not react in a neutral fashion toward the intensive group experience. They regard it as either strikingly worthwhile or deeply questionable. All would agree, however, that it is *potent*. This fact makes it of particular interest to the behavioral sciences since science is usually advanced by studying potent and dynamic phenomena. This is one of the reasons why I personally am devoting more and more of my time to this whole enterprise. I feel that we can learn much about the ways in which constructive personality change comes about as we study this group process more deeply.

In a different dimension, the intensive group experience appears to be one cultural attempt to meet the isolation of contemporary life. The person who has experienced an I-Thou relationship, who has entered into the basic encounter, is no longer an isolated individual. One workshop member stated this in a deeply expressive way:

> Workshops seem to be at least a partial answer to the loneliness of modern man and his search for new meanings for his life. In short, workshops seem very quickly to allow the individual to become that person he

wants to be. The first few steps are taken there, in uncertainty, in fear, and in anxiety. We may or may not continue the journey. It is a gutsy way to live. You trade many, many loose ends for one big knot in the middle of your stomach. It sure as hell isn't easy, but it is a *life* at least—not a hollow imitation of life. It has fear as well as hope, sorrow as well as joy, but I daily offer it to more people in the hope that they will join me. . . . Out from a no-man's land of *fog* into the more violent atmosphere of extremes of thunder, hail, rain, and sunshine. It is worth the trip.

Another implication which is partially expressed in the foregoing statement is that it is an avenue to fulfillment. In a day when more income, a larger car, and a better washing machine seem scarcely to be satisfying the deepest needs of man, individuals are turning to the psychological world, groping for a greater degree of authenticity and fulfillment. One workshop member expressed this extremely vividly:

> [It] has revealed a completely new dimension of life and has opened an infinite number of possibilities for me in my relationship to myself and to everyone dear to me. I feel truly alive and so grateful and joyful and hopeful and healthy and giddy and sparkly. I feel as though my eyes and ears and heart and guts have been opened to see and hear and love and feel more deeply, more widely, more intensely—this glorious, mixed-up, fabulous existence of ours. My whole body and each of its systems seems freer and healthier. I want to feel hot and cold, tired and rested, soft and hard, energetic and lazy. With persons everywhere, but especially my family, I have found a new freedom to explore and communicate. I know the change in me automatically brings a change in them. A whole new exciting relationship has started for me with my husband and with each of my children—a freedom to speak and to hear them speak.

Though one may wish to discount the enthusiasm of this statement, it describes an enrichment of life for which many are seeking.

Rehumanizing Human Relationships This whole development seems to have special significance in a culture which appears to be bent upon dehumanizing the individual and dehumanizing our human relationships. Here is an important force in the opposite direction, working toward making relationships more meaningful and more personal, in the family, in education, in government, in administrative agencies, in industry.

An intensive group experience has an even more general philosophical implication. It is one expression of the existential point of view which is making itself so pervasively evident in art and literature and modern life. The implicit goal of the group process seems to be to live life fully in the here and now of the relationship. The parallel with an existential point of view is clear cut. I believe this has been amply evident in the illustrative material.

There is one final issue which is raised by this whole phenomenon: What is our view of the optimal person? What is the goal of personality development? Different ages and different cultures have given different answers to this question. It seems evident from our review of the group process that in a climate of freedom, group members move toward becoming more spontaneous, flexible, closely related to their feelings, open to their experience, and closer and more expressively intimate in their interpersonal relationships. If we value this type of person and this type of behavior, then clearly the group process is a valuable process. If, on the other hand, we place a value on the individual who is effective in suppressing his feelings, who operates from a firm set of principles, who does not trust his own reactions and experience but relies on authority, and who remains aloof in his interpersonal relationships, then we would regard the group process, as I have tried to describe it, as a dangerous force. Clearly there is room for a difference of opinion on this value question, and not everyone in our culture would give the same answer.

CONCLUSION

I have tried to give a naturalistic, observational picture of one of the most significant modern social inventions, the so-called intensive group experience, or basic encounter group. I have tried to indicate some of the common elements of the process which occur in the climate of freedom that is present in such a group. I have pointed out some of the risks and shortcomings of the group experience. I have tried to indicate some of the reasons why it deserves serious consideration, not only from a personal point of view, but also from a scientific and philosophical point of view. I also hope I have made it clear that this is an area in which an enormous amount of deeply perceptive study and research is needed.

REFERENCES

BENNIS, W. G., BENNE, K. D., & CHIN, R. (Eds.) *The planning of change.* New York: Holt, Rinehart and Winston, 1961.

BENNIS, W. G., SCHEIN, E. H., BERLEW, D. E., & STEELE, F. I. (Eds.) *Interpersonal dynamics.* Homewood, Ill.: Dorsey, 1964.

BRADFORD, L., GIBB, J. R., & BENNE, K. D. (Eds.) *T-group theory and laboratory method.* New York: Wiley, 1964.

CASRIEL, D. *So fair a house.* Englewood Cliffs, N.J.: Prentice-Hall, 1963.

GIBB, J. R. Climate for trust formation. In L. Bradford, J. R. Gibb, & K. D. Benne (Eds.), *T-group theory and laboratory method.* New York: Wiley, 1964.

GORDON, T. *Group-centered leadership.* Boston: Houghton Mifflin, 1955.

HALL, G. F. A participant's experience in a basic encounter group. (Mimeographed) Western Behavioral Sciences Institute, 1965.

Presently: Philip Meyers Professor of Psychology at Brandeis University in Waltham, Massachusetts (since 1951).

Education: Doctor of Philosophy in psychology from the University of Wisconsin (1934).

Current major activity: Writing on values and "meta-motivation."

Future of humanistic psychology: The notion of genuine synergy in society: "eupsychia."

ABRAHAM H. MASLOW

Personal history: Taught at the University of Wisconsin (1930–1935) and at Brooklyn College (1937–1951). At Brandeis University, he was Chairman of the Department of Psychology (1951–1961). Visiting Fellow of the Western Behavioral Sciences Institute in La Jolla, California (1961–1962). President of the American Psychological Association's Division of Personality and Social Psychology (1955–1956) and Division of Esthetics (1960–1961), of the Massachusetts Psychological Association (1960–1961), and of the New England Psychological Association (1962–1963). President of the American Psychological Association (1967–1968).

Writings: Dr. Maslow has been one of the key figures in giving expression and leadership to the development of the humanistic orientation in psychology. His books are *Principles of Abnormal Psychology: The Dynamics of Psychic Illness,* with Bela Mittelman (1941; revised 1951); *Motivation and Personality* (1954); *Toward a Psychology of Being* (1962); *Religions, Values and Peak Experiences* (1964); *Eupsychian Management: A Journal* (1965); and *The Psychology of Science* (1966). He also edited *New Knowledge in Human Values* (1959). Three of his papers are classics in their own right: "A Theory of Human Motivation" (*Psychological Review,* 1943, **50,** 370–396); "Self-actualizing People: A Study of Psychological Health" (*Personality Symposia,* Symposium No. 1 on Values, 1950, 11–34); and "Deficiency Motivation and Growth Motivation" [in M. R. Jones (Ed.), *Nebraska Symposium on Motivation,* 1955].

Present chapter: This essay is adapted from an address given at the Workshop on the Training of Adult Counselors held at Chatham Bars Inn, Chatham, Massachusetts, May 24, 1965. It has not previously been published.

Chapter 29
ABRAHAM H. MASLOW

SELF-ACTUALIZATION AND BEYOND

In this chapter, I plan to discuss ideas that are in midstream rather than ready for formulation into a final version. I find that with my students and with other people with whom I share these ideas, the notion of self-actualization gets to be almost like a Rorschach ink blot. It frequently tells me more about the person using it than about reality. What I would like to do now is to explore some aspects of the nature of self-actualization, not as a grand abstraction, but in terms of the operational meaning of the self-actualizing process. What does self-actualization mean in moment-to-moment terms? What does it mean on Tuesday at four o'clock?

The Beginnings of Self-actualization Studies

My investigations on self-actualization were not planned to be research and did not start out as research. They started out as the effort of a young intellectual to try to understand two of his teachers whom he loved, adored, and admired and who were very, very wonderful people. It was a kind of high-IQ devotion. I could not be content simply to adore, but sought to understand why these two people were so different from the run-of-the-mill people in the world. These two people were Ruth Benedict and Max Wertheimer. They were my teachers after I came with a Ph.D. from the West to New York City, and they were most remarkable human beings. My training in psychology equipped me not at all for understanding them. It was as if they were not quite people but something more than people. My own investigation began as a prescientific or nonscientific activity. I made descriptions and notes on Max Wertheimer, and I made notes on Ruth Benedict. When I tried to understand them, think about them, and write about them in my journal and my notes, I realized in one wonderful moment that their two patterns could be generalized. I was talking about a kind of person, not about two noncomparable individuals. There was wonderful excitement in that. I tried to see whether this pattern could be found elsewhere, and I did find it elsewhere, in one person after another.

By ordinary standards of laboratory research, that is of rigorous and controlled research, this simply was not research at all. My generalizations grew out of *my* selection of certain kinds of people. Obviously, other judges are needed. So far, one man has selected perhaps two dozen people whom he liked or admired very much and thought were wonderful people and then tried to figure them out and found that he was able to describe a syndrome—the kind of pattern that seemed to fit all of them. These were people only from Western cultures, people selected with all kinds of built-in biases. Unreliable as it is, that was the only operational definition of self-actualizing people as I described them in my first publication on the subject.

After I published the results of my investigations, there appeared perhaps six, eight, or ten other lines of evidence that supported the findings, not by replication, but by approaches from different angles. Carl Rogers's findings (1961, etc.) and those of his students add up to corroboration for the whole syndrome. Bugental (1965, pp. 266–275) has offered confirmatory evidence from psychotherapy. Some of the new work with LSD,[1] some of the studies on the effects of therapy (good therapy, that is), some test results—in fact everything I know adds up to corroborative support, though not replicated support, for that study. I personally feel very confident about its major conclusions. I cannot conceive of any research that would make major changes in the pattern, though I am sure there will be minor changes. I have made some of those myself. But my confidence in my rightness is not a scientific datum. If you question the kind of data I have from my researches with monkeys and dogs, you are bringing my competence into doubt or calling me a liar, and I have a right to object. If you question my findings on self-actualizing people (Maslow, 1954, pp. 203–205; Maslow, 1962), you may reasonably do so because you don't know very much about the man who selected the people on whom all the conclusions are based. The conclusions are in the realm of pre-science, but the affirmations are set forth in a form that can be put to test. In that sense, they are scientific.

The people I selected for my investigation were older people, people who had lived much of their lives out and were visibly successful. We do not yet know about the applicability of the findings to young people. We do not know what self-actualization means in other cultures, although studies of self-actualization in China and in India are now in process. We do not know what the findings of these new studies will be, but of one thing I have no doubt: When you select out for careful study very fine and healthy people, strong people, creative people, saintly people, sagacious

[1] See, for example, Chap. 16 in this volume, by Robert Mogar. [Editor]

people—in fact, exactly the kind of people that I picked out—then you get a different view of mankind. You are asking how tall can people grow, what can a human being become? These are the Olympic gold-medal winners—the best we have. The fact that somebody can run 100 yards in less than ten seconds means that potentially any baby that is born into the world is, in theory, capable of doing so too. In that sense, any baby that is born into the world can in principle reach the heights that actually exist and can be described.

Intrinsic and Extrinsic Learning When you look at mankind this way, your thinking about psychology and psychiatry changes radically. For example, 99 percent of what has been written on so-called learning theory is simply irrelevant to a grown human being. "Learning theory" does not apply to a human being growing as tall as he can. Most of the literature on learning theory deals with what I call "extrinsic learning," to distinguish it from "intrinsic learning." Extrinsic learning means collecting acquisitions to yourself like keys in your pocket or coins that you pick up. Extrinsic learning is adding another association or another craft. The process of learning to be the best human being you can be is another business altogether. The far goals for adult education, and any other education, are the processes, the ways in which we can help people to become all they are capable of becoming. This I call intrinsic learning, and I am confining my remarks here entirely to it. That is the way self-actualizing people learn. To help the client achieve such intrinsic learning is the far goal of counseling.

These things I *know* with certainty. There are other things that I feel very confident about—"my smell tells me," so to speak. Yet I have even fewer objective data on these points than I had on those discussed above. Self-actualization is hard enough to define. How much harder it is to answer the question: Beyond self-actualization, what? Or, if you will: Beyond authenticity, what? Just being honest is, after all, not sufficient in all this. What else can we say of self-actualizing people?

B-values Self-actualizing people are, without one single exception, involved in a cause outside their own skin, in something outside of themselves. They are devoted, working at something, something which is very precious to them—some calling or vocation in the old sense, the priestly sense. They are working at something which fate has called them to somehow and which they work at and which they love, so that the work-joy dichotomy in them disappears. One devotes his life to the law, another to justice, another to beauty or truth. All, in one way or another, devote their lives to the search for what I have called (1962) the "being" values ("B," for short), the ultimate values which are intrinsic, which cannot be reduced to anything more ultimate. There are about fourteen of these B-values, including the truth and beauty and goodness of the ancients and perfection, simplicity, comprehensiveness, and several more. These B-values are described in the appendix to my book *Religions, Values and Peak Experiences* (1964). They are the values of being.

Meta-needs and Meta-pathologies The existence of these B-values adds a whole set of complications to the structure of self-actualization. These B-values behave like needs. I have called them *meta-needs*. Their deprivation breeds certain kinds of pathologies which have not yet been adequately described but which I call *meta-pathologies* —the sicknesses of the soul which come, for example, from living among liars all the time and not trusting anyone. Just as we need counselors to help people with the simpler problems of unmet needs, so we may need *meta-counselors* to help with the soul-sicknesses that grow from the unfulfilled meta-needs. In certain definable and empirical ways, it is necessary for man to live in beauty rather than ugliness, as it is necessary for him to have food for an aching belly or rest for a weary body. In fact, I would go so far as to claim that these B-values are the meaning of life for most people, but many people don't even recognize that they have these meta-needs. Part of our job as counselors may be to make them aware of these needs in themselves, just as the classical psychoanalyst made his patients aware of their instinctoid basic needs. Ultimately, perhaps, we shall come to think of ourselves as philosophical or religious counselors.

We try to help our counselees move and grow toward self-actualization. These people are often all wrapped up in value problems. Many are youngsters who are, in principle, very wonderful people, though in actuality they often seem to be little more than snotty kids. Nevertheless, I assume (in the face of all behavioral evidence sometimes) that they are, in the classical sense, idealistic. I assume that they are looking for values and that they would love to have something to devote themselves to, to be patriotic about, to worship, adore, love. These youngsters are making choices from moment to moment of going forward or retrogressing, moving away from or moving toward self-actualization. As counselors, or as meta-counselors, what can we tell them about becoming more fully themselves?

BEHAVIORS LEADING TO SELF-ACTUALIZATION

What does one do when he self-actualizes? Does he grit his teeth and squeeze? What does self-actualization mean in terms of actual behavior, actual procedure? I shall describe eight ways in which one self-actualizes.

First, self-actualization means experiencing fully, vividly, selflessly, with full concentration and total absorption. It means experiencing without the self-consciousness of the adolescent. At this moment of experiencing, the person is wholly and fully human. This is a self-actualization moment. This is a moment when the self is actualizing itself. As individuals, we all experience such moments occasionally. As counselors, we can help clients to experience them more often. We can encourage them to become totally absorbed in something and to forget their poses and their defenses and their shyness—to go at it whole hog. From the outside, we can see that this can be a very sweet moment. In those youngsters who are trying to be very tough and cynical and sophisticated, we can see the recovery of some of the guilelessness of childhood; some of the innocence and sweetness of the face can come back as they devote themselves fully to a moment and throw themselves fully into the experiencing of it. The key word for this is "selflessly," and our youngsters suffer from too little selflessness and too much selfconsciousness, self-awareness.

Second, let us think of life as a process of choices, one after another. At each point there is a progression choice and a regression choice. There may be a movement toward defense, toward safety, toward being afraid; but over on the other side, there is the growth choice. To make the growth choice instead of the fear choice a dozen times a day is to move a dozen times a day toward self-actualization. Self-actualization is an ongoing process; it means making each of the many single choices about whether to lie or be honest, whether to steal or not to steal at a particular point, and it means to make each of these choices as a growth choice. This is movement toward self-actualization.

Third, to talk of self-actualization implies that there is a self to be actualized. A human being is not a *tabula rasa,* not a lump of clay or plastocene. He is something which is already there, at least a "cartilaginous" structure of some kind. A human being is, at minimum, his temperament, his biochemical balances, and so on. There is a self, and what I have sometimes referred to as "listening to the impulse voices" means letting the self emerge. Most of us, most of the time (and especially does this apply to children, young people), listen not to ourselves but to Mommy's introjected voice or Daddy's voice or to the voice of the Establishment, of the Elders, of authority, or of tradition.

As a simple first step toward self-actualization, I sometimes suggest to my students that when they are given a glass of wine and asked how they like it, they try a different way of responding. First, I suggest that they *not* look at the label on the bottle. Thus they will not use it to get any cue about whether or not they *should* like it. Next, I recommend that they close their eyes if possible and that they "make a hush." Now they are ready to look within

themselves and try to shut out the noise of the world so that they may savor the wine on their tongues and look to the "Supreme Court" inside themselves. Then, and only then, they may come out and say, "I like it" or "I don't like it." A statement so arrived at is different from the usual kind of phoniness that we all indulge in. At a party recently, I caught myself looking at the label on a bottle and assuring my hostess that she had indeed selected a very good Scotch. But then I stopped myself: What was I saying? I know little about Scotches. All I knew was what the advertisements said. I had no idea whether this one was good or not; yet this is the kind of thing we all do. Refusing to do it is part of the ongoing process of actualizing oneself. Does *your* belly hurt? Or does it feel good? Does this taste good on *your* tongue? Do *you* like lettuce?

Fourth, when in doubt, be honest rather than not. I am covered by that phrase "when in doubt," so that we need not argue too much about diplomacy. Frequently, when we are in doubt we are not honest./ Our clients are not honest much of the time. They are playing games and posing. They do not take easily to the suggestion to be honest. Looking within oneself for many of the answers implies taking responsibility. That is in itself a great step toward actualization. This matter of responsibility has been little studied. It doesn't turn up in our textbooks, for who can investigate responsibility in white rats? Yet it is an almost tangible part of psychotherapy. In psychotherapy, one can see it, can feel it, can know the moment of responsibility. Then there is a clear knowing of what it feels like. This is one of the great steps. Each time one takes responsibility, this is an actualizing of the self.

Fifth, we have talked so far of experiencing without self-awareness, of making the growth choice rather than the fear choice, of listening to the impulse voices, and of being honest and taking responsibility. All these are steps toward self-actualization, and all of them guarantee better life choices. A person who does each of these little things each time the choice point comes will find that they add up to better choices about what is constitutionally right for him. He comes to know what his destiny is, who his wife or husband will be, what his mission in life will be. One cannot choose wisely for a life unless he dares to listen to himself, *his own self*, at each moment in life, and to say calmly, "No, I don't like such and such."

The art world, in my opinion, has been captured by a small group of opinion and taste makers about whom I feel suspicious. That is an *ad hominem* judgment, but it seems fair enough for people who set themselves up as able to say, "You like what I like or else you are a fool." We must teach people to listen to their own tastes. Most people don't do it. When standing in a gallery before a puzzling painting, one rarely hears "That is a puzzling painting." We had a dance program at Brandeis not too long ago—a weird thing altogether, with electronic music, tapes, and people doing surrealistic and Dada things. When the lights went up everybody looked stunned, and nobody knew what to say. In that kind of situation most people will make some smart chatter instead of saying, "I would like to think about this." Making an honest statement involves daring to be different, unpopular, nonconformist. If we cannot teach our clients, young or old, about being prepared to be unpopular, we might just as well give up right now. To be courageous rather than afraid is another version of the same thing.

Sixth, self-actualization is not only an end state but also the process of actualizing one's potentialities at any time, in any amount. It is, for example, a matter of becoming smarter by studying if one is an intelligent person. Self-actualization means using one's intelligence. It does not mean doing some far-out thing necessarily, but it may mean going through an arduous and demanding period of preparation in order to realize one's possibilities. Self-actualization can consist of finger exercises at a piano keyboard. Self-actualization means working to do well the thing that one wants to do. To become a second-rate physician is not a good path to self-actualization. One wants to be first-rate or as good as he can be.

Seventh, peak experiences (Maslow, 1962; Maslow, 1964) are transient moments of self-actualization. They are moments of ecstasy which cannot be bought, cannot be guaranteed, cannot even be sought. One must be, as C. S. Lewis wrote, "surprised by joy." But one can set up the conditions so that peak experiences are more likely, or he can perversely set up the conditions so that they are less likely. Breaking up an illusion, getting rid of a false notion, learning what one is not good at, learning what his potentialities are *not*—these are also part of discovering what one is in fact.

Practically everyone does have peak experiences, but not everyone knows it. Some people wave these small mystical experiences aside. Helping people to recognize these little moments of ecstasy[2] when they happen is one of the jobs of the counselor or meta-counselor. Yet, how does one's psyche, with nothing external in the world to point at—there is no blackboard there—look into another person's secret psyche and then try to communicate? We have to work out a new way of communication. I have tried one. It is described in another appendix in that same book (*Religions, Values and Peak Experiences*) under the title "Rhapsodic Communications." I think that kind of communication may be more of a model for teaching, and counseling, for helping adults to become as fully developed as they can be, than the kind we are used to when we see teachers writing on the board. If I love Beethoven and I hear something in a quartet that you don't, how do I teach you to hear? The noises are there, obviously. But I hear something very, very beautiful, and you look blank. You hear the sounds. How do I get you to hear the beauty? That is more our problem in teaching than making you learn the ABC's or demonstrating arithmetic on the board or pointing to a dissection of a frog. These latter things are external to both people; one has a pointer, and both can look at the same time. This kind of teaching is easy; the other kind is much harder, but it is part of our job as counselors. It is meta-counseling.

[2] See Chap. 14, by Herbert Otto. [Editor]

Eighth, finding out who one is, what he is, what he likes, what he doesn't like, what is good for him and what bad, where he is going and what his mission is—opening oneself up to himself—means the exposure of psychopathology. It means identifying defenses, and after defenses have been identified, it means finding the courage to give them up. This is painful because defenses are erected against something which is unpleasant. But giving up the defenses is worthwhile. If the psychoanalytic literature has taught us nothing else, it has taught us that repression is not a good way of solving problems.

Desacralizing Let me talk about one defense mechanism that is not mentioned in the psychology textbooks, though it is a very important defense mechanism to the snotty and yet idealistic youngster of today. It is the defense mechanism of *desacralizing*. These youngsters mistrust the possibility of values and virtues. They feel themselves swindled or thwarted in their lives. Most of them have, in fact, dopey parents whom they don't respect very much, parents who are quite confused themselves about values and who, frequently, are simply terrified of their children and never punish them or stop them from doing things that are wrong. So you have a situation where the youngsters simply despise their elders—often for good and sufficient reason. Such youngsters have learned to make a big generalization: They won't listen to anybody who is grown up, especially if the grown-up uses the same words which they've heard from the hypocritical mouth. They have heard their fathers talk about being honest or brave or bold, and they have seen their fathers being the opposite of all these things.

The youngsters have learned to reduce the person to the concrete object and to refuse to see what he might be or to refuse to see him in his symbolic values or to refuse to see him or her eternally. Our kids have desacralized sex, for example. Sex is nothing; it is a natural thing, and they have made it so natural that it has lost its poetic qualities in many instances, which means that it has lost practically everything. Self-

actualization means giving up this defense mechanism and learning or being taught to resacralize.[3]

Resacralizing Resacralizing means being willing, once again, to see a person "under the aspect of eternity," as Spinoza says, or to see him in the medieval Christian unitive perception, that is, being able to see the sacred, the eternal, the symbolic. It is to see Woman with a capital "W" and everything which that implies, even when one looks at a particular woman. Another example: One goes to medical school and dissects a brain. Certainly something is lost if the medical student isn't awed but, without the unitive perception, sees the brain only as one concrete thing. Open to resacralization, one sees a brain as a sacred object also, sees its symbolic value, sees it as a figure of speech, sees it in its poetic aspects.

Resacralization often means an awful lot of corny talk—"very square," the kids would say. Nevertheless, for the counselor, especially for the counselor of older people, where these philosophical questions about religion and the meaning of life come up, this is a most important way of helping the person to move toward self-actualization. The youngsters may say that it is square, and the logical positivists may say that it is meaningless, but for the person who seeks our help in this process, it is obviously very meaningful and very important, and we had better answer him, or we're not doing what it is our job to do.

Put all these points together, and we see that self-actualization is not a matter of one great moment. It is not true that on Thursday at four o'clock the trumpet blows and one steps into the pantheon forever and altogether. Self-actualization is a matter of degree, of little accessions accumulated one by one. Too often our clients are inclined to wait for some kind of inspiration to strike so that they can say, "At 3:23 on this Thursday I became self-actualized!" People selected as self-actualizing subjects, people who fit the criteria, go about it in these little ways: They listen to

[3] I have had to make up these words because the English language is rotten for good people. It has no decent vocabulary for the virtues. Even the nice words get all smeared up. "Love," for instance.

their own voices; they take responsibility; they are honest; and they work hard. They find out who they are and what they are, not only in terms of their mission in life, but also in terms of the way their feet hurt when they wear such and such a pair of shoes and whether they do or do not like eggplant or stay up all night if they drink too much beer. All this is what the real self means. They find their own biological natures, their congenital natures, which are irreversible or difficult to change.

THE THERAPEUTIC ATTITUDE

These are the things people do as they move toward self-actualization. Who, then, is a counselor? How can he help the people who come to him to make this movement in the direction of growth?

Seeking a Model I have used the words "therapy," "psychotherapy," and "patient." Actually, I hate all these words, and I hate the medical model that they imply because the medical model suggests that the person who comes to the counselor is a sick person, beset by disease and illness, seeking a cure. Actually, of course, we hope that the counselor will be the one who helps to foster the self-actualization of people, rather than the one who helps to cure a disease.

The helping model has to give way, too; it just doesn't fit. It makes us think of the counselor as the person or the professional who knows and reaches down from his privileged position above to the poor jerks below who don't know and have to be helped in some way. Nor is the counselor to be a teacher, in the usual sense, because what teachers have specialized in and gotten to be very good at is the "extrinsic learning" I described above. The process of growing into the best human being one can be is, instead, intrinsic learning, as we saw.

The existential therapists have wrestled with this question of models, and I can recommend Bugental's book, *The Search for Authenticity* (1965), for a discussion of the matter. Bugental suggests that we call counseling or therapy "ontogogy," which means trying to help people to grow to their fullest possible height. Perhaps that's a better word than the one I once sug-

gested, a word derived from a German author, "psychogogy," which means the education of the psyche. Whatever the word we use, I think that the concept we will eventually have to come to is one that Alfred Adler suggested a long, long time ago when he spoke of the "older brother." The older brother is the loving person who takes responsibility, just as one does for his young, kid brother. Of course, the older brother knows more; he's lived longer, but he is not qualitatively different, and he is not in another realm of discourse. The wise and loving older brother tries to improve the younger, and he tries to make him better than he is, in the younger's own style. See how different this is from the "teaching somebody who doesn't know nothin' " model!

Counseling is not concerned with training or with molding or with teaching in the ordinary sense of telling people what to do and how to do it. It is not concerned with propaganda. It is a Taoistic uncovering and *then* helping. Taoistic means the noninterfering, the "letting be." Taoism is not a laissez-faire philosophy or a philosophy of neglect or of refusal to help or care. As a kind of model of this process we might think of a therapist who, if he is a decent therapist and also a decent human being, would never dream of imposing himself upon his patients or propagandizing in any way or of trying to make a patient into an imitation of himself.

What the good clinical therapist does is to help his particular client to unfold, to break through the defenses against his own self-knowledge, to recover himself, and to get to know himself. Ideally, the therapist's rather abstract frame of reference, the textbooks he has read, the schools that he has gone to, his beliefs about the world—these should never be perceptible to the patient. Respectful of the inner nature, the being, the essence of this "younger brother," he would recognize that the best way for him to lead a good life is to be more fully himself. The people we call "sick" are the people who are not themselves, the people who have built up all sorts of neurotic defenses against being human. Just as it makes no difference to the rosebush whether the gardener is Italian or French or Swedish, so it should make no difference to the younger brother how his helper learned to be a helper. What the helper has to give is certain services that are independent of his being Swedish or Catholic or Mohammedan or Freudian or whatever he is.

These basic concepts include, imply, and are completely in accord with the basic concepts of Freudian and other systems of psychodynamics. It is a Freudian principle that unconscious aspects of the self are repressed and that the finding of the true self requires the uncovering of these unconscious aspects. Implicit is a belief that truth heals much. Learning to break through one's repressions, to know one's self, to hear the impulse voices, to uncover the triumphant nature, to reach knowledge, insight, and the truth—these are the requirements.

Lawrence Kubie (1953–1954), in "The Forgotten Man in Education," some time ago made the point that one, ultimate goal of education is to help the person become a human being, as fully human as he can possibly be.

Especially with adults we are not in a position in which we have nothing to work with. We already have a start; we already have capacities, talents, directions, missions, callings. The job is, if we are to take this model seriously, to help them to be more perfectly what they already are, to be more full, more actualizing, more realizing in fact what they are in potentiality.

REFERENCES

BUGENTAL, J. F. T. *The search for authenticity*. New York: Holt, Rinehart and Winston, 1965.

KUBIE, L. The forgotten man in education. *Harvard Alumni Bulletin*, 1953–1954, **56**, 349–353.

MASLOW, A. H. *Motivation and personality*. New York: Harper & Row, 1954.

MASLOW, A. H. *Toward a psychology of being*. Princeton, N.J.: Van Nostrand, 1962.

MASLOW, A. H. *Religions, values and peak experiences*. Columbus, Ohio: Ohio State Univer. Press, 1964.

ROGERS, C. R. *On becoming a person*. Boston: Houghton Mifflin, 1961.

Part SIX

THE REUNION OF PSYCHOLOGY
AND THE HUMANITIES

*The terms "humanistic" and the "humanities," of course, have a
common base, although they are often used today to refer
to quite separate concepts. "Humanism" often tends to be a term
set in contrast to "theism," and this is, indeed, one of its
earlier meanings. In a period when learning was chiefly in the realm
of the religious, those who studied the human (as contrasted
with the divine) achievements of Greece and Rome—
language, history, literature, and art—were distinguished by
the title "humanists," and their field of study was the
"humanities." With the passage of time and the secularization
of philosophy, this contrast lost force, and the "humanities" came to
be a way of distinguishing those scholarly disciplines
centering around human thought and relations (almost always
this meant literature and languages; other conceptions
varied as to whether they included the arts, history,
philosophy, and—at times—the social studies). But the meaning
of the "humanities" was clearly becoming a contrasting one
to the "sciences." With the idolatry of science, particularly in this
country, the desertions from the humanities became
wholesale, and the "social studies" became the "social sciences,"
while the trappings of scientism were applied to education, the arts,*

*home economics, physical education, and almost any other
area of learning in sight of the dean's office.*

*Now, perhaps, we are emerging from this adolescent passion and
may begin to recognize that psychology, of all disciplines,
is clearly at the intersection of the humanities, however defined,
and the sciences, whatever that term may come to mean. I think, too,
that this is one of those complicated intersections, for I detect
the crossing of the ancient trail of the religious here also.*

*In Part Six, five authors examine as many implications of this
intersection. Each in his way demonstrates how the interaction of
the particular virtues of the humanities—intuition, aesthetic
sensitivity, and the wisdom of perspective—with the strengths of
science—disciplined observation and hypothesis formation,
an orderly conceptual structure, and procedures for assessing at
least some aspects of observed phenomena—may be highly
productive of insights and enriched understanding of
human experience.*

*Frederick Wyatt, in Chapter 30, regrets the divorce that has
separated psychology and the humanities for too many years, and he
makes a scholarly contribution to healing the breach. The
reader's attention is especially called to Wyatt's treatment of the
problem of naming the subject matter of psychology. The
issue is much more than the superficial one of what word to employ.
As Wyatt points out, "behavior" has its roots in a psychology
that sought to deny the "fact that subjective experience
is inevitably the primary datum of psychology." In important and
subtle ways the names we give our experiences feed back to
influence those experiences. The flat inversion of emphasis (from
the actual centrality of experience) involved in continuing
to speak of psychology as a science of behavior not only is inaccurate
but also perpetuates a fallacy and thus contaminates our thinking.*

*When Albert Camus died in an automobile accident in 1960,
a brilliant and intuitive existential sensitivity was lost.
Szasz, in Chapter 5, and Haigh, in Chapter 22, have already drawn
our attention to Camus's perceptions. Now Thomas Greening
makes a creative and thoroughgoing examination (in
Chapter 31) of the fundamental dimension of human authenticity
versus alienation in the life and work of Camus. This is
a clear example of the sort of scholarly and scientific production
which contributes at once to psychology and to the humanities and
thus demonstrates their basic unity.*

*Bert Kaplan, in Chapter 32, also uses the insights of literature
to illuminate psychological concerns. Concentrating on
Shakespeare's portrayal of King Lear's madness, Kaplan exposes
the relativity of our concepts of sanity and madness. He
challenges much of our complacency when he says, "There is as
much reason to assess critically the value of normal modes
as of abnormal ones." Kaplan is in company with Wilson, in
Chapter 8, and Harman, in Chapter 33, in soberly proposing*

that we might well reexamine some of our best-accepted assumptions about our own natures and the world we experience about us.

This challenge finds its most explicit and most detailed statement in Harman's chapter. What Harman soberly proposes and documents in varied and scholarly fashion is as radical a reconception as any that might occur in science fiction or as Columbus's decision to sail West to get to the East. The reader will, perhaps, have noted a recurrent thread in several parts of our book: For example, Wilson, in Chapter 8, described the "robot" which limits aware functioning; Mogar, in Chapter 15, described the consciousness-expanding experiences associated with the psychedelic substances; and Lifton, in Chapter 20, spoke of the defensive closing-off process by which men limit their awareness. The thread might be phrased something like this: Man's awareness is not a given quantum. It is, rather, subject to much variation, depending on a variety of factors. There is good reason to believe that it is unduly limited as we know it today. If we are able to open our awareness more fully, the whole of our experience of ourselves and of our world may be radically changed. No man today can foresee all that change might entail.

One man today, however, who has an unusually broad perspective on science and man is Ludwig von Bertalanffy. In Chapter 34 he brings our survey of humanistic psychology to a close with a challenge to science to recognize the place of values and valuing in its work. In terms which are explicit and forthright, he overturns some of the current idols of science and education. Bertalanffy's humanistic view is not a softly sentimental one; yet he reaffirms the crucial significance of the individual human being and the social importance of recognizing human worth.

Presently: Director of the Psychological Clinic and Professor of Psychology at the University of Michigan (since 1952).

Education: Doctor of Philosophy in psychology from the University of Vienna (1936).

Current major activities: Teaching, supervising, and practicing psychotherapy and psychoanalysis.

Most rewarding project: Completing a book which aims to translate the experience of many years with psychoanalytic psychotherapy into a characterology of everyday life.

FREDERICK WYATT

Future of humanistic psychology: "I am heartened when I learn that there are many other people who think it vitally important for psychology to find again a relationship to the humanities, especially to literature, history, and philosophy. I am profoundly convinced that man needs to be studied as a *subject* and not only as an *object*."

Personal history: Research associate at Harvard University (1941–1943, 1946–1948). Chief Psychologist at McLean Hospital (1944–1948) and at Cushing Veterans Administration Hospital (1949–1952). Diplomate in Clinical Psychology, American Board of Examiners in Professional Psychology.

Writings: Publications in many different areas including education and guidance, German psychology, projective techniques, literature and psychology, and psychotherapy and the illumination it throws on human experience. Dr. Wyatt has been much in demand as a skillful reviewer of books in many areas of psychology and as a surveyor of developments in the field. In the latter capacity he prepared annual summaries of progress in clinical psychology for the *American Journal of Psychiatry* for a number of years. His perspective is well represented in "The Reconstruction of the Individual and of the Collective Past," in R. W. White (Ed.), *The Study of Lives* (1963).

Present chapter: This is an extensively reworked version of a paper entitled "Psychology and the Humanities: A Study in Misunderstanding," which first appeared in the *Teachers College Record* (1963, **64**, 562–575). It appears here with the permission of the editor of that journal.

Chapter 30
FREDERICK WYATT

PSYCHOLOGY AND THE HUMANITIES: A CASE OF NO-RELATIONSHIP

In the current relationship of psychology to the humanities, there are few areas of contact. The aim of my essay derives from this assessment. At present, only a handful of people in the humanities or in psychology know enough of the other discipline to include it in their scope. Members of this small group are quite naturally those who believe that both disciplines would profit from a closer relationship. The information the two disciplines have about each other at large (inasmuch as it is not part of a folklore of prejudice) frequently depends upon "Names in the News": what Jones says about Freud, or Toynbee about history. Considering the inclination toward collective intellectual enterprise, which is a significant aspect of the life of reason in our time, there have been few ventures of interdisciplinary collaboration between psychology and the humanities. Nor would it be easy to initiate them in the wasteland of indifference and defensive irritability which has grown up between the two camps. The public relationship of the two disciplines involves all the captiousness with which groups protect themselves against self-awareness and change and little of the curiosity and fertile ambiguity that prompt individuals to seize upon new ideas. I am talking, of course, of collective sentiments, not of individual sensibilities. Some channels of communication are open and established among the disciplines, as between literary criticism and history or between psychology and the life sciences, but those between psychology and the humanities are not. The scope of interdisciplinary relationship is defined by the opportunity for meeting each other in print and in person. Interaction depends upon understanding the other discipline's language and basic aims, and for quite some time, neither psychologists nor humanists have known what the other is talking about, and consequently they have not known how to talk to each other.

It would be a big and scurrilous job, full of farce and preposterous self-limitation, to chart the misapprehensions the two disciplines have of each other or to trace them to their historical and ideological origins. The No-Relationship (to borrow an apt construction from E. E. Cummings) of psychology and the humanities presents itself as an aggregate of well-tended misunderstandings and hidden perplexities. Yet this quandary, if appropriately scrutinized, may hold some insight into the collective mythology and the pious stereotypes of both fields. For the typical protestations of No-Relationship unwittingly contain a catalogue of the projections of one group upon the other. The fact of the matter is that psychology and the humanities have more in common than either is willing to admit.

They are concerned with the same subject and derive from the same intellectual history. In spite of the manifest difference in their modern appearance, literature and psychology present responses to the same basic motive, the insistent quest for the "what" and "how" of human experience. Of course, the two subjects may be different in as many respects as they are alike. Still, psychology and the humanities are so obviously concerned with the same vast segment of experience that their endeavors are bound to overlap and coincide.

In order to understand what keeps them apart, it may be useful to examine certain characteristics of both disciplines. I shall first concern myself with the extent of the differences between the two fields and then discuss some idiosyncrasies of modern psychology which appear to isolate it from the humanities. For the sake of contrast, I shall also review some of the metaphysical importunities of one contentious humanist. Throughout, I shall speak of certain problems psychology has created for itself by losing contact with literature, philosophy, and history.

Art and Science The foremost distinction between the humanities and psychology involves the ambiguous polarity of art and science. In English usage, the latter term refers most commonly to the natural sciences. Another, broader meaning of "science"—the systematic investigation of the principles of *any* subject—is less common here than it is in Europe. With the spectacular advances of the natural sciences, and especially of physics, the term "scientific method" has thus increasingly come to denote methods designed according to the prescriptions of the natural sciences. Psychologists have been particularly impressed by the promise of physicalist method. During the last fifty years, psychology, in attempting to make that method its own, has restricted the grasp of its subject over and over again in order to adapt it to the standards of the physical sciences. As a result, psychologists tend to view the humanities as *merely descriptive, historical,* or *ideographic,* thereby relegating them to a lower rank in the hierarchy of knowledge. The humanities are not considered to be sciences because they are not law-declaring or *nomothetic*. Inevitably this suggests that some sciences are better and more effective than others, according to the methods they use. In other words, *method* has become the touchstone of science, so that the rank of a discipline can be established by its approximation to physicalist technique.[1] Finally, this view is extended into the dichotomy of *science* and *art*. To be sure, what is thus called *art* is only vaguely related to the real arts in that it refers to the integration of a variety of impalpable, fleeting cues, as in the "healing arts" or the "art of teaching." In spite of certain undeniable achievements which hardheaded scientists are at a loss to explain, these "arts" come off a poor second when compared with more truly scientific efforts, as in the prediction of events from given premises according to firmly established general principles. Psychology has therefore been projected as a science based entirely on quantitative evidence. It is another matter how much this ideal has so far been approximated and at what cost, if we were to imagine how much the physicalist approach in psychology has succeeded in apprehending the human condition (Wyatt 1957).

THE SUBJECT-MATTER PROBLEM

The subject matter of the humanities is man's culture—his languages and concepts, his symbols and forms, and the history of his actions and ideas. Apart from their historical unity, there is little point in speaking about the humanities collectively. None of the disciplines subsumed under the sciences *or* the humanities was created in order to demonstrate a point of view. They grew from specific cultural and historical circumstances, and their history reflects social needs as well as social accidents. The zest for systematizing arts, letters, and

[1] For a recent demonstration of the importance method has in determining what kind of research will be undertaken, see Levy (1961). For a penetrating analysis of the relationship of the method of the natural sciences to that of the social sciences, see Kaufman (1958), whose book should be much more widely known.

sciences beyond the most obvious differences leads unfailingly to highly abstract speculations and peevish argument. For the rest of this discussion, the term "humanities" will stand for literary criticism, history, and philosophy and will be employed mainly to avoid the tedious repetition of these polysyllabic words. It is obvious that the humanities more often describe ideas or events among people than they formulate universal principles governing their subjects. Thus, Rickert's distinction of ideographic and nomothetic sciences has found a new vogue in psychology,[2] but, at the same time, the meaning he originally intended for that dichotomy seems to have been lost sight of (Messer, 1927; Rickert, 1910; Rickert, 1913). According to Rickert, the *culture sciences* (a term he prefers to *Geisteswissenschaften*) are not merely descriptive but are characteristically concerned with context and meaning (significance). The motives for science (*Erkenntnisdrang*— the drive to know) point as much toward the individual and the unique as toward the universal and generic. In its own endeavor, then, history has as much scientific validity as the natural sciences. Rickert saw clearly, too, that psychology, although it seeks general laws of human behavior, must also be concerned with the unique identity of the individual if it does not want to deny its own character.

In fact, no discipline has succeeded in separating description and the search for general laws so completely as to justify a clear dichotomy between descriptive and law-proposing sciences. Rather, these two approaches represent different stages of any subject. One discipline differs from the next in the stress that it puts on one of these aims rather than the other. Such differences, in turn, will change with time and with the transformation of ideologies. Rickert and others (Dilthey, 1906) emphasized that the humanities are concerned not only with merely linking events in orderly sequences, as they seem to in historical studies, but also with uncovering the *meaning* of these events beyond what they might be declared to "be." This has led to calling the humanities "symbolic," although the term then becomes so inclusive that it loses its point. Still, meaning and symbol have in common that each refers beyond its immediate object and thereby connects with other images and objects. No historical event is of such a kind that it could be unequivocally expressed in one term or exhausted by one definition, even though it is usually abbreviated into a generalized concept and frequently becomes a stereotype (e.g., "war" or "migration"). By itself and in its own right, it is a different event for different observers; and for different people, it will attain a widely divergent significance.[3] Any literary work has many meanings on several levels and always points beyond what it seems to represent concretely.

Thus, the humanities deal with larger contexts or cross-links of reference than psychology, at least in its physicalist conception. The psychologist, being the more analytical and reductionist of the two, frequently tests small aspects of that universal subject; whereas the humanist, engrossed in his more comprehensive aims, will cast it into his mold without taking time to examine all that he has beforehand taken for granted. With the record of human experience as their common matrix, the two disciplines are bound to overlap more often than their partisans are prepared to acknowledge, and would, in fact, complement each other well if their protagonists were able to see and admit it. Meaning and context are essential to man's experience and behavior, as any serious psychology of personality will have to show.

"Behavior" or "Experience" The meaning of the term "behavior" itself provides an apt demonstration of the foregoing point. Customarily used to describe the subject matter of psychology in this country, it has too many hidden implications to serve its purpose well. Originally, behavior referred to the organism in motion. The ideological content of this term is to proclaim a psy-

[3] For a more detailed discussion of this point, see Wyatt (1965).

[2] In Chapter 9, Buhler reviews some of the issues related to this distinction. [Editor]

chology "from the outside" and to exclude and deny the experiential quality of all self-awareness or simply the fact that subjective experience is inevitably the primary datum of psychology. Undeniably, behavior has since then become a more neutral and conciliatory term, so that it can now be extended to reasoning or dreaming, events that can be assessed only very incompletely "from the outside." I have argued on another occasion (Wyatt, 1958) that in employing a term like "behavior," one is bound to acquire also the latent commitments that still secretly inform it. The problem is what word to use instead of behavior. "Experience," no real equivalent of the pertinent German *Erlebnis*, will do to describe the subjective quality of psychological data, but when used too broadly, it also becomes too vague. Perhaps a more extended and more systematic usage of this term in psychology would give it more muscle. "Conduct," as a term to replace behavior, has some advantages, but it is also weighted too heavily with innuendoes of good and bad. For the purpose of this chapter, behavior is used emphatically in its most neutral sense, referring to the "mental events" that people observe in others and in themselves. The nomothetic appearance of much psychological research, on the other hand, either follows from its preoccupation with processes which are physiological and biological rather than psychological or represents the planful isolation of one facet of experience at the expense of all others. This narrowing of scope poses a perennial problem for all social sciences, but a more specific and acute problem is created by the inclination of modern psychology to lose sight of the factitious quality of that isolation and to confuse it with some ultimate kind of reality—as though the tangled web of experience would at once become straight and simple if psychologists only wished it strongly enough.

The Subject Matter of the Humanities If the place of the humanities in our culture is properly assessed, it becomes clear that it, too, can be defined in terms of subject matter. Humanists do more than review books, tally history, and analyze style. Apparently they do something that is not properly comprehended by the terminology of scientific inquiry. Literary criticism and literary history in particular, besides and beyond their researches, act as mediators of a cultural tradition. The study of their subject coincides largely with its cultivation and mediation. Exegesis serves both: the text under study and the continuity of a cultural tradition. Literary criticism in this sense holds out a natural unity of investigation, interpretation, and cultivation.[4] To engage in uncovering yet another meaning of the Homeric poems three thousand years after they were set down in their present form involves the assumption that these works provide an almost inexhaustible repository of latent meanings. It affects us, not just as a work of fiction or as a record of a civilization, but as a singular spiritual force. It is this force that is to be demonstrated and continued by ever-renewed study and interpretation.

The peculiar position of the humanist, who is (at least in principle) the guardian of a cultural tradition while he is its student, lends dignity and perennial vitality to the humanities. This productive ambiguity of role, however, is probably also a deeper cause of the disdain of many psychologists. Characteristically, it is directed against some forms of humanist endeavor (literary exegesis and criticism, literary history, and literary biography) more than against others. The multiple reasons for the prevalent attitudes of one discipline toward the other will have to be examined in a future sociology of knowledge.[5] For the

[4] Culture derives via Latin *cultus*, "worship," from the verb *colere*, "to care for," "tend," "cultivate." For a profound definition of what the humanities are really about, we should turn to Richards (1960): "The humanities . . . are the hardest to teach because wisdom, which they exist to cultivate, cannot be cut and dried. Much in other subjects can." Also: "Literature—a deep enough and leisurely enough familiarity with what the best minds have thought and felt about people. . . ."

[5] For incisive observations of the images the humanities and the natural and the social sciences have of each other, see Riesman (1958).

moment, we shall have to be satisfied with some tentative observations. One could argue that the attitude of psychologists toward the humanities follows from the inclinations which characterize psychologists as people. It could also follow, however, from the prevalent orientation of psychology itself, pointedly at odds with that of the humanities. Let us pursue the second point a little further.

Psychology's Conception of Science   Viewed as an intellectual enterprise, psychology neither represents an integrated system nor can boast a unified ideology. Psychology simply does not have a unified point of view. Its discipline may be described as a number of psychologists addressing themselves to a vast variety of tasks. Their various approaches are determined by the peculiar nature of each task. Contemporary psychology thus presents itself as a congeries of relatively independent viewpoints, of clusters of theory more or less elaborated, of widely differentiated attitudes toward observing, proving, and knowing. In effect, the several major approaches to the subject matter of psychology—experience and behavior—overlap, even though their semantic appearance may proclaim irreconcilable difference.

With such a loose frame of reference, psychology should find it easy to relate to other disciplines that pursue similar ends. Psychology is indeed pluralistic. In order, therefore, to understand its present uneasy relationship to the humanities, it is necessary to look beyond the variety of psychological theories to a much more elementary distinction that pervades contemporary psychology. Psychologists may adhere to different theories or pursue a variety of topics, from animal learning to abnormal behavior, or they may even make a method into a theory, as is the case with factor analysis. Yet all these divergent interests, according to present conviction, will have to submit to similar presuppositions of evidence. The universal task of psychology is to explain (or to understand) how experience and conduct come about. The psychologist on one side of the principal divide may, above all, wish to come close to "real life," whereas his counterpart on the other side will be more concerned with precise concepts and with systemic consistency. The first will put his trust in the discriminating observation of others and of himself and will be wary of the strictures which experiment and quantification impose upon these objectives. The second will be more concerned with rigorous evidence and, in consequence, with what is methodologically manageable. This will make him look for smaller and more isolated segments of experience to address as behavior[6] in the hope of making them more pat and impersonal. The psychologist who wishes to grasp the human condition in its living actuality must be prepared for its ever-changing complexity. His approach is global, and his foremost concern is with understanding human conduct, while his sterner colleague makes scientific rigor his primary goal and occupies himself with the appurtenances of science in psychology.

I suggested before that psychologists in general, but especially the more rigorous ones, tend to consider a kind of physicalism the epitome of science (Richfield, 1954). In token thereof, psychology is deeply committed to measurement and experiment. Both have, in turn, profoundly influenced psychology's conception of itself. Psychological events must be regarded as linear so that they can be isolated and tested experimentally, and the relationship among them must be one of simple and unidimensional cause and effect. The atomism inherent in this approach, far from deterring them, seems to lend laboratory

[6] The real philosophical significance of behavior lies, it would seem, in pointing to the elementary sameness in the conduct of all living things. As such, the concept has undeniable significance. It falls short when applied to a man who lives with other men in a culture; conduct is in practically all respects molded by this elementary condition and can be understood only in relationship to, and in interaction with, it. If a classification is needed, psychology seems to me to be more nearly a *social* than a *behavioral* science. History, for example, has a lot to do with hunger, but nobody has thought to call it a branch of biology for that reason.

(or "tough-minded") psychologists a sense of affinity with the natural sciences. Thus there has been an inclination in the history of psychology to approach experience through the senses and through the physical events which seem to underlie their functioning. Both method and physicalistic inclination have given psychology the quasi-positivist (and sometimes naïvely materialist) cast that characterizes it at present. While many psychologists think of their subject as a biological science for which the vagaries of consciousness are an embarrassment, others may perfectly well conceive of it either in watered-down behaviorist or in outright experiential and introspective terms. The predominance of method, however, remains the same. There are exceptions, of which psychoanalysis (Kohut, 1959) is the most important; otherwise, psychology, biological *or* social, gives obeisance to the same ideal (Frank, 1957).

People select disciplines on the basis of deep-rooted affinities. This applies also to their rejection and refutation. Man tends to rationalize his rancor by relating it to collective causes. He succeeds thereby in transforming his subjective crankiness into objective intellectual indignation and explains the inexplicable—what it really was that riled him—without having to recognize it and so maintains security and avoids uneasiness and guilt. The discipline molds its disciple once he is committed to it. It should not surprise us then that many psychologists find the descriptive or narrative or comprehensive style of the humanities alien and almost reprehensible. Above all, such a style is wanting in the elementary safeguards of scientific objectivity. Criticizing these defects, the psychologist confuses the means of objectivity with the end, and the achievement of sound conclusions with what may, at best, help in attaining them. The peculiar problem of established psychology is that it has made the experimental method absolute, and so psychologists have come to regard its trimmings as indispensable. From such a vantage point it becomes difficult to dis-

tinguish between scientific formalism and the degree of objectivity it really yields.[7] There is, finally, the confusion between the mannerism of scientific writing (an easy target for humanist sarcasm) and the intellectual imperative from which in the last analysis all objectivity springs. Perhaps psychologists recognize in literature and history the early origins of their own science. They may well perceive certain undeniable shortcomings in the propositions of literature and history, but they may also sense in them a greater facility for grasping the essence of human experience. As suggested, both the psychologist and the humanist may, without being quite aware of it, each see himself mirrored in the endeavor of the other. Each misunderstands what the other aims for and projects his own apprehensions onto it; but at the same time, each perceives also something of the real problems of the other discipline.

The Humanities' Involvement in Psychological Issues   No doubt, humanists, too, have their misapprehensions of the social sciences. I do not want to intimate that psychologists would appreciate the humanities more if humanists could only disabuse themselves of some of the notions they hold about psychology. Humanists as historians, as philosophers, and especially as literary critics are in the peculiar position of having to pass judgment on subjects which belong to the social sciences. The historian, unless specialized, will not often speak of scientific and technological developments. He *may* have to consider economics, but he *will* have to judge individual character and the interaction of groups at every turn. By the nature of the task, he will find himself continually occupied with central problems of psychology and sociology. Because literature *must* be concerned with human conduct, the literary critic cannot stay only within his

[7] "For each branch of the science of human and social conditions, rising from a linkage of psychological and comparative-historical insights, develops according to its own principle, which cannot be established by any theory beforehand. Its results will be the more useful, the more accurately psychological understanding renders the sequence of complex psychic events as they actually occur" (Dilthey, 1906).

formal and aesthetic context. When he passes judgment on the presentation of a character or the correctness of his social setting, he is bound to speak of the subject matter of psychology and other social sciences, and he will usually do so with considerable self-assurance. The critic is the only intellectual specialist who still has the freedom to comment on man at large when he comments within his specialty. He has retained something of the universality which, until the end of the eighteenth century, was the prerogative of the truly educated. The vitality of literary criticism may well rest in the conviction that literature contains most of what is known or worth knowing of man. The refusal to be cowed by specialization, both noble and naïve, follows hence.

However, the critic treats of ideas and is therefore subject to the stringency of rational discipline. Does he have the data and the specialized knowledge that his argument demands? Take Ortega y Gasset (1957) writing about love in the great tradition of the literary essayist. He may still have more to say about the topic than any professional psychologist. Yet, it is just possible that he might have done better still *if* he had also read Freud, Reik, and Beach. The humanist is prone to reject an argument that interferes with the comforts of literary intuition and with his cherished beliefs. He will then brush it aside as an absurd presumption or, if it really impresses him, as a dangerous fallacy likely to undermine civilization if it is allowed to go unchallenged.

THE HUMANITIES' VIEW OF PSYCHOLOGY

Joseph Wood Krutch in *The Measure of Man* (1953) offers a view of psychological science from the perspective of a committed and opinionated humanist. His treatise is typical of the attitude of many humanists in that it betrays an exaggerated idea of the near-magical power and presumed public appeal of the social sciences. Many humanists seem to think that the false doctrines of these disciplines have an enormous hold on the public. It is hard to believe that they are so wrong when they can be so persuasive, but no doubt if history has a lesson, it tells how forceful false beliefs can be. Dr. Krutch's book also shows, however, that

much of humanist disdain for the social sciences arises from concern not with their errors and fallacies but with the disturbing impact of their propositions. The fierceness of this criticism may indicate that the critic is not entirely sure of his own position. These new-fangled insights might in the end be right, but just for that reason, he must spurn them even more.

A similar attitude seems to underlie the notion humanists have of the influence of the social sciences on the public. It appears however that they know no more of, say, cultural lag than they do of the second law of thermodynamics, with which C. P. Snow used to test them.[8] "Would it were so," the social scientist might well sigh to himself when he compares the powers attributed to him with those he really has and reflects how far the world is from implementing what the social sciences have to offer. In short, much of the criticism which humanists level against the social sciences arises from a highly intransigent traditionalism which disdains a more realistic view of the human condition insofar as it might force a revision of long-held, much-cherished beliefs. The fulcrum of humanist apprehension in this respect is the demotion of man from the center of creation: for it, social scientists are perpetually reprehended. It is doubtful whether man ever held a higher place than he now does; if he did in theory and rhetoric, certainly it was not so in practice, if we mean *all* men or at least *most* men, and not only a conspicuous but numerically very small elite and its scribes.

Literary sensibility does not always distinguish the noble image of man from his real and frequently ignoble behavior. Social scientists can do no more than try to understand the human spectacle in its peculiarity. They would have little effect in demeaning man even if they were intent upon doing so—compared, for instance, with the

[8] I came to read C. P. Snow's book (1959) only after finishing this essay, but I was impressed by many similar observations, especially regarding the attitude of the humanities toward the newer disciplines.

frightening efficacy that their unscientific brethren can in this respect claim for themselves. It is also hard to understand why the defenders of moral and aesthetic values should prefer a fantasy of human nature to a more realistic grasp of it, even though the psychologist can suggest why the former is so often more comforting.

Psychologists tend to blame the humanities for being more concerned with opinions and values than with facts. This assessment is directed toward a vast diversity of intellectual endeavors; it is therefore parochial and betrays a deplorable ignorance. It may also, however, mootly point to an inherent liability of the humanities which follows from their basic concern with *meaning*. What enables the humanist to perceive experience with more subtlety and depth also makes him liable to confound his idiosyncrasies with his perceptions. When the two disciplines misunderstand each other, the failing of the social scientist is usually indifference and cultural indolence; that of the humanist is a sweeping kind of dilettantism which gives him freedom to judge other people's ideas without sufficient knowledge of their premises. What he does not understand cannot make real sense—or he can at least denounce it as mechanical and soulless and as a sign and portent of barbarism.[9]

PSYCHOLOGY'S NEED FOR THE HUMANITIES

We should reflect now on the cost of the alienation of psychology from the humanities. In the selection of students, graduate departments of psychology are usually

[9] The new aesthetics of diffidence toward an ordered reality, and its spurning in literature and the arts, implies a radical turning away from the image of man which until fairly recently represented the hub of humanist values. It is not likely that we shall find our satisfactions for long with antiheroes and happenings. But when humanists take stock of the passing of their cherished images, they may find it easier than before to use the social sciences for relating the indispensable past to the alienated but irrepressible present.

more concerned with a background in the sciences than in literature or philosophy (Moore, 1957). Of the nearly fifty graduate schools offering doctoral programs in psychology, only one has any formally explicit prerequisites in English, whereas many of them stress the need for a background in the natural sciences. The significance of matter and energy for the problems of human conduct is not immediately apparent, but students selected for psychology because of their interest in physics will probably pursue the physicalist aspects of psychology and draw away from those more directly related to experience, culture, and society. The quality of many psychological publications shows that psychologists have, at least in this respect, succeeded in warding off the intrusion of letters into their subject. All too often, papers are inept in expression, narrow in conception, and so involved in the mannerisms of objectivity that they are insufferable to anybody who does not have a highly specific concern or the attitudinal bias of the author. Style aside, it is an even more potent question whether psychologists who claim to be concerned with the conduct of people would not vastly profit from the universal record of the human condition and its perpetual exploration that literature provides.

Lack of Philosophic Sophistication This applies to philosophy as well as to literature. Present-day psychology is almost without exception devoid of any philosophical sophistication. Psychologists have little awareness of the philosophical problems inherent in almost any psychological proposition. What is the logical status of the working concepts of psychology? Are they as "real" as much experimental work takes them to be, or are they constructs? What follows from either of these positions? How suitable are the data of psychology for quantification? And what, in consequence, are the scope and limits of measurement? Philosophy functions by examining the presuppositions of individual concepts so that they can be fitted into an orderly relationship with one another. Psychologists may argue that it is not their business to expatiate on the problems which philosophy recognizes in the subjects of other disciplines—perhaps hinting thereby that the problems will disappear if one does not bother with them. At this stage of its development, however, psychology can hardly do without a minimum awareness of the philosophical questions peculiar to itself. Mathematics and physics accept that charge as a matter of course, and it is hard to think of a science which would need more awareness of its philosophical implications than psychology. Encompassing all imaginable human experience, psychology has set itself to study (even though it may plead conceptual eyestrain and other disabilities) how man comes by the image of his world in its entire range, from the chemistry of his retina to the recurrent themes of his mythologies. In short, the very scope and complexity of psychology predicates its relationship to the universalism of philosophy.

The Potential Contribution of Literature Of the disciplines collectively referred to as the "humanities," literature surely is the most comprehensive one. In its essence the term comprises the literature of all languages and cultures to which we have general access. It makes little difference that the *Oresteia* will be most extensively taught in the classics department, while, for practical purposes, Don Quixote has his home in Romance languages. Literature is both: the event of creative expression in language itself, the miracle of which has not yet ceased to puzzle and to entrance, and the efforts at understanding it by relating it to history and aesthetic norm, to society and the creative individual. Literature and literary criticism thus have an immense scope. Together they account for the most comprehensive record of the human condition, both by recreating it in concrete images and by reflecting upon it in reason. Literature as creative expression has command of a whole system of devices for its varied purposes. The most characteristic and essential of them is what we may call *poetic language*, the articulation of states of experience as such not directly expressible. Literature succeeds in communicating what could otherwise only be pointed to, though not grasped, by roundabout reference to circumstances, to effects, and to loose analogies. Poetic language achieves its end by total

use of the most recessive potential of language, including the effects of rhythm, sequence, and multiple simultaneous effects. The best way of referring to the extraordinary accomplishments of poetic language as a device of exploration and articulation is perhaps through that semantic manipulation of the more focal and the more marginal meanings of words, of successive messages and allusions, and of the continuous interplay of concrete imagery, abstraction, and symbolization.

A great deal has been said about the similarities and dissimilarities between literature and psychological science. Yet one has the feeling that, next to points which have been made so often that they have become clichés, are others equally important that have not yet been properly stated. If they had been made clear before, we would—at least in theory—not have to spend time demonstrating what psychologists can, and should, get from literature. Let me suggest a simple dichotomy of universal qualities, which would profit psychologists as well as others, and of some more specific qualities that should be indispensable for any psychology of personality and social interaction.

If psychologists are concerned with human behavior, they obviously should know about the genesis, the course, and the comparable varieties of self-awareness in literature. Hegel said that only in philosophy did the human spirit grow fully conscious of itself. But in the sight of literature, that is surely a one-sided and jealous claim. Looking at it differently, if literature is defined as "the best that man has said and thought," obviously psychology should have close contact with it. To be sure, that would be equally true for most other sciences. The relevance of literature can, by its very nature, not be specific to psychology.

There are, however, some qualities in literature which appear to be of a more specific import for psychologists. They should be implemented in graduate training as they would prepare and train psychologists for conditions with which they will be confronted continuously in their work. I shall single out a few at random. Literature is a storehouse of observations. Therefore it is also a continuous inspiration for observing and, if you wish, a school for learning how to look and what to see. With increasing mechanization, the skills of observing—one should better say, the set, the basic attitude —have become more and more neglected, to the obvious detriment of psychology. However, literature and history offer unending opportunities for cultivating the sensibilities of the productive observer.

If thinking or the process of experience is our subject par excellence, then we can never fail to gain from the vast exploration of the modalities of thought and experience in literature. Representing all the stages in the transformation of immediate experience through reasoning and reflection into generalization and abstraction, on the one hand, and into collective images and norms, on the other, literature demonstrates the point by innumerable examples. The language of literature usually comes much closer to the varieties of experience than that of most of our experiments. For an example, see the last chapter of *Ulysses*. If our concern is the conduct of people in ongoing life situations, we could find no better preparation for the continuous shifting back and forth from magical and prelogical to logical thinking, from allusion and analogy to rational confrontation, from fantasy to self-differentiation.

The history of literature from its beginnings to the present also contains an infinitely detailed account of the vagaries of consciousness and the slow, circuitous growth of self-awareness. A book like E. Auerbach's *Mimesis* is really a superb account of the experience of reality and the way it is grasped and pictured at different periods and under different social and cultural circumstances. Our attempts at a differential understanding of identity and the imageries of the self, if they were not supported by a sense of their historical emergence, would be as inadequate as our understanding of sentiments, passions, and con-

flicts would be if we were not keenly aware of their origin in childhood. Again, if we want to grasp the actuality of experience, we have to grant absolute relevance to the allusive and metaphoric quality of so much of our thinking, which the language of literature demonstrates with unsurpassed fidelity.[10]

The Function of History   A concluding word about history. Literature, philosophy, and psychology correspond with one another in a perpetual definition of collective consciousness. In order to explain any aspect of human awareness, it becomes necessary to show how it came about or to produce the history of its antecedents. History as a discipline serves two purposes: the specific one of recording the collective events of civilization and the general one of representing and demonstrating the importance of the historical perspective per se. Psychologists have paid little attention to the fact that history, like literature, is an immense storehouse of the data of human experience. Unlike literature, however, it treats of collective action and large-scale change. History has its own peculiar problems. We can never know *wie es denn eigentlich gewesen*,[11] which Rank defined as the aim of history writing, for all history is a product of reconstruction and as such must forever remain incomplete (Wyatt, 1961; Wyatt, 1965). Yet, despite these limitations, history affords a view of development, a consideration of events from the beginning to the end such as the social sciences can rarely afford. For this reason, psychologists could profitably and properly be more audacious in applying their viewpoint to history, just as Weber has done so fruitfully with sociology. The most important lesson of history, however, coincides with its own endeavor: Nothing in the field of human conduct can be ultimately meaningful unless it is put into context suggesting how the present emerged from the past. It is very nearly a tautology to say that *all* understand-

[10] See Royce's discussion of intuitive and metaphoric sources of knowledge and of the relation of psychology and history in Chapter 3. [Editor]

[11] Freely translated, "how it really was when it happened." See Stein (1956).

ing is in the end *historical*. The antihistoricism of present-day psychology consequently must become one of its major liabilities.

CONCLUSION

The alienation of psychology from the humanities is in all likelihood due to social processes more extensive than the programs of the disciplines and the intellectual proclivities of their members. It is, for one thing, due to the passing of humanist education in our schools and, for another, to the increasing differentiation and specialization of effort which made psychology break away from the discipline of philosophy and the method of literature. Neither of these developments is reversible. Psychology could as little be again an aspect of philosophy as the latter could become once more the handmaiden of theology. It is, however, entirely possible for an autonomous psychology to establish systematically a fruitful new connection with the humanities instead of leaving it to the accidents of individual interest. Psychologists as a group should awake to the fact that the humanities are not a set of antiquated fancies, accepted only for the sake of age and tradition but in essence useless for either life or science. The humanities may occasionally be so absorbed in their own rhetoric that they lose sight of the rest of the world, but they also represent an access to man's consciousness more direct than that of the sciences, and psychologists, by virtue of the breadth and variety of their subject, are in a peculiarly favored position to establish a new, and more meaningful, contact between the sciences and the humanities.

REFERENCES

DILTHEY, W. *Das Erlebnis und die Dichtung.* Leipzig: Teubner, 1906.

FRANK, L. Research for what? *Journal of Social Issues*, Suppl. Series, 1957, **10**, 1–22.

KAUFMANN, F. *Methodology of the social sciences.* New York: Humanities Press, 1958.

KOHUT, H. Introspection, empathy, and psychoanalysis. *Journal of the American Psychoanalytic Association*, 1959, **7**, 459–483.

KRUTCH, J. W. *The measure of man.* Indianapolis: Bobbs-Merrill, 1953.

LEVY, L. H. Anxiety and behavior scientist's behavior. *American Psychologist*, 1961, **16**, 66–68.

MESSER, A. *Philosophie der Gegenwart.* (6th ed.) Heidelberg: Quelle & Meyer, 1927.

MOORE, B. V. Educational facilities and financial assistance for graduate students in psychology. *American Psychologist*, 1957, **12**, 626–647.

ORTEGA Y GASSET, J. *On love.* New York: Meridian Books, 1957.

RICHARDS, I. A. The future of the humanities in general education. In M. Stein, A. J. Vidich, & D. M. White (Eds.), *Identity and anxiety.* New York: Free Press, 1960. Pp. 383–390.

RICHFIELD, J. On the scientific status of psychoanalysis. *Scientific Monthly*, 1954, **79**, 306–309.

RICKERT, H. *Kulturwissenschaft und Naturwissenschaft.* Tubingen: Mohr, 1910.

RICKERT, H. *Die Grenzen der Naturwissenschaftlichen Begriffsbildung.* Tubingen: Mohr, 1913.

RIESMAN, D. *Constraint and variety in American education.* Garden City, N.Y.: Anchor Books, 1958.

SNOW, C. P. *The two cultures and the scientific revolution.* New York: Cambridge Univer. Press, 1959.

STEIN, F. (Ed.) *The varieties of history from Voltaire to the present.* New York: Meridian Books, 1956.

WYATT, F. Orbits of characterology. In H. P. David & H. Von Bracken (Eds.), *Perspectives in personality theory.* New York: Basic Books, 1957. Pp. 336–354.

WYATT, F. A principle for the interpretation of phantasy. *Journal of Projective Techniques*, 1958, **22**, 229–245.

WYATT, F. A psychologist looks at history. *Journal of Social Issues*, 1961, **17**, 66–77.

WYATT, F. The reconstruction of the individual and of the collective past. In R. W. White (Ed.), *The study of lives.* New York: Atherton, 1965.

Presently: Chairman and Partner, Psychological Service Associates, Los Angeles (since 1958).

Education: Doctor of Philosophy in psychology from the University of Michigan (1958).

Current major activity: Practicing psychotherapy, combining psychoanalytic, existential, and humanistic viewpoints.

Most rewarding projects: "Wood carving. Sailing. Collecting material for a book on 'Los Angeles as an experience.' "

THOMAS C. GREENING

Future of humanistic psychology: "Psychology, especially humanistic psychology, will become more and more meaningfully integrated into our national way of life, so that people will regard their psychological education and emotional development as core tasks of living and will freely use psychologists as 'consultants in living.' "

Personal history: Fulbright Scholar at the University of Vienna (1952–1953). Associate of Edward Glaser and Associates and of the Human Interaction Research Institute. Lecturer, Instructor, and Human Relations Trainer at the University of California, Los Angeles (since 1962). Diplomate in Clinical Psychology of the American Board of Examiners in Professional Psychology.

Writings: Dr. Greening has published articles in various areas of psychology, but has developed two particularly: group processes used in training and in therapy and the relation of literature and psychology. In the latter vein, he has written "Existential Fiction and the Paradox of Ethics" (*The Antioch Review*, 1963, **23**, 93–107); "Camus' Unconscious Guilt as a Factor in His Life, Death and Fiction" (presented at the California State Psychological Association, San Francisco, 1963); "The Impact of Fiction on Life" (a paper read at the American Psychological Association in Los Angeles, 1964); and "Candide: An Existential Dream" (*Journal of Existentialism*, 1965, **5**, 413–416).

Present chapter: A further development of the thinking which was first presented in the California State Psychological Association paper listed above, it has not previously been published.

Chapter 31

THOMAS C. GREENING

ALBERT CAMUS: AUTHENTICITY VERSUS ALIENATION

The life of Albert Camus and the lives of the fictional characters he created in *The Stranger, The Plague,* and *The Fall* vividly portray man's deep inner conflicts between emotional relatedness and despairing isolation at the interpersonal level and between personal authenticity and deluded self-alienation at the intrapsychic level.[1] These same conflicts have been given increasing attention in the writings of contemporary psychologists; Bugental (1965), for example, has contributed an extended study of inner authenticity and outward relatedness from an existential-analytic viewpoint. The fourth ontologic given in his analysis is that we are separate from, yet related to, others. He speaks of "the deep satisfactions of intimacy with another and the continuing frustration of being always caught within the envelope of our own individuality . . ." (p. 39). Freud (1943), Buber (1937), and, more recently, Jourard (1964) are examples of other theorists who have been especially concerned with men's efforts to know themselves and to build relationships upon authentic sharing of that being.

These nonfictional studies can do part of the job of helping us confront our human condition. Fiction, such as Camus's, reaches us at another level and thus is an indispensable partner in this enterprise. Finally, there is a need for psychological exploration of literature to catalyze the partnership of psychology and literature into yielding its fullest measure of insight. Humanistic psychology needs studies of great literature and its authors to enrich our perspective on the human experience, on what it really feels like to live a human life in this century. Our own phenomenological experience can give us an individual vision of the human venture, but, in addition, there are the occasional writers who compress and express core themes of life in ways that reflect clearer light back upon our own dim musings. I hope in this chapter to suggest to the reader that Camus can teach us much about ourselves, if we can see that all of us have walked the streets of Algiers, Oran, and Amsterdam with Meursault, Dr. Rieux, and Jean-Baptiste Clamence and that our footsteps have traced a pattern that unites us as humans . . . and demarcates our solitude.

Camus as a man of action and as a writer has captured the public imagination and become a hero. Or, if our age is too jaded for heroes, at least he has become a central figure in our modern drama, symbolizing through his life and writings basic themes

[1] See references to Camus in Chapter 5 (Szasz) and Chapter 22 (Haigh) for supplementation of Greening's views. [Editor]

in the lives of we who now survive him. Camus confronted helplessness, contingency, absurdity, chaos, anomie, and estrangement, and, in spite of these forces, he struggled to live a life of action, creation, commitment, involvement, and relatedness. In his youth he was an athlete; at the age of seventeen he began a lifelong battle with tuberculosis. He opposed the Germans as editor of the underground paper *Combat*, and he worked to rebuild his country during the chaos, rancor, and frustration of postwar French politics. He was noted for his personal charm. In addition to his career as a novelist, he was active as a journalist, political spokesman, playwright, producer, and theater director. Nevertheless, Camus was tormented by a sense of passivity, estrangement, and "unbearable solitude." "Only by a continual effort can I create. My tendency is to drift toward immobility. My deepest, surest inclination lies in silence and the daily routine" (1965b, p. 120).

The same duality predominates in his fictional characters. Meursault, in *The Stranger* (1954), is the ultimate of passivity, boredom, detachment, and emotional flatness. He is overtly unmoved by his mother's death, his boss's offer of a promotion to a job in Paris, his mistress Marie's love, and his own violent murder of an Arab. Meursault, his mother, Marie (his mistress), Raymond (a friend), and Salamano (a neighbor) and his dog all drift about seeking and repelling intimacy. Similarly, ambivalent approach-avoidance feelings about closeness pervade *The Plague* (1948), *The Fall* (1956), and Camus's personal notebooks (1965a; 1965b).

Salamano's dog in *The Stranger* is perhaps one of the most pathetically expressive symbols in Camus's work. The intensely ambivalent attachment of Salamano to his "wretched spaniel" is one of the few examples in this novel of any lasting, deep relationship between two creatures. Salamano got the dog soon after his wife's death to help fill the gap in his life. "For eight years the two had been inseparable," in spite of constant battling. Meursault's mother had been fond of the dog, and the implication

seems to be that the dog, Salamano, the mother, and Meursault are variations on the same theme of ambivalent relatedness and bedraggled loneliness, with the dog having a slight edge as far as his capacity to win loyalty and emotional involvement.[2]

In Camus's world, all closeness ends in loss, and so Salamano loses his dog and weeps. Meursault, who is unable to experience grief at the death of his mother, after hearing Salamano weep for his lost dog, comments, "For some reason, I don't know what, I began thinking of mother" (p. 50). He does not pursue his thoughts and quickly goes to sleep. He cannot consciously acknowledge that he needs Salamano to do his weeping for him or that he is losing his hold on life just as Salamano has lost his dog.

In *The Plague* and *The Fall*, Camus also introduces dogs at critical points to highlight a scene or mood. After the plague and its horrors have receded and the city is full of scenes of reunion and love, the narrator, Dr. Rieux, states: "It is fitting that this chronicle should end with some reference to that man, who had an ignorant, that is to say lonely, heart" (p. 272). He then describes the final death in the book: Embittered, solitary Cottard begins firing his revolver from his shuttered window at the rejoicing people in the street. Then, "a dog, the first dog Rieux had seen for many months," ambles into the street. It is "a draggled-looking spaniel," a symbolic twin of Salamano's. Cottard fires. "The dog did a somersault like a tossed pancake, lashed the air with its legs, and floundered on to its side, its body writhing in long convulsions. . . . Then silence fell again" (p. 274). For Cottard, as for Meursault, human joy and closeness are unbearable, and each must kill and be punished. The rage of the lonely continues to produce its Oswalds.

In *The Fall*, Clamence describes a critical encounter with a dog on a subway platform during the German occupation:

Big, wiry-haired, one ear cocked, eyes laughing, he was cavorting and sniffing the passing legs. I have a very old and very faithful attachment for dogs. I like them because they always forgive. I called this

---

[2] Thomas Mann similarly presented a haunting picture of a lonely man's sadomasochistic investment in a dog (1954).

one, who hesitated, obviously won over, wagging his tail enthusiastically a few yards ahead of me. Just then, a young German soldier, who was walking briskly, passed me. Having reached the dog, he caressed the shaggy head. Without hesitating, the animal fell in step with the same enthusiasm and disappeared with him (pp.121–122).

Dogs disappear, get shot by misanthropes, or desert to the enemy, demonstrating that in Camus's world man can count neither on man nor on man's best friend.

The Stranger　The first line of *The Stranger* announces a loss: "Mother died today." Yet Meursault then proceeds through apathetic words and listless deeds to pretend that he feels no loss. His use of denial and isolation of affect is classical and thorough. Fenichel (1953a) has described a similar case:

> There is a type of patient . . . who produces no fantasies invested with affect, nor indeed any genuine affect at all, and who speaks of the most agitating experiences and recollections without becoming in the least agitated. [Referring to a patient he is treating, Fenichel continues.] . . . this stoical equanimity has always been his most powerful weapon. . . . He has been in the habit of tormenting father-substitutes almost to death; he works them into a violent passion in order that he may express his own superiority by remaining entirely without emotion. . . . The equanimity of the patient is only occasionally disturbed by a feeling of *strangeness* akin to depersonalization. When this comes upon him the whole world seems more than ever a matter of indifference . . . (pp. 32–33; italics supplied).

Only the repeated references to the glare of the sun and the oppressiveness of the heat provide external symbolic cues to Meursault's repressed feelings. The day after his mother's funeral, with his characteristically studied casualness, Meursault decides to swim, meets Marie at the pool, and begins an affair—a mother lost, a mistress gained. Marie soon decides she loves him. Meursault has no reaction. Marie tells him she wants to marry him. Meursault, persisting in his affectlessness, says he doesn't mind.

One weekend at the beach, Meursault and Marie become really close, swimming pleasantly together in the sea and embracing. Meursault seriously thinks he will marry Marie and actually feels "pleasant," but he withdraws into sleep; then he eats and takes a walk with Raymond in the hot sun. "It was just the same sort of heat as at my mother's funeral, and I had the same disagreeable sensations . . ." (p. 75). Moments later, confused and tense, he impulsively kills an Arab and thus unconsciously ensures his separation from the ordeal of intimacy with Marie.

My view of this action closely follows that of Leites in his perceptive explication of the role of the unconscious and the defense mechanisms in Meursault's behavior (1957, pp. 247–267). Similarly, Fenichel (1953b) has written a paper entitled "On the Psychology of Boredom" in which he could well be writing Meursault's unconscious dialogue:

> I am excited. If I allow this excitation to continue I shall have anxiety. Therefore I tell myself that I am not at all excited, that I don't want to do anything. Yet at the same time I feel I do want to do something; but as I have forgotten my original aim I don't know what I want to do. The external world must do something to relieve me of my tension without making me anxious. It must make me do something, and then I shall not be responsible for it. It must divert me, distract me, so that what I do will be sufficiently remote from my original aim. It must accomplish the impossible: it must afford me a relaxation of tension without instinctual action (pp. 296–297).

Meursault seeks the same goal and is by no means a simple, uncomplicated person free from unconscious motivation and intense affect, even though he appears as such in the beginning of the novel. Instead, he must be regarded as the most dangerous and blind type of inauthentic and unrelated man, the kind who claims to know himself and to be content with his relationships. He is thus unaware of the self-alienation and loneliness that really drive him, and when his defenses do finally crumble, his pent-up rage and frustration explode with lethal force:

> Then everything began to reel before my eyes, a fiery gust came in from the sea, while the sky cracked in two, from end to end, and a great sheet of flame poured down

through the rift. Every nerve in my body was a steel spring, and my grip closed on the revolver. The trigger gave. . . . And so, with that crisp, whipcrack sound, it all began. . . . I fired four more shots into the inert body. . . . And each successive shot was a loud, fateful rap on the door of my undoing (p. 76).

This concludes the first half of the novel; the second half is devoted to Meursault as a prisoner, masochistically but invulnerably protected from the risks of freedom and relatedness.

Meursault still does not really face the fact that he is in prison and will probably be condemned to death—until his one and only visit from Marie. ". . . I was hardly conscious of being in prison, I had always a vague hope that something would turn up, some agreeable surprise" (p. 89). Marie comes to see him, and the scene is an epitome of blocked communication and frustrated attempts at closeness. Marie and Meursault face each other across a space of 30 feet, separated by iron grills.[3] A dozen other prisoners are in Meursault's compartment. Meursault and Marie shout to each other, fall silent, shout inanities again, and are drowned out. Finally, the jailer takes Meursault away. Soon after, he receives a letter from her saying that she is not allowed to visit him again. ". . . it was from that day that I realized that this cell was my last home, a dead end, so to speak" (p. 89).

Having effectively cut himself off from life, he now begins to experience intense feelings about life. He moves from his apathetic detachment toward an open avowal of emotion, an assertive commitment to action, and a direct search for contact with the human race. His transition from passive confusion to active engagement parallels the development of his French ancestor, Candide (Greening, 1965). He hopes that the lawyer will like him; he becomes enraged at a meddlesome priest; he experiences a welling up of nostalgic feelings for

[3] At the end of Kafka's *Trial*, Joseph K. sees two babies who are trying to touch each other but who are separated by bars (1956, p. 280).

Marie; he takes pleasure in the realization that his mother had found some happiness in a love affair just before her death; and finally he experiences deep happiness on the eve of his execution.

In his cell at the end of *The Stranger*, Meursault has lost his mother, his mistress, and his friends. He is at last alone. He sleeps and awakens. In his final hours he allows himself to experience a wish for the only form of doomsday relatedness he dares trust in. The closing lines of the novel are " . . . all that remained to hope was that on the day of my execution there should be a huge crowd of spectators and that they should greet me with howls of execration" (p. 154). For lonely, confused, and distrustful men, execution holds out the one hope for reunion and contact with the human race. Rimbaud, in *A Season in Hell*, could be speaking for Meursault when he says, "I contrived to purge my mind of all human hope. On all joy, to strangle it, I pounced with the stealth of a wild beast. I called to the executioners while dying to let me gnaw the butt-ends of their guns" (1945, p. 3). Joseph K., in Kafka's *Trial* (1956), also finds some solace for his confusion and loneliness in the final scene of execution, where he at last establishes contact with his persecutors and receives a "reassuring pat on the back" (p. 284).

More recently, Truman Capote has written a deeply moving nonfictional account of the lonely anguish of two murderers who kill a family which seemed to symbolize happiness, success, and togetherness. One of the murderers, Perry, achieved more relatedness through his talks with Capote than he probably ever experienced before. The execution scene in this book is an almost unbearably vivid picture of closeness and humanness achieved under the most monstrous circumstances (1965, pp. 337–341). The significance of these stories lies in the fact that the authors who feel drawn to write such accounts and we readers who are drawn to read them discover that we share more with the "strangers" in our society than we suspected.

Not only the fictional character Meursault but also the author Camus exemplifies a dangerous inauthenticity and isolation. There is evidence that Camus did not understand the unconscious self-alienation of the character he had created in *The Stranger* and that only later in writing *The Fall* did he demonstrate insight into the self-deluding capacity of an "honest" man. In 1955 Camus wrote in a preface for a new edition of *The Stranger* (originally published in 1942):

> We will have a better idea of, or at least one in conformity with, the intentions of the author, if we ask ourselves in what way Meursault refuses to play the game. The answer is simple: he refuses to lie. Now, lying is not only saying what is not. It's also saying more than *is*, and, in matters of the human heart, more than we feel (1957, p. 355).

Camus describes Meursault as having "a passion for the absolute and the truth . . . the truth of being and feeling" (p. 356). In my perspective, while Meursault may have had a passion for honesty, he has lost contact with his true feelings. Thus, in spite of Meursault's and Camus's well-intentioned attempts at authenticity, psychological analysis of Meursault's supposed "truth of being and feeling" leads us inevitably to the same conclusion as that voiced by the profound preexistentialist philosopher W. C. Fields, who warned, "Never trust an honest man."

The Plague Several of the characters in *The Plague* also act out variations on the themes of separation and reunion, despair and hope, detachment and involvement. In this novel, as in *The Stranger*, the source of man's distress is seen as external, not self-imposed. Just as Meursault blinded himself to his own inner disease of emotional isolation by focusing on his mother, the sun, an Arab, and a priest as causes of his aggravation, so do the characters in *The Plague* experience the plague as causing the frustration of their inner happiness and their isolation from loved ones who are outside the city. Dr. Rieux uses work to avoid confronting his loneliness. He achieves a high degree of existential commitment to involvement and action in the face of estrangement and contingency. He retains his belief in the fundamental importance of personal relationships (Greening, 1963b). But at the end, his wife and his friend Tarrou are dead, Rambert and his mistress are re-united, and Rieux is alone . . . except for his mother.

The Fall *The Fall*, published at the peak of Camus's career (1956) and three years before his death, finally presents us with a protagonist, Clamence, who openly epitomizes the inauthenticity and loneliness that Meursault denied through repression and that Dr. Rieux tried to surmount through hard work. It takes no psychological analysis of Clamence or debunking of a Camus preface for the reader to see the dishonesty and isolation of Clamence's life, because the book is a monologue by Clamence describing his life in just those terms. Camus has clearly gained insight into the darker regions of himself and of man and has undertaken to create a protagonist far more complex than a simple, honest Algerian clerk mistreated by society or a dedicated doctor fighting the plague.

Thody (1957) has noted how the ". . . critical reception [of *The Fall*] in both France and England has reflected the disquiet and uncertainty which the novel produces in the mind of the reader" (p. 75) compared with the relatively clearer significance of *The Stranger* and *The Plague*:

> In his most pessimistic vision of the absurd —in *Caligula* and *Cross-Purpose*—Camus remained a humanist and a defender of man against the absurdity of the world. In *The Outsider* [*The Stranger*], *The Plague* and *The Rebel*, he insisted upon the innocence of man and the natural injustice of the world, and upon the fact that man caused evil and suffering only when he was misled by false ideas. In *The Fall*, all this seems to have been changed. The narrator knows himself to be self-centered, dishonest, cowardly, hypocritical and vain, and has assumed the task of proving to all other men that they are no different from him. His judgments upon mankind are of unrelieved pessimism. . . . Clamence seems to think that, if man suffers, then it is entirely his own fault (1957, pp. 75–76).

Thody wonders whether Camus was so burdened with a sense of sin and unworthiness that he was moving toward the Catholic Church. He notes the similarity of *The Fall* to the Catholic novels of Graham Greene or François Mauriac and considers that *The Fall* may have been "a deeply felt cry *de profundis* for salvation" (p. 77).

Thody expresses his discomfort and reluctance to believe this idea that Camus may have written an intentional or unintentional autobiographical novel revealing his inner sense of tormented inauthenticity. Nevertheless, Thody concludes:

> Coupled, however, with the apparently strong autobiographical elements in it [*The Fall*], and with the disquieting conviction of certain passages, the fact that Camus found the theme important enough to bear such an extensive development is rather significant. . . . Camus wrote it at the age of forty-three, the notorious middle of the journey, when the most sincere and assured men are said to go through a period of doubt and uncertainty (p. 80).

Elsewhere (Greening, 1963a), I have presented the theory that Camus was indeed deeply serious in creating Clamence, that Camus's long-standing pessimism and bitterness were emerging from beneath a lifetime of attempted repression, and that as a result of this emergence Camus may have committed a "subintentioned suicide" (Shneidman, 1963; Tabachnick & Litman, 1966). Despite our admiration for Camus, we would not be enhancing his value or the value he placed on honesty if we allowed our admiration of him to blind us to the strong indication that he may have fallen victim to the inauthenticity he fought so long against.

In this, his final novel, Camus reveals an awesome insight into the entanglements of self-deception, false relatedness, and the desperate cry for contact. From the first paragraph, the reader is assaulted by Clamence's gracious, intrusive, wheedling, deferent, insistent attempt to reach out and establish a bond. Clamence, weighted down with his albatross of guilt, has wandered like a modern mariner to a seaman's bar in the port of Amsterdam and is driven to pour out his

tale to a stranger. Why? Clamence is lonely and devious. Only as his tale unfolds does his goal gradually become apparent.

In Clamence, Camus has presented a thorough portrayal of a phony humanist. Clamence was all things good—at least in his conscious mind and his public image. He was a successful attorney, the champion of innocent victims, and a gracious and beloved social companion:

> I had a specialty: noble cases. Widows and orphans. . . . My heart was on my sleeve. You would really have thought that justice slept with me every night. I am sure you would have admired the rightness of my tone, the appropriateness of my emotions, the persuasion and warmth, the restrained indignation of my speeches before the court (p. 17).

> Familiar when it was appropriate, silent when necessary, capable of a free and easy manner as readily as of dignity, I was always in harmony. Hence my popularity was great and my successes in society innumerable (p. 27). . . . A man at the height of his powers, in perfect health, generously gifted, skilled in bodily exercises as in those of the mind, neither rich nor poor, sleeping well, and fundamentally pleased with himself without showing this otherwise than by a felicitous sociability. You will readily see how I can speak, without immodesty, of a successful life (pp. 27–28).

But in contrast to *The Stranger*, where Camus and his creation, Meursault, both remain unaware of Meursault's inner dishonesty and see society as the source of evil and absurdity, and in contrast to *The Plague*, where Dr. Rieux fights against an external enemy (the plague), in *The Fall* Camus seems at last to have evolved a protagonist who directly confronts himself as the prime source of the evil in his world. At a crucial moment, as in *The Stranger*, Clamence betrays himself and all he thought he stood for. His sin is the same as Meursault's: indifference and inaction in response to a woman's death.

Clamence is forced by his sudden, unexpected treachery against himself and humanity to admit painfully and inescapably that he is not what he seemed. He speaks of how he learned "to see clearly within me and to discover at last that I was not simple" (p. 84). He finally confronts the full extent of his inauthenticity and concludes, ". . . after profound research on myself, I brought out the fundamental duplicity of the human being" (p. 84). "I was absent at the moment when I took up the most space" (p. 87). Twenty years earlier Camus struggled against this pressure toward role playing and wrote despairingly in his journal, "I waste my time all day long, while other people say that I do a great deal" (1965a, p. 9). In the same vein, at the time his first marriage ended Camus wrote, "One goes back into the game. And, without believing in them, everyone smiles at appearances and pretends to accept them" (1965a, p. 17). Through Clamence, Camus pursues this conflict to an attempted resolution. Clamence decides to confess:

> A ridiculous fear pursued me, in fact: one could not die without having confessed all one's lies. Not to God or to one of his representatives; I was above all that, as you well imagine. No, it was a matter of confessing to man, to a friend, to a beloved woman, for example (pp. 89–90).

> I wanted to upset the game and above all to destroy that flattering reputation, the thought of which threw me into a rage . . . (p. 93). In order to reveal to all eyes what I was made of, I wanted to break open the handsome wax figure I presented everywhere (p. 94).

He was embarked upon his "search for authenticity" (Bugental, 1965). But he is not content to admit his guilt to himself, to confess to others, and to seek forgiveness or punishment. His goal is relatedness, not absolution. He prefers fraternity in hell to honor in life or forgiveness in heaven. Clamence wants to rejoin the human race. He is so obsessed with his own inauthenticity and guilt, however, that he believes the only true fraternity is that of the condemned. He points to himself and in effect says, "There, without the grace of God, go all men." Here is a Raskalnikov, an ancient mariner, or a Joseph K. who will not suffer alone, who insists on drawing his accusers and even indifferent spectators into complicity:

> When we are all guilty, that will be democracy. . . . Death is solitary, whereas slavery is collective. The others get theirs, too, and at the same time as we—that's what counts. All together at last, but on our knees and heads bowed (p. 136).

Clamence chooses a bar in Amsterdam as the setting for his confession and his reunion with humanity. The nearby Zuider Zee is "A soggy hell . . . space is colorless, and life dead" (p. 72). "For we are at the heart of things here. Have you noticed that Amsterdam's concentric canals resemble the circles of hell?" (p. 14) He believes that all men must sometime pass through this disreputable seaport bar. He strikes up a conversation with us, his readers. As he nears the end of his tale, he tells us:

> So I have been practicing my useful profession. . . . It consists to begin with, as you know from experience, in indulging in public confession as often as possible. I accuse myself up and down. . . . But let me point out that I don't accuse myself crudely, beating my breast. No, I navigate skillfully, multiplying distinctions and digressions, too—in short I adapt my words to my listener and lead him to go me one better. I mingle what concerns me and what concerns others. I choose the features we have in common, the experiences we have endured together, the failings we share—good form, in other words, the man of the hour as he is rife in me and in others. With all that I construct a portrait which is the image of all and of no one. A mask, in short, rather like those carnival masks which are both lifelike and stylized, so that they make people say: "Why, surely I've met him!" When the portrait is finished, as it is this evening, I show it with great sorrow: "This, alas, is what I am!" The prosecutor's charge is finished. But at the same time the portrait I hold out to my contemporaries becomes a mirror (pp. 139–140).

> Covered with ashes, tearing my hair, my face scored by clawing, but with piercing eyes, I stand before all humanity recapitulating my shames without losing sight of the effect I am producing, and saying: "I was the lowest of the low." Then imperceptibly I pass from the "I" to the "we." . . . Ah, *mon chere*, we are odd, wretched creatures, and if we merely look back over our lives, there's no lack of occasions to amaze and horrify ourselves.

Just try. I shall listen, you may be sure, to your own confession with a great feeling of fraternity (p. 140).

Now it is our turn, if Camus and Clamence have succeeded. We may put down the book, turn away from this raving barfly, and even wonder whether perhaps Camus had sunk into some private pathology. But the voice of Clamence pursues us:

Admit, however, that today you feel less pleased with yourself than you felt five days ago? Now I shall wait for you to write me or come back. For you will come back, I am sure! (p. 141).

And we do come back to Camus, for as Clamence does, he shows us what we fear, deny, and then reluctantly confront in ourselves in order to grow. We must acknowledge our self-alienation and isolation in order to begin our search for authenticity and relatedness. Hopefully we do not need, with Meursault, to wait the eve of our execution, or, like Dr. Rieux, to be forced into solitary work by the separations and deaths caused by a plague, or, like Clamence, to stagger with guilt through the Amsterdam fog. But Camus has shown us the varieties of alienation in unforgettable form, and it becomes our task to create a new "city of man."

REFERENCES

BUBER, M. *I and thou.* New York: Scribner, 1937.

BUGENTAL, J. F. T. *The search for authenticity.* New York: Holt, Rinehart and Winston, 1965.

CAMUS, A. *The plague.* (Tr. by S. Gilbert.) New York: Modern Library, 1948.

CAMUS, A. *The stranger.* (Tr. by S. Gilbert.) New York: Vintage Books, 1954.

CAMUS, A. *The fall.* (Tr. by J. O'Brien.) New York: Vintage Books, 1956.

CAMUS, A. Preface to *The Stranger.* (Tr. by V. Hall, Jr.) *The Nation,* Nov. 16, 1957, 355.

CAMUS, A. *Notebooks: 1935–1942.* (Tr. by P. Thody.) New York: Modern Library, 1965. (a)

CAMUS, A. *Notebooks: 1942–1951.* (Tr. by J. O'Brien.) New York: Knopf, 1965. (b)

CAPOTE, T. *In cold blood.* New York: Random House, 1965.

FENICHEL, O. An infantile, preliminary phase of "defiance by lack of affect." In *The collected papers of Otto Fenichel, first series.* New York: Norton, 1953. (a)

FENICHEL, O. On the psychology of boredom. In *The collected papers of Otto Fenichel, first series.* New York: Norton, 1953. (b)

FREUD, S. *A general introduction to psychoanalysis.* New York: Garden City, 1943.

GREENING, T. Camus' unconscious guilt as a factor in his life, death and fiction. Presented at California State Psychological Association, San Francisco, December, 1963. (a)

GREENING, T. Existential fiction and the paradox of ethics. *Antioch Review,* 1963, **23**, 93–107. (b)

GREENING, T. Candide: An existential dream. *Journal of Existentialism,* 1965, **5**, 413–416.

JOURARD, S. M. *The transparent self.* Princeton, N.J.: Van Nostrand, 1964.

KAFKA, F. *The trial.* (Tr. by Willa & E. Muir.) New York: Modern Library, 1956.

LEITES, N. "The Stranger." In W. Phillips (Ed.), *Art and psychoanalysis.* New York: Criterion Books, 1957. Pp. 247–267.

MANN, T. A man and his dog. In *Death in Venice and seven other stories.* (Tr. by H. T. Lowe-Porter.) New York: Vintage Books, 1954.

RIMBAUD, A. *A season in hell.* (Tr. by Louise Varese.) Norfolk, Conn.: New Directions, 1945.

SHNEIDMAN, E. S. Orientations toward death. In R. W. White (Ed.), *The study of lives.* New York: Atherton, 1963. Pp. 201–227.

TABACHNICK, N., & LITMAN, R. E. Character and life circumstance in fatal accident. *The Psychoanalytic Forum,* 1966, **1**, 66–74.

THODY, P. *Albert Camus: A study of his work.* London: Hamish Hamilton, 1957.

Presently: Professor of Psychology at Cowell College of the University of California, Santa Cruz (since 1965).

Education: Doctor of Philosophy in psychology from the Harvard University Department of Social Relations (1949).

BERT KAPLAN

Personal history: Instructor in clinical psychology at Harvard University (1949–1951). Instructor in mental health at the Harvard School of Public Health (1951–1953). Assistant Professor (1953–1957) and Associate Professor (1958–1963) of Psychology at the University of Kansas. Executive Secretary of the Committee on Primary Records of the National Academy of Sciences–National Research Council (1957–1958). Special Research Training Fellow of the National Institute of Mental Health to the Tavistock Clinic in London (1961). Research Fellow of the Laboratory of Anthropology of the Museum of New Mexico in Santa Fe (1963). Professor and Chairman of the Department of Psychology at Rice University (1963–1965).

Writings: Dr. Kaplan has written *Personality in a Communal Society: An Analysis of the Mental Health of the Hutterites,* with T. Plaut (1956). He edited *Studying Personality Cross-culturally* (1961), a basic work in its field, and *The Inner World of Mental Illness* (1964), a collection of first-person accounts of the experience of emotional or mental illness. His monographs and journal articles reflect his unusual combination of training and interests in clinical psychology and in anthropology, e.g., "A Study of Rorschach Responses in Four Cultures" (*Papers of the Peabody Museum of American Archaeology and Anthropology,* 1954, **42,** No. 2); "Psychological Themes in Zuni Mythology and Zuni TAT's," in W. Muensterberger & S. Axelrad (Eds.), *The Psychoanalytic Study of Society* (1962, pp. 255–262); "An Attempt to Sort Rorschachs from Four Cultures," with Marie Rickers-Ovsiankina & A. Joseph (*Journal of Protective Techniques,* 1956, **20,** 172–180); and "The Social Meaning of Navaho Psychopathology and Psychotherapy," with D. Johnson, in Ari Kiev (Ed.), *Magic, Healing and Culture* (1965).

Present chapter: The ideas in this essay were first presented at the Rice University Shakespearean Festival in the spring of 1964. They were extensively reworked as a result of Dr. Kaplan's spending six weeks with a class reading and discussing *King Lear,* and they are here published for the first time.

Chapter 32
BERT KAPLAN

ON "REASON IN MADNESS" IN KING LEAR

George Bernard Shaw points out in his preface to *Major Barbara* (1907) that the originality of Shakespeare's treatment of madness lies in his taking the lunatic seriously. Although we no longer, as the Elizabethans did, think that the lunatic is funny, modern psychology has not quite gotten to the point of taking him seriously either. In general we have regarded madness simply as something to be cured and gotten rid of, and thus we have been blind to anything within it that might be meaningful and significant. Shakespeare, by contrast, whenever he wanted his characters to be especially serious and universal made them mad. Wyndham Lewis (1955) states that Shakespeare was occupied always with insanity and that most of the major characters of the great tragedies were demented. Lewis considers madness to be an essential factor in all Shakespearean tragedy rather than just a dramatic device. He says, "The natural heightening everywhere in Shakespeare is by way of madness," and we may take it as Shakespeare's implication that whenever experience is intensified and moves toward an extreme form, some kind of madness, with all its paradoxical mixture of "heaven's sense" and nonsense, is immanent.

King Lear is Shakespeare's richest treatment of madness. In this play, considered by many critics to be Shakespeare's greatest, Lear is maddened by the inhuman tormentings of his daughters, and only then, in the depths (or heights) of his madness, is he allowed to utter his deepest and most moving speeches. It is perhaps an understatement to say that Shakespeare loved his fools and madmen. He spoke most personally and "honestly" through them and, one might say, "lived" most "feelingly" in them.

Shakespeare's Genius for Life It is a cliché to speak of Shakespeare as a great psychologist. His mode of being a psychologist, however, is eye-opening for those of us who believe that a "real" psychology is still something to be achieved. Shakespeare is often credited with being a keen observer of human nature, with the implication that his characters represent "truly" the way people "are." This way of being a psychologist, in the modes of understanding and knowledge, does not, I believe, capture Shakespeare's most important achievement as a psychologist. While he does often write about character and often is able to give an acutely perceptive account of a person or an act in small compass, his genius does not consist in his knowledge and understanding of human beings, but in his production of them. He is above all the one who lives the lives of hundreds of powerful and intense characters. The capacity for living thus revealed is not to be confused with that kind of knowledge which seeks to hold up a mirror to human reality, but which itself stands outside it. The genius for life, ordinarily manifesting itself modestly in unobserved lives rather than in literature, and only occasionally in great and significant lives which make history, in Shakespeare expands exuberantly into hundreds of characters who are both literature and person and thus accomplish what the philosophers tell us is impossible: the combination of the immediacy of existence with the reflectiveness of the literary product. These creations of new life forms are presented on the stage for the enlightenment and appreciation of all society, and they become the models and identities that influence whole generations. It is this capacity for the constitution of men and of significant modes of human existence which may be considered to be the mark of the master psychologist.

ON THE MEANING OF "MADNESS"

In *King Lear*, madness is Shakespeare's crucible. At what might be described as the height of Lear's madness, in the climactic Act IV, scene 6, where Lear has entered the stage according to the stage direction "Enter Lear, fantastically dressed with flowers," he reaches his most humane and noble vision. At this point Edgar says, "O, matter and impertinency mix'd! Reason in madness!" What is the meaning of the paradox involved in "reason in madness"? How can madness incorporate reason within it? How can madness reach what Melville calls the "sane madness of vital truth"?

There are at least two interpretations of the phrase. The more conventional interpretation, at least to modern psychology, is that while madness disrupts and disorganizes the reason, it does not do so totally, so that some remnants of reason are left among the ruins of the mind. The imagery is that of a crumbling building in which, despite an overall ruin and unserviceability, certain walls or foundations or columns remain standing. Piranesi, the eighteenth-century Italian engraver, has done hundreds of these crumbling edifices, which critics are inclined to interpret as human mind or culture. Very

often the decay and crumbling are going on simultaneously with construction in other parts of the structures.

Modern psychology has no real conception of *total* madness. The recognition of the humanness and potential capability of mental patients is a recognition of an order of sense and meaning which is the opposite of madness or senselessness. Saneness is not a "natural" state of the human organism. It is an achievement which is constituted by the efforts of the person. As long as any remnant of it is present, there is evidence of the effort being made to live a human life.

Psychology has long been aware that the psychic functioning of psychotic individuals fluctuates greatly and that quite sane and reasonable responses requiring a considerable degree of sensitivity and clear thinking often exist alongside or alternating with a high degree of madness. Such fluctuation of functions is an important clue to the character of psychosis; it suggests that we are not dealing with an organism that is basically damaged but one in which the *capacity* for "good" functioning is intact and, therefore, that the psychosis is action performed in a situation in which the normal alternatives are also possible. The psychosis may be regarded as the preferred course for the individual, the one which is valued more highly and which contains the possibilities that have the superior claim to being transformed into the realm of the real.

This thought leads us to the second sense in which the phrase "reason in madness" may be understood. Instead of taking this phrase to mean the alternation of reason and madness, we may speak of the reason that is to be found in madness itself, or the reason of madness. Many Shakespearean scholars agree, perhaps most notably Robert Heilman in his book *This Great State: Image and Structure in "King Lear"* (1948), that this is the meaning that the phrase has in *King Lear*. In one of its aspects madness has from the times of the Greeks been associated with inspiration. And one continuous theme in Western culture, running from Plato to William James, has been that madness is in some sense in greater touch with the reality of things than the sane state. This is the exact opposite of what we ordinarily think to be the case when we define madness as being "out of touch with reality." This latter definition, which is the one offered to laymen who have asked the question, "What is madness anyway?" has a naïve sound to the ears of anyone who is at all familiar with the Kantian demonstration that any known reality must be a humanly constituted reality. We have all, of course, become considerably less confident that it is the normal world that is in touch with reality, while the mad world is out of touch with it. The related conception that madness is an escape from a reality that is too harsh and burdensome and that it represents a flight from this reality into a fantasy world that is more congenial and amenable to one's wishes is equally dubious in the light of the notion that the world view of any culture is itself such a fantasy product.[1]

Madness and the "Unaccommodated Man"

One of the most striking aspects of madness, and perhaps its main one, is that it is profoundly at odds with prevailing patterns of behavior and with prevailing values. There is nothing in itself inferior or deplorable about a life that stays away from well-traveled roadways, although from the perspectives of sanity and the values that are involved in it, it may seem unhealthy and pathological. Insanity is inevitably a more uncertain, disturbed, and uncomfortable life and one that is dominated by the disapproval of normal people. However, there is probably as much reason to assess critically the value of normal modes as of abnormal ones. In *King Lear*, the two bad sisters, Regan and Goneril, are normal and are able to bring all the apparatus of reason to bear on their lives. They are, nevertheless, seen finally as varieties of monstrousness who move Lear to ask his famous question, "Is there anything in nature that makes these hard hearts?" In *Lear* it is normality that is anatomized and wondered at. The truly normal characters, Kent and Edgar, whose normality consists of a humanitarian sympathy for their fellow men, belong more with the mad Lear than with the sane sisters. In fact it is the mad and cast-out company of Lear —the Fool, Edgar disguising himself as Tom O. Bedlam, and the blind Gloucester— who are the carriers of all that is human.

Shakespeare's explanation of the paradox of reason in madness is that the "unaccommodated man" sees the world in a special way. In the words of Gloucester, he sees it feelingly—not in the light of reason and convention, but in a thoroughly human way. Gloucester contrasts his blindness, in which he can see things feelingly, with his earlier normal condition and says, "I stumbled when I saw." Does the mad person see things feelingly and therefore more truly? I believe that he does; that his experience is less dominated by reason, language, and abstract social forms; and that thus he lives more in a realm of feeling. Lear advises those who would be really human to "Expose thyself to feel what wretches feel." May we not assume that wretches are therefore in some way closer to the bedrock of the real than most of us are who have still to discover or learn what it is that wretches feel?

Psychiatrists who have studied *King Lear* have often made the point that Lear was not driven mad by the treatment of his hard-hearted daughters; rather, they contend that from the outset he was suffering from a form of dementia and that his subsequent actions do not involve the gradual development of nobility but are symptoms of his illness. The usual diagnosis is that of senility. Lear's rash and hasty action in distributing all his wealth and not keeping any for his own protection and his rejection of the honesty of Cordelia in favor of the flattery and "court holy-water" of Regan and Goneril seem foolish in the extreme. But the main error that Lear makes in the distribution scene is that he prefers the false to the genuine. To think that this error is diagnostic of mental disorder is to damn, more or less, the whole human race with this label. As a nineteenth-century writer has said, "An act of folly does not constitute insanity else the world were one great madhouse." One might say it characterizes and is a condition

[1] See Harman's development of a related theme in Chapter 33. [Editor]

of normal life in any society. Lear's madness is not associated with the error of folly but rather with the honesty and clear sight which he develops later in the play. The world of Act I, scene 1, is the normal world. It includes much that is monstrous and seemingly insane, but it is recognizable as an everyday world of social convention.

The first two acts of *Lear* are devoted to a description of a series of blows and traumas to Lear, mainly centering on the theme of the hard daughters' harsh treatment and their stripping him of every protection and resource, culminating in his leaving the court and going out into the storm. Regan, coolly and objectively the voice of reason, notes, "To willful men the injuries that they themselves procure must be their school masters."

The Mad Scenes It is in the climactic Acts III and IV that Lear's madness first shows itself. The scene in Act III is a heath. "For many miles about there's scarce a bush." And a tremendous storm is raging. Into this open, unprotected heath come Lear, the Fool, and Kent, Lear's attendant and friend. The friends try to persuade Lear to take shelter from the storm. The Fool says, "Court holy-water [or flattery] in a dry house is better than this rain water out of doors." But Lear insists on remaining exposed to the elements. He says that the elements are not as pernicious as his daughters are. "I tax not you, you elements with unkindness. I never gave you kingdom, called you children. You owe me no subscription." He does not expect that nature will treat him with special kindness, but he does expect that his own family will and that other human beings will. It is the broken bond between people that is so awful to him, not the rigors of a harsh nature.

And then in his mad, exposed state he discovers something about the world that he did not know before, and he says:

Poor naked wretches, where so ere you are,
That bide the pelting of this pityless storm,
How shall your houseless heads and unfed sides,

Your looped and windowed raggedness defend you,
From seasons such as these? Oh I have taken
Too little care of this! Take physic, pomp;
Expose thyself to feel what wretches feel,
That thou mayest shake the superflux to them,
And show the heavens more just.

In his exposed, naked condition, Lear discovers something that he did not understand when he was king. He "sees things, feelingly," and attains to new wisdom. There is a good deal of the imagery of visual perception in Lear, and there is little question but that Shakespeare meant Lear in his earlier kingly state to be deceived and blind to what was really going on about him, while in his mad state he sees truly "how this world goes." It is the scurvy politician, who with glass eyes, "only seems to see."

Lear then encounters Edgar, Gloucester's son, who has disguised himself as a Tom O. Bedlam. During Elizabethan times, when the mental asylums became too crowded, some of the inmates were periodically cast out of the asylums to make their own way by begging and stealing. In part, they received alms on the basis of putting on a show of madness, and there were a great many pseudo-Tom O. Bedlams who feigned madness as the best way of receiving alms and who wandered through the countryside in rags and tatters, completely unprotected and unsheltered by any social institution. Lear says of Edgar, "Is man no more than this—Thou art the thing itself: unaccommodated man is no more but such a poor, bare forked animal as thou art." At the conclusion of this scene, Lear refers to Edgar as "this philosopher," "this learned Theban," "a noble philosopher," and "good Athenian." It is these references that are generally taken as the first really definite signs that Lear is actually mad. It appears that, through his encounter and sympathy with the apparently mad Edgar, Lear himself becomes mad, or at least Kent and Gloucester think that he does, Kent saying at precisely this point, "His wits begin to unsettle." Gloucester replies, "Thou sayest the king grows mad—I'll tell thee friend I am almost mad myself."

Two scenes later, Lear reaches the height of his madness, when he places Regan and

Goneril on trial before Edgar, the Fool, and Kent as the judges. He enacts the trial as if the two daughters were present, and there is a certain ambiguity in the scene that psychiatrists have seized on to suggest that Lear was having visual hallucinations. Psychiatrists, however, are well known for taking things that their patients say literally and failing to see or accept the poetic license that they are taking. In the midst of this scene, Lear does with much more than ordinary good sense ask, "Then let them anatomize Regan. See what breeds about her heart. Is there any cause in nature that makes these hard hearts?"

The next and last great mad scene is in Act IV, scene 6, when there is a stage direction from Shakespeare hinting of madness, "Enter Lear, fantastically dressed with flowers." There is one short speech which exhibits what psychiatry knows as a typical psychotic flow of incoherent speech. However, immediately after this, Lear begins to make sense again and does not lapse into madness until his exit, which is presumably mad since it is described by a gentleman who is present as "a sight most pitiful in the meanest wretch, past speaking of in a king." In the other mad speeches in this scene, Lear says a number of deep and very powerful things. He realizes that despite the flattery of his court, he has no divinity. "When the rain came to wet me once and the wind to make me chatter, when the thunder would not peace at my bidding, there I found them, there I smelled them out—they told me I was everything. Tis a lie, I am not ague proof." Then in a series of speeches, he exposes sexual corruption and the arbitrariness of justice which is no better than the creatures it judges. He begins to show great sympathy with the underdog and finally concludes, "None does offend, none, I say none." What is clear in this scene is that Lear grows in compassion steadily, and in the final act, when he is reunited with Cordelia, he is no longer either mad or angry but instead is sad, tired, detached, and compassionate. In his ultimate vision he calls himself, with humility, a "very foolish, fond old man" and says to Cordelia:

We two alone will sing like birds i' th' cage
When thou dost ask me blessing, I'll kneel
     down

And ask of thee forgiveness. So we'll live,
And pray, and sing, and tell old tales, and
     laugh
At gilded butterflies, and hear poor rogues
Talk of court news; and we'll talk with them
     too—
Who loses and who wins; who's in, who's
     out—
And take upon 's the mystery of things. . . .

In the end he is restored, but not to his premad condition. Shakespearean scholars have referred to the new state as one of "redemption." What he has reached is not just a "healthier" state, but nothing less than salvation and blessedness. These theological terms signify his rising above a mundane existence to one which is at once new and more truly expressive of the possibilities of being human.

Shakespeare often did associate madness with a loss of humanness and spoke of "too much blood and too little brain," of the "insane root that takes the reason prisoner," of the madness that "deprives your sovereignty of reason," and of "such stuff as madmen tongue and brain not." There can be no denying that madness may have this aspect, but I have come to believe that the madman usually appears unreasonable from the perspectives of someone else's reason and that from the perspective of the madness itself, reason is not overthrown but is in fact present. Polonius, for example, says, "though this be madness yet there is reason in it," and, "how pregnant sometimes his replies are," and also speaks of the "Happiness that often madness hits on which reason and sanity could not so prosperously be delivered of."

One is not ready to say that madness always involves what Melville's Ahab implied when he said, "Now then, Pip, we'll talk this over; I do suck most wonderous philosophies from thee! Some unknown conduits from the unknown worlds must empty into thee!" However, it does seem that madness may sometimes have such an aspect. Perhaps our main error is that we try to define madness as though it were a particular thing or a particular state, when the fact seems to be that there is as much variety in madness as in sanity, and perhaps more. Madness can be and usually is more foolish than normal life; on the other hand, it is sometimes a good deal more wise.

CONCLUSION

The implication of what has been said here is that the notion that madness is a falling away from sanity makes the dual mistake of being overly impressed with sanity and unduly exalting it and of demeaning insanity and failing to see its significance and potential value. I believe that we find in *King Lear* a view of the condition of madness which recognizes its mystery and its strangeness but which nevertheless accepts its relation to the human rather than the bestial. I shall close by quoting that great contemporary of Shakespeare who also found in madness his most important theme. I refer to Cervantes, who wrote, "Melancholy was made, not for beasts, but for men."

REFERENCES

HEILMAN, R. *This great stage: Image and structure in "King Lear."* Baton Rouge, La.: Louisiana State Univer. Press, 1948.

LEWIS, W. *The lion and the fox.* London: Methuen, 1955.

SHAW, G. B. *Major Barbara.* New York: Brentano, 1907.

Presently: Professor in the School of Engineering at Stanford University (since 1952).

Education: Doctor of Philosophy in electrical engineering from Stanford University (1948).

Current major activity: Serving as professor in the new area of engineering-economic systems planning.

WILLIS W. HARMAN

Most rewarding project: A study of the kinds of educational experience which would be most appropriate as preparation for living in the society of twenty years from now.

Future of humanistic psychology: "Exploration of the supraconsciousness, creative unconscious, or whatever we decide to call it."

Personal history: Acting Assistant Professor of Electrical Engineering at Stanford University (1948–1949). Associate Professor of Electrical Engineering at the University of Florida (1949–1952). Director of an Office of Naval Research project on communication theory (1952–1958). Fulbright Lecturer on Communication Theory at the Royal Technical University in Copenhagen, Denmark (1959). Research on the therapeutic and educational aspects of the psychedelic experience for the International Foundation for Advanced Study (1961–1966).

Writings: Dr. Harman has written two graduate texts and one undergraduate text in electrical engineering, published several papers, holds one patent in microwave electronics, and has written one technical report in communication theory. However, his publications from 1962 on reflect his increasing involvement with human rather than electrical potentials: "Self-knowledge: The Third Component of Professional Education" (*Journal of Engineering Education*, 1962, **52**, 225–228); "The Humanities in an Age of Science" (*Main Currents in Modern Thought*, 1962, **18**, 75–83); and "Some Aspects of the Psychedelic Drug Controversy" (*Journal of Humanistic Psychology*, 1963, **3**, 93–107) are examples.

Present chapter: This material was prepared especially for this book. It is based, in part, on the paper, "Discovering the Origins of Responsibility," prepared by W. W. Harman, and copyright 1967 by the Conference on Science, Philosophy and Religion for a forthcoming book to be published by the Conference, and it appears here with their permission.

Chapter 33
WILLIS W. HARMAN

OLD WINE IN NEW WINESKINS

From the study of the past it is evident that, throughout the ages, individuals and communities have repeatedly come upon the creative factors and forces at work in the human psyche. Great philosophies and great religions have time and again come into being as an outcome of such discoveries; and for a while stirred men to the depths. But as often as the discoveries have been made they have again been lost.

In this present age there is the possibility of making the discoveries in a new way: not as an outcome of some special revelation of extraordinary insight on the part of one man or a small body of men, but in the form of direct personal experience of a considerable number of intelligent men and women directing their awareness upon the inner world. For the first time in history, the scientific spirit of enquiry, the free search for truth, is being turned upon the other side of consciousness.

In place of *a priori* dogma there is a growing body of empirically-established experience; experience which can be progressively funded, as our experience of the outer world has been funded, and its meaning learnt. Because of this, there is good prospect that the discoveries can this time be held: and so become, now and henceforward, no longer the lost secret but the living heritage of man (Martin, 1965).

Seldom have the promise and the challenge of humanistic psychology been stated so succinctly and so well. Viewing this area of scientific inquiry as characterized not by monotonic progress but by discoveries made and lost raises questions central to the whole enterprise. What are the characteristics of this knowledge of the "other side of con-

sciousness" which make conceptual ordering so elusive, which make it so difficult to transmit the knowledge gained? Why have these discoveries inspired man's most noble poetry, thoughts, and deeds, and at the same time provoked the most bitter conflicts? Why is it that we find this knowledge at once so valued and yet so threatening? Why is it that, as Maslow (1962) puts it, "It is precisely the god-like in ourselves that we are ambivalent about, fascinated by and fearful of, motivated to and defensive against" (p. 58)?

We shall not answer these questions in a brief chapter, of course, but consideration of them is essential to an understanding of the nature of the enterprise of humanistic psychology.

THE ENCAPSULATED-MAN THESIS

To begin, let us examine a thesis which appears to be as old as our most ancient records of man's attempts to organize his experience. This is the thesis "that man is encapsulated. . . . If man wishes to gain a more inclusive world-view or to approach ultimate reality it will be necessary for him to break through the several cocoons within which he is inevitably encapsulated. The first step in this process is to recognize that he is, in fact, encapsulated. Unfortunately, this first step is the most difficult"[1] (Royce, 1964, p. 3):

> There is a traditional doctrine, usually associated with religion, but now and then in-

[1] See Royce's description in Chapter 3 of how encapsulation is derived. [Editor]

321

vading great literature, that our present waking state is not really being awake at all. . . . It is, the tradition says, a special form of sleep comparable to a hypnotic trance. . . . From the moment of birth and before, we are under the suggestion that we are not fully awake; and it is universally suggested to our consciousness that we must dream the dream of this world—as our parents and friends dream it. . . . Just as in night-dreams the first symptom of waking is to suspect that one is dreaming, the first symptom of waking from the waking state—the second awakening of religion—is the suspicion that our present waking state is dreaming likewise. To be aware that we are asleep is to be on the point of waking; and to be aware that we are only partially awake is the first condition of becoming and making ourselves more fully awake (Orage, 1965, p. 89).

It is our tendency to consider the assertion in this more or less familiar doctrine to be an interesting metaphor. But is it only such a figure of speech, or is it to be taken more literally and more seriously? This is a profoundly important—and challenging—distinction.

The Data of Hypnosis Of all those phenomena whose existence is widely recognized by scientists (whether or not they are felt to be understood), among the most fraught with significance and implication are those associated with hypnosis. The basic facts are generally known, but we have hesitated to draw the conclusions to which they point.

A recent inventory of scientific findings about human behavior (Berelson & Steiner, 1964, pp. 121–123) lists a number of established findings regarding hypnosis, including the following:

Hypnotism works: that is, there is no question today that hypnotism can induce all of the following "unnatural" states:

1 anesthesia and analgesia, local or general

2 positive and negative hallucinations

3 regression to an earlier age

4 unusual muscular strength, rigidity, resistance to fatigue

5 organic effects, normally outside voluntary control. . . .

For example, a hypnotized subject may be induced to perceive an imaginary kitten placed in her lap. She experiences stroking the kitten and hearing it purr; the senses of sight, touch, and hearing seem to corroborate the hypnotist's suggestion. Yet this is a "positive hallucination." There is no kitty there.

Other examples are familiar. A subject accepts the suggestion that a person sitting in a particular chair really is not there; he perceives an empty chair. A hypnotized person is persuaded that a small wastebasket is fastened to the floor; struggling mightily, he is unable to lift it. A subject's body is rendered rigid by appropriate suggestions; he is then used to bridge the space between two chairs, and one or more individuals mount and stand on top of his unsupported chest and abdomen. Blisters and burned spots can be produced by hypnotic suggestion.

In a fascinating series of experiments, Aaronson (1966) has altered the perceptual experience of subjects by giving them hypnotic suggestions such as, "When I wake you up everybody and everything will seem to be moving three times as slowly as usual," or "The dimension of depth will be gone; there will be no depth." By changing the way in which the individual perceived the world—his depth perception, time perception, movement perception, color perception, and so on—major behavior changes, as well as mental states ranging from psychoticlike to euphoric and mystical, were produced.

Now what are the conditions essential to the production of hypnotic phenomena? In their barest simplicity, they are (1) a source of suggestion and (2) the willingness, at a deep level in the personality, to accept suggestions from that source. But surely these conditions are met in our infancy and early childhood. Most of what we commonly think of as the education of the young child amounts to acceptance of suggestions from the parents and from the culture. Extreme willingness to accept the suggestions offered by the environment accounts for the child's success in learning how to get along in the world; it also accounts, in part at least, for his pathology if the environment is unfavorable. The wrong kind of suggestions can lead to such personality defects as exaggerated suspicion and hostility, incapacitating feelings of low self-worth and inadequacy, and phobias.

The inference is as obvious as it is startling: *We are all hypnotized from infancy.*

This proposition is neither bad nor new. It is a necessity of life, our essential adaptation to the culture into which we are born. It is only another way of looking at something we knew all the time and called by some other name, such as "enculturation." But we failed to become sufficiently aware of the implications. The apparent corollary is that we do not perceive ourselves and the world about us as they are but as we have been persuaded to perceive them. Our limitations are primarily not inherent but are those which we have accepted through the suggestions of others. And our usual unawareness that this is so is part of the hypnosis as well.

Now what evidence do we have that this is a reasonable conclusion—that it is to be taken literally and not simply as a metaphor or analogy? We shall consider briefly four sources of such evidence: (1) the behavioral sciences and history, (2) the testimonies of widely recognized men of wisdom in all cultures, (3) the observations of parapsychology, and (4) the comparative descriptions of what William James termed "other forms of consciousness" (1902, p. 379).

Evidence from the Behavioral Sciences and History To begin, then, with the behavioral sciences, we find voluminous research in cultural anthropology, as well as the personal experiences of field workers, substantiating the conclusion that a person immersed in another culture perceives himself and the world very differently from the way we do. The 1898 Cambridge anthropological expedition to Torres Straits found the natives unfooled by optical illusions which uniformly deceived Europeans. Malinowski observed that the Trobriand Islanders, who believed that all characteristics are inherited from the father, regularly failed to see resemblances of the child to the mother's

side of the family. Studies of authoritarian and prejudiced persons have demonstrated that they tend, whether or not the objective data support it, to perceive members of ethnic subgroups as having the characteristics of stereotypes which the perceivers acquired in childhood. Numerous demonstrations in perception (such as the famous ones of Adelbert Ames at Dartmouth) have clearly shown that what we perceive depends in extremely large measure upon our ordering of past perceptions, which in turn is influenced by accepted suggestions. Familiar objects tend to be perceived with normal size, color, and shape as expected, even when these deliberately have been significantly altered. Poor children are found to perceive coins as larger than rich children see them. How a reversible figure-ground pattern will be seen can be influenced by prior pleasant or unpleasant associations with one or the other figure in isolation. The experiments of Asch (Berelson & Steiner, 1964, p. 335) and others indicate the extent to which perceptions are modified by group pressure.

The history of science is replete with examples illustrating that how one sees the world is determined to a large extent by how one expects to see it. To consider the most notorious case, one may recall that Western man in the Middle Ages perceived the earth as a flat plane. He was aware of various phenomena which we would today interpret as demonstrations of the spheroidal nature of the earth's surface—the disappearance of ships at sea over the horizon, the lunar eclipse, the variation of the positions of the stars with change in latitude. On the basis of observations of these same phenomena, Eratosthenes and the Alexandrian astronomers had, many centuries before, computed with remarkable accuracy the earth's circumference and the distance to, and circumference of, the moon. But these phenomena were not perceived to conflict with medieval man's basic perception of the world as flat.

To medieval man, with his teleological preconception, protective coloration in animals was provided for a purpose which was completely obvious. So also were complicated instinctual patterns such as the honey making of bees and the nest making of birds, complex organs of sight and hearing, and so on. But to the post-Darwinian sophisticate of a half-century ago, the world appeared quite differently. To him it was quite apparent that protective coloration and instinctual patterns, eyes and ears were the result of random mutations sorted out by natural selection. Nothing in his observations gave him any reason to suppose that medieval man's perception of meaning and design in life was more than a comforting fiction.

The committee appointed by the French Academy, with Lavoisier as a member, to investigate the frequently reported perception of meteorites as white-hot stones which sometimes fall to the earth and are recovered denied that things could be as they seemed because there are no stones in the sky to fall (Polanyi, 1958, p. 138). The prestige of the committee was such that many museums in Western Europe threw away their meteorite collections since, after all, there were no such things. (Today the considerable publicly available data on "flying saucer" sightings receive scant attention by civilian scientists because there are no such things.) And so it goes. Medieval doctors perceived possession by evil spirits; modern doctors do not. Early chemists perceived phlogiston; early biologists perceived spontaneous generation of maggots in meat. Physicians perceive diseases which were seemingly nonexistent to doctors practicing before they were diagnosed and described. The *Weltanschauung* changes, and as it does man's perception of himself and of his environment changes accordingly. Thus man avoids finding himself in more than mild conflict.

Testimony of the Sages As a second type of evidence, there are the testimonies of those many acknowledged men of wisdom, from diverse cultural backgrounds and scattered along the entire continuum of recorded history, who have concluded that our ordinary perceptions of reality are partial at best and in a very real sense are illusions.

Arthur Koestler describes, in masterful prose, a series of inner experiences during long days of imprisonment in the Spanish Civil War. Of these experiences he writes (1954, p. 353):

> [They] had filled me with a direct certainty that a higher order of reality existed and that it alone invested existence with meaning. I came to call it later on "the reality of the third order." The narrow world of sensory perception constituted the first order; this perceptual world was enveloped by the conceptual world which contained phenomena not directly perceivable, such as gravitation, electromagnetic fields, and curved space. The second order of reality filled in the gaps and gave meaning to the absurd patchiness of the sensory world. In the same manner, the third order of reality enveloped, interpenetrated, and gave meaning to the second. It contained "occult" phenomena which could not be apprehended or explained either on the sensory or on the conceptual level, and yet occasionally invaded them like spiritual meteors piercing the primitive's vaulted sky. Just as the conceptual order showed up the illusions and distortions of the senses, so the "third order" disclosed that time, space and causality, that isolation, separateness and spatio-temporal limitations of the self were merely optical illusions on the next higher level.

Meister Eckhart had said the same in remarking that there are three kinds of knowledge. "The first is sensible, the second is rational and a great deal higher. The third corresponds to a higher power of the soul which knows no yesterday or today or tomorrow." Aldous Huxley makes a similar assertion in summarizing the testimony of scores of sages of all ages and cultures (1946).

Plato summarizes this "universal-hypnosis" view of man's situation in the well-known allegory of the cave, in the seventh book of *The Republic*. It is found in the ancient doctrine of maya in Hinduism, as well as in Sufi tradition: "Humanity is asleep, concerned only with what is useless, living in a wrong world" (Sanai of Afghanistan, 1130 A.D.).

Two, of many possible examples from

more modern writers, will suffice to make the point, one from a modern French psychiatrist and the other from a Russian philosopher: "Our conscious thinking has all the characteristics of a dream; it is a dream. The representation that it gives us of the world is illusory. . . . In the [higher-awareness] state of the Buddha, consciousness is awakened in a way which is no longer exclusive or attached. . . . It is liberated from usual hypnosis" (Benoit, 1962, p. 237). "It must be realized that the sleep in which man exists is not normal but hypnotic sleep. Man is hypnotized and his hypnotic state is continually maintained and strengthened in him. . . . 'To awaken' for man means to be 'dehypnotized' " (Ouspensky, 1949, p. 219).

The Discordant Data of Parapsychology

Third, we come to those anomalous data which are sometimes more and sometimes less completely subsumed under the heading "parapsychology" or "psychical research" (Johnson, 1953; Murphy, 1961; Rhine, 1953; Sudre, 1960). These include those types of phenomena, attested to in many cases by hundreds of observers, which do not "fit in." Yet they seem to speak clearly to the point that something is fundamentally incomplete about a world view which cannot accommodate them.

The mere listing of some of these phenomena, with the implication that perhaps they should be taken seriously, makes some of us squirm: telepathy, clairvoyance, precognition (varieties of extrasensory perception), levitation, teleportation, fire walking, poltergeists, spiritual healing, "seeing" with the fingertips, hypnosis at a distance. The questions raised are as fundamentally challenging as any since the Copernican heresies.

The scientific standing of hypnosis is a case in point. This baffling phenomenon was, less than a century ago, part of the ostracized territory known as "psychical research." So impossible was it considered (since there was no conceivable mechanism to account for it) that even after the analgesic and anesthetic potentialities of hypnosis had been demonstrated in hundreds of apparently painless major operations, some witnessed by scores of physicians, the possibility of the phenomenon's very existence was denied. Medical journals refused to publish papers documenting the work, and patients were accused of "deluding or colluding with" their doctors in pretending to feel no pain while limbs were amputated or abdominal operations were performed (Polanyi, 1958, p. 274). Today the basic phenomenon of hypnosis is widely accepted, as we noted earlier. It is interesting to observe, however, that the earliest scientific definition of hypnosis (Bertrand, 1826) included, besides the "unnatural states" listed at the beginning of this chapter (page 322), telepathic communication; "sight without eyes"; clairvoyant ability to diagnose, prescribe for, and prognosticate about illness; and ability to take on the illness of another and thereby cure him. These phenomena seemingly are no longer observed to occur, and the definition of hypnosis no longer includes or implies them. This could be taken to indicate that they never happened at all, or it may mean instead that the existence of an "a priori impossible" conviction on the part of the hypnotist will preclude their appearing.

Nor should we forget that the phenomena which we presently subsume under the heading "creativity" (having recently become uncomfortable with the connotations of the older term "inspiration") have also only in the recent past come to be considered part of the subject matter of psychology. Prior to that, this topic too was part of "psychical research" (Myers, 1961). The universal testimony of highly creative men has been that their created projects are the result of higher, unconscious processes over which they have only limited control. At approximately the same time that Freud, in Vienna, was developing his theories of the unconscious, Frederic Myers, in Cambridge, was compiling his impressive study of the "subliminal consciousness" containing "a rubbish-heap as well as a treasurehouse" (Myers, 1961, p. 74). This vanguard parapsychological treatise stresses the essential similarities between such phenomena as telepathy and clairvoyance, and the experiences of creative geniuses and of mathematical prodigies.[2]

G. N. M. Tyrrell summarized the implications of the data of the paranormal in *The Nature of Human Personality* (1954, p. 94):

> When we pass beyond the range of our senses, we find evidence that both we and the world we live in have been given a specious appearance of self-completeness. This does not merely mean that the human senses are limited; it means that the practical mind has been formed in such a way that it reinforces the impression given by the senses and takes for granted things which are not true, but which make for simplicity and efficiency in practical life. . . . The great value of psychical research is that it has begun to put perspective into the universe and to show us that neither we nor our world come to an end where we thought they did.

THE "OTHER-FORMS-OF-CONSCIOUSNESS" ISSUE

Finally, we have a fourth source of data which directly challenge the assumption that the world is as we ordinarily perceive it. This is the voluminous literature on transcendental states, on kinds of consciousness other than the usual. One of the earliest studies of these states uses the term "cosmic consciousness" to refer to a broad range of experiences which awaits a satisfactory taxonomy (Bucke, 1905, p. 2):

> The prime characteristic of cosmic consciousness is, as its name implies, a consciousness of the cosmos, that is, of the life and order of the universe. . . . Along with the consciousness of the cosmos there occurs an intellectual enlightenment or illumination which alone would place the individual on a new plane of existence—would make him almost a member of a new species. To this is added a state of moral exaltation, an in-

[2] William James opined that Myers would "be regarded as the Founder of a new science" on the basis of his "concept of the Subliminal Self, by which he colligated and co-ordinated a mass of phenomena which had never before been considered together" (*Proceedings of the Society for Psychical Research*, 1903, **18**, 22).

describable feeling of elevation, elation, and joyousness, and a quickening of the moral sense, which is fully as striking and more important both to the individual and to the race than is the enhanced intellectual power. With these come what may be called a sense of immortality, a consciousness of eternal life, not conviction that he shall have this, but the consciousness that he has it already.

Further documentation may be found in philosophy and the arts, in mystical literature, and in the rapidly accumulating literature on experiences with the psychedelic chemical agents. We shall examine each of these briefly.

The Transcendental in the Humanities Among philosophers, perhaps Baruch Spinoza speaks most unequivocally on the place of the transcendental (Pollock, 1899, p. 269):

> In all exact knowledge the mind knows itself under the form of eternity; that is to say, in every such act it is eternal and knows itself as eternal. This eternity is not a persistence in time after the dissolution of the body, no more than a pre-existence in time, for it is not commensurable with time at all. And there is associated with it a state or quality of perfection called the immediately apprehended love of God.

Again and again we find expressed in the works of the most cherished poets the urging to discover for oneself the supremacy of the transcendental. The forms range from the straightforward statements of the first two examples below to the tantalizingly paradoxical expression exemplified by the latter two:

> If the doors of perception were cleansed, everything would appear to man as it is, infinite.
> For man has closed himself up, till he sees all things thro' narrow chinks of his cavern.
>
> WILLIAM BLAKE,
> "The Marriage of Heaven and Hell"

> Truth is within ourselves; it takes no rise
> From outward things, whate'er you may believe
> . . . and to *know*,
> Rather consists in opening out a way
> Whence the imprisoned splendour may escape,

Than in effecting entry for a light
Supposed to be without.

ROBERT BROWNING,
"Paracelsus"

Die and Become
Till thou hast learned this
Thou art but a dull guest
On this dark planet.

GOETHE, "Spiritual Longing,"
Book I of *West-Eastern Divan*

In order to arrive there,
To arrive where you are, to get from where
   you are not,
You must go by a way wherein there is no
   ecstasy. . . .
And what you do not know is the only thing
   you know
And what you own is what you do not own.
And where you are is where you are not.

T. S. ELIOT, "East Coker,"
Four Quartets

As to the arts, we shall have to allow a single quotation to suffice. It is from J. W. N. Sullivan's biography of Beethoven (1927, p. 159):

All art exists to communicate states of consciousness which are higher synthetic wholes than those of ordinary experience, but in these last quartets Beethoven is dealing with . . . a state of consciousness surpassing our own, where our problems do not exist, and to which even our highest aspirations . . . provide no key.

The Literature of Mysticism   The empirical, mystical element is well recognized to exist in nearly all religions and religious philosophies. To be sure, certain aspects of the Eternal Gospel, the *Philosophia Perennis*, are especially emphasized in the Eastern religious philosophy of Vedanta, others in the mystical tradition of Christianity, and still others in the poetic writings of the mystics of Islam. But its essence is the claim of the possibility of directly apprehended knowledge that is universal and immemorial.

Stace (1960) has provided a particularly helpful analysis of mysticism in various cultures. He concludes that "the mystical consciousness is quite different from [the sen-

sory-intellectual consciousness]. . . . The central characteristic in which all fully-developed mystical experiences agree is that they involve the apprehension of an ultimate nonsensuous unity in all things, a oneness or a One to which neither the senses nor the reason can penetrate. In other words, it entirely transcends our sensory-intellectual consciousness" (p. 14).

Carpenter (1892, p. 156) sums up what might be an appropriate attitude for the humanistic psychologist as follows:

Great have been the disputes among the learned as to the meaning of the word Nirvana—whether it indicates a state of no-consciousness or a state of vastly enhanced consciousness. . . . The important thing is to see and admit that under cover of this and other similar terms there does exist a real and recognizable fact (that is, a state of consciousness in some sense), which has been experienced over and over again, and which to those who have experienced it in ever so slight a degree has appeared worthy of lifelong pursuit and devotion. . . .

The Psychedelic Agents   The rapidly accumulating literature on experiences with the psychedelic ("mind-manifesting" or "consciousness-expanding") chemical agents provides a final array of observations on our central theme.[3] They have been used in the spiritual exercises of many religious groups, both ancient and modern, primitive and sophisticated, to assist man to reveal his mind to himself and to help him reach greatly cherished, heightened levels of awareness and consciousness. In recent years these substances have played an increasingly important role in psychotherapy (Cohen, 1965; Harman, 1963; Masters, 1966; Mogar, 1965; Sherwood, 1962). Their potential theoretical and practical importance has evoked extravagant statements from many of the scientists who have studied them:

Science develops through the development of instruments which make new classes of evidence available. . . . [One such instrument

[3] See Mogar's discussion of these agents in Chapter 15. [Editor]

is] the psychedelics . . . which enhance the sense of meaning or vitality, or beauty and sheer intensity of existence. . . . Quite aside from absolutely all interpretations whatever, to say the very least, these [psychedelic] experiences alter man's conception of himself and the world. . . . They are a way of looking at the cosmos, and therefore belong to the central core of man's needs as a thoughtful being (Murphy, 1965, p. 79).

The very beginning, the intrinsic core, the essence, the universal nucleus of every known high religion has been the private, lonely, personal illumination, revelation, or ecstasy of some acutely sensitive prophet or seer . . . of what I prefer to call "peak experience." . . . In the last few years it has become quite clear that certain drugs called "psychedelic" often produce peak experiences in the right people under the right circumstances (Maslow, 1964, p. 27).

The changes in values and the therapeutic gains which may follow even a partial glimpsing of the psychedelic-mystical perception . . . are suggestive of the part the psychedelic experiences may have to play in helping us to discern the true meaning of the verb "to be" (Sherwood, 1962, p. 79).

Briefly, the evidence of the psychedelics seems to corroborate the testimonies of the men of vision which we examined earlier, to the effect that reality is a far different matter from what we ordinarily imagine it.

Now this is an uncomfortable matter to contemplate. None of us likes to be fooled. It is difficult for us to allow the full significance of this proposition to impinge on our conscious awareness. To an extent far greater than we like to imagine, our perceptions are influenced or determined by what Rokeach (1960) terms the person's "total belief-disbelief system."

The Obdurate Belief System By the term "belief system," Rokeach means not only consciously held beliefs but also "what a person really believes of verbal and non-verbal, implicit and explicit beliefs, sets, or expectancies" (1960, p. 32). Central to this system is a set of unstated but basic beliefs[4]

[4] One might question whether the word "beliefs" is a fortunate choice to refer to inferred determinants of action which are not in the individual's

about the nature of the self, others, and the universe; about what in life is to be highly valued; and about where one looks for ultimate authority. The validity of these basic beliefs and values the individual "does not question and, in the ordinary course of events, is not prepared to question" (p. 40). These basic beliefs are formed early in life. Their nature is strongly influenced by early environment; once formed, they are remarkably resistant to change as one moves through life. Out of this core of basic beliefs the total belief system grows. New perceptions may alter the core beliefs. Much more likely, however, the core beliefs will shape the perceptions to fit in with the existing belief structure.

Viewed in these terms, the lasting and all-pervading effect of the particular suggestions accepted by the infant stands out with clarity. It is thus that the central hypnosis or the core beliefs are shaped. Thenceforth the world tends to be perceived in such a way that the perception supports the image. Always the self-preserving instinct acts to filter incoming data to fit in with the existing belief system. Always the conflict is present between this sanity-maintaining action and the counteroperating growth impulse to remove the distorting lenses, to "cleanse the doors of perception."

We have emphasized so strongly the supporting evidence for this hypothesis of our perceptions of reality being conditioned and limited to a predominant degree because of our natural reluctance to take the proposition seriously. Now the time has come to inquire into some of the consequences of this premise, particularly in relation to the changing character of psychology.

CHARACTERISTICS OF THE NEW PSYCHOLOGY

If there is a perception of reality which is less conditioned, what are its characteristics? We may assume that it includes the commonsense scientific image of reality as a

conscious awareness, since its ordinary usage implies conscious acceptance. However, when persons become aware of these preexistent influences, they often spontaneously express themselves in terms such as "I feel that I have believed this about myself without knowing it."

valid but partial view. It is probable that it cannot be adequately conceptualized with symbols, or in a language, that have been built up mainly out of experience in the hypnotized, conditioned state. (Hence the frequently heard claim that experience of the dehypnotized state is ineffable or that attempts to express it verbally lead to paradoxical statements.) It is not yet clear what metaphors the new psychology will choose for the attempt.

Conceptualizing Man and His Experience We may speculate on the characteristics of the developing humanistic psychology as it comes more and more adequately to deal with the "encapsulated-man" problem and the "other-forms-of-consciousness" issue, as these have been described above. Certain attributes of a liberated psychology seem most probable:

1 It will incorporate some way of referring to the subjective experiencing of a unity in all things [the "More" of William James (1902), "the All" of Bugental (1965), the "divine Ground" of the *Perennial Philosophy* (Huxley, 1946)].

2 It will include some sort of mapping or ordering of states of consciousness transcending the usual conscious awareness [Bucke's "Cosmic Consciousness" (1905), the "enlightenment" of Zen, and similar concepts].

3 It will take account of the subjective experiencing of a "higher self" and will view favorably the development of a self-image congruent with this experience [Bugental's "I-process" (1965), Emerson's "Oversoul" (1950), Assagioli's "True Self" (1965), Brunton's "Overself" (1938), the Atman of Vedanta, and so on].

4 It will allow for a much more unified view of human experiences now categorized under such diverse headings as "creativity," "hypnosis," "mystical experience," "experiences with the psychedelic drugs," "extrasensory perception," "psychokinesis," and related phenomena.

5 It will include a much more unified view of the processes of personal change and emergence which take place within the contexts of psychotherapy, education (in the sense of "know thyself"), and religion (as spiritual growth). This view will possibly center around the concept that personality and behavior patterns change consequent upon a change in self-image, a modification of the person's emotionally felt perception of himself and his relationship to his environment.

Processes of Change We shall adopt here such a conceptual model of personal change resulting from alterations in the self-image because it appears to offer a useful way of summarizing the diversity of techniques which have been used to promote change. The self-image [Self-concept of Bugental (1965), personal construct system of Kelly (1955)] is, of course, a much more complex thing than the name suggests. It is by no means free of inconsistencies and fragmentation, but for our purposes we may oversimplify and speak as though it were a unified pattern of feelings and behavior. It has been likened to the input signal of a feedback control system; the personality and behavior-pattern structure tend to "follow" the self-image. We become as we imagine ourselves to be: "As a man thinketh in his heart, so is he." In a more elaborate metaphor, Lilly (1966) views conscious and unconscious mental processes as a hierarchy of programs available to the brain-computer, with the self-image as a "meta-program" which modifies, controls, and creates the programs giving rise to behavior.

The form of the self-image is part of the original hypnosis. It comprises the feelings and judgments about ourselves which we have accepted from external sources. It is, as we have noted, remarkably resistant to any direct pressures to change. Nevertheless a host of techniques of some effectiveness have been developed and used to try to bring about such changes.

In general, there seem to be four basic techniques for changing the self-image:

CHANGE IN RESPONSE TO CLUES FROM THE ENVIRONMENT, PARTICULARLY OTHER PERSONS Through fortunate life experiences, as well as experiences in the more structured context of therapy or "encounter group" situations,[5] the individual may introject new data resulting in a revision of his self-image. Through a meaningful, emotional relationship with another or with other persons,

[5] See Part Five for a variety of discussions pertinent to this point. [Editor]

and in a supportive environment, he may be able to "see," feel, and alter handicapping and constraining aspects of his basic, preverbal belief structure. Being confronted by awareness of limiting and hurtful aspects of his self-image, and simultaneously supported while he dares to consider reinterpretation and change, the person may use such experiences to revise his basic beliefs and move in the direction of becoming "fully functioning" (Rogers, 1961), "self-actualizing" (Maslow, 1962), and "authentic" (Bugental, 1965). He moves away from resistiveness and defensiveness and toward an increasing awareness of his deeper needs, toward growing confidence in his own inner reactions as a trustworthy guide to behavior, toward increasing sensitivity and openness to all experience with increased ability to form new relationships, and toward being in accord with himself and at one with the world.

CHANGE IN RESPONSE TO CLUES GENERATED BY ONESELF

A second technique involves changing of the self-image by integrative symbols which the person presents, so to speak, to himself. These clues may come through dreams, fantasy, or directed imagination; through the use of psychedelic agents; or in participation in religious ritual or contemplative exercise. Use of such symbols is central to the "constructive technique" of C. G. Jung and to the "psychosynthesis" of Assagioli (1965). It is set forth with particular clarity by one of Jung's students, P. W. Martin (1965, p. 115):

> The principal means by which the creative possibilities of the deep unconscious may be reached is the transforming symbol. Anyone wholeheartedly engaging in the experiment in depth will find, as a normal fact of experience, that the unconscious repeatedly produced shapes, objects, phrases, ideas, which have this peculiar quality: if put to their right use they make possible a re-direction of energy and, by so doing, progressively transform the man who uses them.

Through the emotional and intellectual integration of these symbols, the governing image of the self—the one that is emotionally felt and imagined—may change from one of worthlessness, inadequacy, or precariously pent-up urges, to a self-image centered on an "I," "that of God in every man," whose worth and adequacy are beyond question and whose guidance can be implicitly trusted. The task and joy of life then become that of response to the quiet but insistent demands of this "I" that one actualize his inherent potentialities to know, to be free, and to love—to be oneself.

MODIFICATION BY DELIBERATE CHOICE AND AUTOSUGGESTION

Another technique involves deliberately choosing the characteristics of the self-image to be modified and using autohypnotic techniques to effect the change. Modifications of the self-image, deeply embedded in the personality structure, can be brought about by the persistent vivid imagining that they have already taken place—through a deliberate dehypnotization, as it were. This sort of technique has been one of the secrets of esoteric knowledge for many centuries. "Therefore I tell you, whatever you ask in prayer, believe that you receive it, and you will" (Mark 11:24). It obtained its greatest popularization (and received correspondingly great condemnation) through the work of the French psychologist Emile Coué. More recently Maltz (1960) has given a popular exposition of the technique of rational selection of a desired self-image, with autosuggestive implantation of this image into the deeper levels of the psyche. Assagioli's technique of "ideal models" (1965, p. 166) is similar. The approach is the basis for a number of "personal effectiveness" seminars and training courses. In a superficial form, where it involves a good component of self-deception, it receives much-deserved criticism.

Similar to the autosuggestive techniques are the "autogenic training" of Schultz (Schultz & Luthe, 1959) and Kelly's "fixed-role therapy" (1955). The same basic process would seem to be involved in the influencing of the deeply buried self-image by religious symbol and ritual, by contact with great works of art, and by study of "the best that has been thought and said" in humanities and "great books" courses.

ALTERED CONSCIOUSNESS

The fourth process of character change is described in mystical and occult literature, but it cannot be said to have formed a part of recognized psychotherapeutic procedures in recent times until the advent of psychedelic therapy (Harman, 1963; Sherwood, 1962). It is characterized by the person's image of himself being changed as a result of his having experiences which he perceives as transcendental and valid, as directly revealing to him higher aspects of himself of which he had previously been unaware. Various techniques have been used to facilitate the shift to altered states of consciousness, including prayer and meditation, fasting and asceticism, the various forms of yoga, the shock treatments of Zen, and the use of psychedelic chemicals.

The New Synthesis Knowledge of oneself, of the core of one's being, has throughout history been held before man as his highest goal. Since the Middle Ages in Western civilization, three parallel developments have carried on this tradition, emphasizing their somewhat different techniques and formulating their discoveries in varying ways. With the growth of humanistic psychology, we have the convergence of these three streams—psychotherapy, religion, and liberal (liberating) education. The insights of the psychiatrist's office, of the monastic cloister, of the humanities seminar, and of the artist's studio are now being conceptualized and joined together in practice in ways which promise new levels of effectiveness.

Self-realization, enlightenment, creativity, self-actualization, spiritual development, being authentic, fully functioning—in the end these come mainly to a single essence, to be aware and to respond: to become aware, from one's own immanent, intimate experience, that we are elements of a greater whole and that one has the choice of responding, of saying "yes" to life with the whole of his being, of being responsible (response-able)—and so to choose, and thereby to taste of freedom, to know the origins of love, to find the essence of wisdom, to become authentically man.

We are accustomed to the idea that progress in scientific knowledge is monotonically cumulative. We tend to forget that knowledge can be lost as well as won. It is humbling to realize that that which is newest and most filled with promise in the science of man's psyche is also, in some sense, the most ancient knowledge of all. Perhaps, indeed, the time has come for this knowledge to become not "the lost secret but the living heritage of man."

REFERENCES

AARONSON, B. S. Hypnosis, responsibility and the boundaries of self. Paper read at Conference on Science, Philosophy and Religion, New York, January, 1966.

ASSAGIOLI, R. *Psychosynthesis: A manual of principles and techniques.* New York: Hobbs, Dorman, 1965.

BENOIT, H. *Let go! Theory and practice of detachment according to Zen.* London: Allen & Unwin, 1962.

BERELSON, B., & STEINER, G. A. *Human behavior: An inventory of scientific findings.* New York: Harcourt, Brace & World, 1964.

BERTRAND, A. 1826. Quoted in A. Weitzenhoffer, The nature of hypnosis. *American Journal of Clinical Hypnosis*, 1953, **5**, 296, Part I.

BRUNTON, P. *The quest of the overself.* New York: Dutton, 1938.

BUCKE, M. *Cosmic consciousness.* New York: Dutton, 1905.

BUGENTAL, J. F. T. *The search for authenticity.* New York: Holt, Rinehart and Winston, 1965.

CARPENTER, E. *From Adam's peak to elephanta.* London: Swan & Sonnenschein, 1892.

COHEN, S. *The beyond within: The LSD story.* New York: Atheneum, 1965.

EMERSON, R. W. The oversoul. In *Essays.* New Haven, Conn.: Yale Univer. Press, 1950.

HARMAN, W. W. Some aspects of the psychedelic drug controversy. *Journal of Humanistic Psychology*, 1963, **3**, 93–107.

HUXLEY, A. *The perennial philosophy.* London: Chatto & Windus, 1946.

JAMES, W. *The varieties of religious experience.* New York: Modern Library, 1902.

JOHNSON, R. *The imprisoned splendour.* New York: Harper & Row, 1953.

KELLY, G. A. *The psychology of personal constructs.* Vol. 1. New York: Norton, 1955.

KOESTLER, A. *The invisible writing*. New York: Macmillan, 1954.

LILLY, J. C. The human computer. Paper read at Conference on Science, Philosophy and Religion, New York, March, 1966.

MALTZ, M. *Psychocybernetics*. Englewood Cliffs, N.J.: Prentice-Hall, 1960.

MARTIN, P. W. *Experiment in depth*. New York: Pantheon, 1965.

MASLOW, A. H. *Toward a psychology of being*. Princeton, N.J.: Van Nostrand, 1962.

MASLOW, A. H. *Religions, values and peak experiences*. Columbus, Ohio: Ohio State Univer. Press, 1964.

MASTERS, R. E. L., & HOUSTON, J. *Varieties of psychedelic experience*. New York: Holt, Rinehart and Winston, 1966.

MOGAR, R. E. Current trends in psychedelic research. *Journal of Humanistic Psychology*, 1965, **5**, 147–166.

MURPHY, G. *The challenge of psychical research*. New York: Harper & Row, 1961.

MURPHY, G. Human psychology in the context of the new knowledge. *Main Currents*, March–April, 1965, 75–81.

MYERS, F. W. H. *Human personality and its survival of bodily death*. New York: University Books, 1961.

ORAGE, A. R. *Psychological exercises and essays*. London: Janus, 1965.

OUSPENSKY, P. D. *In search of the miraculous*. New York: Harcourt, Brace & World, 1949.

POLANYI, M. *Personal knowledge*. Chicago: Univer. of Chicago Press, 1958.

POLLOCK, F. *Spinoza's life and philosophy*. London: Duckworth, 1899.

RHINE, J. B. *New world of the mind*. New York: Sloane, 1953.

ROGERS, C. R. *On becoming a person*. Boston: Houghton Mifflin, 1961.

ROKEACH, M. *The open and closed mind*. New York: Basic Books, 1960.

ROYCE, J. R. *The encapsulated man*. Princeton, N.J.: Van Nostrand, 1964.

SCHULTZ, J. H., & LUTHE, W. *Autogenic training*. New York: Grune & Stratton, 1959.

SHERWOOD, J. N., STOLAROFF, M. J., & HARMAN, W. W. The psychedelic experience: A new concept in psychotherapy. *Journal of Neuropsychiatry*, 1962, **4**, 69–80.

STACE, W. T. *The teachings of the mystics*. New York: Mentor Books, 1960.

SUDRE, R. *Parapsychology*. New York: Citadel, 1960.

SULLIVAN, J. W. N. *Beethoven: His spiritual development*. New York: Vintage Books, 1927.

TYRRELL, G. N. M. *The nature of human personality*. London: Allen & Unwin, 1954.

Presently: Professor of Theoretical Biology at the University of Alberta in Edmonton, Canada. He holds appointments in both the Psychology and the Zoology Departments there (since 1961).

Education: Doctor of Philosophy from the University of Vienna (1926).

LUDWIG VON BERTALANFFY

Current major activity: During the 1966 summer, Dr. Von Bertalanffy was in Europe as the guest of the Reimers Foundation for Anthropogenic Research. Meantime he has been preparing the Heinz Werner Inaugural Lectures, which he gave, for publication as a book which will appear in 1967.

Personal history: Born in Vienna. Came to Canada in 1949. Professor at the University of Vienna (1926–1948). Basic contributions to a number of fields, including the foundation of the organismic conception in biology; the Von Bertalanffy growth equations, which are widely used in international fisheries; the Bertalanffy fluorescence method in biochemistry and cancer research; the theory of the open system organism in biophysics and biology; and general system theory. He worked on problems of behavioral science and theoretical psychology, serving as one of the "founding fellows" of the Center for Advanced Study in the Behavioral Sciences at Stanford University in 1954, as one of the founders of the Society for General Systems Research, as a member of study groups of the Mental Health Section of the World Organization, and as a Sloan Visiting Professor at the Menninger Foundation.

Writings: He has, in recent articles, dealt with such topics as the diagnosis of pulmonary cancer, general system theory, the psychopathology of scientism, the biology of mental illness, the postal system of Venice from 1390 to 1797, democracy and education, aggression, the mind-body problem, etc. His books include *Modern Theories of Development* (1933) and *Problems of Life: An Evaluation of Modern Biological Thought* (1952). Both of these have been published in numerous translations. He is an editor of the *Handbuch der Biologie* (twelve volumes since 1942) and of the *General Systems Yearbooks*.

Present chapter: First presented as an address at the Central Washington State College in 1962, this material was published in the *Teachers College Record* (1964, **65**, 496–507). It is presented here in a somewhat revised form with the permission of that journal.

Chapter 34
LUDWIG VON BERTALANFFY

THE WORLD OF SCIENCE
AND THE WORLD OF VALUE

Life and history are no idylls; and when we look back, we find precisely the greatest geniuses—from the Preacher in the Bible to Sophocles, Dante, Michelangelo, and even Goethe—filled with dismay about their times and with what modern philosophers would call existential anxiety, deep-rooted doubts about the meaning and goals of life. Nevertheless, we hardly exaggerate when we say that there never was a deeper, more all-pervading gap between facts—the world which is—and values—the world which ought to be, a more profound insecurity about our directions. The early Christians in the Roman catacombs did not know whether they would see the next day, but they did know that their martyrdom granted the Crown of Life. The Italian Renaissance was politically one of the most atrocious episodes in history, but it sublimated its gore and cruelty into Giotto's frescoes at St. Francis' in Assisi, into the Sistine Chapel, and into the triumphal glory of St. Peter's. The French Revolution slaughtered thousands at the altar of liberty, but it brought a new idea into the world, an idea which would not perish. We, with all our skyscrapers, space vehicles, comfortable homes, economic abundance, cars, and doubled lifespan, are not so fortunate. Whether the abyss of atomic annihilation will devour us or whether we manage precariously to dance at its brink, if everything is said, our creed is that of Iago in Verdi's *Otello—Sento il fango originario in me; e poi? La morte e*

nulla: "I come from primeval slime, and my destiny is death and nothing."

Let us not believe that spiritual questions are superannuated in an age of technology. There is an old saying that God is with the stronger battalions. Modern inventiveness has gone only so far as to replace infantry battalions with atomic bombs. In the last resort, however, it is always a system of values, of ideas, of ideologies that is decisive. We have no reason to assume that this law of history has changed. What has lost its historic meaning will not survive. Military hardware, including the most advanced superbombs, will not save us when the will to live, the guiding ideas or values of life, have subsided. This is one of the few safe conclusions from history.

Poignant Paradoxes   At the risk of appearing ridiculous, I would say that one excellent way to grasp the spirit of the times is to read newspapers and magazines with the eye of the historian (to consider them what he would call "primary sources") and of the naturalist who, in a detached way, looks at the strange ways of ants and termites. On one single page, we may observe all the striking contrasts besetting our time. The report of the latest space exploit is sandwiched between the latest murder and Hollywood divorce, between Red China and war protests, or between the new car model and nuclear annihilation. We can do worse than to contemplate, for a moment, the symbolic meaning of such arrangements. Not only is the conquest of space a most brilliant achievement of science and technology; it is also the fulfillment of a millennial longing of humanity, first expressed in the myth of Daedalus and visionarily anticipated by Utopianists from Leonardo da Vinci to Cyrano de Bergerac, Goya, and Jules Verne. If we accept Oswald Spengler, the philosopher of the *Decline of the West*, space is the *ur-symbol*, the deepest and decisive symbol of the occidental mind, expressed by all manifestations of culture —the longing for space in painting and music, voyages, space-conquering diplomacy, arms, physical theories, and innumerable other areas. Eventually and after centuries, this *ur-symbol* materializes in its definitive, never-before-believed form—and is submerged by trivia, by appeals to what is lowest in human nature, by the cheap sensations provided by an almost subhuman killer and the ephemeral amours of a doll.

Ours is the affluent society, so we read, and we have the highest standard of living ever achieved. We are bombarded with astronomical figures of gross national product —20 billion dollars for the first trip to the moon, 11 billion dollars for packaging wares to make them appetizing to the buyer. But we also read of 100 billion dollars which would be required but is not available for slum clearing; we read that 57 percent of people over age sixty-five live on less than $1,000 a year in cold-water flats, that 10 percent of Americans are functional illiterates. And what is perhaps the most remarkable symptom, economic opulence goes hand in hand with a peak of mental illness, some 50 percent of hospital beds being occupied by mental patients. It goes hand in hand with a continuous increase in the rate of crime, especially juvenile delinquency. And, the psychotherapists tell us, besides the classical neuroses caused by stress, tensions, and psychological trauma, a new type of mental sickness has developed for which they have even had to coin a new term—existential neurosis, mental illness arising from the meaninglessness of life, the lack of goals and hopes in a mechanized mass society.

Society as Patient The psychiatrist is wont to speak of split personality as a classical symptom of mental disease. If anything, our society is a split personality—not split simply into a fine Dr. Jekyll and a hideous Mr. Hyde, but into an enormity of disorganized and antagonistic parts. This is the reason why analyses of modern society are not mere book titles any more, but have become part of everyday language: from the *Decline of the West* to *Brave New World, 1984, Organization Man, Hidden Persuaders, Waste Makers, Status Seekers*, and many others. This literature, in itself, is a symptom or symbol; nothing comparable has existed in history, except perhaps in the analogous time of the decay of the Roman Empire. Like physicians examining an individual patient, these modern diagnosticians of society observe different symptoms, use different tools and terms, and sometimes err or exaggerate their findings. On the whole, however, their analyses are like a battery of laboratory tests, adding up to a consistent picture. It may be expressed in one brief sentence: We have conquered the world, but somewhere on the way, we seem to have lost our souls.

In more realistic terms, this means that we have lost, or lost sight of, those guiding lights for the formation of our lives which are called human values.

A THEORY OF VALUE

At this point, we have to embark on rather abstract considerations, hoping, however, to come back with results which shed light on those disquieting problems.

Unfortunately, the theory of values is one of the most difficult, obscure, and controversial fields in philosophy and behavioral science. The best we can do is start with an operational definition of value and see how far we get; that is, we adapt the definition to our purposes, keeping in mind that, for this very reason, it will not be uncontradictable.

So let us posit: *Values are things or acts which are chosen by, and are desirable to, an individual or to society within a certain frame of reference.* Although it is admittedly tentative, every word matters in this definition. We obviously have to include both objects and acts—material things like dollar bills or Picasso paintings and immaterial qualities like the goodness of a charitable act are obviously values. We further have to introduce the element of choice. Where there is no choice, there is only necessity, not value. In somewhat different terms: Whatever is taken for granted neither is nor has a value. For example, to a perfectly healthy person or animal, health is not a value but is simply taken care of by biological functions. Only if we envisage possible danger and can do something about it, does health become a value. Prolongation of human life is possible; physical immortality is not. The first is a value, not the second. We have to pay for food, but not for breathing air; therefore, the first has value, and the second does not, even though it is equally indispensable for life. To the Aztecs, because gold was abundantly available, it had no particular value. To the Spaniards, it was eminently desirable, so they liquidated Montezuma and his Indians. A postage stamp is worth a few pennies to the letter writer; it may be worth thousands of dollars to the collector because it is particularly desirable within the framework of philately. Our criteria apply equally to actions. In the course of a day, we perform innumerable actions which have no value involvement at all. Only where there is both choice and preferability do value judgments appear. Nobody cares what way I choose to arrive at my office—at least so long as I do not commit an undesirable act like a traffic violation; but my consistently coming late or early may be evaluated. On the other hand, if I fall into the river and save myself by swimming, this is not considered to be a moral act because it is presupposed that there is no choice between drowning and swimming. If another person falls into the river and I save him, I may get a medal because it is presupposed that I did have a choice and took the socially desirable action. And so forth, ad infinitum.

From this infinite array of preferences and evaluations, mankind, starting in some prehistoric stage and continuing to the present day, singled out some very general and abstract notions which became values par excellence. Pleasure, social virtues, goodness, truth, beauty, and deity are a few of them.

It is the objective of a theory of value to elucidate where these values came from, what they mean, from what ultimate concept they can be derived, and what their consequences are for human behavior and society.

One such theory is the naturalistic one. It is a derivative of the philosophical doctrine known as "reductionism," which, in this particular respect, can be formulated as follows: Human values are derived from, and ultimately reduce to, biological needs, drives, and principles. Biological values are essentially maintenance of the individual, survival of the group, and evolution of the species. This basic doctrine can be and has been formuated many different ways. For example, it is the classic philosophical doctrine of hedonism, maintaining that pleasure is the ultimate good. It is also Freud's doctrine that behavior is governed by the pleasure principle and the principle of sustaining the homeostatic equilibrium of the organism in answer to changing environmental influences. Generalizing the original physiological meaning of homeostasis, the terms "psychological homeostasis" and "sociological homeostasis" were introduced; that is, the ultimate goal of behavior is to maintain the psychophysical organism in a biological, psychological, and social equilibrium. Still other terms for the same idea are "psychological and social adjustment" or "adaptation"; from here originate the philosophy of conformity and the ideology of so-called progressive education, both proclaiming social adjustment or equilibrium, with existing society as the ultimate goal.

Man in Two Worlds With leading biologists and psychologists, I am in fundamental disagreement with this theory—not because of theological or metaphysical prejudices, but because it does not fit the facts. Human behavior is not directed simply toward release of tensions; boredom, emptiness, and *taedium vitae* may be psychopathogenic factors. A large part of behavior—play and exploratory activities, creativity, and culture in general—simply does not fit in the scheme. Men (and organisms in general) are not stimulus-response machines, as the theory presupposes; immanent activity going along with so-called function pleasure is an important part of behavior. Life and behavior are not simply utilitarian, trying to come to a so-called equilibrium with a minimum expense of physical and psychic energy. This is not even true of organic evolution, which often produces fantastic formations, behavior patterns, colors, and whatnot, far exceeding mere survival and economic principles of adaptation. It is even less true of man, where not by the wildest flight of fancy can the creativity of an artist, musician, or scientist be reduced to psychological and social adjustment, nor can the self-sacrifice of a martyr be reduced to the principle of utility. The whole of human culture—whether Greek tragedy, Renaissance art, or German music—simply has nothing to do with biological values of maintenance, survival, adjustment, or homeostasis. As far as the idea of any necessary progress of humanity is concerned (the human analog to the biological concept of evolution), any criticism in our time of atomic warfare or any proposal for a return to medieval techniques of statecraft would be an anachronism.

In fact, the answer to our quest is very simple. Man, as the old saying goes, is a denizen of two worlds. He is a biological organism with the physical equipment, drives, instincts, and limitations of his species. At the same time, he creates, uses, dominates, and is dominated by a higher world which, without theological and philosophical implications and in behavioral terms, can best be defined as the universe or universes of symbols. This is what we call human culture; and values—aesthetic, scientific, ethical, religious—are one part of this symbolic universe. This is what man tries to achieve beyond satisfaction of his biological needs and drives; in turn, it governs and controls his behavior.

We have come a rather long way, but I am now prepared to answer the questions which we have left pending. We have spoken of existential neurosis—mental sickness resulting from the meaninglessness and emptiness of life and a lack of desirable goals. Why has life become devoid of meaning and goals at a time of affluence and high standards of living, whereas it apparently had meaning and goals in times incomparably poorer in their economic and technical resources?

The best answer I am able to find is that the complex structure of symbols and values called "human culture" is, besides many other things, an important psychohygienic factor. If man is surely a creature seeking satisfaction of his biological needs—food, shelter, sex, an amount of security for his biological and social existence—he also lives in the higher realm of culture, which is defined by the very fact that it transcends biological needs. Tradition, status in society, full realization of potentialities, religion, art, science—these are a few of the needs deriving from man's cultural existence. Starvation at this symbolic level leads to disturbances of the mental organism, just as starvation at the biologic level leads to disturbances of the physical organism. This is a well-established fact of psychopathology.

The diagnosis of the sick society, then, is quite simply that it provides more or less abundantly for the biological needs but starves the spiritual ones.

The human faculty of rational decision is replaced by biologistic factors, by conditioning like that of laboratory dogs and rats, and by exploitation of the unconscious— all brought to mastery in advertising and by hidden persuaders, motivation research, and human engineering in general. The system works to the profit of business because it is psychologically easier to be pushed by conditioned reflexes than to act with reason. But the loss of psychological freedom is paid for by a loss of goals worth fighting for and, consequently, by a feeling of emptiness and meaninglessness. The need for a value system of religion or at least a secular ideology remains unfilled; the substitute, or ersatz, is Christianity as a social affair or status symbol, or even primitive fetishism, advertised with all tricks of the trade. Art, music—even education, medical facilities, and science—tend to lose their intrinsic value and to retain only their utilitarian or snob value. To a wide extent, they are at the mercy of the whims of the Bureau of

Internal Revenue as they depend on loopholes in the tax structure that make certain donations tax-exempt and profitable.

WHENCE SCIENTISTS?

A few years ago *Life* magazine published an editorial entitled "Can We Produce an Einstein?" observing that the main achievements of modern science were made in Europe or by Europeans. The earlier leaders in American science either came from or studied in Europe. De Tocqueville's famous statement was quoted that the spirit of America, though devoted to practical science, "is averse to general ideas; it does not seek theoretical discoveries." In answer to its question, *Life* referred to the fact that the United States is much more concerned with practical know-how than with theoretical know-why, as is reflected by the fact that 95 percent of the national research budget goes for applied science, and only 5 percent for basic work. *Life*'s recommendation, therefore, was an appeal to provide larger financial resources for the latter.

Although such a recommendation is correct and intelligent, the problem is not that simple. The expectation that we shall produce Einsteins by the simple expedient of putting some additional millions or billions into basic research, bright young scientists, scientific hardware, and large research buildings will remain unfulfilled.

Since Sputnik I was launched, there has been an enormous debate about American education, science, and research. With a gigantic increase in research and development budgets, there has still been—so far as I am able to see—no change in attitude or any reassessment of basic outlook. These past years have seen an increase rather than a decrease of the Russian lead—and by no means in the space race alone. For example, in the fall of 1960, eighty million people in the U.S.S.R. were treated with oral polio vaccine, whereas in the United States it was still in the experimental stage. According to a recent book, little Ivan in the first grade is taught a vocabulary of 2,000 words; little Johnny, 158 words. In the fourth grade, Ivan is prepared for literature, history, and foreign languages, but Johnny still has to babble about "Mommy and Daddy."

If we reject as improbable the hypothesis that Americans are genetically stupider than other people, I believe the answer to *Life*'s question is simple: We do not produce an Einstein because we do not want to—because American universities and institutions of learning are not the place for the breeding and care of such abnormalities as outstanding scientists.

Mr. Khrushchev, who was by no means a mediocre intelligence, gave this an almost classical expression. You will remember what he said after another Russian Lunik was launched: The Americans, he said, should not be disappointed about Russia's conquest of space; after all, they are terribly good at inventing new tail fins.

This is precisely the point: American science excels in designing tail fins of all sorts —in diligently working out new touches, new details or convolutions of an already given body, be it the body of a car or of a theory. It is singularly ineffective in inventing new vehicles of space or of thought.

Why is it so? The answer lies, I believe, in a degradation of the democratic dogma. It starts at the level of the elementary school, when the democratic ideal of equal rights is converted into that of equal intelligence, whence the retardation of little Johnny in comparison with little Ivan. It culminates in universities and scientific production.

While there is a great hue and cry that scientists are needed and wanted, this means the need and desire for trainees to work within a given framework or template of structure and organization—great hustle and bustle, lots of machines and dials to watch, aggressive publicity that so many millions are being spent and new buildings erected, headlines about what often has to be disclaimed, and so forth. It does not mean a genuine welcome for creative individuals who, by definition, are nonconformists, try something new, are sometimes awkward in public relations, and are less interested in quantitative expansion than in being left alone. As a matter of fact, there is a subtle borderline where achievement is penalized. While universities go desperately hunting for junior scientists and can never have enough of them, seniors are left in the lurch because, as the routine phrase goes, "Unfortunately we have no place for a scientist of your reputation, experience, caliber, superior achievements. . . ."

Leadership and Intellect The concise expression of this is the American prima-donna myth. European universities, which, after all, had some six or seven centuries of experience, used to select leaders and pioneers, and it was quite common for students to come to a university not to follow a schedule for a degree but to hear famous Professor X or Y. In the United States a similar personality is apt to be labeled "prima donna"—and regarded as very bad indeed. This attitude misses only one detail: You just cannot play opera without prima donnas, even if they sometimes have difficult personalities and do not care about "togetherness," and you cannot promote science without leaders, individuals who do not fill preconstructed molds but make new ones.

Science depends on men with leadership qualities, initiative, drive, character, and moral courage. It is these qualities which the present system hampers and paralyzes.

Take, for example, the matter of scientific publications and grants for research. Roughly speaking, the principle for evaluation used to be that a scientist, who by his labors over many years had established a certain reputation, is not likely to make a fool of himself. His previous work does not guarantee but does make it more or less probable that his present contribution or project has merit. Our system, however, is totally different. Whether the youngest tyro or an experienced old hand is concerned, everything goes through the same big machinery, just as in the stockyards of Chicago, pigs of all colors and stocks are processed uniformly to make sausages.

What is the outcome of this procedure? Notwithstanding control by supposedly competent committees, our scientific and medical journals are full of superfluous, repetitive, sometimes incompetent and falsified reports. On the other hand, because of this overflood, it often takes years to have important work published—particularly if

it is new and therefore causes headaches to the editorial board. And where grants are concerned, the mildest that can be said is, in the words of Professor Gengerelli, of the University of California at Los Angeles, that "we have a great plethora of $100,000 grants for $50 ideas." For obvious reasons, I cannot quote concrete examples, but, in my admittedly limited experience, I have seen hundreds of thousands of dollars go for research which was simply bogus. I believe that the question of waste makers in science deserves investigation, but I wonder whether it will ever be done.

The interference with scientific productivity goes even further. Professor H. J. Muller has aptly defined freedom as "the condition of being able to choose and to carry out purposes. . . . A person is free to the extent that he has the capacity, the opportunity, and the incentive to give expression to what is in him and to develop his potentialities." I daresay this freedom is strictly limited in American science. To use Riesman's phrase, American science is "other-directed" to a hardly calculable degree—not only applied research with a prescribed practical or commercial goal, but basic science as well, controlled as it is by fashions in science and medicine, grant-giving agencies, financial considerations, and committees of all sorts, all of which often prove much stronger than the "free choice" (in Muller's terms) of the scientist.

The Group Mystique Even more, we see a decay of academic freedom. Mind you, I am careful to keep out matters with any political implication. I do not speak of limitations of scientific communication which may have to be imposed under measures of national security and the like. But I am forced to say that not even in Hitler Germany did I see the thought control and censorship which appear usual in at least *some* American institutions. I have never seen before regulations such as—I quote literally—"All publications, presentations, etc., have to be cleared and approved by the research committee," which, incidentally, was totally incompetent and only a tool of professional intrigue. I could quote examples where this regulation was made to stick and paralyzed the development of important work.

The underlying philosophy of all these

and many other phenomena is the mystical belief in the group, team, committee—and, I should add, the exploitation of this pseudodemocratic idea for personal purposes. Of course, the group or team has an important role in science, particularly modern science, with its high degree of specialization and complicated techniques. Roughly speaking, teamwork will be productive and indeed indispensable wherever elaboration of a given project, discovery, or idea is concerned. The group or team will never, however, replace the individual in inaugurating new developments. There is, I believe, no example in the history of science where a new breakthrough, an essentially novel discovery or theory, was the work of a group. The idea that brainstorming in a bull session will result in new revelations has no factual background. While aware that science is but one limited sector or aspect of modern civilization, I am inclined to believe that it is what the statisticians would call a representative sample.

TWO VIEWS OF HISTORY

Again using the way of gross oversimplification, forced upon us by the need for brevity, there are, in principle, two well-known ways to look at the history of mankind. The one is the theory of progress, seeing in it a continuous upward movement, caused principally by an increasing control of nature. We have gained nearly complete mastery of physical nature. Biological technology, such as control of disease by medicine and control of food by applied biology, is advancing. We now enter the age of psychological technology, that is, of controlling human behavior. When we gain the necessary insight into the laws of society and sociological technology—that is, when education, government, and politics have become thoroughly scientific—humanity will establish the earthly paradise, with the conquest of space and possible colonies on the planets thrown into the bargain.

The other view is different. It is known as the cyclic theory of history, focusing on a sequence of entities called high cultures or civilizations. Instead of continuous progress, each of them goes through a cycle, being born at a certain time and place, growing, flowering, reaching its apex, and eventually

decaying. So it was with the cultures of the past—those of Mesopotamia, Egypt, classical antiquity, China, the Aztecs, and so on. Our own period shows unmistakable symptoms of beginning or advanced decay, and if it does not die a natural death, it may even commit atomic suicide.

To the dispassionate scientist, it looks as if the cyclic model of history were the more realistic one. He would renounce his profession if he could not strongly protest that there has been an enormous progress in one particular sphere of cultural activity, science and technology. However, if he keeps an open mind and does not forget that these are but one sector of culture—that art, poetry, music, religion, and even the modest aspects of customs and styles of living are just as well expressions and needs of humanity as are scientific techniques and that, in our period, we have produced grand science but no grand music, sculpture, or poetry —then he cannot lightheartedly bypass the arguments of the theorists of cultural cycles and decline.

This does not imply, however, cowardly acceptance of historical inevitability. History does *not* repeat itself. Patently, our civilization is different from previous ones in two all-important respects. First, the latter were local phenomena, whereas ours encircles the whole planet. Second, ours is the first consciously to realize its danger and to possess the means to control it.

Here is where education comes in. If I say "education," I mean it in the classical sense of the word as unfolding human potentialities; I do not mean it in the sense of "human engineering," handling human beings with scientific techniques for ulterior purposes. We have already alluded to the fact that, with the help of modern technique, the human animal can be engineered just as well as inanimate and subhuman nature. I believe the main objection is not that of moral indignation about the degradation of man as a free entity, but rather it is the fact that human and social engineering, although efficient for particular purposes of commercialism and politics and over short periods of time, is self-defeating in the long run. A society consisting merely of mechanized or engineered human beings will not survive. Even *Brave New World* needs some marionette players who themselves are above the conditioning and social engineering they impose on the others.

Individuals Reappraised There is no psychological miracle drug or wonder cure; this is about the most certain knowledge modern psychology and psychiatry have taught us. Nevertheless, some of the unpleasant and dangerous aspects of American life and society patently go back to education. It is, of course, not my intention to suggest any practical measures. But it is, I believe, within the competence of the biologist, philosopher, and social critic to recall some principles or maxims upon which practice is and should be based. The introduction or, rather, reintroduction of a proper scale of values is a bald necessity.

It needs no emphasis that a reevaluation in American psychology, in both its theory and its applications, has been going on ever since the first Russian Sputnik disturbed its comfortable and parochial slumber. Less is spoken about Watson, Hull, and Skinner, and much more about Bruner and Piaget. The present volume is a testimony to how widely this need is felt. Nevertheless, theoretical discussion is another thing than practical implementation, and our society is still dominated by a mechanistic, behavioristic, and commercialistic philosophy

One point at which the issue of values is clearly joined is in the worth discerned in the human individual. One perspective insists that all individuals have equal capabilities and intelligence. This, obviously, is a parody of the American Constitution; the Founding Fathers certainly did not envisage or aspire to the manufacture of mass men in a commercialized society. The consequence of that theory, however, is the orientation of education to fit the lowest common denominator, that is, the lowest intelligence level in the group. The results are that Johnny cannot read, that he compares unfavorably with little Ivan, and that college students cannot speak or write decent English.

Intimately connected with this is another

theory fundamental in American psychology and education. It is environmentalism, the hypothesis that all individuals are born equal in their dispositions and that only postnatal influences mold their characters and mental outfits. The theory has a long history in English philosophy. It goes back to Locke's *tabula rasa* and found its classic expression in a statement by Watson, the founder of behaviorism (1959, p. 104):

> Give me a dozen healthy infants, well formed, and my own specified world to bring them up in and I'll guarantee to take any one at random and train him to become any type of specialist I might select—doctor, lawyer, artist, merchant-chief and, yes, even beggarman and thief, regardless of his talents, penchants, tendencies, abilities, vocations, and race of his ancestors.

I do not doubt that Watson is correct; only the bunch will make very poor beggars, lawyers, and doctors indeed.

In a similar vein, Skinner found "surprisingly similar performances" in organisms as diverse as the pigeon, mouse, rat, cat, and monkey. It is interesting to note that the Russians, communism notwithstanding, never fell into this trap. The pope of Russian physiology, Pavlov, reported the enormous variability of his experimental dogs in the conditioning procedure, and if genetic differences are recognized in laboratory dogs, it will be hard to deny them in humans. It is equally characteristic that the existence of hereditary differences—perfectly trivial to the biologist or even to any student who took a science course with *Drosophila* and elementary genetics—appears to come as a revolutionary surprise to American psychologists. Only a short while ago, I received a publication on this topic, cautiously introducing it as "a change in basic philosophy" and asking for correction should the argument be wrong.

Stimulus-Response Reductionism Again connected is still another biological misconception, the stimulus-response scheme: An organism, the human included, responds only to stimuli coming from outside and does so with maximum economy and for maintenance of its homeostatic equilibrium. In other terms, it does nothing if not stimulated or driven by maintenance needs. I have already mentioned that this theory contradicts biological fact, disregarding as it does spontaneous activities, play, and exploratory behavior. I should add that this misconceived theory has had an enormous impact on educational theory. The consequence is that child behavior is conceived essentially as "coping" with an adverse environment, and the task of the humane educator is therefore thought to be to make this coping as painless as possible, reducing to a minimum any tensions and stresses imposed by scholastic requirements. Little use is made of natural curiosity and creativity, the desire for exploration, the child's inherent pleasure in activity and function. This is another background factor underlying the pitiful results of our educational system.

The S-R theory also implies a utilitarian theory of education. Of course, large parts of education are of necessity utilitarian—from the three R's to the training of the doctor and lawyer—and they should be made even more utilitarian by eliminating, in view of the enormous extent of present knowledge, everything that is not of use for the particular purpose. Nevertheless, the goal of education as a whole is not utilitarian. It is not to produce mere social automatons kept in adjustment and submission by conditioning; it is to produce human beings enjoying themselves in a free society. Here, again, current educational philosophy misses the point. I have already pointed out that with respect to one aspect—science—education tends to overemphasize utilitarian know-how against know-why stemming from intrinsic interest in the subject matter. Moreover, in the long run, this apparently practical approach turns out to be not practical at all. This applies even more to the so-called humanities. It is precisely intrinsic to the definition of the cultural values of theoretical science, art, poetry, history, and so forth that they have no short-range, utilitarian values; they are, as the Germans have it, *Selbstzweck*, goals in themselves. Yet for exactly this reason, they have a utilitarian value at a higher level. The poor creature called man, beset with the shortcomings of animal physiology aggravated by domestication, making his living in a continual rat race under a thousand stresses, and chased around in a complex society, becomes some-

thing more than an overburdened Pavlovian dog only by those seemingly useless but factually so indispensable realms of his more-than-animal being.

A last precept: Smash the image of "organization man." In our discussion of science, we have already seen that organization man also belongs to those seemingly eminently practical but, in the long run, self-frustrating ideals. I have no brief to speak about his usefulness and desirability in industry and business. Considering the dangers of regression, recession, inflation, and international competition, the higher efficiency of foreign industry, Volkswagens, Japanese transistors, Russian jets, missiles, satellites —I just wonder. I am pretty sure, however, of just one point: A free society cannot be made out of yes-men. It may be eminently comfortable for business administrations when group-think, togetherness, affability, and prefabricated junior executives predominate, but it is equally certain that it will lead to stagnation everywhere.

On Recognizing Worth   Finally, status symbols must be replaced by status. Democracy grants equal rights, but the pursuit of happiness implies full realization of one's *own* potentialities. Let this be recognized. We must not level down but level up. One need not follow Napoleon's example and make generals and civil servants into fancy counts and princes, or Stalin's example and hang them with gold and silver medals like Christmas trees; but the empty chromium symbol of the Cadillac, the snobbish admiration of European Hollywood counts, must in some way be replaced by recognition of worthiness, of spiritual aristocracy, wherever it is found.

CONCLUSION

In trying to outline what the world of values is, I have rather fully discussed certain shortcomings in contemporary science. An implicit aim has been a reevaluation of the goals of education, looking toward a needed overhauling of our value system if we are to survive in this time of trouble.

Within the small compass of my presentation, I have tried to point out at least a few nooks and ribs in our education and social structure where new timbers should replace old ones. The good old ship is still sailing, even though it is overcrowded and its internal arrangement is uncomfortable at times. Wondrous to see, it has even grown wings and is headed for the abysses of space.

But the new frontiers it is bound to reach —they are not outside somewhere in interplanetary space. They are so near and yet so far: a new continent of the human soul.

REFERENCE

WATSON, J. B. *Behaviorism*. Chicago: Univer. of Chicago Press, 1959.

EPILOGUE AND PROLOGUE

In the physical sciences, much has been made of the dramatic "breakthrough," such as the discovery of the New World or the theory of relativity or the concept of complementarity. Such clear-cut discoveries or inventions are less discernible in the social sciences. Yet major changes in the experiences of countless millions of people have come about from the development of new perspectives on man and his nature. To cite but two examples: The impact of Christianity materially changed the world, and the tidal waves from the psychoanalytic revolution have not yet receded.

I believe, as do a number of others, including many of the authors in the foregoing pages, that we may be in the early stages of such another major evolution in man's perception of himself and thus in the whole nature of the human experience. Abraham Maslow has, characteristically, been one of the first and most insightful observers of this eventuality, and, as so often, he has given us the most facile language for talking about it. Maslow pointed out (1962) that, throughout most of history, man has been principally occupied with meeting the demands thrust upon him by various deficiencies: needs for food and shelter, defense against dangers of all kinds, and so on. Only in very recent times has more than a very small proportion of the world's population been free to turn its attention to what to do with life once its bare maintenance is assured. The former condition Maslow identified as living under conditions of deficiency (D-) motivation, and the newer as a condition of being (B-) motivation.

It seems to me that the tremendous potential significance of Maslow's observation has been too little appreciated. In another volume I have spent some time developing some of the possibilities that particularly impress me (Bugental, 1965). Here I simply want to deal with one aspect, with what some may see as only an analogy, although I feel confident that it is more than that.

Behavioristic psychology is, it seems to me, a product of D-motivation thinking. For example, and as a case in point, it venerates a heuristic convention as though it were a divine law: the principle of parsimony. In worship of this convention, all sorts of astonishing things have been done, including what can only be considered a form of live human sacrifice. Here is what I mean: "Psych-ology" originally meant "knowledge about the soul." D-motivation thinking, wearing the ritual mask of parsimony, wielded "Occam's razor" to cut away the concept of "soul." When this was replaced by other concepts, each in turn was similarly disposed of: "will," "mind," "consciousness," and "self." Man, such thinking seemed to urge, is nothing but a complex of muscle twitches responding to external stimuli—an appropriate image for the soulless, will-less, mindless, unconscious hulk without a self, a decorticated remainder.

However, in a fashion which is a societal enactment of Freud's "return of the repressed," the banished members of man's being are reemerging into polite psychological company. The "self" was revived by Raimy and Rogers and a host of others. "Consciousness" has been kept clandestinely alive by the applied psychologists whether in schools, clinics, or industry. No one seems to know quite in what way "mind" slipped back in past the Hullian censors, but it is increasingly showing up in psychological writings. Rollo May and other existentialists have reproclaimed the once-banished "will," and, confirming the mechanomorphs' worst fears, a host of other exiles have returned with it, "choice," "responsibility," and "guilt" among them. Finally, and this to many a good behaviorist is the ultimate sacrilege, the "soul" is whispered to be on the point of being revived. Man is becoming fully man, fully human again.

Yet that last sentence is misleading. It implies that man knew his fullness and then lost it and that he is now regaining it. I do not think this is so. Some of the more significant aspects of man's experience of himself which he had known and inquired into from his earliest history are now once again being studied by psychologists after a brief hiatus caused by the behavioristic excesses. The rest of mankind has never ceased to deal with most of these issues and has hardly noticed the parochial interruption.

But there is more to the story still. Man's fullness, all that it means and can mean to be human, these are conceptions we are just beginning to explore under the liberating conditions of B-motivation. We really know very little about what lies ahead.

At this stage we can only begin to make some preliminary survey marks. These might be summarized as follows:

1 Man's potential, in nearly every significant psychological dimension, far exceeds that part of it which he presently uses. The development of his ability to use his potential more fully cannot but mean a reshaping of his whole world.

2 The main, and uniquely human, processes of man's being have almost certainly been obscured by living under conditions of D-motivation. What man may be like when this downward-leveling constraint is removed, we can only guess.

3 One of the products of the D-motivation way of being has been a vocabulary for human experiences that emphasizes the regular, the uniform, the predictable—e.g., learning, memory, habits. A new vocabulary which highlights the unique, the creative, the individual, and the artistic may aid us in opening up rich further possibilities to life.

4 There has been an undue attention to, and regard for, the physical, similar to the emphasis on the uniform and predictable, noted above. As D-motivation is replaced by B-motivation, we may expect to recognize with fresh vividness the lesson that history and literature have repeatedly tried to teach: Man often acts much more in terms of the psychological and social values he holds, without regard to, or in actual opposition to, his physical needs. It is probable that in time this recognition may lead to much greater mental control of bodily functions and conditions.

5 The mention of social values reminds us of another area in which we have very little developed our potentials, that of the relations between men (e.g., the family, government, the church, education). Most of the forms of those relations are extremely ancient (and primitive) in origin. They have, until quite recent times, profited but little from the constructive impact of deliberate and dedicated efforts to make them more effective or to replace them with institutions better suited to man's evolving needs.

6 Most of man's most important living and creating is done vicariously (through words, images, and so on); yet our society, our language, and our social institutions are largely organized as though that verbal form of living were inconsequential and only the external, the object-involving, were truly significant. As we give more attention to internal, subjective experiences (e.g., meditation, dreams, reverie, problem solving, inventiveness), we may find a major restructuring of our experience. Such experiments as that conceived in the Esalen Institute residential program (1966) have the potential for more totally revolutionizing the human world than the whole of the man-in-space project.

7 Finally, we need to recognize the probability that man is not altogether subject to the supposed "law of causality" (which, like the "law of parsimony," is actually simply a useful heuristic aid which has been inflated into a would-be canon of science). The fact that man is aware and aware that he is aware introduces a new and qualitatively different element into the scientific enterprise which is not present in any of the physical sciences or in any sciences of animal (subhuman) behavior. Although the proportion may not be high, some part of man's behavior and experience almost surely flows from *reason* and not from *cause*. The difference is revolutionary. Let this difference be accepted and developed, and the torch is lit which will burn away the whole of the mechanomorphic picture of man and illuminate the human enterprise to entirely new levels of realization.

In sum, what I am maintaining—what I feel the chapters of this book begin to document in exciting fashion—is that we are in the

early stages of one of the major revolutions in the human experience.
Once man felt he was the center of the universe. Then science
demonstrated the earth to be far from the center even of our own
galaxy, showed the sun to be the center of the solar system, and
in countless other ways dispossessed man of his sense of specialness
in the cosmos. It was important to our maturity that this occur.
But now the time has come for man to point a new direction to a
process that has overcarried. Not only does man recognize that
he is not the center of the universe, but he has come to put other
matters there: depersonalized, abstracted principles and
supposed laws.

What I argue for is not a man-centered universe, but a man-centered
man in the universe. Let us come home to our own place in our
own lives and set about making our destiny our own.

REFERENCES

BUGENTAL, J. F. T. *The search for authenticity.* New York: Holt, Rinehart and Winston, 1965.

ESALEN INSTITUTE. Residential program brochure. Big Sur, Calif.: Author, 1966.

MASLOW, A. H. *Toward a psychology of being.* Princeton, N.J.: Van Nostrand, 1962.

INDEX

Groups, religious experience in,
    determinants of, 254–255
    examples of, 253–254
    T- (laboratory), 261
    uncontrolled, fear of, 168–169
Growth, establishing climate for, 232
    group (*see* Group growth)
    personal and group (table), 163
Growthful encounter, 215–286
GSR (galvanic skin response), 112
Guilt, existential, existential shame and,
    256–257

Habit, consciousness and, 72–74
    psychotherapy, values and, 247–250
Habit approach to psychotherapy, 247–248
Hachiya, M., 198*n*.
Hackett, T. P., 200*n*.
Hadamard, J., 37
Hagakure, 202*n*.
Haha reaction, 33–34, 36, 37
Haigh, G. V., 8, 162*n*., 216, 218, 219, 232*n*.,
    253*n*., 263*n*., 288, 303*n*.
Hall, C. S., 128, 129
Hall, G. F., 267, 269
Harman, W. W., 8, 288–289, 315*n*., 320,
    321, 327, 331
Harrison, R., 236
Hartley, D., 95
Hartmann, H., 86, 87
Harvey, W., 37
Havel, J., 142
Havighurst, R. J., 88
Hawthorne effect, 139
Hegel, G. W. F., 299
Heilman, R., 314
Herold, V. P., 193*n*.
Heteronomous personality, morality of, 46
Heteronomy versus autonomy, 47
Heuristic research, 80, 101–107
Hibakusha (survivors; explosion-affected
    persons), 195, 197
    identity with, 199, 200
Hierarchy, defined, 183
    in organizational life, 183–184
    six-level simulation, 186
Hilgard, E. R., 129
Hills Beyond, 105
Hiroshima disaster (*see* Death and death
    symbolism: Hiroshima disaster)
Hiroshima University, 195*n*.
Hiss, A., 105
History, behavioral sciences and, evidence
    on encapsulated-man thesis from,
    323–324
    function of, 300–301
    psychology and, 27

History, two views of, 341–343
Hobbes, T., 95
Hochmann, J., 261*n*.
Holt, R. R., 142
Homo patiens, 53–59
Hope, 15
Horney, K., 85, 86
Horror, ultimate, 197
Hug-Hellmuth, H., 85
Hull, C. L., 53, 342, 346
Human beings, fresh look at, 13–18
    requirements of, 14–18
    total, as research method, 103–105
Human experience, the, 41–78
    science and, 5–7
Human life as a whole as central subject
    of humanistic psychology, 83–91
    (*See also* Man)
Human nature, differentiation of aspects
    of, 13–18
Human Potentialities, 130
Human Potentialities Project, 119
Human relationships, rehumanizing, 275
Humanism, 287
Humanistic-behavioristic controversy,
    summarizing, 8–9
Humanistic elements in group growth,
    161–170
Humanistic methodology in personality
    and social psychology, 127–133
Humanistic orientation, 9
Humanistic psychology, breadth and
    inclusiveness of, 127–128
    challenge to, 11
    characterizing, 23–27
    concern with higher human qualities, 130
    contrast between mechanomorphic
        psychology and, 7–8
    emergence of, 22–23
    focus on experiencing person, 129–130
    goal of, 7
    human life as a whole as central subject
        of, 83–91
    life cycle as central subject of, 85–88
    metaphoric knowledge and, 21–28
    methodological problem of, 79–80
    methodology for, 131–132
    model of man for, 45–51
    nature and task of, 1–3.
    preliminary survey, 347
    research products, 147–213
    research techniques for, 89–90
    state of the art, 9–10
    symbolism and intuition in, 23
    task for, 7–9
    of Teilhard de Chardin, 151–158
    values, goals, and purposes of, 130–131
Humanistic research on large social
    organizations, 181–193
    conceptual framework, 181–185

Kohut H., 296
Komatsu, K., 195n.
Krasner, L., 140, 248
Kris, E., 38
Krouss, R. E., 187n.
Krugman, A. D., 138
Krutch, Joseph Wood, 297
Kubie, Lawrence, 285
Kuhn, T. H., 36

Laboratory group (T-group), 261
Laboratory studies in psychedelic research, 137
Laing, R. D., 111
Lange, C. G., 56
Langer, S., 203n.
Langford, N., 105
Laski, M., 144
Lasko, A. A., 8, 217, 246, 247
Laughter, emotional dynamics of, 33–34
    logic of, 33
Lavoisier, A. L., 324
Lawrence of Arabia, 222
Leadership, intellect and, 340
Learning, intrinsic and extrinsic, 280
Lecky, P., 129
Le Corbusier, 39
Leiderman, P., 141
Leites, N., 305
Leonardo da Vinci, 39, 84
Leukemia resulting from Hiroshima
    disaster, 198–199
*Leviathan Documents, Bibliography
    of Project*, 193n.
Leviathan experiments, six-level hierarchy
    simulated in, 186
Leviathan method for research on large
    social organizations (*see*
    Humanistic research on large
    social organizations)
Levine, L. S., 8, 149, 208, 209, 211
Levy, L. H., 292n.
Lewin, K., 128, 129, 131, 132
Lewis, C. S., 283
Lewis, W., 313
"Lie" scale, 112
Life, death as standard for, 202–206
    Shakespeare's genius for, 313–314
Life cycle, as central subject of humanistic
    psychology, 85–88
    phases of, 88
Life magazine, 339
Lifton, R. J., 8, 149, 194, 195, 196n., 197n.,
    199n., 205n., 216, 289
Lilly, J. C., 329
Lim, D. J., 141
Lincoln, A., 65, 105

Lindzey, G., 128, 129
Literature, of mysticism, 327
    potential contribution of, to psychology,
    299–300
Livingston, W. K., 16
Localization of drive, 55
Locke, J., 95, 342
Logic of laughter, 33
Loneliness, 105, 106
Loneliness, study of, 101–107
Lonely Crowd, 105
Lord of the Flies, 26
Love against Hate, 105
Love, place of, in further evolution of
    man, 156–157
Low, B., 203
LSD, 280
LSD research (*see* Psychedelic research)
Lundin, R. W., 131, 132
Lutheran Education Association, 174
Lyerly, S. B., 138

Machiavelli, N., 10
MacKinnon, D. W., 144
Macmurray, John, 15
Mad scenes in *King Lear*, 316–318
Madness, meaning of, 314–318
    reason in (*see King Lear*)
    unaccommodated man and, 315–316
Major Barbara, 313
Malinowski, B. K., 323
Maltz, M., 330
Man, as challenge to man, 5–11
    conceptualizing, and his experience, 329
    existentialist view of, 110
    further evolution of, 156–158
        emergence of new man, 157–158
        modern man and challenge of new
            man, 158
        place of love, 156–157
    in his wholeness, 83–85
    model of, for humanistic psychology,
        45–51
    modern, challenge of new man and, 158
    moral (*see* Moral man)
    new, emergence of, 157–158
    proactive (*see* Proactive man)
    in relation to one another, 211
    in two worlds, 337–339
    unaccommodated, madness and, 315–316
    (*See also* Human life)
Man's nature, preconceptions about,
    210–211
Mann, T., 304n.
Manyoshu, 202n.
Margenau, H., 6
Martin, P. W., 321, 330
Marx, K., 46